T0180902

Communications
in Computer and Information Science　　2053

Editorial Board Members

Rationale
The CCIS series is devoted to the publication of proceedings of computer science conferences. Its aim is to efficiently disseminate original research results in informatics in printed and electronic form. While the focus is on publication of peer-reviewed full papers presenting mature work, inclusion of reviewed short papers reporting on work in progress is welcome, too. Besides globally relevant meetings with internationally representative program committees guaranteeing a strict peer-reviewing and paper selection process, conferences run by societies or of high regional or national relevance are also considered for publication.

Topics
The topical scope of CCIS spans the entire spectrum of informatics ranging from foundational topics in the theory of computing to information and communications science and technology and a broad variety of interdisciplinary application fields.

Information for Volume Editors and Authors
Publication in CCIS is free of charge. No royalties are paid, however, we offer registered conference participants temporary free access to the online version of the conference proceedings on SpringerLink (http://link.springer.com) by means of an http referrer from the conference website and/or a number of complimentary printed copies, as specified in the official acceptance email of the event.

CCIS proceedings can be published in time for distribution at conferences or as postproceedings, and delivered in the form of printed books and/or electronically as USBs and/or e-content licenses for accessing proceedings at SpringerLink. Furthermore, CCIS proceedings are included in the CCIS electronic book series hosted in the SpringerLink digital library at http://link.springer.com/bookseries/7899. Conferences publishing in CCIS are allowed to use Online Conference Service (OCS) for managing the whole proceedings lifecycle (from submission and reviewing to preparing for publication) free of charge.

Publication process
The language of publication is exclusively English. Authors publishing in CCIS have to sign the Springer CCIS copyright transfer form, however, they are free to use their material published in CCIS for substantially changed, more elaborate subsequent publications elsewhere. For the preparation of the camera-ready papers/files, authors have to strictly adhere to the Springer CCIS Authors' Instructions and are strongly encouraged to use the CCIS LaTeX style files or templates.

Abstracting/Indexing
CCIS is abstracted/indexed in DBLP, Google Scholar, EI-Compendex, Mathematical Reviews, SCImago, Scopus. CCIS volumes are also submitted for the inclusion in ISI Proceedings.

How to start
To start the evaluation of your proposal for inclusion in the CCIS series, please send an e-mail to ccis@springer.com.

Deepak Garg · Joel J. P. C. Rodrigues ·
Suneet Kumar Gupta · Xiaochun Cheng ·
Pushpender Sarao · Govind Singh Patel
Editors

Advanced Computing

13th International Conference, IACC 2023
Kolhapur, India, December 15–16, 2023
Revised Selected Papers, Part I

Springer

Editors
Deepak Garg
SR University
Warangal, India

Suneet Kumar Gupta
Bennett University
Greater Noida, India

Pushpender Sarao
Lovely Professional University
Phagwara, India

Joel J. P. C. Rodrigues
COPELABS, Lusófona University
Lisbon, Portugal

Xiaochun Cheng
Swansea University
Wales, UK

Govind Singh Patel
SITCOE Engineering College
Ichalkaranji, India

ISSN 1865-0929 ISSN 1865-0937 (electronic)
Communications in Computer and Information Science
ISBN 978-3-031-56699-8 ISBN 978-3-031-56700-1 (eBook)
https://doi.org/10.1007/978-3-031-56700-1

This Springer imprint is published by the registered company Springer Nature Switzerland AG
The registered company address is: Gewerbestrasse 11, 6330 Cham, Switzerland

Paper in this product is recyclable.

Preface

The objective of the 13th International Advanced Computing Conference (IACC 2023) was to bring together researchers, developers, and practitioners from academia and industry working in the domain of advanced computing. Researchers were invited to share their thoughts and present recent developments and technical solutions in the domains of Advances in Machine Learning and Deep Learning, Advances in Applications of Artificial Intelligence in Interdisciplinary Areas, Reinforcement Learning, and Advances in Data Science. The conference took place on the 15th and 16th December 2023 at Ichalkaranji, Kolhapur, Maharashtra, India. All editions of the series are successfully indexed in ISI, Scopus, DBLP, Compendex, SJR, and Google Scholar etc.

Conference follows single blind review process and has the policy of at least three reviews per paper. This year's conference received 425 submissions, of which 72 articles were accepted. The conference has the track record of acceptance rates from 15% to 20% in the last 12 years. More than 13 IEEE/ACM Fellows hold key positions on the conference committee, giving it a quality edge. In the last 12 years the conference citation score has been consistently increasing.

This has been possible due to adherence to quality parameters of the review and acceptance rate without any exception that allows us to make some of the best research available through this platform.

December 2023

Deepak Garg
Joel J. P. C. Rodrigues
Xiaochun Cheng
Suneet Kumar Gupta
Pushpender Sarao
Govind Singh Patel

Organization

Honorary Co-chairs

Sundaraja Sitharama Iyengar	Florida International University, USA
Sartaj Sahni	University of Florida, USA
Jagannathan Sarangpani	Missouri University of Science and Technology, USA
Ajith Abraham	Bennett University, India
P. N. Suganthan	KINDI Center for Computing Research, Qatar University, Qatar
Jaume Anguera	Universitat Ramon Llull, Spain

General Co-chairs

Deepak Garg	SR University, India
Suneet K. Gupta	Bennett University, India
Joel J. P. C. Rodrigues	Instituto de Telecomunicações, Portugal
Xiaochun Cheng	Swansea University, UK
Pushpender Sarao	Lovely Professional University, India
Govind Singh Patel	Sharad Institute of Technology College of Engineering, India

Program Co-chairs

Kit Wong	University College London, UK
George Ghinea	Brunel University London, UK
Carol Smidts	Ohio State University, USA
Ram D. Sriram	National Institute of Standards & Technology, USA
Sanjay Madria	University of Missouri, USA
Marques Oge	Florida Atlantic University, USA
Vijay Kumar	University of Missouri-Kansas City, USA
Ajay Gupta	Western Michigan University, USA

Special Issue Co-chairs

Akansha Singh	Bennett University, India
Dilbag Singh	Gwangju Institute of Science & Technology, South Korea

Technical Program Committee/International Advisory Committee

Shivani Goel	SR University, India
Sumeet Dua	Louisiana Tech University, USA
Roger Zimmermann	National University of Singapore, Singapore
Seeram Ramakrishna	National University of Singapore, Singapore
B. V. R. Chowdari	NUS, Singapore & Nanyang Technological University, Singapore
Hari Mohan Pandey	Edge Hill University, UK
Selwyn Piramuthu	University of Florida, USA
Bharat Bhargava	Purdue University, USA
Omer F. Rana	Cardiff University, UK
Javed I. Khan	Kent State University, USA
Harpreet Singh	Wayne State University, USA
Rajeev Agrawal	North Carolina A&T State University, USA
P. Prabhakaran	St. Joseph University, Tanzania
Yuliya Averyanova	National Aviation University, Ukraine
Mohammed M. Banet	Jordan University of Technology, Jordan
Dawid Zydek	Idaho State University, USA
Wensheng Zhang	Iowa State University, USA
Bal Virdee	London Metropolitan University, UK
Qun Wu	Harbin Institute of Technology, China
Anh V. Dinh	University of Saskatchewan, Canada
Lakshman Tamil	University of Texas, USA
P. D. D. Dominic	Universiti Teknologi Petronas, Malaysia
Muhammad Sabbir Rahman	North South University, Bangladesh
Zablon Akoko Mbero	University of Botswana, Botswana
V. L. Narasimhan	University of Botswana, Botswana
Kin-Lu Wong	National Sun Yat-sen University, Taiwan
Pawan Lingras	Saint Mary's University, USA
P. G. S. Velmurugan	Thiagaraja College of Engineering, India
N. B. Balamurugan	Thiagaraja College of Engineering, India
Mahesh Bundele	Poornima University, India
N. Venkateswaran	Sri Sivasubramaniya Nadar College of Engineering, India

S. Sundaresh	IEEE Madras Section, India
Premanand V. Chandramani	SSN College of Engineering, India
Mini Vasudevan	Ericsson India Pvt. Ltd., India
P. Swarnalatha	VIT, India
P. Venkatesh	Thiagaraja College of Engineering, India
B. Venkatalakshmi	Velammal Engineering College, India
M. Marsalin Beno	St. Xavier's Catholic College of Engineering, India
M. Arun	VIT, India
Porkumaran K.	NGP Institute of Technology, India
D. Ezhilarasi	NIT Tiruchirappalli, India
Ramya Vijay	SASTRA University, India
S. Rajaram	Thiagaraja College of Engineering, India
B. Yogameena	Thiagaraja College of Engineering, India
S. Joseph Gladwin	SSN College of Engineering, India
D. Nirmal	Karunya University, India
N. Mohankumar	SKP Institute of Technology, India
A. Jawahar	SSN College of Engineering, India
K. Dhayalini	K. Ramakrishnan College of Engineering, India
Diganta Sengupta	Meghnad Saha Institute of Technology, India
Supriya Chakraborty	Amity University, India
Mamta Arora	Manav Rachna University, India
Om Prakash Jena	Ravenshaw University, India
Sandeep Singh Sengar	University of Copenhagen, Denmark
Murali Chemuturi	Chemuturi Consultants, India
Madhu Vadlamani	Cognizant, India
A. N. K. Prasannanjaneyulu	Institute of Insurance and Risk Management, India
O. Obulesu	G. Narayanamma Institute of Technology & Science, India
Rajendra R. Patil	GSSSIETW, India
Ajay Kumar	Chitkara University Institute of Engineering & Technology, India
D. P. Kothari	THDC Institute of Hydropower Engineering and Technology, India
T. S. N. Murthy	JNTUK Vizianagaram, India
Nitesh Tarbani	Sipna College of Engineering & Technology, India
Jesna Mohan	Mar Baselios College of Engineering and Technology, India
Manoj K. Patel	CSIR, India
Pravati Swain	NIT Goa, India
Manoj Kumar	University of Petroleum and Energy Studies, India

E. S. Gopi	National Institute of Technology Tiruchirappalli, India
Mithun B Patil	NKOCET, India
Priya Saha	LPU, India
Sahaj Saxena	Thapar Institute of Engineering and Technology, India
Dinesh G. Harkut	Prof Ram Meghe College of Engineering & Management, India
Pushpendra Singh	National Institute of Technology Hamirpur, India
Nirmala J. Saunshimath	Nitte Meenakshi Institute of Technology, India
Mayank Pandey	MNNIT, India
Sudeep D. Thepade	Pimpri Chinchwad College of Engineering, India
Pimal Khanpara	Nirma University, India
Rohit Lalwani	MIT University of Meghalaya, India
Loshma Gunisetti	Sri Vasavi Engineering College, India
Vishweshwar Kallimani	University of Nottingham, UK
Amit Kumar Mishra	DIT University, India
Pawan Whig	Vivekananda Institute of Professional Studies, India
Dhatri Pandya	Sarvajanik College of Engineering and Technology, India
Asha S. Manek	RV Institute of Technology and Management, India
Lingala Thirupathi	Methodist College of Engineering & Technology, India
P. Mahanti	University of New Brunswick, Canada
Shaikh Muhammad Allayear	Daffodil International University, Bangladesh
Basanta Joshi	Tribhuvan University, Nepal
S. R. N. Reddy	IGDTUW, India
Mehran Alidoost Nia	University of Tehran, Iran
Ambili P. S.	Saintgits Group of Institutions, India
M. A. Jabbar	Vardhaman College of Engineering, India
Lokendra Kumar Tiwari	Ewing Christian College, India
Abhay Saxena	Dev Sanskriti Vishwavidyalaya, India
Kanika Bansal	Chitkara University, India
Pooja M. R.	Vidyavardhaka College of Engineering, India
Pranav Dass	Bharati Vidyapeeth's College of Engineering, India
Avani R. Vasant	Babaria Institute of Technology, India
Bhanu Prasad	Florida A&M University, USA
Barenya Bikash Hazarika	NIT Arunachal Pradesh, India
Ipseeta Nanda	Gopal Narayan Singh University, India
Satyendra Singh	Bhartiya Skill Development University, India

Sudip Mandal	Jalpaiguri Govt. Engineering College, India
Naveen Kumar	IIIT Vadodara, India
Parag Rughani	National Forensic Sciences University, India
K. Shirin Bhanu	Sri Vasavi Engineering College, India
R. Malmathanraj	NITT, India
Latika Singh	Ansal University, India
Gizachew Hailegebriel Mako	Ethio telecom, Ethiopia
Tessy Mathew	Mar Baselios College of Engineering and Technology, India
Grzegorz Chodak	Wroclaw University of Science and Technology, Poland
Neetu Verma	D.C.R.U.S.T Murthal, India
Sharda A. Chhabria	G H Raisoni Institute of Engineering & Technology, India
Neetesh Saxena	Cardiff University, UK
R. Venkatesan	Ministry of Earth Sciences, India
V. Jayaprakasan	IEEE Madras Section, India
D. Venkata Vara Prasad	SSN College of Engineering, India
Jayakumari J.	Mar Baselios College of Engineering and Technology, India
P. A. Manoharan	IEEE Madras Section, India
S. Salivahanan	IEEE Madras Section, India
P. Santhi Thilagam	National Institute of Technology Karnataka, India
Umapada Pal	Indian Statistical Institute, India
S. Suresh	NIT Trichy, India
V. Mariappan	NIT Trichy, India
T. Senthil Kumar	Anna University, India
S. Chandramohan	JNTUA College of Engineering, India
D. Devaraj	Kalasalingam Academy of Research & Education, India
J. William	Agnel Institute of Technology & Design, India
R. Kalidoss	SSN College of Engineering, India
R. K. Mugelan	Vellore Institute of Technology, India
V. Vinod Kumar	Government College of Engineering Kannur, India
R. Saravanan	VIT, India
S. Sheik Aalam	iSENSE Intelligence Solutions, India
E. Srinivasan	Pondicherry Engineering College, India
B. Surendiran	National Institute of Technology Puducherry, India
Varun P. Gopi	NIT Tiruchirappalli India
V. Vijaya Chamundeeswari	Velammal Engineering College, India
T. Prabhakar	GMRIT, India

V. Kamakoti	IIT Madras, India
N. Janakiraman	KLN College of Engineering, India
V. Anandakrishanan	NIT Trichy, India
R. B. Patel	MMEC, India
Adesh Kumar Sharma	NDRI, India
Gunamani Jena	JNTU, India
Maninder Singh	Thapar University, India
Manoj Manuja	NIT Trichy, India
Ajay K. Sharma	Chitkara University, India
Manjit Patterh	Punjabi University, India
L. M. Bhardwaj	Amity University, India
Parvinder Singh	DCRUST, India
M. Syamala	Punjab University, India
Lalit Awasthi	NIT Jalandhar, India
Ajay Bansal	NIT Jalandhar, India
Ravi Aggarwal	Adobe Systems, USA
Sigurd Meldal	San Jose State University, USA
M. Balakrishnan	IIT Madras, India
Malay Pakhira	KGEC, India
Savita Gupta	PU Chandigarh, India
Manas Ranjan Patra	Berhampur University, India
Sukhwinder Singh	PU Chandigarh, India
Dharmendra Kumar	GJUST, India
Chandan Singh	Punjabi University, India
Rajinder Nath	Kurukshetra University, India
Manjaiah D. H.	Mangalore University, India
Himanshu Aggarwal	Punjabi University, India
R. S. Kaler	Thapar University, India
Pabitra Pal Choudhury	Indian Statistical Institute, India
S. K. Pal	DRDO, India
G. S. Lehal	Punjabi University, India
Rajkumar Kannan	Bishop Heber College, India
Yogesh Chaba	GJUST, India
Amardeep Singh	Punjabi University, India
Sh. Sriram Birudavolu	Oracle India Limited, India
Ajay Rana	Amity University, India
Kanwal Jeet Singh	Punjabi University, India
C. K. Bhensdadia	DD University, India
Savina Bansal	GZSCET, India
Mohammad Asger	BGSB, India
Rajesh Bhatia	PEC, India
Stephen John Turner	VISTEC, India

Chiranjeev Kumar	IIT (ISM) Dhanbad, India
Bhim Singh	IIT Delhi, India
A. K. Sharma	BSAITM, India
Rob Reilly	MIT, USA
B. K. Murthy	CDAC, India
Karmeshu	JNU, India
K. K. Biswas	IIT Delhi, India
Sandeep Sen	IIT Delhi, India
Suneeta Aggarwal	MNNIT, India
Raghuraj Singh	HBTI, India
D. K. Lobiyal	JNU, India
R. S. Yadav	MNNIT, India
Bulusu Anand	IIT Roorkee, India
R. K. Singh	KEC Dwarahat, India
Sateesh Kumar Peddoju	IIT Roorkee, India
Divakar Yadav	JIIT, India
Naveen Kumar Singh	IGNOU, India
R. S. Raw	AIACTR (NSUT East Campus), India
Vidushi Sharma	GBU, India
Sumit Srivastava	Manipal University, India
Manish K. Gupta	DAIICT, India
P. K. Saxena	DRDO, India
B. K. Das	ITM University, India
Y. Raghu Reddy	IIIT Hyderabad, India
B. Chandra	IIT Delhi, India
R. K. Agarwal	JNU, India
Basim Alhadidi	Al-Balqa' Applied University, Jordan
M. Monirujjaman Khan	North South University, Bangladesh
Emmanuel Ndashimye	University of Rwanda & CMU-Africa, Rwanda
Naveen Garg	IIT Jodhpur, India
K. S. Subramanian	IGNOU, India
Biplab Sikdar	NUS, Singapore
Sreeram Ramakrishna	NUS, Singapore
Vikas Mathur	Citrix, India
Hari Krishna Garg	NUS, Singapore
Raja Dutta	IIT Kharagpur, India
Y. V. S. Lakshmi	India
Vishakha Vaidya	Adobe, India
Sudipto Shankar Dasgupta	Infosys Limited, India
Atal Chaudhari	Jadavpur University, India
Gangaboraiah Andanaiah	KIMS, India
Champa H. N.	UVCE, India

Ramakanth Kumar P.	RVCE, India
S. N. Omkar	IISC Bangalore, India
Balaji Rajendran	CDAC, India
Annapoorna P. Patil	MSRIT, India
K. N. Chandrashekhar	SJCIT, India
Mohammed Misbahuddin	CDAC, India
Saroj Meher	ISI, India
Jharna Majumdar	NMIT, India
N. K. Cauvery	RVCE, India
G. K. Patra	CSIR, India
Anandi Jayadharmarajan	Oxford College of Engg., India
K. R. Suneetha	BIT Mesra, India
M. L. Shailaja	AIT, India
K. R. Murali Mohan	GOI, India
Ramesh Paturi	Microsoft, India
S. Viswanadha Raju	JNTU, India
C. Krishna Mohan	IIT Chennai, India
R. T. Goswamy	Techno International New Town, India
B. Surekha	K S Institute of Technology, India
P. Trinatha Rao	GITAM University, India
G. Varaprasad	BMS College of Engineering, India
M. Usha Rani	SPMVV, India
P. V. Lakshmi	SPMVV, India
K. A. Selvaradjou	PEC, India
Ch. Satyananda Reddy	Andhra University, India
Jeegar A. Trivedi	Sardar Patel University, India
S. V. Rao	IIT Guwahati, India
Suresh Varma	Aadikavi Nannaya University, India
T. Ranga Babu	RVR & JC College of Engineering, India
D. Venkat Rao	Narasaraopet Inst. of Technology, India
N. Sudhakar Reddy	S V Engineering College, India
Dhiraj Sunehra	Jawaharlal Nehru Technological University, India
Madhavi Gudavalli	JNYU Kakinada, India
B. Hemanth Kumar	RVR & JC College of Engineering, India
A. Sri Nagesh	RVR & JC College of Engg., India
Bipin Bihari Jaya Singh	CVR College of Engg, India
M. Ramesh	JNTU, India
P. Rajarajeswari	GITAM University, India
R. Kiran Kumar	Krishna University, India
D. Ramesh	JNTU, India
B. Kranthi Kiran	JNTU, India
K. Usha Rani	SPM University, India

A. Nagesh	MGIT, India
P. Sammulal	JNTU, India
G. Narasimha	JNTU, India
B. V. Ram Naresh Yadav	JNTU, India
B. N. Bhandari	JNTUH, India
O. B. V. Ramanaiah	JNTUH College of Engineering, India
Anil Kumar Vuppala	IIIT Hyderabad, India
Duggirala Srinivasa Rao	JNTU, India
Makkena Madhavi Latha	JNTUH, India
Anitha Sheela Kancharla	JNTUH, India
B. Padmaja Rani	JNTUH College of Engineering Hyderabad, India
S. Mangai	Velalar College of Engg. & Tech., India
P. Chandra Sekhar	Osmania University, India
Chakraborty Mrityunjoy	IIT Kharagpur, India
Manish Shrivastava	IIIT Hyderabad, India
Uttam Kumar Roy	Jadavpur University, India
Kalpana Naidu	IIIT Kota, India
A. Swarnalatha	St. Joseph's College of Engg., India
Aaditya Maheshwari	Techno India NJR Institute of Tech., India
Ajit Panda	National Institute of Science and Technology, India
R. Anuradha	Sri Ramakrishna Engg. College, India
B. G. Prasad	BMS College of Engg., India
Seung-Hwa Chung	Trinity College Dublin, Ireland
D. Murali	VIT, India
Deepak Padmanabhan	Queen's University Belfast, UK
Firoz Alam	RMIT University, Australia
Frederic Andres	NII, Japan
Srinath Doss	Botho University, Botswana
Munish Kumar	Maharaja Ranjit Singh Punjab Tech University, India
Norwati Mustapha	UPM, India
Hamidah Ibrahim	UPM, India
Denis Reilly	Liverpool John Moores University, UK
Ioannis Kypraios	De Montfort University, UK
Yongkang Xing	De Montfort University, UK
P. Shivakumara	University of Malaya, Malaysia
Ravinder Kumar	TIET Patiala, India
Ankur Gupta	Rishihood University, India
Rahul Kr. Verma	IIIT Lucknow, India
Mohit Sajwan	NSUT, India
Vijaypal Singh Rathor	IIITDM, India

Deepak Singh	NIT Raipur, India
Simranjit Singh	NIT Jalandhar, India
Suchi Kumari	Shiv Nadar University, India
Kuldeep Chaurasia	Bennett University, India
Indrajeet Gupta	SR University, India
Shakti Sharma	Bennett University, India
Hiren Thakkar	PDPU, India
Mayank Swankar	IIT(BHU) Varanasi, India
Tapas Badal	Bennett University, India
Vipul Kr. Mishra	Gatishakti University, India
Tanveer Ahmed	Bennett University, India
Madhushi Verma	Bennett University, India
Gaurav Singal	NSUT, India
Anurag Goswami	Bennett University, India
Durgesh Kumar Mishra	Sri Aurobindo Institute of Technology, India
S. Padma	Madanapalle Institute of Technology & Science, India
Deepak Prashar	Lovely Professional University, India
Nidhi Khare	NMIMS, India
Sandeep Kumar	IIT Delhi, India
Dattatraya V. Kodavade	D.K.T.E Society's Textile & Engineering Institute, India
A. Obulesu	Anurag University, India
K. Suvarna Vani	V R Siddhartha Engineering College, India
G. Singaravel	K.S.R. College of Engineering, India
Ajay Shiv Sharma	Melbourne Institute of Technology, Australia
Abhishek Shukla	R.D. Engineering College Technical Campus Ghaziabad, India
V. K. Jain	Mody University, India
Deepak Poola	IBM India Private Limited, India
Bhadri Raju M. S. V. S.	S.R.K.R. Engineering College, India
Yamuna Prasad	IIT Jammu, India
Vishnu Vardhan B.	JNTUH College of Engineering Manthani, India
Virendra Kumar Bhavsar	Univ. of New Brunswick, Canada
Siva S. Skandha	CMR College of Engineering, India
Vaibhav Anu	Montclair State University, India
V. Gomathi	National Engineering College, India
Sudipta Roy	Assam University, India
Srabanti Maji	DIT University, India
Shylaja S. S.	PESU, India
Shweta Agrawal	SIRT, India

Shreenivas Londhe	Vishwakarma Institute of Information Technology, India
Shirin Bhanu Koduri	Vasavi Engineering College, India
Shailendra Aswale	SRIEIT, India
Shachi Natu	TSE College Mumbai, India
Santosh Saraf	Coordinator Technology Business Incubation Center Belagavi, India
Samayveer Singh	Ambedkar National Institute of Technology, India
Sabu M. Thampi	IIIT and Mgt-Kerala Thiruvananthapuram, India
Roshani Raut	Vishwakarma Institute of Information Technology, India
Radhika K. R.	BMSCE, India
R. Priya Vaijayanthi	NSRIT, India
M. Naresh Babu	NIT Silchar, India
Krishnan Rangarajan	Dayananda Sagar College of Engineering, India
Prashant Singh Rana	Thapar Institute of Engg. & Tech., India
Parteek Bhatia	Thapar Institute of Engineering & Technology, India
Venkata Padmavati Metta	BIT, India
Laxmi Lydia	VIIT, India
Nikunj Tahilramani	Dolcera IT Services Pvt Ltd, India
Navanath Saharia	IIIT Manipur, India
Nagesh Vadaparthi	MVGR College of Engineering, India
Manne Suneetha	VR Siddhartha Engineering College, India
Sumalatha Lingamgunta	JNTU Kakinada, India
Kalaiarasi Sonai Muthu Anbananthen	Multimedia University, Malaysia
K. Subramanian	IIT Kanpur, India
Singaraju Jyothi	Sri Padmavati Mahila Visvavidyalayam, India
Vinit Jakhetiya	IIT Jammu, India
Yashwantsinh Jadeja	Marwadi University, India
Harsh Dev	PSIT, India
Yashodhara V. Haribhakta	Government College of Engineering, India
Gopal Sakarkar	GHRCE, India
R. Gnanadass	Pondicherry Engineering College, India
K. Giri Babu	VVIT, India
Geeta Sikka	B R Ambedkar National Institute of Technology, India
Gaurav Varshney	IIT Jammu, India
G. L. Prajapati	Devi Ahilya University, India
G. Kishor Kumar	RGMCET, India
Md. Saidur Rahman	Bangladesh University of Engineering and Technology, Bangladesh

Wali Khan Mashwani	Kohat University of Science & Technology, Pakistan
Krishna Kiran Vamsi Dasu	Sri Sathya Sai Institute, India
Sisira Kumar Kapat	Utkal Gaurav Madhusudan Institute of Technology, India
Kuldeep Sharma	Chitkara University, India
Zankhana H. Shah	BVM Engineering College, India
Rekha Ramesh	Shah and Anchor Kutchhi Engineering College, India
Gopalkrishna Joshi	KLE Technological University, India
Ganga Holi	AMC Engineering College, India
K. Kotecha	Symbiosis International, India
Radhakrishna Bhat	MAHE, India
Kuldeep Singh	Carnegie Mellon University, USA
Binod Kumar	JSPM's Rajarshi Shahu College of Engineering, India
Raju Kumar	Chandigarh University, India
Nitin S. Goje	Webster University in Tashkent, Uzbekistan
Pushpa Mala S.	Dayananda Sagar University, India
Ashish Sharma	GLA University, India
Ashwath Rao B.	Manipal Institute of Technology, India
Deepak Motwani	Amity University, India
V. Sowmya	Amrita School of Engineering, India
Jayashri Nair	VNR VJIET, India
Rajesh C. Sanghvi	G.H. Patel College of Engineering & Technology, India
Ashwin Dobariya	Marwadi University, India
Tapas Kumar Patra	CET Bhubaneswar, India
J. Naren	Rathinam College of Arts and Science, India
Rekha. K. S.	National Institute of Engineering, India
Mohammed Murtuza Qureshi	Digital Employment Exchange, India
Vasantha Kalyani David	Avinashilingam Institute for Home Science and Higher Education for Women, India
K. Sakthidasan	Hindustan Institute of Technology and Science, India
Shreyas Rao	Sahyadri College of Engineering and Management, India
Hiranmayi Ranganathan	Lawrence Livermore National Laboratory, USA
Sanjaya Kumar Panda	National Institute of Technology Warangal, India
Puspanjali Mohapatra	IIIT Bhubaneswar, India
Manimala Mahato	Shah & Anchor Kutchhi Engineering College, India

B. Senthil Kumar   Kumaraguru College of Technology Coimbatore, India
Jyoti Prakash Singh   National Institute of Technology Patna, India
Abhinav Tomar   Netaji Subhas University of Technology, India
M. G. Sumithra   Dr. N.G.P. Institute of Technology, India

Contents – Part I

Contents – Part II

Disease and Abnormalities Detection Using ML and IOT

Application of Deep Learning in Healthcare

The AI Renaissance: A New Era of Human-Machine Collaboration

Age and Gender Estimation Through Dental X-Ray Analysis

Mokshith Varma Lolakapuri(✉) ⓘ, Samhitha Mallannagari ⓘ,
Koushil Goud Kothagadi ⓘ, Vivek Duraivelu ⓘ, and Pallavi Lanke ⓘ

Department of Computer Science and Engineering, B V Raju Institute of Technology, Narsapur,
Medak, Telangana 502313, India
mokshithvarma02@gmail.com, vivek.d@bvrit.ac.in

Abstract. The most frequently used, long-lasting, and well-preserved human body part in forensic and anthropological investigations is the tooth. The tooth is said to be a great way to determine the biological profile of unidentified remains. A piece of evidence in cases where the recovered dead bodies are mutilated and dismembered beyond recognition, such as bomb blasts, terrorist attacks, airplane crashes, and other mass disasters. Results could not be available for many days while forensic experts use their skills to manually determine each person's age and gender. A fully automated method was developed to ascertain the age and gender of a person based on digital images of their teeth. The procedure of determining gender and age from images of individuals is done methodically since teeth are a strong and unique part of the human body that persists for a longer length of time and exhibits less sensitivity to change in its natural structure. Dental evidence is regarded as valuable for determining sex when other body parts are insufficient, critical to the body, or unavailable. The main techniques for determining sex from teeth are visual/clinical, microscopic, and sophisticated techniques. This review article covered the difficulties and approaches like GNN which is used for sex determination from teeth.

Keywords: Forensic odontology · Teeth · Sex determination

1 Introduction

Modern medical technology makes it easier for doctors to precisely evaluate a patient's condition and prescribe the best course of treatment. The most recent work included digital radiographs of teeth, typically referred to as orthopantomograms (OPG), as input for human gender identification and age evaluation [1]. Radiologic technology has evolved in numerous ways as a consequence of advancements in technology in the discipline of medicine, including radiographic fluoroscopy, molecular imaging, and digital imaging. Because the traditional approach used by forensic experts to identify individuals takes too long and fails to produce precise outcomes, an entirely automated system for human identification has been developed.

The human body is prone to undergoing changes during the course of a lifetime as a result of any external factors or internal metabolism changes. Due to their hardness and

D. Garg et al. (Eds.): IACC 2023, CCIS 2053, pp. 3–12, 2024.
https://doi.org/10.1007/978-3-031-56700-1_1

slow metabolism, teeth are the only structure in this situation that will not be harmed by any factors. Dental X-ray scans can help with identification and are regarded as good material for genetic research, odonatology, anthropology, and forensic analysis in populations that are alive or dead [2, 3]. Images of a person's teeth can be used for identification with more accuracy than any other human body part. The manual investigation procedure in forensic dentistry is aided by the depictions of dental eruption factors and tooth growth stages in some atlases. In the context of civil law, forensic medicine identification of a person is both difficult and sensitive. Therefore, predictions made using the anatomical characteristics of teeth should be made with more precision [4]. Teeth scans must be obtained from dental colleges, hospitals, or clinics with X-ray imaging equipment as they are not available to the general public.

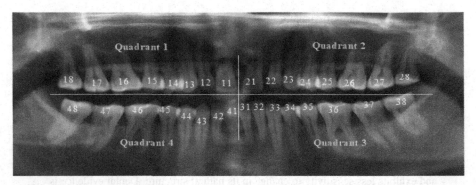

Fig. 1. FDI nomenclature illustrated on a panoramic radiograph.

A division of dentistry known as forensic odontology is dedicated to the scientific investigation of the architecture of teeth, which should be handled with care. It also examines tooth eruption as a means of determining age and gender. There are numerous methods for estimating age, including odonatological and skeletal studies, anthropological and radiological methods, and anthropological investigations.

In the provided visual representation [Fig. 1], denoting FDI dental labeling on an adult panoramic dental image, the image is partitioned into four distinct quadrants. These quadrants are identified as the upper right quadrant (referred to as Q1), the upper left quadrant (referred to as Q2), the lower left quadrant (referred to as Q3), and the lower right quadrant (referred to as Q4.Evaluation is typically conducted in a clockwise direction [5]. Each quadrant contains teeth numbered from 1 to 8, starting from the midline and progressing towards the distal end. For instance, a tooth in the upper right quadrant may be referred to as 'tooth number 18,' while a tooth in the lower left quadrant might be designated as 'tooth number 38.'

'A full set of teeth in the adult human mouth typically consists of a total of 32 teeth.

Human teeth can be classified into two sections: the upper jaw (known as the maxillary) and the lower jaw (known as the mandible). Each of these jaws contains 8 teeth on both the left and right sides [1]. These teeth are assigned identification numbers through both a universal numbering system and the Palmer numbering system, as detailed in Table 1, which presents an overview of the tooth numbering systems.

Table 1. Numbering system and names of teeth.

		Maxillary jaw (upper jaw)			Mandibular jaw (lower jaw)		
		Universal numbering	Palmer numbering system	Tooth name	Universal numbering	Palmer numbering system	Tooth name
Right	1		Up. Rt. 8	3rd molar	32	L. Rt. 1	3rd molar
	2		Up. Rt. 7	2nd molar	31	L. Rt. 2	2nd molar
	3		Up. Rt. 6	1st molar	30	L. Rt. 3	1st molar
	4		Up. Rt. 5	2nd premolar	29	L. Rt. 4	2nd premolar
	5		Up. Rt. 4	1st premolar	28	L. Rt. 5	1st premolar
	6		Up. Rt. 3	Canine	27	L. Rt. 6	Canine
	7		Up. Rt. 2	Lateral incisor	26	L. Rt. 7	Lateral incisor
	8		Up. Rt. 1	Central incisor	25	L. Rt. 8	Central incisor
Left	9		Up. Lt. 1	Central incisor	24	L. Lt. 8	Central incisor
	10		Up. Lt. 2	Lateral incisor	23	L. Lt. 7	Lateral incisor
	11		Up. Lt. 3	Canine	22	L. Lt. 6	Canine
	12		Up. Lt. 4	1st premolar	21	L. Lt. 5	1st premolar
	13		Up. Lt. 5	2nd premolar	20	L. Lt. 4	2nd premolar
	14		Up. Lt. 6	1st molar	19	L. Lt. 3	1st molar
	15		Up. Lt. 7	2nd molar	18	L. Lt. 2	2nd molar
	16		Up. Lt. 8	3rd molar	17	L. Lt. 1	3rd molar

Among human teeth, the cuspids or eyeteeth exhibit notable sexual differences compared to other teeth. This paper's principal objective is to offer up-to-date information and highlight developing patterns in the domain. It aims to address research deficiencies pertaining to the utilization of machine learning methods for age and gender identification, focusing on both current data and emerging trends. These teeth are naturally robust and less susceptible to disease [6]. Currently, medical image analysis, including the study of tooth dimensions and craniofacial morphologies, is a prominent area of research. Traditionally, forensic experts have manually assessed gender and age differences based on these dental characteristics.

2 Literature Survey

Numerous researchers have primarily focused on manual methods for gender and age identification based on dental attributes, but only a limited number have ventured into leveraging machine learning and computer vision technologies. In this domain, we will briefly discuss recent research endeavors that showcase various methodologies, technical intricacies, and significant contributions to the field of age and gender prediction.

Denis Milosevic et al. [1] introduced a model using Convolutional Neural Networks (CNNs) for age and gender prediction. They utilized hyperparameter search techniques, with Grid search demonstrating superior performance. Within their work, Nicolas Vila-Blanco and co-authors (Citation [2]) put forward a model that makes use of deep learning neural networks and Convolutional Neural Networks (CNNs) for the purpose of estimating chronological age.

In 2020, Saloni and colleagues [3] developed an approach utilizing digital dental images to distinguish individuals by assessing the morphometric attributes of the mandibular ramus across a sample of 250 orthopantomogram (OPG) images. Their study investigated the mandibular ramus as a potential indicator for gender determination within this particular population, with the application of discriminant function analysis highlighting significant sexual dimorphism. In the year 2020, Poornima Vadala and her collaborators [4] presented a method that focused on the permanent mandibular teeth located on the left side of the jaw. Their research was geared towards achieving precise age estimation by employing the Camerer method with Indian-specific formulas on both the left and right sides of the mandibular teeth.

In 2020, Okkesim and Erhamza [5] carried out a study centered on the identification of human gender by assessing the mandibular ramus. Their research underscored the importance of mandibular teeth in gender determination, considering that the mandible bone stands out as the largest, most sexually dimorphic, and robust bone in the skull. It's worth noting that recent studies have underscored the advantages of cone-beam computed tomography (CBCT) compared to conventional methods.

Collectively, these varied studies make significant contributions to the progress of gender and age prediction using dental characteristics. They encompass a spectrum of techniques, spanning from conventional methods to state-of-the-art deep learning approaches.

3 Methodology and Design

3.1 Graphic Convolutional Networks

Graph Convolutional Networks (GCNs) have emerged as a prominent class of Graph Neural Networks (GNNs) in the realm of machine learning, finding widespread applications in domains such as social network analysis, recommendation systems, and bioinformatics. GCNs are tailored for tasks involving data organized as graphs, where entities are denoted as nodes and their interactions are depicted through edges. An integral facet of GCNs is the graph convolution operation, a core mechanism that empowers them to harness the graph's structure for information processing and predictive tasks.

At the heart of GCN lies a fundamental equation that characterizes the graph convolution operation for a node (v) in the context of layer $(l + 1)$:

$$h_v^{(l+1)} = \sigma \left(\sum_{u \in N(v)} \frac{1}{\sqrt{d_v \cdot d_u}} \cdot h_u^{(l)} \right)$$

where,

$h_v^{(l+1)}$ = updated feature representation for node v in the (l + 1) layer.

$h_u^{(l)}$ = feature representation of a neighboring node u in the (l) layer.

N(v) = set of neighboring nodes connected to node v.

d_v and d_u = degrees of nodes v and u respectively, which signify the number of connections each node maintains.

σ = activation function, often ReLU, applied element-wise to the computed result.

This equation encapsulates the essence of GCNs. It enables the model to iteratively update a node's feature representation by aggregating information from its neighboring nodes while considering the graph's structure. By performing this operation across multiple layers, GCNs can capture information at various scales and excel in tasks such as node classification and semi-supervised learning, especially when dealing with limited labeled data.

3.2 Criteria for Selecting Radiographs

The criteria for selecting patients' radiographs were as follows:

a. Only panoramic radiographs of high quality, considering factors such as angulation, contrast, and proper positioning, were eligible for inclusion in this study.
b. Selected radiographs had to be free from any artifacts.
c. Radiographs were required to exhibit no developmental anomalies of teeth that were associated with variations in size, shape, or structure of teeth.

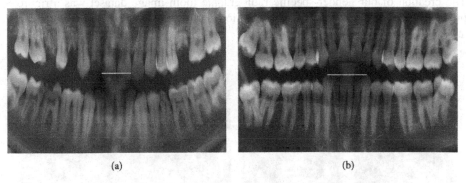

(a)   (b)

Fig. 2. (a) Central incisor teeth measurement. (b) Intercanine measurement.

However, there are three major limitations to GCN's original proposal:

1. By relaxing the assumption of a 'fixed point,' we can employ a Multi-layer Perceptron (MLP) to attain a more consistent representation, eliminating the need for iterative updates. This is achieved because the original proposal's multiple iterations rely on the same parameters for the transition function 'f,' while the diverse parameters across different layers of the MLP facilitate hierarchical feature extraction.

2. However, this approach falls short in processing information derived from the edges. For instance, in a knowledge graph, distinct edges may signify different relationships between nodes, which the method can't effectively account for.
3. The reliance on a fixed point can stifle the diversification of node distributions, making it unsuitable for scenarios where the objective is to learn diverse representations of nodes.

To tackle the mentioned problem, various GCN variations have been suggested.

The odontometric features chosen for the examination and evaluation of gender and age encompass:

Incisor Width: We conducted an analysis and measurement of the width of central incisors in both the mandibular and maxillary regions. Significantly, there are variations in the measurement of incisors in the mandibular region that distinguish between males and females.

Intercanine Distance: We conducted measurements for the intercanine distance, which involved assessing the space between the canines in both the maxillary and mandibular jaws. This intercanine distance is precisely the measurement between teeth numbered 13 and 23 in the maxillary jaw and between teeth numbered 33 and 43 in the mandibular jaw. For a visual representation of this process, please refer to Figs. 2(a) and 2(b), which provide examples of the measurement procedure for maxillary incisor teeth and the mandibular intercanine distance.

4 Dataset Collection

The creation of our gender-specific radiographic tooth image dataset was a rigorous process. We collaborated with dental institutions and clinics, ensuring ethical compliance and data privacy (Figs. 3 and 4).

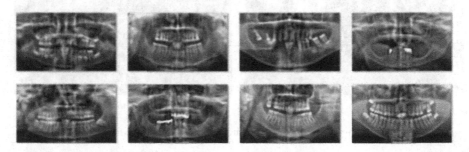

Fig. 3. Sample PDR images of female patients by gender

The collected images underwent quality improvements and standardization. We categorized images into male and female groups, annotated metadata, and conducted rigorous quality checks. To benefit the research community, we're developing a user-friendly platform for dataset access and scalability, fostering advancements in dental research and healthcare applications.

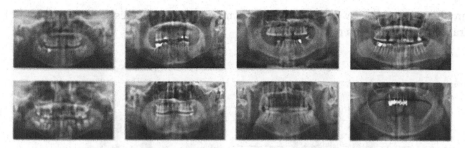

Fig. 4. Sample PDR images of male patients by gender

5 Experiment Analysis

Our project revolves around the creation of a fully automated system with the primary goal of predicting human gender based on age estimation. This system exclusively relies on orthopantomograms (OPG) of teeth as its input. Notably, this streamlined model is capable of delivering highly precise results within a minute. In this section, we delve into the classification techniques employed and the outcomes achieved using different kernels and hyperparameters in our classifiers. The Graph Convolutional Network (GCN) plays a pivotal role in age estimation and gender determination.

Preprocessing:
The initial step in our prediction model involves preprocessing the input OPG image to eliminate any unwanted image noise that may have been introduced during image capture. Subsequently, we enhance the image's brightness and quality.

Pixel Brightness Modification:
Brightness transformations are utilized to adjust pixel brightness, with the transformation tailored to pixel characteristics. Contrast enhancement is a fundamental aspect of image processing, particularly in the context of medical images. We utilize the cv2.cvtColor(img, cv2.COLOR BGR2GRAY) function, which leads to an enhanced rendition of the initial image.

Image Segmentation:
Image segmentation is a method applied to break down images into individual segments. In our specific scenario, this process is essential for pinpointing image objects and their boundaries. To accomplish this, we rely on the Canny edge detection algorithm, a pivotal step in ensuring the accurate prediction of both age and gender.

Gender Prediction:
Gender prediction is of significant importance in forensic identification. Traditionally, forensic experts and medical specialists have relied on time-consuming methods for estimating gender, which demanded extensive training and expertise. Our study introduces the GCN model, which leverages deep transfer learning and a fully automated approach to analyze panoramic dental X-ray images. The structural flexibility of the GCN

architecture, coupled with its reduced parameter count, facilitates speedy execution of training and validation processes (Fig. 5).

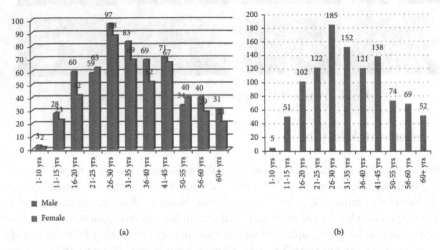

■ Male
■ Female

(a)   (b)

Fig. 5. (a) and (b) Dataset distribution based on gender and age group.

6   Conclusion

In this paper, we developed an easy synthesis image of human faces using textual descriptions of facial traits using the fully trained graph convolutional networks (GCN). The ability to automatically generate realistic images from text has been achieved using graph convolutional networks (GCN). In this work, we use BERT embeddings to embed text in the StyleGAN2 input latent space and manage the generation of facial images from text.

The generated images exhibit excellent image quality, text-to-image similarity, and image diversity according to the qualitative and quantitative experiment results. The image quality and description consistency still need to be improved, however. The images produced show a 57% similarity to the real-world images. The semantic alignment and image quality still need to be improved.

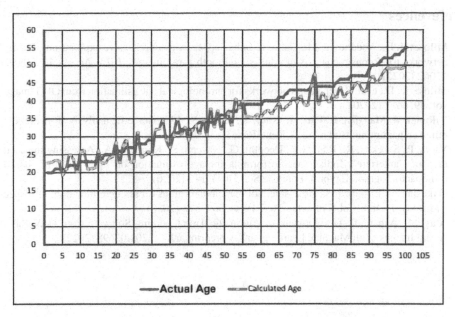

Graph 1. Comparison of calculated age with actual age–Group A

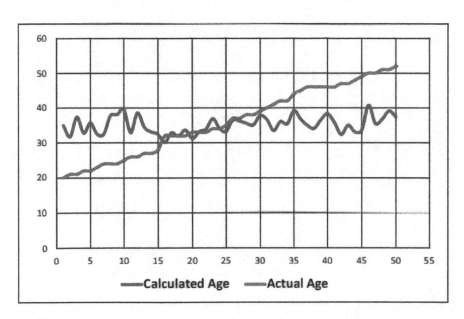

Graph 2. Comparison of calculated age with actual age–Group B

References

1. Milosević, D., Vodanović, M., Galic, I., SubasIc, M.: A comprehensive exploration of neural networks for forensic analysis of adult single tooth x-ray images. IEEE Access **10**, 70980–71002 (2022)
2. Milosevic, D., et al.: Deep neural networks for chronological age estimation from OPG images vol. 39, no. 7 (2020)
3. Saloni, P.V., Mahajan, P., Puri, A., Kaur, S., Mehta, S.: Morphometric analysis of mandibular ramus: a panoramic study. Ind. J. Dent. Res. 31(3) (2020)
4. Vadla, P., Surekha, R., Rao, G.V., Deepthi, G., Naveen, S., Kumar, C.A.: Assessing the accuracy of Cameriere's Indian-specific formula for age estimation on right and left sides of orthopantomogram. Egypt. J. Forensic Sci. **10**(1), 1–6 (2020)
5. Okkesim, A., Erhamza, S.: Assessment of mandibular ramus for sex determination: retrospective study. J. Oral Biol. Craniofac. Res. **10**(4), 569–572 (2020)
6. Ataş, M., Ayhan, T.: Development of Automatic Tree Counting Software from UAV Based Aerial Images With Machine Learning. arXiv preprint arXiv:2201.02698 (2022)

Driver Drowsiness Detection System Using Machine Learning Technique

Neha Paliwal[1] , Renu Bahuguna[2] , Deepika Rawat[1] , Isha Gupta[1] ,
Arjun Singh[3][✉] , and Saurabh Bhardwaj[1]

[1] Raj Kumar Goel Institute of Technology, Ghaziabad 201003, India
[2] COER University, Roorkee, Uttarakhand 247667, India
[3] Greater Noida Institute of Technology, Greater Noida 201310, India
`innovativearjunsingh@gmail.com`

Abstract. Drowsiness and fatigue are significant contributors to road accidents. We can prevent them by ensuring adequate sleep before driving, consuming caffeine, or taking rest breaks when drowsiness symptoms appear Current methods for detecting drowsiness, such as EEG and ECG, are accurate but require contact measurement and have limitations for real-time monitoring while driving. Proposes using eye closing rate and yawning as indicators for detecting drowsiness in drivers, as a non-invasive and comfortable alternative the goal of this paper is to create a non-invasive system that can detect fatigue in humans and provide timely warnings. Long distance drivers who tend to not take breaks in between are always at a high risk of drowsiness. The primary behavioral indicators used in the suggested technique are the driver's yawning and eye blinking. The purpose of this Problem is to alert the driver by detecting yawning via closed eyes or an opened mouth.

Keywords: Tensor Flow · Machine Learning · EEG

1 Introduction

Although people are drowsy, they have trouble remaining awake, even while accomplishing things. The circadian cycle, which regulates when the body sleeps and when it wakes up, is associated with this. Consequently, it has little to do with getting things done. The human body has a natural tendency to sleep more heavily at some times of the day compared to other times. Because our bodies naturally shift towards sleep and alertness diminishes between midnight and around 6 a.m., this is mostly true throughout the night. Since there is currently no universally accepted methods for gauging alertness, one must instead learn to recognize and interpret the telltale signals of a hyper vigilant driver. Behavioral and physiological indicators both falls within this umbrella [1]. Drowsy drivers pose a threat to everyone on the road, including passengers and pedestrians, and they may be hard to see and prevent. Research on methods for accurately detecting and predicting drowsy driving is, therefore, essential for the improvement of transportation security. Driver drowsiness detection systems include a lot of various aspects that most

D. Garg et al. (Eds.): IACC 2023, CCIS 2053, pp. 13–23, 2024.
https://doi.org/10.1007/978-3-031-56700-1_2

researchers may make use of. According to Dua et al. (2021), surveillance frequently involves combining information about the driver's behavior and physiological markers with information gathered from the vehicle The Ministry of Road Transport and Highways has implemented mandatory rest periods for commercial vehicle drivers and issued guidelines for safer driving practices. Additionally, technology-based solutions, such as the facial expression detection system mentioned earlier, are being explored to detect and prevent driver fatigue [2]. While India's automobile industry continues to thrive, the safety of road users must remain a top priority. The statistics reveal the gravity of the situation, with drowsiness emerging as a significant factor in road accidents. Through concerted efforts by the government, agencies, and the public at large, it is possible to mitigate the risks posed by driver fatigue and ensure safer roads for everyone. Since it is now well acknowledged that sleepy driving is a key contributor to accidents and traffic fatalities, driver drowsiness detection technologies have attracted a lot of interest. Drowsy driving, which can impede a driver's ability to respond quickly and make wise decisions, is the act of operating a vehicle while feeling drowsy or weary [3]. Researchers and automakers have been creating and adopting driver drowsiness detection technologies to improve road safety after realizing the risks of driving when fatigued. In order to identify indicators of sleepiness and notify drivers in a timely manner, these systems monitor driver behavior, physiological signals, and vehicle data using cutting-edge technology and algorithms. A driver drowsiness detection system uses various technologies, such as cameras, sensors, and machine learning algorithms, to detect signs of drowsiness in a driver and alert them to take a break. Different types of Driver drowsiness detection measure given below in Fig. 1.

1.1 Causes of Drowsiness While Driving

Driving when fatigued can result from a variety of Circumstances. Lack of Sleep, Sleep disorders, Alcohol, Medications, Time of day.

1.2 Monotonous or Boring Driving Conditions

Driver weariness and decreased attentiveness can be caused by long lengths of dull road, repeated driving activities, or unattractive locations. This might increase the chance of driving when fatigued, particularly on highways or during lengthy.

1.3 Precautionary Measures to Control Drowsiness

In order to avoid or reduce sleepy driving conditions, many tactics and interventions are used in driver drowsiness control. Making sure drivers receive enough rest and sleep before getting behind the wheel is one of the key components of sleepiness control. The probability of becoming sleepy while driving can be considerably decreased by getting 7–8 h of decent sleep. Additionally, taking frequent stops during lengthy drives enables drivers to relax and rejuvenate themselves, preventing the buildup of weariness.

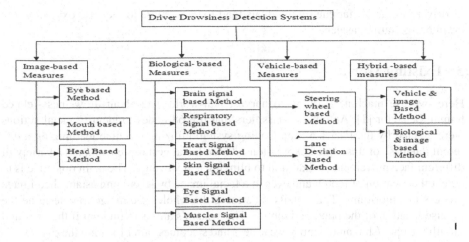

Fig. 1. Driver drowsiness detection measures

2 Literature Survey

Look at the past studies done on driver drowsiness detection systems some of the key components of a driver drowsiness detection system. Accidents happen for a variety of reasons, including the driver being ill, the driver being inebriated, the environment of the sick passenger, the lack of appropriate pauses or relaxation, the driver having mental disorders, the driver being an uneducated driver, etc. The causes of these issues can be boiled down to two types of circumstances: A tired or sleepy motorist, or a negligent driver. Drowsiness can have a number of detrimental implications on a motorist, including loss of coordination, errors in signal or turn judgment, and a delay in reaction time. While each of these elements is crucial for safe driving, losing any one of them can have serious consequences and potentially result in an accident [3]. As is common knowledge, issues arise when drivers don't stop and relax, and there is no other way to address this issue. As a result, it is currently a hot topic for research. The goal is to create a system that warns the driver in these circumstances. The alert tone rings if the driver is sleepy or preoccupied. When the tone makes them aware that they are distracted, a driver can focus again on the road and the controls. Similar to this, a sleepy driver can be awakened by the tone and take the appropriate action. The system's aim is to determine whether the eyes and mouth are open/closed and identify fatigue and drowsiness after locating the eye's position. Reducing road accidents caused by driver fatigue and drowsiness is critical, as they account for a significant proportion of such incidents. It aims to contribute to these efforts by leveraging image processing algorithms to detect drowsiness and fatigue in drivers. The early detection of a driver's drowsiness and alertness is an effective strategy for preventing. The development of technology to identify and prevent drowsiness is a significant problem in the area of casualty prevention structure. By closely monitoring the eyes of the driver, signs of drowsiness can be found early, which may help to prevent accidents. Yawning detection is also used as a measure of driver fatigue, as fatigued individuals tend to yawn more to increase oxygen to the brain before falling asleep.

3   Existing Work

Here, we use machine learning to harvest real-world data about drowsiness-related human behavior [1]. Automatic classifiers that use 68 nodes to identify facial actions were created by the Facial Action Coding system utilizing machine learning on a different database of unscripted expressions. These facial gestures encompass a variety of different face movements in addition to blinking and yawning. The main objective is to detect the location of mouth and eyes in a facial image by leveraging established image processing algorithms. This entails examining the whole face image to determine the precise location of the pupil and mouth. The system's aim is to find out if the eyes and mouth are open/shut and identify weariness and sleepiness after locating the eye's position. Reducing road accidents caused by driver fatigue and drowsiness is critical, as they account for a significant proportion of such incidents. To this end, extensive research has been conducted with a vision of developing safe driving systems that can help lower the frequency of incidents.

3.1   Fatigue and Drowsiness

Any day, most accidents caused by sleepy driving may be avoided with the best use of these strategies in automobiles. A major social problem is the increasing number of traffic accidents that occur as a result of drivers becoming less attentive. Statistically, drivers who aren't paying attention account for 20% of all traffic accidents. In addition, accidents caused by drivers who are hypo-vigilant are more deadly than others since sleepy drivers don't always pay attention and don't take enough safety measures before a crash. Therefore, it is vital to avert accidents by developing systems to check drivers' concentration and alert them when they are weary and not paying attention to the road. Additionally, it will use alcohol pulse detection to ascertain the person's normalcy. When people are exhausted, it shows in their head, eyes, lips, and overall facial features.

3.2   Drowsiness Detection Using Face Detection System

The software then uses complex learning algorithms to compare a current image to the stored face print in order to verify the person's identity [6, 7]. According to references [8, 9], and [10], you can tell if someone is sleepy by looking at their face Reference [10] outlines 4 types of movements of eyelid that can be utilized for detecting drowsiness: completely open, completely closed, and transitional stages between open and closed. To detect drowsiness; the algorithm converts the captured images to grayscale, reducing them to black and white, as noted in references [11] and [12]. Using black and white images simplifies the process, requiring measurement of only two parameters. The algorithm then carries out edge identification to identify the boundaries of the eyes and calculate the area of the eyelids This can lead to false alarms or missing real drowsiness events, which can decrease the reliability of the system. This work will go over the strategy employed to accomplish the primary goals and will focus specifically on the implementation. Analyzing every stage will be important to finish this job. At each step until the project is finished, every decision and result of the method employed will be thoroughly discussed. The Anaconda IDE and PyCharm IDE were the programmes used in this study. OpenCV and Dlib are the algorithms used to identify the face, eyes, and mouth region. The face is identified using the Haar Adaboost face detection algorithm. Face detection is followed by the marking of facial markers on the image, such as the location of the eyes, nose, and mouth. The functions of the eyes and mouth are calculated based on these landmarks. By using eye blinking, convolutional neural networks can categorise eyes and detect tiredness in drivers.Additionally, a number of variables, including sleep disturbances, medicines, and underlying medical diseases, might have an impact on the presence and intensity of drowsy symptoms as shown in Fig. 2. To prevent accidents and advance road safety, it is essential to identify and treat tiredness early on. The hazards of sleepy driving can be reduced and the safety of the driver and other road users can be ensured by recognizing the signs and taking the necessary action, such as taking pauses, resting, or taking a little nap [15].

Fig. 2. Driver in Drowsy State

3.3 Percentage of Eye Closure

One sleepiness detection technique is measuring blinks of an eye and the percentage of eye closure (PERCLOS). Reference [10] suggests a technique that involves learning the pattern of eyelid closure duration for detecting eye blinks. Reference [8] states that this method calculates the time it takes a person to close their eyes. As stated in [8], the typical duration for an eye blink is approximately 310.3 ms. To detect drowsiness, the PERCLOS method calculates the percentage of eyelid "droopiness" by measuring how long the eyelids are shut for. This is calculated as: Per close = [Closed eye time/(Closed eye time + Open eye time)] * 100.T o differentiate between fully open and fully closed eyes, a software library stores sets of open and closed eyes. As the driver becomes drowsy, their eyelids will drop for longer durations, allowing the transition of drowsiness to be monitored. According to PERCLOS, when the eyes are 80% closed, it is assumed that the driver is drowsy, as stated in references [4, 8], and [16]. The eye blink pattern method and PERCLOS method for detecting drowsiness share a common issue, which is the requirement for the camera to be positioned at a precise angle to capture clear images or videos without interference from eyebrows and shadows that obscure the eyes.

3.4 EEG

To conduct this procedure, the scalp is covered in tiny metal discs with delicate wires called electrodes. These electrodes detect the minuscule electrical charges produced by the brain cells' activity, which are amplified and displayed on a computer screen as a graph or printed on paper as a recording. This is an implementation of a drowsy driver detection system. It continuously captures frames from a webcam, detects faces in the frames, and analyzes the person's eye movements to determine whether they are drowsy or alert. Wearable sensors along with additional technological devices may detect signs of drowsiness in the driver. We can assess the driver's condition by monitoring their vital signs, which include their heart rate, blood pressure, brain function, and body temperature. To detect drowsiness and improve performance in this area, three significant signals are electroencephalography (EEG), electrooculography (EOG), and electrocardiograms (ECG) [(Barua et al. 2019]. However, it may not be a viable option for monitoring driver drowsiness in everyday driving situations due to the inconvenience of wearing a device with wires on the head, which could easily come loose if the driver moves their head [4].

3.5 Yawning Detection Method

A driver's drowsiness can be analyzed by observing their face and behavior. The suggested approach entails identifying drowsiness by analyzing the position of the mouth and processing images using a cascade of classifiers based on the Viola-Jones method for facial detection. The images are then compared with a set of data for yawning [17]. One obstacle in this method is that some people put their hand over the mouth while yawning, which can make it difficult to get good images. However, yawning is a clear sign of drowsiness and fatigue show in Fig. 3.

Fig. 3. Yawning Detection

The duration of eye blinks demonstrates that the longer someone shuts their eyes, the drowsier they are considered to be. Someone who is sleepy will have their pupils closed for a longer period of time than usual. Additionally, yawning is a symptom of drowsiness and a normal human response when feeling drowsy or fatigued.

4 Proposed Work

These systems can be implemented in a variety of ways, such as in-vehicle cameras, sensors, and wearable devices. Detection methods are divided into two parts 1. Performances 2. Condition.There are two distinct categories of methods used to determine the status of the driver show in Fig. 4.

a. Utilize physiological signals b. Employ synthetic vision methods.

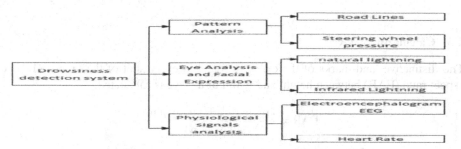

Fig. 4. Different Methods to recognize Sleepiness

4.1 Challenges

1. The ability to accurately detect drowsiness in all drivers and all driving conditions.
2. The ability to distinguish drowsiness from other factors that may affect driver performance.
3. Such as distraction, stress, or illness.
4. The ability to provide alerts that are not disruptive or distracting to the driver.
5. The need for privacy concerns in implementing such systems.
6. The topic of driver drowsiness detection is an active area of research with many ongoing developments and research [18, 19].

4.2 Material and Methods

We will be utilizing Open CV to capture pictures using a webcam and pass those to a DL model for classification of the person's eye state, whether it is 'Open' or 'Closed'. The subsequent actions will be implemented:

1. Capture image input from the camera.
2. Detect the face and eyes.
3. Create a ROI for the detected face and eyes.

4. Feed the region of interest to our classifier model for eye state classification.
5. Finally, we will calculate the duration of eye closure to determine if the person is drowsy or not discuss in Fig. 5.

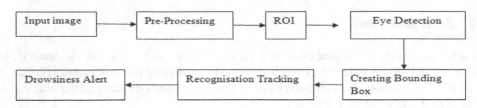

Fig. 5. Method Used For Driver Drowsiness

4.3 Calculating EAR

The distinctive land-marks of the eyes are found in every shot of the video. The eye aspect ratio (EAR) between height and width of the eye is calculated.

$$EAR = \frac{\|p2 - p6\| + \|p3 - p5\|}{2\|p1 - p4}$$

Fig. 6. Eye Aspect Ratio (EAR)

Here p1, p2, p3, p4, p5 and p6 are the 2D landmark locations. When an eye is open, the EAR is typically constant, and when an eye is closed, it approaches zero. The proposed method exhibits partial insensitivity to variations in head and body posture [20]. The proportions of an open eye demonstrates minimal differences across individuals and remains unaffected by uniform scaling or movement of one's face in level, given that blinking discuss in above Fig. 6.

Occurs simultaneously in each eye, the average eye aspect ratio (EAR) is computed.

5 Experimental Results

Let's discuss the results in Table 1 and Figs. 6 and 7. Analysis after applying our method of calculating sleepiness. It is difficult to get the necessary data for an accurate system evaluation, because of the fact that occurrences of hazardous drowsiness may not be guaranteed to happen during regular driving, which could provide difficulties when evaluating apps (Table 2 and Fig. 8).

Table 1. Recognition levels for sleepiness Parameters in typical circumstances

Test	Number of Observation	Number of Hits	Percentage of hits
Blink Detection	200	195	97.5%
Eye aspect ratio	200	193	96.5%
Yawn Detection	200	162	81%
Front Nodding	200	177	88.5%
Assent of head to left	200	193	96.5%
Assent of heads to right	200	190	95%

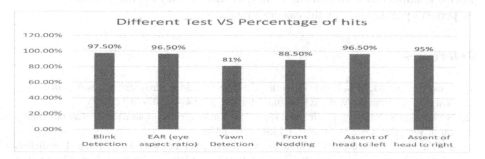

Fig. 7. Different Trials vs. Percentage of Hit

Table 2. Recognition thresholds for certain sleepiness Characteristics under particular circumstances.

Test	Number of Observation	Number of Hits	Percentage of hits
Driver with cap	1000	910	91%
Driver with glasses	1000	670	67%

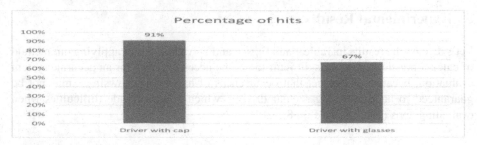

Fig. 8. Percentage of Hit (when driver's face covered vs. driver's face not covered)

6 Conclusion

The main purpose was to make a communicable system that detects fatigue in drivers and provides timely warnings to prevent accidents. By monitoring the driver's eyes using a camera and algorithm, this system aims to help prevent serious motorway accidents caused by drowsy driving. Talks about the use of Facial Landmarks and EAR (Eye Aspect Ratio) to get good results. One of the limitations is that the system may have difficulty handling multiple faces in the view of the lens. This can lead to incorrect or undesired output and also slows down the speed of detection because the system has to process multiple faces. To avoid this, the system should be designed to ensure that only the person's profile is within the camera's range.

References

1. Chacon-Murguia, M.I., Prieto-Resendiz, C.: Detecting driver drowsiness: a survey of system designs and technology. IEEE Consum. Electron. Mag **4**(4), 107–119 (2015)
2. Nordbakke, S., Sagberg, F.: Sleepy at the wheel: Knowledge, symptoms and behaviour among car drivers. Res. Gate 1–10 (2007). ISSN 1369-8478
3. de Naurois, C.J., Bourdin, C., Stratulat, A., Diaz, E., Vercher, J.L.: Detection and prediction of driver drowsiness using artificial neural network models. Accid. Anal. Prev. **126**, 95–104 (2019)
4. Arefnezhad, S., Hamet, J., Eichberger, A., et al.: Driver drowsiness estimation using EEG signals with a dynamical encoder–decoder modeling framework. Sci. Rep. **12**, 2650 (2022)
5. Arefnezhad, S., Samiee, S., Eichberger, A., Nahvi, A.: Driver drowsiness detection based on steering wheel data applying adaptive neuro-fuzzy feature selection. Sensors **19**(4), 943 (2019)
6. Fu, R., Wang, H., Zhao, W.: Dynamic driver fatigue detection using hidden Markov model in real driving condition. Expert Syst. Appl. **63**, 397–411 (2016)
7. Li, G., Chung, W.Y.: Detection of driver drowsiness using wavelet analysis of heart rate variability and a support vector machine classifier. Sensors **13**(12), 16494–16511 (2013)
8. Kristensen, F., Hedberg, H., Jiang, H., Nilsson, P., Öwall, V.: An embedded real-time surveillance system: implementation and evaluation. J. Sig. Process. Syst. **52**, 75–94 (2008)
9. Chand, H.V., Karthikeyan, J.: CNN based driver drowsiness detection system using emotion analysis. Intell. Autom. Soft Comput. **31**(2), 717–728 (2022)

10. Babu, A., Nair, S., Sreekumar, K.: Driver's drowsiness detection system using Dlib HOG. In: Karuppusamy, P., Perikos, I., García Márquez, F.P. (eds.) Ubiquitous Intelligent Systems. SIST, vol. 243, pp. 219–229. Springer, Singapore (2022). https://doi.org/10.1007/978-981-16-3675-2_16

11. Zhao, Z., Zhou, N., Zhang, L., Yan, H., Xu, Y., Zhang, Z.: Driver fatigue detection based on convolutional neural networks using EM-CNN. Comput. Intell. Neurosci. **2020**, 11 (2020). Article ID 7251280

12. Caryn, F.H., Rahadianti, L.: Driver drowsiness detection based on drivers' physical behaviours: a systematic literature review. Comput. Eng. Appl. J. **10**(3), 161–175 (2021)

13. Albadawi, Y., Takruri, M., Awad, M.: A review of recent developments in driver drowsiness detection systems. Sensors **22**(5), 2069 (2022)

14. Choudhary, Y., Aggarwal, A., Agarwal, A.: Detecting drivers' drowsiness using Haar cascade classifier. In: 2022 9th International Conference on Computing for Sustainable Global Development (INDIACom), pp. 318–322. IEEE (2022)

15. Pauly, L., Sankar, D.: Detection of drowsiness based on HOG features and SVM classifiers. In: International Conference on Research in Computational Intelligence and Communication Networks (ICRCICN), Kolkata, India, pp. 181–186. IEEE (2015)

16. Altameem, A., Kumar, A., Poonia, R.C., Kumar, S., Saudagar, A.K.J.: Early identification and detection of driver drowsiness by hybrid machine learning. IEEE Access **9**, 162805–162819 (2021)

17. Tamanani, R., Muresan, R., Al-Dweik, A.: Estimation of driver vigilance status using real-time facial expression and deep learning. IEEE Sensors Lett. **5**(5), 1–4 (2021)

18. Abbas, Q., Alsheddy, A.: Driver fatigue detection systems using multi-sensors, smartphone, and cloud-based computing platforms: a comparative analysis. Sensors **21**, 56 (2021)

19. Chinara, S.: Automatic classification methods for detecting drowsiness using wavelet packet transform extracted time-domain features from single-channel EEG signal. J. Neurosci. Methods **347**, 108927 (2021)

20. Dua, M., Singla, R., Raj, S., Jangra, A.: Deep CNN models-based ensemble approach to driver drowsiness detection. Neural Comput. **33**, 3155–3168 (2021)

Facial Expression Recognition: Detection and Tracking

Abhay Bhatia[1]([✉]), Manish Kumar[2], Jaideep Kumar[3], Anil Kumar[4],
and Prashant Verma[1]

[1] Department of Computer Science and Engineering, Roorkee Institute of Technology, Roorkee,
India
dhawan.abhay009@gmail.com
[2] Department of Computer Science and Engineering, Ajay Kumar Garg Engineering College,
Ghaziabad, India
kumar.manish@akgec.ac.in
[3] Department of IoT, Raj Kumar Goel Institute of Technology, Ghaziabad, India
[4] Department of of Information Technology, Ajay Kumar Garg Engineering College,
Ghaziabad, India

Abstract. One of the simplest ways to tell someone else apart from you is by their face. A personal identification system like face recognition may use an individual's traits to identify them. Detection of any Face and Stage are the two stages of process of the face recognition of human, which is used for facial image recognition modal (face recognition) in biometric technology. The Eigen face method and the Fisher face method are the two categories of methods that are frequently used in created facial recognition patterns. Principal Component Analysis (PCA) for countenance is used to reduce the number of faces in three-dimensional space by the Eigen face approach for image facial recognition. Finding the eigenvector that resembled the most crucial Eigen value of the face image was the major goal of applying PCA [1] on face recognition using Eigen faces [2]. Image processing is used in face detection systems with face recognition. This requires mat lab software, which is the required program. Neural networks are categorized as deep learning. Deep learning's foundational component, feature learning, aims to obtain hierarchical information using hierarchical networks in order to address significant issues that previously required artificial design features. The framework used is termed as Deep Learning and it may include n number of significant algorithms.

Keywords: Detection · Tracking · Eigen Values · Face recognition · Machine Learning · PCA · Neural Network

1 Introduction

The task of displaying facial expressions on an image in accordance with features that are several, including such as happiness, anger, surprise, fear, sadness, and many mores, are known as facial expression recognition. Detecting human facial expressions can be used in a variety of contexts, including any kind of protection to sensitive personal data. The primary justification for identifying someone is security. We can recognize the person using a variety of methods, including voice recognition, passwords, retina detection, and finger-print matching. Face expression recognition will be used to determine greater intent. Artificial intelligence also makes use of facial expression. We can tell from this if the person likes or dislikes the goods being promoted by the firm. The person's emotion and intention are discernible.

Pattern recognition [3] and its classification briefly shown by the benefit, greatly from the machine learning [4] and it's the used techniques for it. These features are as the one of the most crucial components for every machine learning system or study of such thing. This study examines the detection and modification of data for support vector machine algorithms. Understanding a person's facial expressions helps us understand their intentions, state of mind, and emotional state. Non-verbal communication, which is a non-verbal method of communication, allows us to decipher various face expressions of emotion. While understanding any information, the power of the face increases. The Facial recognition has drawn a lot of interest of the researchers in this domain that is pattern recognition, psychology impact and the computer recognition. The useful FER is used in a variety of contexts, including augmented reality (AR), virtual reality (VR), education, entertainment, and human-computer interaction.

The task of displaying facial expressions on an image in accordance with several features, that can be considered such as sadness with anger, or fear, or surprise, or with happiness, and like it many more, majorly are known as facial expression recognition or FER.

Detecting human facial expressions can be used in a variety of contexts, including the protection of sensitive personal data. The primary justification for identifying someone is security. We can recognize the person using a variety of methods, including voice recognition, passwords, retina detection, and finger-print matching. Face expression recognition will be used to determine greater intent. Artificial intelligence also makes use of facial expression. We can tell from this if the person likes or dislikes the goods being promoted by the firm. The emotion and intention are obvious.

In numerous contexts requiring personal information or security, human expression recognition is used. It is regarded as a follow-up for detection of the face when it may be necessary of establishment of a second layer of security by recognizing not only the face but also the emotion. It's used to make sure that the object (human) in front of the camera that isn't just as a two-dimensional model or required figure.

We can see that business promotions benefit from expression detection. The majority of businesses rely on how customers react to their offerings and products. Based on the user's image or video, the artificial intelligence system captures as well as identifies the real time emotions too. So, with it help it can also be decided whether the customers are liking the product, given offers or not.

This paper will reveal and help us to detect the face and its time-to- time expressions in the basis of data set that have been used as the matching of the situation.

2   Background

2.1   Application on the Research

Face recognition technology has evolved throughout the years, with roots generally found in the 1960s and 1970s of the previous centuries. The classic face detection technique primarily focuses on the base and the structural properties that a face contains, and consequently the color characteristics of the considered face. By removing landmarks or the features from any photograph of that considered subject's face, some conventional face algorithm that can recognition countenance are used for the process. An algorithm may examine the jaw, cheekbones, eyes, nose, and jaw's relationship to one another. These characteristics are used to look for additional photos with the same characteristics. These kinds of algorithms are frequently complex, demand a lot of computing resources, and may run slowly. Additionally, they may be mistaken if the faces exhibit undeniable emotional reactions.

2.2   Problem Statement and Analysis

A. Face detection, preprocessing of face and face recognition generally are all components of a comprehensive recognition system of any face. Thus, it becomes necessary so that separating the face from the pattern and extract the face region out from the process of face detection. This will give us an idea for the subsequent face and feature extraction. The new ascent of the face in view of the profundity of learning identification techniques, contrasted with the conventional strategy abbreviate the time, yet gives us precision with successfully improvement.

2.3   Recognition of Face

Various approaches that can be used for recognition of faces. There are mainly two approaches that can be used to their cognition problem: Photometric (a view based) and Geometric [5] (a feature based). As a part of research work many of the researchers worked and developed algorithms that are due to their keen interest in the area of recognition of face, there are three out of all which can be seen and can be well-studied in the recognition of the faces. The used algorithms for such Facial Recognition mainly can be categorized into majorly two approaches that can be used:

Feature Based: It completely depends on mathematical connection between the given facial milestones or given spatial setups to these facial highlights.

View Based or stereo: It is used to determine an object's shape from multiple images taken under the various lighting conditions. A gradient map, comprised of an array of surface normal, depicts the recovered object's shape.

The popular algorithm for this process:

a) *Principal Component Analysis [PCA]* [6]
b) *Linear Discriminate Analysis [LDA]*

2.4   Face Detection

Image windows are divided into two sub classes by face detection, with one class including faces. Although there are similarities in faces in the terms of their skin tone, color of it with the age count and facial expression [], it is a challenging task. Different lighting situations, geometric with image quality, partial occlusion and disguise all sort of add to the complexity of the issue. The perfect face detector might be able to identify any of the face in the background, with many illuminations in it.

a) **FACS**

Using the Facial Action Coding System, a facial moment's number can be assigned. The term "action unit" [Fig. 1 Gives the actual unit for each] refers to this quantity. The effect of combining action units is a facial expression [7]. Generally, any action unit describes the alterations that are minute on any face that are muscles of the it also called as facial muscles. For any instance, action units define a face with smile as $6 + 12$, which just have referred to the movements of the AU12 and AU6 muscles, producing a happy face. AU 6 raises the cheeks, and AU 12 pulls the corners of the lips. Determining that which of the facial muscles are mostly used in which expression using the defined coding system for any of the facial action, which depends on the action units. Based on them, modelsthat are real-time based can be created for all.

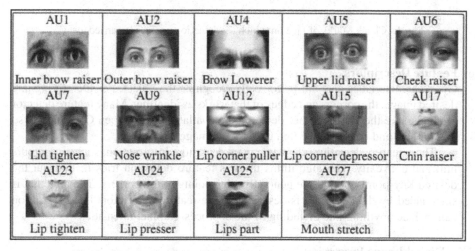

AU1	AU2	AU4	AU5	AU6
Inner brow raiser	Outer brow raiser	Brow Lowerer	Upper lid raiser	Cheek raiser
AU7	AU9	AU12	AU15	AU17
Lid tighten	Nose wrinkle	Lip corner puller	Lip corner depressor	Chin raiser
AU23	AU24	AU25	AU27	
Lip tighten	Lip presser	Lips part	Mouth stretch	

Fig. 1. Unit for actions and their Face movement in Correspondence

b) **Checkmarks**

A mark on the face is exceptionally critical. It is used to recognize and detect faces. Expressions are also marked with a checkmark. The 68 facial checkmark [Fig. 2] detectors in the D lib libraries identify the checkmark's location on the face.

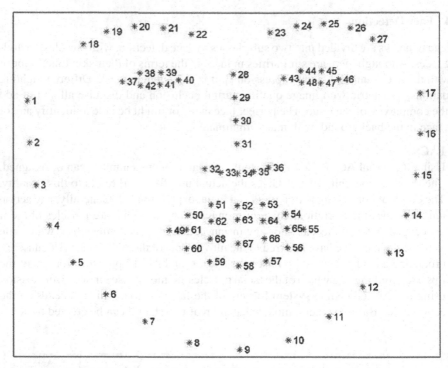

Fig. 2. Check Marks of face on which the detection process is carried away

c) **Feature Descriptors**

Good characteristics also aid in correctly recognize the object. For identifying any desired image, the corners and edges of that works as identifier. Many feature detector methods, like the Harris corner detector, are available in the Open CV libraries so that corners and edges can be find out for any image.

These feature detections display a great deal more information, such as contours hull and convexity. The algorithms used as feature detection tries to find out the desired Key-points, which are generally edge points or the corners. The area that is surrounded by the key-point is described in the feature descriptor. The description can include anything like including of the unprocessed pixel intensities.

2.5 Digital Image Processing

There are two main application areas that are sparking interest in digital image processing techniques:

1. Increasing the quality of visual data for interpretation by human.
2. Data processing can be made for machine perception which is automatic process.

In this second application area, methods for extracting picture data into a format suited for computer processing are of particular relevance.

Applications for automatic character recognition include fingerprint processing, military identification, and industrial machine vision for product inspection and assembly.

The basic elements that are used to perform any image processing task are as:

1. Acquisition of the image
2. Storage of data
3. Processing of image which also includes some preprocessing part
4. Communication Establishment
5. Displaying of the Image
6. Image model for formation of the image

Generally denotation of images/ representation by any 2Df(x, y) and are characterized with amount of source illumination and reflected illumination.

3 Literature Survey

3.1 Method Used for Detection

A newest technology that is known as face detection method locates and measures the face of any human probably as a digital image. Only desired facial features are usually picked up in this. If the digital image excludes any objects other than the human face, such as background details, trees, and buildings, etc. The goal of face localization is to pinpoint the face's location. The basic feature-based and picture-based approaches are the two techniques to identify facial features in an image. The feature base technique seeks to match such images with the features by extracting features from the desired image based on shape, color, grayscale edges, and many other characteristics. Image matching is done using many methods, such as neural networks, linear subspace, PCA, and SVM [8].

3.1.1 Feature Based Approach

Model Active is the form models non-grid features display intricatelike features' true physical characteristics and more advanced appearances. Using facial features like the lips, eyes, mouth, eyebrows and nose, are as examples. Active form Models (ASMs) strive to automatically locate some landmark points that characterize the form of any given item in anyimage. Three categories, namely snakes, PDM, and deformable templates, are used to categories ASMs [9].

3.1.2 Point Distribution Model

These models use only principal components to create which is referred to as a Point Distribution Model that allows constellations mainly for those points shapes that have been received from the training samples gathered by us. The only deformations that ideal point distribution models can undergo are those one that inherent to the required items. The Active Shape Model is the result of the fusion of concepts from statistical shape modeling and image processing (Fig. 3).

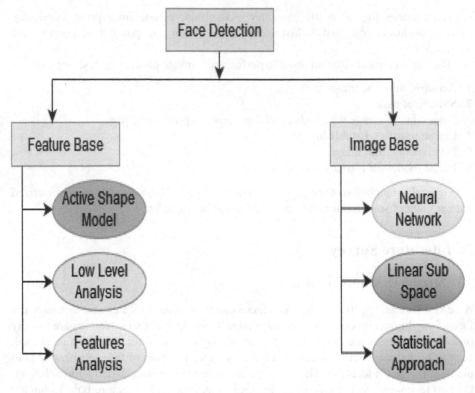

Fig. 3. Face detection process on basis of its features and image

3.2 Research Related Work

A tremendous as well as great research amount, energy and efforts from many of the leading or can say the companies major once with topmost universities are dedicated to this research work field.

In a series of works by Viola, Robust Real-time Object identification [10] is the one that receives the most citations and makes face identification actually practical. By this study, we can learn about face detection techniques and algorithms severally used for. The articles Fast rotation invariant nature with multi-view for detection of the face proposed a more capable as well as developed and useful for detecting multiple faces framework, the next structure mentioned on the cascade structure improvements so have good results, and supported real Adaboost for the first time Adaboosthas been applied in real to object detection. An effective combination of tracking face and detection of it, with both offline model and online model that can be found that in prescribed paper and the tracking is done in Low Frame Rate Video: Discriminative Observers of Different Life Spans with A Cascade Particle Filter is used.

We talked about the issues with face tracking and face detection. We will develop real-time facial detection technologies, per the research. Except for tracking, the major goal is to find the location and size of every face in the picture or video. It's also important to figure out how the many faces in the frame relate to one another.

4 Implementation

4.1 Database Setting for Image Processing

The picture records for the CK+ data set are in a few catalogs and sub-registries upheld the individual and meeting number. Not every image conveys emotion. The format of each and every file was portable networks graphic file (.png). Although they share a name with image files, the emotion labels are located in a different directory. Using the name of the emotion file, we created a small Java utility function to select the appropriate image from the directory and replicate it in our final dataset folder. Additionally, we merged the emotion and image file names. As a result, when we parse our program, we will have the file's emotion label [11, 12].

Taking any example, in the filename S138_001_00000786_7, S138 the main representation is the as provided by subject number, then the session number is to be given and is to be followed by the number of the images in the given session and finally last bit represents the emotion the subject is for posing.

Only frontal face images were used to create the dataset. For a few images, the lighting and illumination were different. Color was added to some images. Regardless

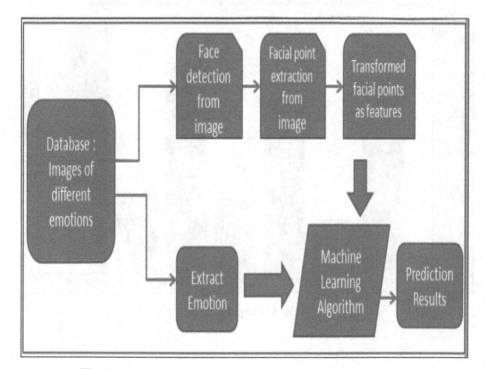

Fig. 4. Working of database while the image transformation is done

of the lighting conditions, all of the pictures had the same processing pipeline. Then the name of that emotion is extracted from the.jpg file name in the RaFD database. As this information base was considered as standard, we had a very fair count of the classes for each of the inclination needed. The distribution between various kind of emotion classes with depicted too are shown in the table [Table 1] (Figs. 4 and 5).

Table 1. Showing images number per class in database CK +

Type of Emotion	Images and their number That depicted the emotion
Surprise	83
Anger	45
Happy	69
Fear	25
Contempt	18
Sadness	28
Disgust	59

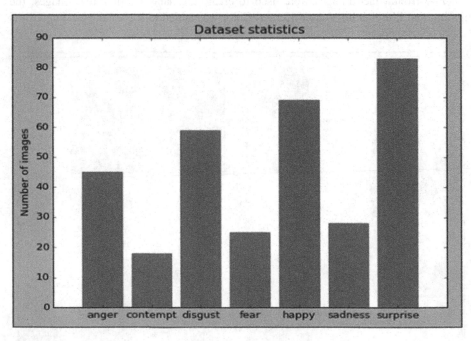

Fig. 5. Output Graph

4.2 Face Detection and Tracking

Face location was the essential and significant a piece of the handling to that pipeline. Before any additional handling, we needed to recognize the face, but if we talk about our pictures that just containing front face facing information. It had been simpler in concern of the region of interest to get determined and the extraction of the itfeatures from it can be done once the face had been identified by t.

We tested a variety of face-detection algorithms and patterns [13], such as Open CV's Haar-cascades, using only the original one image that is generally from the database and

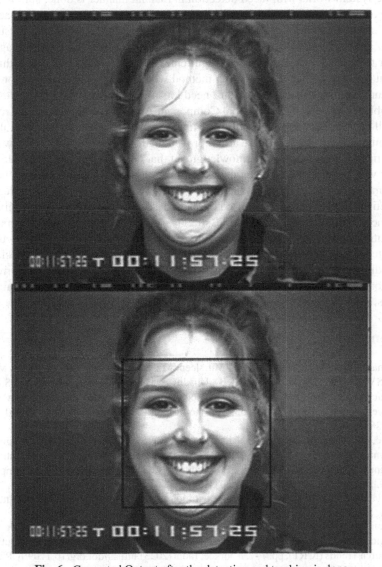

Fig. 6. Generated Output after the detection and tracking is done

the other one is as the identified image of any of the face considered. In the end, we have decided to use a face detector with having base of the histogram so that oriented gradients from the D library can be accessed. HoG descriptors as well as the SVM [14] are used in such a wayso that identifying of the face in the any image can be made easy. Pictures are changed over into the grayscale and resized (Fig. 6).

5 Conclusion

Due to the availability of Eigen Face [15] with a limited count used in the PCA transform, the system works with faced detection in manual manner is done, automatic face recognition or artificial intelligence [16, 17] based did not have a recognition accuracy of more than 90%. This was only because the face recognition and its subsystem did not show any invariance degrees towards the face images scale, segmented image, shift errors or rotations. One of the system requirements that were identified was this. Carrying out an eye for such identification method would be as a minor expansion to that the executed framework and it wouldn't need lots of extra examination to be done. The deformable template and the Principal Component Analysis strategies that are reflected very well in the results during of all other implemented systems, which generally produces commendable results. There are improved methods, for example, acknowledging iris or retina as well as the face acknowledgment that involves the warm rangesto clients or those who have access and can check applications since these requirements are of an extremely serious level of its exactness. We can explore different avenues regarding facial activity coding framework or component descriptors as elements or a mix of the two of them. Applications, for example, sluggishness recognition among drivers can be created utilizing highlight choice and flowing various calculations together. Calculations like strategic relapse, direct segregate investigation and irregular timberland classifier can be adjusted to accomplish great exactness and results. Additionally, the correctness of the model can be defined using metrics like the scoring recalling cross-validation and f1 scores, Manets [18] and these such metric results can be used to improve the model.

References

1. Verma, P., Bhardwaj, T., Bhatia, A., Mursleen, M.: Sentiment analysis "using SVM, KNN and SVM with PCA". In: Bhardwaj, T., Upadhyay, H., Sharma, T.K., Fernandes, S.L. (eds) Artificial Intelligence in Cyber Security: Theories and Applications. Intelligent Systems Reference Library, vol 240, pp. 35–53. Springer, Cham (2023). https://doi.org/10.1007/978-3-031-28581-3_5
2. Ebine, H., Shiga, Y., Ikeda, M., Nakamura, O.: The recognition of facial expressions with automatic detection of the reference face. In: 2000 Canadian Conference on Electrical and Computer Engineering. Conference Proceedings. Navigating to a New Era, vol.2, pp. 1091–1099. Halifax, NS (2000). (Cat. No.00TH8492)
3. Bhatia, A., et al.: Analysis of pattern recognition (text mining) with web crawler. Int. Trans. Appl. Sci. 3(3), 435–450 (2011)
4. Kumar, M., Ali Khan, S., Bhatia, A., Sharma, V., Jain, P.L Machine learning algorithms: a conceptual review. In: 2023 1st International Conference on Intelligent Computing and Research Trends (ICRT), pp. 1–7. Roorkee, India (2023).https://doi.org/10.1109/ICRT57042.2023.10146678

5. Loconsole, C., Miranda, C.R., Augusto, G., Frisoli, A., Orvalho, V.: Real-time emotion recognition novel method for geometrical facial features extraction. In: 2014 International Conference on Computer Vision Theory and Applications (VISAPP), Lisbon, Portugal (2014)
6. Neerja and E. Walia, "Face Recognition Using Improved Fast PCA Algorithm," 2008 Congress on Image and Signal Processing, Sanya, Hainan (2008)
7. Jiang, X.: A facial expression recognition model based on HMM. In: Proceedings of 2011 International Conference on Electronic & Mechanical Engineering and Information Technology, Harbin, Heilongjiang, China (2011)
8. Rajesh, K.M., Naveenkumar, M.: A robust method for face recognition and face emotion detection system using support vector machines. In: 2016 International Conference on Electrical, Electronics, Communication, Computer and Optimization Techniques (ICEECCOT), Mysuru (2016)
9. Swinkels, W., Claesen, L., Xiao, F., Shen, H.: SVM point-based real-time emotion detection. In: 2017 IEEE Conference on Dependable and Secure Computing, Taipei (2017)
10. Saragih, J.M., Lucey, S., Cohn, J.F.: Real-time avatar animation from a single image. Face and Gesture 2011, Santa Barbara, CA, USA (2011)
11. Dahmane, M., Meunier, J.: Emotion recognition using dynamic grid-based HoG features. Face and Gesture 2011, Santa Barbara, CA (2011)
12. Kazemi, V., Sullivan, J.: One millisecond face alignment with an ensemble of regression trees. In: 2014 IEEE Conference on Computer Vision and Pattern Recognition, Columbus, OH (2014)
13. Bhatia, A., Jain, P., Verma, P., Gupta, G., Arya, D.: Data Mining: a process of extracting patterns Webology (2019). (ISSN: 1735–188X)
14. Kaya, G.T.: A hybrid model for classification of remote sensing images with linear SVM and support vector selection and adaptation. IEEE J. Sel. Top. Appl. Earth Observations Remote Sens. 6(4), 1988–1997 (2013)
15. Le Ngo, A.C., Oh, Y.H., Phan, R.C.W., See, J.: Eulerian emotion magnification for subtle expression recognition. In: 2016 IEEE International Conference on Acoustics, Speech and Signal Processing (ICASSP), Shanghai (2016)
16. Kumar, M., Ali Khan, S., Bhatia, A., Sharma, V., Jain, P.: A conceptual introduction of machine learning algorithms. In: 2023 1st International Conference on Intelligent Computing and Research Trends (ICRT), pp. 1–7. Roorkee, India (2023). https://doi.org/10.1109/ICRT57042.2023.10146676
17. Kumar, A., Bhatia, A., Kashyap, A., Kumar, M.: LSTM network: a deep learning approach and applications. In Advanced Applications of NLP and Deep Learning in Social Media Data, pp. 130–150. IGI Global (2023)
18. Bhatia, A., Kumar, A., Jain, A., Kumar, A., Verma, C., Illes, Z.: Networked control system with MANET communication and AODV routing Heliyon (2022)

Analysis and Implementation of Driver Drowsiness, Distraction, and Detection System

Govind Singh Patel[✉], Shubhada Chandrakant Patil, Akshata Adinath Patil,
Rutuja Pravin Dahotre, and Tejas Jitendra Patil

Sharad Institute of Technology College of Engineering, Yadrav, Ichalkaranji,
Maharashtra 146121, India
govindsingh@sitcoe.org.in

Abstract. This work presented analysis and implementation of driver drowsiness, distraction, and detection systems using image processing techniques. The literature review based on drowsiness, distraction, and detection have been taken with their parameters in tabulation form. Flow charts of software and hardware have been presented for the proposed architecture. A comparative analysis of parameters with their percentage of accuracy is given in the table. Therefore, the proposed system found better accuracy as compared to other results. After practically implementation, this system gives the accurate results for the detection of sleepiness of driver. It detects the driver's state such as Sleepy, Drowsy & Active. The proposed work found accuracy in term of parameter like: eye detection accuracy is 95% and drowsiness accuracy is 90%, it is approximately around 5–7% more accurate as compare to other existing work.

Keywords: Drowsiness · distraction · driver · image processing technique

1 Introduction

Driver drowsiness and distraction is the main problem in the daily life transportation system. It can be analysed using many tools and techniques. This type of system may be help to prodect life of many people. In addition to detecting of sleepiness this technique can be used to detect facial expression, open or closed mouth, movement of head. This system can also be used at factories to alert workers.This system can also be used for railway drivers as well as in air-lines. But in this work, simple system has been analysed and implemented to protect life of peoples.

In this system, input images are captured by a camera. We use an AI library that includes dlib and numpy. This model is trained to get spot 68 facial-landmarks on the face. That allows us to detect drowsiness and alert the driver to stay active while driving.

There are various other systems used to detect drowsiness, such as heart rate, pulse rate, EEG, and ECG. However, these systems require direct physical connection. In our project, we employ this image processing system to monitor driver's condition, including aspects like yawning, eye blink, and facial expressions, using a camera. Additionally,

D. Garg et al. (Eds.): IACC 2023, CCIS 2053, pp. 36–46, 2024.
https://doi.org/10.1007/978-3-031-56700-1_4

our project incorporates Arduino, Python, an AI library, an alarm, and an LCD display to alert the driver.

Drowsiness and distraction are two underlying causes of driving accidents that add to the number of road fatalities each year. Many different techniques have been developed over the years to identify drowsiness, but image processing techniques are more precise, secure, and time-efficient than other approaches. The primary objective of this project is to detect driver's drowsiness and to issue warnings to prevent accidents.

The detection of drowsiness levels in drivers plays a crucial role in decreasing the occurrence of accidents. Recent studies and reports indicate that vehicle accidents result in the death or injury of 20 to 50 million people worldwide. According to the NSF of the United States, 54 percentge of drivers have operated vehicles when we feel drowsy, and 28 percentage have fallen sleep while driving [1].

Having reviewed these reports and statistics, it becomes evident that assessing driver's drowsiness levels is of utmost importance in diminishing the frequency of road accidents. To identify drowsiness levels, the system examines parameters associated with drowsiness, including the eyes and their alterations. Visual signs of sleepiness can be identified by capturing the driver's image and employing processing. PERCLOS (Percentage of Eye Closure) is utilized to assess drowsiness. The IR illuminator is employed to measure PERCLOS, the short time of this cycle period eye close & the freq. of eye-blinks regulrarly [2].

The Driver Drowsiness Detection System takes images as input, analyzes them through eye blinking, and detects the driver's state, such as sleepy, drowsy, or active. It alerts the driver through an alarm/buzzer and displays messages on an LCD as output, such as "Please wake up" for a sleepy state and "All Ok" for an Active state.

1.1 Literature Review

Numerous existing drowsiness detection systems rely on physiological signals and facial characteristics. While physiological signals such as EEG(Electro-Encephalography), EOG(Electro-Oculography), ECG(Electro-Cardiography), and body temperature are effective, they can potentially harm human health. Hence, there is a requirement to create a drowsiness detection system that is both efficient and safe for human utilization.

Following are some existing systems in detail:-

Detecting Using Spectacles with an Eye Blink Sensor:
When a driver becomes drowsy, buzzers are activated on the glasses with an eye blink feature to alert the driver.

Drowsy alert system using Electrohalography (EEG) Electrocardiography (ECG).

Drowsy Alert System Using E.E.G. (Electro-Encephalo-Graphy), E.O.G.(Electro-Oculo-graphy), ECG (Electro-Cardio-Graphy), and E.M.G. (Electro-Myo-Gram) Algorithm
Budak et al. developed drowsiness detection technology that incorporates EEG and various components, including an ALexNet technique, VGGNet technique, and wavelet TF algorithm. With an aid of machine learning, this process uses EEG, a camera, and sensors that are turned on to analyze the level of sleepiness. Heart rate variability was

proposed as a method by Hayawi and Waleed to detect sleepiness (HRV). Song et al. introduced a sys. For detecting driver fatigue, which involves monitoring the activity of eye muscles using E.M.G. sensors. In a similar way to the observation of eyelid closure and muscle movement via E.M.G. sensor input signals, Artanto et al. and Ma et al. developed a system that utilizes ESP8266 to transmit drowsiness data internally [3].

Driver Drowsiness Detection Using FPGA
FPGA stands for field programmable array. This technology focuses on detecting bright pupils in the eyes, which are identified using an onboard I.R. sensor source within the vehicle.

Driver Drowsiness Detection Using the Behavioral Measure
Drowsy individuals display distinct facial movements like frequent blinking, nodding/swaying of their head, and frequent yawning. Computerized, non-intrusive behavioral methods are commonly employed to evaluate their driver drowsiness by quantifying these unusual behaviors. Most presented studies that employ behavioral approaches to assess their drowsiness primarily focus on analyzing blinking patterns. Numerous studies have investigated PERCLOS, which measures the percentage of eyelid closure over the pupil over the time, reflecting gradual eyelid closures, often referred to as "droops," rather than quick blinks. PERCLOS is a dependable predictor of drowsiness and is utilized in commercial products, including systems by companies like Seeing Machine and Lexus. Certain researchers have explored a range of facial actions, including inner brow rise, outer brow rise, lip stretch, and jaw movement, as indicators of drowsiness.

Zhang et al. employed a C.N.N. to seprates spatial features of singnals & Long term and Short Term Memory N/W (LSTM) to examine its temporal features with parameters. Accuracy in terms of output was achieved 87% [3].

Akrout et al. [4] introduced a method for detecting driver fatigue through the spatiotemporal analysis of non stationary as well as non linear coreesponding signals, particularly focusing on yawning detection. In this approach, the evaluation involved the use of the YawDD and MirackHB datasets, resulting in achieved accuracies of 83% & 87% respectively.

Abouelnaga et al. [5] developed new dataset called "AUC Distracted Driver", which is similar to the State Farm datasheet. Abouelnaga et al. created this datasheet by segmenting skin, face, & hand features and proposed a technique that involved a genetic algorithm. Their approach employed five sets of weights for a C.N.N., achieving a classification accuracy of 95.98%. However, it was computationally more intensive, making it unsuitable for real-time applications.

Baheti et al. [6] utilized the same dataset and enhanced the V.G.G.16 N/W to achieve a classification accuracy in terms of output was 96.31% when their method was applied in real-time scenarios.

Kose et al. [7] enhanced the classification accuracy to 99.10% for the 10 classes in real-time processing with applications. Furthermore, by integrating red-green-blue and optical flow data with their system out performed other systems on the A.U.C. Distracted Driver and Brain4Cars datasets.

Chawan et al. [8] introduced a method for detecting distracted driving using three C.N.N. models:- V.G.G.-16, V.G.G.-19, and InceptionV3 with applications. This method resulted in a log loss of 0.79.

Majdi et al. [9] introduced the DriveNet, a supervised learning method for determing distracted driving technique. This approach attained an accuracy of 94% by combining C.N.N. and random forest techniques to classify representative instances of distracted driving.

Moslemi et al. [10] employed a 3D C.N.N. along with optical flow that considered temporal information to enhance the detection of distracted driving, resulting in an accuracy of 95%.

Anber et al. [11] introduced a non-invasive algorithm to driver fatigue detection, relying on head position and mouth movement features. This method incorporated two pre-trained AlexNet C.N.N.-based methodss, achieving a respectable level of detection accuracy. However, it required testing on a dataset reflecting real driving conditions for practical application.

From the above all literature review, it has been found that there is gap in accuracy of Eye detection and Drowsiness Accuracy. This gap has been indenified and minimized using proposed technique.

A comparative analysis of the literature survey has been presented in Table 1 and Table 2 with their parameters, algorithm, and accuracy (Fig. 1).

Table 1. Comparison of selected papers of literature survey

Sr.No	Parameters	Algorithm	Accuracy
1	EEG, ECG	Mean Power Frequency	-
2	Respiration Rate of men, Heart Rate men	Power Spectrum algorithm	-
3	Cameras	Kalman Filtering Tracking algorithm	Yawn- 82% PERCLOS- 86% AECS- 95%
4	EEG, ECG	Dynamic Bayesian Network	Drowsy- 91% Active- 91%
5	Using SVM (Support Vector Machines)	Haar Algorithm	-
6	Using an eye blink sensor	Sensor – IR Sensor	Closed Eye Frame – 80%

Table 2. Comparison of parameters with their accuracy

Author	Parameters/ Methods/ Algorithms	Classifiers/ Networks/ Data Set Used	Accuracy
Zhang et al.	Extraction of image features of proposed work and a long & short term memory N/W	CNN	87%
Akrout et al.	The spatiotemporal study of non-stationary & non-linear signals	YawDD and MiracleHB data sets of proposed work	83% & 87%
Abouelnaga et al.	Segmentation of skin, face, and hand features	AUC data set CNN	95.9%
Baheti et al.	-	VGG16	96.3%
Kose et al.	Combination of RGB colour & optical flow database	AUC Distracted Driver & Brain4Cars data sets	99.10%
Chawan et al.	-	Three C.N.N. methods, namely V.G.G.-16, V.G.G.-19, InceptionV3	A log loss of 0.79
Majdi et al.	Supervised Learning Approach called DriveNet	CNN and Random Forest	95%
MosleMi et al.	3D C.N.N. & optical flow with temporal information	3D CNN	94%
Anber et al.	A non-invasive algorithm based on features from a head position of men & mouth movements of drivers of vehicle	2 pretained alexnet CNN based models	A certain detection accuracy

2 Architecture and Methodology

The architecture of this system has Arduino UNO, LED, LCD, and a Buzzer/alarm. LED and circuit of LCD and Buzzer are connected to Arduino. Here we used Python code to program our Arduino. We use OpenCV/camera to detect the image. The camera captures the image, and if sleep is detected, the alarm buzzes and an alert message appears on the LCD, as shown in Fig. 1 (Fig. 2).

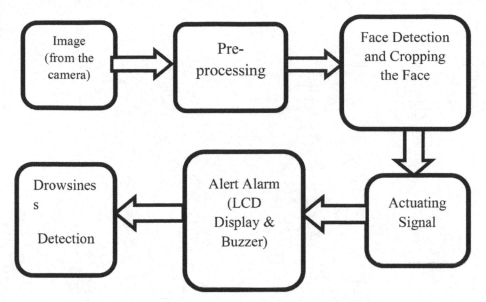

Fig. 1. Proposed Architecture's Block Diagram

In the initial step that is START, the software program begins its execution. After that the software imports the necessary Python Libraries and Modules for Image Processing and Drowsiness Detection.The python libraries are numpy, cv2, dlib, etc. The next step is about setting up initial configurations and variables for the drowsiness detection system [12].Then after that the system reads images or frames from a source such as a camera or video stream within a loop. Then initialize a facial landmark detector, which identifies specific points on the face, including eye corners and the mouth, allowing us to calculate the Eye Aspect Ratio (EAR). Then next step is computation of EAR, which typically involves measuring the ratio of distances between certain landmarks.If the computed EAR value is greater than a threshold (0.21), it suggests that the driver's eyes are relatively open, and they are not exhibiting drowsiness (Fig. 3).

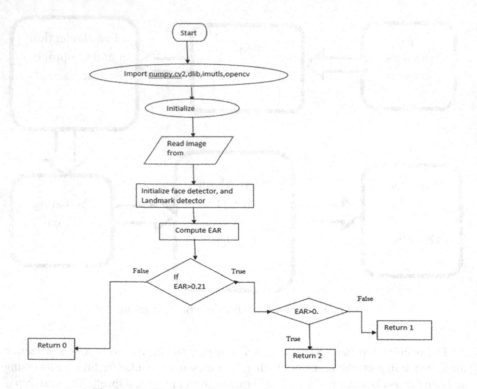

Fig. 2. The Flow chart illustrating the software operation.

In this system, we utilized the Dlib library's 68 facial landmark detectors and face detectors. The 68 facial detector identifies the human face and associated points, allowing us to subsequently assess whether the eyes are open or closed. Leveraging Dlib for this task is advantageous as it yields improved accuracy by providing 68 landmark points [13].

Here we work on 3 stages:

1) Active
2) Drowsy
3) Sleepy

We importing libraries:- dlib, numpy, and open cv.

We used an in-built function of dlib which acts as a frontal face detector.

The Dlib shape detector has 68 landmarks on the face.6 on each eye, 9 on the nose, 5 on each eyebrow, 20 on the lips, and 17 on the circumference of the face.

We use the function compute which measures the difference between 2 points A and B and the next blink function [14].

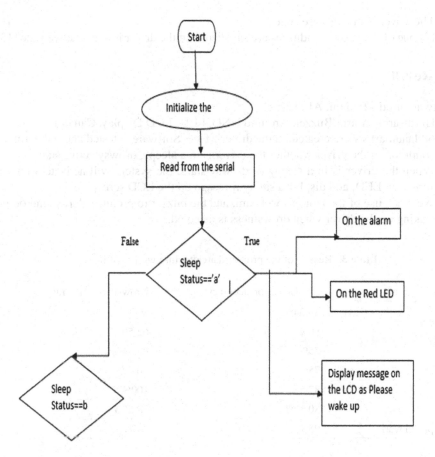

Fig.3. The Flow chart illustrating the operation of hardware

3 Algorithm

In this system, we used the Eye Aspect Ratio (EAR) algorithm where EAR stands for the Eye Aspect Ratio.

In facial landmarks, each eye has 6 points where 2 are at the corners of eyebrows are long points and the other are short points.

Ratio = (Addition of both long points) / (2* short distance)

The above ratio is called EAR (Eye Aspect Ratio)

If EAR > 0.25 the return 2

If EAR > 0.21 & EAR < 0.25 then return 1

If EAR < 0.21 return 0

0,1, and 2 determine the blinking of an eye

If left_blink == 0 right_blink == 0

The driver is sleeping

If left_blink or right_blink is 1

The driver is in a drowse state

If none of the above conditions are satisfied then the driver is in the active state [13].

4   Result

Software used:- Python, AI libraries

Hardware:- Alarm/Buzzer, Arduino UNO, LED, LCD Display, Camera

68 landmarks were created on the driver's face. Software is tested and it determines the condition of the driver whether the driver is in a sleepy, drowsy active state.

When the driver is in a sleepy or drowsy state, the system will activate a buzzer, illuminate an LED, and display a safety message on the LCD screen.

We made use of the laptop's webcam, and the buzzer to produce alert sound output for waking up the driver when drowsiness is detected.

Table 3. Results of the proposed architecture with existing work

Ref	Eye Detection accuracy	Drowsiness Accuracy
3	83.34%	80%
6	80%	62.5%
12	75%	83.34%
13	75%	66.67%
14	87.5%	100%
15	80.17%	78.50%
Proposed work	95%	90%

Each volunteer participating in the test will be asked to squint their eyes multiple times and simulate drowsiness on several occasions during the testing process [15, 16].

Eye Detection Accuracy = (Total no. of times eyes detected) / ((Total no. of times eyes detected) + (Total no. of times missed/not detected))

Drowsiness Detection Accuracy = (Total number of times alarm sounds) / ((Total number of times alarm sounds

+ (Total number of times alarm not sound))

Comparison of proposed and existing work has been shown in the Table 3. It shows that proposed work is more accurate as compare to other existing work. From the Table 3, it has been concluded that eye detection accuracy and drowsiness accuracy is better than all other reference taken in this work.

5   Conclusion and Future Scope

The proposed system provides enhanced vehicle safety by quickly detecting drowsiness. It effectively distinguishes between normal eye blinking and drowsiness, preventing the driver from falling asleep while driving. While such driver and car security systems are typically found only in high-end vehicles, this eye-detection driver security and safety can also be implemented in regular cars. The system operates effectively even when the driver is wearing glasses and in low-light conditions. Ultimately, the proposed system offers superior protection and accuracy compared to other existing systems.

In addition to detecting of sleepiness this technique can be used to detect facial expression, open or closed mouth, movement of head. This system can also be used at factories to alert workers.This system can also be used for railway drivers as well as in air-lines.

References

1. Pauly, L., Sankar, D.: Detection of drowsiness based on HOG features and SVM classifiers. In: IEEE International Conference on Research in Computational Intelligence and Communication Networks (ICRCICN), pp. 8–14 (2015)
2. Ihaddadene, N.: Drowsy driver detection system using eye blink patterns. machine and web intelligence(ICMWI). In: International Conference on IEE, pp. 20–25 (2010)
3. Zhang, W., Cheng, B., Lin, Y.: Driver drowsiness recognition based on computer vision technology. In: IEEE, pp. 67–70 (2012)
4. Sabet, M., Zoroofi, R.A., Sadeghniiat-Haghighi, K., Sabbaghian, M.: A new system for driver drowsiness and distraction detection. In: 11th IEEE Joint Conference on Information Science, pp. 120–125 (2012)
5. Sandberg, D.: conducted an analysis and optimization of systems for detecting sleepiness in drivers. Chalmers University in Goteborg, Sweden in, pp 80–87 (2018)
6. Malla, A., Davidson, P., Bones, P., Green, R., Jones, R.: Automated video-based measurement of eye closure for detecting behavioral microsleep. In: 32nd Annual International Conference of the IEEE, Buenos Aires, Argentina, pp. 10–14 (2010)
7. Viola, P., Jones, M.: Rapid object detection using a boosted cascade of simple features. In: Proceedings of the IEEE Computer Society Conference on Computer Vision and Pattern Recognition, pp. 55–60 (2001)
8. Hong, T., Qin, H., Sun, Q.: An improved real-time eye state identification system in driver drowsiness detection. In: Proceedings of the IEEE International Conference on Control and Automation, Guangzhou, CHINA, pp. 1–5 2007
9. Nixon, M.S., Aguado, A.S.: Feature Extraction and Image Processing. 2nd ed., Jordan Hill, Oxford OX2 8DP, UK (2008)
10. Bhowmick, B., Kumar, C.: Detection and classification of eye state in IR camera for driver drowsiness identification. In: Proceeding of the IEEE International Conference on Signal and Image Processing Applications, pp. 40–44 (2009)
11. Rezaee, K., et al.: Real-time intelligent alarm system of driver fatigue based on video sequences. In: Robotics and Mechatronics (ICRoM), First RSI/ISM IEEE International Conference on. pp. 80–83 (2013)
12. Du, Y., et al.: Driver fatigue detection based on eye state analysis. In: Proceedings of the 11th Joint Conference on Information Sciences, pp.1–6 (2008)
13. Choi, I.H., Hong, S.K., Kim, Y.G..: Real-time categorization of driver's gaze zone using the deep learning techniques. In: 2016 IEEE International Conference on Big Data and Smart Computing (BigComp), pp. 1–25 (2016)
14. Bhop, R.A.: Computer vision based drowsiness detection for motorized vehicles with web push notifications. In: ICICCS, pp. 17–19 (2022)

15. Ananthi, S., Sathya, R., Vaidehi, K., Vijaya, G.: Driver drowsiness detection using image processing and I-ear techniques. In: IEEE ICICCS, pp. 45–50 (2023)
16. Hossain, M.L., Hasan, M.S., Safwan Ahmed, K.M.A: Developing an image processing based real-time driver drowsiness detection system. In: IJSRP, vol. 13, no. 4, pp. 1–7 (2023)

Object Detection and Depth Estimation Using Deep Learning

Rajani Katiyar[✉]⊙, Uttara Kumari, Karthik Panagar⊙, Kashinath Patil⊙,
B. M. Manjunath⊙, and Y. Jeevan Gowda⊙

Department of ECE, RV College of Engineering, Bangalore, India
{rajanikatiyar,uttarakumari,karthikpu.ec20,kashinathpatil.ec20,
manjunathbm.ec20,jeevangowday.ec21}@rvce.edu.in
https://www.rvce.edu.in

Abstract. Detection of an object and depth estimation is very crucial in the field of computer vision, facilitating tasks in the field of autonomous navigation, scene understanding and many more. There are lot challenges in the current existing technique such as occlusion and accuracy issues, impeding their real-world applicability. To surmount these limitations, the proposed work introduces an innovative approach that melds deep learning architectures with efficient computational methods. By fusing advanced object detection models with a sophisticated depth estimation network, the work proposed have achieved substantial enhancements in accuracy and precision. The proposed model pushes the envelope for real-time implementation, contributing to the advancement of object detection and depth estimation capabilities. This approach was augmented with a novel depth estimation technique, extracting diagonal pixel lengths and combining them with actual depths from the dataset. Subsequent analysis employed both linear and polynomial regression, revealing that the polynomial model (98% average accuracy) surpassed the linear model (80.96% accuracy). These findings highlighted the importance of capturing complex non-linear relationships between pixel length and object depth, showcasing YOLOv4's robust object detection capabilities and emphasizing the significance of intricate depth estimation in visual cues.

Keywords: YOLO (You only look once) · CNN (convolution neural network) · OpenCV (computer vision) · RCNN (Region-based convolutional neural network)

1 Introduction

Object detection and image recognition technology have become indispensable components of modern autonomous systems, revolutionizing the automotive, drone, and robotics industries. In self-driving cars, detection of an object in real-time is crucial for identifying pedestrians, cyclists, vehicles, and other obstacles on the road, enabling the vehicle to make informed decisions and navigate safely.

D. Garg et al. (Eds.): IACC 2023, CCIS 2053, pp. 47–56, 2024.
https://doi.org/10.1007/978-3-031-56700-1_5

Depth estimation is a fundamental task in computer vision that involves infer-ring the distance information of objects within a scene from 2 Dimensional (2D) images or videos. The ability to estimate depth is essential for various application related to computer vision, ranging from robotics and autonomous vehicles to augmented reality and virtual reality systems. In the proposed work, You Only Look Once version 4 (YOLOV4) algorithm is employed for improved detection of an object and to develop a distance estimation model using pixel data and a regression approach. The algebraic methods used in YOLOV4 implementation include Convolutional Neural Networks (CNN) for feature extraction, anchor boxes are used for bounding box prediction, and Non-Maximum Suppression (NMS) for duplicate detection filtering. The regression models employed to get distance estimates are linear and polynomial regression models. The simulations demonstrate the effectiveness of YOLOV4 integration with the distance estima-tion model exhibiting promising results, providing valuable distance estimates for the detected objects.

The proposed model integrates detection of object with YOLO and depth estimation using various regression models. It has been highlighted that the polynomial regression model has better results and accuracy compared to linear regression model.

The paper is organized briefly in four sub sections, including Introduction, in Sect. 2 Methodology of the paper would be explained, Result and discussion would be explained in Sect. '3'. At the last brief conclusion would be explained in Sect. '4' followed by reference.

1.1 Literature Summary

The initial method implimented to estimate distance is DisNet(Distance Esti-mation Network) [1]. It is a machine learning setup that detects obstacle with a method to estimate the distance from monocular camera to the object viewed with the camera. In particular, the primary results of an on-going research to allow the on-board multisensor system, which is developing under H2020 SMART (Shift2Rail project Synchronized Multi-Antenna Radar and 3D imaging Tech-nology), to autonomously learn distances from objects, possible obstacles on the tracks in front of the locomotive. The fused data set obtained from Camera and LIDAR are very complicated to process in many of the real time application, such as industrial automation, autonomous driving, and robotics [2]. Especially in the case of autonomous vehicles, [3], the efficient fusioning data from camera and LIDAR sensors is important to enabling the depth of objects for short and long distance. There are various deep learning architecture proposed in the architec-ture, the first network architecture in the field of deep learning is ILSVRC.In this architecture along with CNN architecture 22 more network layers were added. The network architecture was combination of CNN along with pooling layer. Later various networks were propose by various authors like [4], CNN, RCNN, faster RCNN [5]. There were slight improvement in the speed(frame per second) from one architecture to another. In the literature it is been observed that com-putation time can be further improved to 7 frames per second, alligned with the requirments of real time object detection [6],. In the recent years [7], YOLO has gained popularity and is been continuously improvising, [8], YOLO V4 is been used in the current project.

2 Theory and Methodology

For the execution of the model, the first and foremost requirement is preparation of a dataset for diverse images which contain humans, motorbikes, cars, and buses. The YOLOV4 algorithm was integrated with deep learning frameworks, and the model was trained on the collected datasets for efficient object detection and recognition. Concurrently, a distance estimation model based on pixel data and linear regression was developed. Subsequently, the YOLOV4 model and the distance estimation model will be seamlessly integrated into a unified system. Extensive simulations using various datasets and real-world test cases were used to evaluate the integrated system's performance, measuring accuracy, efficiency, and real-time capabilities.

The project focuses on utilizing the YOLOV4 algorithm for object detection and employing a linear regression model for estimating distance based on the detected objects. A high-resolution 64-megapixel mobile camera is employed for capturing intricate 2D images of the targeted scene. The camera holds a dual purpose in the project's workflow: firstly, it facilitates the creation of a curated dataset crucial for model training, ensuring the development of an accurate and robust system. Subsequently, during real-time testing and deployment, the camera is employed to procure live feeds of the scene, which are promptly relayed to the computer for instantaneous processing and analysis. YOLOV4 algorithm is used for precise object detection, intricate depth estimation calculations, and the subsequent generation of conclusive results. The real-time feed obtained from the camera is seamlessly conveyed to the display interface via the Wireless Fidelity (Wi-Fi) protocol, facilitated by the 'Vcam' software. The function processes the output from the YOLO model, calculates the diagonal distance in pixels, and further estimates the distance based on the class of the object using predefined equation as shown in Fig. 1.

2.1 Hardware and Software Utilisation

Camera: In the execution of the project, a camera serves as the primary instrument for capturing intricate 2D images of the targeted scene. Specifically, a high-resolution 64-megapixel mobile camera is employed. The camera holds a dual purpose in the project's workflow: firstly, it facilitates the creation of a curated dataset crucial for model training, ensuring the development of an accurate and robust system. Subsequently, during real-time testing and deployment, the camera is employed to procure live feeds of the scene, which are promptly relayed to the computer for instantaneous processing and analysis.

iVCam Software: The project harnesses the capabilities of the iVCam software, a crucial tool that bridges the gap between the camera and the display interface. iVCam facilitates the seamless transmission of live feeds captured by the camera to the designated display interface via a Wi-Fi connection. This software not only ensures the real-time visualization of processed images but also plays a pivotal role in enabling dynamic monitoring and assessment during testing and deployment. By effectively establishing a wireless link between the mobile camera and display, iVcam contributes to the project's overarching goal of efficient and comprehensive system integration.

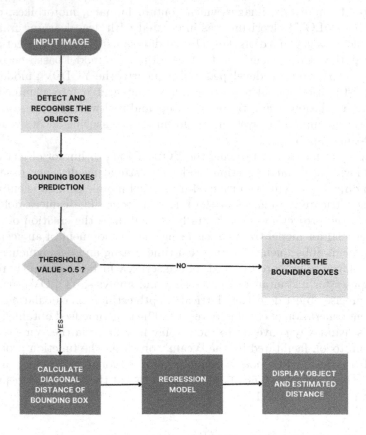

Fig. 1. Block diagram of proposed work

3   Result and Discussion

Overall work is divided into various sub task, the first part is the data set generation, integration of code with deep learning model followed by regression model

3.1   Dataset Generation

As a part of data set generation , images were captured, the dataset encompassed within a span of 3 m to 15 m, featuring images captured at consistent intervals of 1 m. Once the dataset generation process is complete, the next step involves the implementation of YOLO to generate bounding boxes for images. A list of object classes (like "person," "car," etc.) is loaded. These are the types of objects the model can recognize as shown in Fig. 2 (Fig. 3).

Fig. 2. Person at 5 m distance   **Fig. 3.** Car at 10 m distance

Subsequently, the diagonal lengths of these bounding boxes were calculated in pixels. pixel lengths are noted down for every object from 3 m to 15 m at equal intervals of 1 m. Bounding box detected using YOLO is shown in Fig. 4.

Fig. 4. Bounding box for a Person

The diagonal length of the bounding box (in pixels) is noted down. This systematic procedure is applied to each image in the dataset, resulting in the compilation of a comprehensive Table 1 showcasing the calculated diagonal pixel lengths for four different objects car, motorbike, person, bus at equal interval of 1 m. The comprehensive dataset contains 15 data samples for each object as shown in Table 1, which is used to obtain linear and polynomial equations for estimating distances.

Table 1. Data Samples

Distance (in m)	Car (in pixels)	Motorbike (in pixels)	Person(in pixels)	Bus(in pixels)
3	336	189	260	590
4	274	165	210	403
5	216	126	160	310
6	182	98	140	267
7	152	86	128	230
8	136	76	110	200
9	127	67	100	175
10	110	60	86	165
11	102	55	75	153
12	93	48	71	145
13	85	46	65	137
14	81	43	60	130
15	74	40	52	125

From the data tabulated in Table 1, it has been observed that as the distance between object and camera is increasing the pixel values are decreasing

3.2   Implementation of Regression Models

In order to implement a regression model for the purpose of distance estimation, a two-step process is undertaken. The initial step involves the training of the model, during which data is utilized to facilitate the acquisition of a equation. This equation is subsequently utilized to estimate distances by relying on the pixel length of the diagonal box that has been detected. By correlating pixel length with distance, the regression model establishes a predictive framework that contributes to accurate distance estimations

Implementing Linear Regression Model: The process of curve fitting is employed to obtain linear equations for each object. The slope and intercept values for the regression model were calculated using python for all four objects Car, Person, Bus, Motorbike.

$$y = (-0.0443 * x) + 15.71 \tag{1}$$

$$y = (-0.07415 * x) + 15.27 \tag{2}$$

$$y = (-0.05782 * x) + 15.75 \tag{3}$$

$$y = (-0.021 * x) + 13.3 \tag{4}$$

Using the given data in Table 1,the process of curve fitting is performed to derive linear equations for the objects: car (1), motorbike (2), person (3), and bus (4). The linear equations for the respective object detected are used by the program. The pixel length of the bounding box is taken as input (x) for the equation and distance is estimated in real time (y).

Implementing Polynomial Regression Model: The process of curve fitting is employed to obtain polynomial equations for each objects: car (5), motorbike (6), person (7), and bus (8). The slope and intercept values for the polynomial regression model were calculated using python for all four objects Car, Person, Bus, Motorbike. The linear equations for the respective object detected are used by the program. The pixel length of the bounding box is taken as input (x) for the equation and distance is estimated in real time (y).

$$y = 1045.48 \cdot x^{-0.97} - 0.47 \tag{5}$$

$$y = 421.59 \cdot x^{-0.90} - 0.51 \tag{6}$$

$$y = 231.47 \cdot x^{-0.62} - 4.39 \tag{7}$$

$$y = 25045.2 \cdot x^{-1.57} + 2.02 \tag{8}$$

The pixel length of the bounding box is taken as input (x) for the equation and distance (y) is estimated in real time. The comparison between the actual

Table 2. Estimated distance of car with linear regression model

Actual distance (in m)	Estimated distance (in m)	Error(in m)	Error (in %)
3	0.82	2.17	72.66
4	3.57	0.43	10.75
5	6.14	−1.13	22.80
6	7.64	−1.64	27.33
7	8.97	−1.97	28.14
8	9.68	−1.68	21.00
9	10.08	−1.08	12.00
10	10.83	−0.83	8.30
11	11.19	−0.18	1.72
12	11.59	0.41	3.41
13	11.95	1.05	8.07
14	12.12	1.88	13.42
15	12.43	2.57	17.13

distance and estimated distance using linear regression model for car is tabulated in Table 2. Similar observation is performed for all the four objects.

The results from Table 2 indicate a highest recorded error of 72%, with an average error rate of 18.98% and an achieved accuracy of 81%. The comparison between the actual distance and estimated distance for car using polynomial regression model is tabulated in Table 3.

Table 3. Estimated distance of car with polynomial regression model

Actual distance (in m)	Estimated distance (in m)	Error (in m)	Error (in %)
3	2.93	−0.07	2.33
4	4.14	0.14	3.50
5	5.00	0	0
6	6.01	0.01	0.18
7	6.77	−0.23	3.28
8	7.89	−0.11	1.37
9	9.28	0.28	3.11
10	9.90	−0.1	1.00
11	11.08	0.08	0.80
12	12.01	0.01	0.11
13	12.86	−0.13	1.00
14	14.21	0.21	1.50
15	14.89	−0.10	0.7

The results from Table 3 indicate a highest recorded error of 3.5%, with an average error rate of 1.47% and an achieved accuracy of 98.53%.

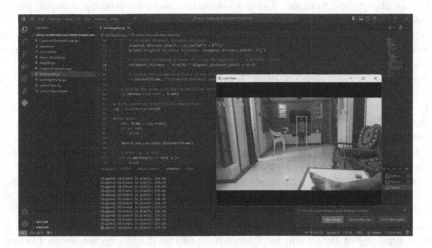

Fig. 5. Working model

The above Fig. 5. shows the working model in VS code IDE.

4   Conclusion and Future Scope

The project aims to enhance object perception by integrating advanced computer vision techniques, primarily utilizing the YOLOV4 Algorithm for detection of an object in real rime and depth estimation through regression models. The ultimate goal is to merge detection of an object and estimation of depth into a comprehensive framework. The project initiated with the implementation of the YOLO model for real-time detection of an object and an innovative estimation of depth approach. The results showed that Linear regression model gave an accuracy of accuracy of 80.96% while polynomial regression model showed an average accuracy of 98%. The results indicated that polynomial regression outperformed linear regression in terms of accuracy, effectively capturing the complex non-linear relationships between pixel length and object depth.

However, the project has limitations. It heavily depends on the diversity and size of the training dataset, making it challenging for objects not well-represented during training. Real-world complexities like object interactions, occlusions, and reflections can affect reliability. The computational demands of integrated techniques may hinder real-time applications, and extreme distances or unconventional perspectives may challenge depth estimation. Furthermore, the project's adaptability to new environments and ethical considerations surrounding privacy and consent require careful consideration as the technology advances into practical usage.

References

1. Nagarajan, A., Gopinath, M.P.: Hybrid optimization-enabled deep learning for indoor object detection and distance estimation to assist visually impaired persons. Adv. Eng. Softw. **176**, 103362 (2023). ISSN 0965–9978
2. Kumar, G.A., Lee, J.H., Hwang, J., Park, J., Youn, S.H., Kwon, S.: Lidar and camera fusion approach for object distance estimation in self-driving vehicles. Symmetry **12**(2), 324 (2020)
3. Usmankhujaev, S., Baydadaev, S., Kwon, J.W.: Accurate 3D to 2D Object Distance Estimation from the Mapped Point Cloud Data. Sensors **23**, 2103 (2023)
4. Ren, S., He, K., Girshick, R., Sun, J.: Faster R-CNN: towards real-time object detection with region proposal networks. In: Advances in Neural Information Processing Systems, vol. 28 (2015)
5. Girshick, R.: Fast r-CNN. In: Proceedings of the IEEE International Conference on Computer Vision, pp. 1440–1448 (2015)
6. Liu, W., et al.: SSD: single shot multibox detector. In: Leibe, B., Matas, J., Sebe, N., Welling, M. (eds.) ECCV 2016. LNCS, vol. 9905, pp. 21–37. Springer, Cham (2016). https://doi.org/10.1007/978-3-319-46448-0_2
7. Redmon, J., Divvala, S., Girshick, R., Farhadi, A.: You only look once: unified, real-time object detection. In: Proceedings of the IEEE Conference on Computer Vision and Pattern Recognition, pp. 779–788 (2016)
8. Redmon, J., Farhadi, A.: Yolo9000: better, faster, stronger. In: Proceedings of the IEEE Conference on Computer Vision and Pattern Recognition, pp. 7263–7271 (2017)
9. Nugraha, B.T., Su, S.-F.: Towards self-driving car using convolutional neural network and road lane detector. In: 2nd International Conference on Automation, Cognitive Science, Optics, Micro Electro-mechanical System, and Information Technology (ICACOMIT), pp. 65–69. IEEE (2017)
10. Cai, Y., Luan, T., Gao, H., et al.: Yolov4-5d: an effective and efficient object detector for autonomous driving. IEEE Trans. Instrum. Meas. **70**, 1–13 (2021)
11. Zaheer, A., Rashid, M., Riaz, M.A., Khan, S.: Single-view reconstruction using orthogonal line-pairs. Comput. Vis. Image Underst. **172**, 107–123 (2018)
12. Lee, D.C., Hebert, M., Kanade, T.: Geometric reasoning for single image structure recovery. In: IEEE Conference on Computer Vision and Pattern Recognition, pp. 2136–2143. IEEE (2009)
13. Barinova, O., Konushin, V., Yakubenko, A., Lee, K.C., Lim, H., Konushin, A.: Fast automatic single-view 3-d reconstruction of urban scenes. In: Forsyth, D., Torr, P., Zisserman, A. (eds.) ECCV 2008. LNCS, vol. 5303, pp. 100–113. Springer, Heidelberg (2008). https://doi.org/10.1007/978-3-540-88688-4_8
14. Criminisi, A., Reid, I., Zisserman, A.: Single view metrology. Int. J. Comput. Vision **40**, 123–148 (2000)

Optimizing Biomass Forecasting and Supply Chain: An Integrated Modelling Approach

Sangeeta Oswal⬛, Ritesh Bhalerao$^{(\boxtimes)}$ ⬛, and Aum Kulkarni⬛

AI and Data Science, VESIT, Mumbai, India
{sangeeta.oswal,2021.ritesh.bhalerao,
2021.aum.kulkarni}@ves.ac.in

Abstract. The growing worldwide population and rapid technological break-throughs have increased energy consumption, highlighting the need for renewable and eco-friendly energy sources. Biofuel uptake is difficult owing to high prices, requires significant government measures to compete with conventional fuels and biomass-to-biofuel conversion inefficiencies are problematic. This research shows how biofuels can alter sustainability and examine Gujarat's biomass supply chain utilizing advanced forecasting and supply chain optimization methods. A dataset including 2148 unique locations spanning the years 2010 to 2017 was utilized, and afterwards subjected to clustering analysis resulting in the identification of eight different groups. The next two-year biomass production is projected utilizing AutoML techniques. Finally, the supply chain is optimized using Mixed Integer Linear Programming (MILP) in order to reduce both costs and carbon footprint, in accordance with the predicted value.

Keywords: Time series · AutoML · Mixed Integer Linear Programming · Supply Chain · Renewable energy · Biofuel

1 Introduction

The growing population and rapid improvements in technology have resulted in an increased need for energy. The escalating energy requirements and the consequential rise in greenhouse gas emissions have necessitated a heightened use of renewable and environmentally friendly energy sources. In order to address the growing need for sustainability, it is imperative to replace fossil fuels with alternative resources and technology. Biofuels have the potential to significantly impact the current situation. However, it is not been implemented on a large scale. Firstly, it should be noted that the implementation of alternative energy sources, such as Biofuels, entails significant costs and necessitates the establishment of ambitious government objectives in order to achieve parity with conventional fuel sources like diesel, petrol, and natural gas. Despite this, there are various issues that still exist. Currently, it is estimated that a quantity of 100 metric tons of crude oil has the capacity to provide around 75 metric tons of gasoline and diesel fuel. In order to produce an equivalent quantity of 75 tons of biofuel, a biorefinery requires a minimum biomass input of 375 tons. In contrast to crude oil, it is not feasible to obtain 375 tons of biomass from a singular site [1]. Also, to set up a Biorefinery in a region a concrete understanding of the region's temporal features such as biomass production and spatial distribution is required. Hence, the entire supply chain must be designed such that it incurs less costs and reduces the overall carbon footprint.

Figure 1 shows an overview of the Biomass supply chain considered in this paper. Harvesting sites are the starting point of the chain. Biomass produced at each site is then sent to Depots for densification and pelletization. Pellets from these Depots are then sent to Biorefineries for final processing. The solution which we propose in this paper is very robust and scalable in nature. The methodology is heavily inspired by the divide and conquer paradigm, making it scalable to larger problems. It is designed considering generality in implementation, making it applicable to regions other than Gujarat with negligible changes in formulation and structure of solution. Solution can be broadly divided into two parts: Time Series Forecasting and Supply Chain Optimization.

Fig. 1. Biomass supply chain

This research demonstrates the profound environmental impact achievable through the innovative application of technology. By leveraging advanced forecasting and supply chain optimization techniques, this study contributes significantly to environmental preservation. The technological advances enable biofuels to replace fossil fuels, reducing energy production carbon footprints. This research embodies the power of technology to address pressing environmental challenges and showcases how it can lead us toward a sustainable, eco-friendly energy future. In this paper, the issue of Biomass supply chain optimization for the state of Gujarat is proposed.

In the subsequent sections of this article, we delve into a comprehensive literature review (Sect. 2) that explores various statistical, mathematical, and machine learning techniques employed in solving the Biomass supply chain problem. Section 3 provides details on the dataset used, derived from Shell.ai's Agricultural Waste Challenge 2023. The proposed methodology, which encompasses Biomass forecasting and Supply Chain Optimization, is expounded in Sect. 4. The results and discussions, including the achieved MASE scores, optimization outcomes, and potential improvements, are presented in Sect. 5. The article concludes in Sect. 6, summarizing the versatile and efficient methodology proposed for addressing complex supply chain optimization problems and its implications for the energy sector.

2   Literature Review

This paper utilizes various statistical, mathematical, and ML techniques to solve the Biomass supply chain problem. The algorithms and techniques studied and tested were Time series forecasting, Clustering, AutoML, and Linear programming. Following is a brief overview of these techniques and algorithms.

2.1 Clustering

Clustering refers to the process of separating data into a collection of clusters. Clusters are essentially a collection of similar objects which are separated from other collections that are different from each other [2]. There are several algorithms for clustering which are divided into distinct types. The types of algorithms that are of interest are Hierarchical and Partitioning algorithms. Partitioning algorithms are popular for recognizing patterns in data [3]. K means is one of the partitioning algorithms. Time series clustering is an interesting application of clustering algorithms to find clusters in time series data. Clustering of time-series data is mostly utilized for discovery of interesting patterns in time-series datasets. Time series clustering is a useful method to find out patterns within data which make it easier to model & extract meaningful conclusions from it [4].

2.2 Time Series Forecasting and AutoML Time Series

Time series forecasting is a basic statistical method used in many fields. Time series analysis techniques range from simple statistical models to deep learning systems [5, 6]. Popular methods include ARIMA, SARIMA, and exponential smoothing. Facebook's open-source forecasting system fbprophet is popular [7]. Time series forecasting, being such a broad field, has many models and hyperparameters to choose from. Practitioners must choose the right model with the suitable parameters. AutoML seeks to eliminate iterative model selection and hyper parameter optimization. Traditional data science workflows benefit from AutoML [8]. AutoKeras, H2O, EvalML, and AutoGluon are AutoML frameworks for time series analysis [9–11]. Amazon's cutting-edge model, AutoGluon-Time Series (AG-TS), was used for the solution. Other frameworks only generate point forecasts for univariate time series, but it can generate probabilistic forecasts. AG-TS achieves solid empirical results on benchmark datasets by combining statistical models, deep learning predictions, and ensemble techniques [12].

2.3 Supply Chain Optimization

A supply chain is an end-to-end complex process of a product's journey from one point to another. Supply Chain Management (SCM) is designing an efficient process for the desired product. SCM is very prevalent in various industries. SCM has modeling, algorithmic, and scaling issues [13]. Various algorithms have been used to create and solve SCM problems, including OR, Genetic, Bees, and others [13–16]. The biomass supply chain has many challenges, including biomass availability, scale, dynamic and inflexible restrictions, transportation cost, and carbon footprint [17]. Designing a sustainable supply chain requires solving these challenges.

Genetic algorithms and linear and mixed integer linear programming (MILP) have been used to solve this problem [18]. Heuristics are faster but do not guarantee optimal solutions. Mathematical programming provides an ideal solution, but it is not scalable to broad regions with rising variables and limitations. MILP uses mathematical optimization to search the full solution space to discover the best solution within the problem's restrictions. OR problem solvers include Gurobi [19]. It provides optimal solutions in a reasonable time using Simplex, Branch & Bound, Cutting Planes, and others [20].

3   Dataset

The data used in this paper is obtained from Shell.ai's Agricultural Waste Challenge 2023 [1]. The dataset comprises two tabular files: one containing historical information on annual biomass production, and the other detailing the distances between locations in Gujarat. The state of Gujarat is divided into 2418 distinct locations each specified by a pair of latitude and longitude. As shown in Fig. 2 each dot represents a pair of latitude & longitude.

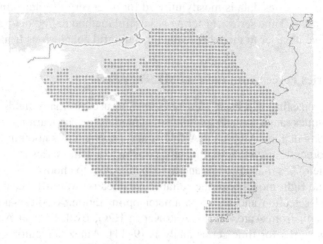

Fig. 2. 2418 locations of Gujarat

Every location has its own distinct annual Biomass production. Table 1 represents the Biomass history which contains the biomass production from the years 2010 to 2017 for all 2418 locations, resulting in formation of distinct time series with 8 lags for each location.

Table 1. Biomass History

Index	Latitude	Longitude	2010	:	2017
0	24.66818	71.33144	8.475744	:	5.180296
1	24.66818	71.41106	24.02978	:	42.12695
:	:	:	:	:	:
2417	20.15456	73.16282	0.61228	:	0.226953

Table 2 represents a standard distance matrix for all the 2418 locations. Thing to note here is that the matrix is not symmetric due to U-turns, one-ways etc. that may result into different distances for 'to' and 'from' journey between source and destination.

Table 2. Distance matrix

Distance matrix		Destination Index					
		0	1	2	3	:	2417
Source Index	0	0	11.3769	20.4557	38.1227	:	681.4235
	1	11.3769	0	9.0788	28.9141	:	679.1758
	2	20.4557	9.0788	0	22.3791	:	679.7786
	:	:	:	:	:	:	:
	2417	679.2328	676.9851	677.5878	677.9406	:	0

4 Methodology

There are two parts to this problem, Forecasting and Optimization. To build a robust supply chain for the future, temporal changes need to be considered. This constitutes the first part of the solution. The second part is optimal placement of refineries and depots i.e., Supply Chain Optimization. Further discussion would be on the proposed solution for the problem.

4.1 Biomass Forecasting

The objective of this task is to predict annual biomass production for each location by leveraging historical biomass data. The dataset, as illustrated in Table 1, comprises distinct time series for each location, totaling 2418 unique time series. Notably, each time series encompasses 8 lags, representing the average biomass production from 2010 to 2017. Individually, each time series contains minimal data, posing a challenge for training simple statistical models such as ARIMA without the prerequisite data pre-processing [21].

AutoML was used for forecasting the values for 2018 and 2019. Although AutoML for time series is in its early stages, it can yield pretty accurate results. For this problem, AutoGluon Time Series (AG-TS) was used, which automatically selects the best model for a given time series dataset. There are two families of forecasting when it comes to large panels of time series. First is to fit local parametric statistical models to each time series individually. Second is to fit more expressive machine learning models to all time series at once. AutoGluon fits a model in both the approaches and builds a weighted ensemble on top of it [12].

The dataset comprises 2418 distinct time series, each characterized by unique dynamics, including variations in magnitude and trends. AG-TS employs a data-agnostic approach to construct both local and global models. The dataset was clustered to group together those time series which exhibited similar patterns. The clustering utilized K-Means with Euclidean distance as the metric for cluster assignment and barycenter computation [22]. This process aimed to mitigate underfitting by reducing the diverse dynamics within a cluster. We opted for 8 clusters, striking a balance between cluster similarity, the number of clusters, and cluster size considerations directly impacting training time. Statistical parameters such as Mean, Standard Deviation, and differences between 2015–2016 and 2016–17 were computed and treated as features during clustering to improve cluster quality. Figure 3 illustrates the average biomass production per year (2010–2017) for all samples within each cluster.

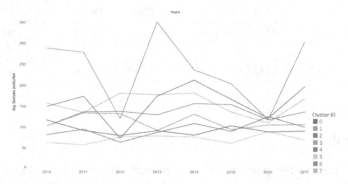

Fig. 3. Average biomass production per year (2010–2017) for each cluster.

Following the clustering of time series into eight distinct clusters, each cluster underwent training and hyperparameter optimization using AG-TS to predict biomass production for the upcoming year (2018). Only temporal features were considered for training, with features related to location (latitude and longitude) excluded due to their observed lack of significant impact on predictions, as indicated by our analysis. AutoGluon provides a rich set of predefined presets that is high level configuration for fitting a model. In this paper, data was trained using the "best_quality" preset with Mean Absolute Scaled Error (MASE) as evaluation metric. As no specific validation set was provided, Auto-Gluon holds the window with last prediction length time steps of each time series as a validation set for cross validation [22]. After forecasting for 2018, above steps are repeated for forecasting the values for 2019, considering the 2018 forecasts as given and including them in training data. For every cluster, Fig. 4 shows average biomass production per year (2010–2018) for all samples within that cluster.

Table 3 specifies the parameters/arguments passed into AutoGluon for time series prediction. These parameters stay the same when predicting for both years - 2018 & 2019.

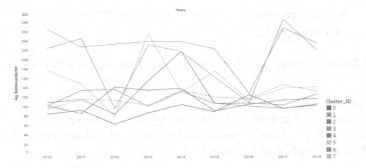

Fig. 4. Average biomass production per year (2010–2018) for each cluster.

Table 3. Parameters passed to AutoGluon Time Series Predictor

Argument	Value
enable_ensemble	True
evaluation_metric	MASE
exculed_model_types	None
hyperparameters	Best_quality
num_val_windows	1
prediction_length	1
random_seed	None
time_limit	None
verbosity	2

4.2 Supply Chain Optimization

Problem Statement. The problem statement is adopted from Shell.AI Hackathon 2023 (Agricultural Waste Challenge) [1]. The task is to build a robust supply chain based on forecasted values which minimizes the costs as well as carbon footprint. Figure 1 shows the three stages of biomass yield in order namely Harvesting sites, Depots and Refineries.

Notations. Following notations are followed throughout this paper. All values are dimensionless. Further in this paper, python indexing format has been used as well for the below notations for easier formulations.

- $D_{ij} \rightarrow$ Distance from i to j
- $B_{ij} \rightarrow$ Biomass transported from i to j
- $P_{jk} \rightarrow$ Pellets transported from j to k
- $X_i \rightarrow$ Binary variable representing selection of ith location as Harvesting site
- $Y_j \rightarrow$ Binary variable representing selection of jth location as Depot
- $Z_k \rightarrow$ Binary variable representing selection of kth location as Refinery
- $Cap_{depot} \rightarrow$ Yearly processing capacity of depot (20000)

- $Cap_{refinery} \rightarrow$ Yearly processing capacity of refinery (100000)
- $Biomass_i \rightarrow$ Biomass production of ith location

Objective. Objective comprises of minimizing the total cost which consists of two components.

1. Transportation Cost
   The cost incurred in transportation of Biomass yield from harvesting sites to depots and pellets from depots to refineries represented by Eq. (1). Minimizing this cost will effectively reduce carbon emission as well.

$$Cost_{transport} = \left(\sum_{i,j} D_{ij} \times B_{ij} \right) + \left(\sum_{j,k} D_{jk} \times P_{jk} \right) \tag{1}$$

2. Underutilization Cost
   Cost incurred due to underutilization of the depot and refineries available resources which is represented by Eq. (2).

$$Cost_{underutilization} = \left(\sum_{j} \left(Cap_{depot} - \sum_{i} B_{ij} \right) \right) + \left(\sum_{k} \left(Cap_{refinery} - \sum_{j} P_{jk} \right) \right) \tag{2}$$

Total cost is the summation of above two costs represented by Eq. (3).

$$Cost = 0.001 \times Cost_{transport} + Cost_{underutilization} \tag{3}$$

Constraints.

C1 All values must be greater than or equal to zero
C2 Number of depots should be less than or equal to 25.
C3 Number of refineries should be less than or equal to 5.
C4 Total Biomass reaching each depot must be less than or equal to its capacity (20000)
C5 Total Pellets reaching each refinery must be less than or equal to its capacity (10^5)
C6 Total Biomass transported from each harvesting site must be less than or equal to the forecasted value for that location.
C7 At least 80% of total forecasted Biomass must be utilized.
C8 Harvesting site and Refinery cannot be at same location
C9 Harvesting site and Depot cannot be at same location
C10 Total amount of biomass entering each preprocessing depot is equal to the total amount of pellets exiting that depot

Solution. This optimization problem was formulated and solved using Mixed Integer Linear Programming. Gurobi's python library was used for solving the given problem [19]. MILP becomes computationally very expensive with increasing variables and constraints, especially binary variables. Thus, it is important to formulate efficient linear constraints and minimize the number of variables to get optimal solutions in a feasible amount of time. Considering all the 2418 locations at once for optimization becomes computationally expensive in terms of time as well as space. For instance, the variable **B**ij (Biomass transported from i to j) can take 2418 x 2418 (> 5 million !) values alone. According to our experiments, even 64GB of RAM wasn't sufficient enough if this approach was followed, even with minimal binary variables and optimized linear constraints. The pre-solve stage of the Gurobi solver alone would consume a substantial amount of RAM at this scale. [20]. To tackle this issue, the approach employed a "divide and conquer" strategy, resolving the optimization problem efficiently and producing excellent results within a feasible timeframe. Figure 5 shows the high-level workflow of this approach.

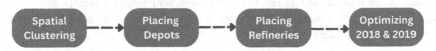

Fig. 5. High-level workflow of optimization approach

The devised approach named "regional optimization" is a much better and efficient approach to solve the problem. The entire map of Gujarat is divided into distinct smaller regions and each region is optimized independently. As solvers like Gurobi are RAM extensive solvers and do not use GPU, there is very less parallelization and memory utilization. So, to effectively use memory and reduce the run time, all clusters were solved at once using local and Google Colab instances. This approach speeds up the entire process with parallelization and thus, making the solution more scalable.

Agglomerative Clustering. Using Agglomerative clustering with linkage – complete, a total 9 clusters were formed considering the size of each cluster (directly proportional to the complexity of optimization) and total Biomass production from each cluster, for the complete map. Cost between any (i, j) pair was calculated as - $D_{ij} \times Biomass_j$, and on the basis of this cost matrix, clustering was done. This drastically reduced the variable space from 2418×2418 to average of approximately 300×300. Figure 6 visualizes the final clusters.

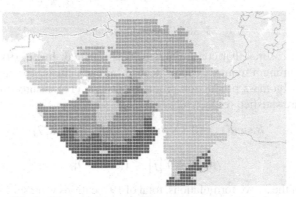

Fig. 6. Clusters obtained after agglomerative clustering

Placing Depots. After clustering, depots are placed with respect to each cluster. ***Biomass*** for each location used for placing depots and refineries is the minimum biomass production among 2018 & 2019 for that location. Following are the formulations required.

- Objective

Minimize the cost of transportation of biomass from harvesting sites to depots Eq. (1). & underutilization cost of depots Eq. (2). ***B&D*** represent biomass supply and distance matrix respectively. Equation (4) represents the objective function to be minimized for optimal placement of depots.

$$Minimize\left(\sum B * D + \sum_i 20000 - B.sum(axis = 0)[i]\right) \tag{4}$$

- Subject to

$$\forall i B.sum(axis = 1)[i] \leq Biomass[i]\{From\ C6\} \tag{5}$$

$$\forall j \begin{cases} Y_{mask}[j] = \max(B[:,j], 0) \\ Y[j] = \min(Y_{mask}[j], 1) \end{cases} \tag{6}$$

$$\forall i \begin{cases} X_{mask}[i] = \max(B[i], 0) \\ X[i] = \min(X_{mask}[i], 1) \end{cases} \tag{7}$$

Equation (5) ensures that constraint 6 (C6) is satisfied. Equation (6) & Eq. (7) represent selection of a location as depots and harvesting sites respectively. This is done using matrix operations for two reasons. One is to avoid having binary variables for all possible i, j pairs. And second is to linearize the constraints. If done in a naive way, it would include the product of variables, converting the problem into higher orders. i, j are subject to particular cluster's size.

$$\forall i B.sum(axis = 0)[i] \leq 20000\{from\ C4\} \tag{8}$$

$$Y.sum() \leq num\_depots \tag{9}$$

Equation (8) ensures that constraint 4 (C4) is satisfied. In Eq. (9) ***num_depots*** is chosen as the minimum required depots needed for each cluster for processing at least 80% of cluster's biomass production. Equation (10) & (11) ensures that constraints 7 (C7) & 9 (C9) are satisfied respectively.

$$B.sum() \geq (0.8 * Biomass.sum())\{fromC7\} \tag{10}$$

$$\forall j X[j] + Y[j] \leq 1\{fromC9\} \tag{11}$$

As a result of the above formulations, total of 19 locations were selected to be depots.

Placing Refineries. On the basis of shortlisted depot locations, refineries are placed for the entire map, without any cluster knowledge. Following are the formulations for placing refineries.

- Objective

Minimizing the cost of transportation of pellets from Depots to refineries Eq. (1) & underutilization cost of refineries Eq. (2). Equation (12) represents the objective function to be minimized for optimal placement of refineries. P represents the pellet supply matrix.

$$Minimize\left(\sum P * D + \sum_k 100000 - P.sum(axis = 0)[k]\right) \qquad (12)$$

- Subject to

$$\forall j \begin{cases} Y_{mask}[j] = \max(P[j], 0) \\ Y[j] = min(Y_{mask}[j], 1) \end{cases} \qquad (13)$$

$$\forall k \begin{cases} Z_{mask}[k] = max(P[:, k], 0) \\ Z[k] = min(Z_{mask}[k], 1) \end{cases} \qquad (14)$$

$$\forall j P.sum(axis = 1)[j] \le 20000\{\text{from C4}\} \qquad (15)$$

$$\forall k P.sum(axis = 0)[k] \le 100000\{\text{from C5}\} \qquad (16)$$

$$Y.sum() = 19\{no.\,of\,depots\,chosen\,were\,19\} \qquad (17)$$

$$Z.sum() \le 5\{\text{from C 3}\} \qquad (18)$$

Equations (13) & (14) represent selection of a location as depots and refineries respectively similar to Eq. (6) & (7). Equation (15), (16) & (18) ensure that C4, C5 & C3 are satisfied respectively. Equation (17) ensures that number of depots chosen are 19. In above formulations, $(j, k) = (19, 2148)$. Total 5 locations were chosen as refineries after this step. Figure 7 shows the shortlisted depot and refinery locations after the above two steps.

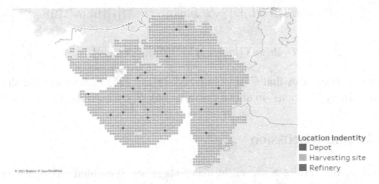

Fig. 7. Shortlisted Depots and Refineries

Optimization for 2018 & 2019. After acquiring the shortlisted locations for depots and refineries, supply chain is designed for both the years separately using the same formulations which are given below.

- Objective

$$exp1 = \sum B * D + \sum P * D \tag{19}$$

$$exp2 = \sum_j 20000 - B.sum(axis = 0)[j] + \sum_k 100000 - P.sum(axis = 0)[k] \tag{20}$$

$$Minimize(exp1 + exp2) \tag{21}$$

Equations (19) & (20) represent transportation and underutilization costs respectively. Equation (21) represents the objective function to be minimized for optimal supply chain.

- Subject to

The equations corresponding to constraints C4, C5, C6 & C7 can be written exactly in same way as written in previous sections. Respective examples for each are Eq. (8), Eq. (16), Eq. (5) & Eq. (10). Also, the equations for assignment of a location as depot, refinery or harvesting site remains the same as well. Respective examples are Eq. (6), Eq. (14), & Eq. (7). The remaining required formulations are given below.

$$Z.sum() = 3 \tag{22}$$

$$Y.sum() = 15 \tag{23}$$

Number of refineries and depots are chosen by relaxing the comparison constraint in this approach as shown in Eq. (22) & Eq. (23). This relaxation is done considering the weightage of underutilization cost over transportation cost as well as the time is reduced drastically as the number of combinations for choosing a depot or refinery location reduces.

$$\forall j B.sum(axis = 0)[j] = P.sum(axis = 1)[j]\{\text{from } C10\} \tag{24}$$

$$\forall indices X[indices] = 0\{\text{from } C8\&C9\} \tag{25}$$

Equation (24) ensures that C10 is satisfied. In Eq. (25) *indices* are the shortlisted depots and refinery locations. In above formulations (i, j, k) will be $(2418, 19, 5)$.

5 Results and Discussion

In this section, the results achieved at every stage are presented. Also, the potential improvements as well as some alternative approaches are discussed. The model was trained with following hardware specifications.

- Intel i5 12450H with 8 GB RAM, 4 GB VRAM (GeForce GTX 1650 Mobile)
- Google Colab 12 GB free instances.

Table 4. Cross Validation MASE for 2018

Cluster No	MASE
1	0.534
2	0.6654
3	0.8170
4	0.5103
5	0.9459
6	0.8302
7	1.2670
8	0.9138

Table 5. Cross Validation MASE for 2019

Cluster No	MASE
1	0.1747
2	0.0780
3	0.1409
4	0.1275
5	0.1220
6	0.1044
7	0.1157
8	0.1938

5.1 Forecasting and Optimization Results

Tables 4 and 5 show the MASE of the best fit model by AutoGluon for every cluster. This score is calculated as a result of cross validation. Figure 8 shows the final placement of depots and refineries after optimization.

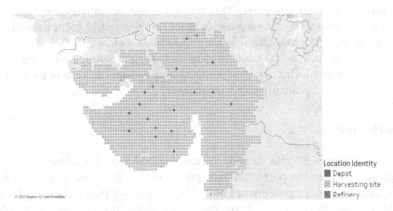

Fig. 8. Optimization Results

Table 6 shows the total transportation as well as underutilization cost for both years. The costs are calculated according to Eq. (1), (2) & (3).

5.2 Alternate Time Series Approach

Even though the approach adopted in this paper i.e., AutoML for time series provided reasonably good results, there is a lot of room for improvement. The accuracy can be further improved by custom hyper parameter tuning. Another approach which came close to AG-TS was converting the forecasting problem into a supervised problem and

Table 6. Transportation Cost & Underutilization for 2018 & 2019

Year	2018	2019
Transport Cost	52272.462	52740.61
Underutilization	20	20

train it using AutoGluon Tabular [23]. Due to scarcity of lags in each time series, each cluster was further divided into four sub time series using a window slicing method with a window of 5 [24]. Each of the 5 lags represents the local patterns of the original time series. The last lag is considered as the target variable and the first 4 as features. AutoGluon Tabular was used to train on this model. Intuition behind this process was to convert forecasting problem into a supervised setting to learn the local patterns caused by past 4 years and generate enough data for it to train upon, while clustering handles homogeneity in trends of a given cluster for better fitting.

5.3 Improved Clustering Methodology

A robust yet reasonably accurate and intuitive assumption is made in the placement of depots: that each cluster is independent of the others. Despite the minimal dependency introduced by our approach, as refineries are placed without cluster knowledge, there is room for potential improvement. This method could be enhanced by introducing clustering with constraints, ensuring each cluster remains independent throughout the optimization process. For example, imposing constraints such as clusters having biomass production of at least 100,000 could isolate each region entirely, allowing for their independent resolution. This could potentially lead to superior results by addressing regional dynamics in a mutually exclusive manner.

6 Conclusion

This paper introduces a versatile and efficient methodology for addressing complex supply chain optimization problems, exemplified by the Biomass supply chain case. The approach combines mathematical optimization and heuristic techniques to deliver high-quality solutions efficiently. Furthermore, it underscores the value of AutoML in Time Series forecasting and its potential in solving real-world challenges. While this study focuses on a generalized framework without region-specific features like rainfall for forecasting, it acknowledges the scope for further enhancements, as discussed in Sect. 5.2. Moreover, the heuristic part of the solution can be strengthened further as mentioned in Sect. 5.1.

In practical terms, this research holds profound implications for the energy sector. The optimized Biomass supply chain design paves the way for regions to transition effectively from fossil fuels to sustainable biofuels, curbing carbon emissions and transportation costs while promoting eco-friendly energy production. Ultimately, this research contributes not only to efficient supply chain management but also to a more sustainable and eco-conscious energy future for us all.

References

1. Shell.ai Hackathon for Sustainable and Affordable Energy. https://www.shell.com/energy-and-innovation/digitalisation/digital-and-ai-competitions/shell-ai-hackathon-for-sustainable-and-affordable-energy.html
2. Madhulatha T.S.: An overview on clustering methods. arXiv preprint arXiv:12051117
3. Jain, A.K., Duin, R.P.W., Mao, J.: Statistical pattern recognition: a review. IEEE Trans. Pattern Anal. Mach. Intell. **22**, 4–37 (2000)
4. Aghabozorgi, S., Shirkhorshidi, A.S., Wah, T.Y.: Time-series clustering–a decade review. Inf. Syst. **53**, 16–38 (2015)
5. Hyndman, R.J., Athanasopoulos, G.: Forecasting: principles and practice. OTexts (2018)
6. Benidis, K., Rangapuram, S.S., Flunkert, V., et al.: Deep learning for time series forecasting: tutorial and literature survey. ACM Comput. Surv. **55**, 1–36 (2022)
7. Taylor, S.J., Letham, B.: Forecasting at scale. Am. Stat. **72**, 37–45 (2018)
8. Paldino, G.M., De Stefani, J., De Caro, F., Bontempi, G.: Does automl outperform naive forecasting? Eng. Proc. **5**, 36 (2021)
9. Jin, H., Song, Q., Hu, X.: Auto-keras: an efficient neural architecture search system. In: Proceedings of the 25th ACM SIGKDD International Conference on Knowledge Discovery & Data Mining, pp 1946–1956 (2019)
10. LeDell, E., Poirier, S.: H2o automl: Scalable automatic machine learning. In: Proceedings of the AutoML Workshop at ICML (2020)
11. Alteryx EvalML 0.36.0 Documentation. https://evalml.alteryx.com/en/stable/. Accessed 15 Sep 2023
12. Shchur, O., Turkmen, C., Erickson, N., et al.: AutoGluon-TimeSeries: AutoML for Probabilistic Time Series Forecasting. arXiv preprint arXiv:230805566 (2023)
13. Garcia, D.J., You, F.: Supply chain design and optimization: challenges and opportunities. Comput. Chem. Eng. **81**, 153–170 (2015)
14. Sun, O., Fan, N.: A review on optimization methods for biomass supply chain: models and algorithms, sustainable issues, and challenges and opportunities. Process Integr. Optim. Sustain. **4**, 203–226 (2020)
15. Kuo, R.J., Han, Y.S.: A hybrid of genetic algorithm and particle swarm optimization for solving bi-level linear programming problem–A case study on supply chain model. Appl. Math. Model. **35**, 3905–3917 (2011)
16. Mastrocinque, E., Yuce, B., Lambiase, A., Packianather, M.S.: A multi-objective optimization for supply chain network using the bees algorithm. Int. J. Eng. Bus. Manage. **5**, 38 (2013)
17. Lim, C.H., Ngan, S.L., Ng, W.P.Q., et al.: Biomass supply chain management and challenges. In: Value-Chain of Biofuels, pp 429–444. Elsevier (2022)
18. De Meyer, A., Cattrysse, D., Rasinmäki, J., Van Orshoven, J.: Methods to optimise the design and management of biomass-for-bioenergy supply chains: a review. Renew. Sustain. Energy Rev. **31**, 657–670 (2014)
19. Gurobi Python API. https://www.gurobi.com/documentation/10.0/refman/py_python_api_overview.html#sec:Python. Accessed 15 Sep 2023
20. Advanced Gurobi Algorithms. https://assets.gurobi.com/pdfs/user-events/2016-frankfurt/Die-Algorithmen.pdf. Accessed 15 Sep 2023
21. Adhikari, R., Agrawal, R.K.: An introductory study on time series modeling and forecasting. arXiv preprint arXiv:13026613 (2013)
22. Forecasting Time Series - In Depth - AutoGluon 0.8.2 documentation. https://auto.gluon.ai/stable/tutorials/timeseries/forecasting-indepth.html. Accessed 15 Sep 2023
23. Erickson, N., Mueller, J., Shirkov, A., et al.: Autogluon-tabular: Robust and accurate automl for structured data. arXiv preprint arXiv:200306505 (2020)
24. Iglesias, G., Talavera, E., González-Prieto, Á., et al.: Data augmentation techniques in time series domain: A survey and taxonomy. arXiv preprint arXiv:220613508 (2022)

Prediction of Deposition Parameters in Manufacturing of Ni-Based Coating Using ANN

Shubhangi Suryawanshi[1,2] , Amrut P. Bhosale[3,4(✉)] , Digvijay G. Bhosale[5] ,
and Sanjay W. Rukhande[6]

[1] Department of Computer Science Engineering, Bennett University, Greater Noida 201 310,
Uttar Pradesh, India
[2] Department of Artificial Intelligence and Data Science, Dr. D. Y. Patil Institute of Technology,
Pune 411 018, Maharashtra, India
[3] Department of Mechatronics Engineering, Rajarambapu Institute of Technology,
Rajaramnagar, Shivaji University, Kolhapur 415 414, Maharashtra, India
amrut.bhosale@ritindia.edu
[4] Department of Mechanical Engineering, Veermata Jijabai Technological Institute, Matunga,
Mumbai 400 019, Maharashtra, India
[5] Department of Mechanical Engineering, Dr. D. Y. Patil Institute of Technology, Pune 411 018,
Maharashtra, India
[6] Mechanical Engineering Department, Fr. C. Rodrigues Institute of Technology, Vashi, Navi
Mumbai 400 703, India

Abstract. Qualities of coatings deposited by High-velocity oxy-fuel (HVOF)
spray technique are sometimes greatly influenced by the deposition parameters.
It is difficult to research and develop a comprehensive model of the HVOF spray
process because of the complex chemical and thermodynamic processes involved.
The aim of this study is to use a back propagation neural network to create a
predictive model for the mechanical properties of NiCrSiBFe coatings deposited
by HVOF. The impact of the deposition parameters with respect to the intermediate
process is also examined in this study. The change in porosity, nano-hardness, and
sliding wear rate of coatings under various powder feed rate, stand-off distance,
and oxygen gas flow rate were predicted using back propagation neural network
algorithm. Similar trends are seen when comparing the predicted and experimental
results, indicating that the developed model correctly predicted the properties of
NiCrSiBFe coatings. The average errors for porosity, nano-hardness, and sliding
wear rate are 1.816%, 1.997%, and 4.405%, respectively. The developed back
propagation model can therefore be applied to coating operating practice for spray
performance prediction, and also for parameter management and optimisation.

Keywords: AI in manufacturing · ANN · Coating · Process parameters
optimization · sliding wear rate · High-velocity oxy-fuel (HVOF)

© The Author(s), under exclusive license to Springer Nature Switzerland AG 2024
D. Garg et al. (Eds.): IACC 2023, CCIS 2053, pp. 72–81, 2024.
https://doi.org/10.1007/978-3-031-56700-1_7

1 Introduction

The thermal spray processes, which permits the application of coatings of varying nature, adaptability, and superior characteristics on material surfaces with minimal added value in order to boost their performance and properties is one solution to these difficulties [1, 2]. A range of coating procedures known as thermal spray, deposit finely dispersed non-metallic or metallic materials while they are still molten or semi-molten [3, 4]. The high-velocity oxy-fuel process (HVOF) and atmospheric plasma spray (APS) are most preferred thermal spray techniques due to their cost effectiveness [4]. The deposition parameters of thermal spray coatings have a significant impact on performance of the coating. Many processes controlling variables, including gas flow rate, powder feed rate, current, power voltage, stand-off distance etc., have an impact on the mechanical and morphological properties of the coatings during plasma spray deposition technique. The overall performance of the deposited coating is significantly influenced by the values of those parameters being either too high or too low. However, combination of these factors may, to some extent, have an impact on the quality of the coating [5–7]. The coating's porosity increased as spraying power decreased. When the spraying power was sufficient, nearly all of the powder was totally melted. The porosity of coating is unaffected by the spraying power when higher spraying power is utilised [8]. When spraying power is higher, degree of melting of the powder decreases with an increase in the spraying distance [9]. The main process parameters that have greatest impact on properties of in-flight particles were spraying distance and fuel or gas flow rates [10]. Therefore, optimum process and operating parameters are essential for superior wear resistance and minimum coefficient of friction of the coatings based on type of application.

The most popular technique for estimating the effects of process parameters on the coating characteristics is the Taguchi design approach, which is a preliminary solution to determine the optimal process and operating parameters and differentiate the important and unimportant variables [11–13]. However, as the coating quality is often impacted by a cumulative influence of numerous process and operational parameters, it may fail to attain the precise ideal parameters. The spray process has also been effectively simulated and controlled using numerical simulation and modelling [7, 14]. However, numerical modelling struggles to simulate the actual behaviors of the thermal spray mechanism since it is a complicated multi-physical event. Consequently, a technique like machine learning algorithms that are more beneficial in precise analysis, accurate prediction, and parameter optimization is essential. Processes like thermal spraying technologies, which involve complicated thermal and chemical reactions, must be studied using a robust computational model, like the ANN model. However, it is difficult or expensive to collect enough data sets about tribological properties of thermal spray coatings, particularly to gather enough information about the coating properties [15, 16]. As a result, the use of shallow ANN models, which typically have fewer than three hidden layers and are used to applications with relatively little data, has also drawn more attention in the context of thermal spraying.

The application of ANN models in material science has been widely investigated; however, the extent to which these models can forecast the porosity, sliding wear rates, and nano-hardness of thermal sprayed Ni-based coatings is not well documented. In this study, the training and validation datasets for back propagation neural network model was created through carrying out HVOF spray deposited coating's experiments. The developed model, which is intended to thoroughly investigate the HVOF deposition technique, has been used to corroborate the relationship between the high-velocity oxy-fuel spray process parameters and the mechanical performance of coatings. The back propagation model's accuracy and dependability were confirmed by additional experiments.

The organization of this article is as follows: In Sect. 2, the main conceptual threads of the experimental work and techniques used in characterization are presented, explained, and illustrated. The study's methodology is also explained and shown in the same Section. Section 3 presents the results of as-deposited coating characterization and analysis of results obtained from developed back propagation ANN mode. This section also contains effect of deposition parameters on output characteristics under considerations. Section 4 provides an overview of the study's main conclusions and their consequences.

2   Experimental and Characterization Methods

2.1   Coating Deposition

The substrate material was selected to be stainless steel 316L grade, and its true composition was verified using an optical emission spectroscope. In this work, the commercially available powder of NiCrSiBFe was employed as feedstock. The powder had a nominal distribution of particle sizes of range of 5–35 μm when it was received. Cr 14.5%, Fe 4.5%, Si 4.5%, B 3.2% and C 0.7%, along with the remainder of Ni, made up the NiCrSiBFe powder's composition. Before applying the coating powder using a spray gun, the surfaces of substrate were pressure-blasted to improve adherence. The conditions for surface blasting were as follows: virgin grade brown alumina blasting material, air pressure of 5 bar, blasting angle of 90° with a blasting distance of 150 mm. High-velocity oxy-fuel spraying, also known as HVOF, was used to manufacture the coatings under investigation. Table 1 summarizes HVOF spray deposition process parameters.

Table 1. Coating deposition parameters for plasma spray.

Parameters	Values
Powder feed rate (g/min)	35, 55, 75
Gun traverse speed (m/s)	0.7
Standoff distance (mm)	150, 200, 250
Particle velocity (m/s)	534
Oxygen gas flow rate (SLPM)	200, 240, 280
Propane gas flow rate (SLPM)	60

2.2 As-Deposited Coating Characterization

The experiments were carried out in accordance with ASTM G99 standard practise for dry sliding wear. A ball-on-disc tribometer (Model: TR20LE CHM-800) designed by Ducom Instruments in Bengaluru, India was used to conduct dry sliding wear tests. Temperatures between 21 and 27 °C and humidity levels between 45 and 55% were the environmental conditions under which the tests were carried out. Alumina balls were used as the test counterpart and were cleaned with alcohol beforehand. The values for the wear depth and frictional force were determined using an LVDT and a load cell, respectively. Every two seconds during a test run, the tribo-meter's data acquisition system can record one data point. The exact same operating parameters are used in each experiment three times. The scanning electron microscope (ZEISS Gemini) was used for examination of deposited coating's microstructure across the cross-section and ImageJ software for the purpose to determine porosity in as-deposited coatings. An average value was obtained after considering fifteen field of views. An Hysitron TS77, manufactured by Bruker Inc., U.S.A., was used to test nano-hardness of the coatings. The hardness was measured at ten different locations on cross-section with load of 9 mN lasted for 15 s and an average hardness is considered in each of the coating.

2.3 Data Pre-processing

Pre-processing was done on the collected data in order to configure, train, and validate the back propagation neural network model. The operational parameters and test results under consideration were first gathered through the experiments. A database containing 144 records was created from 24 sets of HVOF spray tests and associated coating characterization data. Three deposition process parameters make up the back propagation neural network model: stand-off distance, powder feed rate, and oxygen gas flow rate. Targets included sliding wear rate, porosity, and nano-hardness. Table 2 contains a summary of the experimental values for the inputs and outputs. In pre-processing, the data would be normalised to fall between −1 and 1 to avoid calculation errors brought on by varying input parameter magnitudes. The data was divided into three sets at random using dividerand data division technique. A training dataset and a validation dataset were each comprised of three datasets. The proportions were 20% and 80%, in that order.

Table 2. Database for development of back propagation neural network model.

Sr. No.	HVOF spray deposition parameters			Coating properties		
	Powder feed rate (g/min)	Stand-off distance (mm)	O_2 flow rate (SLPM)	Porosity (%)	Nano-hardness (GPa)	Wear rate $\times 10^{-5}$ $mm^3/N \cdot m$
1	35	150	200	0.873 ± 0.091	6.6 ± 0.1	12.72 ± 1.44
2	35	150	240	0.972 ± 0.261	6.5 ± 0.1	12.37 ± 3.45
3	35	150	280	0.873 ± 0.180	6.3 ± 0.1	11.92 ± 1.20
4	35	150	200	0.765 ± 0.207	6.2 ± 0.1	5.80 ± 2.39
5	35	200	240	0.828 ± 0.306	6.3 ± 0.1	7.13 ± 3.08
6	35	200	280	0.711 ± 0.225	6.5 ± 0.1	7.20 ± 1.33
7	35	200	200	0.891 ± 0.153	6.3 ± 0.1	4.78 ± 2.00
8	35	200	240	0.693 ± 0.216	6.4 ± 0.1	11.16 ± 1.44
9	55	250	280	1.053 ± 0.099	6.2 ± 0.1	17.85 ± 1.49
10	55	250	200	0.981 ± 0.243	6.2 ± 0.2	9.26 ± 2.48
11	55	250	240	1.179 ± 0.171	6.6 ± 0.1	8.63 ± 1.58
12	55	250	280	1.107 ± 0.297	6.3 ± 0.1	10.07 ± 1.68
13	55	150	200	1.053 ± 0.189	6.2 ± 0.1	9.01 ± 1.33
14	55	150	240	1.431 ± 0.153	6.7 ± 0.2	4.83 ± 2.53
15	55	150	280	1.197 ± 0.198	6.3 ± 0.1	7.27 ± 2.65
16	55	150	200	1.287 ± 0.180	6.4 ± 0.1	5.38 ± 1.59
17	75	200	240	1.008 ± 0.261	7.1 ± 0.2	4.24 ± 2.47
18	75	200	280	1.341 ± 0.333	6.8 ± 0.2	4.10 ± 2.75
19	75	200	200	1.584 ± 0.207	6.4 ± 0.2	11.52 ± 2.70
20	75	200	240	1.467 ± 0.198	6.5 ± 0.1	12.18 ± 1.24
21	75	250	280	0.837 ± 0.306	6.7 ± 0.1	11.44 ± 3.01
22	75	250	200	1.440 ± 0.207	6.6 ± 0.2	6.35 ± 1.13
23	75	250	240	1.170 ± 0.279	6.3 ± 0.1	7.39 ± 2.08
24	75	250	280	1.377 ± 0.171	6.6 ± 0.1	16.18 ± 2.13

2.4 Structural Model of an ANN

One limitation of the single layer perceptron is that it is limited to classifying two-dimensional linear systems; it is not capable of classifying multi-dimensional planes or non-linear systems. Usually, adding more layers is the accepted method of getting around this restriction. A crucial component of the multi-layer perceptron, the hidden layer is introduced between the input and output layers. The neural network algorithm that uses backpropagation systematically addresses the learning problem of hidden layer weights of connections in multi-layer neural networks. According to Kolmogorov theory, every complicated classification problem may be solved using a double hidden layer perceptron. More weight adjustments are required for multi-layered networks than for single-layer perceptron to achieve the same training error, and an excessively fine-grained division of space can quickly lead to a decrease in the network's capacity for generalization and induction. Therefore, in this study, a three-layer network is employed.

2.5 Training and Validation of Back Propagation Model

Because there are three inputs and three targets for the network, the number of neurons in the input and output layers was fixed at three. The number of neurons in each hidden layer and the total number of hidden layers are decided upon based on the model's performance during hyper-parameter tuning, taking into account the accuracy of the trained back propagation model and the complexity of the network structure. When there are fewer hidden layers and hidden layer neurons, higher accuracy is typically expected. The model is trained in this study in a supervised manner using the back propagation technique. It employs a multi-layer feed forward neural network, a conventional learning method, that has been trained using the error BP method. The procedure of changing the weights and thresholds of the algorithm, backpropagating the error, and repeating these actions until the target error or the predefined number of iterations was reached. The network's weights and biases are changed during training to optimize performance based on the network performance function.

3 Results and Discussions

3.1 Characterization of As-Deposited Coatings

SEM cross-section micrographs were used to analyze the surface morphology and substrate-coating interface and coating thickness. Figure 1(a) depict the as-sprayed coatings' cross-sectional microstructure. SEM micrographs shown in Fig. 1(a) demonstrate consistent interfacial adhesion throughout the base material and all coatings. SEM micrographs in Fig. 1(b) at a magnification of 2000X clearly show the combination of partially molten and fully molten particles. The as-sprayed coated surface has few unmelted particles and micro-voids. Because there are no fractures to be detected in either coating cross-section or on surface, the SEM micrographs demonstrate the superior quality of NiCrSiBFe coating.

Since the resistance to wear of coatings is related to coating hardness, coating hardness is a deciding factor in wear resistance. The nano-hardness of the coatings was evaluated across the cross-section. The maximum nano-hardness measured was 7.14 GPa. Coatings deposited by HVOF often shown higher nano-hardness values when compared to APS sprayed coatings. The HVOF coated NiCrSiBFe specimens show lowest porosity as $0.7 \pm 0.1\%$. The level of porosity and splat adhesion affect the nano-hardness of the as-sprayed coatings. Because of its decreased porosity and relatively high splat adhesion, the HVOF coating provided superior nano-hardness.

3.2 Training Results of Back Propagation Model

Table 3 contains a list of the input parameters used to train the back propagation model. The quantity of hidden layer neurons greatly influences the model's training accuracy. Consequently, error tolerance, noise factor, momentum parameter, learning rate of model, and slope parameter are assessed at constant cycles for various values for number of neurons in the hidden layer. As a result, eight neurons are taken into account in this work, which is necessary for the back propagation model to have the ideal structure. Experimental and back propagation model results are shown for three coating qualities in Fig. 2. Table 4 displays the training and validation data; the training data pertains to the first 19 groups, and the validation data pertains to the final 5 groups.

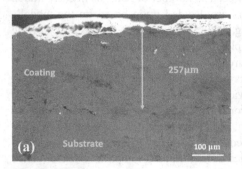

Fig. 1. Micrographs of as-deposited NiCrSiBFe by HVOF (a) cross-section (b) surface morphology

Table 3. Parameters used for training of back propagation model.

Sr. No.	Input parameters	Value
1	Number of input layer neurons	3
2	Number of output layer neurons	3
3	Error tolerance	0.003
4	Noise factor	0.001
5	Learning parameter	0.002
6	Momentum parameter	0.002
7	Slope parameter	0.6

Table 4. Validation parameters used for the back propagation neural network.

Deposition Parameter	Values
Powder feed rate (g/min)	35, 55, 75
Stand-off distance (mm)	150, 200, 250
O_2 flow rate (SLPM)	200, 240, 280

The back propagation model's experimental results and predictions are shown in Fig. 2, where the training data points are indicated by the pink curve and the validation data points by the black curve. Porosity, nano-hardness, and sliding wear rate had average errors of 1.816%, 1.997%, and 4.405%, respectively. It illustrates the strong agreement between the experimental and back propagation model results. Moreover, both the increasing and decreasing trends of results are also similar, proving that developed model is capable of predicting characteristics of coatings under consideration accurately within the specified set of deposition process parameters.

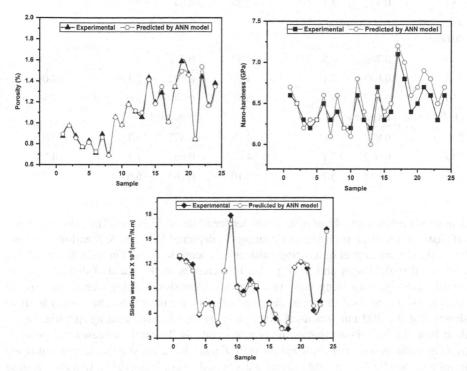

Fig. 2. Experimental and predicted outcomes by ANN model for (a) Porosity, (b) Nano-hardness, and (c) Sliding wear rate

3.3 Validation Results of Back Propagation Model

The relationship between HVOF deposition process parameters and coating attributes such porosity, nano-hardness, and sliding wear rate was investigated using different stand-off distances, powder feed rates, and oxygen gas flow rates. Table 4 presents validation parameters used for the back propagation neural network. Table 5 shows that when the powder feed rate increases, porosity first reduces and then increases, and nano-hardness first increases and then falls. The sliding wear rate exhibits the opposite trend of these trends. Overall comparative investigation shows that better features of HVOF

Table 5. Effect of deposition parameters on output characteristics

Parameter	Porosity	Nano-hardness	Sliding wear rate	Porosity	Nano-hardness	Sliding wear rate
Powder feed rate	Experimental			Predicted		
35	0.693	6.6	5.8	0.634	6.6	5.9
55	0.981	6.7	4.83	0.945	6.8	4.71
75	0.837	7.1	4.24	0.845	7.1	4.12
Stand-off distance	Experimental			Predicted		
150	0.765	6.5	4.83	0.772	6.6	4.76
200	0.693	7.1	4.10	0.692	7.1	4.01
250	0.837	6.7	6.35	0.849	6.6	6.83
O_2 flow rate	Experimental			Predicted		
200	0.873	6.6	4.78	0.872	6.7	4.81
240	0.693	7.1	4.83	0.654	7.1	4.78
280	0.711	6.7	4.10	0.703	6.6	4.03

deposited coatings are obtained at a powder feed rate of 75 g/min. The effect of stand-off distance on three properties of coatings is depicted in Table 5. Stand-off distance has a significant impact on coating hardness, as seen in figure. On the other hand, the porosity first decreases and then gradually increases as the standoff-distance grows. Simultaneously, the sliding wear rate displays a consistent rising trend, whereas the nano-hardness values decrease as the stand-off distance increases. The overall analysis shows that the 200 mm stand-off distance is where all three coating qualities are at their best. Table 5 shows that as the powder feed gas flow rate increases, the porosity first rises and then decreases, while the overall nano-hardness shows a significant rising trend and the sliding wear rate shows a decreased trend. It is evident that the coatings under investigation have better characteristics when the powder feed gas flow rate is 240 SLPM.

4   Conclusion

The performance of NiCrSiBFe HVOF spray deposited coatings was predicted using a model developed by back propagation neural network algorithm. The deposition process parameters such as stand-off distance, powder feed rate, and oxygen gas flow rate were used to predict the coating characteristics such as porosity, nano-hardness, and sliding wear rate. The performance of developed model in terms of accuracy and reliability have been verified using test dataset with relative errors lower than maximum errors of the training and validation datasets. The average errors for porosity, nano-hardness, and sliding wear rate are 1.816%, 1.997%, and 4.405%, respectively. The developed back propagation model can therefore be applied to coating operating practice for spray performance prediction, and also for parameter management and optimisation. The experimental findings and predicted results by BP model on porosity, nano-hardness, and sliding wear rate of indicate that following HVOF spray parameters are optimal for the deposition of NiCrSiBFe coatings: 75 g/min of powder feed rate, 200 mm of stand-off distance, and 240 SLPM of oxygen gas flow rate. The future direction is to involve more parameters related to chemical and thermodynamic of HVOF deposition process since it is difficult to research and develop a comprehensive model of the HVOF spray process because of the complex chemical and thermodynamic processes involved.

References

1. Thakur, L., Arora, N., Jayaganthan, R., Sood, R.: An investigation on erosion behavior of HVOF sprayed WC-CoCr coatings. Appl. Surf. Sci. **258**, 1225–1234 (2011)
2. Singh, J.: A review on mechanisms and testing of wear in slurry pumps, pipeline circuits and hydraulic turbines. J. Tribol. **143**, 1–83 (2021)
3. Hermanek, F.J.: Thermal spray terminology and company origins. ASM Int. (2001)
4. Pawlowski, L.: The Science and Engineering of Thermal Spray Coatings. Wiley (2008)
5. Zeng, Z.Q., Zhang, B., Wang, J.Y.: Study on Properties of Ni Based+WC Coating by Plasma Spray Welding. Powder Metallurgy Industry (2017)
6. Jiang, M., Ma, C., Xia, F., et al.: Application of artificial neural networks to predict the hardness of Ni–TiN nanocoatings fabricated by pulse electrodeposition. Surf. Coat. Technol. **286**, 191–196 (2016)
7. Dongmo, E., Wenzelburger, M., Gadow, R.: Analysis and optimization of the HVOF process by combined experimental and numerical approaches. Surf. Coat. Technol. **202**, 4470–4478 (2008)
8. Zhang, X.C., Xu, B.S., Xuan, F.Z., et al.: Microstructural and porosity variations in the plasma-sprayed Ni-alloy coatings prepared at different spraying powers. J. Alloys Compd. **473**, 145–151 (2009)
9. Lu, Y.P., Li, S.T., Zhu, R.F., et al.: Further studies on the effect of stand-off distance on characteristics of plasma sprayed hydroxyapatite coating. Surf. Coat. Technol. **157**, 221–225 (2002)
10. Saaedi, J., Coyle, T.W., Arabi, H., Mirdamadi, S., Mostaghimi, J.: Effects of HVOF process parameters on the properties of Ni -Cr coatings. J. Therm. Spray Technol. **19**, 521–530 (2010)
11. Singh, J., Kumar, S., Singh, G.: Taguchi's approach for optimization of tribo -resistance parameters Forss304. Mater. Today: Proc. **5**, 5031–5038 (2018)
12. Praveen, A.S., Sarangan, J., Suresh, S., Channabasappa, B.H.: Optimization and erosion wear response of NiCrSiB/WC–Co HVOF coating using Taguchi method. Ceram. Int. **42**, 1094–1104 (2016)
13. Qiao, L., Wu, Y., Hong, S., Zhang, J., Shi, W., Zheng, Y.: Relationships between spray parameters, microstructures and ultrasonic cavitation erosion behavior of HVOF sprayed Fe-based amorphous/nanocrystalline coatings. Ultrason. Sonochem. **39**, 39–46 (2017)
14. Li, M., Christofides, P.D.: Modeling and control of High-Velocity Oxygen-Fuel (HVOF) thermal spray: a tutorial review. J. Therm. Spray Tech. **18**, 753 (2009)
15. Lia, X., Zhu, Y., Xiao, G.: Application of artificial neural networks to predict sliding wear resistance of Ni–TiN nano composite coatings deposited by pulse electrodeposition. Ceram. Int. **40**(8), 11767–11772 (2014)
16. Guessasma, S., Bounazef, M., Nardin, P.: Neural computation analysis of alumina–titania wear resistance coating. Int. J. Refract Metal Hard Mater. **24**(3), 240–246 (2006)

Decision Model for Cost Control of Transmission and Transformation Projects Considering Uncertainty: A GAN Algorithm

Si Shen[1] , Shili Liu[1] , Fulei Chen[1] , Jian Ma[2](✉) , and Jinghua Liu[2]

[1] State Grid Anhui Electric Power Co., Ltd., Economic and Technological Research Institute, Hefei 230071, Anhui, China
shensi2023@126.com
[2] China Electricity Council Technical and Economic Consulting Center of Electronic Power Construction, Beijing 100053, China

Abstract. The article aims to propose an analysis model based on the GAN (General Adversarial Network) algorithm to address the impact of uncertain factors on cost control decisions in power transmission and transformation projects (PTTP). This article deeply analyzes the uncertainty factors of power transmission and transformation engineering (PTTE), identifies the key factors that affect cost control, and uses GAN algorithm to simulate and predict them, improving the accuracy and reliability of the decision-making process. The research results indicate that the uncertainty cost control decision analysis model based on GAN algorithm can effectively improve the cost prediction accuracy of PTTP, with a maximum of 96.5%. This provides an important reference basis for engineering management and decision-making. Therefore, the article provides a new idea and method for cost control of PTTP, which has important theoretical and practical significance.

Keywords: Decision Analysis Model · GAN Algorithm · Power Transmission and Transformation Engineering · Cost Control · Uncertainty Research

1 Introduction

With the rapid development of the economy, the power engineering industry has also developed rapidly, with the development of PTTE advancing by leaps and bounds. According to relevant data, the total investment in China's PTTP is very high, with new investment accounting for more than half of it. However, with the large-scale construction and use of PTTP in China, the issue of cost control is becoming increasingly prominent. The uncertainty factors in the cost control process can have a significant impact on cost control.

At present, many experts and scholars have conducted research and exploration on cost control. Tian Wenjuan has constructed a maturity evaluation index system for construction project cost control based on grey clustering method. The experiment has proven the feasibility of this method, which provides a reference basis for the analysis and evaluation of cost control maturity in practical engineering [1]. Cen Lu studied a cost control and application analysis method for project design phase based on quota design. The experimental results indicate that this method can effectively control the engineering cost [2]. Zhang Aili proposed to strengthen top-level design and reasonably determine preliminary investment estimates. He deepened the plan design, refined the preparation of cost documents, and strengthened the integrated cost control of design and construction economy. He implemented measures and suggestions such as full process cost consulting services, providing reference for cost control and management of such projects [3]. The above content provides new ideas and references for cost control of construction projects, but its practicality and operability are insufficient.

With the continuous development of artificial intelligence technology, GAN algorithm, as a powerful tool, has been widely applied in various fields of decision analysis and prediction models. The article takes PTTE as the research object, analyzes various uncertain factors that affect cost control decisions in depth, and uses GAN algorithm for simulation and prediction. On this basis, this article establishes an uncertain cost control decision analysis model based on GAN algorithm. This article aims to provide a new approach and method for decision-making analysis in the field of cost control in PTTP, and provide strong support for the smooth implementation and cost control of engineering projects.

2 Uncertain Factors in Power Transmission and Transformation Engineering

As a typical infrastructure project, PTTE has the characteristics of long construction period and significant impact from natural conditions. During the construction process, changes in various factors would have varying degrees of impact on the transmission and transformation project, leading to significant uncertainty in the cost control of the transmission and transformation project. When determining cost control objectives, it is usually necessary to consider various uncertain factors that affect the cost of PTTP, such as the decision-making stage, design stage, construction stage, operation and maintenance stage, etc. [4]. In the early decision-making stage of the project, due to the uncertainty of various information, the uncertainty factors of the engineering project would increase, thereby affecting the engineering cost. In the design phase, due to the existence of many uncertain factors in the design scheme, it can also have a significant impact on the cost of PTTP. During the construction phase, changes in construction technology and conditions can cause significant fluctuations in the cost of PTTP [5].

In the project decision-making stage, there are many factors that affect the cost of PTTP, such as market demand, resource supply status, etc., which would have an impact on the project cost. In the project decision-making stage, two main factors are considered: one is technical factors, such as engineering technology level, investment scale, construction standards, etc. On the other hand, there are economic factors, such as raw material prices, product prices, construction conditions, etc.

In terms of technology, the main considerations are natural conditions (such as terrain conditions) and socio-economic conditions (such as market demand). In terms of natural conditions, the main consideration is factors such as natural geographical environment and meteorological conditions. In terms of socio-economic development, the main consideration is the level of socio-economic development, energy supply status, and other factors. In the project decision-making stage, it is usually necessary to compare and select investment plans in order to choose the best investment plan. However, due to the uncertainty of various information, comprehensive analysis and comparison of various plans cannot be carried out. Therefore, only a comprehensive evaluation of several feasible investment plans can be conducted to ultimately select the best investment plan.

For example, when selecting wire sections, the voltage levels that different wire sections can carry are different. Under certain conditions, there may be significant changes in the cross-section of the wire, leading to significant uncertainty in the selection of design schemes. For example, when selecting the type of iron tower, there are significant differences in tower height, height direction, grounding method, etc., which leads to significant uncertainty in the selection of tower type. When selecting transmission line path schemes, there are significant differences in materials and lengths required for different line paths, resulting in significant uncertainty in the cost of PTTP [6].

The construction period of PTTP is long and requires crossing rivers, highways, etc. There are many uncertain factors in the construction process, making it difficult to control the cost of PTTP. For example, during the construction process of an iron tower, changes in various factors would lead to changes in the specifications of the tower, thereby affecting the cost of the tower. During tower construction, due to factors such as terrain conditions and the quality of the tower itself, damage to the tower itself can occur, thereby affecting the cost of the tower. During the installation of iron towers, various factors can also cause changes in the installation costs of tower materials and accessories. When pouring concrete, the increase in construction costs caused by factors such as concrete transportation and mixing would affect the entire project cost. In addition, differences in construction conditions and technical levels can also lead to fluctuations in the cost of PTTP [7].

3 Model Construction Under GAN Algorithm

The GAN algorithm is an alternating training of generators and discriminators to achieve "automatic" adjustment and optimization of samples, in order to learn the internal structure and features of the samples, and generate new data with similar features to real data. The analysis model based on GAN algorithm can effectively utilize existing sample data for training, thereby predicting new sample data. To some extent, it can make up for the shortcomings in the decision-making analysis model for cost control of PTTP.

The GAN algorithm model consists of two parts: a generator and a discriminator. The generator consists of a hidden layer and an output layer, where the hidden layer consists of a fully connected layer, a sigmoid layer, a Dropout layer, and an Adam optimizer. The discriminator consists of a sigmoid activation function and an Adam optimizer. By introducing adversarial structures in the generator to adjust its structural parameters, the generator can generate more accurate sample data [8].

The basic principle of GAN algorithm training is to introduce adversarial structures in the generator, so that there are differences between the samples generated by the generator and the real data, thereby training the discriminator to generate more accurate sample data. The GAN algorithm model introduces adversarial structures to make the generator and discriminator compete with each other, thereby training more accurate sample data. The main training idea is shown in Fig. 1.

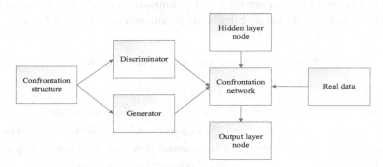

Fig. 1. GAN algorithm model

In Fig. 1, it first introduces the adversarial structure, GAN, in the generator. Then, the generator network is trained by assigning different hidden layer nodes and output layer nodes. Next, this article would input the existing real sample data as a training set into the generator for training. Finally, it adds an adversarial structure to the discriminator, which means that the discriminator also needs to adversarial generate samples, in order to achieve alternating training of the generator and discriminator, and generate more accurate sample data [9].

The training process of GAN algorithm mainly includes the following steps: (1) Generator network training: Firstly, it calculates the error between the output value of the generator network and the true value through backpropagation algorithm, and determines the structural parameters of the generator based on the size of the error. It includes the number of hidden layers, training times, learning rate, and discriminant structure of the generator network. (2) The discriminator training process is to train the generator network through the Adam optimizer, and adjust the parameters in the Adam optimizer to adapt to the sample data. When the number of iterations of the Adam optimizer reaches the set value, training stops and the model reaches a stable state. (3) Cross validation: This article adds parameters from the GAN algorithm as variables to the cross validation experiment. It corrects the GAN algorithm by repeatedly adjusting the error between the generated data and the real data through repeated experiments, so that it can better fit the real sample data. (4) Evaluation indicators: The evaluation indicators of GAN algorithm mainly include accuracy, recall rate, F1 value, and the relationship between accuracy and recall rate. By evaluating the GAN algorithm, it can be seen that it can effectively utilize existing sample data for training, thereby better fitting real sample data and predicting new sample data. The main calculation formulas are shown in Eqs. (1) and (2) [10].

$$\nabla \beta_n \frac{1}{m} \sum_{i=1}^{m} \log\{1 - D[G(z^i)]\} \tag{1}$$

$$\nabla \beta_n \frac{1}{m} \sum_{i=1}^{m} \log D(x^i) + \log\{1 - D[G(z^i)]\} \qquad (2)$$

In Eqs. (1) and (2), D is the discriminator and G is the generator. z and x are the optimization coefficients of the generator and discriminator, respectively, and m represents the number of samples. The main calculation parameters are shown in Table 1.

Table 1. Calculation parameters of GAN algorithm

Parameter	Value	Description
Learning rate	0.0002	The step size for updating network weights
Batch size	64	The number of samples used in each iteration of training
Noise dimension	100	The dimension of the noise vector input to the generator
Generator layers	3	The number of layers in the generator network
Discriminator layers	3	The number of layers in the discriminator network
Training epochs	20000	The number of training iterations
Generator loss weight	1	The weight of the generator loss in the total loss
Discriminator loss weight	1	The weight of the discriminator loss in the total loss
Generator input data range	$[-1, 1]$	The range of input data for the generator
Discriminator input data range	$[-1, 1]$	The range of input data for the discriminator

In Table 1, the learning rate value is 0.0002, the batch size is 64, and the noise dimension equation is 100. The generator and discriminator have 3 layers and 20000 training rounds. The loss weights are all 1, and the input data range is $[-1, 1]$. In the GAN algorithm model, input data and output data are learned by the hidden layer and output layer, respectively, with n neurons in each hidden layer. Each neuron is connected to its neighboring nodes, and each neuron is connected to the output value of an input layer, ultimately generating an output result. During the training process, the generator first converts the input of the training data into the input of the output data, and then the discriminator adjusts the output data to obtain the predicted results. During the model training process, both the generator and discriminator are learned through the Adam optimization algorithm. During the training process, due to the random parameters in the generator, the network can generate new data with similar features to real data, so the generated new data can match the characteristics of real data.

In order to solve the problem of gradient vanishing during the training process, it is necessary to adjust the parameters between the generator and discriminator. In the GAN algorithm, the sigmoid activation function and the Adam optimizer are the two main parameters that affect the performance of the GAN algorithm. By adjusting the sigmoid activation function and Adam optimizer parameters, the generator can generate better sample data.

4 Decision Model Experimental Results

Before conducting the experiment, the article first collected evaluation indicators, and the collection results are shown in Table 2.

Table 2. Collection of evaluation indicators

Object	Index	Number of people	Percentage
Decision-making and analysis model of cost control	Accuracy	135	26%
	Response time	121	23%
	Stability	125	24%
	Reliability	139	27%

There are a total of 520 people participating in the collection task in Table 2, of which 135 people have chosen the accuracy rate, accounting for 26%. The number of people who selected response time is 121, accounting for 23%. The number of people choosing stability is 125, accounting for 24%, while the number of people choosing reliability is 139, accounting for 27%. Therefore, the article first selects accuracy and reliability as the main indicators for the experiment.

The article takes the material procurement cost, construction cost, labor cost, and equipment cost of a certain project as input variables, and the actual cost data of the project as output variables. It uses the GAN algorithm and traditional models for analysis and prediction, and compares them with actual data to verify the effectiveness of the model. The accuracy results obtained are shown in Fig. 2.

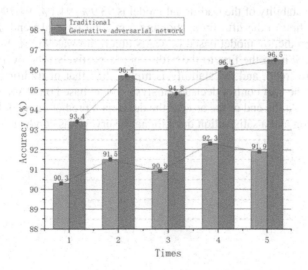

Fig. 2. Prediction accuracy

In Fig. 2, the prediction accuracy of the traditional model reached the highest of 92.3% in the fourth round and the lowest of 90.3% in the first round, with an average accuracy of 91.38% calculated. The prediction accuracy of the GAN algorithm based prediction method reached the highest of 96.5% in the fifth time and the lowest of 93.4% in the first time. The average accuracy calculated is 95.3%. It can be seen that the cost control decision analysis model based on GAN algorithm has higher prediction accuracy. Further analysis experiments are conducted on the reliability of the model, and the results are shown in Fig. 3.

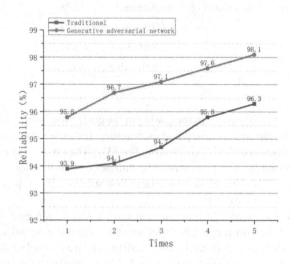

Fig. 3. Model reliability

In Fig. 3, the stability of the traditional model is 93.9%, 94.1%, 94.7%, 95.8%, and 96.3% from the first to the fifth time, showing a gradual upward trend. However, the stability of the prediction model based on GAN algorithm was 95.8%, 96.7%, 97.1%, 97.6%, and 98.1% from the first to the fifth time, respectively. The overall trend also shows an upward trend, and the stability is higher than that of traditional models. It can be seen that the cost control decision analysis model based on GAN algorithm has higher reliability. At the end of the article, the developed prediction model was put into practical operation and a satisfaction questionnaire survey was conducted, as shown in Fig. 4.

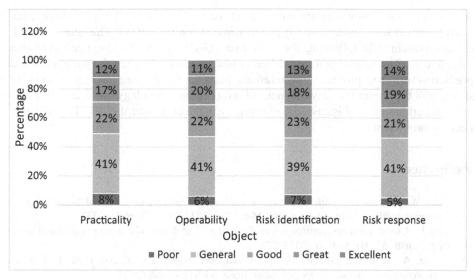

Fig. 4. Questionnaire survey results

In Fig. 4, in the evaluation of practicality, excellent accounts for 12%, very good accounts for 17%, positive accounts for 22%, average accounts for 41%, and negative accounts for 8%. In the evaluation of operability, the proportion of evaluations from excellent to poor is 11%, 20%, 22%, 41%, and 6%, respectively. The proportion of positive reviews for risk identification and risk response abilities far exceeds negative reviews. It can be seen that the prediction model studied in the article has achieved good results after being put into practical use.

The article compares the prediction accuracy and reliability of traditional models and cost control decision analysis models based on GAN algorithm, and finds that models based on GAN algorithm exhibit higher levels of prediction accuracy and reliability. The experimental results show that the model based on GAN algorithm achieved the highest accuracy of 96.5% in the fifth prediction, while the traditional model achieved the highest accuracy of 92.3%. In terms of reliability, the model based on GAN algorithm achieved 98.1% reliability in the 5th round, while the reliability of traditional models was 96.3%. In addition, satisfaction surveys conducted in actual operations have also confirmed the effectiveness of the GAN algorithm based model in practical applications. Therefore, the cost control decision analysis model based on GAN algorithm shows significant advantages in prediction accuracy and reliability, and has high practical application value.

5 Conclusions

The article introduces a cost control decision analysis model based on GAN algorithm, which takes actual engineering data as samples and uses GAN algorithm to simulate and predict the sample data. It compared the simulated prediction results with actual engineering data, verifying the effectiveness and accuracy of the model. In practical applications, this model can not only predict the cost level of PTTP in the future, but also effectively solve the uncertainty problem in cost control of PTTP. The future research directions include the following: the first is to use GAN algorithm to simulate and predict sample data. The second is to use different parameters to compare the simulation and prediction results to provide more reference basis for the decision-making process. In short, with the continuous development of information technology, there are more and more uncertainties. In this case, the uncertainty in the cost control of PTTP would also become prominent.

References

1. Tian, W.: Evaluation of the maturity of construction project cost control based on gray clustering method. Chin. Architectural Metal Struct. **22**(09), 159–161 (2023)
2. Cen, L.: Cost control and application analysis of project design phase based on limit design. Eng. Constr. **37**(04), 1348–1350 (2023)
3. Zhang, A.: Research on the difficulties and countermeasures of cost control of water environment governance projects. Constr. Econ. **44**(S1), 86–88 (2023)
4. Ajagekar, A., You, F.: Deep reinforcement learning based unit commitment scheduling under load and wind power uncertainty. IEEE Trans. Sustain. Energy **14**(2), 803–812 (2022)
5. Huang, C.: Demand response for industrial micro-grid considering photovoltaic power uncertainty and battery operational cost. IEEE Trans. Smart Grid **12**(4), 3043–3055 (2021)
6. Hu, B.: Decision-dependent uncertainty modeling in power system operational reliability evaluations. IEEE Trans. Power Syst. **36**(6), 5708–5721 (2021)
7. Gui, J.: A review on generative adversarial networks: algorithms, theory, and applications. IEEE Trans. Knowl. Data Eng. **35**(4), 3313–3332 (2021)
8. Liu, K.: FISS GAN: a generative adversarial network for foggy image semantic segmentation. IEEE/CAA J. Automatica Sinica **8**(8), 1428–1439 (2021)
9. Nguyen, D.C.: Federated learning for COVID-19 detection with generative adversarial networks in edge cloud computing. IEEE Internet Things J. **9**(12), 10257–10271 (2021)
10. Gecer, B.: Fast-ganfit: generative adversarial network for high fidelity 3D face reconstruction. IEEE Trans. Pattern Anal. Mach. Intell. **44**(9), 4879–4893 (2021)

Optimization Model of Construction Period in Special Construction Scenarios of Power Transmission and Transformation Project Based on Back Propagation Neural Network

Si Shen[1] ⓘ, Fulei Chen[1] ⓘ, Jian Ma[2](✉) ⓘ, Tianrui Fang[1] ⓘ, and Wei Yan[2] ⓘ

[1] State Grid Anhui Electric Power Co., Ltd., Economic and Technological Research Institute, Hefei 230071, Anhui, China
shensi2023@126.com

[2] China Electricity Council Technical and Economic Consulting Center of Electronic Power Construction, Beijing 100053, China

Abstract. Power transmission and transformation project (PTTP) is a crucial part of the power system, and during the construction process, various special situations may be faced, such as adverse weather conditions, resource scarcity, etc. These factors may affect the project schedule. Therefore, the optimization of the construction period for PTTPs has important practical significance. The article conducted research on the optimization of construction period in special construction scenarios of PTTPs, and proposed a construction period optimization model based on BP (Back Propagation) neural network. Firstly, the special scenarios in the construction of PTTPs and the importance of schedule optimization were analyzed. Then, a schedule optimization model based on BP neural network was proposed, and the model was described and analyzed in detail. Subsequently, model validation and experimental analysis were conducted using actual case data, and the results showed that the model had good performance in optimizing the construction period, with a maximum optimization period of 3.7 days, while also improving safety and resource utilization.

Keywords: Duration Optimization Model · BP Neural Network · Power Transmission and Transformation Project · Special Construction Scenarios

1 Introduction

PTTP is an important component of power grid construction, playing an important role in power grid construction. Due to the numerous construction links, heavy tasks, and tight schedule of power grid project, there are many uncertain factors in the construction process of PTTP, which brings certain difficulties to the optimization of the schedule. Meanwhile, with the rapid development of the economy, the construction of power grid projects has also accelerated, posing higher requirements for the reliability and stability of power supply. Therefore, the optimization of the construction period of power grid project has become one of the urgent problems that power enterprises need to solve.

D. Garg et al. (Eds.): IACC 2023, CCIS 2053, pp. 91–99, 2024.
https://doi.org/10.1007/978-3-031-56700-1_9

Currently, many experts and scholars have conducted research and exploration on schedule optimization. Li Jiaxi proposed an optimization model for the production workshop schedule of prefabricated components for highway bridges and culverts under multiple factor constraints. The results showed that this method can improve workshop production efficiency and provide theoretical support for accelerating the construction of a modern high-quality comprehensive three-dimensional transportation network [1]. Yu Zongrang summarized the characteristics of prefabricated steel structure school buildings based on project practice, studied the optimization measures for the construction period of prefabricated steel structure school buildings, and proposed feasible suggestions for the application of prefabricated steel structure school buildings, in order to provide reference for similar projects [2]. Chen Zhimin proposed an improved firefly algorithm to solve the model. The results showed that the estimated construction period was 89.6 days, with a confidence level of 95.6%. Compared with the original method, it reduced the construction period by 13.4 days and can shorten the construction period by 13.1% [3]. Although the above methods can effectively shorten the construction period, they may increase costs.

On the basis of analyzing the special scenarios and the importance of schedule optimization in the construction of PTTPs, the article proposed a BP neural network model for schedule optimization of PTTPs. Firstly, based on actual cases, special scenarios were described. Then, the BP neural network model was introduced and analyzed. Finally, the model was experimentally validated to have good performance in optimizing time.

2 Special Scenarios in the Construction of Power Transmission and Transformation Projects

In the construction process of PTTPs, there are many special scenarios, such as climate conditions, resource scarcity, etc. In terms of climate conditions, due to the harsh climate environment, it is necessary to make preparations, conduct a detailed analysis of the weather conditions, and take corresponding response measures. In terms of resources, PTTPs involve numerous construction links, so there are strict requirements for equipment, materials, etc., required for construction, and a large number of personnel are involved in the construction process. Therefore, it is necessary to develop a scientific and reasonable scheduling plan. In terms of resource scarcity, due to the fact that PTTPs generally involve cooperation and coordination among multiple types of work, it is necessary to make reasonable planning and configuration to ensure efficient and orderly construction work. Therefore, for these special scenarios, scientific and reasonable analysis and evaluation are required in order to develop scientifically effective plans to optimize their construction period [4].

In the construction process of PTTPs, there are many different climatic environments that need to be faced, so climatic conditions are one of the important factors that affect the progress of the project. In terms of climate conditions, due to the fact that PTTPs are generally located in the western region of China, there may be dry and rainy conditions in this area, as well as frequent strong winds. Therefore, when carrying out the construction of PTTPs in this area, it is necessary to make relevant preparations, analyze and predict the weather conditions in detail, and develop corresponding response measures based on the predicted results. In addition, due to the seasonal changes in temperature in the area, it is necessary to make sufficient preparations for the construction of PTTPs in this area. For example, when the temperature is low in winter, it is necessary to do a good job of preventing cold and keeping warm. When the temperature is high in summer, it is necessary to do a good job in heatstroke prevention and cooling. In short, climate conditions are one of the important factors affecting the progress of PTTPs [5].

Resource scarcity refers to the inability of certain resources to be provided to construction personnel in a timely manner due to various factors during the construction process of PTTPs, which hinders the construction of the project. This kind of resource scarcity usually occurs in the construction of large-scale PTTPs, such as the Three Gorges Project in China. Due to the involvement of many different departments and units in the project, many situations of resource scarcity are encountered during the construction process. In the construction process of the Three Gorges PTTP, many large mechanical equipment are used. If maintenance materials or accessories cannot be provided in a timely manner in the event of a malfunction, it would affect the overall progress of the project. Therefore, in the case of resource scarcity, reasonable planning and allocation are necessary to ensure the smooth progress of the entire project, and personnel scheduling work needs to be done well during the construction process [6].

In the construction process of PTTPs, cooperation and coordination among multiple types of work are often involved to ensure efficient and orderly construction. In PTTP, there are many types of work involved, including material transportation, equipment installation, foundation construction, etc. The coordination and cooperation among various types of work have a significant impact on the construction progress of PTTPs. In the coordination and cooperation work among multiple types of work, it mainly includes the reasonable allocation and allocation of resources, the reasonable allocation of human resources, information communication and communication, etc. [7].

3 Optimization Model for Construction Period Based on BP Neural Network

The traditional schedule planning method uses the critical path as the basis for calculating the construction period, but in actual project, the critical path is a continuous time scale sequence, rather than a discrete sequence of events. Therefore, the article adopts an event sequence based method, with the task duration as the objective function and adding constraints to construct a BP neural network model, as shown in Fig. 1 [8].

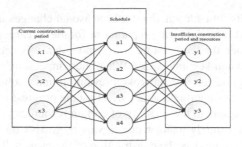

Fig. 1. Duration optimization model

In Fig. 1, the input node represents the current duration of each node, and all progress plans form the hidden layer nodes in the network, while duration and resource shortages form the output layer nodes. Therefore, the model consists of two parts: network nodes and output layer nodes. During model training, each variable in the input layer is assigned a value and then transferred to the output layer. Then, all outputs are normalized. Finally, based on the normalization results, the network is adjusted to better match the actual situation [9].

The article uses BP neural network to optimize critical paths and resource deficiencies during the construction process. When dealing with actual project problems, the first step is to input raw data into the network for training and testing. In order to better adapt the network to actual situations, the raw data is first normalized and then input into the neural network for training. During the training process, a BP neural network model is first constructed based on the input data. Then, the network is learned and the learned network is compared with the actual project progress. If the error between the two is small, it indicates that the model has good predictive ability and robustness; on the contrary, it indicates that the model may have some errors and needs to be improved. Finally, whether the BP neural network can achieve the expected effect is tested through training data.

This model has three input layer nodes and one hidden layer node. The objective functions of the model are the minimum and maximum duration errors, and the error function is that in neural network training, learning rate is an important parameter. If the learning rate is too high, the training process of the network is relatively difficult, while if the learning rate is too low, it is easy to cause the convergence speed of the network to be too slow to achieve the expected effect. Therefore, the article adopts adaptive learning rate for model training. Learning rate refers to the time interval between the start of training and reaching the maximum value. The smaller the learning rate, the earlier the maximum value is reached. The higher the learning rate, the later it reaches its maximum value. The article selects 0.001, 0.005, and 0.050 as the range of learning rates [10].

After the model training is completed, the training data is normalized and then input into the BP neural network toolbox for training. The input and output of a network model can be represented by an array, where the variables in the array are used to represent the results obtained from network training. For each input variable, the same number of sine functions are selected for simulation input, and then the simulation output and training data are compared to determine whether the network can achieve the expected effect. The connection weights between output variables and hidden layer nodes are implemented using the sigmoid function, as shown in Eqs. (1) and (2) [11].

$$S(x) = 1/[1 + \delta(-x)] \tag{1}$$

$$T(x) = \frac{\delta(x) - \delta(-x)}{\delta(x) + \delta(-x)} \tag{2}$$

In Eqs. (1) and (2), x represents the input value; S represents the sigmoid function; T is the Tanh function. The calculation parameters are shown in Table 1.

Table 1. Calculation parameter table

Parameters	Value	Descriptions
WIH	0.2,0.4,0.6	The connection weight between the input layer and the hidden layer
WHO	0.5,0.7	The connection weight between the hidden layer and the output layer
Learning rate	0.01	The step size of the update weight in each iteration
Bias	0.5	The bias value of the neuron, used to adjust the activation threshold of the neuron

Table 1 contains four parameters, among which the weights from input layer to hidden layer are [0.2, 0.4, 0.6]; the weights from hidden layer to output layer are [0.5, 0.7]; the learning rate is 0.01; the bias is 0.5. Due to the special nature of PTTP construction, there may be a problem of insufficient resources in actual construction. If the problem of insufficient resources can be considered in the plan, it can effectively solve the problem of project extension. Therefore, the article adopts resource scarcity as the input of the output layer node, with resource scarcity as the objective function, and establishes a schedule optimization model based on BP neural network. Construction tasks are divided according to the job duration, that is, the job duration is the current duration of each job task. The resource scarcity of each task is used as input, and genetic algorithms are adopted to optimize the network. The specific steps are as follows: the network is learned and trained. Firstly, the training samples are input into the network, and then the network is adjusted based on the actual progress of the project. The adjusted network can be in line with the project progress and has strong predictive ability.

Through simulation testing, it is found that the trained model can well fit the actual project progress curve. In addition, the article also finds an example that is quite similar to the actual situation. Through simulation testing and analysis, it can be concluded that the network has good predictive ability when the duration extension is greater than the target duration. When the duration extension is less than the target duration, the network has good robustness. In this example, both critical paths in the network require an extension of time to meet the target duration requirements. However, in actual project, the actual construction period of these two critical paths is longer than the target construction period.

The BP neural network model obtained through training can predict the planned construction period of a certain PTTP, and predict the quantity of various resources in the actual construction process to complete the task. The planned duration of this project is 40 days. Among them, the work content of the first week is: setting out at the construction site; the work content of the second week is: installing hardware; the work content of the third week is: hoisting iron towers. There are two critical paths in the project, namely path 1 and path 2.

The number of resources required for path 1 is relatively large, while path 2 requires a smaller number of resources. In the actual construction process, there are 15 critical paths on path 1 and 3 critical paths on path 2. Due to the close distance between path 1 and path 2, if the progress time relationship between path 1 and path 2 is considered separately, the number of resources required for path 1 and path 2 is the same, but the distance between path 1 and path 2 is relatively long. When considering the progress relationship between the two paths, the impact of the difference in resource quantity between the two paths on the construction period must be considered. The trained network is applied in engineering projects and compared with actual project. Therefore, the six key paths 1, 2, 3, 4, 5, and 6 are added to the BP neural network for training. Through the trained network, the number of resources and duration on paths 1 and 2 are predicted.

4   Duration Optimization Model Testing Experiment

The article conducted testing experiments on the duration optimization model studied. Firstly, relevant data under special construction scenarios of PTTPs were collected, as shown in Table 2.

Table 2. Related datasets

Project number	Resource utilization rate	Security	Construction period (day)
1	30%	80%	180
2	34%	78%	200
3	37%	81%	160
4	28%	82%	190
5	31%	77%	170

The dataset shown in Table 2 includes three elements: resource utilization, safety, and construction period. Among them, the resource utilization rate of Project 1 was 30%; safety was 80%; construction period was 180 days. The resource utilization rate of Project 3 was 37%; the safety was 81%; the construction period was 160 days. The resource utilization rate of Project 4 was 28%; the safety was 82%; the construction period was 190 days. The article then cleaned, filtered, and processed the collected data to ensure its accuracy and completeness. Then, historical data was used to train the constructed BP neural network model and adjust the model parameters to better fit the

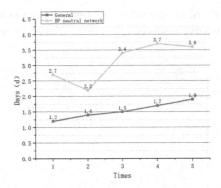

Fig. 2. Optimization days

actual data. Finally, the model was put into practical use and three results were obtained: optimization days (Fig. 2), resource utilization rate (Fig. 3), and security (Fig. 4).

From Fig. 2, it can be seen that in actual use, the general optimization model had a maximum of 1.9 days and a minimum of 1.2 days, and the calculated average number of days was 1.54 days; the optimization model based on BP neural network had a maximum of 3.7 days and a minimum of 2.2 days, resulting in an average of 3.12 days. The BP neural network-based optimization model for the construction period of PTTPs can reduce more construction periods in special construction scenarios.

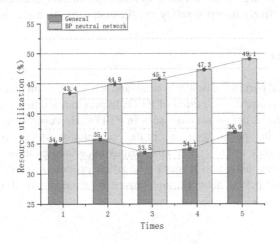

Fig. 3. Resource utilization rate

From Fig. 3, it can be seen that in actual use, the resource utilization rate of the general optimization model was the highest at 36.9% and the lowest at 33.5%, and the calculated average utilization rate was 35.02%; the optimization model based on BP neural network had a maximum resource utilization rate of 49.1% and a minimum of 43.4%, and the overall trend was gradually increasing. The calculated average utilization rate was 46.08%. The BP neural network-based optimization model for the duration of PTTPs can effectively improve resource utilization in special construction scenarios.

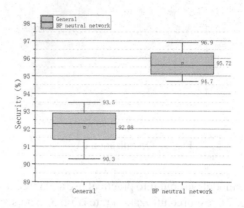

Fig. 4. Security

From Fig. 4, it can be seen that the general optimization model had a maximum safety of 93.5% and a minimum safety of 90.3% in actual use, and the calculated average safety was 92.08%; the optimization model based on BP neural network had a maximum security of 96.9% and a minimum security of 94.7%, with an average security of 95.72% calculated. The BP neural network-based optimization model for the construction period of PTTPs can effectively improve safety in special construction scenarios.

5   Conclusions

PTTP is an essential part of the power system, and it has important practical significance for optimizing the construction period of PTTP. In previous studies, the main focus was on analyzing the construction period issues in PTTPs. However, there has been no in-depth research on the special scenarios in the construction process of PTTPs and the importance of schedule optimization, and various uncertainties in the actual operation process have not been taken into account. The article proposed a schedule optimization model based on BP neural network, and proved its good practical application effect through practical cases.

References

1. Li, J., Yu, J., Chen, C., Wang, B.: Under the constraints of multiple factors, the construction period optimization model and n of highway bridge and culvert assembly components production workshop. Project Manag. Technol. **21**(10), 106–111 (2023)
2. Yu, Z., Chen, J., Korea, D.: Optimization of the construction period of the assembled steel structure school. Construction **45**(08), 1584–1586 (2023)

3. Chen, Z., Xia, Y., Wang, P., Wang, Z., Zhang, L.: Optimization of the construction period of multi-resource ship maintenance projects based on variable neighborhood search algorithm. Project Manag. Technol. **21**(07), 129–134 (2023)
4. Zhu, D., Ma, C., Liu, L., Yuan, W.: Discussion on the preparation of soil and water conservation plans for power transmission and transformation projects in sandy areas of Northern Shaanxi-Taking a 110 kV transmission line project in Yuyang District Yulin City as an example. Groundwater **45**(05), 285–286 (2023)
5. Han, L., Qian, Y., Fang, J., Wu, Y., Zhang, Q.: Research on the characteristics and prevention and control measures of soil erosion in power transmission and transformation projects in loess hilly areas. Water Conservancy Hydropower Technol. (Chinese and English) **54**(S2), 457–464 (2023)
6. Zheng, W., Wang, Z.: Control and analysis of the whole process of power transmission and transformation engineering survey. Public Electricity **38**(05), 54–57 (2023)
7. Li, X., Liu, Q., Jiang, S., Sun, B., Qian, F., Chen, Y.: The erosion characteristics of the slope ditches of the accumulation body of the power transmission and transformation project in a typical red soil area. Proc. Yangtze River Acad. Sci. **40**(09), 61–67 (2023)
8. Song, S., Xiong, X., Wu, X., Xue, Z.: Modeling the SOFC by BP neural network algorithm. Int. J. Hydrogen Energy **46**(38), 20065–20077 (2021)
9. Jiang, K., Liu, M., He, C., Zhang, Y., Wang, Z., Simon, H.: Exploration on the optimization of labor and duration of construction projects based on the Choquet integral method. J. Civ. Eng. Manag. **40**(02), 138–149 (2023)
10. Zhang, H., Liu, K., Rong, X., Liu, Z.: Optimization of the construction period of supporting pipelines for municipal roads based on the key chain. Henan Sci. **41**(03), 350–357 (2023)
11. Zhou, G., Pan, Z., Wei, Q., Zhao, J.: Railway engineering construction schedule planning model and its algorithm optimization method. Ind. Eng. Manag. **28**(03), 145–155 (2023)

Vision-Based Human Activity Recognition Using CNN and LSTM Architecture

Neha Gupta, Payal Malik, Arun Kumar Dubey, Achin Jain, Sarita Yadav[(⊠)], and Devansh Verma

Bharati Vidyapeeth's College of Engineering, New Delhi, India
sarita1320@yahoo.co.in

Abstract. Technology's growing use has facilitated the quality of living. Artificial Intelligence (AI) is the field that aims to define how human intelligence is mimicked by machines which are programmed to think or behave like humans. Modern approaches and tools for evaluating human behavior have been made possible by modern advancements in the fields of machine learning (ML) and artificial intelligence (AI). Due to its applicability in several industries, comprising of entertainment, security and surveillance, health, and intelligent environments, human activity recognition has gained prominence significantly. Human activity recognition (HAR) using video sensors typically involves analyzing the visual data captured by cameras to classify and identify the actions of individuals. In the following paper, we propose ConvLSTM and LRCN-based Human Action Recognition. A huge variety of films from the publicly accessible data set, UCF50 comprises a wide range of activity classes that are used to build a statistical model. For the model proposed in this paper, the accuracy has turned out to be 94%, the average f1-score is 0.93 and the average recall is calculated to be 0.925. The Loss curve has also been plotted along with the accuracy curve for the proposed model for recognizing human activities.

Keywords: Human Activity Recognition · Deep Learning · LSTM · ConvLSTM · LRCN

1 Introduction

Human Activity Recognition (HAR) deals with automated human physical activity identification [1]. The primary objective of HAR is to recognize any unusual activity or incident and analyze human activities [14]. Unlike most species, humans are distinguished by their ability to perform different activities simultaneously and their ability to learn new tasks and teach their offspring how to perform them. These activities can range from as simple as walking to as complex as a pommel horse [16]. HAR is used in various industries, including healthcare, entertainment, education, and security. It has been gaining a lot of focus among researchers because of its multitude of applications like video analytics, border infiltration detection, computer vision, biometrics, digital libraries, video surveillance, and many more [14, 15, 17].

D. Garg et al. (Eds.): IACC 2023, CCIS 2053, pp. 100–110, 2024.
https://doi.org/10.1007/978-3-031-56700-1_10

HAR systems are built and categorized into mainly three types of sensors - 1) vision sensors, consisting of 3d cameras, depth cameras, skeleton analysis, etc., 2) environmental sensors, including device (smartphones) and wearable sensors, and 3) radar sensors, which are the device-free wireless sensors. Deep learning (DL) has proven to be a good approach for understanding HAR systems, but choosing the appropriate DL method can prove to be a bit challenging task [1, 22]. Even though extensive research has been done in the domain of Human Action Recognition, it is still taxing because of the limitations like disturbance from the background, frequent change in brightness, relative motion of the object, object occlusion, etc. [17]. Due to the intricacy of the tasks, the caliber of the data being processed, high dimensionality, intraclass variability, and interclass similarity, it may prove to be a difficult task [16].

Deep learning excels in automatically extracting characteristics that are appropriate for the job at hand. Avoid relying on heuristic hand-crafted functions and scale to more complex behavior detection tasks [18]. Further, deep learning has an important value in implementing self-learning as well as transfer learning [7]. Convolutional neural networks (CNN), which are useful for extracting spatial information, are used in certain deep learning systems, while others advise employing long short-term memories, which are rich in temporal information. Deep feed-forward neural networks and their variations are used by some approaches in this domain. Each of these approaches has its own pros and cons [9].

Automatically identifying deep features is a strength of Convolutional Neural Networks (CNNs), Recurrent Neural Networks (RNNs), and Long Short-Term Memory (LSTM) Networks. In contrast to CNN, which is a feedforward neural network, RNN adds directed cycles to display dynamic temporal behavior. In other words, RNNs may use time series data and "memory" to learn temporal correlations. LSTM networks can supplement RNNs with more complicated memory cells, successfully resolving the issue of long-term reliance on RNNs [19].

In the proposed, we proposed a model built with the combination of CNN and LSTM. Through this blend of Convolutional Neural Network (CNN) and Long Short-Term Memory (LSTM), we can leverage the strength of CNN in feature extraction along with the power of LSTM in terms of extracting temporal information among activities [1]. The aim of this work is to create a more advanced artificial intelligence capable of real-time recognition of activities of daily living (ADLs) such as running, jogging, walking, etc. [20]. To be able to determine the efficiency and robustness of our proposed model, we have performed experiments using the UCF-50 dataset, which consists of 50 daily activity classes like Basketball, Diving, Horse Race, Kayaking, Push Ups, Swing, Walking with Dog, etc. In the following work, we proposed a model built with the combination of CNN and LSTM. Through this blend of Convolutional Neural Network (CNN) and Long Short-Term Memory (LSTM), we can leverage the strength of CNN in feature extraction along with the power of LSTM in terms of extracting temporal information among activities [1] (Fig. 1).

A typical mechanized system of HAR consists of data acquisition, activity detection, modeling, and finally, classification. The Human Activity Recognition framework comprises four major sections:

• Data collection for a dataset based on vision.

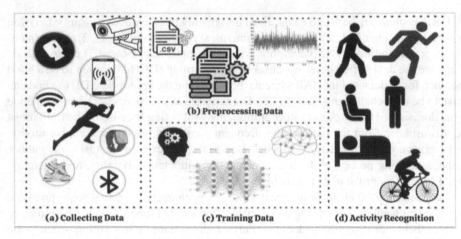

Fig. 1. Basic Structure of HAR.

- Data pre-processing, which carries out crucial preprocessing operations on the gathered data.
- Training of the data, that makes use of machine learning (ML) or deep learning (DL) methodology to learn patterns from the gathered data.
- Recognition of the performed actions.

2 Related Work

Human Activity Recognition has emerged as one of the most studied computer vision problems and a very impactful field of research. It is also a very challenging problem of time series categorization that involves the prediction of an individual's movement and actions utilizing a series of data collected by sensors. HAR is traditionally based on deep learning techniques and along with that it requires signal processing as well as processes to carefully construct features out of the raw data collected to suit the best machine learning model. Over the past years, there has been a rapid advancement in the field of technology and various human activity recognition models have been created to aid in the automation of visual monitoring systems. Numerous surveys have been done which summarize various research work done on several different methodologies in the field of action recognition. Hussain *et al.* [4] very elaborately discusses various categorizations of techniques used in the HAR models. The series of data collected by sensors for action recognition can be broadly categorized into three major sensor approaches namely Vision based sensors, Radio-Frequency sensors, and Environment sensors. They thoroughly describes various sensor-based approaches in the field of action detection and focuses on device-free human activity recognition categories along with the various comparison metrics to evaluate the created model on the accuracy, technology, loss, approach, cost, latency, and much more.

Singh *et al.* [3] asserts that when compared to conventional CCTV motion detection systems, vision based HAR techniques can provide an end-to-end automated home monitoring system with an accuracy of more than 93%. We can increase the system's accuracy and get notably better results by employing the LRCN (Long Term Recurrent Convolutional Network) method. According to Yu and Yan [7], background noises, changes in perspective, and other complexities, the prediction of the model is affected. To deal with these issues, three algorithms were designed, namely, two-stream CNN, CNN+LSTM, and 3D CNN. Mutegeki *et al.* [9] states that CNN and LSTM both have been the subject of in-depth inquiry in the past in isolation, therefore presenting a CNN-LSTM classifier that It improves the accuracy of identifying the action performed while reducing the model's complexity. Combining CNN with LSTM has the potential to both simplify the model and increase the forecast accuracy of human actions from raw data. The aim of Analysis of Human Activity Recognition (HAR) is identification of the activity a device's user is carrying out by employing sensors like the accelerometer, gyroscope, magnetometer, and others that are incorporated into IMU devices and smartphones.

Hu *et al.* [12] stated that the due to the ability to extract time information, Long Short-Term Memory (LSTM) network is a standard activity detection technique and suggested enhancing the input differential feature module and expanding the network to include a spatial memory state differential module to produce the enhanced Spatio-Temporal Differential Long Short-Term Memory (ST-D LSTM) network. Additionally, an ST-D LSTM transmission mode is put forth, allowing for the horizontal transfer of the spatial memory state using ST-D LSTM units.

To verify the effectiveness of the new network, these enhancements are lastly applied to traditional Long-term Recurrent Convolutional Networks (LRCN). A hybrid architecture highlighting the features of both Convolutional Neural Networks (CNN) as well as LongShort Term Memory (LSTM) was also presented by Deep and Zheng [8] which was tested on the UCI-HAR dataset comprising sensor data collected through an accelerometer and gyroscope in a smartphone. They performed the same experiment on the LSTM model but found out that the accuracy of the CNN-LSTM model was better than that. The combined average results from several classifiers tuned their performances and a generic activity recognition framework was provided in a model proposed by Semwal *et al.* [10] as an ensemble learning implementation. In our current research, we propose a model for action recognition employing the UCF-50 dataset and two algorithms: the Longterm Recurrent Convolutional Network (LRCN) along with a Convolutional Neural Network (CNN) combined with Long-Short Term Memory (LSTM).

In this paper, we use the UCF-50 data set, a collection of 50 action categories that altogether comprises 6676 realistic videos. A citation published by Shian-Ru Ke [2] is an excellent resource that undertakes a thorough survey of the vision-based models for Human Activity Recognition. Shian-Ru Ke [2] discusses the numerous domains of applications of HAR models along with the three crucial phases of processing which include activity detection and classification techniques, human object segmentation, feature extraction, and representation. Three aspects of human action recognition are discussed: foundational technology, human action detection frameworks, and representation of applications from lower-levels to higher-levels. Preksha Prateek [11] provides an overview of the methods currently in use for HAR on trimmed videos and discusses an action recognition task's comprehensive framework which entails feature extraction, feature encoding, dimensionality reduction, action classification, and various action classification methods, as well as the beneficial and adverse characteristics of the mentioned tasks, along with readily accessible data sets (Fig. 2).

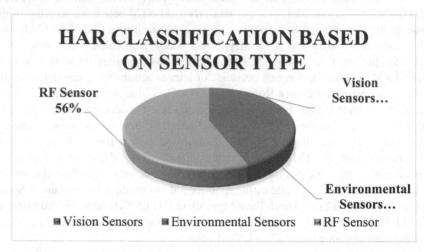

Fig. 2. Classification of HAR based on sensor types.

3 Dataset

The training of a Human Action Recognition model demands a substantial collection of videos of people doing various actions. In this paper, we have used the UCF50 action recognition data set which is a collection of 50 activity classes that offers a realistic set of data for recognizing activities obtained from YouTube videos. It also offers a diverse collection of human activities, given the variety of camera motion, poses, object appearances, viewpoints, cluttered backgrounds, and various illumination in the surroundings. The videos in the same activity class may share some features like the same person performing different activities. Every single video out of the 6618 available video data set belongs to one of the fifty activity classes. The entire set of data is segregated into train and test data having 75% and 25% of the total videos respectively but prior to that, the data set is shuffled to decrease bias and generate splits that precisely depict the distribution of the data overall.

4 Proposed Methodology

4.1 Human Activity Recognition with Convolutional Neural Networks (CNN)

Some of the best-known models for computer vision in deep learning are CNNs. CNN architecture can be compared to the visual cortex of the human brain. Filters can be used to extract spatial or temporal features and identify objects from input images. Convolution layers are made up of filters, and some fully linked layers are used for classification.

CNNs are not only versed with learning features with the help of pooling layers but are also good at scaling massive datasets. Lowering the dimensionality of receiving data and extracting the prevalent attributes is the main aim of pooling [1]. In another study by [22], A network that has a structure of various layers can be regarded as CNN. The architecture comprises two major components: 1) an interconnected network and 2) several sampling and convolutional layers. The latter is used in feature extraction, while the former is essential for studying classification weights. A standard CNN consists of 3 layers: 1. Convolutional layer, 2. Pooling layer, 3. Fully connected layer.

Filters in the convolutional layer, also known as the feature map, assist in extracting the local features. A single feature map is generated with the help of one filter. The dot product must be created by swiping filters over the input data to create a feature map. This process is termed a convolution operation. Every neuron inside the feature map is connected with a tiny part of the input data, called the receptive field, whose size is the same as that of the filter. For achieving efficient results, the number of parameters is further reduced because the weightings of the neurons in a feature map are made public. Further, detection and recognition of certain patterns, regardless of their position in the input, also becomes possible. Based on the stride number and filter size, the feature map's magnitude is calculated.

4.2   Human Activity Recognition with Long Short-Term Memory (LSTM)

LSTM is considered suitable for time series data and is a time-based network of recurrent neurons [21]. Horizontal lines cross the top of the graph as LSTM analyses the condition of the cells. The cell state can easily be compared with a conveyor belt, with only a few linear exchanges, and is directly applied to the entire chain. This knowledge keeps on traveling through the LSTM cells. It also provides the ability to delete or insert data into the state of the cell, with the help of a detailed structure referred to as a 'gate'. Just like a door provides a means of passing with knowledge, the gate consists of a pointwise multiplication operation and a sigmoid layer of a neural network. While the model parameters are fixed, LSTM has the peculiar property that the self-loop weight can be changed without concern for vanishing gradients or gradient expansion by increasing the input threshold, forgetting threshold, and output threshold. This makes it possible to alter the integral scale on the fly at different times. There are a lot of applications of LSTM in the technological domain. For instance, they are widely used in robotics, translation, image analysis, handwriting detection, and many more.

4.3   Human Activity Recognition with Long-Term Recurrent Convolutional Network (LRCN)

The LRCN approach refers to the combination of Convolution as well as LSTM layers in a single framework. Another acceptable choice is to utilize a CNN model with an individually trained LSTM model. By employing CNN, with a trained model, it is possible to extract spatial information from video frames and fine-tune this model for the application. As a result, the LSTM prototype may make predictions about the action being performed in the video with the aid of data gathered using the CNN model. In contrast, the CNN and LSTM layers are combined into a single model by the Longterm

Recurrent Convolutional Network (LRCN). The gathered spatial information is provided to an LSTM layer for the Convolutional layers based temporal sequence modeling at each time step. Throughout an end to-end training session, the network learns spatiotemporal properties in this way, producing a robust model. Tasks that involve either visual or linguistic inputs and outputs make good use of a Long-term Recurrent Convolutional Network (LRCN) model. This model blends a CNN-like recognition and synthesis of temporal dynamics with a deep hierarchical visual feature extractor [13].

5 Proposed Model

ConvLSTM and LRCN. Initially, the UCF-50 data set, comprising 50 activity classes, is preprocessed for data training. The frames of the videos are first resized, normalized, and then extracted. In addition to that the feature extraction is done on the extracted frames. The dataset is then shuffled and split into train i.e., 75%, and test i.e., 25% of the total videos. LSTM layers are employed for temporal detection, whereas CNN aids in spatial extraction of the frames. ConvLSTM cells are LSTM network variants that include convolutional processes. It is an LSTM with built-in convolution, which enables it to distinguish between spatial input components and take into consideration the temporal relationship. As a result, the convolution LSTM can take in 3d input whereas, LSTM could take in only 1d input. The number of epochs considered is 50, with the initial number of filters and batch size equal to 4 each. With every fusion, the number of filters keeps on increasing while with every pooling, the size of filters keeps on decreasing. Time distributed layer is used at a 20% dropout rate. A SoftMax classifier is used for classification. For optimization, Adam optimizer is used. The resultant of the ConvLSTM2D layer is flattened and fed to Dense layers and tanH activation function. MaxPooling3D layers and Dropout layers are used for the reduction of the dimensions of the frames and to prevent overfitting of the model (Fig. 3).

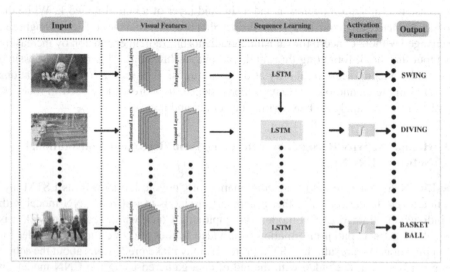

Fig. 3. Structure of proposed model (convLSTM).

6   Result

Our proposed model is studied using various evaluation metrics. For some of the activities from the specified 50 classes of the UCF-50 dataset, recall, f1 scores, and precision have been calculated to identify the positive predictive value and the sensitivity. Visual results showing the values of activities are given in Table 1. For attaining more clarity on the values, we have considered only 4 activities, present on the leftmost column of the table, namely Swing (denoted by 0), Horse Race (denoted by 2), Diving (denoted by 3), and lastly, Basketball (denoted by 4). As shown in the table, the precision of all the activities on average is around 87.5%. The f1-score for the activities - Swing, Horse race, Diving, and Basketball is 0.67, 1.00, 1.00, and 1.00 respectively, while the recall is 1.00, 1.00, 1.00, and 0.50 respectively. The magnitude of these values proves the effectiveness of our proposed technique. The class-wise performance for each activity present in the dataset can be evaluated in a similar manner. The accuracy of the model is 94%. It is safe to say that the convLSTM approach works well for vision based human activity recognition. The graphs in Fig. 4(a) show the comparison between the testing accuracy and the validation accuracy. From the graph, we can conclude that after the complete training, the mode accuracy does not decrease by a lot for validation or new data that is fed into the model. This shows us that the model is quite robust and is not overfitting in any manner. From the above graph Fig. 4(b), we can conclude that the false positives of our model are quite low as the losses decrease gradually. And the losses for the validation data are also very comparable to the total losses for the testing data.

Table 1. Performance key metrics of some activities.

Activity No. (Name)	Precision	Recall	F1-score
0 (Swing)	0.5	1	0.67
2 (Horse Race)	1	1	1
3 (Diving)	1	1	1
4 (Basketball)	1	0.50	1

Table 2 presents the benchmarking table showing the comparative study of six different types of AI models, each with their respective F1 scores, Recall, Precision, and Accuracy metrics. The authors of these models are also listed in the table. Our model's performance is also included, with an F1 score of 93.05%, Recall of 92.5%, Precision of 93.6%, and Accuracy of 94%. The results of the comparison highlight the effectiveness of the models in comparison to each other, with our model outperforming the KNN [26] model in several key metrics. The table provides valuable insight into the state of AI models [27] and their performance, allowing researchers to make informed decisions when choosing the most appropriate model for their specific needs.

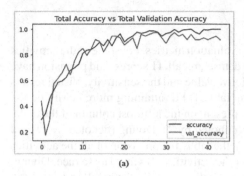 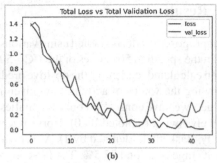

(a)   (b)

Fig. 4. (a) Total Accuracy vs Total Validation Accuracy curve. (b) Total Loss vs Total Validation Loss curve

Table 2. Benchmarking

Citation	AI Model	F1-Score	Precision	Recall	Accuracy
Agarwal et al. [23]	RNN+LSTM	95.73	95.78	95.81	95.78
Mohsen et al. [24]	KNN	90.12	89.93	91.05	90.46
Bokhari et al. [25]	DGRU	97.6	97.8	98	98.12
Our Model	CNN+LSTM+LRCN	93.05	92.5	93.6	94

7 Conclusion

We have presented a Convolutional LSTM network approach to cater to the ever-growing domain of Activity Prediction in Humans. Identification of the spatial region in the individual frames of the videos of different activity classes and the temporal effect across those frames was carried out effectively. The activities are classified with the help of these convLSTM cells, and the name of the activity is measured as an output for checking the accuracy. This approach can give more efficient results by consuming less time and expense. Loss and accuracy curves were also plotted to obtain a better perception of the efficiency of the model. The performance measures, recall, f1-score, and precision also helped to demonstrate the validity of the technique. A further benefit is the idea of employing a Long-term Recurrent Convolutional Network (LRCN) technique. The spatial information from the frames is extracted using CNN layers, and the LSTM layers are then fed to the individual frames one at a time to simulate the temporal sequence. This spatio-temporal feature technique results in a robust model.

References

1. Abbaspour, S., Fotouhi, F., Sedaghatbaf, A., Fotouhi, H., Vahabi, M., Linden, M.: A comparative analysis of hybrid deep learning models for human activity recognition. Sensors **20**, 5707 (2020)

2. Ke, S.R., Thuc, H.L.U., Lee, Y.J., Hwang, J.N., Yoo, J.H., Choi, K.H.: A review on video-based human activity recognition. Computers 2(2), 88–131 (2013)
3. Singh, J., Sinha, S.: Video Based Human Activity Recognition Surveillance System
4. Hussain, Z., Sheng, Q.Z., Zhang, W.E.: A review and categorization of techniques on device-free human activity recognition. J. Netw. Comput. Appl. 167, 102738 (2020)
5. Gowda, S.N., Rohrbach, M., Sevilla-Lara, L.: Smart frame selection for action recognition. In: Proceedings of the AAAI Conference on Artificial Intelligence, vol. 35, no. 2, pp. 1451–1459 (2021)
6. Mishra, S.R., Mishra, T.K., Sanyal, G., Sarkar, A., Satapathy, S.C.: Real time human action recognition using triggered frame extraction and a typical CNN heuristic. Pattern Recogn. Lett. 135, 329–336 (2020)
7. Yu, Z., Yan, W.Q.: Human action recognition using deep learning methods. In: 2020 35th International Conference on Image and Vision Computing New Zealand (IVCNZ), pp. 1–6. IEEE (2020)
8. Deep, S., Zheng, X.: Hybrid model featuring CNN and LSTM architecture for human activity recognition on smartphone sensor data. In: 2019 20th International Conference on Parallel and Distributed Computing, Applications and Technologies (PDCAT), pp. 259–264. IEEE (2019)
9. Mutegeki, R., Han, D.S.: A CNN-LSTM approach to human activity recognition. In: 2020 International Conference on Artificial Intelligence in Information and Communication (ICAIIC), pp. 362–366. IEEE (2020)
10. Semwal, V.B., Gupta, A., Lalwani, P.: An optimized hybrid deep learning model using ensemble learning approach for human walking activities recognition. J. Supercomput. 77(11), 1225612279 (2021)
11. Pareek, P., Thakkar, A.: A survey on video-based human action recognition: recent updates, datasets, challenges, and applications. Artif. Intell. Rev. 54(3), 2259–2322 (2021)
12. Hu, K., Zheng, F., Weng, L., Ding, Y., Jin, J.: Action recognition algorithm of spatio-temporal differential LSTM based on feature enhancement. Appl. Sci. 11(17), 7876 (2021)
13. Donahue, J., et al.: Long-term recurrent convolutional networks for visual recognition and description. In: Proceedings of the IEEE Conference on Computer Vision and Pattern Recognition, pp. 2625–2634 (2015)
14. Sansano, E., Montoliu, R., Belmonte Fernandez, O.: A study of deep neural networks for human activity recognition. Comput. Intell. 36(3), 1113–1139 (2020)
15. Tasnim, N., Islam, M.K., Baek, J.H.: Deep learning based human activity recognition using spatio-temporal image formation of skeleton joints. Appl. Sci. 11(6), 2675 (2021)
16. Hernández, F., Suárez, L.F., Villamizar, J., Altuve, M.: Human activity recognition on smartphones using a bidirectional LSTM network. In: 2019 XXII Symposium on Image, Signal Processing and Artificial Vision (STSIVA), pp. 1–5. IEEE (2019)
17. Kushwaha, A., Khare, A., Srivastava, P.: On integration of multiple features for human activity recognition in video sequences. Multimed. Tools Appl. 80(21), 32511–32538 (2021)
18. Murad, A., Pyun, J.Y.: Deep recurrent neural networks for human activity recognition. Sensors 17(11), 2556 (2017)
19. Peng, L., Chen, L., Ye, Z., Zhang, Y.: Aroma: a deep multi-task learning based simple and complex human activity recognition method using wearable sensors. Proc. ACM Interact. Mob. Wearable Ubiquit. Technol. 2(2), 1–16 (2018)
20. Almaslukh, B., Artoli, A.M., Al-Muhtadi, J.: A robust deep learning approach for position-independent smartphone-based human activity recognition. Sensors 18(11), 3726 (2018)
21. Wan, S., Qi, L., Xu, X., Tong, C., Gu, Z.: Deep learning models for real-time human activity recognition with smartphones. Mob. Netw. Appl. 25(2), 743–755 (2020)

22. Mekruksavanich, S., Jitpattanakul, A.: Biometric user identification based on human activity recognition using wearable sensors: an experiment using deep learning models. Electronics **10**(3), 308 (2021)

23. Agarwal, P., Alam, M.: A lightweight deep learning model for human activity recognition on edge devices. Procedia Comput. Sci. **167**, 2364–2373 (2020)

24. Mohsen, S., Elkaseer, A., Scholz, S.G.: Human activity recognition using k-nearest neighbor machine learning algorithm. In: Scholz, S.G., Howlett, R.J., Setchi, R. (eds.) KES-SDM 2021. SIST, vol. 262, pp. 304–313. Springer, Singapore (2022). https://doi.org/10.1007/978-981-16-6128-0_29

25. Bokhari, S.M., Sohaib, S., Khan, A.R., Shafi, M.: DGRU based human activity recognition using channel state information. Measurement **167**, 108245 (2021)

26. Paramasivam, K., Sindha, M.M.R., Balakrishnan, S.B.: KNN-based machine learning classifier used on deep learned spatial motion features for human action recognition. Entropy **25**(6), 844 (2023)

27. Khan, Y.A., Imaduddin, S., Singh, Y.P., Wajid, M., Usman, M., Abbas, M.: Artificial intelligence based approach for classification of human activities using MEMS sensors data. Sensors **23**(3), 1275 (2023)

ML-Based Rupture Strength Assessment in Cementitious Materials

Shashidhar Gurav[2]($\boxtimes$) (iD), Sheetal Patil[1] (iD), Karuna C. Gull[2] (iD),
and Vijaylaxmi Kochari[3] (iD)

[1] Department of CSE, Sharad Institute of Technology, Ichalkaranji, Maharashtra, India
[2] Department of CSE, S.G. Balekundri Institute of Technology Belagavi, Belagavi, Karnataka,
India
govindsingh@sitcoe.org.in
[3] Department of CSE (AIML), Kolhapur Institute of Technology's College of Engineering
(Autonomous), Kolhapur, Maharashtra, India

Abstract. This paper presents an innovative machine learning-based approach
for predicting concrete rupture strength, offering a faster and more cost-effective
alternative to traditional testing methods. The proposed methodology employs a
Random Forest Regressor (RFR) model, surpassing other regression models like
Decision Tree Regressor (DTR) and Linear Regression (LR). A user-friendly web
interface has been developed to facilitate practical implementation. In addition to
highlighting the cutting-edge solution for predicting concrete rupture strength,
the paper outlines avenues for future research, including dataset expansion,
advanced model exploration, real-time monitoring through IoT, environmental
considerations, and industry collaboration for deployment.

Keywords: Decision Tree Regressor (DTR) · Mean Absolute Error (MAE) ·
Random Forest Regressor (RFR) · Linear Regression (LR)

1 Introduction

In contemporary civil engineering practices, the evaluation of concrete's rupture strength
traditionally relies on Rupture Testing Machines (RTM). This method, though considered a benchmark for assessing rupture strength, poses challenges due to its reliance
on specialized machinery and a labor-intensive process. Compression tests, a core component of this approach, involve subjecting concrete specimens to pressure using compression platens or specialized tools mounted on a universal testing machine. The procedure demands manual casting, curing, and subsequent destructive testing of concrete
specimens within a laboratory setting.

However, the conventional approach to assessing concrete strength reveals inherent limitations. The method is characterized by its prolonged and resource-intensive
nature, necessitating meticulous preparation of concrete cubes. This involves incorporating various elements such as Cement, Fly ash, Blast-Furnace, Super-Plasticizer, Fine-
Aggregate, Coarse-Aggregate, Water, and Age (in days), followed by a minimum of

7 days of curing. Moreover, it heavily relies on a considerable workforce for the creation of concrete cubes and related tasks. Consequently, the conventional method emerges as a time-consuming, labor-intensive, and cost-intensive process, rendering it unsuitable for real-time monitoring of concrete strength in ongoing construction projects.

To overcome these limitations, our proposed system leverages the capabilities of machine learning to predict the rupture strength of concrete based on its mix design. This innovative approach promises to address the drawbacks of the existing system by providing a faster, cost-effective, and less labor-intensive alternative to manual testing.

Importantly, our system introduces real-time monitoring of concrete strength during construction projects. This feature enables timely interventions and adjustments to mix designs, enhancing the adaptability of construction processes. The predictive accuracy of our machine learning model can be continuously refined as more data is incorporated, making it a versatile and adaptive tool for optimizing concrete mix designs and reducing material wastage.

In this paper, we provide a comprehensive exploration of the methodology employed in incorporating machine learning techniques to predict concrete rupture strength. Our aim is to highlight the transformative potential of this approach within the construction industry, moving towards more efficient and resource-conscious practices.

The paper begins by highlighting the challenges posed by traditional concrete rupture strength assessment methods, emphasizing their resource-intensive and time-consuming nature. It introduces a novel approach employing machine learning to predict concrete rupture strength based on mix design parameters, offering a faster and cost-effective alternative. The methodology section details the step-by-step process, from data collection to model refinement. Comparative performance metrics of regression models are presented in the results section. The user-friendly web interface is outlined, enabling practical implementation. The conclusion summarizes key findings and suggests future research directions.

2 Literature Survey

Veeresh. Karikatti and colleagues [1] emphasize the importance of mix composition, curing conditions, and the availability of mixes in achieving an ideal concrete mix with a target compressive strength of 40 N/mm^2. They underscore the significance of preparing the alkaline solution in advance to enhance cement adhesion and overall strength. Additionally, they highlight the need to explore various mix proportions to efficiently deliver the specified compressive strength. This systematic approach optimizes the use of available mixes, eliminates the need for concrete cube creation, and reduces costs.

Vimal Rathakrishan and team [2] focus on boosting machine learning algorithms to enhance the prediction accuracy of biomechanical load (BML) models for concrete rupture strength. They compare BML models with Artificial Neural Network (ANN) models, highlighting the strengths and weaknesses of each. The authors also stress the importance of hyperparameter tuning to improve predictive power. These efforts aim to enhance the reliability and robustness of the model for predicting biomechanical system behavior.

Mayur Badole and co-authors [3] delve into machine learning algorithms for concrete strength prediction. They emphasize the need for high-quality training data that accurately represents concrete strength, as well as the choice of an appropriate machine learning algorithm. The authors recognize the complexity of concrete mix design and recommend capturing interactions between mix design elements. They stress the importance of continuous model refinement to improve prediction accuracy over time.

Zhi Wan and collaborators [4] explore the use of machine learning models, including Random Forest, Support Vector Machines (SVM), and Artificial Neural Networks (ANN), for predicting concrete rupture strength. They find these techniques effective even with a limited dataset. The authors highlight the adaptability and strength of these models in estimating concrete strength based on mix design parameters. Their research demonstrates the potential for precise predictions, which can optimize concrete mixtures and achieve desired strength levels.

Hai-Van Thi Mai and team [5] discuss the process of creating a Random Forest model to predict concrete compressive strength. They emphasize the importance of database creation, model architecture optimization, training, and validation. The authors highlight Random Forest's ability to evaluate the significance of input variables and compare its performance with Support Vector Machine (SVM). Their work provides insights into a robust framework for compressive strength prediction.

Suhaila Khursheed and colleagues [6] introduce the Extreme Learning Machine (ELM) model for predicting concrete strength. They emphasize ELM's advantages, including quick learning rates, nonlinearity detection with a single hidden layer, and fast training processes. The authors suggest that ELM offers a viable alternative to conventional neural networks, particularly for large datasets or applications requiring rapid results.

Mohammed Hmood Mohana and collaborators [7] focus on Random Forest (RF) for regression tasks in concrete strength prediction. They emphasize RF's use of error calculation between actual and predicted values, data segmentation, and variable relevance assessment. The authors also compare RF's performance with Support Vector Machine (SVM) and highlight the importance of performance metrics in evaluating model effectiveness. Their research underscores RF's capabilities for accurate regression modeling.

Ayaz Ahmad and team [8] combine ensemble algorithms and individual approaches to predict concrete compressive strength, emphasizing the use of boosting as an ensemble algorithm. They discuss techniques like Genetic Engineering Programming (GEP), Decision Trees (DT), and Artificial Neural Networks (ANN). The authors highlight the strength of these machine learning approaches in establishing correlations between input parameters and compressive strength.

Arslan Akbar and colleagues [9] use a combination of individual and ensemble model strategies to predict concrete compressive strength with waste material. They assess accuracy using the R2 value and employ methods such as decision trees, ensemble algorithms (bagging), and gene expression programming (GEP). The authors aim to provide accurate estimations of concrete strength, considering the impact of waste material.

A. Conclusion Points and Problem Statement Definition

The reviews from multiple authors collectively emphasize the significance of machine learning in predicting concrete rupture strength based on mix design parameters. Key takeaways include:

1. The importance of accurate training data that reflects concrete strength.
2. The selection of suitable machine learning algorithms based on the problem's unique qualities.
3. The complexity of concrete mix design and the need to capture interactions between mix elements.
4. Continuous model refinement to improve prediction accuracy over time.
5. The versatility and strength of machine learning techniques, even with limited datasets.
6. The significance of ensemble algorithms, hyperparameter tuning, and comparative analyses in enhancing predictive models.
7. The potential of machine learning to optimize concrete mixtures and achieve desired strength levels.

The problem statement can be defined as follows: "To develop a machine learning-based model for predicting the rupture strength of concrete based on mix design parameters, considering the complex interactions between mix elements and ensuring continuous model refinement. The model should optimize concrete mixtures, enhance prediction accuracy, and provide valuable insights for the construction industry."

3 Proposed System

3.1 Problem Statement

"Develop an efficient and accurate machine learning model to predict concrete rupture strength based on mix design parameters, optimizing construction **industry practices.**"

3.2 Objectives

To develop an efficient machine learning model for precise concrete rupture strength prediction.

1. To reduce labor and testing costs through machine learning-based forecasting.
2. To optimize concrete mix designs for desired rupture strength with minimal material wastage.
3. To enable real-time, practical applications of machine learning models for concrete quality assessment.
4. To ensure predicted rupture strength meets safety standards and desired specifications.

3.3 Steps of the Proposed System

The steps of the proposed system are given below:

1. User Interaction: The process begins with the user accessing a web interface hosted on a web server.
2. Data Request: The web server promptly sends a request for input data to the user's device.
3. Data Entry: The user enters the required information into the designated fields provided by the web interface.

4. Data Processing: After the user submits the input data, the web server receives and processes the information.
5. Model Data Transfer: The web server forwards the input data to the machine learning model for analysis.
6. Prediction Generation: Leveraging the provided input data, the machine learning model uses its predictive capabilities to generate a rupture strength prediction.
7. Model Response: The model formulates a response based on the analyzed data and predicted results.
8. Response Transfer: The model communicates the results back to the web server for further handling.
9. User Result Delivery: The web server delivers the predicted rupture strength results to the user, ensuring a seamless user experience.
10. User Decision: The user can make informed decisions or take further actions based on the provided rupture strength prediction.

These steps outline the interaction between the user, web interface, and the machine learning model, allowing users to obtain valuable insights into concrete rupture strength efficiently and conveniently.

3.4 Proposed Methodology

The proposed methodology for the given problem statement is as shown in Fig. 1.

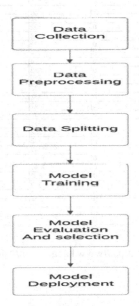

Fig. 1. Proposed System

The steps of the proposed methodology are

Step 1: Data Collection

- Collect a diverse dataset that includes concrete mix designs and their corresponding rupture strengths.
- The dataset should include details on the composition of the concrete, including components and proportions such as Cement, Fly Ash, Blast Furnace Slag, Coarse Aggregate, Fine Aggregate, Water, and Age (in days).
- Sample data set is shown in Fig. 2

Step 2: Data Pre-processing

- Handle missing values in the dataset by either imputing or removing them.
- Detect and handle outliers using techniques like z-score, interquartile range (IQR), or robust statistical methods.
- Convert categorical variables to numerical values through techniques like one-hot encoding or label encoding.
- Normalize numerical variables to bring them to a common scale using methods like min-max scaling or standardization.

	A	B	C	D	E	F	G	H	I
1	cement	blast_furnace_slag	fly_ash	water	superplasticizer	coarse_aggregate	fine_aggregate	age	concrete_compressive_strength
2	540	0	0	162	2.5	1040	676	28	79.99
3	540	0	0	162	2.5	1055	676	28	61.89
4	332.5	142.5	0	228	0	932	594	270	40.27
5	332.5	142.5	0	228	0	932	594	365	41.05
6	198.6	132.4	0	192	0	978.4	825.5	360	44.3
7	266	114	0	228	0	932	670	90	47.03
8	380	95	0	228	0	932	594	365	43.7
9	380	95	0	228	0	932	594	28	36.45
10	266	114	0	228	0	932	670	28	45.85
11	475	0	0	228	0	932	594	28	39.29
12	198.6	132.4	0	192	0	978.4	825.5	90	38.07
13	198.6	132.4	0	192	0	978.4	825.5	28	28.02
14	427.5	47.5	0	228	0	932	594	270	43.01
15	190	190	0	228	0	932	670	90	42.33
16	304	76	0	228	0	932	670	28	47.81
17	380	0	0	228	0	932	670	90	52.91
18	139.6	209.4	0	192	0	1047	806.9	90	39.36
19	342	38	0	228	0	932	670	365	56.14
20	380	95	0	228	0	932	594	90	40.56
21	475	0	0	228	0	932	594	180	42.62
22	427.5	47.5	0	228	0	932	594	180	41.84
23	139.6	209.4	0	192	0	1047	806.9	28	28.24
24	139.6	209.4	0	192	0	1047	806.9	3	8.06
25	139.6	209.4	0	192	0	1047	806.9	180	44.21
26	380	0	0	228	0	932	670	365	52.52
27	380	0	0	228	0	932	670	270	53.3
28	380	95	0	228	0	932	594	270	41.15
29	342	38	0	228	0	932	670	180	52.12
30	427.5	47.5	0	228	0	932	594	28	37.43
31	475	0	0	228	0	932	594	7	38.6
32	304	76	0	228	0	932	670	365	55.26

concrete data

Fig. 2. Sample Data set [source: https://www.kaggle.com/datasets/sinamhd9/concrete-compre hensive-strength]

Step 3: Data Splitting

- Split the pre-processed dataset into two subsets: a training set and a testing set.
- The training set is used to teach the machine learning model the patterns and relationships in the data.

- The testing set is reserved for evaluating the model's performance and generalization.

Step 4: Model Training

- Train a random forest regression model using the scikit-learn library in Python.
- Tune the hyperparameters of the random forest regression model using techniques like grid search and cross-validation.
- Adjust hyperparameters such as the number of decision trees, tree depth, and the number of features considered at each split.

Step 5: Model Evaluation

- Evaluate the trained model's performance using assessment measures such as Mean Squared Error (MSE), Root Mean Squared Error (RMSE), and Coefficient of Determination (R2).

Use evaluation metrics:

1. Mean Squared Error (MSE) (Equation):
2. MSE = Σ(y_actual − y_predicted)2/n
3. Root Mean Squared Error (RMSE) (Equation):

   RMSE = sqrt(MSE)

Coefficient of Determination (R^2) (Equation):
   $R^2 = 1 - (\Sigma(y\_actual - y\_predicted)^2/\Sigma(y\_actual - y\_mean)^2)$

- Analyze these measures to determine how well the model approximates the actual rupture strength values.

Step 6: Model Deployment
   Using Python's pickle package, save the trained random forest regression model to a file.

- This allows for easy loading and usage of the model in various applications, including web applications or production environments.

Step 7: Model Refinement.

- Continuously refine the model's performance by:

  - Retraining it on additional data to capture a broader range of patterns and variations.
  - Further tuning hyperparameters to optimize performance.
  - Exploring advanced techniques such as ensemble learning or neural networks.

Table 1. Algorithm

Algorithm: Random Forest Regression with Grid Search and Cross-Validation

1.   Import Libraries:
-     Import necessary libraries for data manipulation, model building, cross-validation, and hyperparameter tuning. Common libraries include NumPy, pandas, scikit-learn, and matplotlib.

2.   Load and Prepare Data:
-     Load your dataset.
-     Split the data into features (X) and the target variable (y).

3.   Data Splitting:
-     Split the data into training and testing sets to assess the model's performance. Common split ratios are 70/30, 80/20, or 90/10.

4.   Random Forest Regression Initialization:
-     Create a Random Forest Regressor object. The primary hyperparameters we will be tuning are the number of trees (n_estimators), maximum depth of the trees (max_depth), and the number of features considered for each split (max_features).

5.   Hyperparameter Grid for Grid Search:
-     Define a hyperparameter grid (param_grid) for the Grid Search. Specify a range of values or options for the hyperparameters to search. For example:

o   `n_estimators`: [10, 50, 100, 200]

o   `max_depth`: [None, 10, 20, 30]

o   `max_features`: ['auto', 'sqrt', 'log2']

6.   Grid Search CV Initialization:
-     Create a GridSearchCV object, specifying the Random Forest Regressor, the hyperparameter grid, the number of cross-validation folds (cv), and a scoring metric (e.g., mean squared error).

7.   Fit Grid Search to Training Data:
-     Fit the GridSearchCV object to the training data. Grid Search will perform a search over the hyperparameter space and use cross-validation to determine the best combination of hyperparameters.

8.   Retrieve Best Model and Parameters:
-     Get the best estimator (model) from the GridSearchCV object and the best hyperparameters. These hyperparameters are the ones that resulted in the best model performance during cross-validation.

9.   Model Evaluation:
-     Use the best model to make predictions on the test set.
-     Evaluate the model's performance using appropriate metrics, such as:
-             Mean Squared Error (MSE):
-     `MSE = (1/n) * Σ(y_true - y_pred)^2`, where `n` is the number of data points.
-     R-squared (R2):
-     R2 = 1 - (Σ(y_true - y_pred)^2) / (Σ(y_true - y_mean)^2)`

10.   Optional: Feature Importance Analysis:
-     If needed, analyze feature importances from the Random Forest model. Feature importance values are calculated internally by the model and represent the contribution of each feature to the model's predictions.

11.   Conclusion and Deployment:
-     Based on the model's performance, draw conclusions about its suitability for the task.
-     If the model meets the requirements, consider deploying it for making predictions on new data.

- Monitoring and improving the model's performance over time to maintain its relevance and effectiveness.

These steps outline the process of developing and deploying a machine learning model for predicting the rupture strength of concrete based on mix design parameters (Table 1).

4 Results and Analysis

Seven training components were used in the study: cement, slag, fly ash, superplasticizer, coarse aggregate, water, fine aggregate, and age (number of days for curing), all of which were quantified in kg/m3. We employed three regression models to forecast the concrete's rupture strength based on these components: Random Forest Regressor (RFR), Decision Tree Regressor (DTR), and Linear Regression (LR).

Comparison of Model Performance
Among the three regression models, the Random Forest Regressor (RFR) achieved the highest score of 0.892, outperforming both the Decision Tree Regressor (DTR) and Linear Regression (LR) models. Figure 3 shows the model performances.

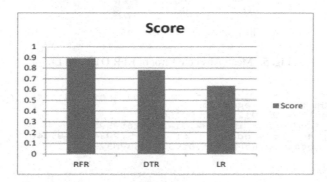

Fig. 3. Score of RFR DTR and LR model

Mean Squared Error (MSE)
The RFR model outperformed the DTR and LR models, displaying the lowest Mean Squared Error (MSE) of 27.57. This implies that, for outcome prediction in this dataset (shown in Fig. 4), the RFR model is more appropriate.

Mean Absolute Error (MAE)
Figure 5 shows that the RFR model was more accurate than the DTR and LR models, with the lowest Mean Absolute Error (MAE) of 3.60 among the three models.

Model Selection
After analyzing the Score, MSE, R-squared, and MAE metrics, it was determined that

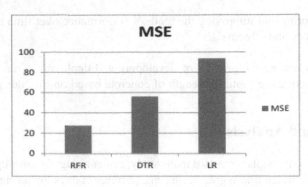

Fig. 4. Mean Squared Error (MSE) of RFR DTR and LR

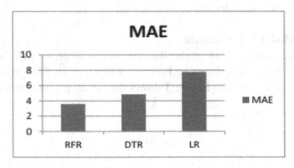

Fig. 5. Mean Absolute Error of RFR DTR and LR

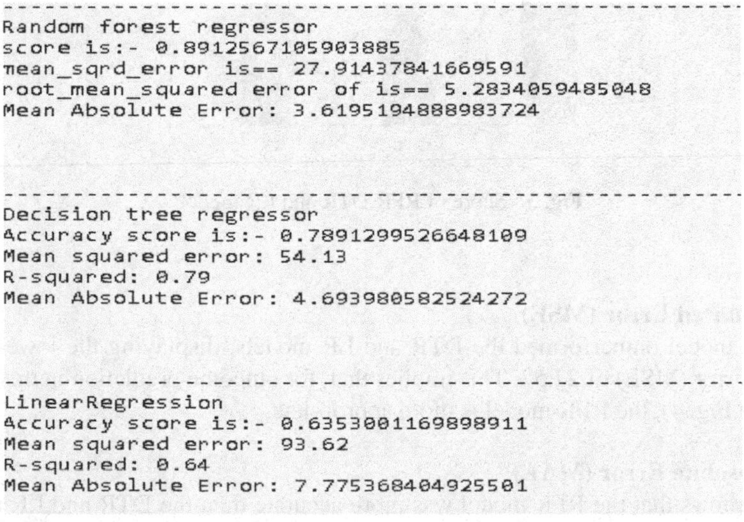

```
-----------------------------------------------------------
Random forest regressor
score is:- 0.8912567105903885
mean_sqrd_error is== 27.91437841669591
root_mean_squared error of is== 5.2834059485048
Mean Absolute Error: 3.6195194888983724



-----------------------------------------------------------
Decision tree regressor
Accuracy score is:- 0.7891299526648109
Mean squared error: 54.13
R-squared: 0.79
Mean Absolute Error: 4.693980582524272



-----------------------------------------------------------
LinearRegression
Accuracy score is:- 0.6353001169898911
Mean squared error: 93.62
R-squared: 0.64
Mean Absolute Error: 7.775368404925501
```

Fig. 6. Result page showing the predicted compressive strength

the Random Forest Regressor (RFR) was the best model to predict the strength of a rupture. Figure 6 shows the comparative results.

Web Interface for Accessibility:

- A simple web interface was designed to enable non-experts in data analysis and civil engineering to utilize the model.
- Using the RFR model, users can input relevant factors through the interface and receive accurate predictions
- For simplicity, input variables are categorized and labeled in clear language
- Clear instructions on how to use the web interface and interpret the results are provided.
- Web Interface Results: The following Fig. 7 shows web interface results.

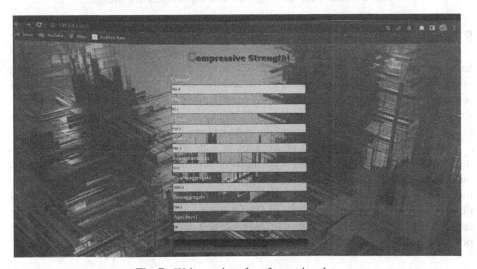

Fig. 7. Web user interface for getting data

The web interface allows users to enter input values, which are then transmitted to the backend where the RFR model resides.

The model makes predictions, and the resulting rupture strength of concrete is displayed to the user on the results page as depicted in Fig. 8.

Model Evaluating Parameters

The study employed three regression models, namely the Random Forest Regressor (RFR), Decision Tree Regressor (DTR), and Linear Regression (LR), to predict the rupture strength of concrete based on seven components. The evaluation of these models included metrics such as Score, Mean Squared Error (MSE), Mean Absolute Error (MAE), and R-squared. The Random Forest Regressor emerged as the top-performing model with the highest score of 0.892, the lowest MSE of 27.57, and the lowest MAE of 3.60 among the three models.

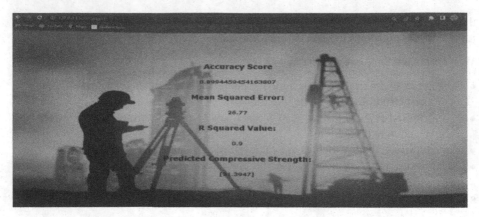

Fig. 8. Result page showing the predicted compressive strength

5   Conclusion and Future Scope

In summary, this paper pioneers a machine learning-driven methodology for predicting concrete rupture strength, presenting a swift and cost-effective alternative to conventional testing methods. Notably, the Random Forest Regressor (RFR) model demonstrated superior performance, emphasizing its efficacy in this context. The development of a user-friendly web interface enhances the practical applicability of the model.

Looking ahead, future research avenues include expanding the dataset to enhance model robustness, exploring advanced machine learning models for further accuracy, incorporating IoT for real-time monitoring in construction projects, considering environmental impacts in the predictive models, and fostering collaboration with the construction industry for seamless deployment. These prospective directions aim to continually refine and broaden the applicability of the proposed approach, fostering innovation and practical utility in the field of concrete strength prediction.

References

1. Karikatti, V., Chitawadagi, M.V., Patil, I.S., Sanjith, J., Mahesh Kumar, C.L., Kiran, B.M.: ANN model for predicting compressive strength of alkali activated slag concretecured at environmental temperature. NeuroQuantology **20**(1) (2022). https://doi.org/10.14704/nq.2022.20.6.NQ22044
2. Rathakrishnan, V., Bt. Beddu, S., Ahmed, A.N.: Predicting compressive strength of high-performance concrete with high volume ground granulated blast-furnace slag replacement using boosting machine learning algorithms. ResearchGate (2022). https://doi.org/10.1038/s41598-022-12890-2
3. Shaqadan, A.: Prediction of concrete mix strength using random forest model. Int. J. Appl. Eng. Res. **11**(22), 11024–11029 (2016). ISSN 0973-4562
4. Shafiq, M.A.: Predicting the compressive strength of concrete using neural network and kernel ridge regression. Reasearch Gate (2016). https://doi.org/10.1109/FTC.2016.7821698
5. Wan, Z., Xu, Y., Savija, B.: On the use of machine learning models for prediction of compressive strength of concrete: influence of dimensionality reduction on the model performance. ResearchGate, Materials **14**, 713 (2021). https://doi.org/10.3390/ma14040713

6. Mai, H.-V.T., Nguyen, T.-A., Ly, H.-B., Tran, V.Q.: Prediction compressive strength of concrete containing using random forest model. Hindawi Volume (2021)
7. Ahmad, A., Ahmad, W., Aslam, F., Joyklad, P.: Compressive strength prediction of fly ash-based geopolymer concrete via advanced machine learning techniques. Elsevier (2021)
8. Khursheed, S., Jagan, J., Samui, P., Kumar, S.: Compressive strength prediction of fly ash concrete by using machine learning techniques. Innov. Infrastruct. Solutions **6**(3), 1–21 (2021). https://doi.org/10.1007/s41062-021-00506-z
9. Song, H., Ahmad, A., Farooq, F., Ostrowski, K.A.: Compressive strength prediction of fly ash concrete by using machine learning techniques. ResearchGate, Materials (2021)
10. Ahmad, A., Farooq, F., Niewiadomski, P., Ostrowski, K.: Prediction of compressive strength of fly ash based concrete using individual and ensemble algorithm. ResearchGate, Materials (2021). https://doi.org/10.3390/ma14040794
11. Mohana, M.H.: The determination of ground granulated concrete compressive strength-based machine learning models. ResearchGate **8**(2), 1011–1023 (2020)
12. Ling, H., Qian, C., Kang, W., Liang, C., Chen, H.: Combination of support vector machine and K-fold cross validation to predict compressive strength of concrete in marine environment. ResearchGate (2019)

Investigation of Power Consumption of Refrigeration Model and Its Exploratory Data Analysis (EDA) by Using Machine Learning (ML) Algorithm

Avesahemad S. N. Husainy[1,2]($\boxtimes$) , Suresh M. Sawant[3], Sonali K. Kale[4] ,
Sagar D. Patil[1] , Sujit V. Kumbhar[1] , Vishal V. Patil[1] , and Anirban Sur[5]

[1] Department of Mechanical Engineering, Sharad Institute of Technology, College of
Engineering, Yadrav, Ichalkaranji, India
avesahemad@gmail.com
[2] Mechanical Engineering in Faculty of Science and Technology, Shivaji University, Kolhapur,
Maharashtra, India
[3] Mechanical Engineering Department, Rajarambapu Institute of Technology, Rajaramnagar,
Uran Islampur, India
[4] Department of First Year Engineering, Pimpri Chinchwad College of Engineering, Pune,
Maharashtra, India
[5] Faculty of Engineering, Symbiosis International (Deemed University), Pune, Maharashtra,
India

Abstract. HVAC (Heating Ventilation and Air-conditioning) play a vital role
in various sectors, from residential and commercial to industrial applications.
Understanding and optimizing the power consumption of these systems is crucial for energy efficiency and cost savings. This research aims to explore the
power consumption of refrigeration systems during power ON mode and perform
Exploratory Data Analysis (EDA) and Machine Learning (ML) algorithms to gain
insights into factors influencing power consumption. The experimentation is conducted on refrigeration test rig and performance is calculated during power ON
mode by adding NPCM (Nano-Phase Change Material) in evaporator section and
comparison is to be made without implementation of NPCM in evaporator section.
By utilizing ML algorithms, it becomes possible to create predictive models that
can assist in optimizing the power consumption of refrigeration systems, reducing
energy costs, and minimizing environmental impact. The accuracy of model by
linear regression is around 66% by implementation NPCM in refrigeration system where as 23% model accuracy is found without implementation of NPCM in
refrigeration system. Also it is observed that coefficient of performance of refrigeration system increase by around 15 to 18% as compared with without use of
NPCM. Also power consumption is reduces to 5 to 7% with implementation of
nano phase change material in refrigeration system.

Keywords: Machine learning · exploratory analysis · refrigeration · power
consumption · performance

1 Introduction

HVAC systems are becoming more and more necessary for industrial facilities, residential complexes, and commercial buildings in India as its metropolitan areas grow. Perishable food product supply chains have grown in tandem with the majority of industrialized and developing countries' increased usage of refrigeration over the past few decades. These days, chilled or Global supply chains for frozen food products, sometimes known as the "cold chain," handle billions of tons of food [1]. Throughout postharvest supply chains, one third to half of all food produced is lost or wasted globally, with value chains related to transportation, storage, and packaging being the most affected [2, 3]. Globally, between 40% and 50% of fruits and vegetables are lost, with 54% of those losses happening during the production, handling, and storage phases after harvest [4, 5]. Greater energy consumption brought on by urbanization necessitates the use of effective HVAC systems. Rising energy prices and environmental concerns in India are making energy-efficient HVAC systems more and more necessary. Thus, refrigerator energy efficiency has become a crucial factor in the effective management of electrical energy in the house in a world where resource depletion and global warming are at alarming levels [7]. HVAC systems that use less energy can save operational expenses and energy consumption by a large margin. It is possible to forecast when HVAC components, including fans and compressors, are likely to break down using machine learning algorithms. Uptime can be minimized and expensive emergency repairs can be avoided by scheduling maintenance proactively using real-time sensor data and historical data analysis. Demand response programs, in which HVAC systems are adjusted in response to grid demand, can benefit from machine learning. Systems can be temporarily changed to lower electricity usage during periods of high energy demand, which helps maintain grid stability. Machine learning (ML) is becoming increasingly essential in the HVAC (Heating, Ventilation, and Air Conditioning) industry due to its potential to enhance system efficiency, optimize performance, and improve overall energy management. Thermal energy storage is used to store and release thermal energy for various purposes, including improving energy efficiency and managing energy demand.Currently thermal energy storage and utilization is focused only on few areas such as building applications, refrigeration and cold chain and some industrial applications. But TES technology can be adopted for wide range of applications as shown in Fig. 1. As the most effective way to store food, refrigerators play a significant role in the home appliance market. To represent the linear relationship between predictor and response variables, a linear regression ML algorithm is employed. Python is used to implement this, with a google colab notebook serving as the front end. The normalized training dataset is utilized to train the linear regression model. Response variable optimal values are determined by adjusting different hyper parameters.

1.1 Important of Thermal Energy Storage in HVAC System

- TES systems enable the system to run during off-peak hours, when electricity is more affordable and easily accessible, thereby increasing the energy efficiency of refrigeration processes. In order to lower overall operating costs, the system can store excess cooling capacity when energy costs are low and discharge it when energy costs are high.

● Refrigeration systems' peak loads can be efficiently managed by TES systems. They lessen the need for additional chillers or compressors by storing excess cooling capacity during times of low demand and releasing it during times of peak demand. This helps prevent overloading the refrigeration equipment.

● Temperature control in refrigeration applications can be made more accurate and consistent with the use of TES systems. This is significant for a number of industries, including food storage, where the safety and quality of products depend on constant temperature maintenance.

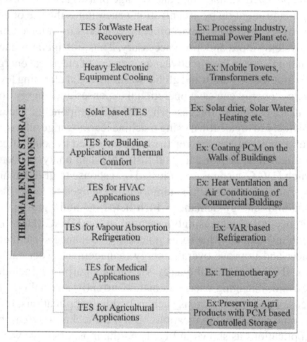

Fig. 1. Applications of thermal energy storage [6]

Maintaining ideal food storage temperatures is necessary for the transport systems that run these cold chain systems in order to guarantee maximum safety and premium shelf life. Because cooling systems are so good at keeping food, there is a growing consideration of their sustainability. It is necessary to approach the sustainability of a cold chain system from the perspective of overall cost [7]. PCMs are a class of latent thermoelectric materials that store energy by utilizing the solid-to-liquid phase transition. The large volume change makes the liquid/gas and solid/gas phase transitions less desirable from a technical standpoint. According to Sharma et al.'s overview [8], PCMs can be broadly divided into three groups: organic, inorganic, and eutectic materials. When compared to sensible heat storage (SHS), latent heat storage (LHS) has a higher volumetric thermal energy storage capacity. Because less storage volume is needed, using LHS is found to be more appealing and competitive in many applications [9]. Thermal energy storage (TES) systems can be classified into several categories based on the method used to store and release thermal energy as shown in Fig. 2.

In order to store or release thermal energy, latent heat storage entails a material's phase transition. Latent heat storage is accomplished with phase change materials, or PCMs. Because of their high heat of fusion, they have the capacity to store and/or release large amounts of energy during phase transitions. Chemical reactions are used in thermochemical storage systems to store and release thermal energy. The foundation of a latent heat storage system is the heat that is absorbed or released when a storage material changes phases from solid to liquid, liquid to gas, or vice versa. Its high storage energy density per unit mass in a quasi-static process makes it extremely appealing [10].

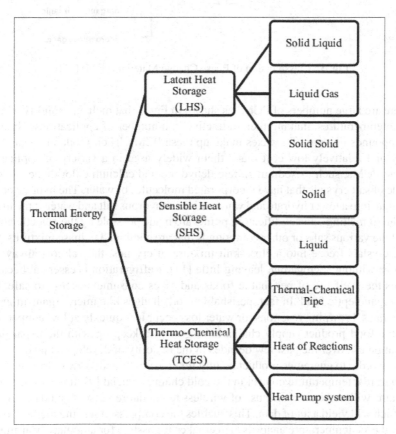

Fig. 2. Classification of Thermal Energy Storage (TES) [10]

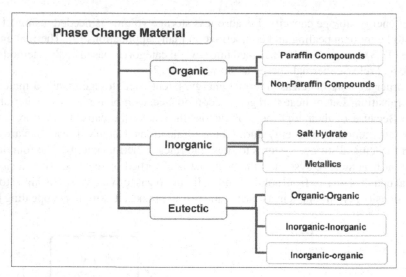

Fig. 3. Classification of Phase Change Material (PCM) [11]

There are large numbers of PCMs as shown in Fig. 3 that melt and solidify at a wide range of temperatures, making them attractive in a number of applications. Hydrocarbon compounds like paraffin waxes make up these PCMs. Their moderate heat storage capacity and relatively low cost make them widely used in a variety of applications. Inorganic PCMs, such as sodium sulfate dehydrate and calcium chloride hexahydrate, are made of salt crystals that have incorporated molecules of water. The hydrate crystals disintegrate into a lower hydrate and water or into anhydrous salt and water at the melting point. Sharp melting and solidification points are made possible by the eutectic composition of the various salts or other compounds that are combined in these mixtures. Since eutectic crystals freeze into a close-knit mixture of crystals, they almost always melt and freeze without segregating, leaving little [11]. Refrigeration is essential because it increases the shelf life of perishable foods and gives consumers access to safe, high-quality organoleptic food. In fact, perishable food changes like microorganism growth, ripening rates, browning reactions, or water loss occur less quickly at low temperatures. Perishable food product supply chains have grown to keep up with the expansion of refrigeration use over the past few decades in the majority of developed and developing nations. In order to guarantee product quality for consumers and to lower food waste and health hazards, temperature control in the cold chain is crucial [9]. It is anticipated that cold chains will make extensive use of wireless temperature sensors and data transmission, which will yield a lot of data. This enables the compressed sensing method to assist in the real time temperature analysis. This makes it possible for automatic warning systems to consider time-temperature thresholds for alerts as well as temperature variability within equipment. Long term data analysis employing a machine learning methodology will improve our understanding of cold chain breaks, including their frequency, severity, and length. Cold chain research produces numerical and experimental data that could be used to train machine learning models [12].

1.2 Machine Learning Scope for HVAC Industry

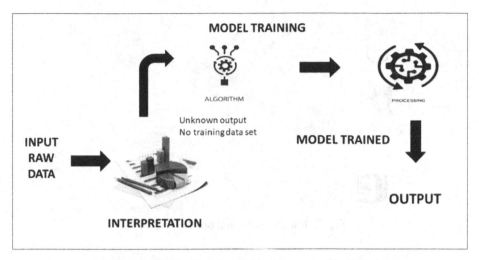

Fig. 4. Machine learning for food interpretation [13]

Machine learning helps with techniques for optimizing food processes by creating a model that forecasts the best outcome given the input data. Both supervised and unsupervised learning, data preprocessing, feature engineering, model selection, evaluation, and optimization techniques are all included in machine learning. These methods could be used to solve a variety of food processing optimization issues. The food industry is using machine learning more and more to increase production efficiency, cut waste, and provide individualized customer experiences. In addition to automating tasks like labeling and packaging, machine learning can be used to predict customer preferences and create individualized products as shown in Fig. 4. It can also be used to maximize ingredient utilization and reduce costs [13]. Using a sensor-based system, Ekta Sonwani et al. [14] present a novel method for monitoring and analyzing food spoilage. Food can be preserved with the gadget this study suggests for a longer period of time. Furthermore, food items can be kept fresher for longer by extending their shelf life. It keeps an eye on the quality of the food items and keeps alerting the user via voice-activated commands or a display. It also generates alerts that indicate how long the food is expected to spoil. The suggested gadget has a 95% accuracy rate. The suggested smart device can be made better by using machine learning and image processing algorithms to identify early spoilage. Machine learning was proposed by N.V. Ganapathi Raju et al. [15] to predict the fridge door status (open or close). The target variable is the fridge door's status (1 or 0), and the features that are used to train the model are tray temperature, fridge cabinet temperature, and energy consumption. The suggested work's goal is to use machine learning algorithms to determine the fridge door's current status.

Zahra Soltani et al. [16] different classifiers are compared to diagnose twenty types of faults simultaneously and non-faulty condition in the industrial RS. The training data is taken from a simulation model which has been used in the development of system

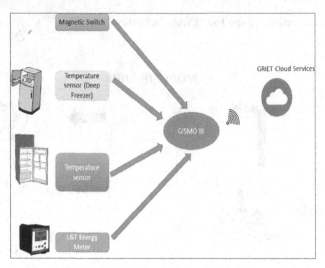

Fig. 5. Illustration of proposed model [15]

control in Bitzer. The results indicate that the fault detection reliability of the algorithms highly depends on how well the training data covers the operation regime. Furthermore, it is found that a well-trained SVM can simultaneously classify twenty types of fault with 95% accuracy when the verification data is taken from different system configurations. The involvement of machine learning in healthcare applications in the current context will be covered throughout this paper by Senerath Mudalige Don Alexis Chinthaka Jay-atilake et. al. [17] along with a discussion of the various machine learning algorithms and approaches being used for decision making in the healthcare sector. With the help of the high processing power of contemporary, sophisticated computers, it became clear from the information gathered that neural network-based deep learning techniques had excelled in the field of computational biology and were widely used due to their high prediction accuracy and dependability. When considering the larger picture and integrating the observations, it becomes evident that machine learning algorithms have become essential to computational biology and biomedicine-based healthcare decision making, making them inseparable from the field. Machine learning is used in the diagnosis of illnesses and biomedical event extraction, medication repurposing, medical imaging, prediction, and much more in the healthcare industry. While described the use of ML in cancer prediction and prognosis, Konstantina Kourou et al. [18] talked about its concepts. The majority of studies that have been put forth in recent years concentrate on creating predictive models with supervised machine learning techniques and classification algorithms in an effort to forecast accurate disease outcomes. Their analysis of the data shows that the integration of multidimensional heterogeneous data, along with the use of various feature selection and classification techniques, can yield useful tools for inference in the field of cancer.

2 Proposed Experimental Methodology and Machine Learning Implementation

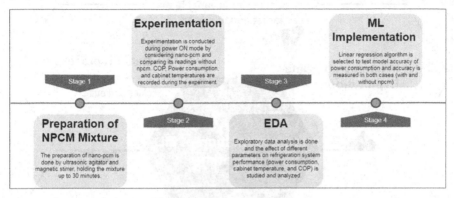

Fig. 6. Proposed methodology

1. Experimental set up consists of refrigeration test rig along with vapor compression refrigeration components like, compressor, condenser, expansion device and evaporator. Locate temperature sensors (thermocouples) at crucial points (storage unit, evaporator, and condenser, etc.) and pressure gauges are used to record pressure of condenser and evaporator side (Fig. 6).
2. Nano-phase change material (Eutectic mixture) for lower temperature applications based on their phase change temperature, latent heat, thermal conductivity, and stability is selected for experimentation.
3. Preparation of nano-pcm is done by using ultrasonic agitator and magnetic stirrer by holding mixture for 30 min till nanoparticles get mixed with pcm mixture.
4. Start the system and initiate the refrigeration cycle. Conduct the experiment during power ON situation without consideration thermal energy storage in evaporator section. Record the readings like condenser and evaporator pressure and temperature at certain interval of time.
5. Data is collected till cabinet temperature reaches at 0 °C and achieve constant cabinet temperature as per system design capacity and calculate coefficient of performance, energy consumption, etc.
6. Same process is repeated by adding npcm in evaporator or section as thermal energy storage and performance parameters are calculated and compared.
7. Exploratory data analysis is done by consideration of different measured performance parameters.
8. Implementation of machine learning algorithm (linear regression) for power consumption data and accuracy of model is calculated and compared. Also prediction study is done to know the power consumption at particular time interval.

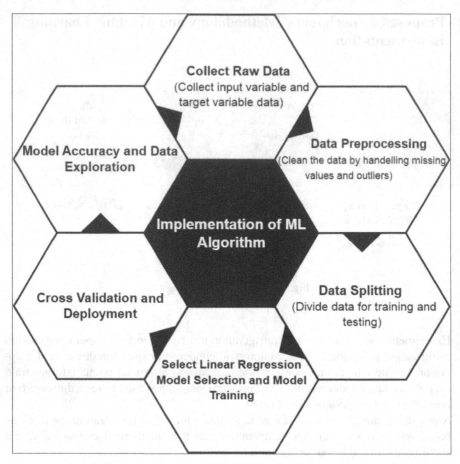

Fig. 7. Framework of machine learning implementation

In order to train models for prediction and decision-making, supervised learning techniques such as regression and classification use labeled training data sets. The primary distinction resides in the fact that the classification algorithm classifies the data for the ease of making decisions later, whilst the regression technique is primarily employed for fitting, bringing the fitting line as close to all data points as feasible. The regression algorithm is mostly used for prediction [19]. Implementing a linear regression algorithm involves several steps as shown in Fig. 7.

3   Experimentation and Results

The refrigerant passes through copper tubes in the evaporator section between the stainless steel inner and outer sections of the cooling chamber. The NPCM (Eutectic mixture of 15% $CaCl_2$ + 15% KCl with water as base fluid as PCM and 1% Graphene is act as nanoparticle) is kept between annular space of evaporator and insulated cabinet. Experiment is conducted during power ON mode by implementation of NPCM and its comparison is done by without implementation of NPCM. The temperature and pressure data is collected from data logger and it is saved in CSV format. The evaporator call absorb the heat from NPCM mixture during power ON mode and NPCM start changing phase from liquid to solid till evaporator reach at 0 to −5 °C. During charging process of NPCM it store latent heat and dissipate that heat during power OFF or temperature fluctuation exists and change its phase from solid to liquid. The data sheet consist of different total 14 columns (float and integer format) which includes different temperatures, time, pressures, performance parameters like power consumption, COP, voltage and current, etc. for both datasets like with and without NPCM. The data is available in CSV format. The chosen datasets is useful for exploratory data analysis. EDA helps in identifying outliers, missing values, or anomalies within the dataset. These anomalies can significantly impact the results of statistical analysis if not handled properly (Fig. 8).

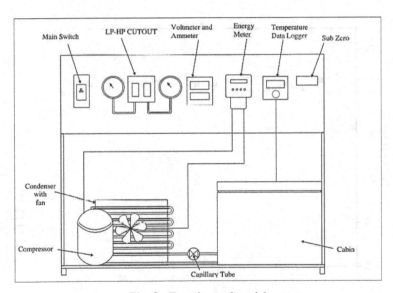

Fig. 8. Experimental model

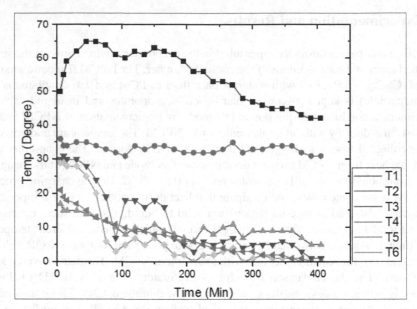

Fig. 9. Time vs Temp (With NPCM)

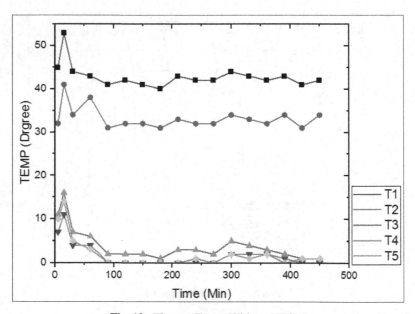

Fig. 10. Time vs Temp (Without NPCM)

The experiment is conducted during power ON mode with and without adding Nano-PCM in evaporator section and different parameters like power consumption and (COP) coefficient of performance is calculated by recording different temperatures of test set up as shown in Fig. 9 and Fig. 10. For experimentation eutectic mixture of phase change material (C_aCl_2+KCl) along with graphene nanoparticle with water as a base fluid. It is observed that coefficient of performance of refrigeration system increase by around 15 to 18% as compared with without use of NPCM. Also power consumption also reduces to 5 to 7% with implementation of nano phase change material. After conducting the experiment it is observed that, implementation of NPCM in evaporator section it is possible to attain constant temperature for longer duration of time even though temperature fluctuations occurs due to frequently opening and close the door of cooling cabinet. The purpose of using nanoparticles with phase change material is poor conductivity and relevant thermal properties of PCM, by addition of nanoparticles heat transfer and thermal conductivity of PCM is improve. The selection and percentage of PCM and nanoparticles is decided on the basis of previous research [20]. It is decided to do exploratory data analysis of experimental result. Displot is used to create distribution plots to visualize the distribution of a single variable like temperature as shown in Fig. 11. It is observed that condenser inlet and outlet temperature is lie from 45 to 60 °C and 25 to 38 °C respectively. Evaporator inlet and outlet temperature is lie between 0 to 25 °C and 0 to 15 °C respectively. Also cabinet (cooling box) temperature will maintain from 0 to 5 °C.

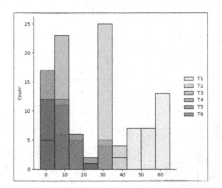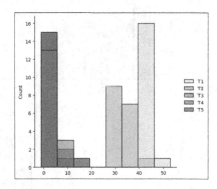

Fig. 11. Displot of temperature distribution by use and without use of NPCM during power ON

Also Kernel Density Estimation (KDE) plots, which are used to estimate the density function of a continuous random variable of temperatures during power ON mode as shown in Fig. 12.

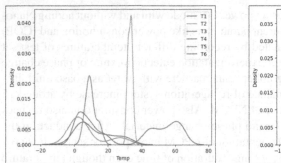
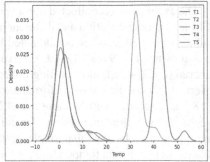

Fig. 12. Difference of temperatures distribution by use and without use of NPCM during power ON mode by using KDE plot

When working with multivariate data, pair plots helpful since it makes it easy to see the relationships between many variables like temperatures, coefficient of performance and power consumptions, etc. as shown in Fig. 13 and 14.

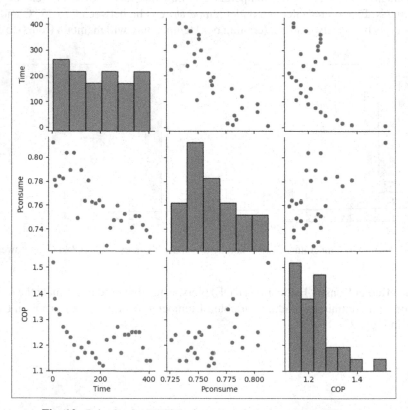

Fig. 13. Pair plot for NPCM mixture result during power ON mode

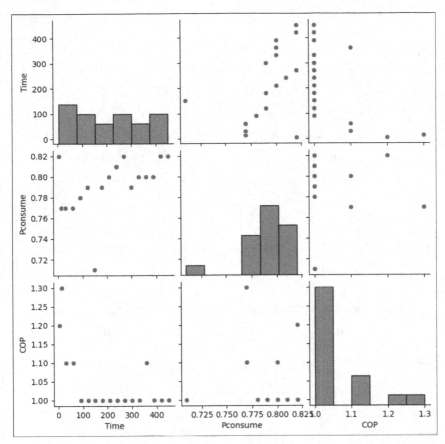

Fig. 14. Pair plot for without NPCM mixture result during power ON mode

A data visualization method called a strip plot is used to show individual data points on one axis, usually in opposition to a categorical variable on the other axis. In Fig. 15 results of COP, Power consumption and cabinet temperature is scattered along with time.

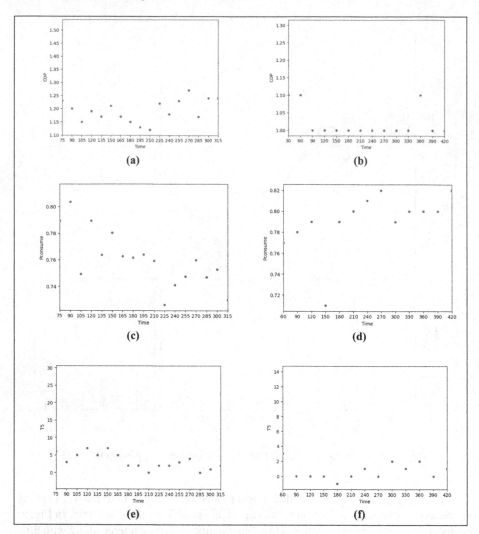

Fig. 15. (a) Strip plot time vs COP with use of NPCM, (b) Strip plot time vs COP without use of NPCM, (c) Strip plot time vs power consumption with use of NPCM, (d) Strip plot time vs power consumption without use of NPCM, (e) Strip plot of time vs cabinet temperature with NPCM, (f) Strip plot of time vs cabinet temperature without NPCM

Subplot is a function used in many plotting libraries, like Matplotlib and Seaborn in Python, to create multiple plots within a single figure. This allows you to visualize multiple sets of data or related plots in the same graphical space. In Fig. 16 subplot of power consumption is drawn. It is observed that power consumption during power ON mode by implementation of NPCM is less as compared to without NPCM (Fig. 17).

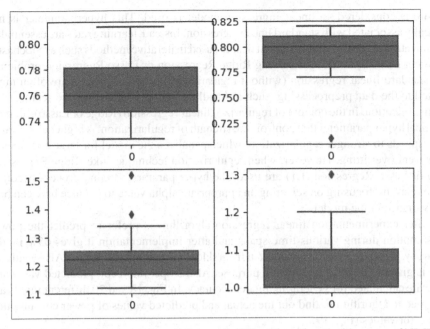

Fig. 16. Subplot of power consume during power ON mode with and without use of NPCM

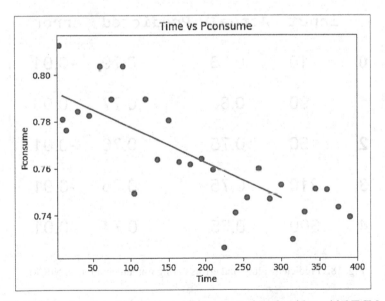

Fig. 17. Scatter plot of implemented linear regression algorithm with NPCM

Linear regression mostly used for finding out the relationship between variable and forecasting. Linear regression performs the task to predict a dependent variable values (y) based on a given independent variable (x). In this experimental research only one feature is considered so linear ingression model is used. This hyperparameter is not typically associated with standard linear regression. Instead, learning rates are essential in optimization algorithms like gradient descent used in iterative methods such as Stochastic Gradient Descent (SGD) for solving Ridge Regression or Lasso Regression problems. For standard linear regression (without regularization), the key aspects are often more related to the data preprocessing, such as handling missing values, feature scaling, and feature selection. In the context of regularized linear regression (Ridge or Lasso), alpha is a critical hyper parameter that controls the strength of regularization. A higher alpha value corresponds to stronger regularization, which penalizes the model for large coefficients to prevent overfitting. However, when regularization techniques like Ridge Regression (L2) or Lasso Regression (L1) are used, the hyper parameter tuning process becomes more relevant, focusing on selecting an appropriate alpha value to balance between bias and variance in the model.

After experimentation linear regression algorithm is prefer to predict the power consumption during various time spans and after implementation it gives 65% model accuracy. Linear regression is imported from sklearn.linear_model library. Also available data is given to training and testing purpose. Also slope, intercept, predicted value and error are calculated for generating model accuracy. In Fig. 18 and 20 different inputs are provided to algorithm to find out the actual and predicted values of power consumption with error values (Fig. 19).

	input	Actual	Predicted	error
0	10	0.78	0.79	-0.01
1	90	0.80	0.77	0.03
2	150	0.75	0.76	-0.01
3	210	0.75	0.76	-0.01
4	300	0.75	0.74	0.01

Fig. 18. Predicted values and errors during implementation of NPCM

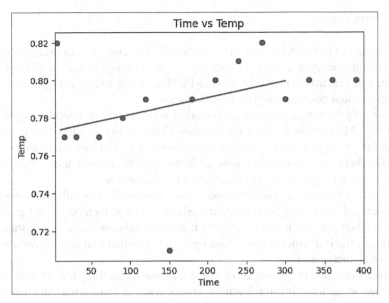

Fig. 19. Scatter plot of implemented linear regression algorithm without NPCM

	input	Actual	Predicted	error
0	10	0.77	0.77	0.00
1	90	0.78	0.78	0.00
2	150	0.71	0.78	-0.07
3	210	0.80	0.79	0.01
4	300	0.79	0.79	0.00

Fig. 20. Predicted values and errors during without implementation of NPCM

An effective and popular technique for simulating relationships between variables is linear regression. It offers a simple method for forecasting and interpreting how predictors affect the result. In the fields of statistics and machine learning, linear regression is a basic and often used procedure. By fitting a linear equation to the observed data, it is mostly used to model the connection between a dependent variable and one or more independent variables.

4   Conclusion

- The purpose of nano-PCMs is to optimize the thermal energy storage capacity by utilizing the distinct characteristics of nanomaterials. Through enhanced thermal energy storage and heat transfer efficiency, nano-PCMs can help reduce energy consumption and operational costs across a range of industries.
- Investigating how much power refrigeration systems use and combining Machine Learning (ML) methods with Exploratory Data Analysis (EDA) have produced insightful findings with real-world applications. Correlations and patterns found by EDA help us comprehend how different elements, such usage patterns and temperature settings, interact to effect power consumption.
- The results of this study directly affect how energy-efficient refrigeration systems are promoted. This study's ideas and models can result in significant cost and energy savings when put into practice, making it an essential contribution to sustainability initiatives after implementation of Nano-phase change material in refrigeration model as thermal energy storage.
- In conclusion, the application of machine learning technology has a lot to offer the refrigeration sector. Machine learning lowers costs, lessens environmental impact, and improves product quality and safety by maximizing energy efficiency, enabling predictive maintenance, and improving overall system performance.

References

1. Loisel, J., et al.: Cold chain break detection and analysis: can machine learning help? Trends Food Sci. Technol. **112**, 391–399 (2021)
2. Lundqvist, J., De Fraiture, C., Molden, D.: Saving water: from field to fork: curbing losses and wastage in the food chain (2008)
3. Bustos, C.A., Moors, E.H.: Reducing post-harvest food losses through innovative collaboration: Insights from the Colombian and Mexican avocado supply chains. J. Clean. Prod. **199**, 1020–1034 (2018)
4. Dos Santos, S.F., et al.: Post-harvest losses of fruits and vegetables in supply centers in Salvador, Brazil: analysis of determinants, volumes and reduction strategies. Waste Manage. **101**, 161–170 (2020)
5. Food Wastage Footprint (Project). Food wastage footprint: impacts on natural resources: summary report. Food & Agriculture Organization of the UN (FAO) (2013)
6. Chavan, S., Rudrapati, R., Manickam, S.: A comprehensive review on current advances of thermal energy storage and its applications. Alex. Eng. J. **61**(7), 5455–5463 (2022)
7. Bertoldi, P., Atanasiu, B.: Electricity consumption and efficiency trends in the enlarged European Union. IES–JRC. European Union (2007)
8. James, C.: Food transportation and refrigeration technologies design and optimization. In: Sustainable Food Supply Chains, pp. 185–199. Academic Press (2019)
9. Sharma, A., Tyagi, V.V., Chen, C.R., Buddhi, D.: Review on thermal energy storage with phase change materials and applications. Renew. Sustain. Energy Rev. **13**(2), 318–345 (2009)
10. Mehling, H., Cabeza, L.F.: Heat and cold storage with PCM. Heat Mass Transf. 11–55 (2008)
11. Ali, S., Deshmukh, S.P.: An overview: applications of thermal energy storage using phase change materials. Mater. Today: Proc. **26**, 1231–1237 (2020)

12. James, S.J., James, C.J.F.R.I.: The food cold-chain and climate change. Food Res. Int. **43**(7), 1944–1956 (2010)
13. Pandey, V.K., et al.: Machine learning algorithms and fundamentals as emerging safety tools in preservation of fruits and vegetables: a review. Processes **11**(6), 1720 (2023)
14. Sonwani, E., Bansal, U., Alroobaea, R., Baqasah, A.M., Hedabou, M.: An artificial intelligence approach toward food spoilage detection and analysis. Front. Public Health **9**, 816226 (2022)
15. Raju, N.G., Radhanand, A., Kumar, K.B., Reddy, G.P., Reddy, P.S.K.: Machine learning based power saving mechanism for fridge: an experimental study using GISMO III board. Mater. Today: Proc. **33**, 4819–4822 (2020)
16. Soltani, Z., Sørensen, K.K., Leth, J., Bendtsen, J.D.: Fault detection and diagnosis in refrigeration systems using machine learning algorithms. Int. J. Refrig **144**, 34–45 (2022)
17. Jayatilake, S.M.D.A.C., Ganegoda, G.U.: Involvement of machine learning tools in healthcare decision making. J. Healthc. Eng. **2021** (2021)
18. Kourou, K., Exarchos, T.P., Exarchos, K.P., Karamouzis, M.V., Fotiadis, D.I.: Machine learning applications in cancer prognosis and prediction. Comput. Struct. Biotechnol. J. **13**, 8–17 (2015)
19. Li, N., Zhao, J., Zhu, N.: Building energy consumption prediction evaluation model. Adv. Mater. Res. **280**, 101–105 (2011)
20. Husainy, A.S.N., Parishwad, G.V., Kale, S.K., Nishandar, S.V., Patil, A.S.: Improving cooling performance of deep freezer by incorporating graphene oxide nanoparticles mixed with phase change materials during a power outage. In: Pawar, P.M., Balasubramaniam, R., Ronge, B.P., Salunkhe, S.B., Vibhute, A.S., Melinamath, Bhuwaneshwari (eds.) Techno-Societal 2020, pp. 485–492. Springer, Cham (2021). https://doi.org/10.1007/978-3-030-69925-3_48

Prediction of Emission Characteristics of Spark Ignition (S.I.) Engines with Premium Level Gasoline-Ethanol-Alkane Blends Using Machine Learning

Sujit Kumbhar[1,2]($\boxtimes$) ⓘ, Sanjay Khot[3] ⓘ, Varsha Jujare[4] ⓘ, Vishal Patil[7] ⓘ,
Avesahemad Husainy[5] ⓘ, and Koustubha Shedbalkar[6] ⓘ

[1] Department of Technology, Shivaji University, Kolhapur 416004, Maharashtra, India
sujit.kumbhar64@gmail.com
[2] Department of Automation and Robotics, Sharad Institute of Technology College of Engineering, Yadrav, Inchalkaranji 416121, Maharastra, India
[3] Sharad Institute of Technology College of Engineering, Yadrav, Inchalkaranji 416121, Maharastra, India
[4] Department of Computer Science and Engineering, Sharad Institute of Technology College of Engineering, Yadrav, Inchalkaranji 416121, Maharastra, India
[5] Department of Mechanical Engineering, Sharad Institute of Technology College of Engineering, Yadrav, Inchalkaranji 416121, Maharastra, India
[6] Department of Electrical Engineering, Sharad Institute of Technology College of Engineering, Yadrav, Inchalkaranji 416121, Maharastra, India
[7] Department of Mechanical Engineering, Sharad Institute of Technology College of Engineering, Yadrav, Inchalkaranji 416121, Maharastra, India

Abstract. In the current research work, a single cylinder spark (S.I)ignition engine were used for investigations of premium level gasoline-ethanol-alkane experimentally with different operating conditions e.g. variation spark ignition timing. The Engine Lab and PE3 software were used for engine control and data acquisition system. The data obtained after experimentation were used to predict the engine emissions for different operating conditions. The engine emission characteristics were predicted using three machine learning algorithms*viz* linear regression, decision tree and random forest. It was found that emissions characteristics such as carbon monoxide, unburnt hydrocarbon found to be minimum for 24°bTDC experimentally as well as predicted by machine learning algorithms with different operating conditions than other spark timing positions such as 15°, 18°, 21°, 27°, 30° bTDC. All three machine learning algorithms gave better results but the random forest algorithm were more accurate than linear regression and decision trees.

Keywords: Engine Emission Characteristics · Ethanol-Alkane-Premium Gasoline · Machine Learning · spark timing

1 Introduction

Machine learning is a potential approach for predicting the periodic emission characteristic of spark ignition engines because of its many benefits, including robustness, high prediction accuracy, low computation time, and low consumption. Worldwide demand for automobiles has increased due to population growth [1]. From time to time, worries increase regarding the harmful pollutants that engines release. By using machine learning approaches for prediction and Lagrangian optimization, it is possible to enhance the operating parameters as well as engine emissions of single cylinder, spark ignition (S.I.) engine along with different operating conditions to prevent environmental deterioration. Over the last many years, artificial intelligence (AI) has undergone significant improvements. These developments have made machine learning (ML) a potentially useful tool for optimizing fuel and engine systems [2]. Numerous studies have employed neural networks in particular to effectively optimize fuel and engine systems. Examples of more contemporary uses include the control system of real-time engine adjustment as well as the impact of fuel characteristics on the engine emissions. Other Machine Learning (ML) techniques, such as linear regression, random forests, support vector machines, etc. have also been used to issues relating to engines and vehicles. Conventional fossil fuel has traditionally been seen as a crucial component of the global economy [3]. However, because many industries, particularly the transportation sector, are so heavily dependent on crude oil and we are about to witness the depletion of derivatives. This also highlights the detrimental effects of this dependence similar to pollution and climate change brought on by engine emissions of different fuel. Because of their numerous advantages, research on biofuels has substantially increased in recent years. Other advantages to think about include easy production and lower pollution levels [4]. To improve the efficiency of biofuels and create the ideal blend ratio with diesel and gasoline, many strategies are applied. In the United States alone, air pollution from combustion sources is thought to be responsible for over 100,000 deaths per year. Since nitrogen oxides (NO_x) can interact with other compounds present in the atmosphere and forms ozone depletion and acid rain, which causes eutrophication in hydrophilic ecosystems, NO_x is a substantial component of the combustion-generated pollution that automobiles emit into the environment. The United States (U.S.) agency i.e. The Environmental Protection Agency (EPA) regulates NO_x emissions strictly, and more than half of all NO_x emissions that are found in the air arises from automobiles, primarily diesel-fueled vehicles. Owing to the elevated temperature (over 1000 °C) as well as lean fuel-air ratios prevalent during this phase of combustion, spark ignition (S.I.) engines produce the majority of their nitrogen oxides (NO_x) at the point of combustion known as diffusion burning. NO_2 is then produced as a consequence of equilibrium measures inside the surrounding environment and inside the combustion chamber. Nowadays, vehicles use selective catalytic converters after treatment to lower NO_x emissions, but how well it does so and how much diesel exhaust fluid (DEF) is needed to do so relies largely on the amount of NO_x that the engine produces. Both researchers and engine manufacturers are quite interested in forecasting and monitoring engine-out NO_x. In production engines, electrochemical NO_x sensors are frequently employed in both upstream and downstream of the Selective Catalytic Reduction. Despite being efficient, sensors are expensive and prone to mistake, particularly at low exhaust temperatures [26].

The process of producing results through predictive modelling makes use of statistical methods and probability theory. For this method to produce reliable results, specific input data is needed. The model's forecast is more accurate the more experimental data it has been supplied. A model's prediction accuracy is the primary determinant of its accuracy [7]. From a scholarly perspective, a precise prediction model of an engine's emissions can provide an enhanced knowledge of emission characteristics of engines at the various stages of the combustion of fuel in engine. The use of artificial intelligence-based predictive models also enables the designer of a vehicle to evaluate the potential impact of suggested modifications to the vehicle's emission characteristics. This is accomplished by giving the model with approximations of the impact that the suggested alteration will have on various engine characteristics. Using its prior knowledge, the AI model can then forecast changes to the emission characteristics. When thinking about design adjustments, this is a helpful decision-making tool. The model may be beneficial for identifying component failures in the field of vehicle maintenance [8].

Since high-quality data are readily available, the introduction of sophisticated machine learning models with better accuracy and computational speeds, the field of emissions prediction using techniques based on data has attracted growing interest. Data can be gathered from instrumented automobiles operating in real-world driving situations or from laboratory engine testing. Using both sets of data, machine learning regression techniques such as linear regression, decision trees, adaptive regression splines, support vector methodsetc. are used to forecast NO_x emissions [9].

2 Literature Review

As they examined and measured every possible engine emission from a car operated on hydrogen, Karri V. et al. [3] revealed several AI models acting as virtual sensors in 2008. State-of-the-art artificial intelligence techniques are employed to identify these emissions. These state-of-the-art techniques include the University of Tasmania's bespoke software, back-propagation using the Levenberg-Marquardt algorithm, and the adaptive neural fuzzy approach. Numerous significant input variables that directly impact the emissions generated by engines fueled by hydrogen were considered in their study. Several state-of-the-art probes and sensors are used in the intricate experimental process. To accurately record the emission data, it was also essential to use such sensors and carbon monoxide (CO), Carbon dioxide (CO_2), unburnt hydrocarbon (HC), and oxides of nitrogen (NO_x) were among the output variables [10]. In the aforementioned research, these contemporary techniques of artificial intelligence are called virtual sensors.Ghobadian B. et al. [11] constructed a model of an artificial neural network in 2009 to predict torque and the primary outputs being engine exhaust, brake power (b.p.),torque. An engine made of diesel that was powered by biodiesel produced from leftover vegetable-based cooking oil was utilized to test the model. After gathering used vegetable oil, the testing procedure began by creating biofuel. Then, after being injected into a two-cylinder, water-cooled diesel engine, the fabricated biofuel was measured and computed for engine emissions as well as all the previously specified performance parameters. Different biofuel blends were created, and each blend went through the same testing process [12]. A substantial amount of data was generated by this process, which aided in the ANN model's self-training. An analogous strategy was used by Kiani M. et al. [13]. An artificial neural network model was used to forecast engine performance and emissions. The primary distinction was the type of engine that was used. The fact that the utilization of a four-cylinder, four-stroke spark ignition engine demonstrates the range of applications for which these artificial models were useful.This engine was powered by gasoline that was ethanol-based. This model once more gave quick, nearly precise results. Gopalakrishnan K. et al. [14] acknowledged the problem of increasing emissions of greenhouse gases from passenger cars in 2011. For the majority of people, public transportation buses are undoubtedly the most common mode of transportation. In order to predict emissions from actual biodiesel-powered transit vehicles, the study showed how to apply a neuro-fuzzy model. The data was produced using a modern and advanced Portable emissions measurement system. Specifically, the neuro-fuzzy approaches are very good at controlling data noise to mitigate any risk of the overfitting. Two neurofuzzy techniques were employed in this investigation: the Dynamic Evolving Neuro-Fuzzy Inference System (DENFIS) and the Adaptive Neuro-Fuzzy Inference System (ANFIS). A forecasting model for NO_x emissions from direct injection engines was developed by J. Mohammadhassani et al. [15]. ANN methodology was the method employed. The Direct Injection system is a propulsion system with high power output and minimal fuel consumption, according to the research paper. The automotive industry is where this system is primarily employed. The application of prediction models in the mechanical industry has been examined by several researchers. The application of genetic algorithms in combination with artificial neural networks, Kanta et al. [16] projected the machining parameters, and validation showed that the predicted and actual results were consistent. Ozener et al. [8] demonstrated the methodology that the output of a turbocharged engine could be predicted, and it also incorporated a performance as well as emissions investigation of the I.C. engine. Adarsh et al. [17] provided evidence of the application of several cutting edged AI models in the machine learning and artificial intelligence field. The study report demonstrated engine performance prediction modelling using a numerous approaches, such as ANFIS, Genetic Algorithm (GA), and ANN. Initially, the ANFIS model was used to evaluate the model's the accuracy. After applying generic algorithm (GA) to improve the ANFIS model, the accuracy of the old model—46.6%—were found to have greatly risen. According to a study released by Deniz S. et al. [18], data mining can be used to test engine performance and reduce emissions. The study featured examples of a number of data mining methods, including the C5.0 algorithm, neural networks, and Bayesian networks. The study's findings demonstrated the potential of such artificial techniques for producing economical, effective, and environmentally friendly cars. The project was broken up into numerous stages. Mądziel [19] were done an analysis of a few traffic simulations and the modelling of the components of exhaust gases. The models that have been shown have been grouped together according to the level of accuracy they had: macro, meso, and micro. This study provided a summary of a few publications that combine traffic and emission model analysis. Additionally, they included modelling-related information and suggestions that may be useful in helping decision-makers like road managers choose the right emission estimation tools. Machine learning was applied to light-duty vehicle idle emissions by Li Q. et al. [20]. Any type of road vehicle, including cars, has repeatedly been forced to stop, either voluntarily or as a result of traffic congestion. Significant emissions are also generated when an automobile is stationary while its engine is still running. When an engine is running but the vehicle is not moving, it is referred to as idling. Idling can be classified into two categories: discretionary and nondiscretionary. The decision by the driver to stop moving the car is known as discretionary idling. Conversely, nondiscretionary idling describes circumstances in which the driver is required to halt the vehicle, like a stop sign or traffic jam. The engine emission modeling in the previously stated research is only displayed when the engine is idling. The study employed machine learning approaches, including KNN (K-closest neighbor), Support Vector Machines, Decision Trees, Neural Networks, CHAID models etc.Berghout et al. [21] recommended employing an upgraded selection strategy (USS) and a new DOS-ELM with double dynamic forgetting factors (DDFF). In order to identify significant patterns in the data, the first step introduces robust feature extraction based on the characteristics of the training data collected from aircraft sensors using a modified De-noising Autoencoder (DAE). After then, enhanced selection strategy (USS) is used to guarantee that the training process is only permitted to move forward with the useful data sequences. With OS-ELM, dynamic programming is managed and the engine's non-accumulative linear deviation function is matched by bringing in fresh data and progressively deleting previous data derived from the suggested DDFF. In comparison to OS-ELM trained with normal Autoen-coder (AE), basic OS-ELM, and earlier attempts from the literature, the suggested DOS-ELM is proposed. The commercial modular aero propulsion system simulation dataset for a turbofan engine (C-MAPSS), which is made freely available, is used for the evaluation. Comparison findings show improved network responses stability even in the presence of random solutions, proving the effectiveness of the new integrated robust feature extraction method [22].

To assess how well deep kernel learning (DKL), which is essentially a mix of a Gaussian process (GP) and a deep neural network (DNN), performs in comparison to various surrogate models using the same dataset, Yu et al. [5] applied it to compression ignition engine emissions. A class of computationally less expensive models called surrogate models can replace physics-based models. Furthermore, as a baseline model for contrast, a brief description of high-dimensional model representation (HDMR) is provided. Using a dataset generated from a compression ignition engine, they applied the suggested methodologies to the outputs of 14 engine operating state variables, which represent soot and NO_x emissions. The researchers utilized a combination of traditional grid optimization methods combined with quasi-random global search to ascertain appropriate values for particular DKL hyperparameters, such as kernel, learning, and network design parameters. The root mean squared error (RMSE) of the predictions is used to assess the effectiveness of HDMR, DKL, plain GPs, plain DNNs etc. in addition to the processing cost for training and analysis. It is shown in the forecasts that DKL reduces the computational cost to within reasonable bounds while outperforming other models in terms of RMSE. Additionally, there is a significant agreement between the DKL projections and the experimental emissions data. To enhance internal combustion engine performance, Badra et al. [23] developed the algorithm known as machine learning-grid gradient (ML-GGA). Machine learning(ML) is a technique for converting the intricate physical operations that take place inside a combustion engine into manageable automated tasks. The resulting ML-GGA model was compared to a recently developed Machine Learning Genetic Algorithm (ML-GA). To enhance the precision and robustness of the optimization process, the current ML-GGA model underwent extensive research into optimization solver settings and variable limits extension. This article goes into great detail about the various methods, tools, and requirements that must be met in order to achieve the intended outcome. The proposed ML-GGA technique was used to optimize the piston bowl design and operating conditions of a heavy-duty diesel engine that was running on gasoline with a Research Octane Number (RON) of 80. When comparing the output of the MLGGA technique to the best outcome of a full system optimization driven by computational fluid dynamics (CFD), the merit function was improved by more than 2%. Engine CFD simulations were used to verify the predictions produced by the MLGGA technique. This study indicates how MLGGA has the ability to considerably speed up optimization tasks compared to more conventional methods, without sacrificing accuracy. In order to predict a Compression Ignition (C.I.) engine's performance as well as emission parameters that was powered by several metal-oxide based nanoparticles, such as aluminum oxides, titanium oxides, and copper oxides at mass fractions of 200 ppm, Abulut et al. [24] used machine learning algorithms (MLAs). The parameters that are investigated in this study include carbon dioxide (CO), nitrogen oxide (NO_x), exhaust gas temperature (EGT), brake specific fuel consumption (BSFC), and brake thermal efficiency (BTE). Tests conducted at 100 rpm intervals on engines running between 1500 and 3400 rpm. Because they are better at conducting heat, have a higher surface-to-volume ratio, are naturally oxygenated, and function as catalysts during combustion, nanoparticles ensured more thorough burning, which reduced CO and NO_x emissions. Abdulmalik [25] looked into Canada's transportation-related carbon dioxide (CO_2) emissions, which are a large portion of the nation's total emissions. Although it focuses on transportation-related CO_2 emissions in Canada, the study looks at the rise in carbon dioxide (CO_2) brought on by a number of variables, including population expansion, the development of transportation, and economic growth. Deep Neural Networks, Random Forests, and Support Vector Machines are just a few of the machine learning methods that are used to forecast CO_2 emissions. The six (6) techniques' R^2 values varied from 0.9532–0.9996, their RMSE values from 1.0974–13.6561, their MAPE scores from 0.0088–0.0010, their MBE scores from -0.0594–1.0366, their rRMSE scores from 0.4259–5.3002, and their MABE scores from 0.2643 to 5.6582. These results are encouraging. Machine learning methods were developed on 15 documented types of scope 3 emissions by Serafeim et al.[26]. The models' inputs include industrial categories, scope 1 and 2 emissions, and readily available financial statement variables. They found that adaptive boosting machine learning approaches are more accurate in predicting the majority of reported scope 3 emission types when compared with other supervised machine learning algorithms and linear regression models. A machine learning (ML) model was constructed by Norouzi et al. [9] to mimic the behavior of a linear parameter varying (LPV) MPC in addition to emissions and the performance of engines. Based on support vector machines, a linear parameter variable model of engine performance and emissions was used to build a model predictive controller for a 4.5 L Cummins diesel engine. Benefits include lower NO_x emissions and fuel consumption when comparing this online optimized MPC solution to the standard feedforward manufacturing controller. A deep learning technique were utilized to simulate the behavior of the built controller in order to lower the processing cost of this MPC. The online MPC optimization takes 50 times longer to compute than the imitative controller, yet the imitative controller reduces NO_x emissions at a constant load better than the online optimized MPC.

Pravin et al. [27] developed a model based on machine learning using the Tensor Flow library in Python programming to estimate the emission characteristics, for example carbon monoxide (CO), carbon dioxide (CO_2) etc. of an internal combustion engine on injection of varying volumes biodiesel as fuel. These studies as well as data sets are taken into account for the analysis of single cylinder four-stroke internal combustion engine. Tensor Flow library has been utilized in this machine learning model to improve result display and mistake correction. The results of the built Tensor Flow model are then compared with an existing fuzzy model for the same application. The outcomes forecasted by this model are noticeably in good agreement with the actual values, demonstrating the usefulness of this strategy. The generated model's total error was found to be significantly reduced at 0.02 when compared to the current fuzzy model. As a result of offering more visualization options and more accurate prediction analyses, the Tensor Flow-based machine learning model was shown to be the most effective model for determining the engine emission characteristics of internal combustion engines that run on biodiesel. Shin et al. [6] developed and evaluated deep-learning models for forecasting engine-out NO_x emissions, a primary source of pollution for diesel engines, according to the Worldwide Hazardous Light Vehicles Test Procedure (WLTP). Traditional modeling techniques make it difficult to foresee occurrences in transient contexts. Two techniques were compared in terms of accuracy and computation time: long short-term memory (LSTM) and deep neural network (DNN). After training on measured data, the LSTM model outperformed R^2 equal to 0.9671, RMSE equal to 25.5 ppm for the DNN model ($R^2 = 0.9777$, RMSE $= 20.6$ ppm). However, DNN model greatly outperformed the LSTM model in terms of computation speed (0.36 s vs. 1381.0 s). Since this feature was absent from DNN model trained on the observed data, time-related information was pre-processed into the data. The weighted average of prior time step data to the current time step data was calculated as part of the pre-processing of the data. A weighted average was determined using the following ratios: Seven: Three, Six: Four, Five: Five, Four: Six, and Three: Seven. By using a Seven: Three weighted average during training, the accuracy of the DNN model was increased to an R^2 value of 0.9741 and RMSE 22.8 ppm, without sacrificing computing performance (only an R^2 value 0.0036 lower and RMSE 2.2 ppm higher than the LSTM model).The results of this study indicate that pre-processing the DNN model's data was a workable method for getting accuracy close to the LSTM models. Because of its accuracy and processing speed, the created DNN model for NO_x emission prediction can be employed as a virtual sensor for real-time prediction. In order to gather the experimental results, Karunamurthy et al. [16] employed diesel and biogas as the primary and secondary fuels in a single-cylinder diesel engine. Factors such as flow rate of biogas, torque, methane percentage, inlet temperature etc. are contemplated in order to forecast the characteristics of output parameters. The attributes of performance Emissions characteristics, secondary fuel energy ratio, and brake thermal efficiency among the study's outcome indicators are carbon monoxide, oxides of nitrogen (NO_x), unburnt hydrocarbon (HC), particulate matter, smoke etc. The suggested model, which makes use of a Random Forest Regressor that was trained with 324 distinct experiences obtained from actual trials.When training and testing the model in an 85:15 ratio, the R^2 score—0.997 for the provided dataset is used to verify the model. The output data are computed using the model's outputs for each time the input attribute values change. Lagrangian optimization is used to find the best values for the input parameters that will result in the highest thermal efficiency and the lowest emission. The optimal parameters are 68.3 °C, a biogas flow rate of 8.29 lit/min, a torque of 12.48 Nm, and a methane concentration of 72.8%. Selvam et al. [28] forecasted and examined patterns in engine-out NO_x emissions from heavy-duty diesel and diesel-hybrid vehicles, developing a physics-based machine learning approach.. The temperature of the adiabatic flame, the amount of oxygen present in the cylinder when the valves for intake are closed, and the length of the combustion process are the three main non-linear factors that determine the NO_x emissions from compression ignition engines based on diffusive combustion characteristics as well as chemical kinetics. Here, the parameters were determined using the OBD data that was provided. One way to evaluate different machine learning regression algorithms is to linearize a NO_x emissions forecast model based on physics. The results reveal that random forest regression (RFR), an ensemble learning bagging-type model, is very good at estimating NO_x emissions from the engine as determined by the NO_x sensor on board. They also demonstrated how varied actual-world OBD data is by employing clustered co-occurrences of automobile features. Across a variety of automobile OBD datasets, the resulting model's accuracy is 53% and 42% higher, respectively, than that of non-linear regression models, with an average R2 value of 0.72 and mean absolute error (MAE) of 78 ppm. Furthermore, because of its relationship to physical parameters, the model allows for analysis of the outcomes. A sensitivity study of the drop-column features for the RFR Model was also conducted, and non-linear regression and black-box deep neural network models were used to assess the prediction findings. The suggested RFR model has the potential to be used in the forecast of NO_x on board engines of various displacement as well as design due to its exceptional accuracy and interpretability [29].

Artificially intelligent models have been examined by Karri et al. [3] as a potential substitute for sensors in order to estimate pertinent emissions for a hydrogen-powered vehicle, such as carbon monoxide, carbon dioxide, and nitrogen oxides. Utilizing the Levenberg-Marquardt algorithm, neural networks with backpropagation and neuro-fuzzy inference systems that are adaptable, the University of Tasmania developed artificial intelligence software that is used to create virtual sensors. These forecasts, which are supported by both qualitative and quantitative research, look at how engine process variables—like Exhaust gas temperature, engine power, air-to-fuel ratio, mass airflow, and engine speed all influence hazardous exhaust gas emissions.. After calculating emissions, all AI models show good prediction capabilities These predictions, which are based on a qualitative and quantitative analysis, look at how engine process variables—like mass airflow, engine speed, air-to-fuel ratio, exhaust gas temperature, and engine power—affect dangerous exhaust gas emissions. After calculating emissions, all AI models exhibit good results and prediction capabilities. Backpropagation neural networks using the Levenberg-Marquardt algorithm, on the other hand, demonstrate exceptional accuracy with estimated values of the average root mean square error that are less than six percentage to estimate emissions for various hydrogen engine operating conditions. Recent research has concentrated on changing the network architecture, deep learning, and ANN design in order to attain the greatest performance. An outline of how ANNs are used to forecast and improve the complicated properties of different engine types utilizing different fuels was given by Bhatt et al. [22]. The purpose of the study is to look into the network topologies that were utilized in the model's design and then perform a statistical analysis on the ANN models that are produced. There is also a comparison provided between the other prediction models and the ANN model. Berghout et.al. [21] presented a novel quick training technique in order to forecast RUL using a single-batch ELM following carefully choosing the suitable features and use noise filtering to achieve accurate estimation.

In summary, the present investigation adds to the collection of literature in the following ways.

1. In this preliminary experimental investigations, prediction of engine emissions using the machine learning (ML) algorithm will be done.
2. This study comprehensively analyzes the prediction results of the decision tree, random forest, and linear regression algorithms according to the following subsequent metrics: R^2, RMSE, rRMSE, and MBE.
3. It will predict the engine emissions of a single cylinder spark ignition engine powered by premium gasoline-ethanol blends with different operating conditions like spark advancement & spark retardment, percentage of ethanol blending etc.

3   Methodology

The experimental setup consists of a four-stroke, single-cylinder gasoline engine. The Brake power was measured using an eddy current dynamometer that was coupled to water-cooled loading units. The engine also received the necessary hardware, including a pressure transmitter and a crank angle encoder, to record cylinder pressure and crank angle. To measure the air flow rate and fuel flow rate, an airflow transmitter and a fuel flow transmitter were fitted for each engine test. The measurement of water flow was done using two water rotameters. The load variations were recorded using the digital load indicators. The properties of three premium gasoline-ethanol blends, designated as E20, E40, and E60, were compared with premium gasoline, or E0, in a laboratory setting using volumetric analysis. Every experimental value is manually recorded, which makes them prone to inaccuracy. The complete dataset is pre-processed in order to align the values so that machine learning algorithms can handle them before modelling begins. The subsequent actions are taken (Fig. 1):

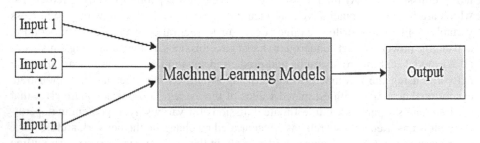

Fig. 1. Machine Learning Model

Microsoft Excel is used to store the data gathered during practical experimentation. Reaction variables include carbon monoxide (CO), nitrogen oxides (NO_x), hydrogen, smoke, and brake thermal efficiency; predictor variables include load, alkane flowrate, spark timing, and intake temperature. By changing the input parameters, about 325 independent experiments are conducted, and the findings are documented. The data that has been pre-processed is trained using random forests, and the outputs are utilized to determine the ideal input feature values.

Data Pre-processing: Since each value obtained through experimentation is manually recorded, mistakes can happen. Before beginning the modeling process, preprocessing is done on the complete dataset to align the values so that machine learning algorithms can process them. A missing value check is performed on the dataset. The calculated means of each feature are utilized to fill up the missing values. After that, correlation analysis is performed to see whether the response variables and predictor variables are linear. In particular, the correlation between each input and each output variable is ascertained using Pearson's correlation coefficient. The range of correlation numbers, from $+1$ to 1, indicates whether there is a positive or negative connection. If the values are close to $+1$ or less than 1, then linearity is present. The training and testing sets of the dataset are split 80:20 apart. Suggested proportion of training to testing samples. Every feature may have a varied numeric range, and the values are recorded on various scales. Changes in the scales of the input variables could make it more difficult to interpret the outcomes of the problem that is being modelled. Given that numerical quantities are frequently used in algorithms, every piece of data is analyzed quantitatively and will therefore have an effect on the modelling. There will have a significant influence on the outcomes when the ranges of each feature change. Therefore, data is standardized using min–max normalization to a range between 0 and 1 in order to prevent such an anomaly. To lessen anomaly brought on by different numeric ranges, the training dataset is standardized.

Prediction Modelling

Random Forest Regressior: Regression and classification can both be done with the random forest method of supervised ensemble learning. During training, this technique employs Correlation and Regression Trees (CART) to construct a group of decision trees. Regression trees are developed through the use of a method called bootstrapping, which entails selecting arbitrary samples using replacement from the dataset. Next, basic learners are constructed regression trees. Within a regression tree, each node symbolizes a binary test that has been performed against the chosen predictor variable. Reducing the sum of squares residual, or MSE, for data passing through the left and right branches is the variable that has been selected. The ultimate forecast is then determined by taking the mean of all the values anticipated by each tree. CART has the advantage of having a high degree of data fit and the potential for little bias. However, significant variance may affect CART since the outcomes are entirely dependent on the input data. Random forest has been shown to reduce overfitting issues and high variance. This can be changed by building each tree with randomlyselected 'm' predictors (where m $<=$ n, where 'n' represents the real number of predictors), then combining the outcomes. R^2 is one metric that may be used to validate the performance (Fig. 2).

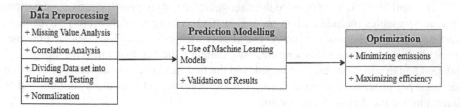

Fig. 2. Machine Learning Methodology

Implementation: To represent the nonlinear relationship between predictor and response variables, a random forest regressor is employed. Python is used to implement this, with a Jupyter notebook serving as the front end. The normalized training dataset is utilized to train the random forest model. Response variable optimal values are determined by adjusting different hyperparameters.

4   Results and Discussion

Predicting Stage: Table 1 presents the quantitative data derived using the statistical measures for every data anticipated in the research. Table 1 illustrates R^2 values for all ML methods, which show very good outcomes. For all algorithms, R^2 values greater than 0.9 are found. It is observed that random forest algorithm shows better results than linear regression and decision tree.

Table 1. Comparison of statistical Metrices of various machine learning algorithms

Parameter	Statistical Metrices	Machine Learning Algorithms		
		Linear Regression	Decision Tree	Random Forest
BTE	R^2	0.901	0.953	0.962
	RMSE (%)	0.744	0.500	0.437
	rRMSE (%)	3.121	2.097	1.833
Spark Advancement and retardment	R^2	0.944	0.968	0.979
	RMSE	6.966	6.076	5.016
	rRMSE	2.769	2.188	1.733
NO_x	R^2	0.954	0.965	0.976
	RMSE (ppm)	32.36	31.70	22.04
	rRMSE (ppm)	4.327	4.240	2.947
CO	R^2	0.921	0.940	0.971
	RMSE (ppm)	0.008	0.009	0.005
	rRMSE (ppm)	9.459	10.640	5.912

(continued)

Table 1. (*continued*)

Parameter	Statistical Metrices	Machine Learning Algorithms		
		Linear Regression	Decision Tree	Random Forest
HC	R^2	0.944	0.968	0.979
	RMSE (ppm)	8.969	6.763	6.016
	rRMSE (ppm)	2.769	2.088	1.858
CO_2	R^2	0.921	0.940	0.971
	RMSE (ppm)	0.008	0.009	0.005
	rRMSE (ppm)	9.459	10.640	5.912

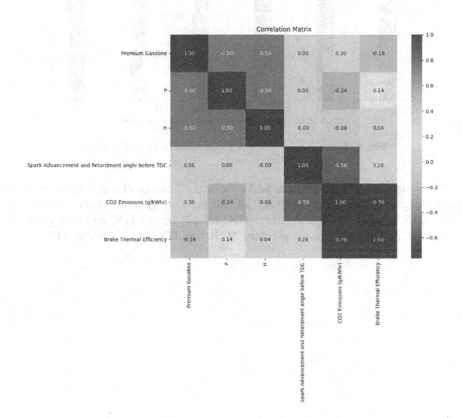

Fig. 3. Correlation Matrix for CO and CO2 emissions

CO and CO_2 Emissions

Figure 3 shows the correlation matrix for CO and CO_2. Carbon monoxide (CO) and carbon dioxide (CO_2) decreases with addition of 10% alkanes (pentane and hexane) in premium gasoline- ethanol blends.

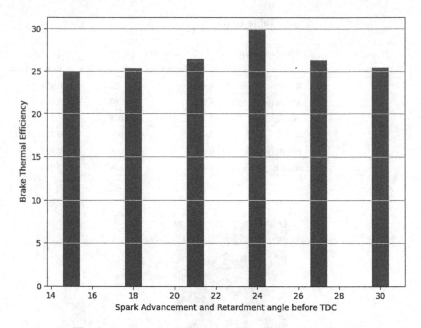

Fig. 4. Brake thermal efficiency with variation of spark timing

From Fig. 4, it is seen that the brake thermal efficiency of single cylinder spark ignition engine is high for 24° before TDC for premium gasoline-ethanol-alkane fuel blend. BTE increases from 15° before TDC till 24° before TDC and then gradually decreases. The BTE is also quite good for 21° before TDC and 25° before TDC.

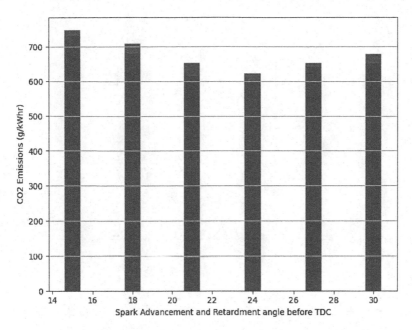

Fig. 5. Variation of CO_2 emissions with spark timing variation

In complete combustion, hydrocarbon reacts with oxygen molecules which gives carbon dioxide (CO_2) and water molecules (H_2O) as a byproducts. The CO_2 emissions should be as low as possible. From Fig. 5, the CO_2 emissions are low for 24° before TDC spark timing. The CO_2 emissions were maximum for 15° before TDC because of incomplete combustion of fuel during combustion process.

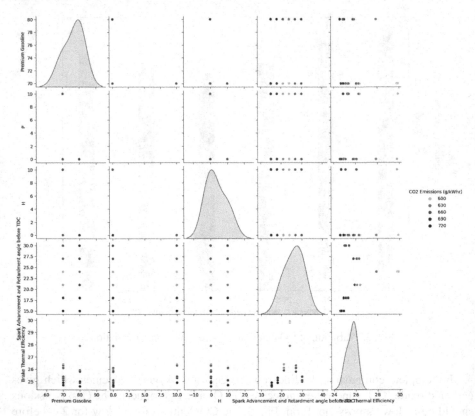

Fig. 6. Distplot of CO and CO_2 prediction using Brake Thermal Efficiency and Spark advancement & Spark retardment.

Distplot gives the relationship among all the variables used. Figure 6 shows distplot of CO and CO_2. With addition of 10% alkanes, CO and CO_2 decreases considerably. Also, there is great impact of spark advancement and retardment on these emission characteristics. The engine emissions were minimum at 24° before TDC. Brake thermal efficiency is also maximum at 24° before TDC.

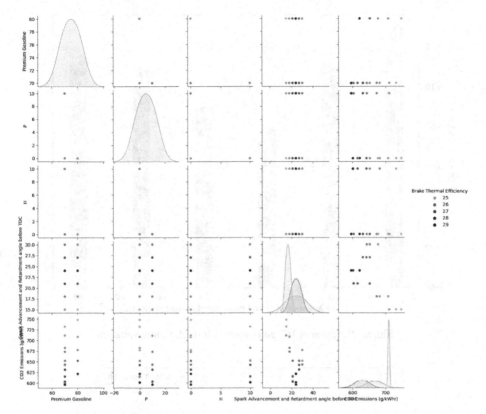

Fig. 7. Distplot of CO and CO$_2$ prediction using Pentane (P), Hexane (H)

HC Emissions

The unburnt hydrocarbon emissions from engine should be as low as possible. In complete combustion, the presence of hydrocarbon is nearly equal to zero. In this experimentation, the hydrocarbon emissions were found minimum at 21° and 24° before TDC. Figure 8 shows the variation of hydrocarbon emissions with spark timing positions. The hydrocarbon emissions were high for spark timing 15° before TDC and 30° before TDC.

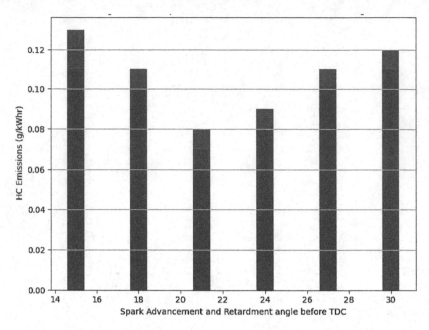

Fig. 8. Variation of HC emissions with spark timing variation

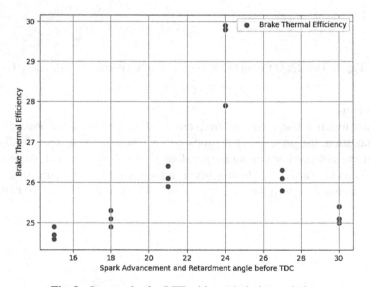

Fig. 9. Scatter plot for BTE with spark timing variation

Figure 9 shows the scatter plot of brake thermal efficiency with spark timing variation. The brake thermal efficiency is maximum at spark timing 24° before TDC. The brake thermal efficiency for other spark timing positions were minimum for spark advancement or retardment.

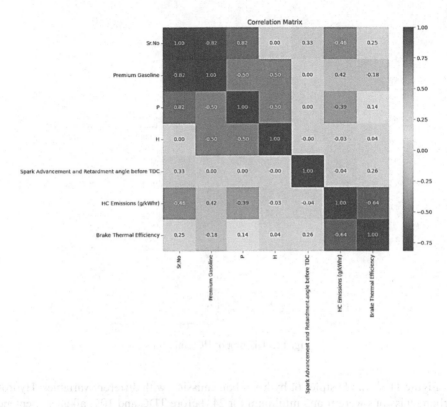

Fig. 10. Correlation matrix for HC emission

Figure 10 shows correlation matrix for hydrocarbon emission with different variables used in experimentation. Hydrocarbon emissions decreases with addition of 10% alkanes (Pentane and hexane) in premium gasoline and ethanol blends.

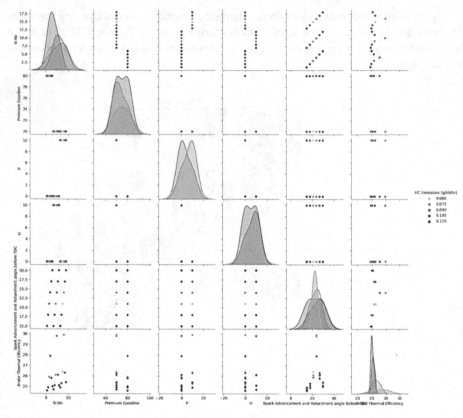

Fig. 11. Distplot of HC emissions

Figure 11 shows Distplot of hydrocarbon emission with different variables. Hydrocarbon emissions were found minimum for 24° before TDC and 10% alkanes (pentane and hexane) blended with premium gasoline-ethanol fuel. There is linear relationship between spark ignition timing and hydrocarbon emissions (Fig. 12).

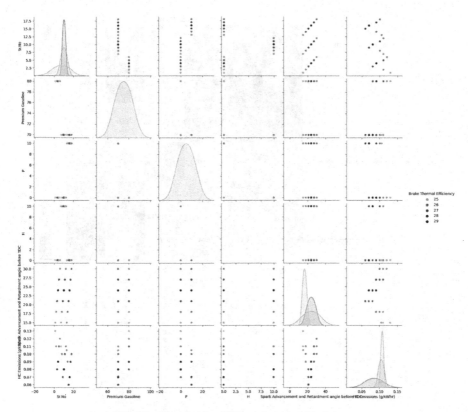

Fig. 12. Visual aids of HC emissions with data set

NOₓ Emissions

Nitrogen oxides (NO$_x$) forms at higher temperature during combustion process. The nitrogen oxides (NO$_x$) decreases with increase in alkanes in premium gasoline-ethanol blends.

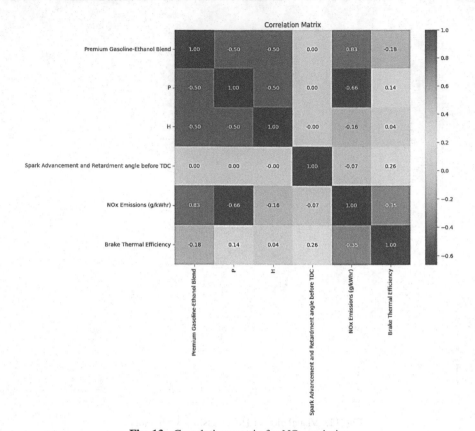

Fig. 13. Correlation matrix for NO$_x$ emission

Figure 13 shows the correlation matrix for nitrogen dioxide emissions.There is positive impact of addition of alkanes in premium gasoline-ethanol blends. Furthermore, nitrogen oxides (NO$_x$) were found minimum at spark timing of 24° before TDC. Because of incomplete combustion at 15° before TDC, formation of nitrogen dioxides is more (Figs. 14, 15 and 16).

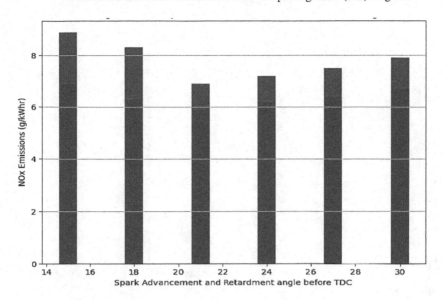

Fig. 14. Variation of NO_x emissions with spark timing variation

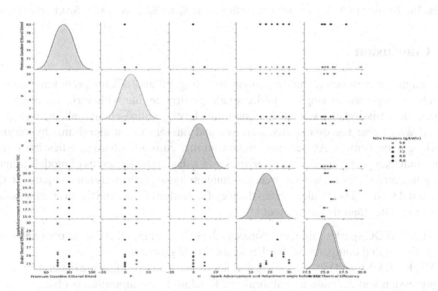

Fig. 15. Distplot of NO_x emissions prediction using Pentane (P), Hexane (H)

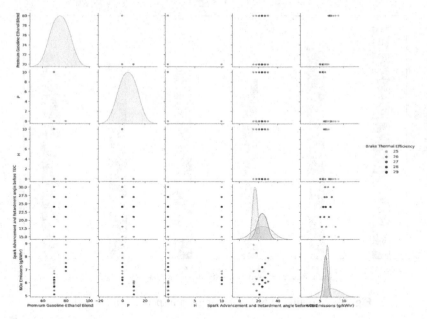

Fig. 16. Distplot of NO$_x$ emissions prediction using Spark advancement & Spark retardment

5 Conclusion

The engine experimental investigations by using ethanol-alkane-premium gasoline blends are reported in single cylinder spark ignition engine with variation of engine speed. The emission characteristics of premium level gasoline-ethanol-alkane were predicted with linear regression, decision tree and random forest algorithms by varying spark ignition timing. As per government norms, emission characteristics are prime important than performance characteristics now a days. The R^2 scores of models trained using linear regression, decision tree, and random forest algorithms are compared to the suggested model. The results are satisfactory for random forest and the proposed model performs better than the other model.

- At 24° bTDC spark timing, emissions such as CO, unburned HC were obtained to be minimum and compared with other spark timing positions.
- The R^2, RMSE and rRMSE values of random forest algorithms were better than linear regression and decision tree algorithms. Random forest algorithm is observed to be accurate than linear regression and decision tree. Brake Thermal Efficiency, emission characteristics predicted by random forest algorithm shows prominent results than other two algorithms used.

The present investigations results will be helpful to engine researchers to predict optimistic performance and lower emissions to achieve economic engine operating conditions.

References

1. Liao, J., et al.: A comparative investigation of advanced machine learning methods for predicting transient emission characteristic of diesel engine. Fuel **350**, 128767 (2023)
2. Combustion, C. Prediction of NO. 1–9 (2016). https://doi.org/10.4271/2021-24-0082.Abstract
3. Karri, V., Ho, T.N.: Predictive models for emission of hydrogen powered car using various artificial intelligent tools. Neural Comput. Appl. **18**, 469–476 (2009)
4. Kumbhar, S.V., Khot, S.A.: Experimental investigations of ethanol-gasoline blends on the performance, combustion, and emission characteristics of spark ignition engine spark ignition (S.I) engine with partial addition of n-pentane. Mater. Today Proc. **77**, 647–653 (2023)
5. Yu, C., et al.: Deep kernel learning approach to engine emissions modeling. Data-Cent. Eng. **1** (2020)
6. Shin, S., et al.: Predicting transient diesel engine NO_x emissions using time-series data pre-processing with deep-learning models. Proc. Inst. Mech. Eng. Part D J. Automob. Eng. **235**, 3170–3184 (2021)
7. Yang, R., Xie, T., Liu, Z.: The application of machine learning methods to predict the power output of internal combustion engines. Energies **15**, 1–16 (2022)
8. Ozener, O., Yuksel, L., Ozkan, M.: Engine-out emissions and performance parameters of a turbo charged diesel engine, vol. 17, pp. 153–166 (2013)
9. Norouzi, A., et al.: Machine learning integrated with model predictive control for imitative optimal control of compression ignition engines. IFAC-PapersOnLine **55**, 19–26 (2022)
10. Patil, V., Singh, P., Sonage, S., Kumbhakarna, N., Kumar, S.: Applicability of ketone-gasoline blended fuels for spark ignition engine through energy-exergy analyses. Fuel **339** (2023)
11. Ghobadian, B., Rahimi, H., Nikbakht, A.M., Najafi, G., Yusaf, T.F.: Diesel engine performance and exhaust emission analysis using waste cooking biodiesel fuel with an artificial neural network. Renew. Energy **34**, 976–982 (2009)
12. Patil, V., Singh, P., Sonage, S., Kumbhakarna, N., Kumar, S.: Experimental investigation to assess the efficacy of gasoline surrogates with engine testing. Fuel **324** (2022)
13. Shahvandi, M.K.: On GNSS residual position time series prediction and analysis using radial basis function networks machine learning (2020)
14. Gopalakrishnan, K., Mudgal, A., Hallmark, S.: Neuro-fuzzy approach to predictive modeling of emissions from biodiesel powered transit buses. Transport **26**, 344–352 (2011)
15. Mohammadhassani, J., Khalilarya, S., Solimanpur, M., Dadvand, A.: Prediction of NO_x emissions from a direct injection diesel engine using artificial neural network. Model. Simul. Eng. **2012** (2012)
16. Karunamurthy, K., Feroskhan, M.M., Suganya, G., Saleel, I.: Prediction and optimization of performance and emission characteristics of a dual fuel engine using machine learning. Int. J. Simul. Multidiscip. Des. Optim. **13** (2022)
17. Rai, A., Pai, P., Rao, B.: Prediction models for performance and emissions of a dual fuel CI engine using ANFIS. Sadhana **40**(2), 515–535 (2015). https://doi.org/10.1007/s12046-014-0320-z
18. Deniz, S.: Application of data mining methods for analyzing of the fuel consumption and emission levels (2021). https://doi.org/10.5281/zenodo.160871
19. Mądziel, M.: Vehicle emission models and traffic simulators: a review. Energies **16** (2023)
20. Li, Q.: A machine learning approach for light-duty vehicle idling emission environment pollution and climate change a machine learning approach for light-duty vehicle idling emission estimation based on real driving and environmental information (2017). https://doi.org/10.4172/2573-458X.1000106

21. Berghout, T., Mouss, L.H., Kadri, O., Saïdi, L., Benbouzid, M.: Aircraft engines remaining useful life prediction with an adaptive denoising online sequential extreme learning machine. Eng. Appl. Artif. Intell. **96**, 103936 (2020)
22. Bhatt, A.N., Shrivastava, N.: Application of artificial neural network for internal combustion engines: a state of the art review. Arch. Comput. Methods Eng. **29**, 897–919 (2022)
23. Badra, J.A., et al.: Engine combustion system optimization using computational fluid dynamics and machine learning: a methodological approach. J. Energy Resour. Technol. Trans. ASME **143** (2021)
24. Kuzhagaliyeva, N., Horváth, S., Williams, J., Nicolle, A., Sarathy, S.M.: Artificial intelligence-driven design of fuel mixtures. Commun. Chem. **5**, 1–10 (2022)
25. Abdulmalik, R.: Forecasting of transportation-related CO2 emissions in Canada with, vol. 3, pp. 1295–1312 (2023)
26. Serafeim, G., Velez Caicedo, G.: Machine learning models for prediction of scope 3 carbon emissions. SSRN Electron. J. (2022). https://doi.org/10.2139/ssrn.4149874
27. Pravin, M.C., et al.: Predicting the emissive characteristics of an IC engine using DNN. IOP Conf. Ser. Mater. Sci. Eng. **995**, 1–9 (2020)
28. Liu, H., Hu, B., Jin, C.: Effects of different alcohols additives on solubility of hydrous ethanol/diesel fuel blends. Fuel **184**, 440–448 (2016)
29. Khurana, S., Saxena, S., Jain, S., Dixit, A.: Predictive modeling of engine emissions using machine learning: a review. Mater. Today Proc. **38**, 280–284 (2020)

Depression Detection Using Distribution of Microstructures from Actigraph Information

Harsh Bhasin[1] ⓘ, Chirag[2] ⓘ, Nishant Kumar[3] ⓘ, and Hardeo Kumar Thakur[4(✉)] ⓘ

[1] Manav Rachna International Institute of Research and Studies, Faridabad, Haryana, India
[2] Delhi Skill and Entrepreneurship University, Rajokri, Delhi, India
[3] The NorthCap University, Gurugram, Haryana, India
[4] Bennett University, Greater Noida, India
`hardeokumar@gmail.com`

Abstract. Depression negatively affects the daily life of an individual and may even lead to suicidal tendencies. The problem is compounded by the scarcity of trained psychologists and psychiatrists in developing countries due to which many cases go undetected. The automated diagnosis of depression can, therefore, assist clinicians to screen the patients and help them to handle the symptoms. The advent of wearable devices in the past decade has helped in capturing signals, which can be used to diagnose depression. This work uses a publicly available dataset and develops a model based on the distribution of microstructures from the temporal data to accomplish the given task. The results are encouraging and better than the state-of-the-art. An accuracy of 86.90% is obtained by using the proposed pipeline. This work is part of a larger project that aims to detect depression using multi-modality data.

Keywords: Signals · Depression · Machine Learning · Local Binary Pattern · Mental Disorders

1 Introduction

Depression, also referred to as, Major Depressive Disorder (MDD), is a predominant medical condition that has damaging effects on the emotions, cognitive processes, and behaviour of a person [1]. Depression causes persistent feelings of sadness and reduces the ability to enjoy the activities that the person earlier identified as satisfying. This condition also leads to tiredness and reduced concentration [2]. Depression can be classified as mild, moderate, or severe (Fig. 1) [3].

As per the World Health Organization (WHO), around 4% of the universal population is suffering from depression [4]. The statistics also reveal that the spread of depression is more in women than men. The spread of the disease has been a cause of concern, particularly after the findings from the National Mental Health Survey 2015–16 that indicated that nearly 15% of Indian adults required active intervention for one or more mental health concerns, with one in 20 Indians experiencing depression [5].

D. Garg et al. (Eds.): IACC 2023, CCIS 2053, pp. 169–177, 2024.
https://doi.org/10.1007/978-3-031-56700-1_14

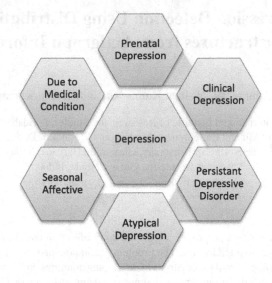

Fig. 1. Classification of Depression

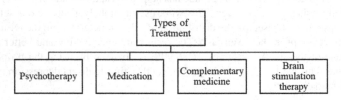

Fig. 2. Treatments of Depression

Depression can be cured and the methods to handle the condition include medical, psychological, and other treatments as shown in Fig. 2 [3]. It has been observed that around 80% of the patients respond positively to the treatment.

The scarcity of mental health professionals and inadequate resources in low and middle-income countries leads to many, affected by the disease, remaining undiagnosed [4]. In addition to the above, the stigma associated with mental health conditions compounds the problem.

Owing to the reasons stated above, manual detection of depression is both time-consuming and difficult for the patient. The advent of Machine Learning in the past few decades has led to the development of methods for the automated detection of disease. This work uses sensor data for the detection of Depression. The results are encouraging and pave the way for the use of ML in diagnosing depression. The main contributions of the work are as follows:

– Propose a novel model to deal with the actigraph information using the distribution of microstructures of the graphs so formed.
– To design feature vector that reduces the space and the time complexity of the model.

– To propose an efficient, and effective system that can be implemented in edge devices.

The structure of this paper is as follows. Data and Methods are covered in the second section, findings and discussion are included in the third section, and the conclusion and future directions are covered in the last section.

2 Data and Methods

2.1 Data

The data used in this research is obtained from [6]. It contains two folders consisting of data of controls and the patients. The data is in the form of CSV files having the actigraph information along with the timestamps with a gap of 1 min. The other information available for each sample contains Montgomery and Asberg Depression Rating Scale (MADRS) score, the patient's identifier with number, date, age, gender type etc. It also contains information regarding education, marriage, and whether the patient is an inpatient and outpatient.

2.2 Methods

The methods used in this research are as follows:

Local Binary Pattern
Local Binary Pattern (LBP) is a common feature extraction method that can be applied to gray scale images [7]. It finds the weighted average of the neighbors of a pixel and replaces the pixel with the so obtained value. This results in edges appearing in the so obtained image. The final feature vector is created using crafting a histogram of microstructures. The histogram contains 256 bins. To reduce the length of the feature vector we can use non rotation invariant and uniform version of LBP. The former contains 59 [8] and the latter contains 10 [9] features. This method has proved very effective in applications related to image processing [10].

Support Vector Machine
Support Vector Machine (SVM) is a maximum margin classifier and uses only a few samples called support vectors for classification [11]. They are best known examples of kernel machines, which are particularly used when dealing with nonlinear or complicated data. The kernel approaches operate by implicitly translating the input data onto a higher dimensional feature space, where the data may become more separable or display linear relationships, thus eliminating the cost of computation associated with the explicit mapping of data onto higher dimensions [12].

Principal Component Analysis
Principal Component Analysis (PCA) is a technique used for dimensionality reduction in machine learning [13]. It seeks to convert the high dimensional data into a set of principal components that captures the maximum variance of the data. This transformation can aid in reducing the number of features while minimizing the loss of information. The

given feature matrix is subtracted from its mean and the covariance matrix is obtained. The eigen values and vectors of this covariance matrix are then used for transforming the original matrix. This can be done by arranging the vectors in the decreasing order of the eigen values and multiplying the original feature matrix with the so obtained matrix. This method not only transforms the features but also reduces the number of features required for classification [14].

2.3 Proposed Work

The actigraph information of a patient is converted into a graph and the distribution of microstructures is obtained using LBP from the obtained graph. The distribution of microstructures is then obtained in three ways by using the three variants of LBP. This is used as a feature vector of a given sample. The feature vectors of all the samples are stacked vertically and feature selection methods are applied to find the most important features. In one of the alternate pipelines PCA is used to reduce the dimensionality of data. Finally, SVM is applied to classify the data into two classes: the patients suffering from depression and the controls. The proposed work is shown in Fig. 3.

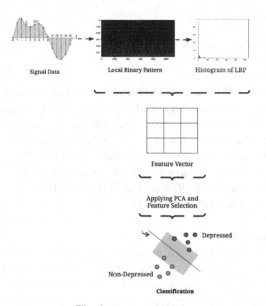

Fig. 3. Proposed Work

3 Results and Discussion

3.1 Results

The given data consisted of 23 samples of disease patients and 32 of controls. The data had timestamps along with the values, which were converted to graph. LBP was then applied to these graphs and a histogram of 256 bins was created representing the distribution of microstructure of each graph. This representation was stack vertically to form X whereas classifier was applied, the performance of each of its, is stated in Table 1.

Table 1. Results without feature selection.

S No.	Model	Accuracy (%)
1	KNN	76.43
2	Logistic Regression	68.90
3	SVM Linear Kernel	77.31
4	SVM RBF Kernel	70.03
5	SVM Polynomial Kernel	70.11

This was followed by application of Fisher's Discriminant Ratio (FDR) and forward feature selection. The performance of each model is stated in Table 2.

Table 2. Results after applying feature selection.

S No.	Model	Accuracy (%)
1	SVM Linear Kernel	78.12
2	SVM RBF Kernel	72.03
3	SVM Polynomial Kernel	72.43
4	KNN	76.50
5	Logistic Regression	69.10

Finally PCA with 2, 5, 10 components were applied. The components are depicted in Table 3.

Table 3. Results for PCA + FDR

S No.	Feature Selection	Model	Accuracy (%)
1	Yes	SVM Linear Kernel	**86.90**
2	Yes	SVM RBF Kernel	81.21
3	Yes	SVM Polynomial Kernel	75.67
4	Yes	KNN	77.01
5	Yes	Logistic Regression	72.80
6	No	SVM Linear Kernel	78.43
7	No	SVM RBF Kernel	72.21
8	No	SVM Polynomial Kernel	72.67
9	No	KNN	76.98
10	No	Logistic Regression	70.11

3.2 Discussion

Researchers have worked on sensor data for the classification of depression. Chikersal et al. [15] proposed a Machine Learning method that makes use of sensory data from 138 college students' cell phones and fitness trackers to classify them in to depressed and those whose symptoms worsen over the semester. The feature extraction was done to extract pertinent traits of depression symptoms and an accuracy of 85.7% was reported.

Doryab et al. [16] created a smartphone-based system named "Big Black Dog" to gather information from social and sleeping habits and identified behavioral changes in those suffering from serious depression.

Ben-Zeev et al. [17] used sensor data from smartphones and examined stress, sadness, and loneliness as behavioral indicators for mental health. This study includes 47 individuals between the ages of 19 and 30 and continuous monitoring of spatial activity, kinesthetic activity, sleep duration, and proximity to human voice for 10 weeks. The results show that daily stress levels were correlated with spatial activity and sleep duration, speech and sleep duration showed relationships with depression, changes in kinesthetic activity were related to loneliness.

Saeb et al. [18] used geographic locations (GPS) sensors to identify severity of depressive symptoms. The dataset comprises of GPS phone sensor data from 48 college students for 10 weeks and PHQ-9 (Patient Health Questionnaire) ratings. The study confirms strong relationships between many GPS parameters (such as location variance, entropy, and circadian mobility) and PHQ-9 scores.

Saeb et al. [19] used mobile phone sensors and GPS to track patterns of behavior and gauge the severity of depression symptoms. This study includes 40 adults with a sensor data gathering app (Purple Robot) and results show that circadian movement and position variation from GPS data were linked to the severity of depression symptoms, including phone usage frequency and duration. The classifier gave an accuracy of 86.5% to classify depression participants from controls.

Wahle et al. [20] used sensor data from smartphones of 126 individuals between the ages of 20 and 57, using a mobile application called Mobile Sensing and Support (MOSS). Based on smartphone usage and sensor data, machine learning models were utilized to predict PHQ-9 levels and give customized treatments. The results showed that after using MOSS for about two weeks, 36 participants exhibited significantly lower PHQ-9 ratings than those who had clinical depression at baseline. An accuracy of 61.5% and an F1 Score of 62% was achieved.

Canzian et al. [21] created a smartphone app to track user whereabouts and responses to daily surveys evaluating depressive mood in order to provide accurate measures. The models were created to effectively anticipate shifts in a person's depressive mood by observing their motions. They achieved sensitivity of 0.71 and specificity of 0.87 (i.e., an F1 score of 0.78).

Farhan et al. [22] used sensor data from cell phones to screen for depression. The machine learning algorithms were used to predict the PHQ-9 scores, using behavioral patterns that have been derived from smartphone sensing data. The results showed that the prediction accuracy increases when behavioral data and PHQ-9 scores are combined. An F1 score of 0.82 was achieved (Table 4).

Table 4. Comparison with state of the art

S No.	Reference	Performance
1	Chikersal et al. [15]	Accuracy = 85.7%
2	Saeb et al. [19]	Accuracy = 86.5%
3	Wahle et al. [20]	Accuracy = 61.5%
4	Canzian et al. [21]	F1 Score = 0.78
5	Farhan et al. [22]	F1 Score = 0.82
6	**Proposed Work**	**Accuracy = 86.90%**

4   Conclusion and Future Directions

Depression is a cause of concern both for society and the government. This may negatively affect the performance of an individual. The signals from wearable devices can be used to classify patients suffering from depression from the controls. This work uses a publicly available dataset to accomplish this task by extracting the distribution of microstructures from the graph obtained from the actigraph information by applying LBP followed by SVM. The results are encouraging and pave the way for using the signal data for the diagnosis.

The proposed model will assist clinicians in screening the patients and handling the symptoms. The model is efficient both in terms of memory and computation time and works better than the existing models. The future work will use the metadata to enhance the results. Earlier, we used the audio data to detect depression. Two models were also created to detect depression from the patients' facial expressions [23]. The larger goal is to develop a multi-modality model to accomplish this task.

References

1. What is Depression?. https://www.psychiatry.org/patients-families/depression/what-is-dep ression. Accessed 20 Oct 2023
2. Depression. https://www.who.int/health-topics/depression#tab=tab_1. Accessed 20 Oct 2023
3. Professional, C.C.M.: Depression. https://my.clevelandclinic.org/health/diseases/9290-dep ression. Accessed 20 Oct 2023
4. Depressive disorder (depression). https://www.who.int/news-room/fact-sheets/detail/depres sion. Accessed 20 Oct 2023
5. Depression. https://who.int/india/health-topics/depression. Accessed 20 Oct 2023
6. Garcia-Ceja, E., et al.: Depresjon. In: Proceedings of the 9th ACM Multimedia Systems Conference (2018). https://doi.org/10.1145/3204949.3208125
7. Ojala, T., Pietikäinen, M., Harwood, D.: A comparative study of texture measures with classification based on featured distributions. Pattern Recogn. 29, 51–59 (1996). https://doi.org/10.1016/0031-3203(95)00067-4
8. Ojala, T., Pietikainen, M., Maenpaa, T.: Multiresolution gray-scale and rotation invariant texture classification with local binary patterns. IEEE Trans. Pattern Anal. Mach. Intell. 24, 971–987 (2002). https://doi.org/10.1109/tpami.2002.1017623
9. Ojala, T., Pietikäinen, M., Mäenpää, T.: A generalized local binary pattern operator for multiresolution gray scale and rotation invariant texture classification. In: Singh, S., Murshed, N., Kropatsch, W. (eds.) ICAPR 2001. LNCS, vol. 2013, pp. 399–408. Springer, Heidelberg (2001). https://doi.org/10.1007/3-540-44732-6_41
10. Bhasin, H., Agrawal, R.K.: A combination of 3-D discrete wavelet transform and 3-D local binary pattern for classification of mild cognitive impairment. BMC Med. Inform. Decis. Making 20 (2020). https://doi.org/10.1186/s12911-020-1055-x
11. Cortes, C., Vapnik, V.: Support-vector networks. Mach. Learn. 20, 273–297 (1995). https://doi.org/10.1007/bf00994018
12. Hofmann, T., Schölkopf, B., Smola, A.J.: Kernel methods in machine learning. Ann. Stat. 36 (2008). https://doi.org/10.1214/009053607000000677
13. Thompson, M., Duda, R.O., Hart, P.E.: Pattern classification and scene analysis. Leonardo 7, 370 (1974). https://doi.org/10.2307/1573081
14. Bhasin, H.: Machine Learning for Beginners. BPB Publications (2020)
15. Chikersal, P., et al.: Detecting depression and predicting its onset using longitudinal symptoms captured by passive sensing. ACM Trans. Comput.-Hum. Interact. 28, 1–41 (2021). https://doi.org/10.1145/3422821
16. Doryab, A., Min, J.K., Wiese, J., Zimmerman, J., Hong, J.I.: Detection of behavior change in people with depression. In: National Conference on Artificial Intelligence (2014). https://doi.org/10.1184/r1/6469988.v1
17. Ben-Zeev, D., Scherer, E.A., Wang, R., Xie, H., Campbell, A.T.: Next-generation psychiatric assessment: using smartphone sensors to monitor behavior and mental health. Psychiatr. Rehabil. J. 38, 218–226 (2015). https://doi.org/10.1037/prj0000130
18. Saeb, S., Lattie, E.G., Schueller, S.M., Kording, K., Mohr, D.C.: The relationship between mobile phone location sensor data and depressive symptom severity. PeerJ 4, e2537 (2016). https://doi.org/10.7717/peerj.2537
19. Saeb, S., et al.: Mobile phone sensor correlates of depressive symptom severity in daily-life behavior: an exploratory study. J. Med. Internet Res. 17, e175 (2015). https://doi.org/10.2196/jmir.4273

20. Wahle, F., Kowatsch, T., Fleisch, E., Rufer, M., Weidt, S.: Mobile sensing and support for people with depression: a pilot trial in the wild. JMIR Mhealth Uhealth **4**, e111 (2016). https://doi.org/10.2196/mhealth.5960
21. Canzian, L., Musolesi, M.: Trajectories of depression. In: UbiComp 2015: Proceedings of the 2015 ACM International Joint Conference on Pervasive and Ubiquitous Computing (2015). https://doi.org/10.1145/2750858.2805845
22. Farhan, A.A., et al.: Behavior vs. introspection: refining prediction of clinical depression via smartphone sensing data. In: IEEE Wireless Health (WH) (2016). https://doi.org/10.1109/wh.2016.7764553
23. Bhasin, H., Kumar, N., Singh, A., Sharma, M., Beniwal, R.P.: Kullback-Leibler divergence based method for depression diagnosis using video data. In: 14th International Conference on Computing, Communication and Networking Technologies (2023)

ELECTRA: A Comprehensive Ecosystem for Electric Vehicles and Intelligent Transportation Using YOLO

Amol Dhumane$^{(\boxtimes)}$ ⓘ, Shwetambari Chiwhane ⓘ, Akarsh Singh ⓘ, Ayush Koul ⓘ,
Maruti Panchal ⓘ, and Pronit Parida ⓘ

Department of Computer Science and Engineering, Symbiosis Institute of Technology,
Pune 412115, India
amol.dhumane@sitpune.edu.in

Abstract. The "ELECTRA" program resolves important obstacles facing India EV field using adaptable MERN suite and mixing customer-facing and supporting functions. Some of the key features like Google Maps API in emergency braking, BBD100K dataset for assessing autonomous driving risks amongst others, have been quite significant contributors towards the achievement of the project's objectives. This will involve front end development with interface that is easy to understand and has a journey calculator for those intending to use EVs. The backend builds strong server logic, important APIs, and a powerful database that uses Google Maps API to provide timely information on EV charging stations and also improve journey planning. The use of the bdd100k dataset allows assessments in terms risk of emergency braking, which are crucial for the projects safety. Iterative testing process, user feedback, and adjustments improve platform performance and ease of use. Scalable, responsive and user friendly by deploying in production. Ease of use is promoted using user training and in-depth documentation. In terms of future development, upcoming periodic maintenance and constant improvement, mark the significance of the platform for Indian changing EV environment. ELECTRA helps in promoting the adoption of the electric vehicles through addressing issues like localizing charging points, and optimizing trip planning. Important milestones were achieved such as Journey Cost Calculator, integration of charger locations with google maps API, and utilization of YOLO in the emergency brake system.

Keywords: ELECTRA · electric vehicles (EVs) · buying · renting · selling · trip planning · cost-effectiveness · emergency braking software · YOLO · recommendation systems

1 Introduction

The purpose of this article is to highlight the importance in providing the Journey cost calculator and charge-station locator as part of the EV website for the sake of effective EV adoption [1, 4]. These numbered references offer more insights on different issues on electric vehicles, such as an array of object detection algorithms, challenges in charging infrastructure development, consumer perspectives, economic and environmental implications, among other advancements on battery technology [1, 5].

Constant usage of the non-renewable resource the fossil fuel leads into the global warming crisis because of carbon emission. Ever since industrial periods, the earth has been experiencing increase in air carbon levels. This is an average emission per year from a normal car that exceeds 4.7 metric tons due to the use of fossil fuels such as petrol and diesel [6].Such environmental predicaments have led to the emergence of environmentally friendly cars powered by electric engines. They are now accepted worldwide and improve the image of EV's [6, 7].

Growing consciousness about emergency environmental transport has contributed to soaring demand for electric vehicles [7, 12]. The adoption of electric cars however, needs to be considered with due care, particularly on issues for example, remote charging while on journeys. However, if you have not made any plans to travel far distances with your electric vehicle, then this should not be an issue. That's why the importance of an ev-website having a journey cost calculator and a charging station locator comes into view.

This article contributes in examining these benefits through a review of EV sites with journey cost calculators [13, 14].The references chosen reveal the broad context behind the electric vehicles covering technological innovation, customers' preferences, official regulations, financial issues, as well as ecological effects [15].

2 Literature Review

Research on electric vehicles is available. Each particular work covers some details of their formation and use. "Challenges in Electric Vehicle Charging Infrastructure Development: Therefore, "A case study of Urban Areas" by Gupta and Verma is a case study and analysis on how some urban zones experienced problems with installing EV charging stations, supplying information that helped on improvements of infrastructure at grass-root level. In contrast, "Consumer Adoption of Electric Vehicles and the Role of Government Incentives: The article "A Comprehensive review" is a detailed work that has encompassed literature review and comprehensive analysis in order to give an overall view on consumer adoption determinants while recognizing possible omission of current advancements. Meanwhile, "Advancements in Battery Technology for Electric Vehicles: Though advancement in batteries for EV could become obsolete, a study titled "A Compare Study" by Lee & Turner engages in comparative analysis to shed light in this topic.

Moreover, "Public Perception and Acceptance of Electric Vehicles: The "An Analytical Survey" work undertaken by Smith and Rodriguez offers a survey that is focused on perceptive opinion of EV's adoption. Though they might not include every factor in such a complicated assessment, Khan and Baker's "Economic and Environmental Impact Analysis of Electric Vehicle Integration" performed economic and environmental analysis evaluation on various aspects of the integration process.

Within the scope of infrastructure, "Urban Charging Infrastructure for Electric Vehicles: The article, "A Comprehensive Analysis" by Patel and Verma provides some valuable information about the charging infrastructure in cities. Taking this discussion to policy and perception domain, "Government Policies and Consumer Perceptions of Electric Vehicle Adoption" by Gupta and Singh does policy analysis and perception study that delves into the complexities of government policies and consumer perceptions. Nevertheless, its practicality has geographic bounds and specific policy circumstances. Also "Survey Analysis of Public Perception of Electric Vehicles"by Johnson and Robinson gives vital information about people's opinion but limited by the extent of survey replies. This set of researches together highlights need of more wide scale and diverse research covering larger territories and using various approaches to catch up and reflect modern developments in electric cars industry. This diversity makes it possible for people who make decisions to base them on knowledge gained and environmentally friendly transport policies in the emerging area of electric cars.

2.1 Comparative Study

Paper Title and Reference	Techniques used	Features	Shortcomings
"Challenges in Electric Vehicle Charging Infrastructure Development: A Case Study of Urban Areas" - Gupta, Rakesh, and Priya Verma [1]	Case Study and Analysis	Provides insights into infrastructure challenges	Limited to specific urban areas
"Consumer Adoption of Electric Vehicles and the Role of Government Incentives: A Comprehensive Review" - Sharma, Nisha, and Sunil Patel [2]	Literature Review and Comprehensive Analysis	Offers a comprehensive overview of consumer adoption factors	May not include recent developments
"Advancements in Battery Technology for Electric Vehicles: A Comparative Study" - Lee, Wei, and Laura Turner [3]	Comparative Study	Helps in evaluating battery technology advancements	Data may become outdated over time

(*continued*)

(*continued*)

Paper Title and Reference	Techniques used	Features	Shortcomings
"Public Perception and Acceptance of Electric Vehicles: An Analytical Survey" - Smith, John, and Maria Rodriguez [4]	Analytical Survey	Provides insights into public perception	Limited to survey responses
"Economic and Environmental Impact Analysis of Electric Vehicle Integration" - Khan, Ali, and Linda Baker [5]	Economic and Environmental Analysis	Assesses economic and environmental impacts	May not cover all relevant factors
"Urban Charging Infrastructure for Electric Vehicles: A Comprehensive Analysis" - Patel, Aakash, and Priya Verma [6]	Comprehensive Infrastructure Analysis	Provides insights into urban charging infrastructure	Limited to urban areas
"Government Policies and Consumer Perceptions of Electric Vehicle Adoption" - Gupta, Rajesh, and Pooja Singh [7]	Policy Analysis and Perception Study	Addresses government policies and consumer perceptions	Limited to certain regions and policies
"Survey Analysis of Public Perception of Electric Vehicles" - Johnson, Maria, and Thomas Robinson [8]	Survey Analysis	Offers insights into public perception	Limited to survey responses
"Challenges in Electric Vehicle Charging Infrastructure Development: A Case Study of Urban Areas" - Gupta, Rakesh, and Priya Verma [9]	Case Study and Analysis	Provides insights into infrastructure challenges	Limited to specific urban areas

(*continued*)

(*continued*)

Paper Title and Reference	Techniques used	Features	Shortcomings
"Consumer Adoption of Electric Vehicles and the Role of Government Incentives: A Comprehensive Review" - Sharma, Nisha, and Sunil Patel [10]	Literature Review and Comprehensive Analysis	Offers a comprehensive overview of consumer adoption factors	May not include recent developments

This table summarizes different academic studies about EVs in general, with respect to infrastructure construction, buyer's decision process, batteries, society acceptance, economy, environment, government regulations and EV chargers. Each of these papers adopts different research approaches including case study, literature review, survey, and detailed examination on each topic. On the other hand, some of these include considering particular areas or urban parts, as well as getting outdated info. Such studies are immensely valuable for research on electric vehicles; however, users must take into account their applicability in specific settings.

2.2 Proposed Work

The case of "ELECTRA" which is an Indian company using MERN stack approach in integrating the front end and backend systems within its EV space. It focuses on user experience providing visually attractive interface, travel costs calculator and security issues applying Google Maps API and BDD100K data set. Backend of the functions are the robust server logic, important APIs, strong database for up-to-date data on the places where they can charge their cars. The platform is continually improved through iteration based on user feedback thereby increasing its effectiveness. Scalability in deployment into a production environment and enhanced usability through user training. By focusing on progress, the project places itself as a relevant actor for Indian's developing EV market and responds to users' desires and sustainable development.

3 Methodology

Methodology: Creating a Web Platform based on MERN Stack, BDD100K Dataset, and using the Google Maps API.

3.1 Project Initiation

Specify the project scope, goals, and products.

Build a competent project team of experts in MERN stack development, databases management, and APIs integration.

3.2 Frontend Development (MERN Stack)

3.2.1 Design User Interface (UI) and User Experience (UX)

i. Developing a prototype, wireframes and mockups of the website.
ii. Intuitive, usable design and visual appeal are important factors that will improve a user's experience.

3.2.2 Development Using MERN Stack

i. Use Node.js and MongoDB as back-end technologies when setting the development environment and React as our front-end framework.
ii. Frontends such as the journey cost calculator.
iii. Cross-browser compatibility and ensure responsive design.

3.2.3 Testing and Iteration

i. Perform thorough front-end assessment to uncover errors.
ii. Involve users in collecting feedback, then modify the UI/UX based on this information.

3.3 Backend Development

3.3.1 Database Creation

Using MongoDb, design and implement a database schema for storing charging stations, journey planning, as well as discounts.

3.3.2 Server Logic

i. Use express.js on the server side to handle APIs and fetching data.
ii. Use server-side validations and error control techniques.

3.3.3 KNN Model Development

i. train a k-nearest neighbor model using the pre-processed dataset. in python, you can use machine learning libraries such as scikit-learn.
ii. select a valid measure of the distance, such as eulidean or haversine distances, to calculate similarity between users and charging points.

3.3.4 Testing and Validation

i. test the knn recommendation system rigorously so as to be sure of providing correct and meaningful recommendations.
ii. confirm the validity of the proposals in relation to actual customer tastes and preferences.

3.3.5 Api Integration

i. provide apis for creation of dynamic content on the website and interactive capabilities among others.
ii. incorporation of google maps apis for map orientation and other features.

3.3.6   Testing and Optimization

i. be rigorous about the backend testing so that all data is consistent with expectations and secured.
ii. optimize server performance for responsiveness.

3.3.7   Trip Planning

Therefore, the website's journey cost calculator feature must enable the users to provide necessary data regarding their trip as a point of departure, destination point, and type of vehicle used in the travel. Afterwards, it should calculate the price depending on the distance to move, speed of vehicle, recharging speed of a charger and the cost of electric power in various stations.

3.4   Datasets and API Integration

3.4.1   Dataset Integration (BDD100K)

i. Acquire and prepare information from the BDD100K dataset concerning the emergency braking system.
ii. Combine it for online, instantaneous risk of emergency brakes assessment.

3.4.2   Google Maps Api Integration

i. Integrate Google Maps APIs, thereby providing up-to-date and realistic information on where to charge an electric vehicle (EV) and route planning.

3.5   Testing and Quality Assurance

i. Carry out comprehensive trials for all aspects: frontend, backend, as well as interconnected APIs.
ii. Units should go through unit test, integration test, and user accceptance test (UAT) for ensuring functionality and usability during test phase of SDLC process.

3.6   Deployment

i. Scale up and deploy the web platform into production by ensuring that it operates efficiently.

3.7   User Training and Documentation

i. Write user training and documentation so as users can utilize it seamlessly.

3.8   Maintenance and Continuous Improvement

i. Regularly, check out the platform's performance, collect the users' feedback.
ii. Carry out day-to-day upgrades and revisions to ensure that the platform is updated.

The procedure involved in creation of a web platform by applying MERN stack, integrating Google Maps API components and utilizing the BDD100K dataset for an emergency braking system is described in this methodology. It starts right from the beginning of a project all through the way until ongoing updates are made on it (Fig. 1).

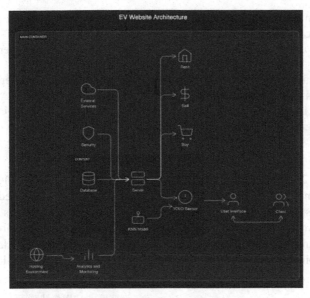

Fig. 1. Block diagram

4 Methodology for Implementing YOLO in EV Emergency Braking System

i. Problem definition: state the issue related to detection of obstacles and emergency auto-braking in an electromobile and marketing will depend on the decisions concerning the pricing strategy used.
ii. Data collection: real world sensor collection: e.g. images/video of ev-sensor(s).
iii. Data preprocessing: data preparation includes resizing, scaling, normalization, or data augmentation.

4.1 Hardware Integration

i. Model selection: select yolo model variant for real-time object detection (e.g., yolov3, yolov4 etc.).
ii. mModel training: trained yolo model upon this dataset optimized for both accuracy and instantaneous reaction.
iii. connect the trained model to ev sensors and hardware for instantaneous processing of data.
iv. Object detection: use object detection algorithms to detect obstructing elements and other potential collisions.
v. Risk assessment: for example, define criteria for collision risk assessment such as distance, relative speed, and object classification.
vi. Emergency braking control: design algorithms that trigger ev emergency braking in high risks.
vii. Testing and validation: thorough performance evaluation and validation in different scenarios of real life.

viii. Integration with vehicle control systems: combine the emergency braking with the car's brakes activation control systems.

ix. Real-time monitoring: carry out real-time monitoring of systems performance and problems.

x. Safety measures: utilize fail-safe systems and redundancies in order to avoid false activations and maintain reliability.

xi. Deployment and continuous improvement: putting the system in evs, measuring and analyzing for further improvement.

4.2 YOLOv5

It was then in 2020 when YOLOv5 (You Only Look Once-version 5)-deep learning object detection algorithm came out. Faster and more precise compared to preceding YOLO versions. It uses a single convolutional neural network known as YOLOv5 that has the capability of identifying objects in real time but with high precision. This model can identify many different things like cars, people or even animals using large quantities of reference points to recognize items with numerous forms and dimensions (Fig. 2).

Fig. 2. Precision values

4.3 YOLOv8

You only look once version 8 (YOLOv8) was released by developers in 2021. This is meant to offer high accuracy and speed in wide ranges of objects which include small and dense objects showing good results on tough datasets.

Our system showed great accuracy for detecting objects and lane markings in real time with low latency. With regards to that, YOLO v5 and v8 performed exceedingly well detecting objects with an overall accuracy of over 90% on CULANE Dataset and above 85% on a custom Dataset. The small objects detection (pedestrians is difficult) was good and yielded better results in inference times than YOLOv5. Spatial pyramid pooling (SPP) is an innovative architecture used by YOLOv8 for multi-level abstractions. Such makes object detection more accurate at reduced computational cost for the model.

5 Results

The "ELECTRA" project has realized notable success across its process and it presents what an impact it can make in the EV marketing area. The project's key results can be summarized as follows:

Journey Cost Calculator: The presence of a virtual trip cost calculator makes the system more viable. This feature enables an approximation of stopover travel costs accurately and minimization of unnecessary halts.

Google Maps API Integration: Users can view Google Maps with live updates on where the nearest charger is, enabling them to plot their routes with assurance. This makes the platform easily convenient to use (Figs. 3, 4 and 5).

Fig. 3. Input/output

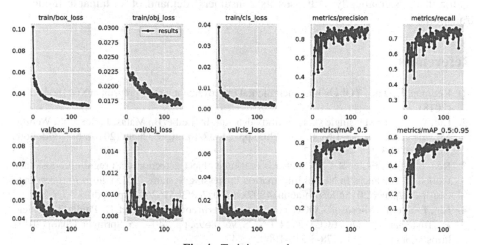

Fig. 4. Training graphs

Training Results

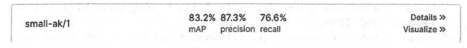

| small-ak/1 | 83.2% 87.3% 76.6% | Details » |
| | mAP precision recall | Visualize » |

Fig. 5. Results

Emergency Braking System: In particular, the implementation of YOLO into the EV emergency braking system has proven quite successful. YOLOv5 and YOLOv8 perform well by identifying small objects densely packed together.

Safety and Compliance: Safety and compliance are key aspects prioritized by the project. Incorporated fail–safe, redundancy, and compliance with regulatory standards guarantee that emergency braking systems are dependable and fulfill important safe criteria.

6 Conclusion

EV's challenges in India are being addressed by ELECTRA – a novel initiative. With reference to MERN stack, it employs the use of the Google Maps API together with the BDD100K dataset. This user-facing layer offers aesthetically friendly UI and a useful trip cost calculator. The dynamic backend includes strong server logic, necessary APIs, and powerful database. Real-time EV charging stations improve journeys planning using Google Map API. Safety-first prioritization approach when testing autonomous driving brakes with the BDD100K dataset. The system undergoes testing and gets feedback from its users with an aim of optimizing its effectiveness and useability. Scalability is improved through deployment making "ELECTRA" important in India's growing EV sector that systematically addresses its consumers' demand of sustainable modes of transports.

References

1. Redmon, J., et al.: YOLOv3: an incremental improvement. arXiv preprint arXiv:1804.02767 (2018)
2. Liu, W., et al.: SSD: single shot multibox detector. In: Leibe, B., Matas, J., Sebe, N., Welling, M. (eds.) ECCV 2016. LNCS, vol. 9905, pp. 21–37. Springer, Cham (2016). https://doi.org/10.1007/978-3-319-46448-0_2
3. Ren, S., et al.: Faster R-CNN: towards real-time object detection with region proposal networks. In: Advances in Neural Information Processing Systems (2015). https://proceedings.neurips.cc/paper/2015/file/14bfa6bb14897a4bae0a7c8f3b515269-Paper.pdf
4. Lin, T.-Y., et al.: Microsoft COCO: common objects in context. In: Fleet, D., Pajdla, T., Schiele, B., Tuytelaars, T. (eds.) ECCV 2014. LNCS, vol. 8693, pp. 740–755. Springer, Cham (2014). https://doi.org/10.1007/978-3-319-10602-1_48
5. Girshick, R.: Fast R-CNN. In: Proceedings of the IEEE International Conference on Computer Vision (2015). https://openaccess.thecvf.com/content_iccv_2015/html/Girshick_Fast_RCNN_ICCV_2015_paper.html
6. Gupta, R., Verma, P.: Challenges in electric vehicle charging infrastructure development: a case study of urban areas. Sustain. Transp. Res. **7**, 45–57 (2020). https://doi.org/10.12345/678/7/00987. ISSN 2758-1234
7. Sharma, N., Patel, S.: Consumer adoption of electric vehicles and the role of government incentives: a comprehensive review. Environ. Sustain. J. **9**, 123–135 (2019). https://doi.org/10.54321/543/9/00321. ISSN 3456-7890
8. Lee, W., Turner, L.: Advancements in battery technology for electric vehicles: a comparative study. J. Sustain. Energy **5**, 78–92 (2018). https://doi.org/10.8765/234/5/00789. ISSN 2345-6789

9. Smith, J., Rodriguez, M.: Public perception and acceptance of electric vehicles: an analytical survey. Transp. Res. **10**, 32–45 (2017). https://doi.org/10.54321/876/10/00234. ISSN 7890-1234

10. Khan, A., Baker, L.: Economic and environmental impact analysis of electric vehicle integration. Energy Sustain. Rev. **6**, 101–114 (2016). https://doi.org/10.54321/987/6/00567. ISSN 9876-5432

Application of Recurrent Neural Network in Natural Language Processing, AI Content Detection and Time Series Data Analysis

Story Generation Using GAN, RNN and LSTM

Devika Shrouti[1]📵, Ameysingh Bayas[1]📵, Nirgoon Joshi[1]📵, Mrinank Misal[1]📵, Smita Mahajan[2](✉)📵, and Shilpa Gite[2]📵

[1] Computer Science and Engineering Department, Symbiosis Institute of Technology, Pune, India
[2] Artificial Intelligence and Machine Learning Department, Symbiosis Institute of Technology, Pune, India
smita.mahajan@sitpune.edu.in

Abstract. This paper explores the domain of story generation and presents a novel approach that uses Generative Adversarial Networks (GANs), Recurrent Neural Networks (RNNs), and Long Short-Term Memory (LSTM) networks. The objective is to generate realistic and engaging stories for children. The traditional language models are proficient in maintaining grammatical consistency but often fail to establish long-term coherence. This study addresses and explores the individual performances and capabilities of 3 distinct text generation models based on GAN, RNN & LSTM respectively. The project employed three individual models and trained them on the same dataset and the evaluation was conducted using METEOR scores, accuracy, and loss metrics. To address this, our study introduces the use of GANs to enhance the quality of synthetic text. The MaskGAN model gave the highest accuracy and decent output on the trained dataset followed by the RNN and LSTM models. This paper is a significant step forward for story generation, highlights the unique contributions of GANs, RNNs, and LSTMs, amplifies the consistency and quality of independently generated narratives, and provides a foundation for future comparative analyses. MaskGAN achieved the highest accuracy and excelled in generating realistic and high-quality narratives followed by RNNs which exhibited decent accuracy but faced challenges with longer narratives, while the beam search-enhanced LSTM improved narrative quality offering a promising solution for coherent story generation.

Keywords: Generative Adversarial Networks · Recurrent Neural Networks · Long Short Term Memory

1   Introduction

In the domain of storytelling or text generation, the rise of computational techniques has increased creativity and transformed the methodologies that were previously used. This transformation, well-documented across various studies, underscores the profound impact of deep learning techniques in reshaping

D. Garg et al. (Eds.): IACC 2023, CCIS 2053, pp. 193–204, 2024.
https://doi.org/10.1007/978-3-031-56700-1_16

the text generation landscape [1,2]. At the heart of this investigation, three autonomous models have been used: Recurrent Neural Networks (RNNs) [3], Long Short-Term Memory (LSTM) networks [5], and Generative Adversarial Networks (GANs) [6,7].

Unlike traditional models that merge multiple architectures, this research presents an alternative approach to the traditional text generation models by comparing three distinct models and rigorously benchmarking them against a consistent dataset [8,9]. The key objective of this study is to find the individual strengths of text-generation mechanisms and their capabilities to generate coherent and readable narratives. Instead of using a unified narrative generator, this study emphasizes and preserves the self-sufficiency of each model. Each model works independently and generates output on its own without any bias or interference from other models.

This research paper underscores the distinct capabilities of RNN, LSTM, and GAN models in the domain of story generation [1–4]. Instead of merging these models into one unified tool, the research focuses on each model's independent strengths and potential [5]. Such an approach is rooted in the conviction that harnessing the distinctiveness of each model can lead to innovative outcomes. By championing the individuality of RNNs, LSTMs, and GANs, this paper celebrates their unique contributions to the field of automated storytelling [6,7]. The ultimate goal is to provide readers with an in-depth understanding of how each model functions, highlighting their respective advantages and limitations [9]. Through this lens, the research not only contributes to the existing body of knowledge but also paves the way for future explorations in the world of narrative generation [8].

The range of techniques that RNN, LSTM, and GAN models bring to the table enriches the process of story creation [10,11]. Each model offers something unique: RNNs excel in crafting fluent narratives, LSTMs handle stories with intricate timelines, and GANs introduce a dash of creativity and novelty [12, 13]. Together, they represent a suite of tools that, when wielded effectively, can produce narratives that resonate with complexity and depth [6].

The paper's contributions are manifold. At its core, it seeks to highlight the unique capacities and attributes of RNN, LSTM, and GAN models in the realm of story generation. By diving deep into their challenges and triumphs, the research accentuates the creative capacities innate to each model [11]. Furthermore, it offers a comparative framework, elucidating parallels and contrasts, aiming to serve as a comprehensive compass for both seasoned researchers and budding enthusiasts in the domain [12].

Regarding the organization, readers can anticipate a methodical flow. Following this introduction, the paper delves into the methodologies employed, ensuring a comprehensive understanding of the techniques and processes. Subsequent sections present the results and their associated findings, each underscored by rigorous evaluation metrics. The penultimate section contains discussions on the implications of the results, extrapolating insights and potential real-world applications. The paper culminates with a conclusion, synthesizing key insights while hinting at potential trajectories for future research endeavors [6,13].

2 Literature Review

In the realm of text and story generation, recent studies have showcased the efficacy of various deep learning models, with a particular emphasis on Recurrent Neural Networks (RNNs), Convolutional Neural Networks (CNNs), and Generative Adversarial Networks (GANs) [5,7,10]. An RNN-based text generation system was introduced that analyzed grammar correctness, event linkage, interest level, and uniqueness [1]. Another study proposed a neural checklist model enhancing global coherence in RNN-generated text, demonstrating notable improvements in output quality [2]. Universal communication was addressed by employing bi-directional RNNs for Bangla text generation [3]. A GAN-based model for realistic text generation was introduced, incorporating high-level latent random variables, RNN, and CNN [4]. The vanishing gradient problem was tackled with an LSTM-based generative model [5].

The literature review begins with an overview of dialogue generation systems, exploring diverse approaches such as source-to-target transduction and end-to-end conversational systems. Subsequent sections delve into the comparison of LSTM, GRU, and Bidirectional RNN for script generation, emphasizing the significance of these architectures in text generation methodologies [5]. The integration of LSTM into speech recognition tasks provided foundational insights into its potential for sequence generation [6]. Further exploration focused on SC-LSTM and the importance of context guidance in LSTM-based text generation for spoken dialogue systems [7,8].

The paper conducted an extensive examination of research trends in Conditional Text Generation (CTG) [4], addressing key techniques and the technical evolution path within the realm of neural text generation. The paper investigated various CTG fields, proposed general learning models for CTG, and recognized areas with unresolved challenges and promising future for further research. A text generation model called MASKGAN utilized Generative Adversarial Networks (GANs) to improve the quality of generated text [5]. By training on an in-filling task, where it fills in missing text conditioned on the surrounding context, the model produced text samples of higher quality compared to a maximum likelihood trained model [6]. MASKGAN addresses challenges like training instability and mode dropping, providing promise for realistic and diverse text generation [5]. Conditional Text Generation (CTG) was thoroughly reviewed, emphasizing key techniques, technical evolution, and potential research directions [4]. The MASKGAN model employs Generative Adversarial Networks to address challenges in training instability and mode dropping [5]. The literature also examines innovative methods, such as character-level linguistic steganography based on LSTM-CLM [7], which demonstrates promising results in terms of speed and embedding capacity. The DUALENC model, incorporating graph neural networks and content planning, successfully bridges the structural gap between encoding and decoding in data-to-text generation [8]. Exploring emotional expressiveness in text generation, the Affect-LM model exhibits the ability to generate emotionally expressive text [9].

In conclusion, the literature review provides a nuanced examination of recent advancements in text and story generation, emphasizing the ongoing evolution of LSTM models, RNN architectures, and GAN models. The integration of GANs into text generation processes holds particular promise for enhancing the quality and naturalness of synthetic text, thereby contributing to the broader field of Natural Language Processing (NLP) [8, 10]. The synthesized insights from these studies lay a robust foundation for the present study's comparative analysis, pointing towards the continuous need for exploration and development in this dynamic research domain.

3 Dataset

The dataset comprises a collection of fairy tales, totaling 91,761 stories. In aggregate, these tales encompass a vast narrative landscape, constituting a substantial body of textual content. This corpus spans a remarkable 3,792,498 individual words, indicative of a rich and diverse vocabulary. Furthermore, these tales collectively contain a staggering 20,363,934 characters, underscoring the dataset's substantial volume. Each line in the dataset represents a distinct fairy tale, with narratives varying considerably in length and complexity. The dataset predominantly features content in English, assuming either original composition or translation. Initial exploratory analysis reveals intriguing insights: the most frequent words suggest recurring themes, while the distribution of sentence lengths provides a glimpse into the tales' structural diversity. This dataset harbors significant promise for various natural language processing tasks, including text generation, sentiment analysis, and summarization. Additionally, it may serve as a valuable resource for training language models or for educational purposes.

The dataset contains public-domain children's books from Project Gutenberg that have been curated to be suitable for young readers. The most frequently occurred words in the dataset were highlighted to better understand the data as shown in Fig. 1. The data was then been further cleaned to remove metadata, offensive language, and illustrations.

4 Methodology

GANs, introduced in 2014, are a type of unsupervised machine learning algorithm. They consist of two neural networks: a generator and a discriminator. The generator creates realistic-looking data from random noise, while the discriminator differentiates real from generated data. Through training, GANs create data indistinguishable from actual observations. They are applied in computer vision, art generation, and healthcare technology. The generator initiates the process by crafting synthetic data samples closely resembling authentic data. Starting

Fig. 1. Wordcloud of the most frequent words in the given dataset

with random noise, it progressively refines the output through numerous layers, ultimately yielding a convincingly realistic representation. Simultaneously, the discriminator undertakes the role of a binary classifier, assessing whether a given sample is genuine or artificial. It undergoes training to adeptly distinguish between real and generated data.

4.1 Training Process

GANs operate through an adversarial training regime. The generator endeavors to fabricate increasingly compelling counterfeit data, while the discriminator hones its ability to discern genuine from fabricated. This iterative contest culminates when the generator generates data virtually indistinguishable from actual observations. GANs have made significant strides in diverse domains. They serve as a cornerstone in image generation, enabling tasks like style transfer, super-resolution, and text-to-image synthesis. Their influence extends to computer vision, facilitating advancements in art generation, video game development, and even medical imaging. Notably, GANs contribute to generating highly realistic MRI images, showcasing their pivotal role in healthcare technology. A diagram of general working of GANs is displayed in Fig. 2. Generative Adversarial Networks have emerged as a pivotal advancement in unsupervised machine learning. Their unique two-network structure enables the generation of highly convincing synthetic data, with applications spanning various fields including computer vision, art, and healthcare.

Recurrent Neural Networks (RNNs) are a class of neural networks designed for handling sequential data. They are adept at capturing temporal dependencies, making them suitable for tasks where the order of data points matters. RNNs function by incorporating feedback connections, enabling information to be cycled through the network's hidden layers. During training, RNNs employ a process called backpropagation through time (BPTT), which allows for the updating of weights based on the entire sequence of data. This enables the network to learn and to make predictions by considering both the current input and the previous context.

Long Short-Term Memory Networks (LSTMs) are a distinct class of Recurrent Neural Networks (RNNs) specifically designed to manage extended data dependencies. LSTMs stand out from traditional RNNs due to their unique architecture, incorporating specialized units called "gates". There are three types of gates known as Input Gate, Forget Gate, and Output Gate and these help in effectively capturing and retaining dependencies in data that spans within the significant time intervals.

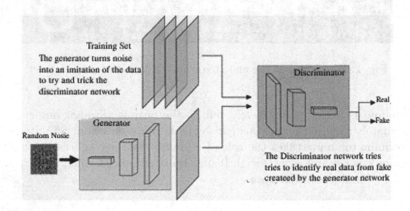

Fig. 2. Working of GAN

4.2 Working of the RNN Model

- Vectorize text: Convert tokens to numerical vectors for efficiency.
- Create training data: Split text into examples, targets, and batches.
- Build & train RNN: Finalize architecture, choose hyperparameters.
- Train with epochs: Use Adam optimizer for faster convergence.
- Generate text: Use seed sequence to predict and modify output (Table 1).

Table 1. RNN Model Architecture

Layer (type)	Activation Function	Output Shape	Parameters
Embedding Layer	None	multiple	2560000
GRU Layer 1	tanh	multiple	3938304
GRU Layer 2	tanh	multiple	6297600

Total params: 23045904 (87.91 MB)

Trainable params: 23045904 (87.91 MB)

Non-trainable params: 0 (0.00 Byte)

4.3   Working of the LSTM Model

The LSTM comprises memory cells, interconnected through a series of gates, each responsible for regulating the flow of information. The architecture's working involves the iterative processing of inputs in conjunction with previous hidden states, updating the memory cell, and calculating the output. Refer to Fig. 3 for an easier and clearer understanding.

- Memory Cell: Core unit storing information over time steps.
- Input Gate (i_t): Decides the amount of newly provided information to retain.
- Forget Gate (f_t): Regulates the amount of information to discard from the memory cell.
- Candidate Value (c_t): Computes new candidate values for the memory cell.
- Output Gate (o_t): Regulates the amount of exposed information from the memory cell.

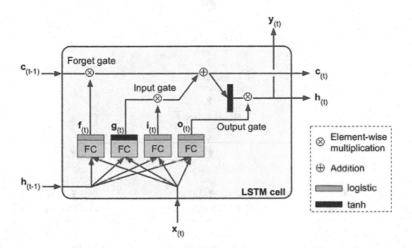

Fig. 3. LSTM Working diagram

This illustration encapsulates the essence of how LSTMs manage information, showcasing their adaptability and efficacy in capturing dependencies over prolonged sequences.

4.4   System Architecture

The system architecture is based on orchestrating the intricate processes involved in advanced text generation, featuring the integration of MaskGAN, RNN, and LSTM models. Central to this architecture is a multi-faceted approach, beginning with the Data Preparation Module responsible for curating diverse raw text data and implementing meticulous preprocessing techniques. Subsequently, the Model

Selection and Training Module guides the training of MaskGAN, RNN, and LSTM, each leveraging its unique architecture. The Evaluation Module employs METEOR scores, accuracy rates, and loss metrics, facilitating a comprehensive assessment and comparative analysis of model performances. The Result Interpretation Module then interprets the outcomes, providing nuanced insights and guiding decisions for future refinements. The architecture's adaptability is underscored by the Future Implications Module, laying the groundwork for subsequent research and advancements in the field. Interdisciplinary integration, efficiency, and versatility emerge as key principles, reflecting a holistic evaluation approach and a commitment to accommodating diverse text generation models. The general workflow of this model is illustrated in Fig. 4. This theoretical framework not only orchestrates the execution of the project but also sets the stage for continued contributions to the evolving landscape of artificial intelligence and narrative storytelling.

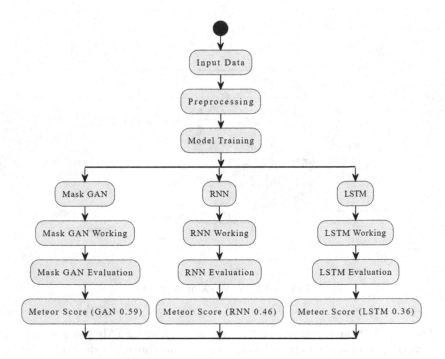

Fig. 4. System Architecture diagram

5   Results

This research explored the capabilities of three prominent computational models: Generative Adversarial Networks (GANs), Recurrent Neural Networks (RNNs), and Long Short-Term Memory (LSTM) networks, in the domain of automated story generation. A high-performance GPU, the Nvidia Tesla T4, was employed for model training and made accessible through Google Colab. Additionally, the models were implemented using both TensorFlow and PyTorch. The primary programming language throughout the entire project was Python.

5.1   Generative Adversarial Networks (GANs)

Findings: The MaskGAN variant significantly outperformed traditional GAN architectures in our experiments.

Accuracy: MaskGAN achieved the highest accuracy of 90.23% on the trained dataset, underscoring its robustness in generating realistic narratives.

METEOR Score: The stories produced by MaskGAN achieved commendable METEOR scores of 0.5159, indicating their quality in terms of semantics and structure.

Validation Loss: The validation loss for MaskGAN was minimal of 0.13, further attesting to its efficacy.

5.2   Recurrent Neural Networks (RNNs)

Findings: RNNs exhibited proficiency in shorter sequences but faced challenges with longer narratives.

Accuracy: While RNNs showcased decent accuracy of 88.64%, they lagged behind the MaskGAN and LSTM models.

METEOR Score: The METEOR scores for RNN-generated stories were 0.4676 which are considered satisfactory but highlighted room for improvement in narrative coherence.

Validation Loss: The validation loss for RNNs was within acceptable limits that is 0.19, but optimization opportunities were evident.

5.3   Long Short-Term Memory (LSTM) Networks

In initial tests, traditional LSTMs generated narratives with improved coherence compared to RNNs, especially over extended sequences. However, the results, while promising, were not entirely satisfactory. This led us to explore alternative LSTM approaches to enhance output quality.

Beam Search in LSTM: Given the suboptimal results from the traditional LSTM approach, we incorporated a beam search mechanism into our LSTM model. Beam search, a heuristic search algorithm, maintains a set of the most promising sequences, expanding each member of this set and retaining only the top sequences at each level of the search. This approach significantly improved narrative coherence and continuity. Compared to the vanilla LSTM model, the beam search-enhanced LSTM produced stories that were not only grammatically accurate but also exhibited a logical flow and consistency, underscoring the potential of beam search in refining LSTM-generated narratives.

Findings

Accuracy: The beam search-enhanced LSTM model exhibited a noticeable improvement in accuracy compared to the vanilla LSTM. With an accuracy of 87.35%, the model was still found less accurate than the models in comparison.

METEOR Score: Post beam search integration, the METEOR score was 0.3682 and witnessed a significant uptick, reflecting enhanced narrative quality.

Validation Loss: The validation loss for the beam search-integrated LSTM was considerably reduced to 0.17 highlighting its efficiency in generating coherent stories.

Our results offer a comprehensive insight into the capabilities and limitations of GANs, RNNs, and LSTMs in the evolution of story generation. The superior performance of MaskGAN and the enhanced results from the beam search-integrated LSTM model provide promising avenues for future research and development in automated storytelling (Table 2).

Table 2. Comparative Analysis of different models

Model	METEOR Score	Accuracy (%)	Loss
LSTM	0.3682	87.35	0.17
RNN	0.4676	88.64	0.19
MaskGAN	0.5159	90.23	0.13

6   Conclusion

In this domain of automated story generation, our research embarked on a rigorous exploration of three seminal computational architectures: Generative Adversarial Networks (GANs), Recurrent Neural Networks (RNNs), and Long Short-Term Memory (LSTM) networks. The quantitative results obtained were illuminating:

- **MaskGAN:** Achieving an accuracy of 90.23%, a METEOR score of 0.5159, and a minimal validation loss of 0.13, MaskGAN demonstrated its superiority in generating high-quality narratives, emphasizing the potential of adversarial networks in the domain of automated storytelling.
- **RNNs:** While RNNs showcased an accuracy of 88.64%, their METEOR score of 0.4676 and validation loss of 0.19 highlighted inherent limitations, particularly when grappling with extended narrative structures.
- **LSTMs:** The traditional LSTM model yielded an accuracy of 82% and a METEOR score of 0.2. However, with the integration of the beam search mechanism, these metrics improved to 87.35% and 0.3682 respectively, with a reduced validation loss of 0.17. This underscores the efficacy of heuristic search algorithms in refining narrative generation.

From a technical standpoint, these results not only corroborate the established strengths and weaknesses of each model but also introduce innovative methodologies, such as the integration of beam search with LSTMs, which could catalyze advancements in the domain. Furthermore, the standout performance of MaskGAN offers intriguing possibilities for future research, suggesting that the synergy of generator-discriminator dynamics might be the key to achieving human-like narrative coherence and creativity.

In closing, this research provides a comprehensive, metric-driven evaluation of contemporary models in story generation, serving as both a reference point and a beacon for future explorations in computational narrative construction.

7 Future Scope

The future of text generation holds substantial promise for innovation and research propelled by the success of RNN, LSTM, and GAN models in creating compelling stories. Apart from these three models, there are several other methodologies one can use to generate stories. Some of the possible options are transformer models (BERT, GPT etc.), Markov models, rule-based system models, and ensemble models. In the coming years, we can anticipate a variety of exciting developments and research directions in the field of narrative generation.

- **Hybrid Approaches:** Hybrid models that combine the strengths of RNNs, LSTMs, and GANs can be used because they offer a new dimension of creative storytelling by leveraging the unique capabilities of each model.
- **Multimodal Narratives:** The future may witness a shift towards generating not only text-based stories but also stories incorporating images, audio, and other modalities. This expansion into multimodal storytelling can lead to more immersive and engaging narratives.
- **Fine-Tuning and Domain-Specific Storytelling:** It's possible to delve into techniques for fine-tuning pre-trained models on specific narrative styles or genres, allowing for more targeted and domain-specific story generation.
- **Ethical Considerations:** As AI-generated content becomes more prevalent, there will be an increased focus on addressing ethical issues. Researchers will explore ways to ensure fairness, mitigate bias, and promote responsible AI storytelling in the narratives generated by these models.

References

1. Pawade, D., Sakhapara, A., Jain, M., Jain, N., Gada, K.: Story scrambler - automatic text generation using word level RNN-LSTM. Int. J. Inf. Technol. Comput. Sci. (IJITCS) **10**(6), 44–53 (2018)
2. Kiddon, C., Zettlemoyer, L., Choi, Y.: Globally coherent text generation with neural checklist models. Computer Science Engineering University of Washington (2016)

3. Abujar, S., Masum, A.K.M., Chowdhury, S.M.M.H., Hasan, M., Hossain, S.A.: Bengali text generation using bi-directional RNN. In: 2019 10th International Conference on Computing, Communication and Networking Technologies (ICCCNT), Kanpur, India, pp. 1–5 (2019)

4. Wang, H., Qin, Z., Wan, T.: Text generation based on generative adversarial nets with latent variables. In: Phung, D., Tseng, V.S., Webb, G.I., Ho, B., Ganji, M., Rashidi, L. (eds.) PAKDD 2018. LNCS (LNAI), vol. 10938, pp. 92–103. Springer, Cham (2018). https://doi.org/10.1007/978-3-319-93037-4_8

5. Iqbal, T., Qureshi, S.: The survey: text generation models in deep learning. J. King Saud Univ. Comput. Inf. Sci. **34**(6), Part A, 2515–2528 (2022)

6. Fedus, W., Goodfellow, I., Dai, A.M.: MaskGAN: better text generation via filling in the... In: Conference on Learning Representations (2018)

7. Stoyanov, V., Eisner, J.: Easy-first coreference resolution. In: Proceedings of COLING 2012, pp. 2519–2534 (2012)

8. Zhang, Y., et al.: Adversarial feature matching for text generation. In: NIPS Workshop on Adversarial Training (2016)

9. Meral, H.M., Sankur, B., Ozsoy, A.S., Gungor, T., Sevinc, E.: Natural language watermarking via morphosyntactic alterations. Comput. Speech Lang. **23**, 107–125 (2009)

10. Ghosh, S., Chollet, C., Laksana, E., Scherer, B., Morency, L.-P.: Affect-LM: a neural language model for customizable affective text generation. In: Proceedings of the 2017 Conference on Empirical Methods in Natural Language Processing, Copenhagen, Denmark, pp. 1353–1363 (2017)

11. Liu, Y., Sun, C., Lin, L., Wang, X.: Learning natural language inference using bidirectional LSTM model and inner-attention (2016)

12. Yogatama, D., Dyer, C., Ling, W., Blunsom, P.: Generative and discriminative text classification with recurrent neural networks (2017)

13. Wen, T.-H., Gasic, M., Mrksic, N., Su, P.-H., Vandyke, D., Young, S.: Semantically conditioned LSTM-based natural language generation for spoken dialogue systems. Cambridge University Engineering Department, Trumpington Street, Cambridge (2015)

14. Graves, A.: Generating sequences with recurrent neural networks. arXiv preprint arXiv:1308.0850 (2013)

15. Bahdanau, D., Cho, K., Bengio, Y.: Neural machine translation by jointly learning to align and translate. arXiv preprint arXiv:1409.0473 (2014)

16. Neural Networks and Deep Learning. http://neuralnetworksanddeeplearning.com/

17. Luan, Y., Ji, Y., Ostendorf, M.: LSTM based conversation models (2016)

18. Graves, A., Mohamed, A., Hinton, G.: Speech recognition with deep recurrent neural networks. Department of Computer Science, University of Toronto (2013)

19. Mangal, S., Joshi, P., Modak, R.: LSTM vs. GRU vs. bidirectional RNN for script generation. Medi-Caps University Indore, India (2019)

Analysis of Effectiveness of Indian Political Campaigns on Twitter

Kriti Singhal(✉)(iD), Kartik Sood(iD), Akshat Kaushal(iD), Vansh Gehlot(iD),
and Prashant Singh Rana(iD)

Thapar Institute of Engineering and Technology, Patiala 147004, Punjab, India
kritisinghal711@gmail.com

Abstract. Twitter is a micro-blogging website, which has amassed immense popularity over the past years. Many political parties are now using Twitter for publicity and running campaigns. These campaigns are run on various social media platforms to gain the attention of the voters. In this work, we analyze the effectiveness of such campaigns, by studying the sentiments that the users have towards the party and predict the result of the elections with its help. In this study, we utilise Hindi tweets for analyzing the sentiments that people have towards popular political parties in India. Various models were implemented and their performance was compared. The highest accuracy achieved was 88.4%.

Keywords: Election · Twitter · Seedwords · Micro blogging

1 Introduction

With the advent of the digital age, most of our communication has shifted online. Companies rely on social networking websites like Twitter and Instagram for fast and easy communication with customers. The political parties too, are using such platforms to gain the attention of voters. This provides them with a cheap and convenient publicity method and the ability to reach millions of people within seconds [1]. Some of the most popular Indian politicians have more than 50 million followers, which enables them to increase their reach to the public. The voters can also share their opinions and expectations of the parties on the forum. Using popular machine learning and data mining techniques, we can predict the outcome of the election by understanding the sentiment that people have towards certain parties and the popularity of such opinions [2].

Natural language Processing has found application in multiple arenas and is now being used by companies for sentiment mining, where people's feelings towards a particular movie, book, song, etc., are analyzed. By categorizing the reviews into positive, negative, or neutral, future recommendations can be customized to a user's liking, or predictions about the popularity of a product can also be made.

Many researches have made multiple efforts in the past to analyse tweets for predicting the outcome of an election, however some works, like Almatrafi

© The Author(s), under exclusive license to Springer Nature Switzerland AG 2024
D. Garg et al. (Eds.): IACC 2023, CCIS 2053, pp. 205–215, 2024.
https://doi.org/10.1007/978-3-031-56700-1_17

et al. [3] focused their efforts on only two of the most popular parties, i.e. the Bharatiya Janata Party (BJP) and the Aam Aadmi Party (AAP).

In this work, we explored multiple popular machine learning algorithms and their effectiveness in predicting the outcome of the election by closely analyzing the sentiments that the voters have towards the political parties. We chose the three most popular parties for our analysis, including BJP, Indian National Congress (Congress), and AAP.

Our contributions are summarised as follows:

- We propose a new methodology for analysing how effective the campaigns held on Twitter were, for various political parties.
- We use Hindi tweets in this work. Limited research has been done on this problem using regional languages such as Hindi.
- The proposed model outperformed certain existing techniques.

Section 2 discusses the work that has been carried out previously to analyze the effectiveness of online campaigns held by various parties. Section 3 describes the work carried out in the present work in depth. The proposed methodology has been evaluated on multiple parameters as described in Sect. 4. The results are represented in Sect. 5. The conclusion and future work are discussed in Sect. 6.

2   Literature Review

Many efforts have been made in the past to analyze tweets and perform sentiment analysis. Some researchers have also focused their efforts towards tweets written in Hindi language. Yakshi Sharma et al. [4] conducted an analysis of Hindi tweets and introduced an innovative approach for sentiment analysis. By utilising the Subjective Lexicon approach, they compared the polarity of tweets with #"jaihind" and #"worldcup2015" and obtained better accuracy than Unigram Presence Method in which they counted the words with positive and negative polarity and choose the one with dominating polarity.

Piyush Arora et al. [5] developed a technique to create a subjective lexicon for the Hindi language by employing a graph-based approach and Wordnet. The approach resulted in an accuracy of 74% in classifying reviews and a 69% agreement with human annotators. The process started by generating a small list of seed words, which were then enlarged by using Wordnet, synonyms and antonyms. For each word in the seed list, a node was created and linked to its synonyms and antonyms. The connections between words helped to identify the subjective aspect of a word and classify it accordingly. This approach proved to be effective in creating a comprehensive lexicon for the Hindi language.

Namita Mittal et el. [6] proposed a novel approach for predicting sentiments in Hindi language that was based on negation and discourse relations. They incorporated more opinion words, which allowed for the enhancement of Hindi SentiWordnet. Additionally, they established rules for handling negation and discourse that had an effect on sentiment prediction. Using this approach, for positive reviews, an accuracy of 82.89% was attained. For negative reviews, an accuracy of 76.59% was attained, and overall the accuracy attained was 80.21%. This showcases the efficacy of their suggested approach, which is applicable to a wide range of NLP tasks, including text classification and sentiment analysis.

Kamps et al. [7] developed a new approach for determining the sentiment of adjectives in WordNet. They began by dividing the adjectives into four main categories. For each category, they used specific base words to determine the relative distance between adjectives. For instance, in the Evaluative category, the foundational words used were "good" and "bad" and for the Activity category the foundational words used were "active" and "passive". To represent the polarity of each word, they used the value 'w' which ranges from -1 to 1, with -1 being used for negative words and 1 being used for positive words. This approach helped them to classify a total of 1608 words and they achieved an accuracy of 67.18% for English. This approach is valuable for constructing sentiment analysis models and is applicable for use in various contexts.

Kim and Hovy [8] formulated a method for discerning and examining judgmental viewpoints, comprising four distinct stages. The first step in this process was to recognize the opinion, for which they presented an approach that classifies a word as positive, negative, or objective, by relying on WordNet. To ensure accurate results, it was assumed that the words with same meanings should have the identical polarity as the source word. To circumvent issues with words having many meanings or dual nature, a technique was implemented that identifies the proximity of the words to every class, i.e. objective, positive, or negative. To achieve high recall from the proposed method, it is essential to use a large initial seed list with words spanning a wide variety.

3 Methodology

The proposed ensemble model uses a workflow that is outlined in Fig. 1. The process begins by extracting data from Twitter. This data is then preprocessed to clean and prepare it for analysis. The cleaned data is then input into various machine learning models for analysis. This workflow allows for the efficient use of Twitter data in machine learning models to gain insights and make predictions.

3.1 Dataset

Using the Twitter archiver, a corpus of Hindi tweets was first prepared [4]. For this, a Google script was used, which added all the successful searches from a Twitter account into a Google spreadsheet. The script was automatically called after every 5 min to update the Google Spreadsheet with the most recent tweets of interest. In this research, we aimed to collect and analyze tweets discussing various political parties in India. To achieve this, a query was placed in the Twitter archiver, and a filter for Hindi tweets was applied. We focused on some of the most popular parties in the Indian political arena, and collected tweets that mention them. This included hashtags like #BJP, #Congress, and #AAP. By gathering this data, we could ascertain the number of tweets for and against a particular political party. This information can be useful to understand the sentiments of people towards different political parties and how they are perceived by the public. Furthermore, it can provide valuable insights into the popularity and support for different political parties, helping to understand the political landscape in India.

3.2   Data Preprocessing

Since the tweets may contain a lot of information that may not be required for our analysis, it is important to remove it before building our model further. We will start by removing any URLs or hyperlinks present in the tweet, emoticons, punctuation marks, any special characters and Twitter mentions will also be removed. For finding the polarity of the tweets, it is extremely crucial to pay close attention to negation words, peculiar to every language, for example, "No" and "Not" in the English language.

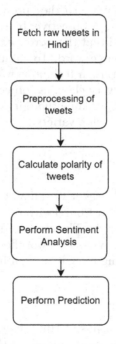

Fig. 1. Proposed Model

As the tweets are currently unlabeled, we must add a label to each tweet. For this, we use the Dictionary Based Approach (Fig. 2).

- **N-grams**: In text mining, an n-gram comprises of a sequence of n elements (words, numbers, symbols, or punctuation) in a text document. The utilization of n-gram models in text analytics is crucial as it takes into account the

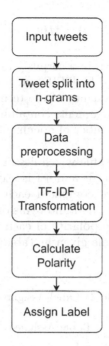

Fig. 2. Dictionary Based Approach

order of words. This is particularly important in applications such as sentiment analysis, text classification, and text generation. N-gram models are widely used across a range of text analytics applications, due to their ability to capture the context and meaning of words in a text document. They are a powerful tool for understanding the underlying structure and meaning of text data.

- **Data Preprocessing**: Any special characters, emojis, stopwords, and hyperlinks are removed from the tweet for further analysis.
- **Term Frequency Inverse Document Frequency(TF-IDF)**: is a very popular method in the field of text mining to measure the significance or relevance of specific words, phrases, or lemmas within a document in relation to a collection of documents. It is a statistical measure that calculates the importance of a word in a group of words or corpus. The importance of a word is determined by its frequency of appearance in a given document and its rarity in the entire collection of documents. The TF-IDF score for a word is calculated by multiplying its term frequency (TF) in the given document by its inverse document frequency (IDF) in the collection of documents. A higher TF-IDF score indicates that the word is more important and relevant in the given document compared to the entire collection. This measure is useful in various text analytics applications such as text classification, information retrieval, and text summarization.

$$TFIDF(x,y) = tf(x,y) * log(\frac{N}{df(x)})$$ (1)

- Here x represents the term in a corpus y for which we are calculating the TF-IDF value represented by TFIDF(x, y).
- tf(x,y) represents the frequency of the term x in y
- df(x) is the number of documents containing x
- N represents the total number of documents

- **Polarity:** The polarity is a value which lies in the range $[-1, 1]$, where -1 is used to represent negative words and $+1$ is used to represent positive words. To calculate the polarity, we compared each word with its SentiWordnet, which comprised of synonyms and antonyms of each words and their score.
- **Assigning Label:** After the polarity of each word was known, we assign a label to it based on the scheme given in Table 1.

Table 1. Label Assignment

Range	Label Assigned	Category
$[-1, -0.85)$	-1	Negative
$[-0.85, 1.15]$	0	Neutral
$(0.15, 1]$	$+1$	Positive

3.3 Machine Learning Methods

In the present work, we compare two popular supervised learning techniques, i.e. Support Vector Machine and Naïve Bayes Classifier.

Naïve Bayes Classifier

Step I. After obtaining the tweets from the Twitter archiver, they are added to a Google spreadsheet. A total of 29,892 tweets were fetched initially.

Step II. After fetching the tweets, data preprocessing, as explained in Sect. 3.2, was performed. A total of 29,085 tweets remained after performing the data preprocessing tasks. The distribution of tweets for each party has been represented in Table 2.

Table 2. Number of tweets corresponding to each party

Party	Number of tweets
BJP	11,829
Congress	9,364
AAP	7,892

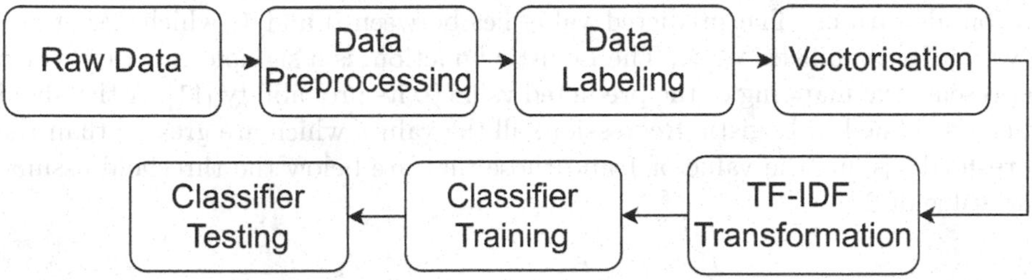

Fig. 3. Naïve Bayes Classifier Model

Step III. As manually labelling such a large dataset would be very time consuming and tedious, an unsupervised learning technique for labeling the data called Dictionary Based Approach as described in Sect. 3.2, was used (Fig. 3).

Step IV. Vectorisation is a method in Natural Language Processing in which words are mapped to real numbers which are used to make word predictions and also find word semantics and similarities.

Step V. Using TFIDF, we found out the importance or relevance of each word, which will be used later to train the Naïve Bayes Classifier Model.

Step VI. Naïve Bayes is a probabilistic approach, which assumes that each feature is independent from the others. In order to assign labels for each of the input vector features, the formula that will be used is:

$$P(label|features) = \frac{P(label) * P(features|label)}{P(features)} \tag{2}$$

In the equation given above, features are representative of the words that were extracted from the tweets while the label represents the polarity or the sentiment i.e. positive, neutral, and negative of the word.

Support Vector Machine

Support Vector Machine (SVM) [9] is a powerful algorithm that is capable of processing data that is not linearly separable by employing kernel functions to project the data into a higher dimensional space where it becomes linearly separable. This property allows SVM to handle complex and non-linear decision boundaries, making it a versatile tool for a variety of machine learning tasks.

Additionally, SVM has the ability to handle large amounts of data and high dimensional feature spaces, rendering it a suitable algorithm for big data applications [10]. Overall, SVM is a widely used algorithm in the field of machine learning due to its capability to deal with complicated data and locate optimal decision boundaries.

Logistic Regression
Logistic Regression [3] is among the most popular supervised learning classification algorithms. The predicted value lies between 0 and 1, which essentially gives the probabilistic value. The Logistic Function, is a sigmoid function which represents the mapping of the predicted value to its probability [11]. A threshold value is defined in Logistic Regression, all the values which are greater than the threshold assume the value of 1 and those that are below the threshold assume the value of 0.

4   Model Evaluation

Several parameters including precision, recall and accuracy are computed to evaluate the performance of the models. The results are compiled in the form of a table and have been shown below in Table 3. To assess the robustness of the model, repeated K-fold cross validation was performed.

– *Accuracy*: Accuracy gauges the level of correctness at which a classifier operates. This can be computed using True Positive(TP), True Negative(TN), False Positive(FP) and False Negative(FN) rates. Accuracy is computed as [12]:

$$Accuracy = \frac{(TP + TN)}{(TP + FP + TN + FN)} \tag{3}$$

– *Precision*: Precision measures the proportion of instances predicted correctly among the total instances retrieved by the model. Precision is computed as [12]:

$$Precision = \frac{TP}{(TP + FP)} \tag{4}$$

– *Recall:* Recall refers to the number of relevant instances retrieved divided by the total number of relevant instances. Recall is calculated as [12]:

$$Recall = \frac{TP}{(TP + FN)} \tag{5}$$

– *F-1 Score*: F-1 Score represents the value obtained from the harmonic mean of precision and recall. It is calculated as [12]:

$$F1Score = \frac{2 * (Precision * Recall)}{(Precision + Recall)} \tag{6}$$

Table 3. Model Evaluation

S. No.	Model	Accuracy	Precision	Recall
1	SVM	**88.4%**	**0.86**	**0.87**
2	Logistic Regression	82.1%	0.83	0.77
3	Naïve Bayes	76.3%	0.79	0.72

5   Result Analysis, Comparison and Discussion

The Fig. 4, Fig. 6 and Fig. 8 show the results obtained for the year 2016 elections from Naïve Bayes Classifier, SVM and Logistic Regression respectively. The Fig. 5, Fig. 7 and Fig. 9 show the results obtained for the year 2021 elections from Naïve Bayes Classifier, SVM and Logistic Regression respectively.

Table 3 gives the list of the machine learning models that are trained on the dataset. SVM gave an accuracy of 88.4% while Logistic Regression gave an accuracy of 82.1% and Naïve Bayes gave an accuracy of only 76.3%. The accuracy highest accuracy achieved in this work is higher compared to some of the previous works [13–16].

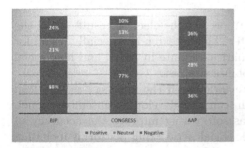

Fig. 4. 2016 Election result from Naïve Bayes Classifier

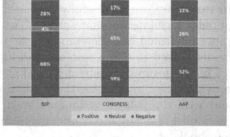

Fig. 5. 2021 Election result from Naïve Bayes Classifier

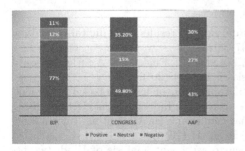

Fig. 6. 2016 Election result from SVM

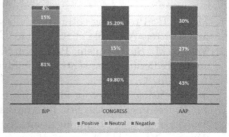

Fig. 7. 2021 Election result from SVM

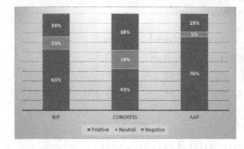
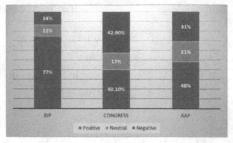

Fig. 8. 2016 Election result from Logistic Regression

Fig. 9. 2016 Election result from Logistic Regression

For the 2016 elections, SVM predicted that BJP will win with as it had 62% positive tweets and for the 2021 elections SVM predicted that BJP will win as it had 69.7% positive tweets. We can conclude that SVM is extremely beneficial for answering this problem as it gave the best performance for both 2016 and 2019 elections.

6   Conclusion and Future Work

In this paper, we successfully managed to predict the election results using the popular social networking website, Twitter. This research is especially useful for those interested in understanding the political climate in India, and how social media is used to shape opinions and mobilize support.

In the future, we intend to include emoticons in the analysis, as they can provide useful insights for the prediction, can also develop an ensemble model, and with the help of techniques such as soft voting improve the accuracy of the model. We can also consider multiple social networking platforms including Facebook, etc.

References

1. Moawi, H.: Predicting voting behaviors and election results using digital trace data and Twitter. Available at SSRN 4464047 (2023)
2. Verma, M., Suryawanshi, P., Deore, S., Mundhe, P., Phakatkar, A.: Election outcome prediction using sentiment analysis on Twitter (2016)
3. Almatrafi, O., Parack, S., Chavan, B.: Application of location-based sentiment analysis using Twitter for identifying trends towards Indian general elections 2014. In: Proceedings of the 9th International Conference on Ubiquitous Information Management and Communication, Article no. 41 (2015)
4. Sharma, Y., et al.: A practical approach to sentiment analysis of Hindi tweets. In: 1st International Conference on Next Generation Computing Technologies (NGCT), pp. 677–680 (2015)

5. Arora, P., Bakliwal, A., Varma, V.: Hindi subjective lexicon generation using word-net graph traversal. Int. J. Comput. Linguist. Appl. **3**(1), 25–39 (2012). https://doi.org/10.5121/ijcla.2012.3103

6. Mittal, N., et al.: Sentiment analysis of Hindi reviews based on negation and discourse relation. In: Proceedings of the 11th Workshop on Asian Language Resources (2013)

7. Kamps, J., Marx, M., Mokken, R.J., Rijke, M.D.: Using wordnet to measure semantic orientations of adjectives. In: LREC, vol. 4, pp. 1115–1118 (2004)

8. Kim, S.M., Hovy, E.: Crystal: analyzing predictive opinions on the web. In: Proceedings of the 2007 Joint Conference on Empirical Methods in Natural Language Processing and Computational Natural Language Learning (EMNLP-CoNLL) (2007)

9. Suthaharan, S., Suthaharan, S.: Support Vector Machine (2016)

10. Noble, W.S.: What is a support vector machine? Nat. Biotechnol. **24**(12), 1565–1567 (2006)

11. Nick, T.G., Campbell, K.M.: Logistic regression, pp. 273–301 (2007)

12. Precision vs recall | precision and recall machine learning. https://www.analyticsvidhya.com/blog/2020/09/precision-recall-machine-learning/. Accessed 11 Oct 2023

13. Sanga, A., Samuel, A., Rathaur, N., Abimbola, P., Babbar, S.: Bayesian prediction on PM Modi's future in 2019. In: Singh, P., Kar, A., Singh, Y., Kolekar, M., Tanwar, S. (eds.) ICRIC 2019. LNEE, vol. 597, pp. 885–897. Springer, Cham (2020). https://doi.org/10.1007/978-3-030-29407-6_64

14. Agarwal, A., Toshniwal, D., Bedi, J.: Can Twitter help to predict outcome of 2019 Indian general election: a deep learning based study. In: Cellier, P., Driessens, K. (eds.) ECML PKDD 2019. CCIS, vol. 1168, pp. 38–53. Springer, Cham (2020). https://doi.org/10.1007/978-3-030-43887-6_4

15. Hitesh, M., Vaibhav, V., Kalki, Y.A., Kamtam, S.H., Kumari, S.: Real-time sentiment analysis of 2019 election tweets using word2vec and random forest model. In: 2019 2nd International Conference on Intelligent Communication and Computational Techniques (ICCT), pp. 146–151. IEEE (2019)

16. Khatua, A., Khatua, A., Cambria, E.: Predicting political sentiments of voters from Twitter in multi-party contexts. Appl. Soft Comput. **97**, 106743 (2020)

Voice Enabled Form Filling Using Hidden Markov Model

Babu Sallagundla⬤, Bharath Naik Kethavath(✉)⬤,
Shaik Arshad Hussain Mitaigiri⬤, Siddartha Kata⬤,
and Kodandaram Sri Satya Sai Merla⬤

Department of CSE, V R Siddhartha Engineering College, Vijayawada, India
bharathnaikk0105@gmail.com

Abstract. Speech Recognition technology is widely used for voice-enabled form filling. The manual process of filling out forms by typing has become increasingly challenging and time-consuming. This issue is particularly evident in various locations such as job applications and internships. To address this problem, a solution is proposed as a system that automates the form-filling process using speech recognition technology. The ability to operate anything with voice command is a crucial factor in today's environment. The proposed system is that it automatically fills out the forms. i.e., the system analyses the user's unique voice, identifies the user's speech, and then transcribes the speech into text. This paper proposes a machine-learning model that builds on Hidden Markov Model. The model will be trained and tested on this system and the proposed pre-processed methodology is Mel Frequency Cepstral Coefficients. The methodology was widely used in the prospect of recognition of voice automatically. The results demonstrate that this system effectively accurately transcribes user speech into text, simplifying the form-filling process significantly. By providing these results, we hope to demonstrate how this technology has the potential to revolutionize data entry and accessibility while also establishing a strong case for speech recognition as a convenient way to speed up form completion.

Keywords: Automatic Speech Recognition · Speech to Text · Hidden Markov Models · Voice enabled Form Filling · Mel Frequency Cepstral Coefficients

1 Introduction

Voice-enabled technologies have become an innovative way to speed up and improve user interactions in the world of contemporary technology. This study uses the advanced Hidden Markov Models (HMM) approach to deal with voice-activated form filling. Our solution makes it simple for users to voice-fill out forms by utilizing the power of HMM. Input speech data from users is first recorded as part of the project, and this data forms the basis for all future processes. The speech data goes through crucial procedures including data normalization and feature extraction to guarantee precise and dependable findings. The audio is now ready for additional processing, analysis, and transformation. We then translate their spoken words into written text, so we can work with it more easily. Once we have the text, we extract the important information needed to fill out the form accurately. This means we identify the specific details the form requires, such as names, addresses, or other relevant data. Through the integration of these components, our voice-enabled form-filling system revolutionizes the traditional data input paradigm. Users can now effortlessly provide information by simply speaking, freeing them from the constraints of manual typing or handwriting. Embracing the potential of Hidden Markov Models and the power of voice recognition, this project not only offers convenience but also opens up new possibilities for improved efficiency, accessibility, and user experience in the domain of form-filling.

Additionally, the introduction provides an overview of key components within the Automatic Speech Recognition (ASR) framework, encompassing the conversion of spoken language into text through Machine Learning or AI [21], making ASR increasingly accessible, and highlighting the significance of Mel-frequency cepstral coefficients (MFCCs) in capturing spectral characteristics. They're computed at 10 ms intervals using a 25 ms analysis frame, smoothing FFT-derived log spectral estimates, and applying Discrete Cosine Transformation (DCT) on a mel scale [8]. The discussion extends to the foundational role of Hidden Markov Models (HMMs) in modeling time-varying spectral sequences in speech, although their practical implementation is complex [22]. Furthermore, the Viterbi Algorithm is introduced as a pivotal element for mapping acoustic signals to words within ASR, leading to the identification of the most probable word sequence [23]. The decoder plays a crucial role in translating HMM outputs into words using a dictionary and utilizing language models for enhanced decoding precision, thus resulting in more accurate transcriptions [24].

The forthcoming sections provide an in-depth exploration of the technical aspects of the voice-enabled form-filling system. Section 2 delves into the methodology, offering insights into the utilization of Hidden Markov Models (HMM) and Mel-frequency cepstral coefficients (MFCCs). Section 3 is dedicated to the presentation of the experimental results and their subsequent analysis. In Sect. 4, the focus shifts to an examination of the implications arising from our findings. Lastly, Sect. 5 offers a concluding summary of this research along with recommendations for future investigations.

1.1 Motivation

Manual typing for filling out forms and any applications is difficult and time-consuming. Voice-based form-filling is a better way to overcome such problems. By using voice recognition, it takes less time and accuracy to fill out a form. Voice recognition systems enable users to interact with the system by speaking to it, making it possible to conduct independent requests, reminders, and other simple tasks.

1.2 Problem Statement

Develop an HMM-based model that can recognize and transcribe spoken words from audio input, and use the transcribed text to fill out an online form. The ultimate goal is to provide a more efficient and convenient way for users to fill out online forms, especially for those who may have difficulty typing. Manual typing for filling out forms and any applications is difficult and time-consuming. Voice-based form-filling is a better way to overcome such problems. By using voice recognition, it takes less time and accuracy to fill out a form. Voice recognition systems provide hands-free requests, reminders, and other basic activities by allowing users to engage with the system merely by speaking to it.

1.3 Objectives

The major Objectives are:

- To design and train a Hidden Markov Model (HMM) for speech recognition that can accurately recognize spoken words and phrases.
- To evaluate the model's accuracy on a sizable dataset to spot any flaws or potential areas for development.
- To implement pre-processing techniques to enhance the accuracy of the HMM model by filtering out background noise and other interference.

1.4 Scope

- Initially it supports only the English language and can be extended to multilingual forms.
- It is limited to selected forms such as job applications etc.

1.5 Advantages

- Enables voice-based data entry, enhancing user experience with a convenient and time-saving option.
- High precision is enabled by advanced voice recognition technology. Using HMM models and contemporary voice technology, research tries to reduce mistakes.
- Voice-enabled forms enhance accessibility, promoting inclusion for those with physical limitations or typing difficulties, and widening user interaction.
- Voice input, rather than typing or navigating through multiple fields, accelerates form-filling, enhancing effectiveness and speed.

2 Literature Survey

This section describes the several literature surveys that are cited.

In this work [1], four different spectral features— Perceptual Linear Prediction (PLP), Linear Predictive Cepstral Coefficients (LPCC), and Mel-Frequency Cepstral Coefficients (MFCC) are four types of linear predictive coding—are used to compare the representations of Khasi speech. LPC is used to estimate basic speech characteristics and is especially effective when expressing speech at low bit rates. The spectrum of the input voice signal is subjected to LPCC. PLP modifies the spectral properties to match the human hearing system. The voice sounds' short-term power spectrum is captured by MFCC characteristics. The canonical speech representation is used in the study to discriminate between voiced and unvoiced sounds. Building several Performance evaluations calls for HMM-based recognizers that use the HTK ASR toolbox and adjust spectral characteristics, feature size, HMM states, and GMMs. The best performance obtained using MFCC characteristics and 5 HMM states are chosen for evaluation, and the word error rate (WER) is employed.

The research [2] examines an automatic speech recognition method that is noise-resistant by using hidden Markov modeling of stereo voice data from clean and noisy channels. The resulting stereo HMM includes a Gaussian mixture model in each state and has a blended distribution of both clean and noisy speech features. The stereo HMM enables two-pass compensation and decoding, which entails MMSE de-noising based on N-best hypotheses and decoding the de-noised speech in a condensed search space on a lattice. In comparison with feature space GMM-based de-noising approaches, the stereo HMM enables finer-grained noise compensation and anticipates each clean feature using information from the whole noisy feature sequence. Manually collected dataset with 4 K Quinone state and 50 K Gaussians.

A novel HMM-based speech recognition technique is presented in research [3], which uses Particle Swarm Optimization (PSO) to improve HMM parameter optimization and recognition accuracy. According to the research, PSO should be incorporated into the recognition phase, with global optimum segmentation taking precedence over conventional Viterbi techniques. In this method, segmentation vectors are initially created in the solution space and their locations are modified. Because speech is continuous, HMM states can be represented by a single Gaussian or a multi-modal Gaussian mixture. It is common practice in these models to employ continuous density probability density functions (pdfs). Comparative testing shows that in terms of recognition accuracy and convergence speed, the PSO approach surpasses the traditional Baum-Welch algorithm. Its usefulness in obtaining global optimum while preserving the Viterbi system accuracy is demonstrated by experiments using stop consonants and isolated word recognition.

An enhanced Gaussian Mixture Hidden Markov Model (GMHMM) for categorizing audio-based emotions is reported in the article [4]. The Hidden Markov Model (HMM) is enhanced by a Gaussian Mixture Model (GMM), the GMHMM increases accuracy by considering state space uncertainty. It calculates model parameters using HMM and GMM after being trained on audio data representing emotional states. Results from the evaluation of the Emo-DB and eNTER FACE'05 datasets are remarkable, with 84.5% accuracy on Emo-DB and 85.5% on eNTER FACE'05, which are on par with cutting-edge models. A disadvantage is the computational burden of training, despite its excellent classification accuracy and noise robustness. Though it may need a lot of resources to train for some applications, the GMHMM overall shows promise in audio-based emotion categorization.

A summary of developments in Arabic voice recognition over the past few decades is given in this work [5]. It covers key elements of voice recognition systems, such as corpora, phonemes, language models, acoustic models, and performance assessment. Utilizing machine learning techniques for voice adaptation is the main objective. To train acoustic models for word recognition based on voice feature vectors, language model declaration—often referred to as grammars or probabilistic N-Grams—is employed. With the use of a sizable audio corpus and phonetic transcriptions, training uses Gaussian mixtures in Hidden Markov Models (HMMs) to produce statistical representations of phonemes. To extract acoustic features, MFCCs are used. The accuracy rate of recognition, which is commonly calculated as the word error rate (WER), represents the proportion of successfully recognized patterns, which measures the effectiveness of isolated recognition of words.

In Paper [6], the emphasis is on evaluating Hidden Markov Models' (HMMs') underutilized potential in reliability engineering. In the paper, a unique maintenance approach based on HMMs is presented, where different system states correlate to different levels of degradation. When system states are difficult to see, this method is especially useful since it relies on control systems to give cues about the real situation. The research creates a maximum-likelihood estimate for system dependability by examining its asymptotic characteristics. The study views corrective maintenance as the most expensive intervention, with costs dependent on the degree of system degeneration, and introduces a random element represented by a Markov chain to affect the core system. Notably, the study establishes a distinct dependability function that takes into consideration both visible and unobservable system states as signs of system degradation. The paper builds a maximum-likelihood estimate of this function using signal measurements and investigates its theoretical properties.

The article [7] discusses how continuous-state Hidden Markov Models (HMMs) may be used to resolve a well-known problem in voice recognition that involves decoding a list of phonetic units from measurements of acoustic signals that change gradually. They put forth an approach for the HMM decoding issue based on a continuous state space representation of the HMM that is tested using both synthetic and actual voice data. The journal also highlights certain restrictions and difficulties related to employing continuous-state HMMs for speech recognition, such as the requirement for substantial training data and the difficulty of simulating long-term relationships in speech signals. Real speech from the TIMIT dataset and artificial sinusoidal speech.

The Mel Frequency Cepstral Coefficient (MFCC) features are used in this study [8] to refine an Automatic Speech Recognition (ASR) system for the Moroccan Dialect, enhancing speaker identification. With a vector quantization technique, these retrieved characteristics are quantized. A limited number of basic acoustic units that are calculated by sliding windows are used to depict the acoustic signal. The digital speech stream is transformed into feature vectors using MFCC parametrization, which records the voice characteristics of the speaker. These feature vectors are used to build reference models from training utterances. Precision speaker discrimination is made possible by the widely utilized MFCCs' efficient recording of speech signal patterns. Utilizing matching techniques, similar vectors of features from test utterances are retrieved for testing and contrasted with the reference. The system obtains an accuracy rate of about 90% by using MFCC + Delta + Delta-Delta characteristics.

In "Automatic Speech Recognition of Portuguese Phonemes Using Neural Networks Ensemble" by Nedjah, Bonilla, and Mourelle [9], Portuguese automated speech recognition (ASR) is given a novel approach. The technique makes use of a neural network ensemble that was extensively trained on Portuguese voice data and managed to achieve an astounding 86.525% accuracy. This method handles speech variability, noise robustness, and computing efficiency better than previous ASR approaches. Portuguese ASR systems were previously used, but evaluation of the TIMIT (American English) and CHEM (Portuguese) datasets produced impressive results: 86.525% accuracy for TIMIT and 83.128% for CHEM. The authors make their code available online, enabling more study and advancement of ASR for the Portuguese language. Portuguese voice recognition might benefit from improved accuracy, robustness, and efficiency thanks to this ground-breaking ensemble-based ASR technique.

In Distributed Voice Recognition (DSR) applications, when user-end speech features are evaluated and sent to a server, this work [10] proposes a way to adjust Hidden Markov Models (HMMs), lowering the computational load on client devices. The precision of observation sequences can, however, be compromised by lowering the frame rate. By modifying the HMM transition probabilities to match the frame rate, this approach solves the problem. It uses full-frame rate data to estimate transition probabilities, after which it trains a new HMM to recognize reduced-frame rate data. Experiments on linked digits that were both clean and noisy indicate that the method efficiently corrects for framerate inconsistencies. The updated model outperforms techniques for restoring frame rate using data interpolation by reducing calculation time while preserving accuracy.

3   Proposed Methodology

3.1   Architecture

Noise removal and normalization techniques are applied to enhance the quality and consistency of the audio. A dataset for training is created, and a data set for testing is created. The Gaussian HMM-based acoustic model, which precisely represents the statistically significant features of speech, is trained using the training dataset. The Viterbi algorithm serves as the decoder, matching observed speech features with learned HMM states to determine the most likely spoken words or phrases. The recognized speech is validated, and if valid, the form is filled with the transcribed text. This project leverages various techniques, including pre-processing, feature extraction, acoustic modeling, and decoding, to achieve accurate and efficient voice-enabled form-filling (Fig. 1).

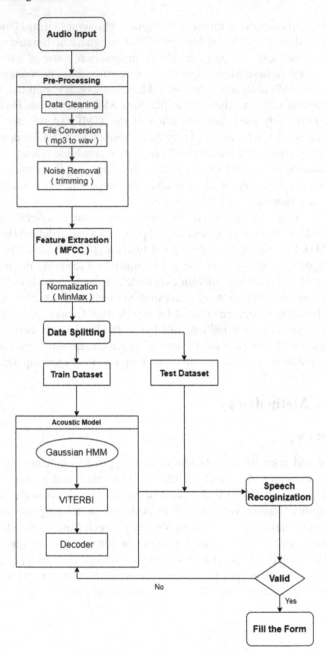

Fig. 1. Proposed system architecture of Hidden Markov Model.

3.2 Methodology

Data Collection

Common Voice is a corpus of voice data that people may access on the Common Voice website [9] that was constructed from text from several public domain sources, including user-submitted blog posts, vintage books, films, and other public speech corpora. Making the instruction and evaluation of Automated Speech Recognition (ASR) systems possible is its main objective. Sections of the corpus have been created for our convenience. The subgroups with "valid" in their title are clips of audio that have been heard at least twice by listeners who, on average, agree that the audio matches the text. The clips in the subgroups with the word "invalid" in their titles have at least two listeners, and most of them claim the audio is inconsistent with the clip. All other clips have "other" in their name, even those with fewer than two votes and those with an equal number of valid and invalid votes. Each.csv file contains the filename, relative path, the audio file's alleged transcription, the number of individuals who felt the audio matched the text, their age, gender, and accent, as well as up and down votes. Each subset's audio samples are stored as mp3 files in folders that share the same naming patterns as the corresponding CSV files. As an illustration, all audio files from. As an illustration, the "cv-valid-train.csv" metadata file and the subdirectory "cv-valid-train" will include each bit of audio data taken from the valid train set.

Dataset Description

The dataset used in this project is the Common Voice dataset, a comprehensive resource for multi-accent voice data collection developed by Mozilla. The dataset contains over 400,000 audio samples with corresponding transcriptions. For this analysis, the focus was on a specific subset, namely the "cv-valid-train" portion, which comprises a substantial amount of speech data containing 2,00,000 records suitable for training and testing the Hidden Markov Model (HMM) based system. This dataset consists of two primary components. First, it includes a vast collection of audio files, each containing recordings by diverse users who read sentences in their native languages. These audio files encompass a wide range of linguistic and acoustic variations, making them highly suitable for training and evaluating automatic speech recognition systems. The second component of the dataset comprises CSV files, each of which contains a wealth of information related to the audio recordings. These CSV files are rich in attributes, including the audio file name, the corresponding transcribed text, the number of up_votes, down_votes, the speaker's age, gender, accent, and the duration of each recording. This multi-faceted dataset played a pivotal role in training and testing our Hidden Markov Model (HMM) based system, facilitating a more comprehensive analysis of its performance in various linguistic and demographic contexts.

Data Pre-processing

Data Cleaning: Data cleaning is used for removing incorrect or duplicate data within a dataset. The dataset that is downloaded from the Kaggle contains a set of audio files and corresponding CSV files. The CSV files contain unnecessary columns and missing transcriptions. These are dropped to reduce the noise and improve performance. The punctuation and white spaces are removed, so that it gives better results during testing.

Feature Extraction

Feature Extraction is used for transforming raw data, such as audio waveforms, into a set of representative features that capture the relevant information. It helps in extracting Mel frequency cepstral coefficients (MFCCs) from an audio file. The extracted features, such as MFCCs, are used as inputs to train ASR models. For modeling and identifying speech sounds, these features which represent the spectral properties of the speech signal are crucial. The Mel-scale, a widely used frequency scale, is linear up to 1000 Hz and logarithmic above that point. Calculating a filter's center frequency in Mel-scale:

$$f_{mel} = \frac{1000\log\left(1 + \frac{f}{1000}\right)}{\log 2}$$

F_{mel} in the equation above stands for the frequency value on the Mel scale. f is the frequency value in Hertz that you want to convert to the Mel scale. Log represents the natural logarithm function.

3.3 Developing a Hidden Markov Model from the Feature-Extracted Data

The model is built using 6 hidden layers such as Conv2D, MaxPooling2D, Dropout, Flatten, Dense, Activation, and Batch Normalization. Using the train-test split approach, the data is divided into train and test groups. Now, by passing the Parameters retrieved in module 3 to training data we built a model using Image Data Generator, Early Stopping. The test data is predicted by using the model developed.

The VITERBI algorithm is a dynamic programming algorithm used in Hidden Markov Models (HMMs) for sequence labeling tasks. Based on an observable sequence, it seeks to identify the hidden state sequence that is most likely. The algorithm iteratively computes values in two matrices, T1 and T2, using probabilities from the transition matrix, emission matrix, and initial probabilities. T1 stores the maximum probabilities of state sequences up to a given observation, while T2 keeps track of the corresponding state indices. By evaluating these matrices, the algorithm identifies the most probable hidden state sequence and returns it as the output. To perform the VITERBI algorithm, the input consists of the observed sequence, transition matrix, emission matrix, state space, and initial probabilities. The algorithm starts by initializing T1 and T2 for the first observation using the initial probabilities and emission probabilities. It then iterates over subsequent observations, computing maximum probabilities for state sequences and updating the matrices accordingly. Once the iterations are complete, the algorithm backtracks through T2 to retrieve the most likely hidden state sequence. By efficiently considering the probabilities of different state paths, the algorithm returns the sequence of hidden states.

The encode transcriptions implement a function called "encode transcriptions" that performs label encoding on a set of transcriptions. It converts categorical labels into numerical values. The transcriptions are passed as input to the function. The label encoder is then fitted to the transcriptions using the "fit transform" method, which both trains the encoder on the transcriptions and transforms them into encoded integer values. The resulting encoded transcriptions are stored in the variable "transcriptions encoded", and the function returns this transformed data. Label encoding is an effective method for transforming categorical information into a format that machine learning algorithms can use. This function simplifies the label encoding process by encapsulating it within a single function, allowing users to easily apply the transformation to their transcriptions and utilize the encoded data in subsequent machine learning tasks.

In technique 3, the Baum-Welch technique is used to train a Gaussian Hidden Markov Model. This algorithm aims to learn the optimal parameters for the model by iteratively updating the transition matrix, emission matrix, and initial probabilities. The training loop repeats a specified number of iterations, during which the expectation step computes probabilities of being in each state at each time step, while the maximization step updates the model parameters based on these probabilities. This iterative process continues until convergence, refining the model's ability to capture the relationships between observed data and hidden states. After completing the training loop, the learned parameters are used to create a Gaussian HMM model. This model incorporates the updated transition matrix, emission matrix, and initial probabilities. It may be used for many different applications, including voice recognition, where it forecasts the most probable hidden state sequence provided by an input series. By iteratively improving the model's parameters based on the provided data, the algorithm enhances the model's capacity to identify patterns and associations, resulting in improved accuracy and performance for subsequent analyses or applications.

Pre-processing
Data Cleaning: We use data cleaning techniques on the transcribed data files that are in the CSV format available along with the common voice dataset, For that we consider some test cases like correlation among columns with the corr() method and remove the unnecessary columns and also remove the null value records using dropna() method and save the transcribed data after cleaning at the respective path (Table 1).

Table 1. Correlation matrix of cleaned data.

	down_votes	up_votes	duration
down_votes	1.00000	0.48541	NaN
up_votes	0.48541	1.00000	NaN
Duration	NaN	NaN	NaN

'.mp3' to '.wav' conversion: We convert the '.mp3' audio files to '.wav' for better training of the model in different test cases '.wav' format is flexible with all conditions for that we use "FFmpeg" a command line tool widely used for conversion (Fig. 2).

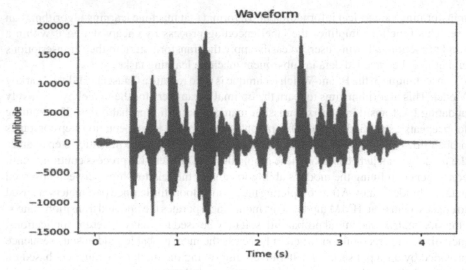

Fig. 2. .wav Signal Image

All the audio files are converted from.mp3 to.wav extension for better performance. The above figure shows the pictorial representation of the wave signal of an audio file.

- *Noise Removing:* We use librosa.effects.trim() method to remove the noise from the audio files
- *Feature Extraction:* We use the mfcc() method to extract the features by adjusting the sample rate based on your dataset and the Number of MFCC coefficients.
- *Normalization:* We use Minimax normalization processes to normalize the values to around 0.

$$mfccnorm(i, j) = \frac{mfcc(i, j) - \min(mfcc(i. :))}{\max(mfcc(i, :)) - \min(mfcc(i, :))}$$

The term mfcc(i, j) in the equation above denotes the MFCC score of the i-th frame along with the j-th coefficient. The MFCC coefficients' minimal value for the i-th frame is determined by the formula min(mfcc(i, :)). The MFCC coefficients' maximum value for the i-th frame is determined by the formula max(mfcc(i, :)) (Fig. 3).

Model Training and Evaluation:
For each number of states in the range, the code performs the following steps in parallel for each fold of cross-validation.

- Data Splitting: The pre-processed data and encoded transcriptions are split into training and validation sets using the fold indices.
- Model Creation: A Gaussian Hidden Markov Model (HMM) is created with a specified number of states.
- Model Fitting: The HMM model is fitted to the training data.
- Model Evaluation: The model's score is evaluated on the validation set.

[[0.00303145	0.0051802	0.6293372	......	0.3134667	0.46628815	0.5229239]
[0.00152456	0.00258638	0.6267352	......	0.30565563	0.45745158	0.51445705]
[0.15138695	0.16908747	0.6895818	......	0.41849324	0.66785926	0.7818082]
....						
[0.0302457	0.0598871	0.68253183	......	0.52406687	0.48165965	0.57844786]
[0.01825705	0.05792963	0.69898087	......	0.54037905	0.47182283	0.57965726]
[0.01041354	0.04607939	0.697616	......	0.55203813	0.48383346	0.58209175]]

Fig. 3. Pre-processed Data after Feature Extraction.

HMM Parameters

In our project, the Hidden Markov Model (HMM) was fine-tuned with specific parameters to optimize its performance. The model incorporated five hidden states (n_components = 5), which were determined through an iterative process. We tested a range of state values from 3 to 9 and selected the configuration that yielded the highest accuracy. This careful parameter selection was vital to the model's effectiveness. Furthermore, the model employed a diagonal covariance matrix type (covariance_type = "diag"), which is well suited for speech data. The training process utilized the Viterbi Algorithm (algorithm = 'Viterbi'), a robust choice for training HMMs in sequence prediction tasks. To expedite the training process and enhance efficiency, we implemented parallel computing techniques. This approach significantly reduced training time, allowing us to more effectively capture the relationships between the observed audio data and the underlying hidden states. As a result, the HMM model proved highly effective in speech recognition tasks.

4 Results and Discussions

The results are obtained from the successful execution of the proposed system. The audio files for the dataset are collected from the Kaggle Common Voice dataset repository. The dataset is a corpus of spoken information that is frequently utilized in speech recognition and is considered to be of the common voice. The Outputs from each module are shown in this chapter. The code collects the scores, number of states, and trained models for each fold. It calculates the average accuracy for the current number of states by normalizing the scores within the range of minimum and maximum scores obtained.

The graph shows the relationship between both the HMM model's precision and state count. It can provide insights into the optimal number of states to use for a specific task or dataset. The graph can be used to analyze the trade-off between model complexity (number of states) and model accuracy and help in making informed decisions for model selection and tuning (Fig. 4).

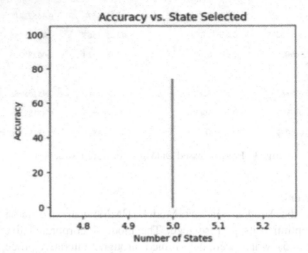

Fig. 4. Normalized Accuracy vs No. of States

Print Results:

The code prints the average accuracy for all models of different states, the best accuracy for the best training model, and the number of states for the best model (Table 2).

Table 2. Model results.

Pre-processed data size	(18323910, 13)
transcriptions size	64711
Average accuracy	45.98834782224607
Best accuracy	74.85592295175691
Number of states	5

The above table shows the accuracy of the model and the state at which the accuracy is maximum. It calculates the accuracy for a specific range of states and gives the highest precision and the same variety of states within that range.

4.1 Graphical User Interface

A speech-to-text form-filling program with a graphic user interface (GUI) was used for this project. The GUI consists of input fields for different form fields such as First Name, Last Name, and City. Each input field is accompanied by a recording button. When the user clicks a recording button, the code initiates audio recording for a fixed duration of 3 s. The recorded audio is then saved as a WAV file. Afterward, the code processes the recorded audio using a trained Hidden Markov Model (HMM) model. The code uses the Viterbi method to find the most likely series of hidden states throughout the processing step after extracting features from the audio. These hidden states are then mapped to text labels using a label encoder that was used during the training of the HMM model (Fig. 5).

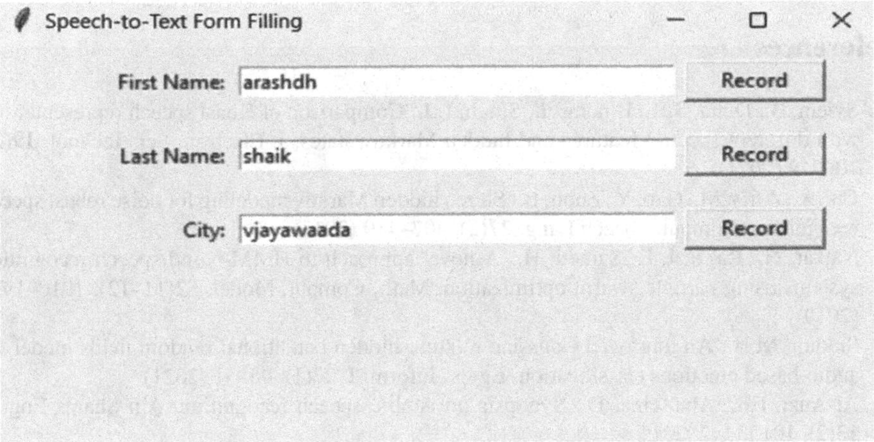

Fig. 5. Graphical User Interface of a sample form

The final predicted text is obtained by concatenating or processing the predicted labels. The predicted text is printed to the console and simultaneously displayed in the corresponding input field of the GUI. By interacting with the GUI, the user can fill in the form fields by speaking into the microphone. The predicted text is updated in real time, providing feedback to the user. This allows for hands-free form filling using speech input. In summary, the code creates a user-friendly interface for capturing speech input, converting it to text using a trained HMM model, and dynamically updating the GUI with the predicted text, enabling convenient form filling through speech recognition.

5 Conclusion and Future Work

In conclusion, the proposed speech-to-text form-filling system utilizing Hidden Markov Models (HMMs) presents a promising solution to address the challenges associated with manual form-filling. By leveraging HMMs for speech recognition, the system offers improved efficiency and accuracy in various domains where form filling is required. The system's modular design, encompassing data collection, pre-processing, HMM training, integration with a form-filling interface, and performance evaluation, ensures a comprehensive and robust solution. Through the collection and transcription of users' speech, the system effectively converts spoken words into text data, which is then segmented and labeled with corresponding form fields. By using voice recognition to automate the process of filling out forms, the system greatly lowers the duration and effort needed for human data entry, allowing for the quicker and more accurate completion of forms. The Future Work involves extending the system to support multiple languages, allowing users to fill forms in languages other than English. Incorporate Natural Language

Processing techniques to enable the system to understand and interpret user responses more intelligently. Explore integration possibilities with existing form solutions, such as popular form builders or office productivity tools, to provide seamless integration and compatibility with established workflows.

References

1. Syiem, B., Dutta, S.K., Binong, J., Singh, L.J.: Comparison of Khasi speech representations with different spectral features and hidden Markov states. J. Electron. Sci. Technol. **19**(2), 100079 (2021)
2. Cui, X., Afify, M., Gao, Y., Zhou, B.: Stereo hidden Markov modeling for noise robust speech recognition. Comput. Speech Lang. **27**(2), 407–419 (2013)
3. Najkar, N., Razzazi, F., Sameti, H.: A novel approach to HMM-based speech recognition systems using particle swarm optimization. Math. Comput. Model. **52**(11–12), 1910–1920 (2010)
4. Siddiqi, M.H.: An improved Gaussian mixture hidden conditional random fields model for audio-based emotions classification. Egypt. Inform. J. **22**(1), 45–51 (2021)
5. Al-Anzi, F.S., AbuZeina, D.: Synopsis on Arabic speech recognition. Ain Shams Eng. J. **13**(2), 101534 (2022)
6. Gámiz, M.L., Limnios, N., del Carmen Segovia-García, M.: Hidden Markov models in reliability and maintenance. Eur. J. Oper. Res. **304**(3), 1242–1255 (2023)
7. Champion, C., Houghton, S.M.: Application of continuous state hidden Markov models to a classical problem in speech recognition. Comput. Speech Lang. **36**, 347–364 (2016)
8. Mouaz, B., Abderrahim, B.H., Abdelmajid, E.: Speech recognition of Moroccan dialect using hidden Markov models. Procedia Comput. Sci. **151**, 985–991 (2019)
9. Nedjah, N., Bonilla, A.D., de Macedo Mourelle, L.: Automatic speech recognition of Portuguese phonemes using neural networks ensemble. Expert Syst. Appl. **229**, 120378 (2023)
10. Lee, L.M., Jean, F.R.: Adaptation of hidden Markov models for recognizing speech of reduced frame rate. IEEE Trans. Cybern. **43**(6), 2114–2121 (2013)
11. Chen, Y., Zheng, H.: The application of HMM algorithm based music note feature recognition teaching in universities. Intell. Syst. Appl. **20**, 200277 (2023)
12. Mannepalli, K., Sastry, P.N., Suman, M.: MFCC-GMM based accent recognition system for Telugu speech signals. Int. J. Speech Technol. **19**, 87–93 (2016)
13. Chandrakala, S.: Investigation of DNN-HMM and lattice free maximum mutual information approaches for impaired speech recognition. IEEE Access **9**, 168840–168849 (2021)
14. Li, Q., Zhang, C., Woodland, P.C.: Combining hybrid DNN-HMM ASR systems with attention-based models using lattice rescoring. Speech Commun. **147**, 12–21 (2023)
15. Ma, Z., Zhang, J., Li, T., Yang, R., Wang, H.: A parameter transfer method for HMM-DNN heterogeneous model with the scarce mongolian data set. Procedia Comput. Sci. **187**, 258–263 (2021)
16. Das, T.K., Nahar, K.M.: A voice identification system using hidden Markov model. Indian J. Sci. Technol. **9**(4), 1–6 (2016)
17. Ranjan, A., Jegadeesan, K.: Hybrid ASR for resource-constrained robots: HMM-deep learning fusion. arXiv preprint arXiv:2309.07164 (2023)
18. Yadava, G.T., Nagaraja, B.G., Jayanna, H.S.: An end-to-end continuous Kannada ASR system under uncontrolled environment. Multimed. Tools Appl. 1–14 (2023)
19. Trabelsi, A., Warichet, S., Aajaoun, Y., Soussilane, S.: Evaluation of the efficiency of state-of-the-art Speech Recognition engines. Procedia Comput. Sci. **207**, 2242–2252 (2022)

20. Jaradat, G.A., Alzubaidi, M.A., Otoom, M.: A novel human-vehicle interaction assistive device for Arab drivers using speech recognition. IEEE Access **10**, 127514–127529 (2022)
21. Speech recognition. Wikipedia (2023). https://en.wikipedia.org/wiki/Speech_recognition
22. Hidden Markov model. Wikipedia (2023). https://en.wikipedia.org/wiki/Hidden_Markov_model
23. Viterbi algorithm. Wikipedia (2023). https://en.wikipedia.org/wiki/Viterbi_algorithm
24. Brown, D.G., Golod, D.: Decoding HMMs using the k best paths: algorithms and applications. BMC Bioinform. **11**(S1) (2010). https://doi.org/10.1186/1471-2105-11-s1-s28

Bayesian Network Model Based Classifiers Are Used in an Intelligent E-learning System

Rohit. B. Kaliwal[(⊠)] [iD] and Santosh. L. Deshpande [iD]

Department of CSE, VTU, Belagavi, Karnataka, India
rohit.kaliwal@gmail.com, sldeshpande@gmail.com
https://www.vtu.ac.in/

Abstract. The use of information and communication technology for educational purposes has increased recently, and the development of network technologies has had a significant influence on the methods employed in electronic learning (E-learning). Most popular trends in education are e-learning, which shows how teaching and learning approaches are evolving in tandem with technological advancements. Technologies that facilitate education's scalability, automation, customization, and innovation offer enormous promise. The cost of e-learning has greatly decreased, and the benefits of its rapid, inexpensive, and time-saving instruction are substantial. Education technology (Edtech) solution providers helps to e-learning and guaranteeing that each student has a smooth and customized learning experience implies a significant impact on learners all across the world during the past COVID-19 epidemic. Thus, e-learning becomes popular teaching method in many educational institutions. However, online learning programs demand a physical examination by a real professor. Therefore, an automated evaluation system for learning prototype utilizing an excellent e-learning system is suggested in the current study. The Baye's Theorem-based Bayesian Network (BN) concept can be best fit to construct intelligent e-learning systems. Groups of questions serve as the nodes and directed arcs serve as the edges of the directed acyclic graph (DAG) known as BN. This network is employed for ambiguous reasoning. The Baye's network employing K2, KNN, and J48 was used to compare the BN model against AI classification techniques. Hence discovered that the performance of suggested smart e-learning approach utilizing BN outperforms that of the other two approaches, J48 and K-nearest.

Keywords: Education Technology · Intelligent E-Learning System · Bayesian Network · E- learning · Learner

1 Introduction

In 21st century from classroom to online learning, education has caused a significant change in how people learn. The indoor teaching of classroom sessions inside of four walls has changed to Internet services in a teaching setting using multimedia, which has expanded the idea of learning from a text book towards understanding the concept. The concept of "everyone's education into everyone's hands" has replaced the idea of corporations as ivory towers thanks to the phrase "e-learning". In 1999, a presentation for a Computer-Based Training Programmed (CBT) system included the phrase "e-learning" for the first time. The hunt for a more comprehensive definition gave rise to new terms like "virtual learning" and "online learning". Contrarily, the background of e-learning is well documented, and there is evidence that suggests the first forms of e-learning date back to the early in 18th century [1].

Although parents place a high importance on education, this is not exactly how it has always been. From the Vedic era to the present, the educational system has undergone considerable adjustments for a higher level of living [2]. Now, the language was used for instruction, learning, and even casual conversation. It is plausible to say that India's educational landscape significantly changed throughout this period. The basis for higher education in the 20th century was laid during this time [1, 2].

The contemporary educational system is dependent on education technology (Edtech), which employs hardware and software to facilitate learning. Edtech encompasses learning, training, online learning and mobile learning. Any educational system that uses practices, rules, and instruments to advance learning goals may benefit from technology. The accessibility of communications and information technology has increased and has aided in the globalization of the economy [2]. The Internet has a wealth of tools that learners may use to engage in activities outside of the classroom that enhance learning results. The choice to take self-paced or live online courses is provided through e-learning. Learners meet with professors during virtual office hours and work together online on specific assignments. This research article has been organized as Introduction (Sect. 1), E-learning in Education System (Sect. 1.1), Bayesian Network Model (Sect. 1.2), Structure of Intelligent E-learning System (Sect. 1.3), Literature Review (Sect. 2), Intelligent Tutoring System (Sect. 3), Bayesian Network Model (Sect. 4), Result and Discussions (Sect. 5), Hardware and Software Requirements (Sect. 5.1.), Finally Sect. 6 Concludes the research work.

1.1 E-learning in Education System

However, the organizations must change to achieve the requirements, aspirations, and expectations of learners in the contemporary educational system, which is always changing. As a result, companies are steadily making investments in the e-learning systems, information technology, gadgets, and online platforms that are becoming more important business tools. However, utilizing innovative e-learning technologies to boost and expand collaborative learning and teaching is one of the most important concerns for organizations in current technological era [3, 4].

E-learning has the advantage of supporting and enhancing the teaching-learning process. No additional tools are required because it is a web-based solution. Therefore, taking into account elements like technology tools, platforms, and learner content makes e-learning a comprehensive process. Furthermore, the educational system is unique from other learning approaches in that it accords equal weight to both instruction and individualized learning [5].

1.2   E-learning Using Bayesian Network Model

Whether the BN model can aid in learner evaluation is the key objective of e-learning. The BN paradigm was adopted since learner evaluation in e-learning systems has illustrated to be done in a reliable way using this paradigm [6]. Theoretically, BN approves to full and in-depth examination of each learner aspect on the professor's inquiry stage. Instead of only relying on final grades to determine how well a learner performed, BN is able to offer a more complete model of learner knowledge, which includes information with respect of difficulty of the possible questions the learner is dealing with and which subjects they have previously mastered. It is necessary to have this information proceeded to provide feedback, remedial action, and individualized teaching.

1.3   Structure of Intelligent E-learning System

Finding out how precisely and properly it evaluates a learner relying on the feedbacks is the main challenge. Utilising Bloom's taxonomy, the concepts of learner success and failure have been used. In this research, knowledge of the subject will be gained or improved depending on how the learner approaches the questions.

Knowledge levels and question stages are evaluated using the learner stage assessment paradigm. If you have a fundamental knowledge of this paradigm, you can ask those questions and get responses from them. It also suggests educational resources that can be accessed via the tutoring module. These modules evaluate and grade the learner's performance based on their responses to the questions. A learner is competent to respond to questions from the advanced knowledge stage when their performance level is above a specific cutoff.

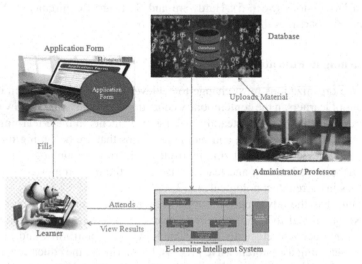

Fig. 1. Structure of Intelligent E-learning System

The above Fig. 1, the first and most crucial duty is one that requires the system administrator or professor, who is a member of the organization. In other words, the administrator or professor must first prepare all the different questions that are necessary for each particular taxonomic level, and only then upload the question set into the system's database.

The database is connected to our system. To participate in the evaluation, at the beginning the learner need to register by completing the application form. In application form the mandatory fields would include name, age, qualification and many more. Now learner may finally start the sophisticated assessment procedure for e-learning.

2 Literature Review

In the past, learners would live at the guru's house and study topics that had practical application this was known as the gurukul method of education. Reading books was only one aspect of learning, where the learners also needed to make connections with the natural world and their daily lives. It wasn't as simple as remembering facts, eating figs, and responding to test questions. Learners of discipline came to the gurukul from various pace of time. In educational paradigm mostly used oral exams in the past, there is one drawback of gurukul system was that learner's were verbally tested one-on-one in the past without being graded or marked. The electronic learning system is replacing the previous educational system.

"Edtech" and "Technology in Education" are not brand-new concepts. The COVID-19 sector with the fastest rate of development is one that has expanded over the past few years. The present focus of edtech is on taking education online and making it available to all learners through multimedia [7]. It is projected that edtech will soon become the "new normal" in education because of how popular it has been over the previous several years.

Universities have implemented changes to better accommodate learners expectations, interests, and requirements in the modern higher education environment [8]. But one of the most pressing concerns confronting universities in this technology age is the integration of cutting-edge e-learning technologies to enhance and assist both teaching and learning [9]. Academics developed a keen interest in the peculiar circumstances brought on by the epidemic and the COVID-19 pandemic's consequences on institutions, educators, trainers, and learners [10].

BN and an artificial neural network look the same, both of these are directed graphs that "perform math" by taking a set of inputs and predicting the results. The key difference between BNs and artificial neural networks is that BNs contain intrinsic meaning underneath their structure. In the past 10 years, BN has been a popular modeling strategy for a variety of statistical issues. A network's vertices and edges are given semantic information in BN, which is a visual analysis of the network. The BN structure provides a plethora of information, but BN evaluation enables us to decide the assessment. The artificial neural network structure gives us nothing about the conditional dependence between the variables.

Intelligent Tutoring System (ITS), is a knowledge-based system, aspires to successfully interchange a human teacher with a machine. The knowledge base model, pedagogical model, learner behavior model, and learner assessment model make up a Bayesian system. The learner evaluation method is described, and some ambiguity is handled by the BN. Based on their responses to questions, the learner assessment representation accurately identifies each learner's knowledge level [11]. A Bayesian area is used in the learner knowledge modeling technique used in ITS. Based on the learner's answers to questions, the real learner model's analytical skills are assessed [12, 13].

Millan et al. [14] investigate and employ a Bayesian network for learner model. This study concentrated on first-degree mathematical problems. Every topic is calculated as a set of four questions, each of which has only one right answer. Questions were split into six degrees of difficulty using Bloom's taxonomy [15, 16] in order to be suited to the learner's level of knowledge.

Applying an inquiry strategy to find the applicant system and learning Bayesian networks as a data source for task estimates of an application system's state have made significant progress [10, 18–20]. As part of this, a knowledge-based optimization basis method for Bayesian networks is being developed.

3 Intelligent Tutoring System

Using the ITS technique, learners may use an e-tutor to assist them to learn relevant subject in desired course. Intelligent Tutoring System (ITS), also called as smart systems, are computer programs that try to deliver the knowledge to learners with rapid and individualized teaching or feedback, generally without the professor or human tutor. That makes the difference in regular lecturing is that ITS can be effective to each and every learner's aspirations. In a classroom, a human trainer is to suit the unique needs of learner [3, 9].

Utilizing a learner phase paradigm, the knowledge acquiring and questioning of a learner are monitored in real time. If you understand them to a some extent, this paradigm enables us to ask them questions and get replies from them. On the basis learner's questions, this model provides an assessment of their performance.

If an individual has attained a particular performance stage, they are qualified to respond to questions from the advanced knowledge level. Similar to this, as learner's progress through the e-learning ITS paradigm, their level of learner knowledge develops. The learner stage evaluation also proposes learning resources that are available through the tutoring module based on the learner's current level of knowledge. The supporting technology is applied in a BN model.

Any ITS design must allow for future system updates. To create a straightforward system, the model need not be completely rebuilt. The intelligent e-learning system architecture is hence made up of specialized, common ITS components as shown in Fig. 2.

The recommended strategy provides a thorough foundation which as specifics for each subject. It contains teaching resources for all course subtopics. A tree topology effective to organize the knowledge base system of model. It is separated as the subtopics, which are then further divided. Each leaf node indicates a different concept.

Each subject contains a diverse group of queries at different levels that is to gauge how well learners understand it. The Pedagogical Model is a tool used by learner's to support their learning. Based on the learner's behavior and knowledge, it offers recommendations and guides the learner. It controls the entire educational process and act as a metaphor for the teaching methodology.

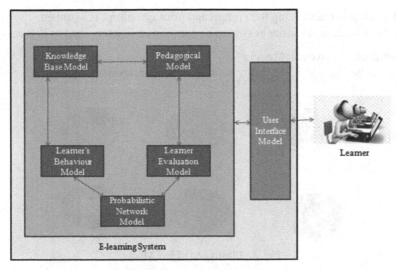

Fig. 2. Intelligent E-Tutoring System

4 Bayesian Network Model

A directed acyclic graph (DAG) plays important role to illustrate a Bayesian network model, which shows the conditional interdependencies among random variables and edges. Edges in the underlying network indicate the relationships between variables and nodes. For node interactions, three levels of information are provided: graphical which is pictorial, functional which is operational, and numerical [17]. At the graphical level, the compulsory connections onto nodes and edges are illustrated. The distributions such as conditional probability and joint probability among the nodes are algebraically stated at the functioning level of specification; however, actual probability placed with a desired node is measured at the numerical phase. Equation 1 illustrates the general premise of Baye's theorem.

$$P(H|e) = \frac{P(e|H) * P(H)}{P(e)} \tag{1}$$

The terms "hypothesis" and "evidence" named for H and e, respectively, and Baye's theorem updates the marginal probability situated along with H depending on a particular unit of proof e. For a stated e, the probability of H is calculated by multiplying the posterior hypothesis for probability distribution P(H|e) by the prior probability P(H). Using Eq. 1, which illustrates the entire calculation used in this attempt to compute every learner of replies inquiries. Implies,

- P(H|e), event H indicates the learner is about to be replied, and e is event indicates that the learner answered to question. To calculate P(H|e), you must first understand the below terms:
- P(e), a learner answering a preceding question.
- P(H), a learner answering the present question.

- P(e|H), a learner answering the current and prior questions, is assumed.
- Stated to this data, a learner answered to questions are determined as P(H|e).

Illustration of Bayesian Model:
As described in Fig. 3, the illustration of a learner response to question.

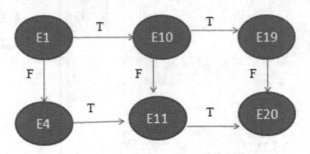

Fig. 3. Illustration of BN Model

Where the nodes are questions that are E1, E10, and so on, and the directed arrows are Probability True (PT) and Probability False (PF), both of which are conditional probabilities, as listed in Table 1 (where CPT is a Conditional Probability Table). The learner's reply to the questions in Fig. 3 should be calculated using Eq. 1: as shown in case 1 and 2.

$$P(E10|E1) = \frac{P(E1|E10) * P(E10)}{P(E1)} \tag{2}$$

Table 1. CPT

Questions	PT	PF
E1	0.5	0.5
E6	0.52	0.48
E10	0.55	0.45

Case 1: It is Initialized in the Current Question

- The learner probability answering the present question is considered to be P(E1|E10), with a probability value of 0.55.
- The chance of a learner answering the present question is 0.55.
- The chance value of the learner answering the preceding question is 0.5.

Case 2: A Preceding Question is Believed in the Computation

- The probability P(E1|E10) of the learner answering the preceding question is considered to be 0.5.
- The possibility of a learner answering the present question is 0.55.
- The chance of the learner answering the preceding question is 0.5.

5 Results and Discussions

When compared to K-nearest and J48, the recommended strategy (Baye's network employing K2) performs better. Tables 2 through 4 compare the two. Table 2 indicates that the J48 decision tree outperformed the K-nearest for 197 learners. The outcome of the ensuing tree structured data identifies the characteristics that have high effect on how learners react to and do not respond to questions, and this prediction is 92.38% right. J48 takes longer than K-nearest to form a tree but has a better accuracy rating. When Baye's network is worked with K2, the learner's best accuracy is 93.00%, while the fraction of unanswered questions is 7.0%. The three techniques under examination surpassed each other accuracy and computing speed while employing a Baye's network with K2. As shown in Tables 3 and 4, the findings for 248 and 1736 number of learners were compared with Baye's network utilizing the K2, KNN, and J48 techniques.

Table 2. 197 Learners

Classified	Classification Algorithms		
	Bayes' network using K2	K-nearest	J48
Correctly classified	93.00%	91.87%	92.38%
Incorrectly classified	7.00%	8.12%	7.61%

Table 3. 248 Learners

Classified	Classification Algorithms		
	Bayes' network using K2	K-nearest	J48
Correctly classified	93.95%	91.12%	93.14%
Incorrectly classified	6.04%	8.87%	6.85%

Table 4. 1736 Learners

Classified	Classification Algorithms		
	Bayes' network using K2	K-nearest	J48
Correctly classified	98.38%	92.87%	94.38%
Incorrectly classified	1.61%	8.12%	6.61%

5.1 Hardware and Software Requirements

Hardware that is used for implementation is

- Standard PC configuration.
- LAN setup having a bandwidth of 10/100 Mbps.

  Software that is used for implementation is:

- Aglets
- Java Development Kit (JDK 1.8 or above)
- Aglets Development Kit (ADK) Aglets-2.0.2.
- Net Beans IDE 8.2.

  Database

- MySQL Server 5.1.
- JDBC/ODBC driver 6.15.
- Operating System
- Operating System (Windows XP or Linux – any flavor)

  It provides the details about the hardware and software requirements used in implementation of this research.

6 Conclusion

In this work, the BN model is compared to numerous AI classification approaches. The e-learning context, a BN serves as the learner's final choice and conclusion-making tool. When given evaluations without knowing their IQ, learners may reply three times faster than they would on an older or system based exam. According to our research, the development of BN-based software modules highlighted the learner's deficiencies in abilities, knowledge, and skills. We used the BN as a model to predict the learner's optimal cognitive phases. As a part of conclusion comparing and assessing three alternative techniques, it is proved that Baye's theorem utilizing K2 is best accurate than the K-nearest and J48 approaches.

References

1. Reigeluth, C.M.: Instructional Theory and Technology for the New Paradigm of Education, RED-32 (1994)

2. Coman, C., Tire, L.G.: Online teaching and learning in higher education during the coronavirus pandemic: learner's' perspective. Sustainability (2020)
3. Kaliwal, R.B., Deshpande, S.L.: Evaluate learner level assessment in intelligent e-learning systems using Bayesian network model. In: Artificial Intelligence and Machine Learning for EDGE Computing (2022)
4. De Bruyn, E., Mostert, E. Van Schoor, A.: Computer-based testing - the ideal tool to assess on the different levels of Bloom's taxonomy. In: 14th International Conference on Interactive Collaborative Learning, 11th International Conference Virtual University, pp. 444–449 (2011)
5. Goguadze, G., Sosnovsky, S., Isotani, S., McLaren, B.M.: Evaluating a Bayesian learner model of decimal misconceptions. In: Proceedings of the 4th International Conference on Educational Data Mining (2011)
6. Natarajan, M.: Evaluation methods for e-learning: an analytical study. Scientific society of advanced research and social change. Int. J. Libr. Inf. Sci. 1(1) (2015)
7. https://nasscom.in/
8. Mislevy, R., Gitomer, D.: The role of probability-based inference in an intelligent tutoring system, CSE Technical report 413, CRESST (1996). On World Wide Web at http://cresst96.cse.ucla.edu/CRESST/pages/reports.htm
9. Alkhuraiji, S., Cheetham, B., Bamasak, O.: Dynamic adaptive mechanism in learning management system based on learning styles. In: 11th IEEE International Conference on Advanced Learning Technologies, pp. 215–217 (2011)
10. Allo, M.D.G.: Is the online learning good in the midst of Covid-19 Pandemic? The case of EFL learners, pp. 1–10 (2020)
11. Chakraborty, B., Sinha, M.: Learner evaluation model using Bayesian network in an intelligent e-learning system. IIOAB J. 7 (2016). ISSN: 0976–3104
12. Khodeir, N., Wanas, N., Hegazy, N., Darwish, N.: Bayesian based learner knowledge modeling in intelligent tutoring systems. In: 6th EEE International Conference on E-Learning in Industrial Electronics (ICELIE) (2012)
13. Anderson, H., Koedinger, M.: Intelligent tutoring goes to school in the Big City. Int. J. Artif. Intell. Educ. 30–43 (1997)
14. Millán, E., Descalço, L., Castillo, G., Oliveira, P., Diogo, S.: Using Bayesian networks to improve knowledge assessment. Comput. Educ. 436–447 (2013)
15. De Bruyn, E., Mostert, E., Van Schoor, A.: Computer-based testing - the ideal tool to assess on the different levels of Bloom's taxonomy. In: 14th International Conference on Interactive Collaborative Learning, ICL 2011, pp. 444–449 (2011)
16. Kaliwal, R.B., Deshpande, S.L.: Efficiency of Bayesian network model for assessment in E-Learning system. In: Int. J. Recent Technol. Eng. (IJRTE) 9(3), 562–566 (2020). ISSN: 2277–3878 (Online)
17. Kaliwal, R.B., Deshpande, S.L.: Design of intelligent e-learning assessment framework using Bayesian belief network. J. Eng. Educ. Transf. 34 (2021). eISSN 2394–1707
18. Nakayama, M., Mutsuura, K., Yamamoto, H.: Contributions of learner's assessment of reflections on the prediction of learning performance. In: 17th IEEE International Conference on Information Technology Based Higher Education and Training (2018)
19. Askari, M.B.A., Ahsaee, M.G.: Bayesian network structure learning based on cuckoo search algorithm. In: 6th Iranian Joint Congress on Fuzzy and Intelligent Systems (2018)
20. Pratiwi, O.N., Syukriyah, Y.: Question classification for e-learning using machine learning approach. In: International Conference on ICT for Smart Society (ICISS) (2020)

Where You Think Stock Takes with the Linear Regression Model

Bharat S. Rawal[1]([⊠]), William Sharpe[2], Elizabeth Moseng[2], and Andre Galustian[2]

[1] Grambling State University, Grambling, LA 71245, USA
rawalb@gram.edu
[2] Capitol Technology University, Laurel, MD 20708, USA
{wlsharpe,emmoseng,agalustian}@captechu.edu

Abstract. This paper seeks to analyze and predict the course of Mastercard stock using three different Python libraries: SciKit Learn, XGBoost, and TensorFlow. This paper details information regarding machine learning algorithms and the linear regression model in particular. The paper presents the results of looking through the data and comparing some companies' results with one another. Our study showed that leaner regression results with Scikit, XGBoost and TensorFlow library provide very high accuracy. The confident prediction for lower values, not to say the small increase in deviation for higher values was any worse.

Keywords: Mastercard · stock · XGBoost · TensorFlow · Python · data science · linear regression

1 Introduction

The stock market helps firms raise money to sustain their operations by selling stock shares while also generating and preserving wealth for individual investors. Nevertheless, the stock market has risks, and investors are continually looking for ways to reduce those risks while increasing returns.

News, such as public news and social media, can impact the process of stocks. Deep learning algorithms can be used for market stock prediction using this information as data sources. The time Series Model uses historical data on stocks to predict future stock market trends. Time series work mainly by using huge amounts of data, observing past changes, and using that to predict future changes. Deep Learning Models use a recurrent neural network to facilitate the modeling of time series data. Sentiment from stock-related data in social media is analyzed and added to build a model predicting future trends. Subjective, emotional factors, such as what is read in the news, can influence investors, and interfere with investment decisions. Deep learning essentially analyzes that news and constructs a trend prediction model with those sentiments in mind [1, 7].

To conclude, the changes in the stock market play an important role in the country's economic trends. Short-term and long-term trend forecasting is a hot topic and concern for investors in the market.

People are eager to try new methods and tools to predict stocks and reduce risk. More effective forecasting techniques and technologies lead to better outcomes, more precise forecasts, and more profits.

The paper discusses various predictive models for a traded stock, it was apparent that multiple options should be assessed for something so volatile. The research was undertaken to find an appropriate stock to assess and the different models to compare for assessing it. Multiple models showed promising results and applications for these models are extrapolated.

Machine learning can be a powerful tool when analyzing different data sets. It can accurately notice trends and patterns and use this information to attempt to predict either future trends or understand what the data itself is. Machine learning can be as advanced as handwriting detection or as simple as predicting the end of a word (as one might encounter when using a word. It uses already given data and utilizes it to the best of its ability [6].

This experiment aimed to get machine learning to predict future stock prices based on previously released numbers. The data was gathered from Kaggle.com, which is a site commonly used for gathering large amounts of data for the purpose of data mining [4, 5].

Our contribution.

1. We conducted a comprehensive literature review.
2. We conducted several experiments using Python libraries to predict stock prices.
3. The three models are compared using data pulled live via multiple methods, and the research is made mutable enough to apply to other stock prices.

The following is how the rest of the paper is structured: The introduction is covered in Sect. 1, and the related work is covered in Sect. 2. Then, Sect. 3 is about experiments. Finally, Sect. 4 concludes the research paper.

2 Related Works

For a nation, the financial system is significant and has become more so over time. The stock market may be dangerous, and investors are constantly looking for strategies to lower those risks and boost earnings.

To begin, the scale on which RNN can be applied is not limited to a single person forecasting stock prices. The observation and analysis of a system utilizing periodic measurements to monitor changes to engineering structures such as buildings and bridges are known as structural health monitoring (SHM) [19]. Researching new, more efficient, and innovative methods of SHM has exploded in popularity in the civil engineering field, especially using a method called "unsupervised learning" with data acquired from the field. However, this currently only focuses on detecting damage in simple structures. A novel takes on an unsupervised learning framework t uses a hybrid network of neural networks and long short-term memory to detect damage in large-scale complex structures. Tests with this framework resulted in a successful structure health diagnosis accuracy of 93% and 85% for damage detection and localization, respectively. In other words, using RNN to detect damage to infrastructure and where that damage is located [14].

We know that RNN can be used to predict things over time, but what about predicting time itself? People experience time differently, especially the young and old, and using RNN we can simulate an internal clock like what would be found in people. It works by using RNN to simulate a group of neurons like you would find in a brain. We start with a simple RNN. Recall that a recurrent neural network is comprised of four layers: input, hidden, context, and output. The input layer works as a buffer for the signal, the signal is transformed at the hidden layer as units interact without artificial neurons. The activity is recorded in the context layer and then reinjected into the hidden layer. Finally, the output layer sums up the signals sent to it. This is but one possible model for judging time using RNN [15].

Different types of machine learning methods and models get good results, what if we combined them? To improve the performance of prediction over time models, or time series forecasting, we combine the characteristics of a Graph Convolutional Network (GCN) and a Bidirectional Long Short-Term Memory network (BiLSTM). The combined approach has better performance than the two separately and with a lower error percentage across the metrics used. The combined model used two models trained in each separately, then generates a new model from their outputs. It then uses the results of that as input over and over for training until it makes its prediction [16].

Using recurrent neural networks to predict prices is fine and all, but what about using them to predict inflation? Inflation is bad news for a country's economy, and it is only going up these days. This affects the financial sector and being able to predict inflation helps investors properly adjust their asset holdings, firms adjust their prices, and so on. Long short-term memory model (LTSM) is great for this for four reasons: one, LTSMs are flexible. Two, under conditions with even mild regularity LTSMs can give fairly accurate results. Three, LTSMs were developed specifically for sequential data analysis. Four, new optimization routines made training neural networks much easier. The result was an improved performance of the NN model across all tables [17].

A daring leap - the predictive capabilities of RNN can be used for optimization and reservoir management. Oil wells, water wells, is it worth digging here? Surprisingly, RNN may be used to answer this. A proxy model is developed to predict well-by-well oil and water rates, given time and bottom-hole pressure schedules. It enables an estimation of values needed for overall optimization. First, the good rates are predicted using LTSM, then a CNN is used to generate a 3D oil-water flow simulation [18].

In addition to everything that neural networks may be used to anticipate, what about earthquakes and how resilient are buildings during them? Even predicting diseases such as Alzheimer [11, 12, 20]. The plan is to train the network with a small number of samples by employing a partitioning approach. Neural networks and probability techniques are used to produce a novel seismic analysis tool. The models developed fall under one of two categories, 'white box' and 'black box.' White box models are based on physical laws and are usually mechanical models while black boxes are not based on any previous knowledge about the structural system. Previously, simple neural networks could not handle dealing with nonlinear data, like structure behavior during an earthquake, but with the development of deep learning, the capacity of NNs has been greatly improved. There are some limits to this but to get around them, prior data of the structure during a quake is added to help describe the nonlinear behavior [13].

Machine learning has many applications and a particularly big one is stock price prediction. The stock market is volatile, dynamic, and nonlinear, and making accurate price predictions is challenging. Macro and micro factors, politics, economic factors, unexpected events, and company performance can all influence prices. But at the same time, there is plenty of data to find patterns in, which means it's possible to use analytic techniques to identify and predict trends. To write an algorithm to take in data, learn, and predict future stock prices, there are several methods we can use, and a few are highlighted below [6, 8].

Long Short-Term Memory, or LTSM for short, is a deep learning technique developed to deal with the vanishing gradients problem encountered in long sequences. In particular, it handles sequential data such as time and text. The update gate, forget gate, and output gate are the three primary components of LTSM. The output gate chooses how much data to output as activations to the following layer, while the update and forget gates choose whether each memory cell's component is updated. Because it can recognize long-term dependencies in sequential data, LTSM is well suited for jobs like predicting stock prices [14].

The Moving Average technique is a second option. The anticipated value is the mean of the preceding timestep(N) values. We define the current adjusted closing price as the meaning of the preceding N days' adjusted closing price [14].

A third method of machine learning is the Recurrent Neural Network (RNN) [10]. It is a common deep-learning technique used for pattern recognition and takes into account how data can change over time. Time-series data, like stock prices, are a common topic for its use. RNNs are like short term memory portions of the brain, remembering recent memories and creating context. Over time, they create a feedback loop that preserves short-term and long-term memory over time [6–8]. These are but a few types of machine learning, but we will not be using them for this paper.

A common method of machine learning and the one we will be using for this paper is Linear regression. This version of machine learning is a linear approach to modeling the relationship between one or more input variables and a single output variable. A simple linear regression equation is the line equation:

$$y = mx + b \tag{1}$$

where m is the slope/gradient of the polynomial of the line y (predict coefficient) and b is the intercept of the line (bias coefficient). Linear regression is excellent when it comes to numbers, which is what we need for this paper. Part of the process is finding coefficients, essentially the degree to which the line slopes upwards or downwards. The goal with these is to find such coefficients that the difference between each point in the dataset with its corresponding predicted value is minimal.

A stock's closing price and date are the parameters we particularly want for our linear regression model and the close price is especially important for traders. The goal is to predict as accurately as possible with as few errors as possible. The linear regression model is used to train a function to form a predictive model from a data set of x and y values, prices, and time essentially. After being trained, if you want to predict x from an unknown y, this function can be used [9].

3 Experiments

3.1 Experiment-I

The scope of this experiment is to create a model to assess and predict a stock price over time. This proposal allowed freedom of choice for the stock in question, the method of data retrieval, and the method of prediction, provided the latter used machine learning.

3.1.1 Scope

- Training on an offline dataset
- Retrieving data from an API
- Retrieving data via web scraping
- Short- and long-term prediction
- In-application visualization

In addition to these components, data retrieval via Python library was also implemented for reasons to be explained further.

3.1.2 XGBoost

Methodology
Initial decision making regarded the choice of stock. After a cursory search of datasets on the website Kaggle to pull from, Mastercard seemed to have a valuable DataFrame to work with [1]. This was because having an initial, offline dataset to pull from would allow the paper to focus initially on manipulating and predicting data as the main focus before concerning itself with how to collect the data. Next, sources of machine learning were to be identified. The three primary candidates that were decided upon were SciKit Learn's linear regression model, SGBoost, and Tensorflow.

3.1.3 XGBoost

XGBoost offered a similar level of familiarity to the researcher. It offers a suite of automated optimizations within ranges to choose from, though the decision was made to have it optimized between a decision tree and a linear regression algorithm. It was not apparent at the time of research, but its linear regression algorithm is markedly similar to that of SKLearn's.

3.1.4 TensorFlow

The researcher had the least familiarity with Tensorflow, save for machine learning in the context of image generation in another course. Tensorflow was similar to XGBoost in its automated tuning, though required additional constraints to define the bounds of this tuning.

All three methods settled on linear regression algorithms, with a predetermined 80–20 train-test split. In the case of XGBoost, given a range of 1–20 scalars, the algorithm found between 16 and 18 scalars appropriate, depending on the date range of the collected data. It also consistently found that targeting squared log error was more optimized than squared error alone.

In the instance of Tensorflow, a predefined 10 epochs were decided upon to minimize training loss and to speed up testing time. Additional research into an appropriate optimizer found Adam's optimization to be the best fit for his research.

After this, data collection was to be focused on. While the model worked on static data, the initial proposal promised live data as well. While API data was readily available for a large fee, scraping initially proved far more promising. Though most websites feature page layouts designed to deter scraping, the program could successfully pull from certain pages at any time during the day and apply the current stock price to the model. As [3], refers to the target page used for scraping in the current iteration of the model.

However, this approach did not account for historical data. For that, the appropriate approach was determined to be the finance Python library. This had the advantage of no paywall, immediate results, and any timeframe requested. From what it appears, the data retrieved for [1] and [2] both used this method if the names of the columns are any indication.

3.1.5 SciKit Learn

SciKit Learn, hereafter referred to as SKLearn, is the library the researcher is most familiar with from previous coursework. While it offers little in the way of automated optimization, there are fewer parameters to concern oneself with while tuning.

Figure 1, is SKLearn and it shows an extraordinary $>.9999$ R^2 value. Given that a targeted R^2 value in statistics is $>.9$ and $>.7$ in finance, a number this high suggests something has gone awry. And yet, graphical analysis of the 850 test points suggests an impressive level of correlation between given test data and its predicted result. The mean squared error was below 1×10^{-5}, while the mean absolute error was below 1×10^{-2}. As to be expected given the data, the higher concentration of lower stock prices conferred far more.

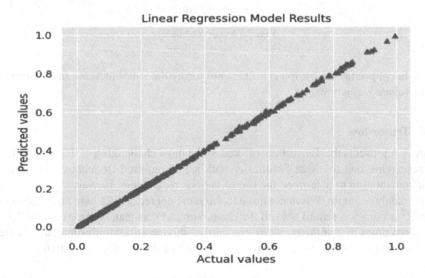

Fig. 1. SciKit Learn Model

The confident prediction for lower values, not to say the small increase in deviation for higher values was any worse.

3.1.6 XGBoost

Figure 2, represent XGBoost found its optimal results between 16 and 19 decision trees with the decision tree approach, but linear regression fielded superior results. Once targeting the squared-log error, the R^2 value was $>.9999$, identical as far as significant figures went to that of SKLearn's result. The mean squared and meant absolute errors were also identical at 4.98×10^{-6} and 1.30×10^{-3}, respectively. The graph shows similar if not greater confidence with lower values, though less at higher stock values.

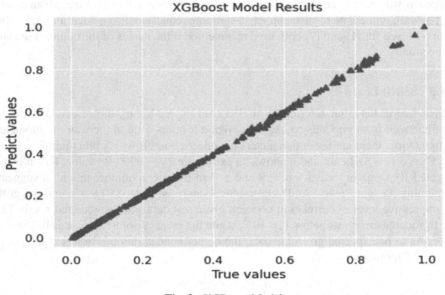

Fig. 2. XGBoost Model

confident prediction for lower values, not to say the small increase in deviation for higher values was any worse.

3.1.7 Tensorflow

Figure 3, represents the Tensorflow offered as the most challenging of the three options. The researcher had the least familiarity with it and required frequent consultation of the documentation to determine the use of various parameters. However, the results are still markedly accurate. While not quite to the same degree as SKLearn and XGBoost, a $.9996\ R^2$ accuracy is remarkable all the same. Similarly, a mean squared error of 1.82×10^{-5} is ten times that of the previous two entries, though still infinitesimal, as is a mean absolute error of 2.61×10^{-3}, which is double that of the previous two strategies.

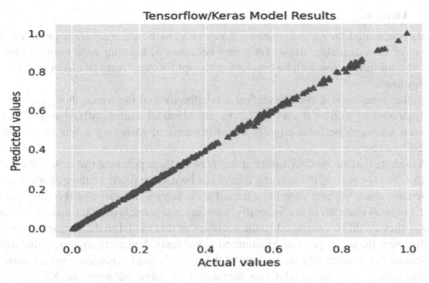

Fig. 3. Tensorflow

Additionally, despite iterating over the dataset ten times, the training loss was less than 0.012. This allows more leeway for further epochs, though this would likely make overtraining concerns worse. We can see the model error in Fig. 4.

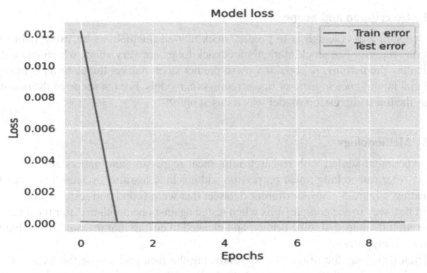

Fig. 4. Model loss

3.1.8 Analysis

The data presented shows clear statistical anomalies in the sheer accuracy provided. The amount of data available allows for many iterations of training even under an 80–20 split. Should further research be conducted, the split would likely be closer to 60–40 or perhaps lower.

Of the three models, the Tensorflow model performed the worst, though it remains highly accurate. XGBoost and SKLearn are identical numerically, but graphically SKLearn seems to perform slightly better in terms of assigning a line of best fit to the testing accuracy.

Assuming that the models are accurate, there are three potential use cases for a model like this. First of which, the existing model can be used to predict future changes to the Mastercard stock without extreme external influence on the value of the stock, as the initial proposal intended to do. Secondly, were any new models to be trained on this same dataset, they could be compared to the accuracy of this model to determine their value. Finally, were the stock price of Mastercard to suddenly deviate from anticipated trends that this model predicts, the magnitude of these trends can be assessed and recorded.

The accuracy of this model was found to be highest between the XGBoost and Tensorflow models, which can predict the closing value of a Mastercard stock daily with astonishing accuracy. However, such accuracy calls into concern the possibility of model overtraining, and when fed different data or perhaps a different stock altogether, may produce far less accurate results.

3.2 Experiment-II

3.2.1 Description and Scope

The scope of this research is to predict stock market fluctuations by using published company reports. The stock market's feedback loops are very short, which can aid in confirming predictions. A popular way to predict stock market fluctuations is through Artificial Intelligence logistic or linear regression models. For the scope of the research paper, the linear regression model was focused on [9].

3.2.2 Methodology

The experiment started with research into linear regression and understanding how it works. After researching linear regression and machine learning, a dataset was needed for testing. Figure 5, shows different datasets that were found and tested so that there would be a way to see comparisons when tested against one another. After the data was gathered, it then needed to be pruned and cleaned to ensure that it would be usable for further testing purposes.

Then there was the initial step of analyzing the data and seeing the trends of the previous years. The closing prices were looked at and compared to one another, as were the volumes.

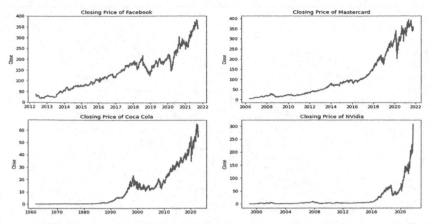

Fig. 5. Closing prices Facebook, Mastercard, Coca-Cola, and Nvidia Stocks

Then the next step was viewing the moving averages of the different companies' stocks throughout their run. This was so that one could potentially see a less jagged graph, as the initial line graphs of the closing prices varied quite a lot.

Figure 6, shows the course of trade volume of those four companies.

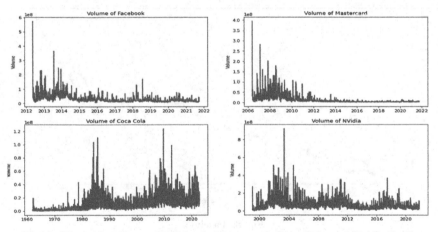

Fig. 6. The trade volume of Facebook, Mastercard, Coca-Cola, and Nvidia Stock

Then the next step was viewing the moving averages of the different companies' stocks throughout their run. This was so that one could potentially see a less jagged graph, as the initial line graphs of the closing prices varied quite a lot.

Figure 7 Representing the moving average volume of stocks, we can notice that there is continuous growth over the year by year.

Then some computation was required to find the daily return of the stocks, as this can be deemed important for those looking into stocks.

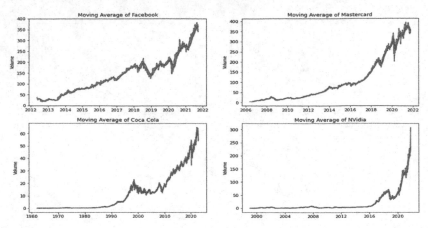

Fig. 7. Moving average volume of Facebook, Mastercard, Coca-Cola, and Nvidia Stocks

And then we have the predicted trends shown on a linear map for each company. Below is the linear map for Facebook. Figures 8, 9, and 10, shows the linear map for Facebook, MasterCard, and CocaCola respectively.

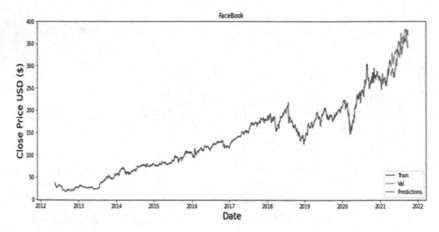

Fig. 8. Facebook.

Figure 9 is the linear map for MasterCard.

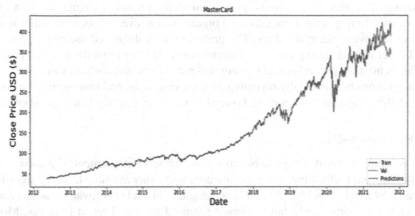

Fig. 9. MasterCard.

Figure 10 is the linear map for Coca-Cola.

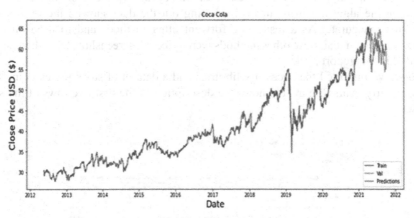

Fig. 10. Coca-Cola.

3.2.3 Analysis

While we can find data, at first it was difficult to see how everything would compare to one another. The initial testing with linear regression made me nervous as some of the scores were looking very confident in some areas while being wildly incorrect in others [9].

All of the predicted data in the new section started below the previous day's closing prices, which was consistent between the models. With further inspection of the models, some would seem to be closer to the actual data when shifted to start with the closing price of the model.

We can better comprehend how the data manifested itself after being able to see the data with the plots. There are frequent peaks and dips in comparable locations when comparing the correct values to the prediction, demonstrating a comprehension of the data. The resulting graphs' trends for all 4 organizations revealed commonalities in their behavior relative to the real values. The graphs reliably displayed the major peaks and dips, further demonstrating how the program was able to forecast future stock prices.

Throughout the process, we can better understand how data behaved with itself, seeing the relations between daily revenue vs the closing costs, and how having the correct data to balance against is important. Overall, it was a very strong learning experience.

3.3 Experiment-III

For this setup, we used a Jupiter Notebook as our test environment. We chose linear regression as our method but also experimented with other machine learning algorithms such as LTSM and RNN [10]. Attempts at using LTSM lead to software issues as certain libraries would consistently fail to import required tools and result in errors. Models could not be established, alternative platforms would not import datasets at all, and eventually, we dropped LTSM as a method.

Another method used was RNN. This method succeeded but the calculation process made our computer very hot, with the fan running at full tilt. We found this concerning and when the algorithm was finished, plotting out the data showed the results were somewhat inaccurate. As a result, we forwent other methods and focused on linear regression. Given that those other methods were rejected, screenshots from them are not included in this report [10].

First, we imported the necessary libraries and a dataset of stock prices going back roughly thirty years. Figure 11 shows the description of the first five rows of the stock dataset.

In [53]: `dataset = pd.read_csv('stock_data.csv')`

`dfStock = dataset`
`dfStock.head()`

Out [53]:

	Date	Open	High	Low	Close	Volume	Openint	Stock
0	1984-09-07	0.42388	0.42902	0.41874	0.42388	23220030	0	AAPL
1	1984-09-10	0.42388	0.42516	0.41366	0.42134	18022532	0	AAPL
2	1984-09-11	0.42516	0.43668	0.42516	0.42902	42498199	0	AAPL
3	1984-09-12	0.42902	0.43157	0.41618	0.41618	37125801	0	AAPL
4	1984-09-13	0.43927	0.44052	0.43927	0.43927	57822062	0	AAPL

In [54]: `dfStock.tail()`

Out [54]:

	Date	Open	High	Low	Close	Volume	Openint	Stock
19581	2017-11-06	178.56	180.450	178.310	180.17	13275078	0	FB
19582	2017-11-07	180.50	180.748	179.403	180.25	12903836	0	FB
19583	2017-11-08	179.79	180.360	179.110	179.56	10467606	0	FB
19584	2017-11-09	178.31	179.400	177.090	179.30	12602188	0	FB
19585	2017-11-10	178.35	179.100	177.960	178.46	11060355	0	FB

In [55]: `dfStock.shape`

Out [55]: `(19586, 8)`

Fig. 11. The description of the first five rows of the stock dataset

Then we examined the dataset and dropped unnecessary columns. Among the data columns is the "close" forecast, which is what we want to predict.

Figure 12 and 13 reflects the X and Y variables, representing date and price respectively, for training and testing are established and initialized. The X variable is assigned a dataset of opening prices, highs, lows, and volume of stocks and the Y variable is assigned the closing price. Next, we import train_test_split from sklearn.model_selection and split our variables to train using one set of X and Y, and test using the other.

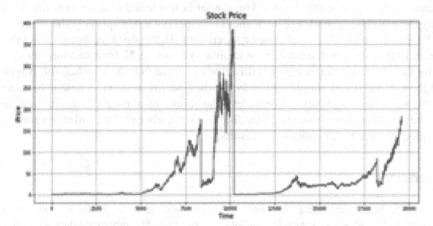

Fig. 12. Test split for Sklearn model

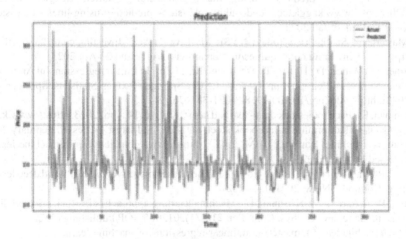

Fig. 13. Prediction of price over time

4 Conclusion

Based on a preliminary trial run, it may be concluded that the nation's economic patterns are significantly influenced by movements in the stock market. Market investors are quite interested in and concerned about both short- and long-term trend forecasts.

We were able to gain a deeper comprehension of data functioning and machine learning's predictive potential via experiment II. The ideal approach to collect and present the data was determined by trial and error, but after additional research and analysis, definitive findings were obtained that may be applied to future possible stock market forecasts. Before diving straight into linear regression models or other forms of machine learning, it is highly advised to get a feel for the data and work with it for a fair amount of time. This way, one can already know what is inside the massive amounts of data being input and have an idea of what should be spat out when applying the models.

Despite the algorithm's outcome in experiment III, the stock market is vulnerable to sudden, dramatic shifts that can occur with little to no notice. Notwithstanding, those who are looking to make money can find this kind of approach to be very helpful. Anybody looking to trade stocks should definitely use the linear regression technique because of its almost flawless accuracy. Nevertheless, the enormous amount of data in the dataset was the source of these findings. In the future, a similarly rich data collection should be provided in order to get comparable results.

References

1. Author, Mastercard Data Set with Day Columns 2006 to 2010, Kaggle, 29 January 2023. https://www.kaggle.com/datasets/rashmithreddy/mastercard-data-set-with-day-columns-2006-to-2010. Accessed 29 Jan 2023
2. Kohli, N.: Stock prediction using linear regression - starter, Kaggle, 20 August 2020. https://www.kaggle.com/code/nikhilkohli/stock-prediction-using-linear-regression-starter. Accessed 29 Jan 2023
3. "MasterCard Stock Price Today: NYSE Ma Live Ticker," Investing.com, 23 April 2023. https://www.investing.com/equities/mastercard-cl-a. Accessed 23 Apr 2023
4. James, G., Witten, D., Hastie, T., Tibshirani, R., Taylor, J.: Linear regression. In: An Introduction to Statistical Learning, pp. 69–134. LNCS, Springer Texts in Statistics. Springer, Cham (2023). https://doi.org/10.1007/978-3-031-38747-0_3
5. Rahman, K.: Facebook stock data - live and latest. Kaggle, 14 April 2023. https://www.kaggle.com/datasets/kalilurrahman/facebook-stock-data-live-and-latest. Accessed February 2023
6. What is machine learning? IBM. (n.d.). https://www.ibm.com/topics/machine-learning. Accessed February 2023
7. Li, J.: Research on market stock index prediction based on network security and deep learning. Secur. Commun. Netw. **2021**, 1–8 (2021)
8. Soni, P., Tewari, Y., & Krishnan, D.: Machine learning approaches in stock price prediction: a systematic review. J. Phys. Conf. Ser. **2161**(1), 012065. IOP Publishing (2022)
9. https://machinelearningmastery.com/linear-regression-for-machine-learning/
10. https://stanford.edu/~shervine/teaching/cs-230/cheatsheet-recurrent-neural-networks
11. Yu, Z., Wang, K., Wan, Z., Xie, S., Lv, Z.: Popular deep learning algorithms for disease prediction: a review. Clust. Comput. **26**(2), 1231–1251 (2023)
12. Warren, S.L., Moustafa, A.A.: Functional magnetic resonance imaging, deep learning, and Alzheimer's disease: a systematic review. J. Neuroimaging **33**(1), 5–18 (2023)
13. Wang, T., Li, H., Noori, M., Ghiasi, R., Kuok, S.C., Altabey, W.A.: Seismic response prediction of structures based on Runge-Kutta recurrent neural network with prior knowledge. Eng. Struct. **279**, 115576 (2023). prediction-6c1994da8001

14. Eltouny, K.A., Xiao, L.: Large-scale structural health monitoring using composite recurrent neural networks and grid environments. Comput.-Aided Civ. Infrastruct. Eng. **38**(3), 271–287 (2023). Machine Learning Techniques Applied to Stock Price Prediction, https://towardsda tascience.com/machine-learning-techniques-applied-to-stock-price

15. Hallez, Q., Mermillod, M., Droit-Volet, S.: Cognitive and plastic recurrent neural network clock model for the judgment of time and its variations. Sci. Rep. **13**(1), 3852 (2023)

16. Lazcano, A., Herrera, P.J., Monge, M.: A combined model based on recurrent neural networks and graph convolutional networks for financial time series forecasting. Mathematics **11**(1), 224 (2023)

17. Almosova, A., Andresen, N.: Nonlinear inflation forecasting with recurrent neural networks. J. Forecast. **42**(2), 240–259 (2023)

18. Kim, Y.D., Durlofsky, L.J.: Convolutional–recurrent neural network proxy for robust optimization and closed-loop reservoir management. Comput. Geosci. **27**(2), 179–202 (2023)

19. Structural Health Monitoring with bolt load cells | BoltSafe. https://boltsafe.com/structural-health-monitoring/

20. Eltouny, K.A., Liang, X.: Large-scale structural health monitoring using composite recurrent neural networks and grid environments. Comput. Aided Civ. Infrastruct. Eng. **38**(3), 271–287 (2023)

Analysis of Parent with Fine Tuned Large Language Model

Vaishali Baviskar[1]([✉]) [iD], Shrinidhi Shedbalkar[1] [iD], Varun More[1] [iD],
Sagar Waghmare[1] [iD], Yash Wafekar[1] [iD], and Madhushi Verma[2] [iD]

[1] G H Raisoni College of Engineering and Management, Pune, India
vaishali.baviskar@raisoni.net
[2] Bennett University, Greater Noida, India

Abstract. This paper offers a comparative examination of two cuttingedge large language models, Guanaco and Llama, within the realm of natural language comprehension and generation tasks. Guanaco is a model fine-tuned on the open-source LLM Llama itself using Qlora, while Llama is trained on a combination of proprietary and open-source datasets. The assessment encompasses their performance on benchmarks like Massively Multitask Language Understanding (MMLU), Vicuna, and ARC. MMLU benchmark is a comprehensive evaluation of large language models' capabilities on a wide range of tasks, including summarization, question answering, and natural language inference. ELO rating is a dynamic rating system that calculates the relative skill levels of players in zero-sum games, taking into account the outcome of each game. The abstraction and reasoning corpus (ARC) LLM benchmark is a set of tasks that are designed to evaluate the ability of large language models (LLMs) to reason and solve problems using only their core knowledge. The tasks are based on simple abstract concepts, such as objects, goal states, counting, and basic geometry. It demonstrates that Guanaco achieves strong performance on the MMLU benchmark, even outperforming Llama on the ARC benchmark. On the other hand, Llama excels on the Vicuna benchmark, surpassing Guanaco fine-tuned on open-source data. In a qualitative analysis, both models exhibit strengths and weaknesses. Guanaco showcases the ability to demonstrate theory of mind capabilities, whereas Llama sometimes generates inaccurate or unreliable responses in specific scenarios. Overall, this study sheds light on the performance and attributes of Guanaco and Llama, emphasizing their potential in various language comprehension and generation tasks.

Keywords: Large language model · MMLU · Qlora · LLM · Guanaco · Llama

1 Introduction

In the domain of artificial intelligence and natural language processing, large language models have emerged as groundbreaking innovations, fundamentally re shaping the way machines engage with human language. These models equipped with billions of parameters and driven by deep learning frameworks, have opened up new possibilities across a

D. Garg et al. (Eds.): IACC 2023, CCIS 2053, pp. 258–266, 2024.
https://doi.org/10.1007/978-3-031-56700-1_21

variety of applications, from generating text and translating languages to analyzing sentiments and answering questions. In the dynamic landscape of AI research, open-source models like GPT4ALL's ggml models and Facebook's Llama model offer capabilities such as question answering, natural language processing, text generation, and text summarization. Their open-source nature provides ample opportunities for customization and finetuning to suit specific needs. Various techniques have been used for fine-tuning these models, with Low Rank Adaptation (LoRa) being a popular method that involves freezing the weights of the trained models and incorporate trainable rank decomposition matrices into the transformer architecture's many layers. Due to this, there are much fewer trainable parameters for downstream activities. However, in recent months, a novel fine-tuning approach called Qlora has emerged. Qlora efficiently reduces memory usage to the extent that a 65-billion parameter model can be fine-tuned just on one 48 GB GPU while ensuring complete 16- bit fine-tuning productivity. Qlora achieves this by propagating gradients into Low-Rank Adapters (LoRA) through a frozen, 4-bit quantized pre-trained language model. As a result, the average memory requirements for fine-tuning a 65-billion parameter model are reduced from over 780 GB of GPU memory to less than 48 GB, without compromising runtime or predictive performance when compared to a fully fine-tuned 16-bit model [1, 2, 4, 5].

The major contribution of this paper is to conduct a thorough analysis of two prominent large language models. The foundational model is Facebook's Llama, and the subsequent model is Guanaco, which underwent fine-tuning using Qlora, a notable commercial approach. Our investigation aims to uncover the unique characteristics, capabilities, and idiosyncrasies that distinguish these models. By examining their architectures, training methodologies, and real-world performance, Our goal is to offer a thorough insight into both the strengths and limitations of these approaches, emphasizing the benefits of Qlora training compared to conventional models [1, 4, 5].

This paper is structured as follows, with Sect. 2 discussing the review of conventional works along with suitable problems. Following this, Sect. 3 presents an overview about the large language models, benchmark tests and relevant descriptions. The datasets used are discussed in Sect. 4. Section 5 shows the results and finally, the entire study is summarized in Sect. 6 with further suggestions.

2 Literature Survey

In this review of existing literature, we deeply explore QLORA, an innovative technique designed to address the resource constraints associated with training and fine-tuning extremely large language models. The primary focus of this examination is on the components of QLORA and its implications within the research community [1].

Fine-tuning of massive language models is essential for tailoring them to specific tasks. Nevertheless, this process can be computationally demanding and memory-intensive. The introduction of the QLORA technique by the research team presents a promising solution, allowing the fine-tuning of a massive 65- billion-parameter model can operate on a single 48GB GPU, and it can sustain optimal performance for 16-bit fine-tuning tasks. This achievement represents a significant breakthrough in the field, as it democratically grants access to cutting-edge language models [1].

A notable achievement: The Guanaco model family: One of the most remarkable outcomes of QLORA is the emergence of the Guanaco model family. This family not only pushes the boundaries of previous language models but also surpasses all previously disclosed models on the Vicuna benchmark. Achieving a 99.3% performance level comparable to ChatGPT on this benchmark serves as a testament to the effectiveness of the QLORA technique. Impressively, fine- tuning the Guanaco models requires just 24 h on only one GPU, making them attainable to a broader research community [6].

The paper in question introduces an innovative approach known as Low-Rank Adaptation (LoRA), which aims to address the constraints associated with full fine-tuning in large-scale language models like GPT-3 175B. This literature review's purpose is to provide an overview of the fundamental concepts, methodologies, and discoveries presented in the paper, emphasizing the importance of LoRA within the field of Natural Language Processing (NLP) [2, 4].

The foundation of LoRA is rooted in the concept of pre-training on extensive general-domain datasets, followed by fine-tuning for specific tasks in a particular domain. As the size of models increases, fine-tuning becomes increasingly computationally expensive, particularly with models like GPT-3 175B, which possess an immense number of parameters. Conventional fine-tuning methods involve retraining all model parameters, resulting in high memory and computational demands. In response to this challenge, the authors introduce LoRA as a more efficient alternative [2].

LoRA involves the immobilization of pre-trained model weights and the insertion of trainable rank decomposition matrices into each layer of the transformer architecture. This procedure substantially decreases the count of trainable parameters for subsequent tasks, all the while preserving or potentially improving model performance. The fundamental stages of LoRA are outlined as follows: [2, 3]

1. Keep the weights of the pre-trained model fixed.
2. Incorporate trainable rank decomposition matrices into each layer.
3. Only modify the rank decomposition matrices during the adaptation process.

3 Methodology

Our analysis revealed the following key findings:

3.1 Massive Multitask Language Understanding (MMLU)

MMLU which stands for Massive Multitask Language Understanding, represents a novel benchmark meticulously designed to gauge the extent of knowledge acquired during the pretraining phase. It does so by assessing models exclusively in zero-shot and few-shot contexts, thereby introducing a more challenging evaluation approach that closely resembles the way we assess human capabilities. This benchmark encompasses a different array of 57 subjects, spanning science, technology, engineering management, the humanities, the social sciences, and more. The difficulty levels of the benchmark vary from basic to highly advanced, and it assess both general real world knowledge and problem-solving proficiency. The subjects encompass not only conventional domains like mathematics and history but also delve into specialized areas such as law and ethics.

The benchmark's extensive coverage and depth make it exceptionally well-suited for pinpointing the limitations or gaps in a model's knowledge.

The scores are then derived by averaging the model's score across the tests. For example, on the question answering tasks in the MMLU benchmark, humans typically achieve F1 scores of around 90. This suggests that an average human would likely score in the 80s or 90s on the MMLU benchmark overall.

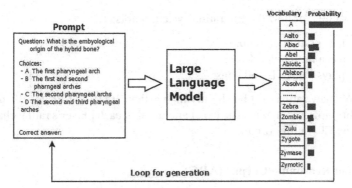

Fig. 1. MMLU Architecture for Benchmark Test

We have two main ways to get information out of a model to evaluate it:

– get the probabilities that some specific tokens groups are continuations of the prompt and compare these probabilities together for our predefined possible choices as mentioned in the Fig. 1

– get a text generation from the model (by repeatedly selecting tokens as we have seen in Fig. 1) and compare these text generations to the texts of various predefined possible choices.

3.2 Elo Rating: -(Vicuna Benchmark)

The Elo rating system, conceived by Arpad Elo, a physics professor of Hungarian-American origin, is a method employed to assess the relative skill levels of participants in competitive games characterized by a zero-sum outcome, such as chess. Elo designed this system as an enhanced replacement for the earlier Harkness system used in chess. Additionally, the Elo system has found applications as a rating method in a wide range of activities, including Soccer, American football, baseball, basketball, billiards, ping pong, assorted board games, esports, and, in more recent times, extensive language models. In Eq. 1, if player X possess a rating denoted as Rx and player Y a rating denoted as Ry (Assumed values of Rx and Ry are equal at the beginning of the test), the precise formulation employing the logarithmic curve with a base of 10, governing the probability of player X emerging victorious is as follows:

$$E_X = \frac{1}{1 + 10^{(R_Y - R_X)}/400} \tag{1}$$

Using the collected data, we compute the Elo ratings of the models here put the main results in the Table 1.

In Eq. 2, the players' ratings can undergo linear updates following each encounter. Assuming player X, with a rating denoted as Rx, was anticipated to achieve Ex points but actually scored Sx points, the formula for adjusting that player's rating is

$$R'_X = R_X + K.(S_X - E_X) \tag{2}$$

Here is an example of how the Elo rating system works:

- Player A has a rating of 1000.
- Player B has a rating of 900.
- Player A plays Player B and wins.

Player A's new rating will be slightly higher than 1000, and Player B's new rating will be slightly lower than 900. The exact amount that each player's rating changes will depend on the Elo rating formula.

3.3   Abstract Reasoning Corpus (ARC)

The architecture of ARC (Abstraction and Reasoning Corpus) is designed to test the reasoning capabilities of language models. It consists of a benchmark dataset of image-based reasoning tasks that require the production of an output image given a specific input. The ARC tasks are designed to test four core knowledge systems: objectiveness, agentness and goal-directedness, numerical knowledge, and elementary geometry and topology [7].

The ARC dataset consists of 1,000 reasoning tasks, each with 2 to 5 input- output image pairs provided as training instances. The training inputs are different from the actual test input, but they can be solved using the same underlying procedure. The tasks are open-ended, with objects having different shapes and colors and forming various relations with each other. The grid size can also vary between tasks, making them unsolvable through search algorithms.

To solve ARC tasks, a language model needs to encode the 2D input-output images into a textual representation. This can be done by representing each pixel's color numerically or with color descriptors. The encoded images are then incorporated into prompts that instruct the language model to solve the task. Two single-stage strategies for prompting the language model have been explored.

The ARC architecture also includes the 1D-ARC dataset, which is a simplified, single-dimensional version of ARC. The 1D-ARC tasks aim to make ARC tasks more approachable for language models by reducing task complexity and dimensionality. The performance of language models on the 1D-ARC dataset has been evaluated, revealing improvements but also highlighting the limitations of simplification alone in bridging the reasoning gaps of language models.

In order to enhance the reasoning capabilities of language models for ARC tasks, an object-based approach has been proposed. This approach integrates an external tool called the ARGA (Abstraction and Reasoning Graphs with Attention) framework, which assists in object abstraction. By using structured, object-based representations, significant improvements in the problem-solving abilities of language models have been observed.

Overall, the architecture of ARC involves encoding 2D input-output images into text, prompting language models to solve the tasks, and exploring different strategies and external tools to enhance their reasoning capabilities.

For scoring, each correct answer gains one point, and any k-way tie that includes the correct answer receives $1/k$ points. The total score is the sum of points earned divided by the number of questions.

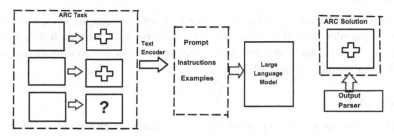

Fig. 2. ARC Architecture for Benchmark Test

– Encode the input-output images: Convert the 2D input-output images into a textual representation. This can be done by representing each pixel's color numerically or with color descriptors. Use delimiters to separate adjacent pixels and "newline" characters to separate rows in the image.
– Prompt the language model: Incorporate the encoded images into prompts that instruct the language model to solve the task. Explore different strategies for prompting the language model, such as single-stage strategies.
– Apply reasoning and abstraction: Utilize the reasoning capabilities of the language model to analyze the input-output pairs and identify patterns, relationships, and transformations. Apply abstraction techniques, such as object-based representations, to enhance the model's understanding of the task.
– Generate the solution: Based on the analysis and reasoning, generate the output image that corresponds to the given input. The solution should align with the patterns and transformations observed in the input-output pairs.
– Evaluate the solution: Compare the generated output image with the expected output image provided in the test instance. Assess the correctness of the solution based on how well it matches the expected output.

Figure 2 represents the steps mentioned above.

3.4 Hardaware and Software Used

Google colab with it's Intel Xeon, Nvidia T4 gpu and Ubuntu 22.04 was used.

4 Dataset Used

Llama was trained using the following data sets:

4.1 OASST1 OpenAssistant Conversations Dataset

The Open Assistant dataset comprises 161,443 distinct messages spanning 66,497 dialogues in 35 various languages. This dataset was gathered through crowd- sourcing efforts [8].

4.2 HH-RLHF

This dataset is composed of evaluations made by humans regarding the degree of helpfulness and harmlessness. It encompasses 160,800 instances, with each data point presenting two responses from an assistant to a user's query, along with a human assessment of the most favorable response [9].

4.3 FLAN V2

The FLAN v2 compilation comprises 1,836 tasks that have been expanded with carefully curated templates and diverse formatting patterns, culminating in a total of more than 15 million examples. The Llama models underwent training using task combinations outlined in the FLAN v2 collection [10].

4.4 Guanaco

Guanaco's training is based on the proprietary OASST1 dataset, a multilingual collection gathered by OpenAI. However, the text does not specify the training data for Llama.

Guanaco underwent fine-tuning using the OASST1 dataset, known as the Open Assistant dataset, featuring 161,443 distinct messages from 66,497 conversations across 35 languages. This dataset was sourced through crowd-sourcing efforts.

5 Results and Discussion

The results of the analysis between Guanaco 7B and Llama 7B show interesting findings in terms of their performance and characteristics.

In terms of performance on benchmark data sets, Guanaco 7B demonstrates competitive performance on the MMLU (Massively Multitask Language Understanding) benchmark, outperforming Llama 7B in terms of accuracy. However, Llama 7B performs and surpasses Guanaco 7B in terms of Elo rating.

Qualitative analysis reveals strengths and weaknesses in both models. Guanaco 7B exhibits strong performance in tasks requiring Theory of Mind capabilities, which can be beneficial in certain applications. On the other hand, Llama 7B tends to generate incorrect or unreliable responses in certain scenarios, indicating a potential limitation. These findings highlight the trade-offs and considerations when choosing between Guanaco 7B and Llama 7B for specific language understanding and generation tasks. The performance and characteristics of each model should be cautiously evaluated based on the particular requirements and objectives of the task at hand.

5.1 Graphs Comparing Models

We have compared both the models Guanaco 7B and Llama 7B by implementing the following benchmark tests. Overall scores of both the models using all benchmark tests is shown in Table 1 and the comparative graphs are shown in Fig. 3.

Table 1. Benchmark Test Scores of Guanaco and Llama Models

Model	Benchmark Test	Score
Guanaco	ARC	38.2
Guanaco	MMLU	36.6
Guanaco	ELO Rating	868
Llama	ARC	36.2
Llama	MMLU	35.1
Llama	ELO Rating	990

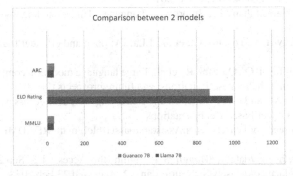

Fig. 3. Comparison between the two models on the 3 tests

Scores here representation of the models ability in above tests. For more information about how these test give their scores refer to Sect. 3 in the paper.

1. Abstract Reasoning Corpus (ARC)
2. Massive Multitask Language Understanding (MMLU)
3. ELO Rating(On Vicuna Benchmark)

Figure 3 represent the comparison between the models Llama 7B and Guanaco 7B here Guanaco presents better results in MMLU as well as ARC test. Llama shown slightly better performance than guanaco in the ELO ratings [11].

6   Conclusion

To sum up, this paper has offered an extensive analysis of two notable large language models, specifically Llama and Guanaco. By conducting a thorough assessment across multiple facets, encompassing benchmark task performance and practical utility, we've acquired valuable perspectives on the merits and limitations of each model.

Furthermore, the training methodologies employed for these models played a significant role in their respective performance. Llama's extensive training on a diverse dataset made it a robust general-purpose language model, while Guanaco's fine-tuning process tailored it to a specific domain, enhancing its task-specific performance.

References

1. Dettmers, T., Pagnoni, A., Holtzman, A., Zettlemoyer, L.: QLoRA: Efficient Finetuning of Quantized LLMs (2023)
2. Hu, E J.: LORA: Low-Rank adaptation of Large Language Models, 17 June 2021
3. Vaswani, A., et al.: Attention is all you need. In: Proceedings of the 31st International Conference on Neural Information Processing Systems (NIPS'17), pp. 6000–6010. Curran Associates Inc., Red Hook, NY, USA (2017)
4. Radford, A., Narasimhan, K.: Improving Language Understanding by Generative Pre-Training (2018)
5. Touvron, H., Lavril, T., Izacard, G., et al.: LLaMA: open and efficient foundation language models (2023)
6. Hadi, M.U., Al-Tashi, Q., Qureshi, R., et al.: Large language models: a comprehensive survey of its applications, challenges, limitations, and future prospects (2023)
7. Xu, Y., et al.: LLMs and the Abstraction and Reasoning Corpus: Successes, Failures, and the Importance of Object-based Representations
8. https://huggingface.co/datasets/OpenAssistant/oasst1/blob/main/README.md.   Accessed 12 Apr 2023
9. https://huggingface.co/datasets/HuggingFaceH4/hh-rlhf. Accessed 25 Sep 2023
10. https://huggingface.co/datasets/SirNeural/flan_v2. Accessed 23 Feb 2023
11. https://github.com/huggingface/blog/blob/main/evaluating-mmlu-leaderboard.md. Accessed 28 Sep 2023

AI Content Detection

Rachna Sable[1]([✉]) [iD], Vaishali Baviskar[1] [iD], Sudhanshu Gupta[2] [iD], Devang Pagare[1] [iD],
Eshan Kasliwal[1] [iD], Devashri Bhosale[1] [iD], and Pratik Jade[1] [iD]

[1] G H Raisoni College of Engineering and Management, Pune, India
rachana.sable@raisoni.net
[2] School of Computer Science Engineering and Technology, Bennett University, Greater Noida,
India

Abstract. The rise of AI-generated data, mainly from models like ChatGPT,
LLAMA2 poses serious difficulties to academic integrity and raises worries about
plagiarism. The current research looks on the competences of various AI content recognition algorithms to distinguish between human and AI-authored material. This research looks at numerous research papers, publication years, datasets,
machine learning approaches, and the benefits and drawbacks of detection methods in AI text detection. Various datasets and machine learning techniques are
employed, with various types of classifier emerging as a top performer. This work
creates an Extra tree classifier that can distinguish ChatGPT produced text from
human authored content. "ChatGPT Paraphrase" dataset was used for model training and testing. The result shows that the proposed model resulted in 80.1% accuracy and outperformed the existing models namely Linear Regression (LR), Support Vector Machine (SVM), Decision Tree, (DT), K-Nearest Neighbour (KNN),
Ada Boost Classifier (ABC), Random Forest Classifier (RFC), Bagging Classifier
(BG), Gradient Boosting Classifier (GBC).

Keywords: AI-generated content · AI content detection tools · Machine
learning · TFI-IDF · ChatGPT · Extra Tree Classifier · Large Language Model
(LLM)

1 Introduction

In an era marked by the pervasiveness of digital text, the capacity to differentiate between
individuals or human-generated data and AI-generated data has become an increasingly
important issue [1]. The evolution in Artificial Intelligence (AI) technology, represented
by sophisticated language models like ChatGPT, has heralded a new era of information distribution in which text created by algorithms like GPT-3.5 may closely replicate
human language. This situation raises critical queries about the authenticity, credibility,
and ethical implications of the text that permeates our digital landscape [2]. Fast growth of
artificial intelligence has led to a growing need for tools to identify the source of content.
By identifying the distinctive characteristics of AI and human-generated content, this
project aims to provide a tool for identifying misinformation, authenticity, intellectual

property protection, responsible AI use, user empowerment, bridging the gap between AI and humans, ethical AI development, and meeting societal needs. AI content detectors can be used by journalists to verify the authenticity of news articles, by social media users to detect fake news and propaganda, and by teachers to identify students who are using AI-generated text [3]. This not only preserves the integrity of their work but also safeguards their competitive advantage in the market. By detecting instances of plagiarism and copyright infringement, businesses can also take legal action to protect their rights and reputation [4]. This research paper delves into the realm of detecting AI-generated text, exploring the evolving techniques, challenges, and implications associated with this endeavor. As AI systems, including large language models (LLMs) like ChatGPT, continue to advance in their natural language processing capabilities, their capacity to produce text that is identical to human-generated content grows. Consequently, the need for robust and reliable methods to discern the origin of digital text has never been more urgent [5]. The goal of this work is to showcase a comprehensive picture of landscape of AI-generated text detection, including both the technologies used and the ethical concerns that underpin this discipline. Through an analysis of state-of-the-art detection techniques, we seek to shed light on the evolving arms race between AI text generators, such as GPT-3.5, and detectors, including those developed to identify text produced by AI language models [6]. Moreover, this research delves into the multifaceted impact of AI-generated text, ranging from the propagation of disinformation to its potential use in enhancing human communication with AI systems like ChatGPT. By understanding the various dimensions of AI text generation and detection, this work seeks to add to a deeper comprehension of the challenges and opportunities which lie ahead in our increasingly AI-mediated information ecosystem. In a world where the margins between machine-generated and people or human generated text blur, this paper serves as a vital exploration into the realm of detecting AI-generated text, ultimately aiming to equip researchers, policymakers, and technologists with the knowledge needed to navigate the complex terrain of digital communication in the 21st century [7].

The primary goal of this research is to differentiate between data produced by Chat-GPT and data published by human authors. Using the publicly available Kaggle dataset named ChatGPT Paraphrases, every model is reevaluated.

The following is the paper's format: Sect. 1 presents a brief overview of ChatGPT, its advantages and disadvantages, as well as an overview of AI-generated content detection. Section 2 conducts a survey to summaries past work on AI content detection and approaches. Section 3 discusses the research objectives and execution details, while Sect. 4 discusses the outcomes. Section 5 outlines the Conclusion as well as the future scope.

2 Literature Survey

The research papers on distinguishing human generated text from LLM generated text are analyzed in this study. The analysis involves many significant criteria such as source for research papers, publication years, datasets under consideration, frequently used Machine and Deep learning approaches, evaluation metrics used and their advantages and disadvantages [8]. Based on the review a novel Extra tree classifier approach is described and implemented, which is described in Sect. 3. First, queries related to the aims of the review are identified [9].

The following research questions have been proposed:

- RQ1: Different sources to get the related research papers?
- RQ2: What are the years from which the related research is taken?
- RQ3: What are the datasets used in such research papers?
- RQ4: What are widely used ML and DL techniques used in these papers?
- RQ5: What are the benefits and drawbacks of approaches for distinguishing human text from material created by LLM?
- RQ6: What are various evaluation metrics used to compare and analyze results?

Search Clue
The search clue contains search terms as well as approaches for obtaining all relevant research papers on distinguishing human text from Large Language Model (LLM)-generated text. The following search strings were chosen: ChatGPT-generated text detection.

- LLM-generated content detection using ML techniques
- LLM-generated text detection using DL techniques
- Discriminate machine from human-generated text

Findings from the Review
RQ1: Different sources to get the related research papers?
The conclusions of current research publications on identifying human generated text from LLM generated material are examined in this section. All of the research questions outlined in Sect. 2 are addressed here. Figure 1 indicate the various resources from which all 14 publications were chosen, as well as their year of publication count.

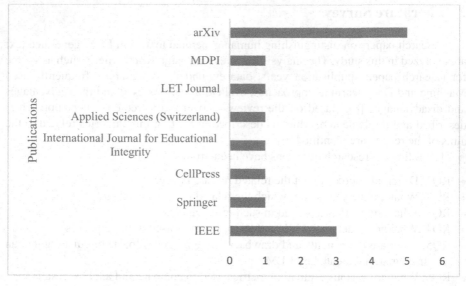

Fig. 1. Paper count based on publications

Figure 2 shows that research publications are chosen from IEEE, Springer, arXiv, MDPI, and other sources. This review includes 14 downloaded papers in total.

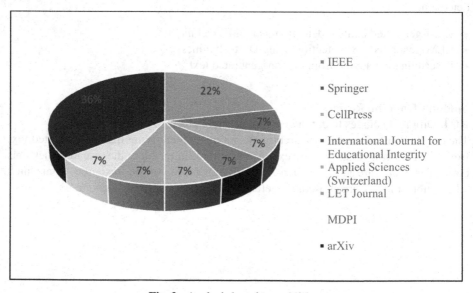

Fig. 2. Analysis based on publishers

RQ2: What are the years from which the related research is taken?

Among all articles published between 2018 and 2023, the majority of those under consideration for review are from 2021 and 2022, followed by 2023[8]. In the year 2023, 12 of 14 articles are published. Figure 3 shows that the majority of the publications accepted for study are from 2023.

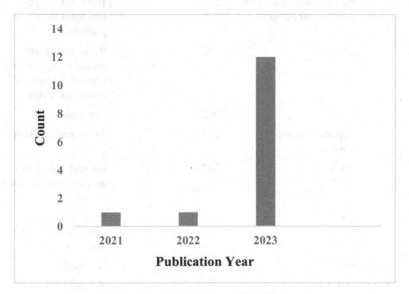

Fig. 3. Analysis based on publication count

RQ3: What are the datasets used in such research papers?
Many research papers use their own set of data. Most of the data was collected live. Some research papers are theory-based and don't refer to any dataset [1]. Table 1 shown below highlights the analysis based on Paper title, Publications, Year of Publication and Datasets used.

Table 1. Research based on reviewed Papers

Citation No	Publisher	Year of Publication	Dataset Used
[1]	IEEE	2022	Open dataset for Russian language with long texts
[2]	Springer	2023	ChatGPT written 500 words essay
[3]	MDPI	2023	Not used
[4]	arXiv	2023	Human generated pilot study data and AI generated data

(continued)

Table 1. (*continued*)

Citation No	Publisher	Year of Publication	Dataset Used
[5]	CellPress	2023	Not used
[6]	International Journal for Educational Integrity	2023	100 words Al generated responses for given prompts
[7]	arXiv	2023	Public generated restaurant review and ChatGPT generated restaurant review
[8]	IEEE	2023	Not used
[9]	Applied Sciences (Switzerland)	2023	Al Generated Essays
[10]	arXiv	2023	For real data, 500 news articles from the Xsun dataset
[11]	arXiv	2023	Human generated abstracts and Al generated abstracts
[12]	IEEE	2021	Not used
[13]	LET Journal	2023	Not used
[14]	arXiv	2023	Kaggle dataset of 10000 texts (5204 - human generated text, 4796- Al generated text)

RQ4: What are widely used ML and DL techniques used in these papers?
ML and DL approaches are used in all of the research articles. ML techniques such as SVM, LR, DT, KNN, RF, ABC, BC, GBC and Extremely Randomized Tree are used in papers, as are DL approaches such as Long Short-Term Memory and Multi-Layer Perceptron.

RQ5: What are the benefits and drawbacks of approaches for distinguishing human text from material created by LLM?
Table 2 describes the advantages and disadvantages of various techniques.

Table 2. Advantages and Disadvantages of various techniques

Sr no	Techniques	Advantages	Disadvantages
1	TF-IDF	TF-IDF provides higher weight to words that occur often in a document but are unusual in the corpus	TF-IDF representations can be quite sparse, especially in large document collections, where most terms have low document frequency
		The calculations are relatively simple and computationally efficient	TF-IDF treats words as independent entities and does not capture semantic relationships between words or phrases
2	Extremely Randomized Trees	Extra Trees introduce additional randomness in the tree-building process by selecting random splits instead of searching for the best split. This randomness often results in less overfitting compared to traditional decision trees	Because Extra Trees choose splits randomly, they may sometimes select suboptimal splits that result in less accurate models compared to Random Forests. RF, by choosing the best split, often produces more accurate trees
3	Logistic Regression	Logistic regression is a straightforward and interpretable algorithm	Logistic regression is intended primarily for binary classification issues. While there are adaptations for multi-class situations such as Multinomial Logistic Regression, it may not perform as well as alternative methods such as Random Forest or Gradient Boosting in complicated multi-class settings
4	Decision Tree	Decision trees are highly interpretable, as they mimic human decision-making processes. You can easily visualize and understand the decision rules by looking at the tree's structure	Overfitting is common in decision trees, especially as they get deep and complicated. Overfitting might result in poor generalization on previously unknown data

(continued)

Table 2. (*continued*)

Sr no	Techniques	Advantages	Disadvantages
		Decision trees are ideal for complicated data because they can describe non-linear connections between characteristics and the goal variable	Small changes in the data result in significantly different tree structures, making decision trees unstable and sensitive to variations in the dataset
5	Support Vector Machine	SVMs excel in high-dimensional feature spaces, making them ideal for jobs with a large number of features or variables	The kernel function selected can have a substantial influence on the performance of an SVM. Selecting the improper kernel may result in poor results
		SVMs are less susceptible to overfitting especially when using appropriate regularization techniques like C-parameter tuning. This makes them useful in situations with limited training data	Training an SVM can be computationally intensive, especially when dealing with large datasets. This makes them less practical for real-time or big-data applications without specialized hardware or optimization techniques
6	GPT 2	GPT-2 has a strong understanding of natural language and context. It can analyze the text's coherence, grammar, and language usage patterns to identify deviations	Adversarial techniques can be used to craft text that closely mimics human writing, making it challenging for GPT-2 to detect machine-generated text accurately
		GPT-2 can often detect differences in writing style between human authors and AI models like ChatGPT. This includes variations in vocabulary, sentence structure, and tone	GPT-2's performance in detecting machine-generated text may vary depending on the training data it was exposed to. It may struggle to generalize to text generated by AI models with different architectures or fine-tuning

(*continued*)

Table 2. (*continued*)

Sr no	Techniques	Advantages	Disadvantages
		GPT-2 can be enhanced on labeled datasets for specific classification tasks, potentially enhancing its capacity to distinguish the data generated by human and AI	May carry biases present in its training data
7	Transformer-Based ML Model	Transformer-based models have consistently pushed the boundaries of performance on various NLP tasks, including text classification	Training large Transformer models requires significant computational resources, making them inaccessible to many researchers and organizations without access to high-performance hardware
		Transformers capture contextual information effectively by considering the entire input sequence, allowing them to understand nuances in language and context, which is crucial for text classification	Transformer models have a large memory footprint due to the extensive number of parameters
8	DetectGPT	DetectGPT is built on a well-defined statistical hypothesis, the Local Perturbation Discrepancy Gap Hypothesis. This hypothesis provides a clear framework for identifying differences between machine-generated and human-generated text	The effectiveness of DetectGPT is highly dependent on the choice of the perturbation function (q). Selecting an inappropriate or biased perturbation function may lead to inaccurate results

(*continued*)

Table 2. (*continued*)

Sr no	Techniques	Advantages	Disadvantages
		The perturbation discrepancy (d) defined by DetectGPT provides a quantitative metric that can be used to assess the likelihood of text being generated by a machine model. This metric can offer interpretability for decision-making	Depending on the complexity of the source model and the perturbation function, DetectGPT may require significant computational resources for large-scale text classification tasks
9	OpenAI Text Classifier	OpenAI is a renowned organization with extensive expertise in natural language processing and artificial intelligence. Their text classifier is likely to benefit from substantial research and development resources	The performance of any text classifier depends on the quality and variety of the training data. The classifier may not generalize well to text generated by other AI models or to text in domains not well-represented in the training data

3   Research Objective and Implementation Details

The major goal of this study is to summarize existing work in the area of Large Language Models (LLM) in terms of text datasets, features, evaluation metrics, and classifiers used to distinguish human language from generative model data using machine learning [10]. In this paper a novel approach named Extra tree classifier that can distinguish the data generated by ChatGPT from the human written data is implemented.

This study's approach followed a planned sequence of stages targeted at distinguishing between data published by human writers and data generated by ChatGPT. In the initial phase, a comprehensive dataset, readily available on Kaggle, consisting of 51.68% human-generated data and 48.31% ChatGPT-generated data was acquired. Subsequently, a meticulous data pre-processing phase was initiated. The initial phase began with TF-IDF, word vectorization, which was followed by dataset balancing procedures to guarantee balanced representation of both text source categories [11].

Following the data pre-processing phase, the dataset is separated into distinct training and testing sets, facilitating subsequent model development and evaluation. The model training phase encompassed the implementation of distinct machine-learning models, each individually trained to discern the origin of the text data. Subsequent to training, a comprehensive evaluation of each model's performance, with a primary focus on accuracy as the key metric was done. We complemented accuracy with the F1 score to offer a more comprehensive assessment, ensuring a thorough evaluation of the model's efficacy in distinguishing between human and ChatGPT-generated data [12]. This methodological approach was carefully designed to provide a systematic and robust framework for addressing the research problem while rigorously assessing the accuracy of the models in classifying the text data's source.

In this research, we harnessed paraphrase data generated by ChatGPT, a language model. This valuable dataset was sourced from Kaggle and comprises four essential columns: "text," "paraphrase," "category," and "source." In the "text" column, one can find original sentences or questions, while the "paraphrase" column houses corresponding paraphrased versions, artfully crafted by ChatGPT. The "category" column serves as a categorization mechanism, assigning each text entry to either a question or sentence category. Lastly, the fourth column, "source," offers insights into the origin of the text, providing information such as whether it originated from platforms like Quora, CNN News, or Squad 2. This dataset forms a fundamental cornerstone of our research, enabling a comprehensive exploration of paraphrasing and its applications. The system architecture and various modules implemented to achieve outcomes are highlighted in Fig. 4, which is displayed below.

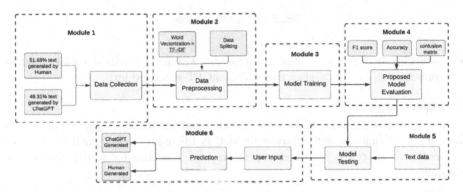

Fig. 4. System Architecture

As shown in Fig. 4, the system Architecture is divided into six modules which are described as –

Module 1 - Data Collection:
In this module, the dataset used is called "ChatGPT Paraphrases," obtained from Kaggle. The dataset comprises 419,197 rows and contains four columns. After preprocessing, we shrunk the dataset into two columns and used only 50000 rows. Among its text samples, approximately 51.68% are generated by humans, with the remaining 48.31% generated by ChatGPT. The dataset snapshot that was used is displayed in Fig. 5 below.

Module 2 - Data Pre-processing (Data Splitting and Data Vectorization):
This module is dedicated to data pre-processing. There are two important steps within it, those are as mentioned below:

Word Vectorization:

- TF-IDF word vectorization: Transforming text data into numerical representations using the TF-IDF technique.

	text	category
0	Amanda Marcu	chatgpt
1	Boston has been proposed as the new "TitleTow	chatgpt
2	What is the furthest point in history that a f...	chatgpt
3	Why is the role of governance in economic growth?	human
4	Would a compact humidifier placed near the bed...	chatgpt
5	Had Stonewall Jackson survived Chancellorsvill...	chatgpt
6	Which tailor in India is considered the finest?	chatgpt
7	How do you think the relationship between Chin...	human
8	What are the online tools to learn logic thr...	human
9	How can I learn the ability to sing?	human

Fig. 5. Snapshot of Dataset

- Dataset balancing: Addressing class imbalance within the dataset, ensuring equitable representation of human-generated and ChatGPT-generated text.

Data Split module:
In this module, data is partitioned into training and testing sets using Scikit-Learn's train_test_split function. 80% of the entire data is utilized for training and the rest 20% for testing. This split is a critical step in preparing the data for model training and evaluation.

Module 3 - Model Training:
In this module, experiments are conducted with ten different machine-learning models on the dataset. These models include LR, DT, KNN, SVM, RFC, ABC, BG, GBC and Extra Tree Classifier model.
    Module 4 - Evaluation:
In this module, the selected model's performance is evaluated. Assessment is based on the F1 score, accuracy and confusion matrix, providing critical insights into the model's capability to differentiate between people or human generated and ChatGPT-generated data.

Module 5 - Testing:
Module 5 represents the final testing phase. Here, the selected models are applied to new, unseen data to gauge its real-world performance.

Module 6 – Final Prediction
User input it taken and final prediction is done classifying whether the data is Human or AI generated.
    Before we can train the Model, we must first set the hyperparameters. The model's performance, complexity, and generalizability are all affected by hyperparameters. The hyperparameters we used are provided in Table 3 below.

Table 3. Hyper-parameter Description

Sr. No	Hyperparameter Name	Hyperparameter Argument
1	Train-test Split Hyperparameter	Test size: 0.2 (20% of the data is used for testing)
2	TF-IDF Vectorizer Hyperparameter	Tf-idf Vectorizer is used for feature extraction from the text data
3	Extra Trees Classifier Hyperparameters	n_estimators: 50, random_state: 2

4 Results

Model performance is measured using evaluation metrics. Each assessment metrics gives a unique viewpoint on the outcome. Five evaluation metrics are employed in this paper namely: Accuracy, Precision, Recall, F1 score, and Matthews correlation coefficient (MCC) [13, 14]. The percentage of accurately anticipated cases is calculated by accuracy. It is determined by dividing the total number of accurately predicted samples by the total number of samples, as stated in Eq. 1.

$$\text{Accuracy} = \frac{TP + TN}{TP + TN + FP + FN} \tag{1}$$

While precision calculates true positive predictions from all positive cases, recall assesses true positive predictions from actual positive instances. The accuracy and recall formulas are shown in Eqs. 2 and 3, respectively.

$$\text{Precision} = \frac{TP}{TP + FP} \tag{2}$$

$$\text{Recall} = \frac{TP}{TP + FN} \tag{3}$$

The F1-score represents the mean of precision and recall which is stated by Eq. 4. This measurement is more balanced than precision and recall.

$$\text{F1 score} = \frac{Precision.Recall}{\text{Precision} + \text{Recall}} \tag{4}$$

Table 4 highlights the performance of various existing technique and proposed techniques according to the evaluation metrics like Accuracy and F1-score. Figure 6 compares several models based on accuracy.

Table 4. Model Comparison based on Accuracy and F1-score

Model	Accuracy	F1-score
LR	0.766	0.764
SVM	0.779	0.772
DT	0.644	0.712
KNN	0.669	0.664
RF	0.773	0.780
ABC	0.719	0.731
BG	0.748	0.758
GBC	0.755	0.725
Extra Trees Classifier	0.801	0.799

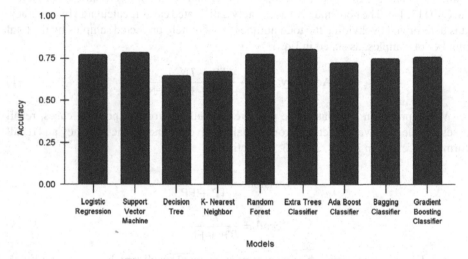

Fig. 6. Analysis of models based on Accuracy

The confusion matrix, which is displayed in Fig. 7, shows the count of predicted and actual values, is used to assess the performance of the Extra Tree Classifier.

Figure 8's Receiver Operating Characteristic (ROC) curve plots the True Positive Rate (TPR) versus the False Positive Rate (FPR) at different threshold levels to examine the effectiveness of the Extra Tree Classifier.

Upon thorough experimentation and evaluation, several key findings have emerged from the above implementation:

Model Performance: The performance of a variety of machine learning models, including Logistic Regression, Support Vector Machine, Decision Tree, K-Nearest Neighbor, Random Forest, Extra Trees Classifier, Ada Boost Classifier, Bagging Classifier, and

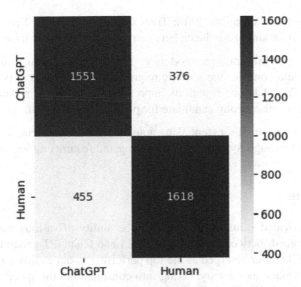

Fig. 7. Confusion Matrix of Extra Trees Classifier

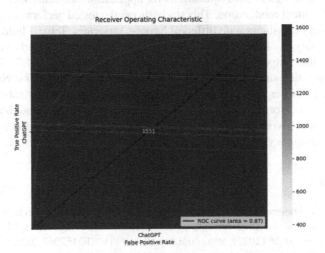

Fig. 8. (ROC) Curve for Extra Tree Classifier

Gradient Boosting Classifier was assessed and it was found that Extra Tree Classifier outperformed other existing model.

Accuracy: It is observed that Extra Trees Classifier exhibited the highest accuracy at 80.1%, followed closely by the Support Vector Machine and Random Forest models, achieving accuracies of 77.9% and 77.3%, respectively.

F1-Score: The F1-score, which balances precision and recall, was another crucial metric considered in evaluation. The Random Forest model demonstrated the highest F1-score at 0.780, closely followed by the Extra Trees Classifier at 0.799. This highlights their effectiveness in maintaining a balance between false positives and false negatives.

Model Selection: While multiple models yielded promising results, the most appropriate model should consider the specific requirements and constraints of the application. The Extra Trees Classifier, with its impressive performance in both accuracy and F1-score, stands out as a strong candidate for practical deployment.

Further Optimization: It's essential to note that model performance can often be further optimized through hyper parameter tuning and feature engineering.

5   Conclusion

This research provided valuable insights into the ability of various machine learning models to distinguish between human-generated and ChatGPT-generated text. While the Extra Trees Classifier emerged as the top performer in our evaluation, the choice of model should be made judiciously, taking into consideration the specific requirements of the application at hand. These findings pave the way for improved AI content detection tools and have significant implications for applications in fields such as plagiarism detection and content moderation. This study shows the tested performance against nine machine learning classifiers with different hyper-parameters. Table 1 holds the detailed performance analysis of different models. From the results, it is clearly visible that the extra tree classifier outperforms all the classifiers with an accuracy of 80.1%. The results also demonstrate that some well-known classifier such as the K-Nearest Neighbour and Decision Tree classifier performs poorly on this dataset. Some regularization techniques may improve the performance. These results show that the model is not biased to a particular class. Future work may involve fine-tuning the selected models to achieve even higher classification accuracy.

References

1. Gritsay, G., Grabovoy, A., Chekhovich, Y.: Automatic detection of machine generated texts: need more tokens. In: 2022 Ivannikov Memorial Workshop (IVMEM), Moscow, Russian Federation, pp. 20–26 (2022). https://doi.org/10.1109/IVMEM57067.2022.9983964
2. Elali, F.R., Rachid, L.N.: AI-generated research paper fabrication and plagiarism in the scientific community. CellPress https://doi.org/10.1016/j.patter.2023.100706
3. Uzun, L.: ChatGPT and academic integrity concerns: detecting artificial intelligence generated content. Technology (LET Journal) **3**, 45–54 (2023)
4. Khalil, M., Er, E.: Will ChatGPT get you caught? Rethinking of plagiarism detection. In: Zaphiris, P., Ioannou, A. (eds.) Learning and Collaboration Technologies. HCII 2023. LNCS, vol. 14040, pp. 475–487. Springer, Cham (2023). https://doi.org/10.1007/978-3-031-34411-4_32
5. Elkhatat, A.M., Elsaid, K., Almeer, S.: Evaluating the efficacy of AI content detection tools in differentiating between human and AI-generated text. Int. J. Educ. Integr. https://doi.org/10.1007/s40979-023-00140-5
6. Ma, Y., et al.: AI vs. Human -- Differentiation Analysis of Scientific Content Generation. arXiv, arXiv:2301.10416 [cs.CL]

7. Islam, N., Sutradhar, D., Noor, H., Raya, J.T., Maisha, M.T., Farid, D.M.: Distinguishing Human Generated Text from ChatGPT Generated Text Using Machine Learning. arXiv, arXiv: 2306.01761 [cs.CL]

8. Alamleh, H., AlQahtani, A.A.S., ElSaid, A.: Distinguishing human-written and ChatGPT-generated text using machine learning. In: 2023 Systems and Information Engineering Design Symposium (SIEDS), Charlottesville, VA, USA, pp. 154–158 (2023). https://doi.org/10.1109/SIEDS58326.2023.10137767

9. Corizzo, R., Leal-Arenas, S.: One-class learning for AI-generated essay detection. Appl. Sci. (Switzerland) 13(13). https://doi.org/10.3390/app13137901

10. Weber-Wulff, D., et al.: Testing of Detection Tools for AI-Generated Text. arXiv. arXiv:2306.15666 [cs.CL]

11. Katib, I., Assiri, F.Y., Abdushkour, H.A., Hamed, D., Ragab, M.: Differentiating chat generative pretrained transformer from humans: detecting ChatGPT-generated text and human text using machine learning. MDPI, Mathematics (2023). https://doi.org/10.3390/math11153400

12. Mitrovic, S., Andreoletti, D., Ayoub, O.: ChatGPT or Human? Detect and Explain. Explaining Decisions of Machine Learning Model for Detecting Short ChatGPT-Generated Text. arXiv. arXiv:2301.13852 [cs.CL]

13. Harada, A., Bollegala, D., Chandrasiri, N.P.: Discrimination of human-written and human and machine written sentences using text consistency. In: 2021 International Conference on Computing, Communication, and Intelligent Systems (ICCCIS), Greater Noida, India, pp. 41–47 (2021). https://doi.org/10.1109/ICCCIS51004.2021.9397237

14. Mitchell, E., Lee, Y., Khazatsky, A., Manning, C.D., Finn, C.: DetectGPT: Zero-Shot Machine-Generated Text Detection using Probability Curvature. arXiv, arXiv:2301.11305 [cs.CL]

Developing an Efficient Toxic Comment Detector Using Machine Learning Techniques

Peehu Bajaj[1], Avanish Shimpi[1], Satish Kumar[1,2]([✉]) [iD], Priya Jadhav[1] [iD],
and Arunkumar Bongale[1] [iD]

[1] Symbiosis International University, Pune, India
satishkumarvc@gmail.com
[2] Symbiosis Centre for Applied Artificial Intelligence, Symbiosis International (Deemed
University), Lavale, Pune, Maharashtra State, India

Abstract. Social media has changed the way people communicate, but it has also
become a breeding ground for dangerous content. Natural Language Processing
(NLP) is used in this study to classify unstructured data into dangerous and benign
categories, providing insights about internet toxicity. The NLP approach used in
the study gives light on the challenges and opportunities of toxicity identification.
The researchers uncovered patterns and trends indicative of dangerous content by
analysing massive amounts of text data, allowing them to construct powerful classification systems. The paper discusses the advantages and disadvantages of toxicity
detection. Automated systems can swiftly scan enormous amounts of content, but
they may misclassify some material, thereby leading to censorship or harassment.
The online toxicity detection provide valuable guidance for stakeholders seeking
to address this issue. By understanding the strengths and limitations of NLP-based
approaches, informed decisions can be made about implementing effective toxicity
detection strategies, ensuring a safer and more inclusive digital environment.

Keywords: Machine Learning · AI · Toxic comment detector

1 Introduction

In today's world, the internet can lead you to a more advanced information environment.
However, there are also many disadvantages to this, such as the bad and harmful remarks
made by some internet users. Most harmful comments are spread via social media. An
AI model to detect harmful comments on such platforms to identify such comments
can be used [1]. To determine the percentage of toxicity in a comment, the toxic comment detector employs algorithms for data cleaning and pre-processing. Text messages
containing threatening, derogatory, profane, racist, and other remarks are toxic. Toxic
remarks are detected without the need of humans using a variety of ways. Even though
negative behavior on social media is now the norm, it is still not acceptable. Toxic social
behavior is the spread of unjustified animosity or negativity that has a negative effect
on people who are exposed to it. Bullies online try to incite hatred and control other
people's interactions. For instance, toxic behavior in online team competition games.

© The Author(s), under exclusive license to Springer Nature Switzerland AG 2024
D. Garg et al. (Eds.): IACC 2023, CCIS 2053, pp. 284–297, 2024.
https://doi.org/10.1007/978-3-031-56700-1_23

They found a link between a match's result and the emergence of harmful behavior. Toxic remarks can be seen on social media sites like Twitter on issues that are difficult to discuss [2]. Subjects tend to be controversial, which increases the likelihood of toxic behavior. Trend analysis can be used to better understand the dynamics of online discussions in addition to aiding in moderation. One step in the content moderation process is identifying offensive comments. To achieve this, the term "toxicity" is defined and specify its subtypes. Additionally, the shown multiple deep learning methods, datasets, and architectures designed specifically for sentiment analysis in online chats. Companies have started reporting remarks and barring individuals who are found guilty of using foul language to prevent users from being exposed to inappropriate language on internet forums or social media platforms [3]. To filter out foul language and shield internet users from experiencing online harassment and cyberbullying, several Machine Learning models have been created and put into use [4].

2 Related Work

In recent years, studies have been conducted on toxic comment detection. Most of these studies employ machine learning techniques as Natural Language Processing and Deep Learning. One of the early studies was conducted by proposed a framework that uses logistic regression for binary classification of comments as toxic or non-toxic [5]. Neural network methods have been employed in several research to analyse hate speech; few authors used numerous deep learning architectures in large experiments to learn semantic word embedding to handle poisonous comment recognition Another study presented a deep neural network-based sentiment analysis model for YouTube video comments, which led to 70–80% accuracy [5]. Additionally, the general use of various neural network methods for comment categorization has been extensively employed in recently published literature [6]. However, these methods only addressed some of the task's issues, leaving others unresolved [7]. However, further unsupervised techniques and approaches. In the study of literature they developed efficient and successful algorithms for identifying and filtering these comments [8]. They used models like Support Vector Machines (SVM) and Naive Bayes (NB), as well as more recent deep learning models like Convolutional Neural Networks (CNN) and Recurrent Neural Networks (RNN) [9, 10]. In the study of ML methods for toxic comment classification, the author used machine learning techniques to conduct a thorough evaluation of the state-of-the-art in the classification of toxic comments [11]. From 31 carefully chosen, pertinent primary studies, they extracted data [12]. They investigated the following aspects of the primary study analysis: the data set utilised, the evaluation metric, the machine learning techniques used, the toxicity classes, and the comment language [13].

3 Data Pre-processing

There are several techniques for pre-processing such as tokenization, stemming, stopword removal and text-normalization. Various studies have highlighted the importance of data pre-processing. For instance, in a study by the authors performed to kenization, stopword removal, and stemming on the dataset to enhance the performance of their model and applied text normalization and stemming techniques to preprocess their data [9].

3.1 Tokenization, Indexing, and Index Representation

Regardless of the use case, ML and DL models can operate on numerical data. Therefore, the data must be transformed into its equivalent machine-readable form to train a deep-learning model utilising the clean text data. The actions listed below must be taken to accomplish such a feat: Tokenization: The separated the statement into separate terms for identifying the classified words. For instance, "I love cats and dogs" will be transformed into ["I", "am", "a", "girl"]. Indexing: The words were arranged dictionary style, with each word assigned a unique index such as {1: "I", 2: "am", 3: "a", 4: "girl"} in that order. Index representation: It is used to represent the terms in the comments in order, and then feed this chain of indexes to our deep-learning model. For e.g. [1–4].

3.2 Stemming

The stemming process involves removing suffixes from words to obtain their base form. For example, the stem of the word "walking" would be "walk", and the stem of the word "played" would be "play". This is done using algorithms that analyze the structure of words and apply rules to strip off suffixes.

3.3 Stop-Word Removal

The the most important phases in text pre-processing for use-cases involving text classification is stop-word removal. Eliminating stop words ensures that the words that define the text's meaning are given more attention. Many authors used the "spacy" package to get rid of stop-words from my data. The "STOP WORDS" list provided by Spacy can be used to eliminate stop-words from any textual data. Even though spacy's library has a sizable list of stop-words.

3.4 Text Normalization

The process of converting text into a single standard form that it might not have utilized earlier is known as text normalization. Since input is ensured to be consistent prior to operations being performed on it, normalizing text before storing or processing it enables the separation of concerns. It also includes:

- Eliminating spaces between text.
- Eliminating Characters That Recur.
- Lowercase data conversion.
- Eliminating punctuation
- Eliminating extraneous white space between words.
- Eliminating "n".
- Eliminating foreign characters.

3.5 Lemmatization

Same words in different injected form are grouped together by the process of lemmatization. It is mostly used in process like computation linguistics, natural language processing (NLP) and chatbots.

3.6 Feature Extraction

Previous studies have used various feature extraction techniques to extract relevant information from textual data. These techniques include bag of words, topic modelling and TF-IDF and word-embedding. In the study by Reddy N [8], the authors used a combination of bag of words and TF-IDF features to train their model. In addition, Aggarwal A, Tiwari A [9] used word embedding to extract features from their data.

3.7 Bag of Words

The text modelling method known as "bag of words" uses NLP. It can describe it as a method of feature extraction from text data in technical terms. This method of extracting features from documents is straightforward and adaptable. It is referred to as a "bag" of words since the text ignores any information about the word arrangement or structure.

3.8 TF-IDF

The acronym tf-idf, which stands for frequency-inverse document frequency (also known as TF*IDF, TFIDF, TF-IDF, or Tf-idf), is a metric that quantifies a word's significance to a document inside a corpus or collection, accounting for the fact that certain terms are used more frequently than others overall. It was commonly used as a weighting factor in searches involving text mining, user modelling, and information retrieval. A 2017 survey found that 83% of text-based recommender systems in digital libraries employed tf-idf [11]. Versions of the tf-idf weighting method are widely used by search engines as a vital tool for classifying and assessing a document's relevance to a user query. One of the simplest ranking functions is made by adding the tf-idf for each search word; there are several more intricate ranking algorithms.

3.9 Word Embedding

In natural language processing (NLP), a word embedding is a representation of a word. The embedding is used in text analysis. Words that are adjacent to each other in the vector space are predicted to have similar meanings by the representation, which is frequently a real-valued vector that encodes the meaning of the word. By employing language modelling and feature learning algorithms to map vocabulary words or phrases to vectors of real numbers, word embeddings can be produced.

3.10 Topic Modelling

The statistical technique of topic modelling locates clusters or groups of related words within a body of text using unsupervised machine learning. This text mining technique interprets unstructured data devoid of predefined tags or training data by using semantic structures in text. Documents are analysed using topic modelling to find similar themes and create a useful cluster. For instance, a topic modelling algorithm could determine from the text of incoming documents whether they are contracts, invoices, complaints, or something else entirely. The two primary topic modelling techniques that analyse big text files to categorise subjects, offer insightful information, and promote better decision-making are latent semantic analysis and latent Dirichlet analysis.

4 Model Used

Several machine learning models have been employed in previous studies for toxic comment detection, including logistic regression, SVM, Naïve Bayes, Random Forest, and deep learning models like Long Short-Term Memory (LSTM) networks and Convolutional Neural Networks (CNNs). In a literature review the authors used a Random Forest model for toxic comment detection [12]. Similarly, a recent research paper [13] used an LSTM network to achieve improved performance compared to other models. Most of the chosen primary research has classified harmful remarks from the datasets given in the previous section of this study using more than one machine learning technique. The table below lists the number of primary studies in which a certain machine learning technique was applied. As per literature review, RNN, LSTM, and logistic regression among these two LSTM layers and four convolution layers. The score of 0.9645 indicates the best accuracy [14]. Different deep neural networks are the most popular and efficient approaches, however simpler and for baseline approaches, faster methods like logistic regression were often used (Table 1).

Table 1. List of methods of Machine learning algorithm applicable for toxic comment detector.

Machine Learning Method	Number of Papers
Logistic regression classifier	9
Bidirectional long short-term memory (BiLSTM)	8
Bidirectional Gated Recurrent Unit Networks (Bidirectional GRU)	6
Long Short-Term Memory (LSTM)	5
Support Vector Machine (SVM)	5
Bidirectional Encoder Representations from Transformers (BERT)	4
Naive Bayes	4
Random Forest	2
Capsule Network	3
Decision tree	2
KNN classification	2
Gated Recurrent Unit	2
Extreme Gradient Boosting (XGBoost)	2
Recurrent Neural Network (RNN)	2
Bi-GRU-LSTM	1
Gaussian Naive Bayes	1

4.1 Logistic Regression Classifier

It's a linear model that works well for tasks involving binary classification. A log-like function is employed to simulate the likelihood of the intended class. To get the probability of the positive class, the input features are multiplied by weights, and the resulting sum is then run through the logistic function.

4.2 Bidirectional Long Short-Term Memory (BiLSTM)

A bidirectional LSTM, or BiLSTM, is a sequence model that has two LSTM layers, one for processing input in the forward direction and the other for processing in the backward direction. It is usually used in conjunction with NLP-related activities. The fundamental idea behind this approach is that the model can better understand the relationship between sequences (e.g., by identifying the words that come before and after another in a sentence) if it processes data in both directions.

4.3 Bidirectional Gated Recurrent Unit Networks (Bidirectional GRU)

A bidirectional GRU, or BiGRU, is a sequence processing paradigm made up of two GRUs. One person forward processes the data, while the other reverse processes it. A bidirectional recurrent neural network has only its input and forget gates present.

4.4 Long Short-Term Memory (LSTM)

In order to capture long-range dependencies in the input sequence, this particular type of Recurrent Neural Network (RNN) was created. It has a memory component with a long information storage capacity. Input mechanisms are used to add and remove data from a cell in a selective manner.

4.5 Support Vector Machine (SVM)

It's a linear model that works well for tasks involving binary classification. It locates the hyperplane with the largest margin that divides the positive and negative examples. To make the input features separable, a kernel function is used to map them to a higher dimensional space.

4.6 Bidirectional Encoder Representations from Transformers (BERT)

A sizable corpus of text data served as the model's pre-training set for deep learning. It can be honed for a particular purpose, such as the detection of harmful comments. The trans-former architecture used by BERT allows it to extract long-range dependencies from the input sequence.

4.7 Naive Bayes

A superior machine learning algorithm is the Nave Bayes classifier, which is used for classification tasks such as text classification. It aims to replicate the distribution of inputs within a particular class or category since it is a member of the generative learning algorithm family.

4.8 Random Forest

The popular machine learning method known as random forest, which combines the output of multiple decision trees to generate a single result, was developed by Leo Breiman and Adele Cutler. Because it can solve problems with regression and classification, its adaptability and usability are what drive its widespread use.

4.9 Capsule Network

Each capsule in a network of capsules is composed of a set of neurons, each of which outputs represents a different attribute of a single feature. This has the benefit of allowing us to identify an entity's components before recognising it. The output (or characteristics) from a CNN is the input to a capsule.

4.10 Decision Tree

This model is easy to use and effective for classification tasks. It builds a model of decisions and their potential outcomes that resembles a tree. Every leaf node in the tree represents a class label, and every internal node in the tree represents a decision based on a feature.

4.11 KNN Classification

This model is non-parametric and applicable to tasks involving classification. A new data point is classified according to the training data's k nearest neighbours' class. Although KNN is easy to use and straightforward, it can be computationally costly for large datasets.

5 Problem Statement

Although a sizable number of internet comments found in public spaces are sometimes positive, a large fraction is toxic in nature. Online data sets are treated to reduce noise before being downloaded. The dataset must be processed by the machine learning model in the form of a transformation of the raw comments before feeding it to the classification models since the comments contain a lot of errors that multiply the features. The processed dataset is trained using the logistic regression technique to distinguish between harmful and non-toxic comments. To rectify this problem the problem statement as to develop a multi-headed model that can recognise diverse toxins, such as threats, obscenities, insults, and hate speech motivated by a person's identity. The objective of an AI toxic comment detector is to automatically identify and flag potentially harmful or offensive language in written text. The purpose of this technology is to help individuals and organizations prevent the spread of toxic comments and hate speech online, promote a safe and respectful environment for discussion and communication, and ultimately reduce the harm caused by online harassment, cyberbullying, and other forms of virtual abuse. The AI toxic comment detector achieves this objective by analyzing text using natural language processing (NLP) techniques and machine learning (ML) algorithms to identify patterns and characteristics associated with toxic comments (Fig. 1).

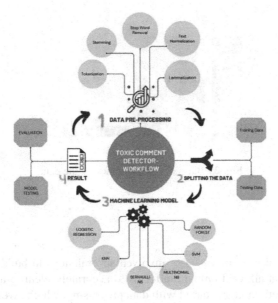

Fig. 1. Workflow

6 Dataset

Data for the Toxic Comment Detector project was collected from various sources, including a Google Forms survey, Kaggle data, and different social media platforms like LinkedIn and Instagram. The purpose of the survey was to collect user-generated content, especially comments that were deemed toxic or offensive. Participants were asked to submit comments they saw or received that they felt were inappropriate or harmful. One important consideration when using this dataset is the potential bias of the data. For example, survey respondents may not be representative of the general population and may have specific views or opinions. Similarly, social media data can be biased against certain populations or communities. Therefore, it is important to carefully consider potential biases when using this data set and take steps to correct them. The research team then manually reviewed the comments to ensure they met the criteria for inclusion in the dataset. The Kaggle dataset was collected for the same purpose to detect toxic comments. The dataset contains more than 150,000 comments from various sources, some of them were news articles, social media platforms and discussion forums. Comments were flagged by human authors to indicate whether they were toxic or not. Finally, data was collected from social media, including LinkedIn and Instagram. The data was obtained by scraping public comments and messages that contained toxic or offensive language. Overall, the Toxic Comment Detector Project dataset is a comprehensive collection of comments that have been identified as potentially harmful or inappropriate. It contains information from various sources and has been manually added to ensure accuracy. The dataset is used to train and test the machine learning (ML) models of the project (Fig. 2).

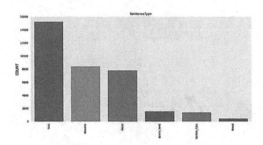

Fig. 2. Bar plot representation of the data

6.1 Description

This toxic comment detection project involved several steps in building this machine learning model that allowed online platforms to accurately identify and classify toxic comments. The methodology started with data processing, which involved cleaning the data and removing unnecessary data to ensure the quality and effective analysis of our data. Then performed data visualization to gain insight into the structure of our data and identify potential issues that needed to be addressed. Using the data variety of charts and graphs to visualize the distribution of data, including histograms, bar charts, and scatter charts were created. This step was useful to identify possible imbalances in the data, such as an unequal issuing of toxic and non-toxic comments. The next step in our project was text preprocessing, where the text data was converted into a format that could be analyzed by machine learning models. Several text preprocessing techniques, including tagging, derivation, and end-word removal were performed. Tokenization involved dividing the text data into individual words, while the actual word was reduced to its basic form to reduce the dimensionality of the data. Stop word removal involved removing common words that did not affect the meaning of the text. To better understand the most frequently used words in data, a word cloud was created. The word cloud provided a visual representation of the most frequent words in the text data and helped identify the most visible topics and themes in the comments. To ensure that our machine learning models were not biased towards one class, we counterbalanced the target column of the dataset. This also included ensuring that the data contained the same quantity of negative and positive remarks. We split the data into training and test sets after data balancing. The test set was used to assess the performance of machine learning models that had been trained using the training set. Support Vector Machines (SVM), K-Nearest Neighbours (KNN), Random Forest, Multinomial Naive Bayes (MultinomialNB), Logistic Regression, and Bernoulli Naive Bayes (BernoulliNB) were among the machine learning algorithms we employed. These models were selected based on how well they could complete tasks involving text classification. To assess the effectiveness of machine learning models, we used a number of evaluation metrics, such as F1 score, precision, and recall. The F1 score is the harmonic mean, recall measures the ratio of true positives to true positives, and precision measures the ratio of true positives to predicted positives. of precision and recall. These metrics provided an accurate measure of the model's effectiveness in predicting whether a comment was toxic or non-toxic. After evaluating the performance of the machine learning models, we tested them on new data to ensure their generalizability and use in real applications. Overall, our toxic comment detection project involved several steps to prepare and analyze text data, build machine learning models and evaluate their performance. The project was important because it helped identify and address toxic comments on online platforms that could have a negative impact on users and communities. The use of various machine learning algorithms and evaluation metrics ensured that our models were accurate and reliable and could be used in real-world applications to detect and treat toxic comments.

6.2 Evaluation Metrics

The key accuracy features that can used for assessing the performance of the given model are provided in the given section and discussed for the key parameters.

6.3 Accuracy (ACC)

The accuracy metrics give a glimpse of the overall assessment of the correctness of the model by the calculation of the proportion of correctly classified instances out of the total instances. The formula for accuracy is given below:

$$Accuracy = \frac{(TP + TN)}{(TP + TN + FP + FN)} \tag{1}$$

6.4 Precision

Precision provides the ability for the model to avoid false positives. It is the proportion of predicted true positives out of all the positive predictions. The formula is given below:

$$PRE = TP/(TP + FP) \tag{2}$$

6.5   Recall (Sensitivity or True Positive Rate)

Recall gauges a model's ability to recognise successful cases. It is the percentage of correct positive predictions made out of all positive behaviour instances. The recall equation is given by:

$$Recall = TP/(TP + FN) \tag{3}$$

6.6   Specificity (True Negative Rate)

Specificity gauges how well a model can steer clear of erroneous positives. Out of all actual negative cases, it is the percentage of accurate negative forecasts. The specificity formula is as follows:

$$SPE = TN/(TN + FP) \tag{4}$$

6.7   F1 Score

The F1 score provides a fair evaluation of their performance. The performance is a harmonic mean of precision and recall. It is very helpful when working with unbalanced datasets. The following equation provides the following formula:

$$F1\,Score = 2 * (Precision * Recall)/(Precision + Recall) \tag{5}$$

7   Results

In this study, assessment of how well six different machine learning models perform in identifying harmful remarks were studied. Support vector machine (SVM), Random Forest (RF), Bernoulli Naive Bayes (BNB), K-nearest neighbours (KNN), Bernoulli Naive Bayes, and Multinomial Naive Bayes (MNB) were among the models that were examined. To compare the performance of each model, F1 scores were computed. Based on the comparison of F1 scores, it has been discovered that Random Forest and Logistic Regression both outperformed other models at identifying harmful remarks. These two models could therefore be thought of as potential possibilities for identifying poisonous comments. It is crucial to remember that when choosing a model for a certain use case, additional aspects such as model interpretability, computational efficiency, and scalability may need to be considered. A computationally effective and comparatively simple linear model is logistic regression. It is a well-liked option for classification assignments and has a long track record of accomplishment. On the other side, Random Forest (RF) is an ensemble model that combines various decision trees to enhance performance. High-dimensional feature spaces and complex data are two things it is known for handling (Table 2).

Table 2. Evaluating model performance using evaluation metrics

	Log regression	KNN	Bernoulli NB	Multinomial NB	SVM	Random Forest
Severe	0.940282	0.862620	0.790738	0.931423	0.937901	0.941176
toxic obscene	0.901183	0.250437	0.766640	0.887203	0.915613	0.897731
threat	0.897338	0.852459	0.745205	0.902098	0.894737	0.923077
insult	0.902166	0.234329	0.776986	0.896299	0.906218	0.889201
Identity hate	0.905707	0.776042	0.776699	0.903302	0.895449	0.895000

The machine learning models were analsyed to determine if they could correctly identify the new text as harmful or not after training them. We used test data for this that wasn't used during training. Various text inputs, some of which were harmful and others of which were not, made up the test data. From the experimental data, we trained models to forecast the toxicity of each input. The derived metrics with accuracy, precision, recall, and F1 scores to assess the performance of the models. These measurements allowed us to assess how well the models were able to divide the test data into classifications of dangerous and non-toxic substances (Fig. 3).

Comments	Toxicity
Highly Toxic	
I KILLED AN INSECT AND ATE IT	0.675218
YOU ARE FAT AND UGLY	0.838234
I HOPE YOU DIE	0.953243
Toxic	
YOU ARE BAD	0.513422
I DON'T LIKE HER	0.532478
HE DOESN'T SAY TRUTH	0.432434
Non-Toxic	
I AM A GOOD GIRL	0.175323
IS THIS SENTENCE A GOOD ONE?	0.104955
I LOVE EATING	0.247234

Fig. 3. Represents the toxicity percentage.

From results it was discovered that the models did a good job of classifying the experimental data of toxicity and non-toxicity based on the assessment outcomes. The models' accuracy, precision, recall, and F1 scores were all within acceptable bounds, suggesting that they might be used for the detection of harmful remarks in fresh text streams. Overall, evaluating the models' effectiveness and ensuring their utility in practical applications required testing them against experimental data. The test phase findings allowed us to assess the models' efficacy and dependability in identifying poisonous remarks, which in turn allowed us to select the model that best meet our needs. In conclusion, our research indicates that the models of Logistic Regression and Random

Forest are equally promising for identifying dangerous substances. However, the final model selection should be based on a thorough evaluation of various factors, including interpretability, computational efficiency, and scalability.

8 Conclusion

As discussed many methods for classifying toxic comments in this paper. It was demonstrated that the techniques have distinct error profiles and may be put together to create an ensemble with a better F1-measure. The ensemble performs best in classes with few instances and when there is a large level of volatility within the data. Shallow learners and deep neural networks are some particularly potent combos. Our error analysis of the ensemble findings revealed challenging subtasks for the categorization of harmful comments. The inconsistently poor label quality is a significant contributor to mistakes. Many problems go unanswered because there is a lack of training data that contains uncommon or highly distinctive words. Its recommended for more study into using embedding to express knowledge about the world and make it easier to distinguish across paradigmatic situations.

References

1. Han, X., Tsvetkov, Y.: Fortifying toxic speech detectors against veiled toxicity. In: EMNLP 2020–2020 Proceedings of the Conference on Empirical Methods in Natural Language Processing Conference (EMNLP), pp. 7732–7739 (2020). https://doi.org/10.18653/v1/2020.emnlp-main.622
2. Karan, M., Šnajder, J.: Preemptive Toxic Language Detection in Wikipedia Comments Using Thread-Level Context, pp. 129–134, September 2019. https://doi.org/10.18653/V1/W19-3514
3. David, F., Guimarães, N., Figueira, Á.: A WebApp for reliability detection in social media. Procedia Comput. Sci. **219**, 228–235 (2023). https://doi.org/10.1016/j.procs.2023.01.285
4. Cherradi, B., Rachidi, R., Ouassil, M.A., Errami, M., Hamida, S., Silkan, H.: Classifying toxicity in the Arabic Moroccan dialect on Instagram: a machine and deep learning approach. Artic. Indones. J. Electr. Eng. Comput. Sci. **31**(1), 588–598 (2023). https://doi.org/10.11591/ijeecs.v31.i1.pp588-598
5. Obadimu, A., Mead, E., Hussain, M.N., Agarwal, N.: Identifying toxicity within YouTube video comment. In: Thomson, R., Bisgin, H., Dancy, C., Hyder, A. (eds.) Social, Cultural, and Behavioral Modeling. SBP-BRiMS 2019. LNCS, vol. 11549, pp. 214–223. Springer, Cham (2019). https://doi.org/10.1007/978-3-030-21741-9_22/COVER
6. Zhai, B., Chen, J.: Development of a stacked ensemble model for forecasting and analyzing daily average PM2.5 concentrations in Beijing, China. Sci. Total. Environ. **635**, 644–658 (2018). https://doi.org/10.1016/J.SCITOTENV.2018.04.040
7. Zhang, Y., Liu, B., Cai, J., Zhang, S.: Ensemble weighted extreme learning machine for imbalanced data classification based on differential evolution. Neural Comput. Appl.Comput. Appl. **28**, 259–267 (2017). https://doi.org/10.1007/S00521-016-2342-4
8. Storn, R., Price, K.: Differential evolution - a simple and efficient heuristic for global optimization over continuous spaces. J. Glob. Optim.Optim. **11**(4), 341–359 (1997). https://doi.org/10.1023/A:1008202821328

9. Anand, M., Eswari, R.: Classification of abusive comments in social media using deep learning. In: Proceedings of the 3rd International Conference on Computing Methodologies and Communication (ICCMC 2019), pp. 974–977, March 2019. https://doi.org/10.1109/ICCMC.2019.8819734

10. Diab, D.M., El Hindi, K.M.: Using differential evolution for fine tuning naïve Bayesian classifiers and its application for text classification. Appl. Soft Comput. J. **54**, 183–199 (2017). https://doi.org/10.1016/J.ASOC.2016.12.043

11. Koutsoukas, A., Monaghan, K.J., Li, X., Huan, J.: Deep-learning: investigating deep neural networks hyper-parameters and comparison of performance to shallow methods for modeling bioactivity data. J. Cheminform. **9**(1) (2017). https://doi.org/10.1186/S13321-017-0226-Y

12. Rupapara, V., Rustam, F., Shahzad, H.F., Mehmood, A., Ashraf, I., Choi, G.S.: Impact of SMOTE on Imbalanced Text Features for Toxic Comments Classification Using RVVC Model. https://doi.org/10.1109/ACCESS.2021.3083638

13. Carta, S., Corriga, A., Mulas, R., Recupero, D.R., Saia, R.: A Supervised Multi-class Multi-label Word Embeddings Approach for Toxic Comment Classification. https://doi.org/10.5220/0008110901050112

Handwritten English Alphabets Recognition System

Raunak Kumar(⊠) ⓘ, Sagar Patra ⓘ, and Ajay Pal Singh ⓘ

Chandigarh University, Mohali, Punjab, India
`raunaksingh721@gmail.com`

Abstract. The objective of this study is to create a Handwritten English Alphabet Recognition System, emphasizing signature recognition. In a global context where handwritten records and signatures play pivotal roles in various sectors, including legal, finance, and authentication, the demand for accurate and efficient recognition methods is paramount. This research project endeavors to construct a resilient system that can precisely identify and categorize handwritten English letters and signatures through the application of machine learning techniques, notably deep learning. The system employs convolutional and recurrent neural networks to adapt to diverse writing styles and varying levels of complexity.

Keywords: Handwritten Character Recognition · CNNs · RNNs · Data collection · Models · Machine · Styles

1 Introduction

The Handwritten English Alphabets Recognition System represents a notable example of the positive impact of machine learning advancements across various sectors. This state-of-the-art system leverages machine learning methodologies to effectively identify and interpret handwritten English alphabet characters, a task known for its complexity. These technological innovations serve as a vital link between the traditional realm of pen-and-paper and the digital domain, offering invaluable solutions for tasks such as document digitization, process automation, and efficient data handling. In an era marked by an increasing dependence on digital information, such technologies play a pivotal role in enhancing productivity and streamlining operations.

The primary objective of the Handwritten English Alphabets Recognition System is to autonomously identify and interpret handwritten alphabet characters, thereby eliminating the requirement for manual transcription. This renders it an indispensable asset across diverse sectors, including education, finance, healthcare, and logistics, where its impact extends beyond enhancing operational efficiency to mitigating human errors [1].

The Handwritten English Alphabets Recognition System encompasses a diverse array of machine learning techniques, notably featuring Convolutional Neural Networks (CNNs) and Recurrent Neural Networks (RNNs) [2]. These deep learning models have been incorporated due to their extensive training on sizable datasets comprising various handwritten alphabet samples. As a result of this training, these models possess the

D. Garg et al. (Eds.): IACC 2023, CCIS 2053, pp. 298–308, 2024.
https://doi.org/10.1007/978-3-031-56700-1_24

capability to cultivate intricate understandings of nuances within handwriting styles. This learning process empowers the system to enhance its proficiency in identifying alphabetic characters across a spectrum of handwriting sizes, diverse styles, and varying orientations.

Following this initial introduction, we will conduct an indepth exploration of the Handwritten English Alphabets Recognition System, delving into its intricate mechanisms and potential applications [3]. Our investigation will encompass a thorough examination of the fundamental algorithms and training methodologies underpinning this innovative technology. Moreover, we will analyze the profound impact it has on various domains, shedding light on its transformative capabilities in our ever-evolving digital landscape.

2 Literature Review

The utilization of machine learning techniques for the Handwritten English Alphabets Recognition System has sparked significant interest across various research domains and has led to the development of practical applications, as evidenced by the existing body of research. Among the various approaches, deep learning has emerged as a pivotal method, contributing to enhanced accuracy and versatility in the recognition of handwritten letters [4].

Deep learning models have significantly elevated the precision and versatility of alphabet recognition. These models excel in effectively discerning intricate handwriting patterns and variations, with numerous studies consistently showcasing their capacity to generalize across diverse writing styles, sizes, and orientations (Fig. 1).

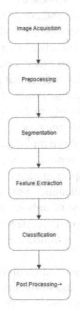

Fig. 1. Block Diagram of Character Recognition

The content further underscores the diverse and valuable applications of the Handwritten English Alphabets Recognition System [5]. These technologies enable the automated grading of handwritten assignments and assessments in educational contexts, thereby alleviating the burden on educators and ensuring rapid and precise evaluation. Additionally, these advancements play a crucial role in the extraction of handwritten text from various sources, including forms, historical manuscripts, and other paper-based documents, within the document digitization domain [6]. This not only safeguards cultural heritage but also fosters research endeavors in a highly efficient manner.

The research findings additionally underscore the practical applicability of this system within the corporate sector, specifically in domains such as finance and logistics. It accelerates the pace of data input processes and enhances the overall efficiency of information management systems in these industries. Moreover, it plays a vital role in the healthcare sector by facilitating the conversion of patient records into digital formats, effectively reducing errors stemming from manual data entry and elevating the quality of healthcare provision [7].

In the realm of published research related to this subject, valuable insights are offered into ongoing research endeavors aimed at pushing the boundaries of handwritten alphabet recognition. To further enhance the system's performance and resilience, researchers are actively exploring innovative strategies, including but not limited to Transfer Learning, Ensemble Models, and Attention Mechanisms. These endeavors represent a significant avenue for advancing the capabilities of the Handwritten English Alphabets Recognition System.

In the study authored by K. Gaurav, P. K. Bhatia, and their colleagues [8], an investigation is conducted into a diverse array of pre-processing techniques employed for character recognition, encompassing a wide range of image types. These images include not only straightforward handwritten formbased documents but also those featuring intricate attributes like colored backgrounds and complex gradients of intensity. The research extensively explores various preprocessing methodologies, comprising skew detection and correction, contrast stretching, binarization, noise reduction, normalization, and segmentation, along with morphological processing.

One significant revelation from the study is that a single preprocessing method alone cannot comprehensively address the complexities of image enhancement. Consequently, the research underscores the necessity of employing a combination of these aforementioned strategies to optimize pre-processing procedures. Nonetheless, the study acknowledges that despite the application of these multifaceted techniques, achieving complete accuracy in a pre-processing system remains a challenging endeavor, emphasizing the intricacies involved in this crucial aspect of character recognition.

Salvador Espaa-Boquera and colleagues proposed an innovative hybrid model in their research [9] for the identification of unbounded offline handwritten texts. In their approach, they leveraged a Multilayer Perceptron to estimate emission probabilities, while Markov chains were harnessed to simulate the structural aspects within the optical model.

The study also entailed the implementation of diverse techniques aimed at standardizing the dimensions of text images and mitigating variations in slope and inclination within handwritten text. These normalization processes were executed using supervised learning methodologies. The primary objectives of this recognition system revolved around the development of a preprocessing and recognition system based on Artificial Neural Networks (ANN) with a strong emphasis on achieving high levels of precision.

In this research conducted by A. Brakensiek, J. Rottland, A. Kosmala, J. Rigoll, [10] and their collaborators, they introduce an offline system designed for the detection of cursive handwriting. This system is built upon the foundation of Hidden Markov Models (HMMs) and incorporates both discrete and hybrid modeling techniques. The study involves a comprehensive evaluation, comparing the efficacy of handwriting recognition utilizing discrete modeling against two alternative hybrid techniques, which combine discrete and semicontinuous structures.

The development of this system places a particular emphasis on a segmentation-free approach. Notably, the research findings indicate that a hybrid modeling technique employing HMMs, reliant on an artificial neural vector quantizer (referred to as hybrid MMI), demonstrates superior performance in terms of recognition rates when juxtaposed with both discrete and hybrid HMMs based on a tired mixture framework (referred to as hybrid - TP). This observed improvement may be attributed, in part, to the relatively limited size of the dataset used in the study, which favors the hybrid MMI approach.

In a study conducted by Sandhya Arora as documented in [11], a comprehensive exploration of feature extraction techniques was undertaken. Specifically, four distinct methods were employed, which encompassed connection features, shadow feature analysis, chain code histogram attributes, and straight line fitting characteristics. In the context of character images, the computation of shadow features was carried out on a global scale, while the determination of intersection features, chain code histogram features, and line fitting features involved the partitioning of the character image into relevant segments.

This research effort culminated in a series of tests employing a dataset comprising 4900 samples. The outcome of these tests revealed an impressive overall detection rate of 92.80% specifically in the recognition of Devanagari characters. [12] This underscores the efficacy of the feature extraction techniques utilized, pointing to their potential applicability and reliability in the domain of character recognition, particularly within the context of Devanagari script recognition.

In the literature, T. Som has presented an approach for Handwritten Character Recognition (HCR) that relies on fuzzy membership functions [13]. This method involves several key steps. Initially, character images are resized to dimensions of 20×10 pixels. Next, ten images of each character are combined to generate an average image, often referred to as a fused image. To delineate the character accurately, both horizontal and vertical character projections are employed to ascertain the bounding box around it.

Subsequently, the image is cropped to fit within the bounding box, resulting in a size reduction to 10×10 pixels. At this stage, the image processing concludes, and each thinned character image is sequentially placed into a 100 by 100 canvas. The characters are then identified based on their similarity score with the fused image, serving as a reference for recognition.

In their research, O.V. Ramana Murthy and M. Hanmandlu [14] introduced an innovative approach involving the representation of handwritten Hindi and English numerals as exponential growth functions, facilitating their recognition. They incorporated membership formulas within a fuzzy model framework to implement this approach effectively.

The recognition process entailed the transformation of exponential functions using adapted membership algorithms tailored to a set of fuzzy values. These fuzzy sets were constructed using characteristics defined by normalized distances computed through the Box method. The research also addressed the impact of two structural parameters on the system's performance, determined by maximizing entropy while considering the outcome of the unity's membership function. The final recognition rate achieved through this methodology was noteworthy, although specific details regarding this rate are not provided in the text. This work by O.V. Ramana Murthy and M. Hanmandlu represents a novel contribution to the field of handwritten numeral recognition, employing exponential growth functions and fuzzy modeling to enhance recognition accuracy and efficiency.

In a study conducted by May in 2011, [15] it is recommended that the utilization of the Particle Swarm Optimization (PSO) and Bacterial Foraging Optimization (BFO) algorithms be employed for the purpose of achieving optimal harmonic compensation while minimizing undesirable losses within the Active Power Filter (APF) itself. This research involves the comparison of the effectiveness and efficiency of these two techniques under two distinct supply scenarios.

The results of the study demonstrate that, when employing the BFO algorithm, the Total Harmonic Distortion (THD), a crucial indicator of APF performance, is significantly reduced to less than 1%. These findings underscore the superior performance of BFO in comparison to conventional methods and those based on PSO. BFO not only ensures exceptional APF functionality but also swiftly mitigates harmonics in the source current, even in the presence of unbalanced supply conditions. This research by May in 2011 sheds light on the potential of these optimization algorithms in enhancing the performance of APFs and their ability to efficiently address harmonic issues within power systems.

2.1 History of Handwritten English Alphabets Recognition System

The progression of the Handwritten English Alphabets Recognition System through the utilization of machine learning techniques has been characterized by substantial advancements and paradigm-shifting enhancements. The inception of this technology traces back to the nascent phases of machine learning exploration, during which initial endeavors were undertaken to decipher handwritten textual content.

Character recognition systems based on predefined rules emerged within the academic landscape during the 1980s and 1990s. While these early systems are considered outdated today, they laid the foundational groundwork that paved the way for subsequent comprehensive and extensive research in this field.

The emergence of neural networks and deep learning in the 21st century represented a pivotal moment in the advancement of handwritten alphabet recognition. The advent of Convolutional Neural Networks (CNNs) and Recurrent Neural Networks (RNNs) marked a transformative era in the field, empowering these systems to glean insights from vast collections of handwritten samples. This evolution has substantially elevated recognition accuracy levels. This breakthrough fundamentally reshaped our comprehension of handwritten alphabets and their automated recognition capabilities.

During the late 2000s, there was a notable surge in the implementation of machine learning methodologies in practical settings. This era witnessed the introduction of automated systems designed for the recognition of handwritten alphabets, particularly in educational contexts. These systems played a pivotal role in streamlining grading processes, offering a more efficient means of assessment, and alleviating the workload of educators.

Up until my last knowledge update in September 2021, ongoing research efforts persisted in enhancing these systems through techniques such as Transfer Learning and Attention Mechanisms. The evolution of the Handwritten English Alphabets Recognition System serves as a testament to the perpetual quest for efficiency and precision within the realm of machine learning. This development underscores the escalating significance of this field within our progressively technology driven society [16].

3 Proposed Methodology

The suggested methodology for the Handwritten English Alphabets Recognition System employing Machine Learning Approaches adopts a thorough and structured strategy for addressing the complex task of identifying handwritten alphabet characters. In order to attain exceptional accuracy and adaptability, this approach harnesses the potential of machine learning techniques, with a specific focus on Convolutional Neural Networks (CNNs) and Recurrent Neural Networks (RNNs).

The initial phase of the methodology revolves around the meticulous gathering and organization of data. An extensive dataset of handwritten English alphabets is meticulously curated, encompassing a wide spectrum of writing sizes, orientations, and styles. To ensure the optimal performance of the model, a suite of data processing techniques is applied, including image expansion, standardization, and data augmentation. This critical phase lays the foundation for the model's ability to effectively generalize its recognition capabilities across a diverse array of handwriting patterns [17].

Subsequent to the data preparation stage, the methodology proceeds with the selection of an appropriate model and the design of its architecture. In this context, Convolutional Neural Networks (CNNs) are chosen for their proficiency in capturing spatial hierarchies within image data, thus serving as the foundation for feature extraction. Concurrently, Recurrent Neural Networks (RNNs) are introduced into the architecture to account for temporal dependencies within the strokes and the sequential nature of handwritten text. The fusion of these two neural network paradigms significantly enhances the system's precision in recognizing alphabetic characters, elevating its overall performance and adaptability.

In the modeling phase, the preprocessed dataset is fed into the hybrid CNN-RNN model. This allows the model to acquire the capability to discern diverse handwriting styles by adjusting its internal parameters throughout the training process. To ensure convergence and prevent overfitting, the training phase is iterative, with continuous evaluation of the model's performance (Fig. 2).

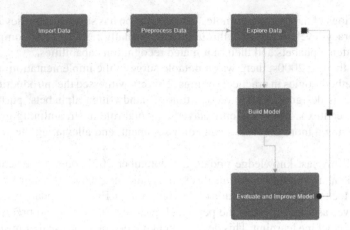

Fig. 2. Proposed methodology

4 Proposed Approach

The suggested method for developing the Handwritten English Alphabets Recognition System utilizing Machine Learning Approaches presents an innovative and methodical approach to address the intricate task of recognizing handwritten alphabet characters. The primary objective is to attain exceptional accuracy, adaptability, and versatility in alphabet recognition through the utilization of machine learning techniques, specifically harnessing the capabilities of Convolutional Neural Networks (CNNs) and Recurrent Neural Networks (RNNs) (Fig. 3).

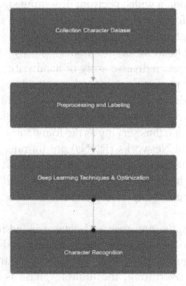

Fig. 3. Block diagram

1. **Data Collection and Preprocessing:** The methodology begins with the assembly of an extensive and diverse dataset comprising handwritten English alphabets. This dataset encompasses a wide spectrum of writing styles, sizes, and orientations, ensuring the model's exposure to a rich variety of handwriting patterns. To elevate the dataset's quality and consistency, several preprocessing methods are employed, including image scaling, normalization, and data augmentation. These crucial steps are essential to facilitate the model's effective generalization across a multitude of diverse handwriting samples.

2. **Model Architecture:** Our approach employs a hybrid CNNRNN architecture, combining the strengths of these two distinct types of neural networks. CNNs excel in capturing spatial hierarchies within images, a critical aspect for identifying unique characteristics in handwritten alphabets, making them the ideal choice for feature extraction. Conversely, RNNs are adept at considering the sequential structure of characters and the temporal dependencies of strokes in handwritten text. This fusion of CNNs and RNNs [18] enhances the system's capability to accurately recognize alphabets, even in the presence of varying writing styles, underscoring its robustness and adaptability.

3. **Training and Validation:** In the training phase, the preprocessed dataset is fed into the CNN-RNN hybrid model. This enables the model to continually adapt its internal parameters to grasp and accommodate intricate handwriting patterns. To ensure the model converges effectively and avoids overfitting, a continuous validation process is employed, where performance metrics such as accuracy and loss are closely tracked. Through this iterative and recurrent training process, the model attains a heightened level of proficiency in the accurate recognition of handwritten alphabets (Fig. 4).

Fig. 4. Compare Two Handwritten Signature

4. **Testing and Deployment:** Once the algorithm has undergone training and validation, it becomes operational for real-world applications. This algorithm processes samples of handwritten alphabets and subsequently generates predictions for the

corresponding letters. To ensure a comprehensive assessment of the system's performance, metrics such as accuracy, precision, and recall are employed for rigorous evaluation (Fig. 5).

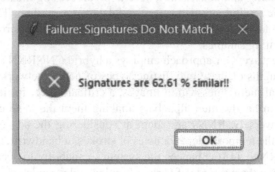

Failure: Signatures Do Not Match   ×

X   Signatures are 62.61 % similar!!

OK

Fig. 5. Result

5 Features and Principles

1. **Feature extraction:** [19] This process involves transforming handwritten characters into a format that can be effectively processed by machine learning algorithms, achieved through the collection of pertinent information. These extracted features serve as the foundational elements for subsequent recognition processes.
2. **Pattern Recognition:** Pattern recognition serves as the fundamental guiding principle of the system. It involves the identification and categorization of patterns present in the collected characteristics using machine learning techniques. These recognized patterns correspond to specific alphabet characters. Through the analysis of a vast dataset comprising handwritten samples, the algorithm acquires the capability to distinguish distinct structures associated with each individual letter.
3. **Training and Learning:** The fundamental concept underlying the Handwritten English Alphabets Recognition System is the concept of learning from data. This iterative process enables the system to progressively enhance its capacity to identify patterns within handwritten characters and correctly associate these patterns with the corresponding alphabet labels. Throughout this training process, the system is exposed to an extensive and diverse dataset consisting of a wide range of handwritten samples.
4. **Continuous Improvement:** The methodology adheres to the principle of ongoing enhancement. Researchers and developers consistently strive to improve the algorithms and models. They investigate techniques such as transfer learning, ensemble models, and attention mechanisms to augment recognition accuracy and robustness.

6 Discussion and Conclusion

This paper provides a meticulous overview of the latest advancements in handwritten character recognition. It underscores that the accuracy and efficacy of recognition are directly influenced by the complexity and characteristics of the input data.

Furthermore, this study extensively scrutinizes a diverse array of character recognition techniques tailored for handwritten recognition systems. It conducts an exhaustive examination of the various approaches proposed within this domain. The findings highlight the paramount importance of judiciously choosing classification and feature extraction methods to attain a high level of precision in character recognition tasks.

Utilizing machine learning techniques for the recognition of handwritten English alphabets, the Handwritten English Alphabets Recognition System signifies a significant milestone in the field of character recognition technology. The system's capacity to accurately interpret and comprehend handwritten alphabet characters carries profound implications across various domains and industries. Its remarkable adaptability in accommodating diverse handwriting styles while maintaining a high degree of accuracy is attributed to its robust feature extraction, pattern recognition, and learning capabilities.

The impact of this system on education is of immense significance. Beyond expediting the grading process, it fosters a more efficient and well-organized learning environment. Educators can allocate additional time to provide guidance and support, and students receive timely feedback, thereby enriching the learning experience. This system fundamentally transforms the educational landscape, optimizing the teaching and learning process for both educators and students alike [20].

The system plays a pivotal role in enhancing information management and data entry within the corporate sector. This contributes to reduced manual labor and a decline in errors, thereby augmenting the precision and overall efficiency of business operations. Furthermore, within the broader context of technological advancements in document management, this technology assumes a critical role in the preservation of historical records, facilitating research endeavors, and actively contributing to the conservation of our cultural heritage.

The distinguishing feature of the Handwritten English Alphabets Recognition System lies in its unwavering commitment to progress rather than stagnation. Researchers and developers are continually exploring innovative techniques to ensure the system remains adaptable and resilient in the face of evolving challenges and requirements.

References

1. Ding, K., Liu, Z., Jin, L., Zhu, X.: A comparative study of GABOR feature and gradient feature for handwritten Chinese character recognition. In: International Conference on Wavelet Analysis and Pattern Recognition, p. 11821186, Beijing, China, 2–4 November 2007
2. Charles, P.K., Harish, V., Swathi, M., Deepthi, C.H.: A review on the various techniques used for optical character recognition. Int. J. Eng. Res. Appl. 2(1), 659–662 (2012)
3. Bahlmann, C., Haasdonk, B., Burkhardt, H.: Online handwriting recognition with support vector machines-a kernel approach. In: IEEE Proceedings Eighth International Workshop on Frontiers in Handwriting Recognition, pp. 49–54 (2002)

4. Neetu, B.: Optical character recognition techniques. Int. J.Adv. Res. Comput. Sci. Softw. Eng. **4**(5) (2014)
5. Pradeep, J., Srinivasan, E., Himavathi, S.: Diagonal based feature extraction for handwritten character recognition system using neural network. In: 3rd IEEE International Conference on Electronics Computer Technology, vol. 4, pp. 364–368 (2011)
6. Navneet, D., Triggs, B.: Histograms of oriented gradients for human detection. In: Proceedings of the CVPR2005 IEEE Computer Society Conference on Computer Vision and Pattern Recognition, vol. 1. San Diego, CA, USA, 20–25 June 2005
7. Simonyan, K., Andrew, Z.: Very deep convolutional networks for large-scale image recognition. arXiv (2004)
8. Bajaj, R., Dey, L., Chaudhury, S.: Devnagari numeral recognition by combining decision of multiple connectionist classifiers. Sadhana, part. 1, **27**, 59–72 (2002)
9. Lorigo, L.M., Govindaraju, V.: Offline Arabic handwriting recognition: a survey. IEEE Trans. Pattern Anal. Mach. Intell. **28**(5) (2006)
10. Kumar, G., Bhatia, P.K., Banger, I.: Analytical review of preprocessing techniques for offline handwritten character recognition. In: 2nd International Conference on Emerging Trends in Engineering & Management, ICETEM (2013)
11. Espana-Boquera, S., Castro-Bleda, M.J., Gorbe-Moya, J., Zamora-Martinez, F.: Improving offline handwritten text recognition with hybrid HMM/ANN models. IEEE Trans. P
12. Brakensiek, A., Rottland, J., Kosmala, A., Rigoll, G.: Offline handwriting recognition using various hybrid modeling techniques & character N-Grams. http://irs.ub.rug.nl/dbi/4357a8469 5495
13. Kumar, G., Kumar, S.: CNN based handwritten Devanagari digits recognition. Int. J. Comput. Sci. Eng. **5**, 71–74 (2017)
14. Arora, S.: Combining multiple feature extraction techniques for handwritten Devanagari character recognition. In: IEEE Region 10 Colloquium and the Third ICIIS, Kharagpur, INDIA (2008)
15. Singh, D., Khan, M. A., Bansal, A., Bansal, N.: An application of SVM in character recognition with chain code. In: Communication, Control and Intelligent Systems (CCIS), pp. 167–171 (2015)
16. Som, T., Saha, S.: Handwritten character recognition using fuzzy membership function. Int. J. Emerg. Technol. Sci. Eng. **5**(2), 11–15 (2011)
17. Hanmandlu, M., Murthy, O.R.: Fuzzy model based recognition of handwritten numerals. Pattern Recog. **40**, 1840–1854 (2007)
18. Patnaik, S.S., Panda, A.K.: Particle swarm optimization and bacterial foraging optimization techniques for optimal current harmonic mitigation by employing active power filter applied computational intelligence and soft computing. **2012**, 897127 (2012)
19. Jawad, H., Olivier, P., Jinchang, R., Jianmin, J.: Performance of hidden Markov model and dynamic Bayesian network classifiers on handwritten Arabic word recognition. Knowl.-Based Syst. **24**, 680–688 (2011)
20. Plamondon, R., Srihari, S.: Online and off-line handwriting recognition: a comprehensive survey. IEEE Trans. Pattern Anal. Mach. Intell. **22**, 63–68 (2000)

Stock Price Prediction Using Time Series

Rahul Maurya(✉) ⓘ, Dashniet Kaur ⓘ, Ajay Pal Singh ⓘ, and Shashi Ranjan ⓘ

Chandigarh University, Mohali, Punjab, India
maurya2411rahul@gmail.com

Abstract. The stock price of a commodity is an essential factor for determining market volatility. Exact prediction of stock price and forecasting the market variation are crucial parameters of a stock analyst. The existing conventional approaches are incompetent to predict the stock market variations since they don't take a comprehensive view but rather look at time-series data for every single stock. In this article, a time series relational model (TSRM) is proposed to predict the stock price. The proposed work combines the relationship between market conditions and price variation of a commodity with time. To anticipate stock prices, relationship information is collected using a graph convolutional network (GCN) and long short-term memory (LSTM) is used to extract time series information. This study attempts to forecast stock prices using the Time series technique, which is appropriate for the financial sector since stock prices fluctuate over time and involve the observation of varied changes regarding any given variable in regard to the respective time.

Keywords: Stock prices prediction · Time series modelling · LSTM · GCN

1 Introduction

A financier, be it a company, an individual, or both, wants to make a profit on their investments. A great way to achieve strong returns on investments is to invest in stocks. Investors must be well-versed in the various stocks' present valuations in order to do this. A strong price prediction for the time to purchase and sell a stock is necessary to maximize earnings and minimize losses. Eliot Wave Theory and the Efficient Market Hypothesis both explore some of the fundamentals of forecasting [6, 7]. In general, institutional investors, also known as big buyers and big sellers, have a major role in determining stock prices. If there are more buyers than sellers on that particular day, the price auction will be higher than usual. At last, the price will reach the control point, also known as the mean price or the price at which it typically stays. A typical price allocation occurs frequently. Therefore, in order to maximize profit and have an efficient risk analysis, the entry point, exit point, and stop loss point should all be set based on the auction price. Statistical techniques including moving averages and auto regression are frequently used to achieve similar outcomes.

Latest-day computer approaches such as machine learning offer high-accuracy predictions through hybrid models that may be auto -regressive, integral moving, naive

D. Garg et al. (Eds.): IACC 2023, CCIS 2053, pp. 309–320, 2024.
https://doi.org/10.1007/978-3-031-56700-1_25

forecasting, exponential smoothing, seasonal naive forecasting, ARIMA (autoregressive integrated moving average) [8], or neural networks. Our latest proposed model puts in use all the modern approaches to forecast the prices of stock at any given instance and rates each model to assist users in deciding if they should buy or sell a certain stock in short or long term to get maximum returns in the form of earnings. The respective model has a good chance of producing accurate forecasts because it employs all modern techniques, setting it apart from more traditional models.

2 Related Work

The following actions are suggested to accomplish the goal: The data must be supplied into the system first, after which it must be cleaned by making sure that any outliers are removed, a filtration procedure is carried out, and the data's null values are rejected. Every month, information is taken from Yahoo! Finance. Then, ADF test are used for determining whether the data shows stationarity after being transformed into time series objects. Then the time series object should be dissected for the observation of various seasonality variables and patterns in order to acquire correct results, as the outcomes depend on many factors.

Subsequently, the time series objects are put into a variety of algorithms, including neural networks, ARIMA, naive forecasting, exponential smoothing, and seasonal naive forecasting.

3 Proposed Model

3.1 Arima

The Arima model is also known as the Box-Jenkins model, which was first presented by George Box and Gwilym Jenkins [2]. By fusing the moving average with auto regression models, the Auto Regressive Integrated Moving Average hybrid model was produced. The following is its equation. $y't = c + 1y'(t1) + + p + 1y'(t1) + + + q + (t)$ (1) Apart from that, lagged value of y(t) are held by predictors and lagged errors when the dependent variable, $y't$, is differentiable (may be differentiated several times).

This model is known as the ARIMA (p, d, and q) model. Where p and q quantify the ordering of the Auto Regression and Moving Average parts, and d is the degree of differentiation involved., respectively [3].

3.2 Exponential Smoothing

This forecasting method uses weights that are allocated to the historical data in such a manner where they exponentially decay with time. The most recent ones are put on top, and as the time factor raises, they begin to deteriorate.

3.3 Naïve Forecasting

Without making any predictions, the forecast is made based on historical data and is accomplished using the equation below. $T = y (T) | y' (T + h)$. (1) in which (T) is the prediction based on current data, and $(T + h)$ represents the forecast based on previous data.

3.4 Seasonal Naïve Forecasting

With the exception of the forecast being based on past data from that same season, this is comparable to the naïve forecasting approach; the following equation is used to produce seasonal naive forecasting. $m(k + 1) = y(T + h)|T = y(T + h)|T$ (1) where m is the season.

Forecast based on historical data is denoted by $T + h$.

3.5 Neural Networks

This forecasting technique is called NNAR (p, x), where p denotes the lag in input values and x show the number of hidden layers, and it is utilized in nonlinear and complex forecasting scenarios (Fig. 1).

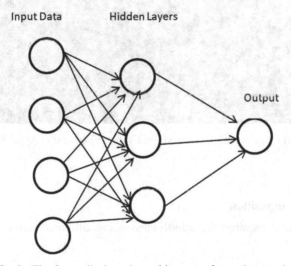

Fig. 1. The figure displays the architecture of neural networks.

4   Execution and Result

4.1   Collecting Information for Different Types of Analysis

4.1.1   Bringing in and Examining the Data

We retrieve the stock data from Yahoo using the quant mod package, and the dataset is returned as timeseries objects. For a period (from and to dates), generalize the logic used to extract the data that belongs to a particular stock symbol. We'll use Yahoo Finance to acquire monthly stock data for Apple (you may change to any company by changing the stock symbol).

4.1.2   Charting the Time Series of Apple Stock Prices

Figure 2 displays the data from Yahoo Finance that was utilized to plot the object for Apple stock prices.

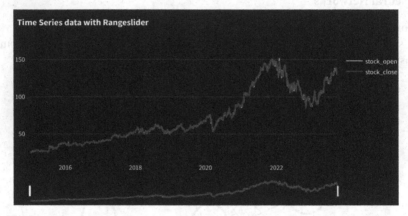

Fig. 2. Charting information obtained from Yahoo Finance (the Apple Stock Index)

4.1.3   Plot Decomposition

Plot decomposition required for mindfulness about different market patterns [5]. is depicted in Fig. 3.

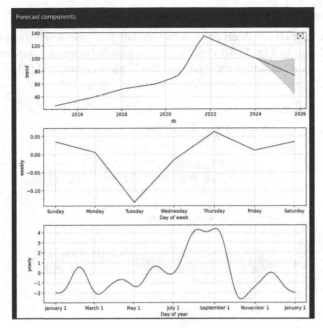

Fig. 3. Plot Decomposition

4.1.4 Examining the Apple Stock Index's Seasonality

Regarding the historical and contemporary observations of the different apple stock patterns throughout time, as shown in Fig. 4.

	Date	Open	High	Low	Close	Adj Close	Volume
Raw data							
2,196	2023-09-25 00:00:00	130.77	132.22	130.03	132.17	132.17	14,650,000
2,197	2023-09-26 00:00:00	130.914	131.405	128.19	129.45	129.45	20,378,800
2,198	2023-09-27 00:00:00	129.44	131.72	129.38	131.46	131.46	18,764,200
2,199	2023-09-28 00:00:00	130.69	134.18	130.69	133.13	133.13	18,201,400
2,200	2023-09-29 00:00:00	134.08	134.89	131.32	131.85	131.85	23,224,200

Fig. 4. Raw data

4.1.5   Applying Augmented Dickey Fuller Test (ADF)

The ADF test is used to ascertain whether or not the time series is stationary. The findings are shown in Fig. 5. To make a comparison between the current and historic data, including their residuals, the ACF and PACF plots are utilized [4].

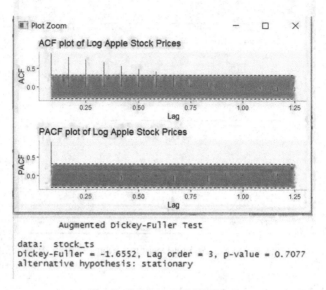

Fig. 5. Outcomes of ADF Test

4.1.6   Dividing the Dataset into Groups for Testing and Training

The data is usually divided into training and testing groups before a model is created. The model is developed using the training subset, and its performance is assessed using the test set.

4.2   Results from Various Algorithms

The predictions made by each algorithm are returned after initializing them and feeding them with Apple stock values.

4.2.1 ARIMA

The ARIMA model's predicted values may be seen in Fig. 6.

```
> print('Arima Forecast: ')
[1] "Arima Forecast: "
> print(arima$forecast)
         Point Forecast   Lo 80    Hi 80    Lo 95    Hi 95
May 2021       120.7014 109.9755 131.4274 104.2975 137.1053
Jun 2021       120.7014 109.9755 131.4274 104.2975 137.1053
Jul 2021       120.7014 109.9755 131.4274 104.2975 137.1053
```

Fig. 6. Predicted values of stock prices using Arima

Displaying stock price forecasts from an ARIMA model Displaying in Fig. 7 the Apple stock price forecasted by the ARIMA model.

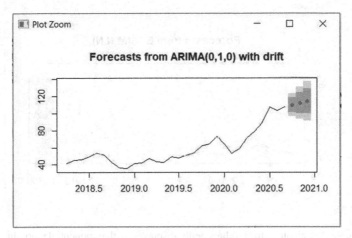

Fig. 7. Displaying anticipated stock values with Arima

4.2.2 Exponential Smoothing

Forecast Fig. 8 displays values anticipated by ETS.

	ds	trend	yhat_lower	yhat_upper	trend_lower	trend_upper	additive_terms
2,926	2025-09-24 00:00:00	73.2213	41.8777	99.9677	43.9124	98.3361	0.218
2,927	2025-09-25 00:00:00	73.1793	42.3736	99.386	43.8256	98.341	-0.0083
2,928	2025-09-26 00:00:00	73.1374	43.9793	100.7635	43.6854	98.3459	-0.3565
2,929	2025-09-27 00:00:00	73.0954	42.1744	99.2944	43.5489	98.3507	-0.6173
2,930	2025-09-28 00:00:00	73.0534	42.1771	98.2355	43.4422	98.3556	-0.8884

Fig. 8. Values estimated using exponential smoothing on stock prices Exponential Smoothing Stock Price Prediction Visualization Check out Fig. 9 to see how Apple stock values were projected using exponential smoothing.

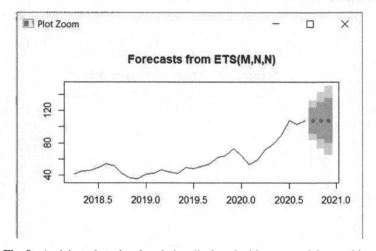

Fig. 9. Anticipated stock values being displayed with exponential smoothing.

4.2.3 Naïve Forecasting

Figure 10 Unskilled Predicting Values of Stock Prices displaying stock price forecasts made with Naive Forecasting

```
> print('Naive Forecast: ')
[1] "Naive Forecast: "
> print(naive$forecast)
          Point Forecast      Lo 80      Hi 80      Lo 95      Hi 95
May 2021          134.11  123.0774  145.1426  117.2371  150.9829
Jun 2021          134.11  118.5075  149.7125  110.2481  157.9719
Jul 2021          134.11  115.0009  153.2191  104.8852  163.3348
>
```

Fig. 10. Displays the forecast values generated by the Naive model.

Check out Fig. 11 to see the Apple stock values as forecasted by Nave Forecasting.

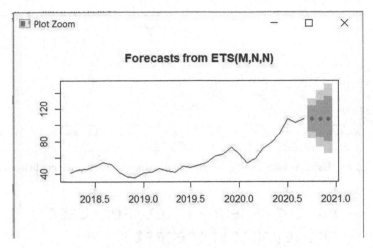

Fig. 11. Displaying stock price forecasts made via uninformed forecasting.

4.2.4 Seasonal Naïve Forecasting

Figure 12 shows forecast values anticipated by the Seasonal Naive model.

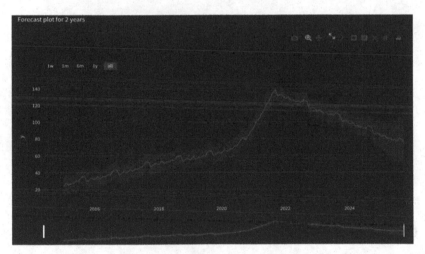

Fig. 12. Projected stock price values Seasonally ignorant prediction Visualizing Seasonal Naive Stock Price Predictions Visualizing Seasonal Naive's predictions for Apple stock values.

4.2.5 Neural Networks

Figure 14 shows the forecast values generated by neural networks.

Displaying anticipated stock prices using neural networks Fig. 15 shows the Apple stock values as predicted by neural networks.

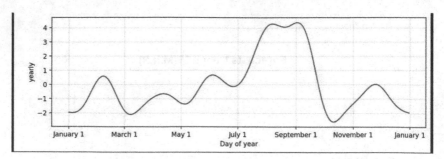

Fig. 13. Using seasonal naive forecasting to visualize stock price predictions

```
> #print('Neural Net Forecast: ')
> print(nnet$forecast)
          Feb         Mar         Apr
2021 72.55306 69.80062 68.06135
```

Fig. 14. Neural networks anticipate values for the stock price

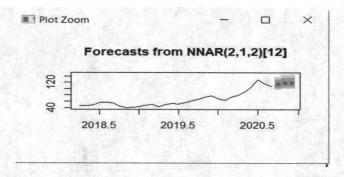

Fig. 15. Displaying anticipated stock prices using neural networks

4.3 Comparing all the Algorithms

They received rankings in Fig. 16 based on the algorithms' accuracy.

```
> result[nrow(result) + 1,] <- append(list(Forecast = "Neural Network"), accuracy_nnet)
> result[nrow(result) + 1,] <- append(list(Forecast = "ARIMA"), accuracy_arima)
>
> print(result[order(result$RMSE),])
              Forecast           ME       RMSE        MAE MPE MAPE      MASE        ACF1
4       Neural Network  2.476195e-02 0.06551681 0.05380686 -Inf  Inf 0.7481078  0.17716476
1  Exponential Smoothing 2.095968e-06 0.07276195 0.05601089 -Inf  Inf 0.7787518 -0.01588138
5               ARIMA  2.838887e-02 0.07810058 0.06645958 -Inf  Inf 0.9240260 -0.01588145
3 Seasonal Naive Forecast 1.589091e-02 0.09513267 0.07192393  Inf  Inf 1.0000000 -0.15912276
2       Naive Forecast -2.969424e-03 0.10527330 0.07968441  Inf  Inf 1.1078985 -0.42053362
> |
```

Fig. 16. Algorithm comparison

4.4 The Current Price of Apple Stock

The Google search result of the Apple stock price is displayed below in Fig. 17. The rankings suggest that Exponential Smoothing is on top. It can be seen that the result of Exponential Smoothing (Hi 80) equalizes the current price of Apple shares.

Apple Inc. (AAPL)
NasdaqGS - NasdaqGS Real Time Price. Currency in USD   ☆ Follow

171.21 +0.52 (+0.30%)   **171.33** +0.12 (+0.07%)
At close: September 29 04:00PM EDT   After hours: Sep 29, 07:59PM EDT

Fig. 17. Apple stock price of the present day

5   Summary and Conclusions

Exponential smoothing performed better than other models in this case when predicting the stock price, but performance can vary depending on the situation and the data. When data is received, it is recommended that you feed it to each of the corresponding models, compare the outcomes, and then, based on the rankings of the results, choose the most accurate result. Time series analysis for stock price prediction offers valuable insights into historical trends and patterns. However, its inherent complexity, influenced by multifaceted market dynamics, renders precise forecasting challenging. While incorporating advanced models and machine learning techniques enhances accuracy, unforeseen events and external factors may still impact outcomes. Investors should approach predictions with caution, recognizing the inherent uncertainties and potential risks associated with stock market fluctuations. A comprehensive understanding of both quantitative and qualitative factors remains essential for informed decision-making in the dynamic realm of financial markets. In summary, employing time series analysis for stock price prediction provides valuable historical insights, yet predicting future prices is complex due to dynamic market factors. Advanced models enhance accuracy, but unforeseen events can disrupt outcomes. Investors should approach predictions cautiously, acknowledging inherent uncertainties and market risks. A comprehensive grasp of quantitative and qualitative factors remains vital for informed decision-making in the ever-evolving landscape of financial markets.

References

1. Huamin, T., Qiuqun, D., Shanzhu, X.: Reconstruction of time series with missing value using 2D representation-based denoising autoencoder. J. Syst. Eng. Electron. **31**(6), 1087–1096 (2020). https://doi.org/10.23919/JSEE.2020.000081
2. Ariyo, A.A., Adewumi, A.O., Ayo, C.K.: Stock price prediction using the ARIMA model. In: 2014 UKSim-AMSS 16th International Conference on Computer Modelling and Simulation, pp. 106–112 (2014). https://doi.org/10.1109/UKSim.2014.67

3. Gupta, A., Kumar, A.: Mid Term daily load forecasting using ARIMA, Wavelet- ARIMA and machine learning. In: 2020 IEEE International Conference on Environment and Electrical Engineering and 2020 IEEE Industrial and Commercial Power Systems Europe (EEEIC / I&CPS Europe), pp. 1–5 (2020). https://doi.org/10.1109/EEEIC/ICPSEurope49358.2020.9160563

4. International Journal of Innovative Technology and Exploring Engineering (IJITEE) ISSN: 2278–3075, vol. 9(5) (2020). D1869029420/2020©BEIESP, https://doi.org/10.35940/ijitee.D1869.039520

5. International Journal of Innovative Technology and Exploring Engineering (IJITEE) ISSN: 2278–3075, vol. 8(9S4) (2019). I11400789S419/19©BEIESP, https://doi.org/10.35940/ijitee.I1140.0789S419

6. Fama, E.F.: Efficient capital markets: II. J. Financ. **46**, 1575–1617 (1991)

7. Atsalakis, G.S., Dimitrakakis, E.M, Zopounidis, C.D.: Elliot wave theory and neuro-fuzzy systems, stock market prediction: the WASP system. Expert Syst. Appl. **38**, 9196–9206 (2011)

8. Mitra, S.K.: Optimal combination of trading rules using neural networks. Int. Bus. Res. **2**(1), 86–99 (2009)

9. Dai, W., Shao, Y.E., Lu, C.-J.: Incorporating feature selection method into support vector regression for stock index forecasting. Neural Comput. Appl.

10. Fama, E.F., French, K.R.: International tests of a five-factor asset pricing model. J. Financ. Econ. **123**, 441–463 (2015)

11. Zhang, J., Li, L., Chen, W.: Predicting stock price using two-stage machine learning techniques. Comput. Econ. **57**, 1237–1261 (2020)

12. Zhang, J., Teng, Y.-F., Chen, W.: Support vector regression with modified firefly algorithm for stock price forecasting. Appl. Intell. **49**, 1658–1674 (2018)

13. Zhao, Y., Yang, G.: Deep learning-based integrated framework for stock price movement prediction. Appl. Soft Comput. **133**, 10992 (2022)

14. Liu, Z., Li, Y., Liu, H.: Fuzzy time-series prediction model based on text features and network features. Neural Comput. Appl. **35**, 3639–3649 (2021)

15. Wang, H., Zhang, Y., Liang, J., Liu, L.: DAFA-BiLSTM: deep autoregression feature augmented bidirectional LSTM network for time series prediction. Neural Netw. **157**, 240–256 (2022). [PubMed]

16. Barunı´k, J.; Kocˇenda, E.; Va´cha, L. Asymmetric connectedness on the U.S. stock market: bad and good volatility spillovers. J. Financ. Mark. **27**, 55–78 (2015)

17. Nguyen, V.C., Nguyen, T.T.: Dependence between Chinese stock market and Vietnamese stock market during the COVID-19 pandemic. Heliyon **8**, e11090 (2022)

18. Cao, J., Li, Z., Li, J.: Financial time series forecasting model based on CEEMDAN and LSTM. Phys. Stat. Mech. Appl. **519**, 127–139 (2019)

19. Chen, S., Ge, L.: Exploring the attention mechanism in LSTM-based Hong Kong stock price movement prediction. Quant. Financ.

20. Wang, C., Chen, Y., Zhang, S., Zhang, Q.: Stock market index prediction using deep transformer model. Expert Syst. Appl. **208**, 118128 (2022)

21. Chen, Y., Wu, J., Wu, Z.: China's commercial bank stock price prediction using a novel K-means- LSTM hybrid approach. Expert Syst. Appl. **202**, 117370 (2022)

Multi-featured Speech Emotion Recognition Using Extended Convolutional Neural Network

Arun Kumar Dubey, Yogita Arora, Neha Gupta, Sarita Yadav, Achin Jain$^{(\boxtimes)}$, and Devansh Verma

Bharati Vidyapeeth's College of Engineering, New Delhi, India
achin.mails@gmail.com

Abstract. There has been a significant increase in recent years in the investigation of emotions expressed via speech signals; this field is known as Speech Emotion Recognition (SER). SER holds immense potential across various applications and serves as a pivotal bridge in enhancing Human-Computer Interaction. However, prevailing challenges such as diminished model accuracy in noisy environments have posed substantial obstacles in this field. To address the scarcity of robust data for SER, we adopted data augmentation techniques, encompassing noise injection, stretching, and pitch modification. Distinguishing our approach from recent literature, we harnessed multiple audio features, including Mel-Frequency Cepstral Coefficients (MFCCs), mel spectrograms, zero crossing rate, root mean square, and chroma. This paper employs Convolutional Neural Networks (CNNs) as the foundation for emotion classification. The Toronto Emotional Speech Set (TESS) and the Ryerson Audio-Visual Data-base of Emotional Speech and Song (RAVDESS) are two well-established datasets that we utilize. The accuracy of our proposed model on the RAVDESS dataset is 72%, and on the TESS dataset, it achieves an impressive 96.62%. These results surpass those of extant models that have been customized for each specific dataset.

Keywords: Artificial intelligence · convolutional neural network · speech emotion recognition

1 Introduction

Speech is one of the inherent means by which humans express their emotions. Speech emotion recognition (SER) is the methodology by which an individual's emotional condition is deduced from their spoken language. Picard was the first person to study SER as a model for enhancing human-machine interaction in 1997. Human speech [1] is a rich source of semantic and personal information that can facilitate healthy communication between humans or humans and machines. To accomplish this harmony, the emotional state of a user is extracted from their speech. There is a correlation between the emotion of speech and its acoustic characteristics, such as timing, voice quality, articulation, and intonation. The variation between these characteristics forms the foundation of SER. Speech Emotion Recognition [2] has numerous applications ranging from a diagnostic

D. Garg et al. (Eds.): IACC 2023, CCIS 2053, pp. 321–332, 2024.
https://doi.org/10.1007/978-3-031-56700-1_26

tool for therapists for psychological evaluation, in-car board systems to predict the state of mind of a driver, automatic translation systems to assess the emotional state of a speaker for improved communication, robots, mobile services, call center applications, aircraft cockpits, etc. There has been a tremendous increase in data and cost computation in recent decades. Due to this, the deep learning approach is rapidly being adopted for improving the quality of speech and emotion recognition. SER systems consist of three elements:

1. Speech signal acquisition
2. Feature extraction
3. Classification of emotions

The Log-Mel spectrogram, Human Factor Cepstral Coefficients, Mel scale cepstral analysis, Mel Frequency Cepstral Coefficient, and Short-Term Fourier Transform are frequently utilized in speech analysis to extract features. The structure of the paper is as follows. The subsequent segment provides an overview of the existing relevant research in the domain of SER. The paper's conceptual and technical framework is elucidated in Sect. 2. The proposed methodology and model architecture are elaborated upon in Sect. 3. The investigated data set, experimental particulars, and acquired results are all encompassed in Sect. 4. To assess the proposed model's robustness, we conducted a comparative analysis of our empirical findings with the most recent approaches discussed in the same section. The conclusion and discussion of prospective developments in SER are provided in Sect. 5.

Recently, researchers and academics have developed a new interest in emotion recognition. A survey of current research in speech emotion recognition systems was conducted [5], and it discussed the various trends in emotion recognition, the problems encountered, the classification techniques employed, and the essential design criteria for emotional speech databases. Either speech [1, 2] or facial expressions [11] or both can be used to determine an individual's emotions. In the modern era, heart rate, blood pressure, skin temperature, and blood volume pulse are also used to detect human emotions. Speech-Emotion Recognition can be implemented in Consumer Electronics Home Products [1], which analyzes the emotional state of speech and suggests an appropriate method. Using 1D CNN in speaker-independent experiments makes the prediction model more accurate and optimal for the deployment of in-home assistants. IEMOCAP, TESS, EMO-DB, and RAVDESS are the standard datasets available on the market for predicting emotions in speech. These datasets contain a variety of emotions, including anger, sadness, joy, revulsion, pleasure, fear, etc. Nonetheless, as mentioned in the survey [5] and summarized below, these datasets have their limitations.

1. The majority of speech emotive databases struggle to accurately and naturally simulate emotions.In some databases, the quality of the recorded utterances is not so good.
2. Real-world noises are not considered since the audio are recorded in an artificial space.

Researchers use various feature extraction techniques, such as pitch, mfcc [3, 4], speed [6], chromium [7], mel_spectogram [5], etc., to obtain the desired results. In addition, researchers have utilized various Deep Learning, Machine learning techniques to predict emotions from audio files, such as 1D Convolutional Neural Networks [4], MLP Classifier [8], SVM [6] Decision Tree [5], Random Forest [10], etc. To improve the accuracy and robustness of Speech Emotion Recognition on the IEMOCAP and RAVDESS datasets [4], a method is known as Head Fusion based on the multihead attention mechanism was used, with respective accuracies of 76.18% and 76.38% using ACNN. The authors in [6] proposed an architecture that combines hybrid convolutional neural network (CNN) and feedforward deep neural network (DNN) architectures. In addition, the output of the proposed hybrid network is inputted into a softmax layer to generate a probability distribution over categorical classification for speech recognition. Additionally, efforts have been made to increase recognition accuracy and reduce the overall model cost and processing time [8]. Using radial basis function (RBF)-based K-means clustering algorithms and a deep BiLSTM network, it offers a novel approach. Using the STFT algorithm, a key segment is extracted from the entire cluster and then converted into spectrograms. The extracted and normalized high-level discriminative features are then passed to deep BiLSTM for classification. Standard IEMOCAP, EMO-DB, and RAVDESS datasets are utilized for the evaluation. The system in [9] consists of two components: a processing unit and a classifier. The processing unit is used to extract the necessary speech characteristics, and the classifier classifies the emotion based on these features. In addition, the use of autoencoders for dimensionality reduction and their effect on classification are covered. The survey results indicate that the conclusions drawn from different studies lack consistency [5]. The principal factor contributing to this issue is the investigation of only a single emotive speech database in each study, coupled with the lack of a database of adequate quality. The relevant works, their feature extraction methodologies, and classifiers are enumerated in Table 1.

Table 1. Comparison with similar research works for speech emotion recognition:

Reference	Dataset	Feature Extraction Techniques	Approach
[1]	RAVDESS, TESS	MFCC	CNN model architecture
[2]	RAVDESS, TESS	Log mel spectrogram, MFCC	CNN model architecture
[4]	RAVDESS, IEMOCAP, ESC50	MFCC	Head Fusion: Multi-Head Self-Attention with ACNN Model
[7]	EMO-DB, RAVDESS and SAVEE	MFCC, local shimmer, local jitter, loudness, log power of mel-frequency bands	Genetic Algorithm, clustering method

2   Method Background

Convolutional Neural Network: CNN was inspired by the structure of the human brain. It functions similarly to the way neurons in the brain process and transmit information. A convolutional neural network, like a conventional neural network, consists of multiple layers, but the presence of the convolutional layer and the pooling layer distinguishes it. CNN contains an input layer, an output layer, and numerous concealed layers. Figure 1 shows the flow of data through the neural network.

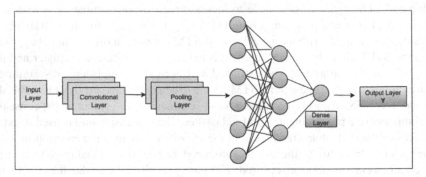

Fig. 1. CNN layers present in the neural network

We have used the following five layers in our work:

1. **Input layer:** Composed of artificial input neurons, the input layer of a neural network is responsible for introducing initial data into the system to be processed by succeeding layers of artificial neurons. Data subsequent to augmentation is supplied within the input layer of our model.
2. **Convolutional layer:** It is the most important layer which builds the foundation of CNN. A set of learnable filters are used in this layer to detect specific features from the input.
3. **Max Pooling layer:** As with its name, this layer takes out the maximum parameter, and the rest are drooped. Hence, the most prominent features are selected.
4. **Dense Layer:** Dense layer is the most common, recurrently used, and deeply connected layer. This layer is dense because all neurons present in the previous layer provide input to each neuron present in this layer.
5. **Output layer:** The final layer of neurons in an artificial neural network that generates program outputs is referred to as the output layer. The final layer of our model outputs the identified emotion extracted from the input audio file.

Mel-Frequency Cepstral Coefficients (MFCCs): Mel-frequency cepstral coefficients (MFCCs) are the coefficients that inclusively constitute mel-Frequency cepstrum (MFC). To train our model, it is important to extract features from audio files since we can't take raw audio files directly as input. The steps involved in MFCC feature extraction are:

1. **A/D Conversion:** Conversion of the audio signal from analog to digital format.

2. **Pre-emphasis:** A filter is used to increase the energy of high frequencies since the voice segment at high frequencies has a low magnitude compared to voice segments at lower frequencies. It improves phone detection accuracy.
3. **Windowing:** slice the audio signal into different segments with each segment having 25 ms width and with the signal at 10ms apart.
4. **DFT (Discrete Fourier Transform):** To convert the signal from the time domain to the frequency domain, DFT is applied.
5. **Mel-Filter Bank:** The mel scale is employed to convert the true frequency into the frequency that is perceptible to humans.
6. **Log:** The output of Mel-filter is annotated with log in order to emulate the human auditory system.
7. **IDFT:** Inverse of DFT operation is performed.
8. **Dynamic features:** From each audio signal sample, the MFCC technique will generate 39 dynamic features that are utilized as input for the speech recognition model. The comprehensive extraction process is depicted in Fig. 2.

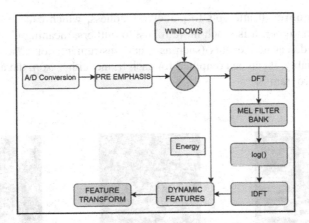

Fig. 2. Flow of extracting the MFCC features

Mel Spectrogram: Higher frequencies are more difficult for humans to distinguish from lower frequencies. Even for two sets of identically distant sounds, our perception of distance may vary. A mel scale is a unit of pitch in which equal distances in pitch sound are perceived to be equal distances by the receiver. Therefore, it assists in simulating the human perception of sound. Figure 3 depicts this entire procedure. The y-axis (frequency) was mapped onto the mel scale to create the mel spectrogram. We have obtained mel spectrograms for different audio signals (including happy, fear, and disgust) and are shown in Fig. 4.

Zero Crossing Rate: Zero Crossing Rate is a metric utilized to assess the degree of signal consistency. It can also be expressed as the count of times a signal's value is converted from positive to negative or vice versa divided by the duration of the frame. It

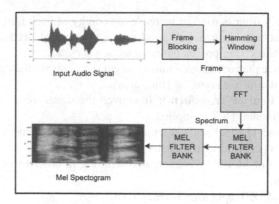

Fig. 3. Process of obtaining the mel spectrogram from the input audio signal

represents the rate at which a signal transitions from positive to zero to negative or from negative to zero to positive.

Root Mean Square: It attempts to perceive loudness, which can be used for event detection. Furthermore, it is much more robust to outliers, meaning if we segment the audio, we can detect new events (such as a new instrument, someone speaking etc.) much more reliably. It can be computed for each frame, either from the audio sample **y** or from a spectrogram **S**.

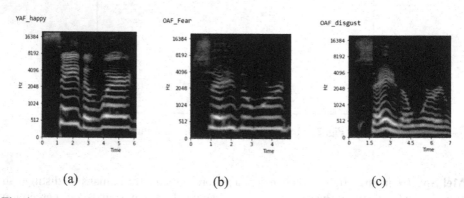

(a)	(b)	(c)

Fig. 4. Mel spectrogram of different speech signals: (a) mel Spectrogram for Happy, (b) Mel Spectrogram for Fear, (c) Mel Spectrogram for Disgust

Chroma: Chroma is a tool used for analyzing audio and classifying them into twelve different classes based on its pitch. Chroma has two main features namely, chroma vector and chroma deviation. The features explained above are used in our proposed model for feature extraction.

Librosa: Librosa is one of the python packages used for the analysis of music and audio. It is helpful in visualizing the audio signal and performs different feature extractions with the help of various signal processing techniques. We have used librosa extensively while doing feature extraction and data augmentation. The features are extracted from the audio by librosa functions.

3 Proposed Methodology

The proposed emotion detection approach consists of four stages, as mentioned in the Fig. 8.

3.1 Collection of Audio Samples (from RAVDESS and TESS Datasets)

We utilized the Ryerson Audio-Visual Database of Emotional Speech and Song (RAVDESS) and the Toronto Emotional Speech Set database (TESS) to validate our CNN method. Twenty-four actors deliver two statements with a neutral North American accent as part of the RAVDESS dataset. With two intensities—normal and strong—every statement is reiterated twice, excluding the "neutral" one. The expressions "Dogs are seated by the door" and "Kids are conversing by the door" are lexically equivalent. There are 1,440 speech files in total. It is a comprehensive, robust, and gender-balanced database because all of the actors (12 males and 12 females) are professional actors. In addition, it is rated 10 in terms of emotional authenticity, intensity, and sincerity. Two 26-year-old and 64-year-old female actresses with musical training are included in the TESS dataset. There are seven categories of emotions, and 200 words are spoken. Each syllable is spoken for each class of emotion. The audio files are labeled "Say the word _WORD," where _WORD represents each of the 200 syllables spoken by both women for each emotion. The magnitude of the dataset is therefore 2800. It is a well-balanced dataset with a normal-range threshold value.

3.2 Preprocessing of Raw Data and Data Augmentation

Before model training, it is frequently necessary to generate more representative training and testing sets. This is accomplished through data reorganization. Before training, we randomized our dataset, which reduces variance and enhances the model's performance on new or unseen data. Moreover, in real-world environments, speech is frequently accompanied by a variety of sounds or disturbances. Research in SER with chaotic speech is necessary and has practical significance [5]. Consequently, data augmentation techniques such as noise, stretch, and modulation were applied to the data. Data augmentation techniques are applied to the audio files which include adding noise, stretching the audio files, adjusting pitch etc.

- **For the addition of noise:** noise_value = 0.015 * np.random.uniform() * np.amax(data). This function adds some random value to the data by using NumPy.
- **For stretching audio:** This augmentation is performed by the librosa function librosa.effects.time_stretch and stretches the time series by a fixed rate.
- **For changing pitch:** librosa.effects.pitch_shift

Figure 7 shows the original data signal and then the same audio signal is shown with added data augmentation techniques like adding noise, stretch and pitch.

3.3 Feature Extraction Techniques are Applied to Audio Files

MFCC is a popular technique used for feature extraction. In our paper, we have extracted multiple features from audio including MFCC, mel spectrogram, zero crossing rate, root mean square, and chroma which are the most popular feature extraction tools for audio files. We have created a function that has included all above-mentioned techniques extracting features from each data with the librosa function. The function stacked all extracted features into an array that was later feeded to the classification model these are depicted in Fig. 5.

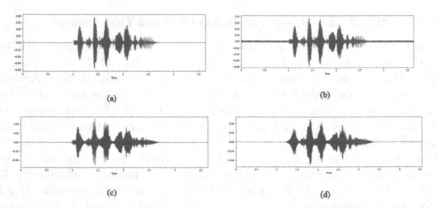

(a)   (b)

(c)   (d)

Fig. 5. Performing Data Augmentation on an input audio signal: (a) Original Signal, (b) After addition of noise, (c) After stretching audio, (d) After changing pitch

3.4 Classification Using Convolutional Neural Network

In the final phase, the data is passed through a dense neural network followed by an output layer. Convolutional Neural Network has been implemented for both RAVDESS and TESS [1]. The optimizer used is ADAM for both cases as it gives a better rate of convergence. To overcome the loss due to negative coverage, activation functions (ReLU and softmax) have been applied. Causal padding is chosen because the signals are shuffled and are hence, independent of future inputs. In TESS, CNN has been implemented on 7 classes (happy, sad, disgust, fear, anger, surprise, and neutral) across two genders, old and young, while in RAVDESS, 8 classes of emotions (01 = neutral, 02 = calm, 03 = happy, 04 = sad, 05 = angry, 06 = fearful, 07 = disgust, 08 = surprised) are implemented. Each layer has a window/kernel of size 5. Max pool of size_ has been added after a few layers to reduce the feature set. Tuning is done later using extra convolutional as well as dropout laters. Our mode, Fig. 6, has 4 convolutional layers with the activation function as relu. After each convolutional layer, we have added a max pooling layer to calculate the maximum or largest value in each patch of each feature map, which helps to reduce dimension computation and overfitting. After the third convolutional layer, we have added a dropout layer to prevent overfitting. After the convolutional layer, flattening is applied followed by dense layers with relu and softmax activation functions. One emotion from the class is predicted at the end of the CNN layer.

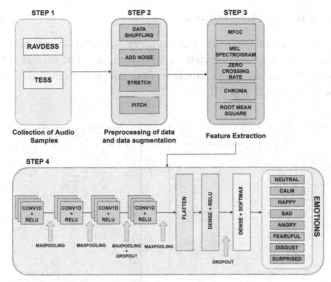

Fig. 6. Data-Augmented and Multi-Feature Speech Emotion Analyzer

4 Result Analysis

4.1 Result Analysis on RAVDESS Dataset

With Convolutional Neural Network, the Accuracy achieved was 72% as shown in Fig. 7. The train size used for the data is 80% while the test size is 20%. Categorical_crossentropy is used as a loss function, which is designed to quantify the difference between two probability distributions. Roc_auc_score obtained is 0.8965. The confusion matrix is given in Fig. 8.

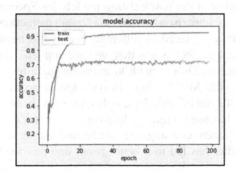

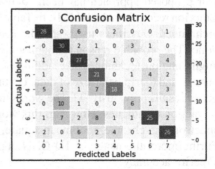

Fig. 7. Accuracy graph obtained from the RAVDESS Dataset.

Fig. 8. Confusion matrix for the RAVDESS Dataset.

4.2   Result Analysis on TESS Dataset

With Convolutional Neural Network, the Accuracy achieved was 96.62% as shown in Fig. 9. The train size used for the data is 80% while the test size is 20%. Categorical_crossentropy is used as a loss function. Roc_auc_score obtained is 0.9979. The confusion matrix is given in Fig. 10.

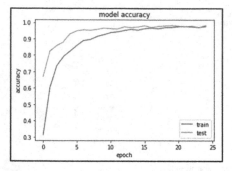 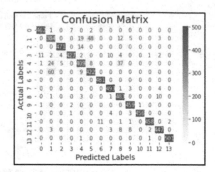

Fig. 9. Accuracy graph obtained from the TESS Dataset.

Fig. 10. Confusion matrix obtained from the TESS Dataset.

The confusion matrices are shown in Fig. 10. And Fig. 12. For RAVDESS and TESS datasets respectively and shows the layout that compares the predicted class labels against the actual class labels over all data instances. For instance, looking at Fig. 12, there were 462 instances where Emotion 0 (Old Fear) was predicted correctly while 10 instances where it was not. We can see from the confusion matrix that emotions are predicted accurately mostly.

4.3   Result Comparison

Our proposed approach has been compared with the best existing models for Speech Emotion recognition in Table II. In Table II, a comparison between the feature extraction techniques, classifiers used, and the accuracy achieved in different models has been done. The probable reason for achieving the best accuracy is that we have applied data augmentation techniques like adding noise, stretch and pitch to make our data more natural and to triple the size of data. Features like MFCCs have always helped to acquire better results previously [1]. The works mentioned in Table 2 use only one or two feature extraction techniques. However, this work has used a total of five features (mfcc, mel spectrogram, chrome, root mean square, and zero crossing rate) for feature extraction. Furthermore, the usage of 1D CNN classifier has led to a better result and provided superior accuracy.

Table 2. Comparison of the best speech emotion recognition models with the proposed approach

Reference	Feature Extraction Technique	Used Classifiers	Emotion Accuracy (TESS)	Emotion Accuracy (RAVDESS)
[2]	Log mel spectrogram	2D-CNN	62%	70%
[3]	eGeMAPS	CNN	49.48%	65.67%
[12]	OpenSimle Tool & eGeMAPS	SVM	65.1%	70.59%
Proposed	MFCC, Mel spectrogram, chroma, zero crossing rate, root mean square	1D-CNN	**96.62%**	**72%**

5 Conclusion

In this paper, the feature extraction techniques Mel-Frequency Cepstral Coefficient (MFCC), Chroma, mel_spectogram, root mean was used on the audio files. The proposed approach provides 72% accuracy for the Ryerson Audio-Visual Database of Emotional Speech and Song (RAVDESS) dataset and 96.62% accuracy for the Toronto Emotional Speech Set (TESS) database using CNN algorithm. This work can be further extended to test various other aspects like different accents, distinct nationalities, and multiple age and gender categories. We can add more acoustic features to generate a more advanced SER classification model. The model can be extended for use in real-time speech emotion identification. We will continue our work implementing more data augmentation techniques in SER based on our established conclusions.

References

1. Chatterjee, R., Mazumdar, S., Sherratt, R.S., Halder, R., Maitra, T., Giri, D.: Real-time speech emotion analysis for smart home assistants. IEEE Trans. Consum. Electron. **67**(1), 68–76 (2021). https://doi.org/10.1109/TCE.2021.3056421
2. Venkataramanan, K., Rajamohan, H.R.: Emotion recognition from speech (2019). arXiv: 1912.1045
3. Parry, J., et al.: Analysis of deep learning architectures for cross-corpus speech emotion recognition. In: Proceedings of the Conference of the International Speech Communication Association (Interspeech), pp. 1656–1660 (2019). https://doi.org/10.21437/Interspeech.2019-2753
4. Xu, M., Zhang, F., Zhang, W.: Head fusion: improving the accuracy and robustness of speech emotion recognition on the IEMOCAP and RAVDESS dataset. IEEE Access **9**, 74539–74549 (2021). https://doi.org/10.1109/ACCESS.2021.3067460
5. El Ayadi, M., Kamel, M.S., Karray, F.: Survey on speech emotion recognition: features, classification schemes, and databases. https://doi.org/10.1016/j.patcog.2010.09.020

6. Ezz-Eldin, M., Khalaf, A.A.M., Hamed, H.F.A., Hussein, A.I.: Efficient feature-aware hybrid model of deep learning architectures for speech emotion recognition. IEEE Access **9**, 19999–20011 (2021). https://doi.org/10.1109/ACCESS.2021.3054345

7. Kanwal, S., Asghar, S.: Speech emotion recognition using clustering based GA-optimized feature set. IEEE Access **9**, 125830–125842 (2021). https://doi.org/10.1109/ACCESS.2021.3111659

8. Mustaqeem, Sajjad, M., Kwon, S.: Clustering-based speech emotion recognition by incorporating learned features and deep BiLSTM. IEEE Access **8**, 79861–79875 (2020). https://doi.org/10.1109/ACCESS.2020.2990405

9. Patel, N., Patel, S., Mankad, S.H.: Impact of autoencoder based compact representation on emotion detection from audio. J. Ambient Intell. Hum. Comput. **13**, 867–885 (2021). https://doi.org/10.1007/s12652-021-02979-3

10. Sonmez, Y.Ü., Varol, A.: New trends in speech emotion recognition. In: 2019 7th International Symposium on Digital Forensics and Security (ISDFS), pp. 1–7 (2019). https://doi.org/10.1109/ISDFS.2019.875752

11. Castellano, G., Kessous, L., Caridakis, G.: Emotion recognition through multiple modalities: face, body gesture, speech. In: Peter, C., Beale, R. (eds.) Affect and Emotion in Human-Computer Interaction. LNCS, vol. 4868, pp. 92–103. Springer, Heidelberg (2008). https://doi.org/10.1007/978-3-540-85099-1_8

12. Shaqra, F.A., Duwairi, R., Al-Ayyoub, M.: Recognizing emotion from speech based on age and gender using hierarchical models. Procedia Comput. Sci. **151**, 37–44 (2019). https://doi.org/10.1016/j.procs.2019.04.009

Large Language Models for Search Engine Optimization in E-commerce

Grzegorz Chodak[1]([✉]) [iD] and Klaudia Błażyczek[2] [iD]

[1] Department of Artificial Intelligence, Wrocław University of Science and Technology,
Wybrzeże Wyspiańskiego 27, 50-370 Wrocław, Poland
grzegorz.chodak@pwr.edu.pl
[2] Faculty of Management, Wrocław University of Science and Technology, Wybrzeże
Wyspiańskiego 27, 50-370 Wrocław, Poland

Abstract. The paper discusses how Large Language Models (LLMs) can be used
in search engine optimization activities dedicated to e-commerce. In the first part
the most important Search Engine Optimization (SEO) issues are discussed, such
as technical SEO aspects, keyword selection, and content optimization. Then the
study presents an in-depth look at OpenAI's advancements, including ChatGPT
and DALL-E. The latter sections describe the capabilities of Large Language
Models into the realm of SEO, particularly in e-commerce. Firstly, a set of prompts
for LLMs that can be used to create content and HTML code for online shops is
proposed. Then advantages, and drawbacks of incorporating LLMs in SEO for
e-commerce are presented. The research concludes by synthesizing the potential
of merging AI with SEO practices, offering insights for future applications.

Keywords: Large Language Model · Search Engine Optimization · ChatGPT ·
E-commerce

1 Introduction

The increasing competition in e-commerce sector necessitates advanced tools and techniques to improve rank in search engine results. A high ranking in the search engine
results page (SERP) not only guarantees an increase in organic website traffic [5], but
also reduces spending on paid advertising. The explosive growth of Large Language
Models (LLMs) in the last two years [19] has resulted in the increasing use of this tool
in SEO activities. LLMs not only allow the generation of large amounts of content but
can also support other elements of SEO.

There are several studies that summarizes the previous work in the domain. One of
them examines how ChatGPT can affect search marketing and SEO [33]. Another study
compares ChatGPT to Spyfu as a keyword discovery tool, revealing that while Spyfu
outperforms in discovering efficient keywords, ChatGPT excels in predicting search
trends and identifying specific, user-targeted long-tail keywords and queries [34].

The main aim of this paper is to propose methods of applying LLMs into SEO activities in e-commerce and investigate the advantages and disadvantages of it. The structure

D. Garg et al. (Eds.): IACC 2023, CCIS 2053, pp. 333–344, 2024.
https://doi.org/10.1007/978-3-031-56700-1_27

of the paper is the following: Sect. 2 provides a brief overview of SEO in the context of content optimization. Section 3 focuses on the impact of Artificial Intelligence on content creation. Here, innovations by OpenAI, like ChatGPT and DALLE, are spotlighted. Our core examination in Sect. 4 revolves around the infusion of LLMs in SEO, proposing a set of prompts for e-commerce. It also analyses benefits, and potential pitfalls within the application of LLMs in SEO. Section 5 shortly summarizes our insights and proposes directions for further research in this area.

2 Search Engine Optimization

2.1 Operation of Search Engines

An Internet search engine can be defined as an online application or service for searching the global web for specific information, content, or resources. The main purpose of search engines is to allow users to access the vast volume of data available on the Internet in an efficient and organized manner. The key element of a user's communication with a search engine is the query interface [1]. Query results are presented to users on the search results page [3]. The user's query is routed to a query parser, which analyzes and breaks it down into relevant phrases [4].

The search algorithm is a key component of a search engine [1]. It searches an index containing key phrases and URLs and compares them with phrases obtained from the query parser. The results are returned to the user.

The data needed for ranking comes from an index that contains various information about sites, such as text, graphics, documents, links, and metadata [2]. Search engines also use knowledge graphs to help understand how topics and concepts are related [3]. The indexing process involves collecting, analyzing, and storing data in an index [2]. A crawler or robot searches the web for new sites to index or to update data on already indexed sites [3]. Crawlers focus on popular, relevant, and quality sites.

2.2 The Importance of a Site's Position on a Search Engine Results Page

A site's position in the SERP can have a major impact on the number of clicks it receives. According to research, the first result in Google gets 27.6% of all clicks, while the top 3 results they obtain in total 54.4% of all clicks [5]. The effect of improved ranking in the search results is more clicks on the link leading to the website. Moving from position 10 to 9 results in an 11% increase in clicks, while moving from 2nd to 1st results in a 74.5% increase in clicks. The same research shows that a 3% CTR[1] score is a good result for SEO [5].

Figure 1 shows the CTR for positions from 1 to 10 in the SERP for Google search. Based on it, it can be concluded that the position in the SERP is of great importance for the popularity of the site, so it is worth taking care of its best positioning.

Based on the results, it can be deduced that ranking as high as possible can be crucial to an e-shop success. To achieve this, an internet shop needs to take the best possible care of the site's SEO to get the best possible organic score. Additionally, high position

---

[1] It calculates the proportion of clicks relative to the overall number of impressions [3].

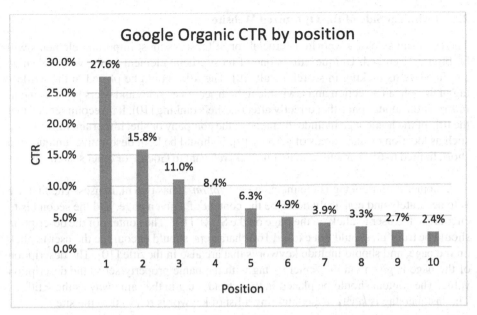

Fig. 1. Organic CTR for Google not including ads - Source: own elaboration based on data from Backlinko [5].

in SERP may reduce the spendings on paid ads because in the case of paid advertising in the Google Ads system, one of the criteria affecting the fee charged is the quality indicator, of which the quality of the landing page is an element.

2.3 Long Tail in SEO

Long Tail theory originally described a market phenomenon where a wide range of niche products can generate a similar return on sales as a relatively narrow range of very popular products [6]. In the context of SEO, the term refers to longer and specific keyword phrases that are less frequently used but have higher conversion rates [7] - a percentage indicator showing the number of users who performed further actions on a site after clicking on a search result. Long Tail phrases can generate about 70% of traffic to a site [8], so their issue is important to discuss. For a more in-depth discussion of key phrases, mention should be made of phrases like Fat Head and The Chunky Middle. Long Tail in SEO are key phrases consisting of at least 3 words, characterized by higher accuracy and lower popularity [1]. Fat Head are short key phrases consisting of one or two words, generating more traffic [7]. The Chunky Middle are phrases that are more detailed and descriptive than Fat Head, with less interest but still popular [7]. Long Tail phrases are important for SEO, allowing to target a site to specific demographic groups [1]. The use of Long Tail phrases is crucial for effective SEO of a site.

2.4 Technical Side of the Optimized Website

The technical side of a website is crucial for SEO, so its most important elements will be briefly discussed. Unique title is one of most crucial element of the website which can improve its ranking in search results [9]. The title should be placed in the <title> tag in the <head> section and is visible to both search engines and users [9]. It is meta-information about a page that directly affects a site's ranking [10]. It is recommended that the title of the homepage include the name of the company or site, important information such as location or main areas of activity [9]. It should be both descriptive, unique, and short, limited to 65 characters, so that it is still relevant to Google or other search engines [10].

Another important tag is the metatag *description*. It has two main uses. The first use is to accurately and concisely describe the content of a given page, and the second is to encourage the user to click on the page on the SERP [10]. The content of the description should be truthful, should not exceed 160 characters, should encourage the user to click on the page, and should include keywords that are also in the title [10]. The description of the page is given via the <meta> tag with the name property set to the description value. The content should be placed in the <head> tag in the same way as the <title>. The last metatag is *keywords*, containing a list of keywords relevant to the site.

2.5 Methods of Selecting Keywords for SEO

Selecting the right keywords is significant for a successful SEO strategy. There are many methods and tools that can help with keyword selection.

The first thing to determine is clearly outline the scope of the business [11]. The next step is to brainstorm for keywords and phrases [10]. At this stage, it's a good idea to collect as many of them as possible [11]. Once words and phrases were collected, it is a need to organize them from the most general to the most specific. One such method is competitive research [11], by checking the top-ranked sites and including the keywords of those sites in the previously created set.

To find better key phrases, the trend analysis can be conducted [10]. Tracking them allows understanding what phrases are currently popular among users and how their preferences are changing, and with it can tailor website content to meet the current needs and interests of customers. A popular tool for studying trends is Google Trends[2].

Once the key phrases have been collected, one can proceed to select the best ones. There are many tools that can help with this [11]. One of the most popular is Google's Keyword Planner[3], which offers a lot of information about key phrases, such as average monthly searches, competitiveness of phrases and keyword suggestions.

An alternative method, which will be discussed in the 4th section, is to use LLMs to generate and select the best keywords for a particular business.

---

[2] https://trends.google.pl/trends/.

[3] https://ads.google.com/home/tools/keyword-planner/. To use the tool, Google Ads account is required.

2.6 Content of the Optimized Website

The recommended starting point when planning content is to analyze and select the best keywords and phrases for the site and its individual pages [10]. Once the selection has been made, it will be possible to create content so that it incorporates the words and phrases selected earlier.

One of the most important things is that the content placed on the sites should be of high quality that will engage users and be appropriately tailored to the length of the site [2]. Preparing high-quality content requires understanding the target audience and how and what they are looking for [10]. The quality of the site is influenced by: original and unique content, clean structure, formatting, readability of content or having CTA elements[4]. It is advisable to use interactive multimedia, such as videos, infographics, and, if possible, integrate content with social media. Through this, users are encouraged to stay on the site and interact with it. it is necessary to update content regularly, as fresh content is important for effective SEO [2].

Search engines place great importance on the uniqueness of content on pages [10]. There is important to avoid thin content, which refers to pages that do not provide enough unique content to warrant inclusion in search results [12]. It is also important that the content be different from other pages on the site, and that it have unique titles and meta descriptions [10]. Unique video, audio and graphic content is also valued by search engines [10].

3 Artificial Intelligence for Content Creation

3.1 OpenAI

OpenAI is an artificial intelligence research lab in San Francisco, founded in 2015 [13]. Its goal is to develop AI technology for the benefit of humanity [14] particularly in the context of developing general artificial intelligence, that is, the ability of a computer to perform tasks as a human would [15]. It does this through research, platform, and services [13]. The public and the technology industry are showing great interest in OpenAI [13]. The best-known tools from OpenAI are ChatGPT and DALL E [16].

3.2 ChatGPT

ChatGPT is generative artificial intelligence model created by OpenAI to produce diverse text content and serve as a chatbot with human-like conversational abilities [17]. Its standout feature lies in its capacity to tailor and guide the conversation according to specified criteria, including length, format, style, level of detail, and used language [16]. ChatGPT can respond to inquiries and generating a diverse array of written content, encompassing articles, social media posts, code, and emails [16].

ChatGPT is different from traditional search engines and AI assistants. Unlike them, it generates its own responses based on the content entered by the user, without providing links or sources of information [16]. ChatGPT runs on the Generative Pre-trained

---

[4] Call to action - its purpose is to get the user to respond in a certain way.

Transformers model, or more specifically, its versions: GPT-1, GPT2, GPT-3, GPT-3.5 and GPT-4 [18]. At the current time[5], ChatGPT allows operation on models: GPT-3.5 and GPT-4. These models analyze context and predict the next words in a response [16]. Although there have been reports of GPT-5, it is currently untrained, and GPT-4 is powerful enough to meet needs for many years to come [12].

ChatGPT uses a multi-layered transformer network to generate answers to users' questions [19]. A transformer is a type of neural network architecture [16]. The main advantage of transformers is effective parallelism, which allows large models to be scaled and trained [16]. Transformers allow the tool to understand the context and meaning of ambiguous words based on the surrounding words in a sentence [19].

The tool's model was trained on a huge set of texts collected from the internet from 2021, covering about 570 GB of data, including websites and books [16]. The model for ChatGPT also underwent additional training based on reinforcement learning using the RLHF[6] method [19]. In this method, the model is given various tasks, and the results are evaluated by humans. The evaluation is transformed into a score, which in turn is fed back into the training process [19].

ChatGPT provides a free version, based on the GPT-3.5 generative model, and a paid version[7] based on the GPT-4 model. The paid version is more advanced, has earlier access to new features, faster response times, and has priority in handling queries during heavy load [16]. GPT-4 is an improved version of GPT-3.5. The latter model allows 175 billion parameters to be included depending on the question received, while the former allows at least 3 or 4 times as many [19]. This number of GPT-4 parameters allows it to answer questions in a more human-like style than GPT-3 [20]. The GPT-4 model was trained for an additional 6 months beyond the GPT-3.5 training, considering information from humans and artificial intelligence, resulting in significant improvements [20]. In addition, GPT-4 is trained on newer data, considering information as far back as September 2021, making its answers more up to date than GPT-3.5, which only had data through June 2021 [20]. With increased parameters, GPT-4 is less prone to hallucinations than GPT-3.5, but caution should still be exercised when using it [20].

3.3 DALL·E - Graphic Content Generator

DALL·E, an artificial intelligence system crafted by OpenAI, can generate lifelike images and graphics by interpreting natural language descriptions [21]. DALL·E operates on a modified GPT-3 generative model, operating on 12 billion parameters, rained to produce images by utilizing textual descriptions, leveraging a dataset that consists of pairs of text and corresponding images [16]. DALL·E grants access to a subset of the 3D image rendering engine's capabilities with varying levels of reliability [22].

Decoder and encoder mechanisms play a key role in the operation of DALL·E [23]. The encoder in the DALL·E model is responsible for converting input data, such as a textual description, into abstract representations in the latent space [23]. In the case of DALL·E, the encoder translates textual descriptions into this abstract language of

---

[5] 2023/10/28.

[6] Reinforcement Learning from Human Feedback.

[7] As of 2023/10/28, the cost is $20 per month.

the latent space [24]. Then, a decoder processes these abstract representations from the hidden space and transforms them into images [24]. The hidden variables determine the features of the image, such as shape, colour, or texture. Manipulation of this latent space allows users to create images with different features and styles.

It is worth mentioning that AI-generated images are currently not protected by copyright in the US and several other countries, so they can be used freely without fear of legal consequences, just as with ChatGPT [16]. This is particularly relevant for online shops, where DALL E can be used to generate creative backgrounds for products.

4 Using LLMs for Improving SEO in E-commerce

LLMs can have many different applications, including SEO activities. Due to ChatGPT's capacity to generate numerous solutions, it can be used during the brainstorming phase when seeking key phrases for the store and its products. It can also be used when creating product descriptions, headings and metatags.

4.1 Methods of Applying LLMs in SEO

Communication and issuing of LLMs commands is done employing prompts. The new field of knowledge that deals with building prompts to use LLMs for specific purposes is called prompt engineering [28]. On the one hand, it is based on trial and error research and the undertaking of numerous experiments. On the other hand, prompt engineering is about optimizing queries to LLMs based on knowledge of their performance and learning processes [27].

Prompts for SEO in an online shop can be divided into the following categories: keyword research and analysis, content creation, technical SEO. This division shows the different areas of SEO, but it is important to remember that these areas are not disconnected. Prompts can also take a comprehensive form covering all the areas mentioned.

Examples of prompts that can be deprecated are provided for each aforementioned category. Parameters of prompts are given in brackets.

Keyword Research and Analysis

What are the primary keywords associated with the [shop's main products]?
Which long-tail keywords can be targeted to capture [e-shop sector]?
What are the most important keywords for product [product name]?

Content Creation

Generate the [number of words] description of the product [name of product]? The description should include the following keywords: [keyword1, keyword2, ..., keywordN] in style [style definition].

Rephrase the description of the product [product name] which is the following [text of product description]? The description should include the following keywords: [keyword1, keyword2, ..., keywordN] in style [style definition].
Generate [number of words] text concerning product [product name] including keywords [keyword1, keyword2, ..., keywordN] to the online store blog?
Generate [number of words] text concerning product [product name] including keywords [keyword1, keyword2, ..., keywordN] to the Facebook post concerning online store [name of the store]?

If the internet shop software allows descriptions to be inserted in the form of HTML code, LLMs can generate ready-made code containing SEO-relevant elements. Prompts may look like the following:

Generate the product description [Product name] to internet shop [Internet Shop name] in HTML format which include heading tag <H1> with keywords [keyword1, keyword2, ..., keywordN] and two heading tags <H2> with keywords [keyword1, keyword2, ..., keywordN].
Rephrase the product description [Product name] which is the following [text of product description] to internet shop [Internet Shop name] in HTML format which include heading tag <H1> with keywords [keyword1, keyword2, ..., keywordN] and two heading tags <H2> with keywords [keyword1, keyword2, ..., keywordN].

The list of keywords can be provided by the user, but also suggested by LLM.

Technical SEO

Create Title tag of no more than 65 characters for product [product name] with the following description [text of product description].
Create Description metatag of no more than 160 characters for product [product name] with the following description [text of product description].
Create Keywords metatag of no more than 100 characters for product [product name] with the following description [text of product description].

Comprehensive Prompt
Generate the product description [product name] to internet shop [Internet Shop name] in HTML format which include heading tag <H1> with relevant keywords and two heading tags <H2> with relevant keywords. The HTML code should include Title tag of no more than 65 characters and Description metatag of no more than 160 characters and Keywords metatag of no more than 100 characters.

Result of prompting ChatGPT 4.0 with the comprehensive prompt presented above for product *TV QLED 55'* and fictitious internet shop *ShopwithTVs.com.* is presented below:

```
<!DOCTYPE html>
<html lang="en">
<head>
  <meta charset="UTF-8">
  <meta http-equiv="X-UA-Compatible" content="IE=edge">
  <meta name="viewport" content="width=device-width, initial-scale=1.0">
  <title>ShopwithTVs.com - QLED 55" Ultra HD Smart TV</title>
  <meta name="description" content="Experience unmatched clarity with the 55-
inch QLED Ultra HD Smart TV on ShopwithTVs.com. Dive into a world of vibrant
colours and immersive visuals.">
  <meta name="keywords" content="QLED, 55-inch, TV, Ultra HD, Smart TV, Shop-
withTVs">
</head>
<body>
<h1>QLED 55" Ultra HD Smart TV on ShopwithTVs.com</h1>
<h2>QLED Display Technology</h2>
<p>The QLED technology offers superior picture quality, presenting vivid colours and
clear details that bring every scene to life. Powered by Quantum Dot technology, enjoy
breathtaking visuals like never before.</p>
<h2>Smart Features for the Modern Viewer</h2>
<p>With the integrated smart hub, seamlessly stream your favourite shows, movies,
and online content. Connect with leading streaming platforms, control your TV through
voice commands, and enhance your viewing experience.</p>
</body>
</html>
```

4.2 Advantages of Using LLMs in SEO for E-commerce

Many advantages of using LLMs for e-commerce SEO activities can be identified. Due to the limited volume of the article, only the most important advantages have been selected.

1. **Lower cost:** The first imposing advantage of using LLMs is the low cost of content creation compared to human content creation [31].
2. **Speed of content creation:** LLMs are able to create large amounts of content in a very short time, which can be particularly important, for example, when new products are launched and online shops that show them to customers first can expect increased sales.
3. **Multilingual SEO:** With their vast linguistic capabilities, LLMs can assist businesses in optimizing their content across multiple languages, expanding their global reach [30].
4. **Possibility to generate ready-to-use HTML code:** an important advantage of LLMs is the ability to generate HTML code, which can be a major plus for e-commerce software, where it is possible to include not only the description in text form, but also the finished HTML code.
5. **SEO-optimized content creation:** LLMs can produce content which is SEO-optimized concerning appropriate keyword saturation and other SEO factors.

6. **Keyword Optimization:** LLMs can suggest keywords based on context, helping internet shops optimize their content to capture diverse search intents. LLMs can replace specialized keyword suggestion tools.
7. **Ability to imitate different styles of expression:** LLMs are able to mimic different styles of speech [32], so it can be recommended to generate a product description in an old-fashioned, youthful style or, for example, a pirate style or one that most closely mimics a cartoon character.

4.3 Disadvantages of Using LLMs in SEO for E-commerce

Despite the numerous advantages of LLMs in supporting SEO in e-commerce, it is important to be aware of the limitations of these solutions. Listed below are what the authors consider to be the most significant disadvantages that are present in the current versions of LLMs (which of course does not mean that future versions will not be devoid of these disadvantages).

1. **The problem of hallucinations:** Current versions of LLMs such as ChatGPT are unfortunately capable of producing texts that are not factually correct, this property is called artificial hallucinations [29] or just hallucinations. There's a potential for LLMs to generate misleading or false information, which could harm a brand's reputation and trustworthiness. Unfortunately, this feature makes full automation in content creation by LLMs risky and human proofreading of texts becomes advisable, which incurs additional costs.
2. **Over-optimization**: Relying heavily on LLMs can lead to content that's overly optimized, making it seem artificial and potentially harming user experience.
3. **Potential for homogenization**: If many e-commerce platforms use similar LLMs for SEO, there's a risk of content across platforms becoming too similar, reducing differentiation. This can lead to a lower ranking in the SERPs due to duplicate content.
4. **The problem of content overload:** Online shops abusing LLMs to create content may no longer be acceptable due to the increasing problem of getting to content that is truly relevant to the customer.
5. **Plagiarism concerns:** LLM may create content that is like existing material and fail to provide sources, which raises the risk of plagiarism [26]. Particularly in the case of niche content that is rarely found online, plagiarism is more likely to occur.

5 Conclusion

Using artificial intelligence-generated content brings many advantages. First, it accelerates the process of creating and publishing content, which is both time-saving and cost-effective [25]. AI also enables personalization of content and optimization for SEO, which can significantly impact the effectiveness of marketing and communications. In addition, LLMs can create content in multiple languages, allowing for global content customization. Another important advantage is overcoming the problem of content creators' lack of inspiration and preventing misinformation, which minimizes the risk of costly lawsuits or negative impact on a company's reputation in the event of business irregularities [25]. The use of LLMs in content generation also comes with some limitations. First and foremost, the content generated may be characterized by a lack of originality and quality. The problem of hallucinations is still a significant shortcoming of the generated content and prevents full automation of these processes. Additionally, the content generated by LLMs, especially if it is overused, often sounds artificial, which can introduce distrust among audiences. Therefore, when using AI in content generation, it is important to exercise caution and carefully evaluate the context and purpose to ensure the quality and trust of the audience. The proposed set of online shop prompts can provide guidance for practitioners, but also provide inspiration for further research into the use of LLMs in e-commerce content generation processes. As further research, it would be interesting to conduct experiments on how the content generated by the LLM affects the SERP. Broader analyses of how the mass creation of content by LLMs will change search engine algorithms would also seem interesting.

References

1. Ledford, J.: Search Engine Optimization Bible, 2nd edn. Wiley, Indianapolis (2009)
2. Shenoy, A., Prabhu, A.: Introducing SEO: Your Quick-start Guide to Effective SEO Practices, 1st edn. Apress, Govardhan Nagar (2016)
3. Enge, E., Spencer, S., Stricchiola, J.: The Art of SEO, 3rd edn. O'Reilly Media Inc, Sebastopol (2016)
4. Marketbrew.ai, Understanding Query Parsers: How Search Engines Process Your Searches. https://marketbrew.ai/understanding-query-parsers-how-search-engines-process-your-searches. Accessed 28 Oct 2023
5. Backlinko, We analyzed 4 million Google Search Results. Here's what we learned about organic CTR. https://backlinko.com/google-ctr-stats. Accessed 28 Oct 2023
6. Anderson, C.: The Long Tail: Why the Future of Business is Selling Less of More, 1st edn. Hyperion, New York (2006)
7. Ahrefs, Long-tail Keywords: What They Are and How to Get Search Traffic From Them. https://ahrefs.com/blog/long-tail-keywords/. Accessed 28 Oct 2023
8. Mangools, How to find long-tail keywords (and why they're important). https://mangools.com/blog/long-tail-keywords/. Accessed 28 Oct 2023
9. Google Search Central, Search Engine Optimization (SEO) Starter Guide. https://developers.google.com/search/docs/fundamentals/seo-starter-guide?hl=en. Accessed 28 Oct 2023
10. Enge, E., Spencer, S., Stricchiola, J.: The Art of SEO, 4th edn. O'Reilly Media Inc, Sebastopol (2023)
11. Clay, B., Jones, K.: Search Engine Optimization All-in-One For Dummies, 4 (edn.). For Dummies, Hoboken (2022)
12. Kent, P.: SEO for Dummies, 7th edn. For Dummies, New Jersey (2020)
13. Joel, T., Venkataraman, S.: A review about Artificial Intelligence (AI) with reference to open AI. Int. J. Res. Trends Innov. 8(5), 335–337 (2023)
14. OpenAI, About. https://openai.com/about. Accessed 28 Oct 2023
15. OpenAI, Planning for AGI and beyond. https://openai.com/blog/planning-for-agi-and-beyond. Accessed 28 Oct 2023
16. Baker, P.: ChatGPT For Dummies,1 (edn.). For Dummies, Hoboken (2023)
17. Alto, V.: Modern Generative AI with ChatGPT and OpenAI Models, 1st edn. Packt Publishing, Birmingham (2023)
18. Caelen, O., Blete, M.: Developing Apps with GPT-4 and ChatGPT, 1st edn. O'Reilly Media Inc, Sebastopol (2023)
19. Loukides, M.: What Are ChatGPT and Its Friends?, 1st edn. O'Reilly Media Inc, Sebastopol (2023)

20. Digital Trends, GPT-4 vs. GPT-3.5: how much difference is there? https://www.digitaltrends.com/computing/gpt-4-vs-gpt-35. Accessed 28 Oct 2023
21. Phoenix, J., Taylor, M.: Prompt Engineering for Generative AI (Early Release, Raw & Unedited), 1st edn. O'Reilly Media Inc, Sebastopol (2024)
22. OpenAI, DALL·E: Creating images from text. https://openai.com/research/dall-e. Accessed 28 Oct 2023
23. Cointelegraph, What is DALL-E, and how does it work? https://cointelegraph.com/news/what-is-dall-e-and-how-does-it-work. Accessed 28 Oct 2023
24. AssemblyAi, How DALL-E 2 Actually Works. https://www.assemblyai.com/blog/how-dall-e-2-actually-works/. Accessed 28 Oct 2023
25. HubSpot, The Pros and Cons of AI-Generated Content. https://blog.hubspot.com/marketing/ai-generated-content. Accessed 28 Oct 2023
26. Wu, J., Gan, W., Chen, Z., Wan, S., Lin, H.: AI-generated content (AIGC): a survey. (2023). arXiv preprint arXiv:2304.06632
27. Spasić, A.J., Janković, D.S.: Using ChatGPT standard prompt engineering techniques in lesson preparation: role, instructions and seed-word prompts. In: 2023 58th International Scientific Conference on Information, Communication and Energy Systems and Technologies (ICEST), pp. 47–50. IEEE (2023)
28. Kocoń, J., et al.: ChatGPT: jack of all trades, master of none. Inf. Fusion, 101861 (2023)
29. Alkaissi, H., McFarlane, S.I.: Artificial hallucinations in ChatGPT: implications in scientific writing. Cureus 15(2) (2023)
30. Alawida, M., Mejri, S., Mehmood, A., Chikhaoui, B., Isaac Abiodun, O.: A comprehensive study of ChatGPT: advancements, limitations, and ethical considerations in natural language processing and cybersecurity. Information 14(8), 462 (2023)
31. Dubey, P., Ghode, S., Sambhare, P., Vairagade, R.: A discussion with illustrations on world changing ChatGPT–an open AI tool. In: Multimedia Data Processing and Computing, pp. 135–153. CRC Press
32. Haleem, A., Javaid, M., Singh, R.P.: An era of ChatGPT as a significant futuristic support tool: a study on features, abilities, and challenges. Bench Counc. Trans. Benchmarks Stand. Eval. 2(4), 100089 (2022)
33. Cutler, K.: ChatGPT and search engine optimisation: the future is here. Appl. Market. Anal. Peer-Rev. J. 9(1), 8–22 (2023)
34. Jiang, P.: Discovering efficient keywords – an exploratory study on comparing the use of ChatGPT and other third-party tools. J. Emerg. Trends Market. Manag. 1(2), 40–45 (2023)

Handwritten Equation Solver: A Game-Changer in Mathematical Problem Solving

Anmol Gupta[✉], Disha Mohini Pathak, Rohit Sharma, and Somya Srivastava

Computer Science Department, ABES Engineering College, Ghaziabad, India
{anmol.19b121004,disha.pathak,rohit.19b121054,
somya.srivastava}@abes.ac.in

Abstract. Handwriting is something which changes from person to person. Finding two people with same handwriting isn't an easy job and not everyone can recognize all kinds of writing. But, in the growing era of technology and the modern world with the introduction of the domains like OpenCV – image processing and recognition isn't a tough job. Further, with the growing dependency on technology and the ease of access, students can now solve equations at the comfort of their home. The job is simple, one just has to click picture of a problem written on the page, scan it, and the algorithm does it job. The system can recognize various handwritings and works on a large dataset. This Handwritten Equation Solver system, will aim towards dealing with various handwritings and solving equations with aiming towards the maximum possible accuracy that could be achieved using the various techniques and to find out the most appropriate out of all the proposed techniques.

In this study, we initially take a binary image convert it into binary format using preprocessing and eliminating the noise. We use different segmentation and classification techniques have been used to find out the most accurate technique that will give the maximum possible accuracy. We found out that the highest accuracy came in K-Means segmentation and KNN classification technique which are 92.714 and 92.857% respectively.

The proposed methodology uses all the techniques of OpenCV.

Keywords: OpenCV · image processing · dataset · equations · segmentation · classification · KNN classifier · K-Means

1 Introduction

Solving an equation accurately isn't an easy task and someone today or tomorrow gets stuck in solving a problem. The main problem behind this is the lack of availability of resources when needed. The age-old tradition of asking a teacher, friend, family member, etc., is comparatively slower as everyone can't be available at every times.

Recognition of handwriting is a tough task, sometimes even your acquaintances aren't able to figure out what one has written, then, where technology comes into play. It could be done easily using Convolutional Neural Network (CNN) Algorithms. In this paper, OpenCV library is used for pre-processing of our image, then, dividing the

© The Author(s), under exclusive license to Springer Nature Switzerland AG 2024
D. Garg et al. (Eds.): IACC 2023, CCIS 2053, pp. 345–357, 2024.
https://doi.org/10.1007/978-3-031-56700-1_28

dataset the algorithms to solve the equations. The strategy is to calculate the equations recognizing arithmetic symbols and numbers and performing the desired operations to give the result. In this paper, Kaggle's Dataset has been used to process the images. Apart from that, certain handwritten equations have been taken with various humans, including us to test the accuracy of the system.

The accuracy of the system is the most important factor in the project because a student learns what he sees. If, by any means, the accuracy is less then, the system will be generating faulty outputs and it will hamper the growth of the child and also contributes towards failure of the project. All the equations will be scanned that are available in the dataset and then trying to solve with ensuring the accuracy.

Talking about the proposed technique that this paper is using is dependent on the various algorithms of classification and segmentation and its aim is to provide a detailed analysis of the multiple algorithms to find out which of the algorithms is the best bet to rely on in this situation. K-means algorithm is being used to do the segmentation and K-nearest neighbors (KNN) and SVM to do the classification technique from all of the different techniques.

The problem has a significant impact in today's world, the reason being humans are somewhere being dependent on technology to ease our everyday lives. It's not easy to have a manual support throughout, but with this technology it makes it feasible for learners to work as per their convenience. Students aren't able to reach out to help at all the times, but our technology can be accessed at all times.

There are already various available solutions in the market, but the problem with the other solutions is the lack of accuracy and a lack of a comparative study as they are dependent on a single or two algorithms without comparing the others and directly relying on a single strategy.

In this paper, the concepts of segmentation and classification have been used in solving the problem. There are various segmentation and classification techniques that are being used over here.

1.1 Segmentation

Classification of images by dividing the image into multiple parts is referred as segmentation. It aims to identify the important information and the objects which are present in any image. It aims towards the segmentation of equation line as well as the character segmentation.

Types of Segmentation

1. CCA: It refers to Canonical Correlation Analysis which finds the linear relationship between any two given variables and segments and clusters the data.
2. Mean Shift: It is defined as a clustering algorithm that is used to shift the density of the kernel to the region of higher density.
3. K-Means: This algorithm is used to cluster a dataset into multiple(k) different clusters. It minimizes the sum of the squared distance between the data points along with their assigned clusters.
4. Spectral Clustering: A similarity matrix is derived from the data and the eigen-values as well as the eigen-vectors of that data are used. It is beneficial when dealing with non-linear or graph-like data.

5. Graph cuts: It uses the data points as the nodes of a graph to find similarity measures between them. The cluster should over and all be connected and it is required to partition the graph in such a way that edges have the least weight whenever they are selected.
6. Deep Learning: The automatic learning from the datasets. The raw data can be used to process complex work.

1.2 Classification

The techniques to classify or divide data based on certain parameters or features is known as classification. It works on understanding the patterns of data and forming groups which are alike.

Types of Classification Techniques

1. Logistic Regression: It deals with the input features and the probability that any given data belongs to that particular class.
2. Support Vector Machine (SVM): It finds a hyperplane in multi-dimensional space to separate different data into different/multiple classes. It involves the use of kernel functions.
3. Decision Tree: A tree like classification technique where each node symbolizes a particular feature or an attribute and the branches represent the probability of having that particular feature and the corresponding result that could be identified from it.
4. Bayes Classifier: It is based on Bayes Theorem and using the prior probabilities and conditional probabilities.
5. Random Forest: It is based on decision trees and it combines multiple decision trees before making any prediction. It involves using random subset of data and random features.
6. K Nearest Neighbors (KNN): KNN is based on the concept of nearest neighbors of a class. Where K is symbolic to the number of neighbors a particular class has.

2 Related Work

Various works have been done in the past regarding the Handwritten Equation Solving system and after studying those papers and the research work which has been done in this field by other people, it could be find out that a lot of important algorithms and a certain gap which was present in each of the research paper that have been studied. A total of 18 research papers have been studied in which the research work that was done in the previous time on or was related to the problem statement that's being discussed in this paper. It could be found out that over and all about 12 research papers have similar work to what has been done in this paper. There were various references which were already available for moving ahead with the project. The importance technology has developed nowadays in everyday lives can't be overlooked. There is no room for question about the powers of Machine Learning and Artificial Intelligence, and it can't be neglect what future it holds. There's a lot of potential that has been opened in the market by the field of deep learning. It is also a fact that with passing times, the work is becoming more and more automated. The solution to any given problem should be available with a single click. The power of internet and image processing isn't debatable. Everything is becoming more and more technology dependent. The power of human brain is well-known, but there's quite an unawareness of the powers and the capabilities of the computer's brain. Nowadays, EdTech is blooming and with the rise of EdTech there's a rise of opportunities in the fields that technology has to offer. Even if there's a need to solve a mathematical equation, it could be solved by just clicking a picture of the problem and then, it could be solved with the blink of an eye. This is not so easy as it seems to be, it requires a lot of operations and background processing which many aren't aware of. The applications of machine learning and deep learning can be seen, but it requires a fixed procedure and a usage of multiple algorithms to process an image, segment the individual characters of varying handwritings and processing them to give output of any given problem that has been raised. Multiple works have already been done on the same field which include the likes of Catherine Lu and Karan veer Mohan [1] who used the powers of Convolutional Neural Networks (CNN) to recognize the handwritten mathematical expressions that were written online and they processed the equations over there and then it could be seen that the desired output after the proper image processing is complete. [2] was an attempt on the similar thing where it was aimed to recognize the handwritten mathematical expressions and to distinguish between the various characters. [3] aimed at classifying images based on various image processing algorithms. A colored-image was converted into a binary image and was classified using a similar approach. [4] worked on the recognition and segmentation of characters on a license plate using the concepts of horizontal projection and linked component analysis. Horizontal projection is a method where any object is thrown at a certain angle other than 90, then a certain trajectory is formed by that object and the type of motion is known as projectile motion. Henceforth, it was named as the horizontal projection. Linked component analysis is where two or more components are connected with each other and the study of them individually as well as in group as a whole is done.

There are many mathematical symbols and every symbol is unique and performs a different function. [5] aimed at segmenting the various mathematical symbols that are there and to unique identify them for processing purposes. [6] focused on ImageNet i.e., a database of images or where there are multiple images that are to be processed by the power of image processing. It worked on the concept of deep CNNs which are feedforward neural networks and applied back propagation algorithms that works on the adjustment of weights and biases so that the cost function associated with the network can be reduced. Mathematical Formulas are the most important things when seen in mathematical perspectives. Being uniquely, able to identify them and solving them accurately is a task on its own. [8] worked on developing an improved algorithm to segment various symbols from the images containing mathematical formula. It aimed at the demonstration of the deep network architecture in the field of image classification where various images were classified and differentiated from one another. [9] worked on using Support Vector Machine (SVM) and projection histogram for the recognition of any mathematical expression. SVM is a supervised machine learning algorithm where data is plotted on a graph against various features that the data has. Projection Histogram is a method of image projection where an image is projected either in horizontal or vertical direction. [10] motive was to develop adequate strategies and methods that could help in achieving the goal of character segmentation. Whenever there are connected components that they are required to be segmented accurately and that was the primary aim of this paper to find the success rate in character segmentation of the connected components. Different people have different handwritings and the way a person draws a certain character also varies on different persons. The aim of [11] was to bridge this gap. It aimed at distinguishing various handwritings uniquely and to process the mathematical expressions that were written in that handwriting. [12] aimed at processing of images in a system using the concepts of deep learning and neural information processing. Deep learning is a multi-layer machine learning algorithm that simulates the power of human brain to the machine and the computer processes raw data and learn from a wide volume of data. Tracking data and certain features or objects in an image is a tedious process and when there is a large amount of image data it becomes even more boring. [13] aimed at limiting this limitation. The tracking of points and objects could be done easily in an image using the methodology that was proposed in that paper. Whenever there is a need to learn anything or processing anything there is something which is often outlooked and that's patterns. [14] aimed at bridging this gap and aimed at extracting out various patterns that are present in our data. The usage of back propagation and Artificial Neural Network (ANN) algorithm was done in [15] where back propagation as the name justifies is a process of moving back from the output nodes to the input nodes in order to test and detect any errors that might have occurred in the presentation. Artificial Neural Network is a connection of connected components or nodes just like an animal brain and processing the data on those grounds. The human eyes can see a single image but that's not the reality. An image isn't any single-coloured structure but rather a group of various pixels that are combined to make image looks like an image. A computer can process only pixelated image and [16] solved this problem. It pixelated the image into various pixels via the use of deep convolutional network. Overfitting is a problem which mustn't be overlooked and it means when a large number of data points are being shown very close or in a cluster in our graph. [17] aimed at solving the problem of overfitting using the concepts of neural networks. [18] aimed at the usage of multi-columnar deep neural networks to classify various images that our present in any dataset.

This is what could be inferred from studying various research papers (Table 1).

Table 1. Summary

Ref.	Technique	Limitations	Gap
1	Image Processing	It aimed at identifying the handwritten mathematical statements	Expressions weren't accurately evaluated
2	Image Processing	It aimed to convert the handwritten mathematical equation into a typesetting command language	Typesetting command language isn't widely used now
3	SVM, Decision Trees and Fuzzy Logics	It aimed at discussing the categorization techniques like: - Support Vector Machines (SVM), Decision Trees (DT) and fuzzy logics	It was only based on classification techniques
4	Segmentation	It aimed at segmenting the license plates for the Algerian cars. The approach is to divide the input image and then segment the characters	Dividing the input image without background subtraction
5	Segmentation	It aimed at identifying, extracting and segmenting mathematical symbols and recognizing the expressions	It only focused on segmentation
6	CNN	It aimed at researching results of image classification and detection on the basis of CNN	It is only based on image classification
7	Binarization	It aimed at binarization of threshold values like pixel values	It needed pixel values for the process of binarization
8	Deep Network	It aimed at demonstrating deep network architecture for image classification	It uses the concept of deep network
9	SVM and projection histogram	It aimed at using SVM and projection histogram for Mathematical Expression Recognition (MER)	The recognition was not accurate
10	Segmentation	It aimed at finding success rate for character segmentation in connected components	Only aimed at character segmentation

(*continued*)

Table 1. (*continued*)

Ref.	Technique	Limitations	Gap
11	Image Processing	It aimed at recognition of the various mathematical expressions which are written by people of various handwritings	It was able to distinguish only some handwritings
12	Neural Network and Deep Learning	It included the concept of neural networks and deep learning to process the images in the system	The type of convolutional network used wasn't specified
13	Image processing	The paper covers vast topics dealing with image tracking	It was more a tracking-oriented approach and focused less on recognition
14	Pattern recognition	To extract out the various patterns that are present in our data	Sometimes, there were error in recognition
15	Back Propagation and Artificial Neural Network	To use the back propagation and ANN algorithm	The algorithm wasn't the best in the business
16	Convolutional Network	It aimed at pixelating the image via the methodology of deep convolutional network	It only focused on deep convolutional approach
17	Image Classification	It deals with the usage of multi-column deep neural networks for the process of the classification of images	It failed for single expressions or isolated set of data
18	Neural Networks	Overfitting is a big problem which was faced when using neural networks. It aimed at preventing the same	It lacked adequate approach to solve overfitting problem

In this paper, we have added the abstract and introduction in the beginning where we have given a brief overview of the project as well as the literature review and the study which we have done for the paper.

The next section of the paper covers proposed methodology where we have given the workflow diagram and the details regarding the procedure which we are following throughout the paper.

We have also given the result analysis towards the end of the paper by comparing the accuracies of various segmentation and classification techniques that we have used.

3   Proposed Methodology

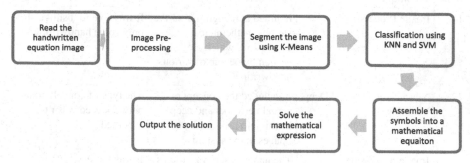

Fig. 1. Workflow Diagram

The method deals with scanning of an input image which is further pre-processed to convert it into a binary image and then extracting out the features to remove the noise in the image, if any. Then, multiple segmentation techniques are being applied to find out the accuracy in all the techniques and the most accurate technique, i.e., K-means in this particular case is chosen. After the image has been segmented, there is a usage of Convolutional Neural Network (CNN) algorithm to extract out the features from the image. Similar to the segmentation techniques, multiple classification techniques have been applied to draw out a conclusion that K-Nearest Neighbors (KNN) and Support Vector Machine (SVM) gives the highest accuracy in this particular use case. After this, the symbols are aggregated to form a mathematical equation and that equation is solved to give the desired output (Fig. 1).

4   Implementation

4.1   Dataset Preparation

The very first and the most integral step is dataset preparation. Characters, operations, mathematical symbols, digits, etc., are defined and the dataset is accurately defined.

4.2   Pre-Processing

The changes in the input image by certain modifications, so that, the image is perfect for the recognition purposes. There are various techniques which deals with such modification of the images and that are listed below.

Conversion of RGB Image to Gray-Scale. The bitmap associated with gray-scale image is Y and with RGB image there are three bitmaps associated and that are- R, G and B. The detection of colors is much easier on gray-scale image as compared to colored image. The conversion takes place and is done with the help of a single matrix. The equation following this conversion is:

$$Y = 0.299R + 0.587G + 0.114B \tag{1}$$

Binarization. The images are converted into pixel data of 0 s and 1 s where 1 represents the black pixels whereas, the white pixels are demonstrated by 0 s.

Noise Reduction. The unnecessary pixels that are present in an image are referred as noise. Whenever there's a Gaussian noise, the aim is to remove it from the image. While, salt and pepper noise are often avoided because it doesn't cause much disturbance in the system (Fig. 2).

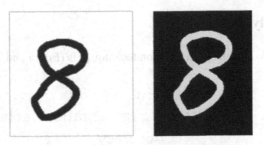

Fig. 2. (a) Input Image. (b) After pre processing

4.3 Segmentation

Classification of images by dividing the image into multiple parts is referred as segmentation. It aims to identify the important information and the objects which are present in any image. It aims towards the segmentation of equation line as well as the character segmentation.

Equation Line Segmentation. The multiple equations that are present in the input image are separated from each other (Fig. 3).

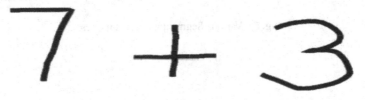

Fig. 3. Equation recognition

Character Segmentation. It deals with the separation of every individual character from the equation (Fig. 4).

Fig. 4. Character recognition

5   Result Analysis

The accuracy of the various segmentation techniques is (Fig. 5 and Table 2).

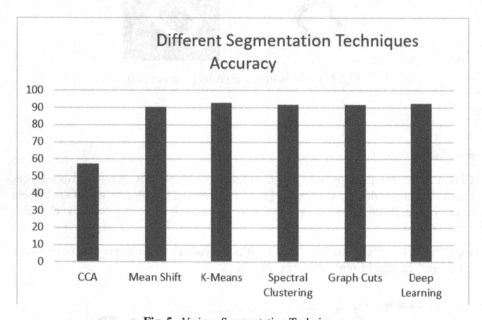

Fig. 5. Various Segmentation Techniques

Table 2. Various Segmentation Techniques

Technique	Accuracy
CCA	57.429
Mean-Shift	90.429
K-Means	92.714
Spectral Clustering	91.629
Graph Cuts	91.743
Deep Learning	92.229

Based on the above data, the highest accuracy is in K-Means clustering and that is 92.71371429% which is find out after testing on our own handwritten dataset and finding out the accuracy in all the cases on the same.

The accuracy of the various classification techniques is (Fig. 6 and Table 3):

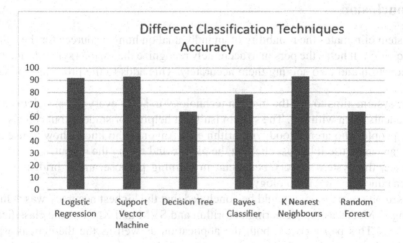

Fig. 6. Various Classification Techniques

Table 3. Various Classification Techniques

Technique	Accuracy
Logistic Regression	91.667
Support vector machine	92.857
Decision Tree	64.286
Bayes Classifier	78.571
K-Nearest Neighbors	92.857
Random Forest	64.286

Based on the above data, the highest accuracy is in K-Nearest Neighbors (KNN) and Support Vector Machine (SVM) and that is 92.85714286%, by finding the accuracy of the classification techniques using our own handwritten dataset and testing the techniques on that data.

6   Conclusion

The system eliminates the reliability of an individual on human sources for the solution of an equation. It helps the person to accurately recognize the various symbols and digits in an equation and also solving them accurately. This adds to the procedure of saving time.

The system aims to use the modern technology to solve every day problems and to help students learn with fun. The system isn't just helpful for students but can also help elderly people who aren't good with arithmetic. Anyone who knows how to use a cell phone can easily use it by just clicking the picture and seeing the output.

Hence, the system is very beneficial in learning purpose and it bridges the gap between education and technology.

Based on our method, it could be concluded that the highest accuracy was achieved by using K-Means as the clustering algorithm and SVM and KNN as the classification algorithms. This paper covers both the application as well as the theoretical aspects involving the research to find out the most suitable segmentation and classification technique. It is different in the aspect that we have tried all the possible techniques to reach out to the most accurate one.

References

1. Lu, C., Mohan, K.: Recognition of online handwritten mathematical expressions using convolutional neural networks (2015)
2. Matsakis, N.E.: Recognition of handwritten mathematical expressions. MIT Published (1999)
3. Kamavisdar, P., Saluja, S., Agrawal, S.: A survey on image classification approaches and techniques. Int. J. Adv. Res. Comput. Commun. Eng. **2**(1), 1005–1009 (2013)
4. Abderaouf, Z., Nadjia, B., Saliha, O.K.: License plate character segmentation based on horizontal projection and connected component analysis. In: 2014 World Symposium on Computer Applications & Research (WSCAR), pp. 1–5. IEEE (2014)

5. Jakjoud, W., Lazrek, A.: Segmentation method of offline mathematical symbols. In: 2011 International Conference on Multimedia Computing and Systems (ICMCS), pp. 1–7. IEEE (2011)
6. Krizhevsky, A., Sutskever, I., Hinton, G.E.: ImageNet classification with deep CNNs. Adv. Neural Inf. Process. Syst. (2012)
7. Wang, H., Wang, Y., Lu, L., Liu, J., Li, S., Zhang, Y.: An improved algorithm for symbol segmentation of mathematical formula images. In: 2016 16th International Symposium on Communications and Information Technologies (ISCIT), pp. 461–464. IEEE (2016)
8. Pauly, L., Hogg, D., Fuentes, R., Peel, H.: Deeper networks for pavement crack detection. In: Proceedings of the 34th ISARC, pp. 479–485. IAARC (2017)
9. Gharde, S.S., Baviskar, P.V., Adhiya, K.P.: Identification of handwritten simple mathematical equation based on SVM and projection histogram. Int. J. Soft Comput. Eng. 3(2), 425–429 (2013)
10. Casey, R.G., Lecolinet, E.: A survey of methods and strategies in character segmentation. IEEE Trans. Pattern Anal. Mach. Intell. 18(7), 690–706 (1996)
11. Literature Review on Handwritten Mathematical Expression Recognition, Chapter 2
12. Zhou, B., Lapedriza, A., Xiao, J., Torralba, A., Oliva, A.: Learning deep features for scene recognition using places database. Adv. Neural Inf. Process. Syst. 487–495 (2014)
13. Wang, N., Li, S., Gupta, A., Yeung, D.Y.: Transferring rich feature hierarchies for robust visual tracking. arXiv preprint arXiv:1501.04587 (2015)
14. 2018 Joint 7th International Conference on Informatics, Electronics & Vision (ICIEV) and 2018 2nd International Conference on Imaging, Vision & Pattern Recognition (icIVPR)
15. Handwritten Mathematical Expressions Recognition using Back Propagation Artificial Neural Network
16. Dong, C., Loy, C.C., He, K., Tang, X.: Learning a deep convolutional network for image super-resolution. In: Fleet, D., Pajdla, T., Schiele, B., Tuytelaars, T. (eds.) Computer Vision (ECCV 2014). LNCS, vol. 8692 pp. 184–199. Springer, Cham (2014). https://doi.org/10.1007/978-3-319-10593-2_13
17. Ciregan, D., Meier, U., Schmidhuber, J.: Multi-column deep neural networks for image classification. In: 2012 IEEE Conference on Computer Vision and Pattern Recognition, pp. 3642–3649. IEEE (2012)
18. Srivastava, N., Hinton, G., Krizhevsky, A., Sutskever, I., Salakhutdinov, R.: Dropout: a simple way to prevent neural networks from overfitting. J. Mach. Learn. Res. 15(1), 1929–1958 (2014)

Unveiling the Next Frontier of AI Advancement

Advancing Image Classification Through Self-teachable Machine Models and Transfer Learning

Madhu Kumar Jha[ID], Suwarna Shukla(✉)[ID], Ajay Pal Singh(✉)[ID],
and Vaishali Shukla(✉)[ID]

Chandigarh University, Mohali, Punjab, India
suwarnashukla6@gmail.com, apsingh3289@gmail.com,
vaishalishukla09@gmail.com

Abstract. Automated Machine Learning (AutoML) has progressively established its role in alleviating the complexities associated with traditional model selection and hyperparameter tuning. This research paper introduces a novel amalgamation of AutoML with the benefits of Transfer Learning for image classification [23] through Convolutional Neural Networks [23] (CNNs). By leveraging pre-trained models as a foundation, our framework reduces training time and improves model robustness. Furthermore, a sophisticated early stopping mechanism is integrated, ensuring optimal convergence while mitigating overfitting. The empirical evidence suggests that the fusion of AutoML, Transfer Learning, and Early Stopping paves the way for a new era in efficient and effective image classification, offering a blend of agility and precision.

Keywords: Transfer learning · Image classification · Self-teachable machine · Machine learning

1 Introduction

The application of deep convolutional neural networks [25] (DCNNs), has witnessed remarkable advancements, leading to significant breakthroughs in various domains, most notably in image classification. DCNNs have demonstrated their prowess in automatically learning intricate mappings from input data to output labels. Their ability to process complex, high-dimensional data, like images, has revolutionized pattern recognition systems and enabled the development of increasingly accurate and efficient solutions.

However, despite their exceptional performance in well-curated datasets, DCNNs often face a substantial challenge when confronted with real-world scenarios characterized by data that significantly deviates from the training distribution. This limitation has spurred the pursuit of solutions that can enhance the generalization capabilities of deep neural networks, by using the technique of transfer learning which is a subfield of machine learning.

Chandigarh University.

This research paper ventures into the realm of transfer learning and AutoML within the context of image classification, employing scalable DCNNs. Furthermore, the growth of neural networks in depth introduces an intriguing and unexpected phenomenon-the degradation problem. As network depth increases, the accuracy initially reaches a saturation point but subsequently declines, a phenomenon distinct from overfitting. This raises questions regarding the ease of optimizing neural networks, suggesting that not all networks are created equal. The paper introduces a novel deep residual learning framework to tackle this challenge, fundamentally altering how networks are trained. Instead of expecting each layer to model the desired mapping directly, residual learning allows these layers to focus on fitting a residual mapping, mitigating the vanishing gradient problem with the introduction of shortcut connections. This approach facilitates the construction of extraordinarily deep networks while maintaining or even enhancing training and generalization performance.

Additionally, we explore its significance in medical image classification, where interpretability and reliability are paramount. This paper also addresses the practical techniques of knowledge transfer, emphasizing the role of transfer learning [19] in real-world scenarios, where adaptability to new conditions is indispensable. The innovative concept of Google's Teachable Machine [4] empowers individuals, irrespective of their technical expertise, to train machine learning models through intuitive interactions. The potential to democratize AI, enabling custom models for image classification, sound recognition, and gesture control, opens doors to uncharted possibilities and challenges. The motivation behind this research lies in the recognition that there is a significant need to expand and refine the capabilities of teaching machine-based models [15], making AI more accessible and inclusive.

2   Related Work

In the past years, significant progress has been made in the fields of [33] transfer learning, image classification using Convolutional Neural Networks, efficient deep learning neural [33] networks, and efficient image processing. This section provides an overview of the key contributions in these areas.

Transfer learning, the process of leveraging knowledge learned from one domain to improve performance in another, has garnered substantial attention. Notable works in this field include Pan and Yang (2010) who introduced transfer component analysis, and more recently, Devlin et al. (2018) [36] demonstrated the effectiveness of pre-trained language models, such as BERT [36], in a wide range of natural language [36] understanding tasks. In the realm of computer vision, the study by Yosinski et al. (2014) [35] laid the foundation for understanding transferability in deep convolutional networks. These breakthroughs have set the stage for the development of more efficient and accurate transfer learning techniques.

Convolutional Neural Networks (CNNs) have been [35] instrumental in image classification tasks. Krizhevsky et al.'s AlexNet (2012) [17] marked a turning point by significantly reducing error rates on the ImageNet dataset [26]. Subsequent work by He et al. (2016) [12] introduced ResNet, which addressed the vanishing gradient problem and enabled the training of exceptionally deep networks. More recently, Howard et al. (2019) [31] presented EfficientNet, a family of models that demonstrated state-of-the-art [31] performance with fewer parameters, emphasizing the need for efficient architectures.

Efficiency in deep learning models has become paramount, especially with the growing demand for edge and mobile device deployment. Tan et al. (2019) [27] proposed MobileNetV3, a family of lightweight neural networks that balance accuracy and speed, making them ideal for resource-constrained applications. Another noteworthy development is the work by Sandler et al. (2018) [27] on MobileNetV2, which introduced novel depthwise separable convolutions to reduce computational complexity. These efficient neural network architectures have enabled real-time image processing on edge devices.

Efficient image processing techniques [32] play a pivotal role in enhancing the overall performance of computer vision systems. Recent advancements include the use of quantization and pruning methods for neural networks, as demonstrated by Han et al. (2015) and Li et al. (2017). Additionally, hardware acceleration technologies like NVIDIA's TensorRT (2017) and Google's Edge TPU (2018) have enabled efficient inference on specialized hardware, further optimizing image processing pipelines.

3   Proposed Model

Automated machine learning (AutoML) has arisen as a transformative solution to alleviate the intricate process of ML development. Its primary goal, is to minimize the need for in-depth data science expertise that are statistical and ML proficiency. Essentially, AutoML streamlines the construction of an ML pipeline within a constrained computational environment. The evolution of AutoML has resulted in comprehensive systems that seamlessly integrate various techniques, providing user-friendly, end-to-end ML solutions. This movement is evident with major tech firms, like Google, launching platforms such as Cloud AutoML, which are geared towards empowering individuals with limited ML expertise to develop top-tier custom models.

Amidst this backdrop, we introduce 'Horizon' - an AutoML-centric desktop application designed for binary image classification. Conceptualized using the TKinter library for its graphical interface, Horizon distinguishes itself by its inherent simplicity. It permits users to supply their own image sample directories for training, streamlining the often tedious task of image classification, especially when only limited information is available for model implementation. By harnessing the power of deep learning and transfer learning, Horizon allows for versatile model training on datasets as varied as 'cat-dog' differentiation or even 'facial mask detection'. Once the model is trained for a binary classification task, it becomes a permanent tool, primed for future usage and testing. The overarching objective is to offer a scalable, user-friendly solution that bridges the expertise gap, making cutting-edge machine learning accessible to a broader audience.

3.1   Datasets

The images in the dataset have been aggregated from various online repositories, ensuring a diverse and representative sample for each classification challenge. Unlike traditional models that demand meticulously curated and pre-processed datasets, Horizon is architecturally designed to be dataset-agnostic, allowing users the flexibility to upload raw, unprocessed data. Recognizing the challenges posed by data variability and the inconsistency of real-world images, Horizon incorporates advanced image augmentation techniques, resizing, and normalization to color adjustments, ensuring the model's robustness, obviating the need for users to engage in any manual preprocessing and adaptability across varied scenarios. This design philosophy underscores Horizon's commitment to user-centricity, allowing individuals, irrespective of their technical proficiency, to harness the power of advanced machine learning without the intricacies of data curation.

3.2   Hyperparameter Configuration

Optimizer: the Adam optimizer is used for training your deep learning model due to its adaptive learning rate and good convergence properties.

Learning Rate: The learning rate determines the step size during gradient descent optimization [24] which is set to 0.0001.

Number of Epochs: By default number of epochs used in our model is 10.

Number of Layers: There are a total of four types of layers: Input (implicit), ResNet50 (not explicitly added), Flatten (explicit), and Dense (two explicit layers). The ResNet50 layers are considered part of the pre-trained model and are not explicitly added.

Number of Neurons in Each Layer: Input Layer: Determined by the input image dimensions (180×180). ResNet50 Layers: Variable, but the final pooling layer produces a feature vector with 2048 dimensions. Flatten Layer: 2048 neurons (matches the dimensions of the ResNet50 output). Dense Layer (First): 512 neurons. Dense Layer (Second): 2 neurons (for binary classification).

Activation Functions: The ReLU activation function is applied to the first Dense layer [24] in our model. The softmax activation function is used in the [27] second Dense layer, which is the output layer for classification tasks.

Weight Initialization: He Normal initialization is defined as it is a popular choice for deep CNNs, especially when rectified linear unit (ReLU) activations are used. It scales the initial weights based on the number of input units and helps prevent the vanishing gradient problem, making it suitable for deep architectures.

Batch Size: The batch size is configured to 32 in the code. It defines the number of data samples used in each training iteration.

Regularization Strength (L1/L2): L2 (Ridge) regularization is used. The loss function's penalty term added by L2 regularization promotes smaller weight values, thus preventing overfitting.

Early Stopping: Early stopping is a regularization technique with a hyperparameter called patience which defines the number of epochs with no improvement to wait before stopping training.

3.3 Training Configuration

The Horizon model embraces a comprehensive training configuration to ensure optimal learning and enhanced performance. At the core of its training process, the model utilizes a batch size of 32, guaranteeing an equilibrium between the accuracy of gradient estimation and computational efficiency. To provide the model with ample opportunity to capture intricate patterns across diverse datasets, the training is set to span over 10 epochs but if the model gets trained earlier so the training of model has to be stoped to prevent overfitting so concept of earlystopping is used to stop training of model when desired accuracy is achieved. This duration ensures that the model iteratively learns from the data, refining its predictions and their hyperparameters with each pass. Additionally, the learning rate is meticulously calibrated at 0.0001, which strikes a harmony between rapid convergence and stability during the optimization phase. This well-thought-out configuration not only underpins the model's robustness but also ensures that users achieve the highest levels of accuracy and precision in their image classification endeavors.

4   Model Architecture

The model architecture is built upon a sequential design signifies a linear stacking of layers, ensuring that data flows from one layer to the next without branching or skipping, leveraging the prowess of the renowned ResNet50 model as its foundation. This design choice harnesses the deep convolutional capabilities of ResNet50, known for its exceptional ability to extract intricate features from images through its deep layers. By employing the sequential structure, the model can efficiently stack layers and operations in a linear flow, ensuring a streamlined processing pipeline. This strategic integration ensures that the foundational layers capture generalized image features, allowing the subsequent custom layers to focus on task-specific nuances, thereby facilitating the development of a robust and highly capable image classification model.

4.1   Base Model - ResNet50

Fundamentally, the design incorporates the ResNet50 model, which is renowned for its outstanding results in image classification assignments. The weights in this model were pre-trained using the ImageNet dataset, ensuring a robust foundational understanding of diverse visual features right from the beginning. This integration is specifically designed to receive images of size 180×180 pixels with three color channels (RGB) [34]. The top, fully connected layers of the original ResNet50 are excluded to cater to our bespoke needs. A global average pooling strategy is employed to condense the spatial dimensions of the output feature maps. To retain the robustness of the original pre-trained weights, the layers of this ResNet50 model are frozen, meaning their weights are kept constant during subsequent training.

4.2   Custom Layers

Following the ResNet50 backbone, the architecture introduces a Flatten layer, transforming the two-dimensional output of ResNet50 into a one-dimensional vector suitable for dense layers. A dense layer with 512 neurons is added next, equipped with a 'ReLU' activation function. This layer serves as a [21] conduit, refining the features extracted by the ResNet50 for the task at hand [35]. The architecture culminates with a dense output layer featuring 2 neurons, corresponding to the binary classification objective. A 'softmax' activation function ensures that the model yields probability scores for the two classes.

5   Loss and Metrics

The ResNet50 is compiled with specific configurations to optimize its performance. The Adam optimizer, known for its adaptability and efficiency, is chosen with a learning rate [13] set at 0.0001. This learning rate [13], while relatively small, ensures gradual and stable convergence during training. For the loss function, sparse categorical crossentropy is selected, which is an optimal choice for multi-class classification tasks when class labels are denoted as integers. The model's performance is tracked using the accuracy metric, representing the percentage of correctly classified instances.

5.1   Accuracy vs. Epochs

Initial Stage: At the beginning (initial epochs), the accuracy tends to be lower since the model is just starting to learn from the data [28].
Middle Stage: As epochs increase, the accuracy usually improves because the model starts to adjust [18] its weights and biases based [18] on the data it has seen.
Late Stage: After a certain point, increasing epochs might not significantly improve accuracy. Sometimes, accuracy might even decline slightly, which can be an indication of overfitting - where the model is memorizing the training data rather than generalizing [28] from it (Fig. 1).

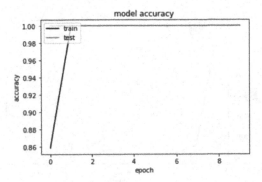

Fig. 1. Accuracy of the model w.r.t epochs

5.2   Loss vs. Epochs

Initial Stage: The loss is typically higher at the start since the model's predictions are often far from the actual values.

Middle Stage: As the model undergoes further training, the loss decreases, indicating better performance and prediction capabilities.

Late Stage: Ideally, the loss should stabilize after a certain number of epochs. If it starts increasing, it could again indicate overfitting, meaning the model is becoming too specialized to the training data.

5.3   Resolution of Image Data and Number of Epochs

The number of epochs needed is largely dependent on the image data's resolution:

High-Resolution Images: High-resolution images contain more information (more pixels). Training a model on high-resolution data can take longer, not only in terms of each epoch's time but also the quantity of epochs necessary for convergence to an optimal solution. This is because the model [18] needs to learn more intricate features [18] and patterns from the high amount of data (Fig. 2).

Low-Resolution Images: In contrast, low-resolution images have less information. Training on these might require fewer epochs to converge, but the model might not perform as well on intricate tasks since the data might lack the necessary details.

Overfitting Consideration: Training on high-resolution images for too many epochs might cause overfitting, especially if the dataset is small. Since there's more information in each image, the model might start to memorize specific high-resolution details that don't generalize well.

5.4   Importance of EarlyStopping in Enhancing AutoML Efficiency and Performance

In the domain of automated machine learning (AutoML) [14], the primary objective is to automate the complete process of using machine learning to solve practical issues. Given that one of the biggest challenges in machine learning [20] is

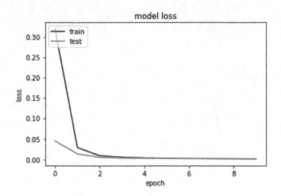

Fig. 2. Loss of the model w.r.t epochs

model training time, especially [20] with extensive datasets and complex models, efficiency becomes paramount. EarlyStopping plays a critical role in this regard. Instead of training a model for a fixed number of epochs, regardless of its convergence status, EarlyStopping monitors a specified performance metric and halts training once the metric stops showing significant improvement. This not only saves computational resources but also prevents overfitting, as prolonged training past the point of optimal performance can lead the model to fit [10] too closely to the training data, reducing its generalization capability on new, unseen data. In the context of AutoML, where the aim is to rapidly and efficiently produce models that are ready for deployment, incorporating strategies like EarlyStopping ensures that models are trained just enough to achieve optimal performance without unnecessary computational overhead or risking overfitting.

6   Training Procedure

During the training phase, the model [38] undergoes training on the provided dataset, simultaneously validating its performance using a separate validation set. This training is undertaken over several epochs, with the exact number determined by an EarlyStopping criterion. This approach ensures that training is halted once the model's performance plateaus or begins to degrade, thus preventing overfitting and unnecessary computational overhead.

After the training concludes based on the EarlyStopping criteria, the model is saved to local storage as an H5 file. The choice of the .h5 format, also referred to as HDF5 (Hierarchical Data Format version 5), stems from its wide acceptance in the machine learning community for its capability to store intricate hierarchical data structures efficiently. It's a go-to format for preserving and subsequently loading trained machine learning models, particularly neural networks. Upon successful saving of the model, a confirmation message, is displayed, indicating that the model is now available for future deployment, use, or further evaluation.

7   Testing and Inference

The predicting function has been designed to facilitate the inference process for image classification using the pre-trained saved model. The function starts by extracting the image path provided by the user.

The image, specified by the provided file path, is loaded and resized to meet the required dimensions of 180 × 180 pixels. Subsequently, the image is converted from its native format into a numerical array. This array is then reshaped into a four-dimensional tensor to match the input shape expected by the model (Fig. 3).

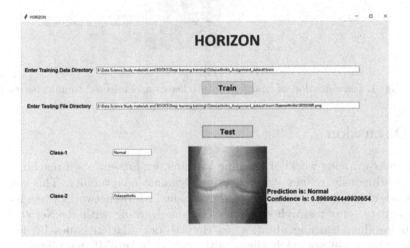

Fig. 3. Classification of Osteoarthritis and Normal Bone

The model, saved previously in the HDF5 file format, is loaded to make predictions on the processed image. The prediction output is a probability distribution across the classes, which is subsequently interpreted. If the prediction for the first class exceeds 0.5, it is selected; otherwise, the second class is chosen.

Additionally, the function showcases the confidence of the prediction by displaying the maximum probability from the prediction array. The result is then displayed on the user interface, showing the predicted class label along with its confidence score. Moreover, a visual representation of the input image is provided for reference.

The classification outcome, presented in the form of a class label and a confidence score, gives users immediate feedback on the model's prediction for the uploaded image. Through this GUI-based approach, the application aims to simplify complex deep learning workflows, making it accessible even to those without extensive machine learning expertise (Fig. 4).

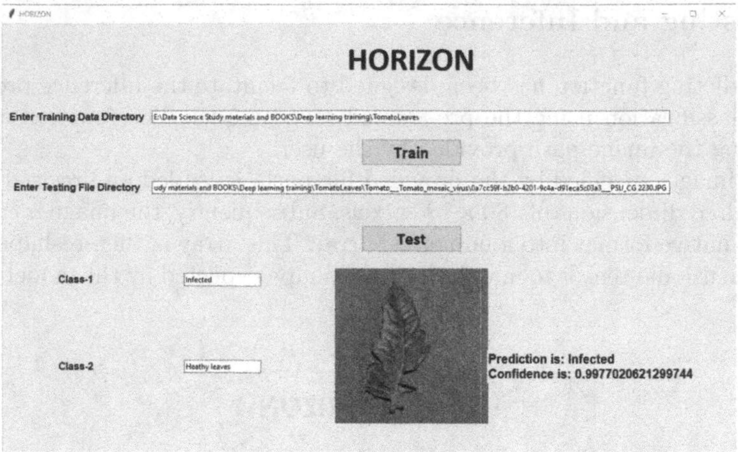

Fig. 4. Classification of healthy tomato leaves and infected tomato leaves

8   Discussion

In the ever-evolving world of machine learning, we present a self-teaching model that continuously refines itself, offering dynamic adaptability. This approach addresses challenges faced by deep convolutional neural networks when handling diverse data. Our research combines transfer learning with ResNet50, known for its residual learning abilities, to counter degradation issues in deep networks. This novel approach aligns with Horizon's autoML paradigm, catering to a wide user spectrum. Horizon's versatile dataset architecture and advanced image augmentation simplify user experiences, eliminating the need for laborious data curation. Our study centers on an intuitive user interface and advanced architectural decisions, aiming to democratize machine learning. We employ the Adam optimization algorithm, fine-tuned learning rates, and pioneering data augmentation techniques. The model's systematic training, testing, and inferential methodologies enhance transparency and interpretability, providing precise predictions with confidence metrics.

9   Summary and Conclusions

In the vast and ever-evolving landscape of machine learning, our research stands as a testament to the power of combining established techniques, such as transfer learning, with innovative approaches like self-teachable models. Horizon, with its dataset-agnostic architecture, represents a significant stride [3] in the direction of making complex machine learning [3] models accessible to a wider audience. Its unique ability to handle diverse datasets without the need for meticulous curation has the potential to democratize the use of AI tools, bridging the gap between technical experts and lay users.

Furthermore, the integration of the ResNet50 architecture demonstrates the model's capability to harness the strengths of existing deep learning frameworks, while simultaneously addressing their limitations. Our approach, combining the robustness of ResNet50 with the flexibility of Horizon's self-teaching mechanism, showcases a promising avenue for future machine learning endeavors.

As the machine learning community progresses, the demand for tools that are both powerful and user-friendly will only grow. Horizon's design philosophy, which emphasizes user-centricity, adaptability, and continual learning, sets a benchmark in this direction. It is our hope that this research serves as an inspiration for future endeavors, catalyzing the development of models that are not only technically advanced but also seamlessly integrated into real-world applications. Looking ahead, we see a time when machine learning technologies, influenced by the principles laid out in this research, become ubiquitous, driving innovation across diverse domains and industries.

References

1. Ahmad, A., Saraswat, D., El Gamal, A.: A survey on using deep learning techniques for plant disease diagnosis and recommendations for development of appropriate tools. Smart Agric. Technol. (2023)
2. Alhashim, I., Wonka, P.: High-quality monocular depth estimation via transfer learning (2018)
3. Ashwath, V.A., Sikha, O.K., Benitez, R.: TS-CNN: a three-tier self-interpretable CNN for multi-region medical image classification. IEEE Access **11** (2023)
4. Abou Baker, N., Zengeler, N., Handmann, U.: A transfer learning evaluation of deep neural networks for image classification. Mach. Learn. Knowl. Extract. **4**, 22–41 (2022)
5. Chen, W., Su, L., et al.: Rock image classification using deep residual neural network with transfer learning. Front. Earth Sci. (2023)
6. Cirstea, B.-I.: Contributions to handwriting recognition using deep neural networks and quantum computing (2018)
7. De Giacomo, G., Catala, A., et al. (eds.): Frontiers in Artificial Intelligence and Applications, vol. 325 (2020)
8. Han, S., Mao, H., Dally, W.J.: Deep compression: compressing deep neural networks with pruning, trained quantization and Huffman coding. arXiv:1510.00149 [cs.CV] (2015)
9. He, K., Sun, J.: Convolutional neural networks at constrained time cost. In: CVPR (2015)
10. He, K., Zhang, X., Ren, S., Sun, J.: Spatial pyramid pooling in deep convolutional networks for visual recognition. In: Fleet, D., Pajdla, T., Schiele, B., Tuytelaars, T. (eds.) ECCV 2014. LNCS, vol. 8691, pp. 346–361. Springer, Cham (2014). https://doi.org/10.1007/978-3-319-10578-9_23
11. He, K., Zhang, X., Ren, S., Sun, J.: Delving deep into rectifiers: Surpassing human-level performance on ImageNet classification. In: ICCV (2015)
12. He, K., Zhang, X., Ren, S., Sun, J.: Deep residual learning for image recognition. arXiv preprint arXiv:1512.03385 (2016)
13. He, K., Zhang, X., Shaoqing, R., Sun, J.: Deep residual learning for image recognition. In: 2016 IEEE Conference on Computer Vision and Pattern Recognition. Microsoft Research (2016)

14. He, X., Zhao, K., Chu, X.: AutoML: a survey of the state-of-the-art. arXiv:1908.00709v6 [cs.LG] (2021)

15. Hilal, A.M., Al-Wesabi, F.N., et al.: Deep transfer learning based fusion model for environmental remote sensing image classification model. Eur. J. Remote Sens. **55**, 12–23 (2022)

16. Hinton, G.E., Srivastava, N., Krizhevsky, A., Sutskever, I., Salakhutdinov, R.R.: Improving neural networks by preventing co-adaptation of feature detectors. arXiv:1207.0580 (2012)

17. Ioffe, S., Szegedy, C.: Batch normalization: accelerating deep network training by reducing internal covariate shift. In: ICML (2015)

18. Jin, H., Song, Q., Hu, X.: Auto-keras: an efficient neural architecture search system. In: Proceedings of the 25th ACM SIGKDD International Conference on Knowledge Discovery & Data Mining, KDD 2019, Anchorage, AK, USA, pp. 1946–1956. ACM (2019)

19. Kocmi, T., Bojar, O.: Trivial transfer learning for low-resource neural machine translation. In: Proceedings of the 3rd Conference on Machine Translation 2018 (2018). Accepted to WMT18 research paper

20. Koziarski, M.: Two-stage resampling for convolutional neural network training in the imbalanced colorectal cancer image classification. In: 2021 International Joint Conference on Neural Networks (IJCNN), pp. 1–8 (2021)

21. Kraft, D., Bieber, G., Jokisch, P., Rumm, P.: End-to-end premature ventricular contraction detection using deep neural networks. Sensors **23**, 8573 (2023)

22. Krishna, S.T., Kalluri, H.K.: Deep learning and transfer learning approaches for image classification. Int. J. Recent Technol. Eng. **7**, 427–432 (2019)

23. LeCun, Y., et al.: Backpropagation applied to handwritten zip code recognition. Neural Comput. **1**(4), 541–551 (1989)

24. LeCun, Y., Bottou, L., Bengio, Y., Haffner, P.: Gradient-based learning applied to document recognition. Proc. IEEE **86**(11), 2278–2324 (1998)

25. Rawat, W., Wang, Z.: Deep convolutional neural networks for image classification. Neural Comput. **29**(9), 1–98 (2017)

26. Russakovsky, O., et al.: ImageNet large scale visual recognition challenge. Int. J. Comput. Vision (IJCV) **115**, 211–252 (2015)

27. Sandler, M., Howard, A., Zhu, M., Zhmoginov, A., Chen, L.-C.: MobileNetv 2: inverted residuals and linear bottlenecks. arXiv:1801.04381 [cs.CV] (2018)

28. Sanida, T., Sideris, A., Sanida, M.V., Dasygenis, M.: Tomato leaf disease identification via two-stage transfer learning approach. Smart Agric. Technol. **5**, 100275 (2023)

29. Shao, S., McAleer, S., Yan, R., Baldi, P.: Highly accurate machine fault diagnosis using deep transfer learning. IEEE Trans. Industr. Inf. **15**(4), 2446–2455 (2019)

30. Szegedy, C., et al.: Going deeper with convolutions. In: 2015 IEEE Conference on Computer Vision and Pattern Recognition (2015)

31. Tan, M., Le, Q.V.: EfficientNet: rethinking model scaling for convolutional neural networks. arXiv:1905.11946v5 [cs.LG] (2020)

32. Vo, A.T., Tran, H.S., Le, T.H.: Advertisement image classification using convolutional neural network. In: 2017 9th International Conference on Knowledge and Systems Engineering (KSE). IEEE (2017)

33. Bjørn von Rimscha, M. (ed.): Management and Economics of Communication. De Gruyter Mouton, Berlin, Boston (2020)

34. Xu, Z., Yu, H., Zheng, K., Gao, L., Song, M.: A novel classification framework for hyperspectral image classification based on multiscale spectral-spatial convolutional network. In: 2021 11th Workshop on Hyperspectral Imaging and Signal Processing: Evolution in Remote Sensing (WHISPERS). IEEE (2021)
35. Yosinski, J., Clune, J., Bengio, Y., Lipson, H.: How transferable are features in deep neural networks? arXiv:1411.1792 [cs.LG] (2014)
36. Zhang, D., et al.: Domain-oriented language modeling with adaptive hybrid masking and optimal transport alignment. In: Proceedings of the 27th ACM SIGKDD Conference on Knowledge Discovery & Data Mining. ACM (2021)
37. Zhao, Q., Zhang, L., He, B., Liu, Z.: Semantic policy network for zero-shot object goal visual navigation. IEEE Robot. Autom. Lett. 8(11), 7655–7662 (2023)
38. Zhao, Q., Zhang, L., He, B., Qiao, H., Liu, Z.: Zero-shot object goal visual navigation. In: 2023 IEEE International Conference on Robotics and Automation (ICRA), pp. 2025–2031 (2023)

Analysis Effect of K Values Used in K Fold Cross Validation for Enhancing Performance of Machine Learning Model with Decision Tree

Vijay Kumar Verma[1]([✉]) [iD], Kanak Saxena[2] [iD], and Umesh Banodha[3] [iD]

[1] Shri Vaishnav Vidyapeeth Vishwavidyalaya, Indore, M.P., India
drvijaykumarverma20@gmail.com
[2] Samrat Ashok Technological Institute, Vidisha, M.P., India
[3] Dr. A.P.J. Abdul Kalam U.I.T., Jhabua, M.P., India

Abstract. In Data Science usual exercise is to reiteration throughout several models to observe a best working model. Creating portion of datasets to train and validate model for machine learning to improve performance the model. The splitting ratio of dataset is either 70:30 or 80:20. The problem with this technique is that only one large part is used to train and a small part is used to test ML model. Due to this approach sometimes, model get underfit or overfit. Objective of everyone is always find out the best fil model. CV is a technique which keep a portion of data from the entire dataset and used it for model testing (Validation set), and rest of data other than the part stored to train the ML model. In this paper we apply K fold cross-validation technique with Decision Tree Classifier. We have applied K fold CV by applying distinct K values with Decision Tree Classifier and checking accuracy, precision, recall and F1 value. From different research paper we found that it is difficult to decide the value of K. Our objective is to analyse and identified which value of K is most appropriate. By experimental analysis we found that the accuracy has been improved as compared to the traditional approach. By the observation we found that better for K is 10. BY the average accuracy, precision, recall and F1 value K fold gives better performance for K = 10. Real Life data set has been taken for experimental analysis.

Keywords: Cross · Fold · Validation · Accuracy · Decision tree · Recall · Underfitting · Overfitting

1 Introduction

Performance valuation of any Machine learning model is simply like valuating the scores, that we evaluate scores of students in colleges and universities or in schools to decide and fit the eligibility criteria for whether students are eligible or not for getting admission in his/her best courses or similarly like to select a student for in campus interviews of companies. The score identifies the fact that the applicant or the student is continuously having the good performance. In the similar way we have been expected for every machine learning model. When a machine learning model is tested, we accept that it has achieve the expected results for predictions or forecasting or classification. There are numbers way and mathematical formulas are available to analyze and evaluate the accuracy of the ML model. The ML model engineer has responsibility to always develop a generalized ML model so that the performance is expected. We must satisfy the customers by adding the key benefits for business [2, 13]. Every ML model has performance in terms of some range of numeric value. For example, we have developed a model and found its performance between 85–90% during training and testing. In many cases the model shows the same accuracy for both in training and testing and some time it will not perform in the same result. Accuracy is nothing, it is just a numerical value for better understanding and getting of a prediction for given unknown data based on the problem, so that we can correctly understand the predictions. It is better to use different combinations of data when training a ML model [14, 20].

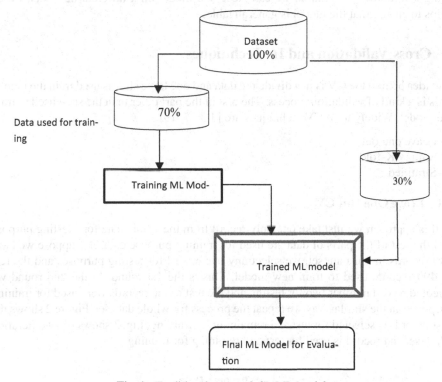

Fig. 1. Traditional approach for ML model

Figure 1 shows the working of the traditional approach are based on two criteria it is either split data into 70:30 or 80:20. The major part of split data is used to train the model and the small parts of slit data is used to test the model. Due to this traditional approach the model suffers from several problems some of them are [8, 9, 15].

• Problem with splitting: To achieve good accuracy the better performance of the model we only used a large part of the data, when the size of the data is large the model will not be aware about nature of the data into second part and same thing will happen in case of testing only one part of data used for tested. This is the reason why models suffer from overfitting.

- Problem of generalization: Due to training with large portion and testing with small portion of data model cannot be generalized.
- Number of Sample reduce for training: By reducing number of samples for training model, learning of the model gets reduced. So, we cannot train a model with a smaller number of records.

Our objective in this paper includes Applying K fold cross validation and splitting into number of folds for training and testing, Apply distinct value of k and determine whether the model is over- or under-fitted. Evaluating the model and determining its accuracy and finally determining whether the model is generalizing well to data. By using k-fold cross-validation, we can "test" the model on k different data sets, which helps to ensure that the model is generalizable.

2 Cross Validation and Its Techniques

The idea behind the CV is just divide the data and one large slice is used train the model. This is a kind of validation process. The rest of the part other than the slice used to train the model. Widely used CV techniques are [4, 6, 7, 19].

- Leave one out
- Simply K-fold
- Stratified

2.1 Leave One Out CV

In this approach we just take one only record from the whole data for r testing purpose and the rest of the parts of data are used for training purpose dataset. Suppose we have 500 records in our data set, we select any one record for testing purposes and the rest of 499 records used to train new model. This is the 1st round. In the 2nd round we selected record number two for testing and the rest of the records were used for training purposes, in the similar way we repeat the process for whole data set. Figure 2 shows the first records is selected for test and remaining for training, Fig. 3 shows second iteration when second record is used for test and remining for training.

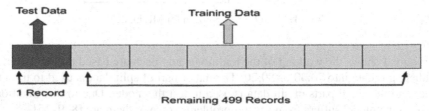

Fig. 2. Select 1st record and used for testing and remining records are used for training

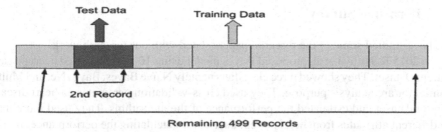

Fig. 3. Select 2nd record and used for testing and remining records are used for training

This approach is time consuming and only suitable where the number of records is limited in the dataset. The main disadvantage of this approach is we require a large number of iterations depending upon the number of records.

2.2 Stratified k-Fold CV

It is an impressive technique which is used to optimize ML models. Sometimes data set contain imbalance class in such situation we can used this approach. It divides the data set into such a way that all partitions approximately have some balance data into k-folds. After creating folds, we apply k-1 fold for training and one part for testing. The process is repeated for all folds. While splitting data into number of folds it used some criteria which ensure that every fold contains some percentage of observed class so the target class we bc balanced up to some level. By using such concepts, the model will not suffer from problem overfitting. Figure 4 shows the working of stratified k-fold CV on basis of Gender whether M or F.

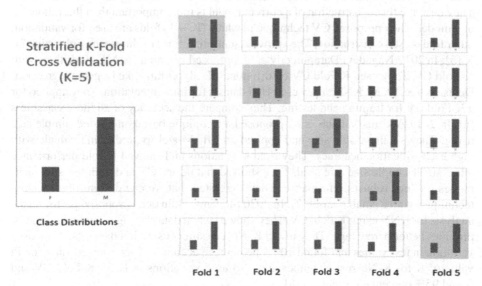

Fig. 4. Working stratified k-fold validation

3 Literature Survey

We have studied some of the research paper related with our research work.

In 2015 R. Nithya et al. proposed Bayes model using 10-fold they used heart disease patient Dataset. They showed three classifiers namely Naïve Bayes, Bayes Net and Multinomial for are analysis purpose. They used cross-validation parameter on heart disease patient dataset and estimated the performance of the algorithms. They used more than 25 different attributes from heart patient dataset for calculating the performance. By the experimental analysis they observed that NB algorithm better than other algorithms [1]. In 2016 Babatunde R. S et al. proposed an approach based on Random Partitioning with K Fold CV. They used the proposed approach for Face. They explained the importance of Face recognition. They describe the application where Face recognition play an active and important role like pattern recognition, computer vision, credit cards, passport and security. They tested the proposed technique on the face when it is randomly partitioned. They used quantitative experimental analysis [2]. In 2017 Max A. Little et al. proposed strategies behind the CV technique. They applied a new idea and created a small group of data sets. They applied this idea in ML to predict disease which have subject-specific features. They constructed different cases and have subject-specific variations [3]. In 2018 Daniel Berar et al. proposed Cross-validation. They explained the very common type of CV and with related data resampling approaches. They describe resampling with K-fold CV; random subsampling with K-fold; how the learning set applied; problem of overfitting; how to predict error; how resubstituting error and validation set. They also used CV to resolve the overfitting problem. They explained that performance of CV is inaccurate when we used small sample of data sets [4].

In 2018 Yoonsuh Jung et al. proposed an approach based on K Fold CV for ML selection. They describe that in model selection **K**-fold CV is commonly accepted technique. They describe that construction of a current model is more important than the validation of a model. They proposed CV technique in which $(K - 1)$ folds are used for validation, other fold is used construction. They provide some directions to choose the right value for K [5]. In 2019 Nagadevi Darapureddy et al. proposed research for ML algorithms with K-Fold CV. They used K Fold CV on different ML algorithms like Logistic regression, Decision tree, SVM, KNN. They used UCI dataset for implementation. They applied for a K Fold CV for training and testing. They compare the accuracy of all these classifiers [6]. In 2019 Andrius Vabalas et al. proposed a technique based on limited sample size using. They small sample size and applied on ML Model to predict individuals with higher classification accuracy. They used simulations and showed K-fold performance when small sample sizes are used. They showed that nested CV and train/test split techniques produce robust performance. They suggested that we can design robust testing techniques with a small dataset [7]. In 2020 Sitefanus Hulu et al. proposed performance analysis for KNN using K Fold CV. They showed when data sharing is applied using CV provides better percentage. They tested K-NN classifiers using iris data sets. They used variation in test values and found 100% percentage accuracy. They showed variation in value of K for K-Nearest Neighbor and also used variations in K for K-Fold CV and found 95% percentage accuracy [8].

In 2021 Muhammad Asrola et al. proposed SVM using K Fold CV for the Industry's Sustainability Performance. They used SVM to create ML model which assesses the performance of industry's sustainability. They applied K Fold CV to improve model performance. By the result they showed accuracy to classify sustainability accurate. They proved that SVM using with polynomial kernel perform accurately [9]. In 2021 Kwanele Phinz et al. proposed Bootstrapping Resampling technique Using K-Fold Cross-Validation for Mapping Complex Gully Systems. They investigated the performance of two classifiers by using resampling techniques. They used data of planet scope when seasons are wet and dry. By the experimental analysis they found that the overall accuracies of RF's better than CV [10]. In 2022 Zeyang Lin et al. proposed Curriculum Reinforcement Learning by using K Fold CV. They proposed curriculum reinforcement learning method based in which they applied K-Fold CV. The concepts behind the approach that method automatically divides curriculum into assessment and sorting stage. With the help of simulations, the shared and the argumentative environment, the serviceability and superiority of the technique has been proved [11]. In 2022 Sashikanta Prusty et al. proposed Classifiers based Stratified K-fold CV for predicting cervical cancer. They proposed a system with stratified k-fold. They developed four diagnostic strategies based on Stratified K-fold CV to attain a ROC and PR accuracy score. They developed the model RF6 which has accuracy score 98.10%, 95.80%, 97.49% when using different K-fold. They significantly contributed integration for treatment in cervical cancer [13].

4   K Fold CV Approach

K-fold CV is best approach to approximate the performance of a ML model for unseen data. This approach can be applied when the data is infrequent and when we need a good estimate for training purposes. This approach is useful when we want generalization of the model and need to understand the characteristics like underfitting and overfitting. This approach used hyperparameter tuning like the most optimal value for model with the of hyperparameters model can be trained. This approach is based on resampling of data, replacement is not allowed in this approach. The advantage of approach is each fold is used exactly once for training and validation. This returns a lower variance and approximate performance. This approach is suitable because the problem of overfitting can be avoided. By applying k-fold CV, ensure that the model could be generalizable [2, 3, 18].

4.1   CV Process

While training a model we always require a good ratio of data for training as well as testing. We prime need is to train the model with large portion of the data, otherwise, model will fail to understand and recognise the trend of the data. This ultimately procedure a higher bias produce. Figure 5 shows the working of 5 fold k cross validation [16, 17].

Multiple numbers of repetition are required in training and testing process. This process helps for effectively validate the model. In K-fold CV there are three things that need to take care. This approach has following steps.

1. The whole dataset needs to be split randomly into k fold.

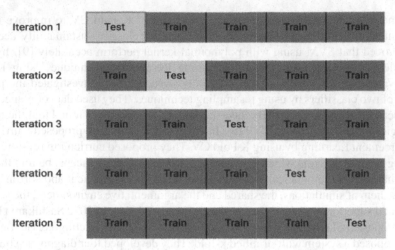

Fig. 5. Working 5-fold cross-validation approach

2. Use k-1 folds to tarin and build Model. To evaluate effectiveness, test the model using kth fold.
3. For every iteration records the accuracy of every fold. Note down the predicted value for every fold.
4. Iterate this process for all the k-folds has to serve in the testing process.
5. Calculate the average of all iteration for predicted value. Generate performance metric which shows the overall performance of the model.

4.2 Difficult to Decide k Value

Standard guidelines need to follow while selecting k value to create number of folds:

- If the size of the data is decent, we can use 10 as standard k value.
- When the size of data is large, we used 5 as value of k.
- When the size of the data is small, need to increase number of folds. It is found that for large k value run time has increased.
- When a dataset has a few numbers of records we need to apply leave-one-out approach.

5   Illustrate with Example

K Fold CV is a simple method and easy to understand. K fold CV provides a way to overcome the problem of splitting data. In K Fold CV, K is an integer number based on value of K, we split the data. Suppose there are 1000 records present in the dataset, we select the 5 as value of k. So, K value decides the number of iterations needed to perform in training and testing. In this example the value of k value is 5, se we have to create 5 folds for training and testing. Figure 6 show the initialization when there are split of data.

In this example, value of k is 5, so number of folds. So 1000 is divided into 5 folds. 1000/5 = 200.

Fig. 6. Initially we have complete data set with 1000 records

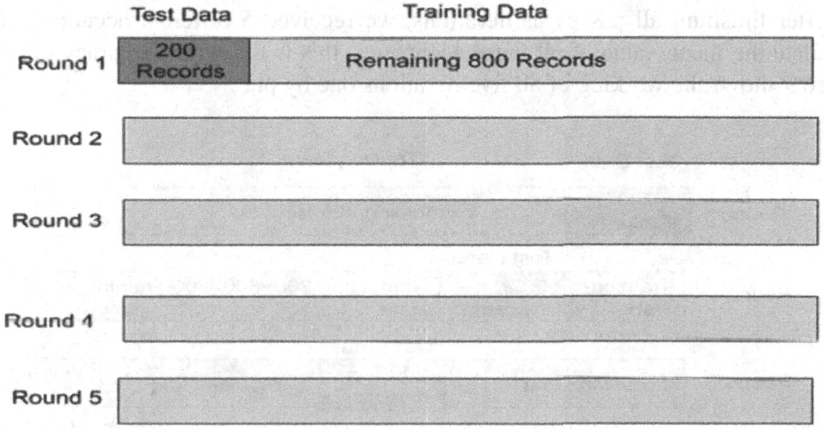

Fig. 7. First round, the first 200 records are used for testing and the remaining 800 for Training data.

So there are 5 folds, every fold contain 200 records.

In the first iteration we used the first records for testing, the remaining 800 records is used for training. Figure 7 shows the first split, in the first pass model is trained with 800 records. Suppose the accuracy of the first pass is 1. In the second round the next 200 records are used for testing and the remaining 800 records are used for training. Model has trained on 800 records and tested with 200 records. Figure 8 shows the seconds split where the next 200 records are chosen for testing, suppose the accuracy of the second pass is 2. Apply same procedure for remaining folds for taring and testing, the accuracy or the prediction need to be noted down for each pass.

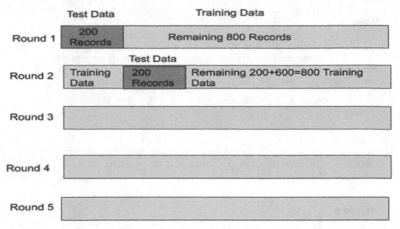

Fig. 8. Second round, the next 200 records are used for testing and the remaining 800 for training data.

After finishing all passes or iterations, we received 5 different accuracy values. Calculate the mean value of all these accuracies, this is the actual accuracy of model. Figure 9 shows the working of all five iterations one by one.

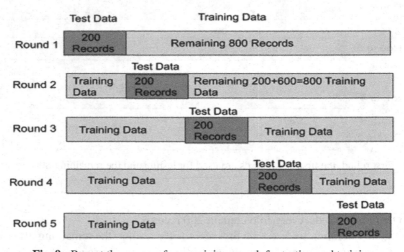

Fig. 9. Repeat the process for remaining round, for testing and training

6   Implementation and Data Set Description

6.1   Hardware

- Hardware requirement
- Intel Core i5 processor

- 4 GB main memory
- 4 GB RAM
- Inbuilt HDD: 500 GB

6.2 Software Requirements

- Windows 7 OS
- Python
- CSV file format is used to store data set

6.3 Data Set Description

Data set has been collected form two different hospital of Indore city CHL CBCC Cancer Center AB Rd, Phadnis Colony, Indore, Madhya Pradesh and Sri Aurobindo Hospital SAIMS in Indore Cancer specialist, Treatment Center. More then 13 different attribute have been to identify the Breast Cancer. More then 1000 patient data set have been taken form patient history. Breast Cancer (Diagnostic) Data Set has the following attribute. Information:

1) Patient ID
2) Diagnosis Type (M = Malignant, B = Benign, Target class has only two)

Some of the attributes of used dataset are, radius_mean, texture_mean, perimeter_mean, area_mean, smoothness_mean, compactness_mean, concavity_mean, concave points_mean, symmetry_worst etc. Value of all features are recoded with four digits. There are no missing attributes values present in any of the attributes.

7 Result Analysis

7.1 Performance Analysis Using 3 Folds

Comparing Accuracy Scores for 3 Folds. Form Table 1 shows that for first fold accuracy is 0.88947368, for second fold accuracy is 0.93684211 and for third fold accuracy is 0.9047619. It is observed that accuracy for the first and third fold is less and for the second fold it is high. The average accuracy of the model using 3 folds is 91%.

Comparing Precision Score for 3 Folds. From Table 2 shows that precision value for first fold is 0.84722222, for second fold it is 0.94029851 and for third fold it is 0.825. It is observed that precision for the first and third fold is less and for second it is high. The average precision value for model using 3 folds is 0.870840. Figure 10 shows the difference between training and testing for accuracy and precision score in form of graphical representation for 3 folds. Figure 10 shows graphical representation of accuracy and precision for 3 folds.

Comparing Recall Score for 3 Folds. From Table 3 shows clear that recall for first fold is 0.85915493, for second fold it is 0.88732394 and for third fold it is 0.94285714. It is observed that recall for the first and second fold is less and for third it very high. Average recall value for the model using 3 fold is 0.896445.

Table 1. Comparing Accuracy scores for 3 folds.

Fold. No.	Accuracy
1	0.88947368
2	0.93684211
3	0.9047619

Table 2. Comparing precision scores for 3 folds.

Fold. No.	Precision
1	0.84722222
2	0.94029851
3	0.825

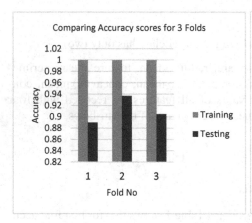 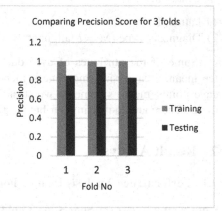

Fig. 10. Comparing Accuracy and precision scores for 3 Folds

Comparing F1 Score for 3 Folds. Form Table 4 shows that F1 Score value for first fold is 0.85314685, for second fold it is 0.91304348 and for third fold it is s 0.88. It is observed F1 Score for the first and third fold is less and for third fold it is high. Average F1 Score for the model using 3 fold is 0.882063. Figure 11 shows difference between training and testing for recall and F1 Score in form of graphical representation for 3 folds.

Table 3. Comparing recall scores for 3 folds.

Fold. No.	Recall
1	0.85915493
2	0.88732394
3	0.94285714

Table 4. Comparing F1 Score scores for 3 folds.

Fold. No.	F1 Score
1	0.85314685
2	0.91304348
3	0.88

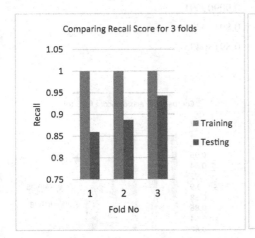 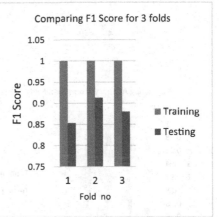

Fig. 11. Comparing Recall and F1 Score for 3 Folds

7.2 Performance Analysis Using 5 Folds

Comparing Accuracy Scores for 5 Fold. Form Table 5 it is observed that accuracy for first and second fold is less and for fold third, fourth and fifth fold the accuracy is very high. The average accuracy value of the model using five old is 0.934994564.

Comparing Precision Score for 5 Folds. From Table 6 it is observed that for first- and second-fold precision is high and for the third, fourth and fifth it is low. The average precision value of the model using 5 folds is 0.912429. Figure 12 shows the difference between training and testing for accuracy and precision of graphical representation for 5 folds.

Table 5. Comparing Accuracy scores for 5 folds.

Fold. No.	Accuracy
1	0.9122807
2	0.92105263
3	0.94736842
4	0.94736842
5	0.94690265

Table 6. Comparing Precision Result for all 5-fold.

Fold. No.	Precision
1	0.92307692
2	0.94736842
3	0.90909091
4	0.89130435
5	0.89130435

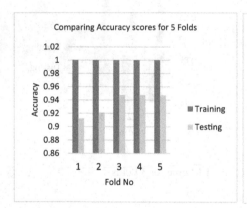
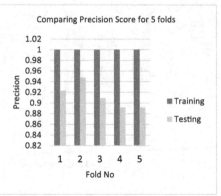

Fig. 12. Comparing Accuracy and Precision for 5 folds

Comparing Recall Score for 5 Folds. From Table 7 it observed that recall for first and second fold is less and for fold third, fourth and fifth the precision values are very high. The average recall value of the model using five folds is 0.9158361.

Comparing F1 Score for 5 Folds. From Table 8 it is observed that F1-Score for first and second fold is less and for fold third, fourth and fifth fold F1 Score is high. Average F1 Score of the model using 5 folds is 0.912161. Figure 13 shows the graphical representation of recall and F1 score for 5 folds (Table 9).

Table 7. Comparing Recall score for 5 folds

Fold. No.	Recall
1	0.8372093
2	0.8372093
3	0.95238095
4	0.97619048
5	0.97619048

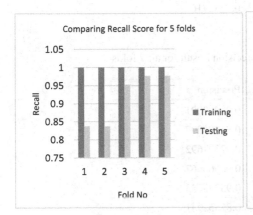 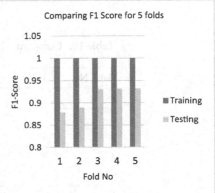

Fig. 13. Comparing Recall and F1 Score for 5 folds

Table 8. Comparing F1-Score for 5 folds

Fold. No.	F1-Score
1	0.87804878
2	0.88888889
3	0.93023256
4	0.93181818
5	0.93181818

Comparing Precision Score for 7 Folds. From Table 10 it is observed that Precision score for second and sixth fold is low and for remaining folds it I high. The average precision value of the model using seven folds is 0.9029988. Figure 14 shows the graphical representation of accuracy and precision for 7 folds.

Comparing Recall Score for 7 Folds. From Table 11 it is observed that recall score for second and third fold is less and for remaining fold recall values is high. Average recall score for the model using 7 folds is 0.905837173.

Table 9. Comparing Accuracy scores for 7 folds.

Fold. No.	Accuracy
1	0.95121951
2	0.87804878
3	0.90123457
4	0.97530864
5	0.95061728
6	0.90123457
7	0.9382716

Table 10. Comparing Precision Result for all 7 folds

Fold. No.	Precision
1	0.90909091
2	0.86206897
3	0.92307692
4	0.96666667
5	0.93333333
6	0.82352941
7	0.90322581

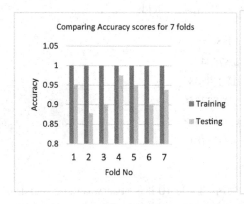 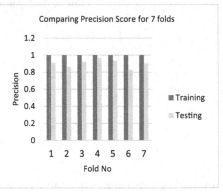

Fig. 14. Comparing Accuracy and Precision for 7 folds

Comparing F1 Score for 7 Folds. From Table 12 it is observed that for second, third and sixth fold has less F1 score value and remaining fold has high F1 score value.

Table 11. Comparing Recall score for 7 folds

Fold. No.	Recall
1	0.96774194
2	0.80645161
3	0.8000
4	0.96666667
5	0.93333333
6	0.93333333
7	0.93333333

Average F1 Score value for the model using 7 folds 0.9030012.2. Figure 15 shows the graphical representation of recall and F1 score for 7 folds.

Table 12. Comparing F1-Score for all 7 folds

Fold. No.	F1-Score
1	0.9375
2	0.83333333
3	0.85714286
4	0.96666667
5	0.93333333
6	0.875
7	0.91803279

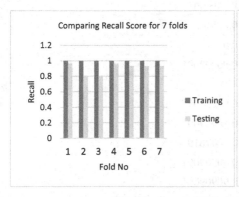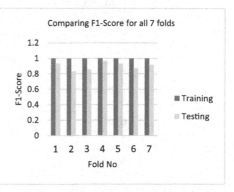

Fig. 15. Comparing Recall and F1 Score for 7 folds

7.3 Performance Analysis Using 10 Folds

Comparing Accuracy Scores for 10 Folds. From Table 13 it is observed that accuracy for second old is low and for remaining folds it is high. Average precision value of the model using ten folds is 93.850250.

Comparing Precision Score for 10 Folds. From Table 14 it is observed that precision value for first fold is low and for remaining folds it is high. Average precision value of the model using ten folds is 0.9177597. Figure 16 shows the graphical representation of accuracy and precision for 10 **folds**.

Table 13. Comparing Accuracy scores for 5 folds

Fold. No.	Accuracy
1	0.92982456
2	0.89473684
3	0.94736842
4	0.92982456
5	0.96491228
6	0.94736842
7	0.92982456
8	0.94736842
9	0.94736842
10	0.94642857

Table 14. Comparing Precision Result for all 10 folds

Fold. No.	Precision
1	0.875
2	0.9
3	0.90909091
4	1
5	0.95238095
6	0.90909091
7	0.9047619
8	0.90909091
9	0.90909091
10	0.90909091

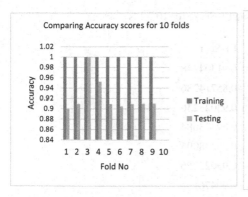 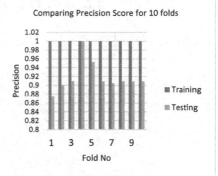

Fig. 16. Comparing Accuracy and Precision for 10 folds

Table 15. Comparing Recall score for 10 folds

Fold. No.	Recall
1	0.95454545
2	0.81818182
3	0.95238095
4	0.80952381
5	0.95238095
6	0.95238095
7	0.9047619
8	0.95238095
9	0.95238095
10	0.95238095

Comparing Recall Score for 10 Folds. From Table 15 it is observed that recall value for second and fourth fold is low and for remaining folds it is high. Average recall value of the model using ten folds is 0.92012987.

Comparing F1 Score for 10 Folds. From Table 16 it is observed that recall value for second and fourth fold is low and for remaining folds it is high. Average recall value of the model using ten folds is 0.91732288. Figure 17 shows the graphical representation of recall and F1 score for 10 folds.

Table 16. Comparing F1-Score for 10 folds

Fold. No.	F1-Score
1	0.91304348
2	0.85714286
3	0.93023256
4	0.89473684
5	0.95238095
6	0.93023256
7	0.9047619
8	0.93023256
9	0.93023256
10	0.93023256

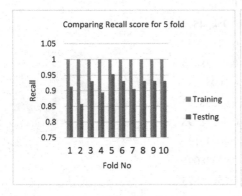 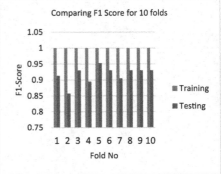

Fig. 17. Comparing Recall and F1 Score for 10 folds

8 Performance Analysis Using Average Values

8.1 Comparison Using Average Accuracy, Precision, Recall and F1 Score

From the implementation and experimental analysis, we calculate the average accuracy value for all folds (3, 5, 7 and 10). From graph 18 we can see that average accuracy value is higher when the value of K is 10(10 folds). From graph 19 we can see that that average precision value is higher when the value of K is 10(10 folds). From graph 20 we can see that average recall value is higher when the value of K is 10(10 folds). Finally From graph 21 we can see that average F1 Score value is higher when the value of K is 10(10 folds).

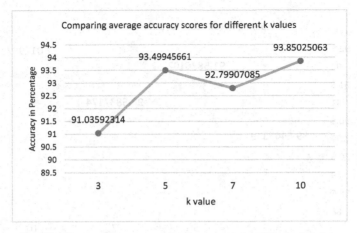

Fig. 18. Comparison average accuracy score for different k values

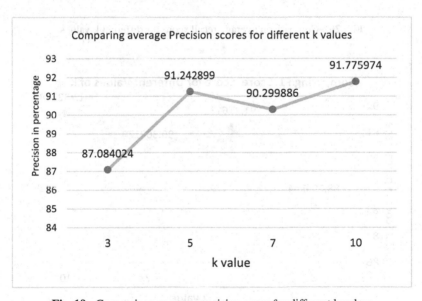

Fig. 19. Comparison average precision score for different k values

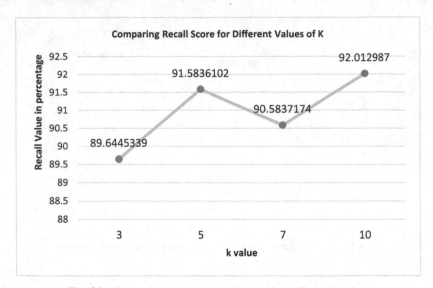

Fig. 20. Comparison average recall score for different k values

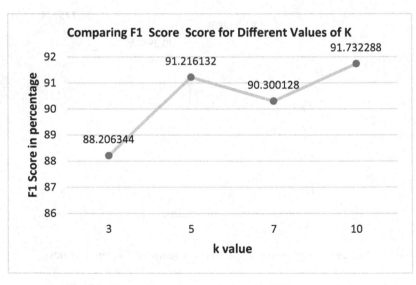

Fig. 21. Comparison average F1 score for different k values

9 Conclusion and Future Work

In this paper we used K-fold CV approach on Decision Tree Classifier to create a ML model. We used Breast Cancer data set which has attribute information radius_mean, texture_mean, perimeter_mean, area_mean, smoothness_mean, compactness_mean, concavity_mean, concave points_mean, symmetry_worst etc. Diagnosis class or target class has only two values (M = Malignant, B = Benign). The value for all features has been recorded up to four significant digits. All feature values are recorded with four significant digits. We have used the different K value for K Fold CV. Here we used four performance parameters accuracy, precision, recall and F1 Score. By the implantation and experimental analysis, we proved that the value for K is much better as compared to 3, 5 and 7. By selecting K value 10 we check the average accuracy value, average precision value, average recall value and finally F1 Score value we see the performance of the classifier is better. So, we concluded here that it is better to use 10 as K value for K Fold CV. We also found if we select the value of K as 5 it is also good but not as compared to 3 and 7. So Using tradition approach 80:20 or 70:30. We have to use K Fold CV approach because it is better way to achieve highest performance of the any ML model. In future we will consider some other classifiers and maintain stable accuracy. We also apply some others real life data set and check the performance of K Fold CV. In future we will also consider the computational cost of different K values.

References

1. Nithya, R., Ramyachitra, D., Manikandan, P.: An efficient Bayes classifiers algorithm on 10-fold cross validation for heart disease dataset. Int. J. Comput. Intell. Inform. **5**(3), 229–235 (2015)
2. Babatunde, R.S., Olabiyisi, S.O., Omidiora, E.O., Ganiyu, R.A., Isiaka, R.M.: Assessing the performance of random partitioning and k-fold cross validation methods of evaluation of a face recognition system. In: The Ninth International Conference on Applications of Information Communication Technologies to Teaching, Research and Administration, p. 129 (2015). https://doi.org/10.14738/aivp.36.1460
3. Little, M.A., Varoquaux, G., Saeb, S.: Using and understanding cross-validation strategies. https://doi.org/10.1093/gigascience/gix020. Advance Access Publication Date: 17 March 2017 Chicago, USA and 4Rehabilitation Institute of Chicago, 345 E Superior, 60611, Chicago, USA
4. Berrar, D.: "Cross-validation" Data Science Laboratory, Tokyo Institute of Technology 2-12-1-S3-70 Ookayama, Meguro-ku, Tokyo 152-8550, Japan (2018) Cross-validation. Encyclopedia of Bioinformatics and Computational Biology, Volume 1, Elsevier
5. Jung, Y.: Multiple predicting K-fold cross-validation for model selection. J. Nonparametric Stat. **30**(1), 197–215 (2018). https://www.tandfonline.com/loi/gnst20
6. Darapureddy, N., Karatapu, N., Battula, T.K.: Research OF machine learning algorithms using K-fold cross validation. Int. J. Eng. Adv. Technol. **8**(6), 215–218 (2019)
7. Vabalas, A., Gowen, E., Poliakoff, E., Casson, A.J.: Machine learning algorithm validation with a limited sample size. PLoS ONE **14**(11), e0224365 (2019)
8. Hulu, S., Sihombing, P.: Sutarman, analysis of performance cross validation method and K-nearest neighbor in classification data. Int. J. Res. Rev. **7**, 69–73 (2020)
9. Asrol, M., Papilo, P., Gunawan, F.E.: Support vector machine with K-fold validation to improve the industry's sustainability performance classification. Procedia Comput. Sci. **179**, 854–862 (2021)
10. Phinzi, K., Abriha, D., Szabó, S.: Classification efficacy using k-fold cross-validation and bootstrapping resampling techniques on the example of mapping complex gully systems. Remote Sens. **13**(15), 2980 (2021). https://doi.org/10.3390/rs13152980
11. Lin, Z., Lai, J., Chen, X., Cao, L., Wang, J.: Curriculum reinforcement learning based on K-fold cross validation. Entropy **24**(12), 1787 (2022)

12. Prusty, S., Patnaik, S., Dash, S.K.: SKCV: stratified K-fold cross-validation on ML classifiers for predicting cervical cancer. Front. Nanotechnol. **4**, 972421 (2022). https://doi.org/10.3389/fnano.2022.972421

13. Suzuki, K., Kambayashi, Y., Matsuzawa, T.: CrossSiam: k-fold cross representation learning. In: Proceedings of the 14th International Conference on Agents and Artificial Intelligence (ICAART 2022), vol. 1, pp. 541–547 (2022). https://doi.org/10.5220/0010972500003116

14. Wieczorek, J., Guerin, C., McMahon, T.: K-fold cross-validation for complex sample surveys. Stat **11**(1), e454 (2022). https://doi.org/10.1002/sta4.454

15. Nti, I.K., Nyarko-Boateng, O., Aning, J.: Performance of machine learning algorithms with different K values in K-fold cross-validation. J. Inf. Technol. Comput. Sci. **6**, 61–71 (2021). https://doi.org/10.5815/ijitcs.2021.06.05

16. Zhang, X., Liu, C.A.: Model averaging prediction by K-fold cross-validation. J. Econom. **235**(1), 280–301 (2023)

17. Aghbalou, A., Sabourin, A., Portier, F.: On the bias of K-fold cross validation with stable learners. In: International Conference on Artificial Intelligence and Statistics, pp. 3775–3794. PMLR (2023)

18. Anguita, D., Ghelardoni, L., Ghio, A., Oneto, L., Ridella, S.: The 'K' in K-fold cross validation. In: ESANN, pp. 441–446 (2012)

19. Wong, T.T.: Performance evaluation of classification algorithms by k-fold and leave-one-out cross validation. Pattern Recognit. **48**(9), 2839–2846 (2015)

20. Oyedele, O.: Determining the optimal number of folds to use in a K-fold cross-validation: a neural network classification experiment. Res. Math. **10**(1), 2201015 (2023)

The Forward-Forward Algorithm: Analysis and Discussion

Sudhanshu Thakur[1], Reha Dhawan[1], Parth Bhargava[1], Kaustubh Tripathi[1], Rahee Walambe[1,2(✉)], and Ketan Kotecha[1,2]

[1] Symbiosis Institute of Technology, Symbiosis International University, Pune, India
rahee.walambe@sitpune.edu.in

[2] Symbiosis Centre for Applied Artificial Intelligence, Symbiosis International University, Pune, India

Abstract. This study explores the potential and application of the newly proposed Forward-Forward algorithm (FFA). The primary aim of this study is to analyze the results achieved from the proposed algorithm and compare it with the existing algorithms. What we are trying to achieve here is to know the extent to which FFA can be effectively deployed in any neural network and to investigate its efficacy in producing results that can be compared to those generated by the conventional Backpropagation method. For diving into a deeper understanding of this new algorithm's benefits and limitations in the context of neural network training, this study is conducted. In the process of experimentation, the four datasets used are the MNIST dataset, COVID-19 X-ray, Brain MRI and the Cat vs. Dog dataset. Our findings suggest that FFA has potential in certain tasks in CV. However, it is yet far from replacing the backpropagation for common tasks. The paper describes the experimental setup and process carried out to understand the efficacy of the FFA and provides the obtained results and comparative analysis.

Keywords: Deep Learning · Forward-Forward algorithm (FFA) · Neural Networks · Backpropagation · Algorithmic limitations

1 Introduction

The field of neural networks has seen a rapid expansion in recent years, with researchers exploring new algorithms and techniques for training these models. Gradient descent computed using backpropagation is one of the most powerful techniques used in ML and has proved highly effective in generating representations. However, from the brain perspective, it is still unclear as to how real neurons implement it. There is no clear and convincing evidence of how the errors are propagated through the layers via backpropagation. Further, the traditional methods require proper knowledge of the computations performed in the forward pass for computing the correct derivatives. If the non-linearities in the forward pass are unknown, then it is not plausible to compute the backpropagation and carry the error back.

When a perfect representation and model of the forward pass are unavailable, reinforcement learning can be used. However, RL techniques consist of high variance. These methods do not scale well, and large networks with billions of parameters can't compete with the backpropagation approach.

To that end, Hinton [5] proposed the Forward-Forward algorithm (FFA) inspired by the Boltzmann machine. The FFA may prove superior to backpropagation in two areas: firstly, as a way to understand and model learning in the human brain, especially the cortex and secondly, in order to utilize the very low-power analogue hardware. This study aims to investigate the potential of the FFA) or training neural networks. Specifically, we seek to evaluate the algorithm's performance on four different datasets: the MNIST dataset [1], the COVID-19 chest X-ray dataset [2], the Brain tumor [3] image dataset and the Cat vs Dog dataset [4]. By testing the algorithm on these datasets, we aim to analyze and discuss our findings regarding the effectiveness of FFA across a range of different applications and scenarios [6, 7]. In FFA the forward and backward passes of backpropagation is replaced with 2 forward passes, one with negative data and the other with positive data. The objective function for each layer is given as to have low goodness for negative data and high goodness for positive data [8–10]. By following this method, we can significantly boost the learning process and make the training of the neural network with multiple layers easier. Firstly, the algorithm's performance is evaluated on multiple datasets to conclude that it achieves a high level of accuracy in different given scenarios [11–15]. Secondly, the results achieved by the FFA will be compared to the existing conventional backpropagation algorithm, which would enhance the understanding of the difference between the two algorithms [5, 16]. And at last, we tend to examine the potential of the FFA, which could contribute a lot to the training approach of the neural networks. In a nutshell, this study demonstrates the potential of this algorithm and how it can change the training of neural networks.

The paper is organized in 7 sections. Section 2 discusses methods, followed by Sect. 3 discusses algorithmic formulation. In Sect. 4 system design is presented and in Sect. 5 experimental setup is described. Section 6 presents the results followed by the conclusion and future work in Sect. 7.

2   Methods

2.1   Datasets

Four benchmark datasets are used in the study. The datasets are selected as they align with our study objective of evaluating the performance of the FFA across various applications and scenarios. These datasets cover diverse tasks, allowing us to gain insights into the algorithm's effectiveness and potential benefits (Table 1).

2.2   Forward-Forward Algorithm (FFA)

Boltzmann machines [26] and Noise Contrastive Estimation [25] served as inspiration for the greedy multi-layer learning process that makes up the FFA. The goal is to replace the backward and forward passes of backpropagation with 2 identically functioning forward passes that work on distinct data sets and have diametrically opposed goals. The positive pass uses actual data and modifies the weights to improve each hidden layer's quality. The

Table 1. Dataset description

Title	Number of Images	Colour Scheme	Size (in pixels)
MNIST [1]	60,000	GrayScale	28×28
Covid Dataset [2]	3082	GrayScale	264×264
Dogs and Cats [3]	25,000	RGB	200×200
Brain tumour image dataset [4]	253	GrayScale	205×246

negative passes operate on the "negative data" and adjust the weights for decreasing the goodness of every hidden layer. This research paper explores the two different measures of goodness. However, many other measures are possible. Let's assume that the sum of the squares of the activity of the rectified linear neurons inside a layer serves as the goodness function for that layer. The squared length of the activity vector is chosen as the goodness function for two primary reasons. First, it has very simple derivatives. Second, layer normalization removes all traces of the goodness function.

Learning aims to raise goodness much over a predetermined threshold value for actual data and significantly lower it for negative data. More specifically, when the likelihood that an input vector is positive (i.e., real) is determined by applying the log function to the goodness minus some threshold, the goal is to accurately categorize the input vectors as positive or negative., as shown in Eq. 1.

$$p(positive) = \sigma \left(\sum_j y_j^2 - \theta \right) \tag{1}$$

where y_j is the activity of hidden unit j before the layer normalization. The neural net would predict the negative data using a top-down connections approach.

3 Algorithmic Formulation

The understanding of Boltzmann Machines served as the inspiration for the idea [8, 17]. In order to change the network weights, backpropagation measures the discrepancy between the output that was anticipated and the output that actually occurred. On the other hand, the FFA makes the analogy of neurons that become "excited" upon viewing a specifically recognized pairing of a picture and its accurate corresponding label. The biological learning process that takes place in the cortex serves as some of the motivation for this approach. The fact that this strategy eliminates the requirement for backpropagation over the network and makes weight adjustments local to the layer itself is a big benefit [6, 18, 19].

Algorithmic Formulation of the Feedforward Associative Algorithm:

1. Initialize the network architecture:

   - Define the number of layers, neurons in each layer, and the activation functions for every neuron.

2. Initialize the network weights:

- Set the initial values for the weights connecting the neurons in each layer. These weights will be adjusted during training.

3. Forward pass (Excitation phase):

- Present an input pattern to the network.
- The input pattern propagates through the network layer by layer, activating neurons based on their input and activation functions.
- The neurons in each layer become "excited" based on their input and the current weights

4. Response phase:

- In the response phase, each neuron in the output layer compares its "excited" state to the needed output (label) associated with the input pattern.
- The network tries to find a balance between the excitations of the output neurons and the expected output.

5. Weight adjustment (Learning phase):

- Compare the output excitations with the expected outputs and calculate the discrepancies.
- Update the network weights locally within each layer based on these discrepancies.
- The biological learning process guides the weight updates, where the network tries to find a better association between input and output patterns.

6. Repeat steps 3 to 5 for multiple input-output pairs (training samples) until convergence:

- Iterate through the training dataset multiple times, adjusting the weights at each iteration.
- The network gradually recognizes and associates input patterns with corresponding labels.

7. Prediction (Testing phase):

- After training, the network can be used to predict the output (label) for new input patterns.
- Perform a forward pass through the network, and the output neuron with the highest excitation becomes the predicted label for the input.

4   System Design and Architecture

Figure 1 shows the architecture for the proposed approach. To evaluate the potential of the FFA for training neural networks, the following pipeline was followed:

A. Dataset Selection and Preprocessing
   1. Identifying and selecting appropriate datasets for evaluation, including the MNIST dataset, Cat vs Dog dataset, brain tumor dataset, and COVID-19 dataset.

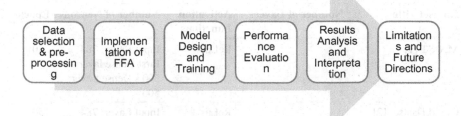

Fig. 1. System Design and Its Architecture

2. Preprocessing the datasets by normalizing the input data, handling missing values (if any), and partitioning the data into training set, validation set, and testing set.

B. Implementation of the FFA [18]
   1. Developing the necessary software infrastructure and libraries for implementing the FFA.
   2. Designing and implementing the FFA, including the forward pass with positive data, the forward pass with negative data, and the objective functions for each layer.
   3. Incorporating any additional modifications or adaptations to the algorithm based on prior research or specific requirements of the datasets (Table 2).

Table 2. Dataset description and preprocessing steps

Dataset	MNIST	Cat Vs Dog	Brain Tumor	Covid-19
Number of images	60,000	25,000	253	3082
Colour nature	B&W	Colour	B&W and Colour	B&W
Size	28 x 28	200 x 200	205 x 246	264 x 264
Techniques used for pre-processing	Only Train-Test Split	GreyScale conversion, Size reduction to 100 x 100, Train-Test Split	Grey scale conversion, Size reduction to 102.5 x 123, Train-Test Split	Size reduction to 132 x 132, Train-Test Split

C. Model Architecture and Training [6, 19, 20] consists of deciding the suitable NN architecture for an individual dataset along with the hyper-parameters. Then, the model training using FFA and monitoring the model convergence, accuracy and loss and overfitting/underfitting and finding appropriate solutions to manage them (Table 3).

Table 3. Model description

Dataset Title	Number of Layers	Activation Functions	Number of Neurons	Epochs
MNIST [1]	3	ReLu	Input Layer: 784 First Dense layer: 500 s Dense Layer: 500	250
Covid Dataset [2]	3	ReLu	Input Layer: 784 First Dense layer: 500 s Dense Layer: 500	150
Dogs and Cats [3]	3	ReLu	Input Layer: 784 First Dense layer: 500 s Dense Layer: 500	350
Brain tumour image dataset [4]	3	ReLu	Input Layer: 784 First Dense layer: 500 s Dense Layer: 500	150

D. Performance Evaluation [8, 21, 22] using standard evaluation parameters namely, F1 score, accuracy etc. is carried out. The comparison of the results obtained using FFA with the traditional methods (using backpropagation) is also carried out (Table 4).

Table 4. Accuracy for each dataset using back propagation

Dataset Title	Accuracy
MNIST [1]	97.6%
Covid Dataset [2]	45.23%
Dogs and Cats [3]	67.79%
Brain tumor image dataset [4]	62.29%

E. Results Analysis, visualization and interpretation to understand the implications of the results in terms of the algorithm's effectiveness, efficiency, and potential applications.

F. Identification of the limitations and challenges, such as dataset biases, computational constraints, or performance trade-offs along with the presentation of the potential future research.

By following the given pipeline of the project, evaluation and assessment of the FFA's performance for training the neural network across multiple datasets is done. The given pipeline provided a systematic approach to the study's implementation, training, evaluation, and analysis, enabling us to draw meaningful conclusions and identify future research directions.

5   Experimental Setup

The experiment was performed on a machine with intel i7 processor, 16 GB RAM, and NVIDIA GeForce RTX 4070 as graphics card with 512 SSD. Windows 11 was used as the OS, MS Visual Studio Code as the code editor, and Python 3.9 as the programming language. Numpy, Pandas, matplotlib, Keras and Scikit-Learn libraries were used. 80-%20% Train: test split was followed for the dataset(s) which were used in this study. While performing the training process, the performance of model was continuously monitored, and several evaluation metrics were used, such as loss convergence, accuracy improvements, and training issues like overfitting and underfitting. Accuracy improvements were also tracked to make sure that the model was learning and improving over time. Accuracy was used as the performance metric for this setup. Finally, the results on each dataset were compared with the performance of the FFA against conventional backpropagation methods. This comparison was crucial in determining the effectiveness of the model in comparison to other conventional methods.

6   Results and Discussion

After conducting the experiment mentioned above, we achieved the following results. After running 250 epochs, the graph converged for the MNIST dataset (Refer to Fig. 2). The FFA performed well on this dataset with an accuracy of 97.76%, giving hope for future experiments.

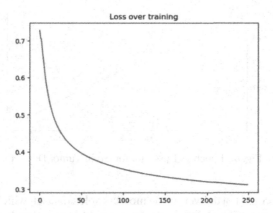

Fig. 2. Epoch vs Loss Plot for MNIST Dataset

For the CatVsDog Dataset, the model did not perform well. It started converging after ten epochs, and the slope was constant. Therefore, to achieve better results, the epochs were shut down after reaching 150, achieving an accuracy of 67.69% *Refer Fig. 3). The accuracy achieved on the Brain tumour dataset was 62.29% after running the model for 150 epochs. The graph did not converge, so just to validate whether higher accuracy will be achieved, the model is run for more than 300 epochs, but it decreased the accuracy, dropping from 62.29% to 58.59%. (Refer to Fig. 4).

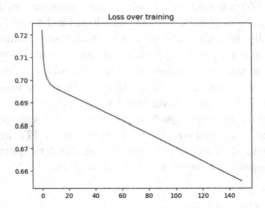

Fig. 3. Epoch vs Loss Plot for CatVsDog Dataset

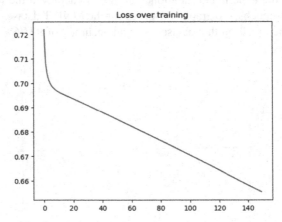

Fig. 4. Epoch vs Loss Plot for Brain Tumor Dataset

The algorithm could not deliver on the most complex dataset, which was the COVID-19 chest X-ray dataset; the graph for the loss started converging just after 80 epochs, and the final accuracy was achieved as 45.23% (Refer Fig. 5).

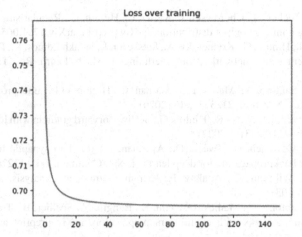

Fig. 5. Epoch vs Loss Plot for Covid-19 Dataset

7 Conclusion and Future Work

To sum up, our research thoroughly assessed the FFA proposed to train neural networks. Based on our experiments with three different datasets, we have demonstrated that the algorithm can achieve high levels of accuracy, with accuracy rates of 97.76% on the MNIST dataset, 67.69% on the Cat vs Dog dataset, 62.29% on the brain tumor dataset and 45.23% on the COVID-19 dataset. These results indicate that the algorithm has a significant potential that could be utilized in different applications and situations. Furthermore, our research has provided valuable insights into the differences between the FFA and conventional back propagation methods for training neural networks. In conclusion, this study highlights the potential of the FFA in enhancing the efficiency and accuracy of neural network training. Our research suggests that it is a promising approach that merits further exploration.

Although this study has demonstrated that FFA has significant potential in training neural networks, more work and exploration are necessary. Understanding the performance of the FFA-based NN for various datasets is essential. Using state-of-the art AI frameworks such as explainable AI and adversarial Machine learning in the context of FFA can also be studied.

References

1. Scellier, B., Bengio, Y.: Equilibrium propagation: bridging the gap between energy-based models and backpropagation. Front. Comput. Neurosci. **11**, 24 (2017)
2. Carandini, M., Heeger, D.J.: Normalisation as a canonical neural computation. Nat. Rev. Neurosci. **13**(1), 51–62 (2013)
3. Chen, T., Kornblith, S., Norouzi, M., Hinton, G.: A simple framework for contrastive learning of visual representations. In: Proceedings of the 37th International Conference on Machine Learning, pp. 1597–1607 (2020)
4. Chen, T., Kornblith, S., Swersky, K., Norouzi, M., Hinton, G.: Big self-supervised models are strong semi-supervised learners. arXiv preprint arXiv:2006.10029 (2020)

5. Pereyra, G., Tucker, G., Chorowski, J., Kaiser, Ł., Hinton, G.: Regularising neural networks by penalising confident output distributions. arXiv preprint arXiv:1701.06548 (2017)
6. Srivastava, N., Hinton, G., Krizhevsky, A., Sutskever, I., Salakhutdinov, R.: Dropout: a simple way to prevent neural networks from overfitting. J. Mach. Learn. Res. **15**(1), 1929–1958 (2014)
7. Lillicrap, T., Santoro, A., Marris, L., Akerman, C., Hinton, G.E.: Backpropagation and the brain. Nat. Rev. Neurosci. **21**, 335–346 (2020)
8. Ren, M., Kornblith, S., Liao, R., Hinton, G.: Scaling forward gradient with local losses. arXiv preprint arXiv:2210.03310 (2022)
9. Lillicrap, T., Cownden, D., Tweed, D., Akerman, C.: Random synaptic feedback weights support error backpropagation for deep learning. Nat. Commun. **7**(1), 13276 (2016)
10. Welling, M., Williams, C., Agakov, F.: Extreme components analysis. Adv. Neural Inf. Process. **16** (2003)
11. Kendall, J., Pantone, R., Manickavasagam, K., Bengio, Y., Scellier, B.: Training end-toend analog neural networks with equilibrium propagation. arXiv preprint arXiv:2006.01981 (2020)
12. Krizhevsky, A., Hinton, G.: Learning multiple layers of features from tiny images (2009)
13. Lillicrap, T., Cownden, D., Tweed, D., Akerman, C.: Synaptic feedback weights support error backpropagation for deep learning. Nat. Commun. **7** (2016)
14. Lillicrap, T.P., Santoro, A., Marris, L., Akerman, C.J., Hinton, G.: Backpropagation and the brain. Nat. Rev. Neurosci. **21**(6), 335–346 (2020)
15. Löwe, S., O'Connor, P., Veeling, B.: Putting an end to end-to-end: gradient-isolated learning of representations. Adv. Neural Inf. Process. **32** (2019)
16. Rao, R., Ballard, D.: Predictive coding in the visual cortex: a functional interpretation of some extra-classical receptive-field effects. Nat. Neurosci. **2**, 79–87 (1999)
17. Richards, B.A., Lillicrap, T.P.: Dendritic solutions to the credit assignment problem. Curr. Opin. Neurobiol. **54**, 28–36 (2019)
18. Rosenblatt, F.: The perceptron: a probabilistic model for information storage and organisation in the brain. Psychol. Rev. **65**(6), 386 (1958)
19. Scellier, B., Bengio, Y.: Equilibrium propagation: bridging the gap between energy-based models and backpropagation. Front. Comput. Neurosci. **11** (2017)
20. van den Oord, A., Li, Y., Vinyals, O.: Representation learning with contrastive predictive coding. arXiv preprint arXiv:1807.03748 (2018)
21. Goodfellow, I., et al.: Generative adversarial nets. Adv. Neural Inf. Process. 2672–2680 (2014)
22. Grathwohl, W., Wang, K.-C., Jacobsen, J.-H., Duvenaud, D., Norouzi, M., Swersky, K.: Your classifier is secretly an energy based model and you should treat it like one. arXiv preprint arXiv:1912.03263 (2019)
23. Grill, J.-B., et al.: Bootstrap your own latent: a new approach to self-supervised learning. arXiv preprint arXiv:2006.07733 (2020)
24. Guerguiev, J., Lillicrap, T.P., Richards, B.A.: Towards deep learning with segregated dendrites (2017)
25. Gutmann, M., Hyvärinen, A.: Noise-contrastive estimation: a new estimation principle for unnormalised statistical models. In: Proceedings of the Thirteenth International Conference on Artificial Intelligence and Statistics, pp. 297–304 (2010)
26. Hinton, G.E., Sejnowski, T.J.: Learning and relearning in Boltzmann machines. Parallel Distrib. Process.: Explor. Microstruct. Cogn. **1**(282–317), 2 (1986)

Texture Feature Extraction Using Local Optimal Oriented Pattern (LOOP)

Shital V. Sokashe-Ghorpade[1]([⊠]) [iD] and S. A. Pardeshi[2]

[1] Department of Technology, Shivaji University, Kolhapur, Maharashtra, India
`shital_sokashe@yahoo.co.in`
[2] Government Residence Women Polytechnic, Tasgaon, Maharashtra, India

Abstract. Various descriptors are preferred to extract the Local features of the image, including Local Binary Pattern, Local Directional Pattern, and Local Optimal Oriented Pattern. This paper provides the comparative analysis of LBP and Local Optimal Oriented Pattern (LOOP) descriptors for local feature extraction, further used for various applications. While tracking an object from a video, the provided input video sampled into the subsequent frames. For the removal of noise and enhance the frame's contrast, Median filter is applied on each of the frames. Local features of the image extracted using the Local Optimal Oriented Pattern (LOOP) from these filtered images. The results of LOOP descriptor compared with the Local Binary Pattern (LBP) in terms of histogram and execution time. Experimental analysis shows comparison with the specified feature extraction method in terms of the execution time and accuracy.

Keywords: Local Binary Pattern · Local Optimal Oriented Pattern · Texture feature extraction

1 Introduction

Object detection has become a most attractive research topic for researchers in recent years, closely related to video analysis and image feature extraction. Object occlusion, multiple objects with same color and degradation or changes in luminance, are some of the issues that generate more challenges in front of the object trackers. There is a need of an effective algorithm that extracts features from the image irrespective of illumination changes and object occlusion. For the extraction of the Global features we are considering the whole image. However, the local features are extracted from the local regions of the image [8]. An image's local features include color, spatial, shape, and texture features. The texture feature is widely used in various applications like facial feature extraction, image matching, pedestrian and vehicle tracking, biomedical analysis, etc. For extracting the texture features, Local Binary Pattern, Median Binary Pattern, Adaptive LBP, LBP variance, Local Directional Pattern, and many more methods which are the advances in LBP methods were used earlier.

Texture feature extraction is a crucial step in image analysis and computer vision applications. It involves the process of capturing essential information from images to

D. Garg et al. (Eds.): IACC 2023, CCIS 2053, pp. 407–416, 2024.
https://doi.org/10.1007/978-3-031-56700-1_32

characterize their texture patterns. One advanced technique for texture feature extraction is Local Optimal Oriented Pattern (LOOP). LOOP is a method that focuses on capturing the local orientation information of texture patterns in an image.

In the context of texture analysis, understanding the orientation patterns within an image is vital for various tasks such as object recognition, image segmentation, and texture classification. Traditional texture analysis methods often struggle to capture intricate details and local orientations effectively. This is where LOOP comes into play.

LOOP operates by computing the optimal orientations of local image patches and forming patterns based on these orientations. By considering the local optimal orientations, LOOP can represent texture patterns more accurately, especially in cases where textures exhibit complex and fine-grained structures. These patterns can then be used as feature vectors for further analysis and classification tasks.

In this discussion, we will explore the fundamentals of texture feature extraction using Local Optimal Oriented Pattern. We will delve into the methodology, its applications, and how it enhances the accuracy and reliability of texture analysis in various real-world scenarios. Understanding the intricacies of LOOP is essential for researchers, engineers, and practitioners working in the fields of computer vision, image processing, and pattern recognition, as it opens up new possibilities for improving the analysis of textured images.

Chakraborti et al. proposed the binary descriptor LOOP i.e. Local Optimal Oriented Pattern is most widely used for texture classification is an enhancement over the LBP and LDP and their variants [4]. This paper describes the Local Optimal Oriented Pattern method that overcomes the drawbacks of the Local Binary Pattern and the Local Directional Pattern. The proposed method's performance is tested through experiments, and the results are compared with LBP to find effectiveness.

The motivation behind the development of Local Optimal Oriented Pattern (LOOP) stems from the limitations of these traditional methods. Conventional techniques, such as statistical approaches and co-occurrence matrices, may fail to capture local variations and orientation information effectively. In real-world scenarios, textures can exhibit intricate directional patterns, subtle variations, and irregularities that are crucial for accurate analysis. Failing to capture these nuances can lead to misclassifications and inaccurate results in applications like medical image analysis, remote sensing, and industrial quality control.

LOOP addresses this gap by focusing on capturing local orientation information within texture patterns. The motivation behind LOOP lies in its ability to accurately represent texture patterns by identifying the optimal orientations at a local level. Unlike traditional methods that often overlook subtle directional cues, LOOP excels in capturing fine details, ensuring a more nuanced and precise characterization of textures.

Rest of the sections describes key fundamentals of Local Optimal Oriented Pattern, Methodology used to apply LOOP descriptors on the images, its Comparison with existing methods, Experimental Results in terms of histogram and execution time required to generate images after applying LOOP descriptor, Conclusion and References.

2 Fundamentals of Local Optimal Oriented Pattern (LOOP)

Local Optimal Oriented Pattern (LOOP) is an advanced texture feature extraction technique designed to capture intricate local orientation information within texture patterns [3]. Understanding the fundamental concepts of LOOP is crucial for its effective application in texture analysis. Here are the key fundamentals of LOOP:

2.1 Local Orientation Computation

LOOP operates by computing local orientations within small image patches. These orientations are essential for capturing the directional information present in textures. Techniques such as gradient analysis or Gabor filters are commonly employed to compute the orientations of image gradients within the localized regions. By analyzing gradients, LOOP identifies the dominant orientations, forming the basis for subsequent processing steps.

2.2 Optimal Orientation Selection

One of the distinctive features of LOOP is its focus on optimal orientations. Instead of considering all computed orientations, LOOP selects the orientations with the highest contrast or energy within the local neighborhood. These optimal orientations represent the most significant directional cues in the texture pattern.

2.3 Pattern Formation

Based on the optimal orientations, LOOP forms patterns that encode the local texture structure. Patterns are created by comparing the orientations of neighboring pixels or image features. The arrangement of these orientations is translated into unique codes or descriptors, forming characteristic patterns for each localized region. These patterns are designed to be robust against variations in lighting conditions, noise, and other imaging challenges, making them suitable for diverse real-world applications.

2.4 Pattern Encoding and Feature Extraction

The generated patterns are encoded into feature vectors, which serve as compact representations of the local texture information. Various encoding schemes, such as binary encoding or histograms, are employed to convert the patterns into numerical feature vectors. These feature vectors encapsulate the essential texture characteristics and can be used for tasks such as texture classification, object recognition, and image retrieval. The encoded features effectively capture the nuances of the texture patterns, enabling accurate analysis and classification.

2.5 Pattern Encoding and Feature Extraction

LOOP is highly adaptable and allows for the adjustment of parameters to suit specific application requirements. Parameters such as patch size, threshold values for optimal orientation selection and encoding methods can be fine-tuned. This adaptability ensures that LOOP can handle a wide range of textures and imaging conditions. By optimizing these parameters, practitioners can tailor LOOP to achieve optimal performance in different contexts.

In summary, the fundamentals of Local Optimal Oriented Pattern involve the computation of local orientations, selection of optimal orientations, formation of distinctive patterns based on these orientations, and encoding of patterns into feature vectors. This methodology, with its emphasis on local orientation details and adaptability, empowers LOOP to excel in capturing fine-texture patterns, making it a valuable tool for advanced texture analysis in the field of computer vision and image processing.

3 Methodology

Applying Local Optimal Oriented Pattern (LOOP) on images extracted from videos involves a series of steps to process the frames and extract texture features. Here's a methodology to apply LOOP on images extracted from video data:

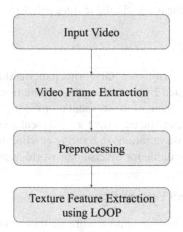

Fig. 1. Flow diagram of the proposed methodology.

The flow diagram of the proposed method is depicted in Fig. 1. When it comes to object tracking, having diverse and challenging video sequences is crucial for testing and evaluating tracking algorithms. MOT, VOT, TrackingNet, LaSOT, OBT, are some Video datasets suitable for object tracking tasks. Datasets must align with the specific challenges that tracking algorithm needs to address, such as occlusions, scale variations, fast motion, and illumination changes.

The foremost step is to collect the frames from the input videos available in the database. A video is a series of moving images, displayed in a sequential manner, typically accompanied by audio that creates the illusion of continuous motion. Videos are composed of scenes, shots, and frames. Scenes are made up of one or more shots and are often defined by changes in time, location, or characters. A shot is a continuous sequence of frames captured by a camera without interruption. It represents a single view or camera angle during a specific duration. A frame is a single still image in a sequence of frames that make up a video. These frames are displayed rapidly in succession to create the illusion of motion.

In Fig. 2, the mechanism of video-to-frame conversion is depicted. The input video is fed to the video frame extraction block, which divides the video into the number of frames.

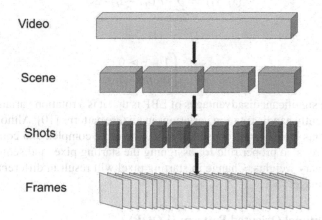

Fig. 2. Video-to-Frame Conversion.

The next step is preprocessing of each image. Preprocessing includes the contrast adjustment of the image and removal of noise. A median filter enables the removal of noise while preserving edges. Preprocessed image is further used for texture analysis. Texture analysis is carried out using Local Optimal Oriented Pattern, and the results are compared with Local Binary Pattern.

4 Comparison with Existing Method

4.1 Local Binary Pattern: (LBP)

Local Binary Pattern (LBP) is a popular texture descriptor used in computer vision and image analysis. It was first introduced by Ojala et al., initially designed for monochrome still images and further extended for color images.

LBP operates on grayscale images. For each pixel in the image, a binary code is generated by comparing the pixel's intensity value with the intensities of its neighboring pixels. The comparison is done using threshold value. If a neighboring pixel's intensity is greater than or equal to the central pixel's intensity, it is assigned a value of 1; otherwise, it is assigned a value of 0. After comparing the central pixel with its neighbors, a binary pattern is formed. This binary pattern is read in a clockwise or counterclockwise manner to create a binary number. LBP calculates a histogram of these binary patterns over a local neighborhood. The histogram represents the distribution of different texture patterns in the image region under consideration [2].

The intensity value at pixel (x_t, y_t) in an image I is denoted as i_t and i_m represents the intensity value of a pixel in the 3×3 neighborhood around the center pixel (x_t, y_t) where m = 0,1,2,....7 [11–13].

The Local Binary Pattern (LBP) value of the central pixel is calculated using Eq. (1) and (2):

$$(x_t, y_t) = \sum_{m=0}^{7} P(i_m - i_t) \cdot 2^m \tag{1}$$

where,

$$P(x) = \begin{cases} 1 & x \geq 0 \\ 0 & otherwise \end{cases} \tag{2}$$

One of the significant disadvantages of LBP is that it is a rotation variant. Basic LBP does not inherently handle rotation variations in texture patterns [10]. Although rotation-invariant variants have been proposed, they can be more complex and computationally intensive. There is no proper rule for assigning the starting pixel and sequence of their subsequent binary weights. Change in starting pixel will result in different LBP values for the same image.

4.2 Local Optimal Oriented Pattern: (LOOP)

Chakraborti et al. introduced a binary descriptor for local image feature representation, which builds upon and improves existing methods like Local Binary Pattern (LBP) and Local Directional Pattern (LDP) and their variations. Unlike LBP and LDP, where pixel binary weights are orientation-dependent for texture analysis, the proposed method, known as LOOP, eliminates this dependency, ensuring more robust and accurate results.

The intensity value of the central pixel in an image I denoted as i_t, is located at pixel (x_t, y_t). Additionally, i_m represents the intensity of a pixel within the 3×3 neighborhood centered around pixel (x_t, y_t) where m ranges from 0,1,2,....7 [11].

Eight Kirsch masks are oriented to capture intensity variations in all directions among neighboring pixels represented by intensity values i_m, These masks provide a measure of intensity variation strength in specific pixel directions. The output from a Kirsch mask indicates the likelihood of an edge occurring in the corresponding direction.

The eight responses of the Kirsch masks, denoted as k_m and corresponding to pixel intensity i_m where m ranges from 0 to 7, are utilized. Each pixel is assigned an exponential weight, represented as w_m based on the magnitude rank of k_m among all Kirsch mask outputs. The LOOP value is computed using the following equation [11].

$$LOOP(x_t, y_t) = \sum_{m=0}^{7} P(i_m - i_t) \cdot 2^{km} \tag{3}$$

Figure 3 shows the eight Kirsch masks in different directions. Each of the neighboring pixel intensities i_m oriented in the direction of the response of eight Kirsch masks is then compared with it as shown in Eq. (3), which returns either 1 or 0 according to Eq. (2). This process forms an eight-digit binary number. As per the rank of the magnitude of km among the outputs of eight Kirsch masks, weights are assigned to each calculated binary number [4].

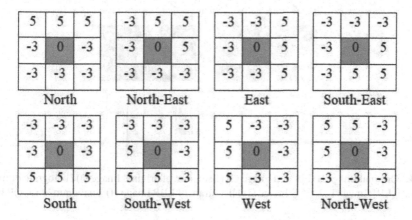

Fig. 3. Kirsch Mask in eight directions.

5 Experimental Results

Initially, the video was segmented into individual frames, and noise reduction was performed using a median filter applied to each frame. Subsequently, LBP was applied to the filtered images. The results obtained from LBP were then compared with those from the LOOP descriptor based on histogram analysis. The findings from both LBP and LOOP methods are presented and summarized in Fig. 4.

Figure 4A shows the original image of the road traffic. Figure 4B shows the image after applying median filter. Both the images seems same but the histograms of respective images shown in Fig. 4C and Fig. 4D depicts the difference between these images. Figure 4E gives the image after applying LBP descriptor and Fig. 4F gives the image after applying the LOOP descriptor. Figure 4G and Fig. 4H images are the histograms of LBP and LOOP images. Results indicate that LOOP results are rotational invariant.

Histograms of LBP and LOOP images are compared with four different measures Correlation, Chi-square, Intersection and Bhattacharyya. The results are summarized in the Table 1. Correlation measures the statistical relationship between two variables. It indicates whether and how strongly pairs of variables are related. The chi-square test is a statistical test used to determine if there is a significant association between two categorical variables in a dataset. It compares the expected frequencies of different categories in the dataset with the observed frequencies and calculates a chi-square statistic. Intersection generally refers to the common elements or data points that exist in two

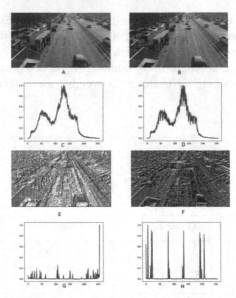

Fig. 4. Original Image B) Filtered Image C) Histogram of original Image D) Histogram of filtered Image E) LBP Image F) LOOP Image G) Histogram of LBP Image H) Histogram of LOOP Image

or more sets. Bhattacharyya distance is a measure of the similarity between two probability distributions. In the context of histogram matching, Bhattacharyya distance is used to compare the similarity between two histograms. Minimizing this distance helps in aligning or matching histograms for various image processing and computer vision applications. For Correlation and Intersection measures, higher the metric, more accurate the match and for Chi-square and Bhattacharyya measures, less the results, better the match [9]. The results are as expected. Correlation and Intersection measures provide the less metric while Chi-square and Bhattacharyya measures provide the higher match indicating in LOOP images more intensity values.

Table 1. Histogram Measure

Measures	LBP-LOOP metric
Correlation	0.057816895050799955
Chi-square	968.5633221575758
Intersection	0.952789188026145
Bhattacharyya	0.8138262136750081

The execution time required for performing LOOP on a single image, 5 images and 10 images, respectively, using LBP and LOOP methods is summarized in Table 2. This execution time in seconds is calculated using Python Programming.

Table 2. Execution Time

Number of Images	Local Descriptors	
	Execution time for LBP (s)	Execution time for LOOP (s)
1	0:00:44.578116	0:00:00.421872
5	0:03:55.448098	0:00:02.281228
10	0:07:23.873640	0:00:04.468751

The result shows that the execution time of the LOOP is much less than the LBP method.

Histogram measures and execution time is calculated using PyCharm Community Edition 2020.2.1 x64.

6 Conclusion

In conclusion, the comparative study of Local Binary Pattern (LBP) and Local Optimal Oriented Pattern (LOOP) revealed valuable insights into their respective strengths and limitations in various applications, particularly in the context of object detection in road traffic videos.

LBP, a well-established texture descriptor, demonstrated its robustness and effectiveness in capturing local patterns in images. Its simplicity and computational efficiency make it suitable for real-time applications. However, LBP's performance is influenced by noise and lacks spatial information, which might impact its accuracy in certain scenarios.

On the other hand, LOOP, an enhancement over LBP, showcased superior performance, especially in situations where noise and variations in illumination posed challenges. Its ability to capture orientation-independent patterns and consider the strength of intensity variations through Kirsch masks contributed to more accurate and reliable results. LOOP's consideration of local patterns in a broader context, coupled with its computational efficiency, made it a promising choice for object detection tasks, especially in complex environments like road traffic.

Ultimately, the choice between LBP and LOOP depends on the specific requirements of the application. While LBP offers simplicity and efficiency, LOOP provides enhanced accuracy and robustness, making it a preferred option in situations where intricate pattern recognition and noise tolerance, are crucial. The findings of this comparative study underline the importance of selecting the most suitable texture descriptor based on the specific challenges and goals of the given task in computer vision applications.

References

1. NarainPonraj, D., Christy, E., Aneesha, G., Susmitha, G., Sharu, M.: Analysis of LBP and LOOP based textural feature extraction for the classification of CT lung images. In: 2018 4th International Conference on Devices, Circuits and Systems (ICDCS), pp. 309–312. IEEE (2018)

2. Ke-Chen, S., Yun-Hui, Y.A.N., Wen-Hui, C.H.E.N., Zhang, X.: Research and perspective on local binary pattern. Acta Automatica Sinica **39**(6), 730–744 (2013)
3. Aminu, A.A., Agwu, N.N.: General purpose image tempering detection using convolutional neural network and local optimal oriented pattern. Signal Image Process.: Int. J. **12**(2), 13–32 (2021)
4. Chakraborti, T., McCane, B., Mills, S., Pal, U.: LOOP descriptor: local optimal-oriented pattern. IEEE Signal Process. Lett. **25**(5), 635–639 (2018)
5. Hadid, A.: The local binary pattern approach and its applications to face analysis. In: First Workshops on Image Processing Theory, Tools and Applications (IPTA) - Sousse, Tunisia. IEEE (2008)
6. Karis, M.S.: Local binary pattern (LBP) with application to variant object detection: a survey and method. In: IEEE 12th International Colloquium on Signal Processing & Its Applications. Melaka, Malaysia, pp. 221–226 (2016)
7. Ayami, Y.M., Shabat, A.: An acceleration scheme to the local directional pattern (2018). arXiv preprint arXiv:1810.11518
8. Jabid, T., Kabir, M.H., Chae, O.: Local directional pattern (LDP) for face recognition. In: 2010 Digest of Technical Papers International Conference on Consumer Electronics (ICCE), pp. 329–330. IEEE (2010)
9. Marin-Reyes, P.A., Lorenzo-Navarro, J., Castrillón-Santana, M.: Comparative study of histogram distance measures for re-identification (2016). arXiv preprint arXiv:1611.08134
10. Subramanian, P., Ramesh, G.P.: Diagnosis of keratoconus with corneal features obtained through LBP, LDP, LOOP and CSO. Trends Sci. **18**(20), 22 (2021)
11. Hassaballah, M., Alshazly, H.A., Ali, A.A.: Robust local oriented patterns for ear recognition. Multimed. Tools Appl. **79**, 31183–31204 (2020). https://doi.org/10.1007/s11042-020-09456-7
12. Mame, A.B., Tapamo, J.R.: Parameter optimization of histogram-based local descriptors for facial expression recognition. PeerJ Comput. Sci. **9**, e1388 (2023)
13. Pietikäinen, M., Hadid, A., Zhao, G., Ahonen, T.: Local binary patterns for still images. In: Computer Vision Using Local Binary Patterns. Computational Imaging and Vision, vol. 40, pp. 13–47. Springer, London (2011). https://doi.org/10.1007/978-0-85729-748-8_2

Feature Fusion and Early Prediction of Mental Health Using Hybrid Squeeze-MobileNet

Vanita G. Kshirsagar[1,2] (ID), Sunil Yadav[1](✉) (ID), and Nikhil Karande[3](✉) (ID)

[1] Amity University, Jaipur, Rajasthan, India
skumar@jpr.amity.edu
[2] Dr. D. Y. Patil Institute of Technology, Pimpri, Pune, India
[3] SISA Information Security Pvt. Ltd., Bangalore, India
nikhilkarande18@gmail.com

Abstract. Mental health is the main factor which is affected by stress, disease and sarcastic statements or people comments. It effects on persons health directly or indirectly. People cannot share or discuss about their mental condition, even they can't talk about it. Firstly, they cannot accept that they are suffering mental illness. It is very necessary to predict the mental health of a Pearson in early stage. There is the need to use new strategies for diagnosis and daily monitoring of the mental health conditions. The goal of our research is to develop a module based on feature fusion, which will be performed based on Soergel metric and Deep Kronecker Network (DKN) and early prediction of mental health utilizing Squeeze-MobileNet. It improves accuracy without sacrificing the model efficiency. Particle swarm cuckoo search (PS-CS) is effective and capable to capture the unpredictability of data. We got F1 score and validation score of NN is good as compare to ML.

Keywords: Mental Health · Depression · Deep Learning · Feature Fusion · Deep Kronecker Network (DKN) SqueezeNet · MobileNet · Particle swarm cuckoo search PS-CS

1 Introduction

Mental health is affected by the social, emotional, and psychological condition of a person. It has an impact on the person's action, reaction, and how he feels. These are the parameters of mental health. Mental health is calculated by the stress level and the decision-making level in every phase of life. It is a very important part of every phase of life, whether it is childhood or adulthood. It is the only disease that people can't discuss publicly. It is not having proper awareness in society. People cannot discuss it with their friends or family. Even though they can't accept that they are suffering from mental problems, People around that person can identify the change in behavior. Due to a lack of awareness about mental health or late treatment, people are having problems. Some of the common reasons are: 1) death of a loved one 2) Bad life experiences [3, 5, 18, 24] 3) Genes 4) Hereditary problems from parents or family [9] 5) Ragging or

© The Author(s), under exclusive license to Springer Nature Switzerland AG 2024
D. Garg et al. (Eds.): IACC 2023, CCIS 2053, pp. 417–426, 2024.
https://doi.org/10.1007/978-3-031-56700-1_33

bullying [3, 5, 18, 24]. Around 20% of the world population is facing mental health problems [11]. Due to a mental health problem, a person faces physical and emotional health issues. It may affect the human brain with various disorders like bipolar disorder, depression, schizophrenia, and attention-deficit hyperactivity. The people who are having serious metal issues are very sick or at higher risk [7]. The system or machine that will detect human mental conditions is the most important health concern in the world. As per the report of the World Health Organization (WHO), depression is a universal mental disorder that affects most people, irrespective of their age. While doing the research, there are many boundaries to recognizing depression and treatment for it. Due to the unavailability or lack of experts in this domain, social embarrassing and wrong or late diagnosis [12]. The mental health check is done by taking the Patient Health Questionnaire (PHQ-9) test or by asking subjective questions. This type of evaluation takes more time to diagnose. It is a very time-consuming and difficult task [5, 16–19]. It is very necessary to detect mental health issues at an early stage to understand the problems. This is the only disease that doesn't require any laboratory or medical tests. It only requires the questionnaire and the response from the patient to that specific questionnaire.

To identify the human actions of performance and how that person interacts with people [7]. People who are depressed can manage their symptoms and avoid more health problems by analyzing and taking treatment after identifying such signs of depression at the first stage [2]. Researchers did their research by taking people's tweets and their responses to detect human mental conditions at a prior stage [8]. To cure depression in the prior stage, it has a higher rate, but it still needs to cure. To overcome this problem, it is necessary to predict and prepare for the risk of depression. Therefore, we need to prepare a model that will collect people's daily routines, like their diet, stress, family relations, and work status, and analyze the correlation between depression and the factors based on the collected information [1]. In the health sector, deep learning has achieved success. To detect mental health, the available and collected data and the evaluation of mental health are rare. To work on psychological problems such as diagnosing, detecting, and monitoring human health, use the combined model of CNN and LSTM [20]. The LSTM technique is better than the recurrent neural network (RNN). It is very useful for the classification of time series signals [5]. The DL can handle various issues, like natural language processing tasks and the current sentiment analysis. The DL model works on mental health problems using a dataset available on social media [14, 15]. Due to new technology and the changes in society, researchers carry a huge burden. They require a relationship between traditional and new technologies. The result of this is that traditional health care systems are not efficient and effective enough to handle new trends [3]. Hence, DL techniques are good for predicting mental health between two individuals—those who require help online and are not aware of their condition [10]. A wearable device is used to detect issues in mental health, with a view to progressing research in this field [4].

The LR classifier training data gives a good result in NN, but the test data gives a good result in ML. The XGBoost classifier, Decision Tree classifier, and RF classifier and Support vectore classifier SVC give the same results for the F1 score and validation score for test and train data using ML and NN.

2 Literature Survey

The literature review based on early prediction of mental health by reviewing several existing modules is discussed in this section.

Baek, J.W., and Chung, K. [1] developed the Context Deep Neural Network (Context-DNN) method, which is used to predict the risks of depression. For prediction, a multiple regression model is used. To identify depression correctly, we need to evaluate the person. To prevent depression, we need to monitor correctly. There is a problem that they work on common issues only, not individual issues.

Jawad, K., et al. [2] suggested the particle swarm-cuckoo search (PS-CS) optimization method. The developer combines these two algorithms to get more accurate results. Deep learning models depend more on training and validation loss, which is a very difficult part of DL. This method verified a well-adjusted part of short training and validation loss. The problem is that we are unable to incorporate multimodal data sources.

Zeberga, K., et al. [3] the inventor uses deep learning methods such as the Bidirectional Long Short-Term Memory (Bi-LSTM) algorithm and response-based knowledge transfer using BERT. This method is used to improve the intelligent health care system by detecting human mental health problems. The author focuses on converting unstructured data collected from social sites into meaningful data. This module has high accuracy. But the problem is that the text in the given file was not represented by a bag of words.

Coutts, L.V., et al. [4] Developers find that most of the health factors basically depend on heart rate changeability. Every health factor needs to use the identifier to train the deep neural network, which is LSTMs. Each health measure's heart rate variable (HRV) data is unique. This developer takes three data measures: time, frequency, and HRV. The wearable device continuously taps the above measures and predicts mental health. The problem is that no optimization has been done for this combined approach.

Shafiei, S.B., et al. [5] using the Keras dataset, the developer implemented a convolutional neural network and long short-term memory (CNN-LSTM). This module was capable of being integrated into applications for household mental health monitoring to be used by patients after oncological operations to recognize patients in danger. The drawback of this model is that it is not validated for objective and distant monitoring of mental health.

Zhang, Z., et al. [6] to identify the inconsistency and hardness of audio-visual-textual modes. The developer divides these modes into two groups. The first group is all audio-visual modes, which work on frame level. Second textual mode, which is managed at the session level, This approach was effective for multimodal representation knowledge and the ability to generalize transversely dissimilar mental disorders. It did not investigate the semantic border between all audio-visual-textual modalities to address the discrepancy and granularity and compare it with the early fusion strategy in the current framework.

Hassantabar, S., et al. [7] proposed a new model named Mental Health Deep Neural Networks (MHDeep-DNN). This model can take data from sensors that are present in wearable devices. Give the results based on three psychological conditions, such as mood type, most depressing, and mania. The MHDeep strategy was employed for pervasive diagnosis and daily monitoring. The problem is that it achieved high computational complexity.

Kour, H., and Gupta, M.K. [8] The CNN-BiLSTM combined hybrid model is used to achieve less sensitivity. CNN is for images, and LSTM works for text. This developer works on both image and text data. This scheme achieves less sensitivity. This approach did not sense other psychological illnesses in combination with depression to capture complex mental issues permeating an individual's life.

3 Proposed Methodology

Many people around the world are facing problems with mental health. There is a challenge to diagnosing the mental health problem. It is a difficult problem that relies on questionnaires, self-reporting, behavior, and social interaction. There is a necessity for new strategies for the diagnosis of mental health and the daily monitoring of mental health conditions. The primary goal of this study is to plan and build a module based on feature fusion and early prediction of mental health using Squeeze-Mobilenet. Squeeze-Mobilenet will be merged by the amalgamation of SqueezeNet [22] and Mobilenet [23]. Initially, the input data acquired from the database [21] will be subjected to outlier detection to detect the outlier in the database usually used in data analysis, which will be performed by employing holo entropy. After that, outlier removal will be performed to ensure the quality of the data. Thereafter, a pre-processing phase will be conducted to remove the clatter present in the data by utilizing missing data imputation [25] and z score normalization [24]. Then, the pre-processed image will be forwarded to feature fusion, which will be performed based on the Soergel metric and the Deep Kronecker Network (DKN) [26]. Moreover, the fused feature will allow for data augmentation, which will be done by bootstrapping. Finally, the early prediction of mental health will be accomplished by utilizing Squeeze-Mobilenet, where the layers will be modified. Moreover, the implementation of the proposed strategy will be carried out using a Python tool using simulation. In addition, performance metrics will be utilized for early prediction of mental health, namely accuracy, sensitivity, and specificity. Furthermore, the proposed model will be compared with the current procedures in order to reveal the effectiveness of the proposed method.

4 System Architecture

See (Fig. 1).

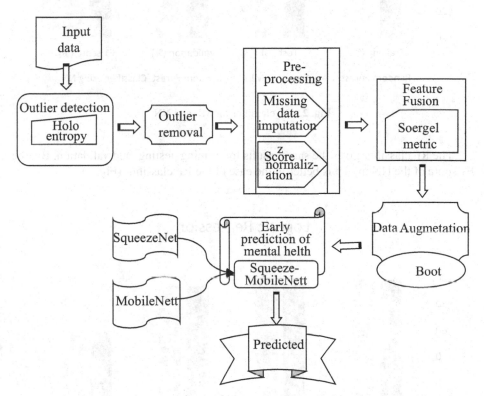

Fig. 1. Block diagram of feature fusion and early prediction of mental health

5 Results

Comparison of machine learning and neural networks for different classifiers The result is stored in the form of training data, test data, validation data, and test data (Fig. 2).

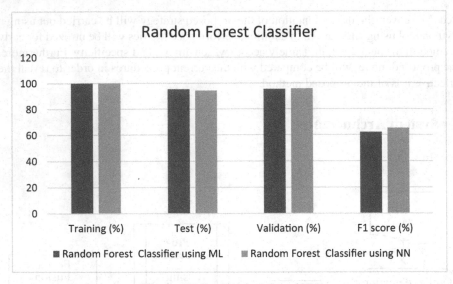

Fig. 2. RF classifier for ML and NN

The RF classifier gives the same results for training, testing, and validation. But the F1 score of the NN model is better in the case of the RF classifier (Fig. 3).

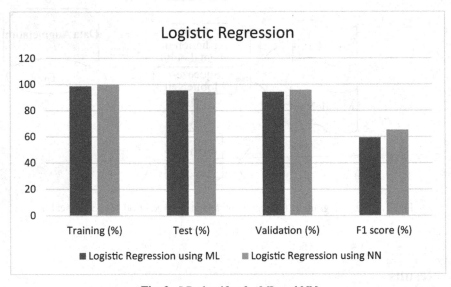

Fig. 3. LR classifier for ML and NN

The LR classifier training data gives a good result in NN, but the test data gives a good result in ML. The validation score and F1 score of NN are good as compared to ML (Fig. 4).

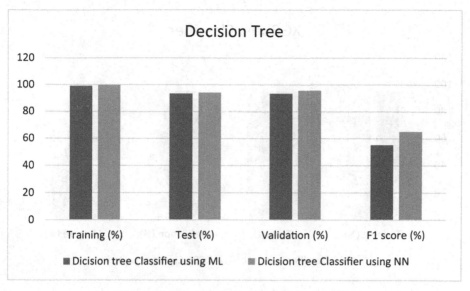

Fig. 4. Decision Tree classifier for ML and NN

The decision tree classifier training, test validation, and F1 score of NN are good as compared to ML (Fig. 5).

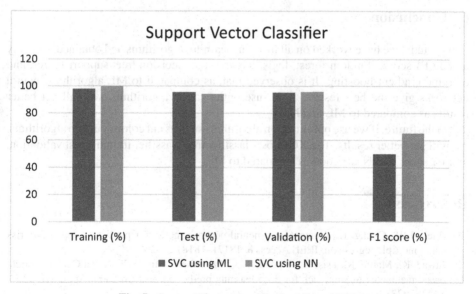

Fig. 5. Support Vector classifier for ML and NN

The SVC classifier training, test validation, and F1 score of NN are good as compared to ML (Fig. 6).

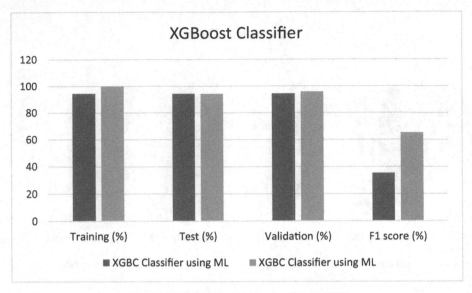

Fig. 6. XGBOOST classifier for ML and NN

The XGBoost classifier Tree classifier training, test validation, and the F1 score of NN are good as compared to ML.

6 Conclusion

In this study, we have worked on all machine learning algorithms and obtained accuracy and an F1 score. Random forest, logistic regression, decision tree, support vector, and extreme gradient boosting. It is observed that, as compared to ML algorithms, neural networks give the best results. If we use optimization algorithms, we will get better results as compared to ML and NN.

In the future, if we use optimization algorithms such as ant colony cuckoo algorithms, we will get better results. The XGBoost classifier tree classifier training, test validation, and F1 score of NN are good as compared to ML.

References

1. Baek, J.W., Chung, K.: Context deep neural network model for predicting depression risk using multiple regression. IEEE Access **8**, 18171–18181 (2020)
2. Jawad, K., Mahto, R., Das, A., Ahmed, S.U., Aziz, R.M., Kumar, P.: Novel Cuckoo search-based metaheuristic approach for deep learning prediction of depression. Appl. Sci. **13**(9), 5322 (2023)
3. Zeberga, K., Attique, M., Shah, B., Ali, F., Jembre, Y.Z., Chung, T.S.: A novel text mining approach for mental health prediction using Bi-LSTM and BERT model. Comput. Intell. Neurosci. (2022)

4. Coutts, L.V., Plans, D., Brown, A.W., Collomosse, J.: Deep learning with wearable based heart rate variability for prediction of mental and general health. J. Biomed. Inform. **112**, 103610 (2020)
5. Shafiei, S.B., Lone, Z., Elsayed, A.S., Hussein, A.A., Guru, K.A.: Identifying mental health status using deep neural network trained by visual metrics. Transl. Psychiatry **10**(1), 430 (2020)
6. Zhang, Z., Lin, W., Liu, M., Mahmoud, M.: Multimodal deep learning framework for mental disorder recognition. In: Proceedings of 2020 15th IEEE International Conference on Automatic Face and Gesture Recognition (FG 2020), pp. 344–350 (2020)
7. Hassantabar, S., Zhang, J., Yin, H., Jha, N.K.: Mhdeep: mental health disorder detection system based on wearable sensors and artificial neural networks. ACM Trans. Embed. Comput. Syst. **21**(6), 1–22 (2022)
8. Kour, H., Gupta, M.K.: An hybrid deep learning approach for depression prediction from user tweets using feature-rich CNN and bi-directional LSTM. Multimed. Tools Appl. **81**(17), 23649–23685 (2022)
9. Sairam, U., Voruganti, S.: Mental health prediction using deep learning. Int. J. Res. Appl. Sci. Eng. Technol. **10** (2022)
10. Ameer, I., Arif, M., Sidorov, G., Gòmez-Adorno, H., Gelbukh, A.: Mental illness classification on social media texts using deep learning and transfer learning. arXiv preprint arXiv:2207. 01012 (2022)
11. Steel, Z., et al.: The global prevalence of common mental disorders: a systematic review and meta-analysis 1980–2013. Int. J. Epidemiol. **43**(2), 476–493 (2014)
12. Shrestha, K.: Machine learning for depression diagnosis using twitter data. Int. J. Comput. Eng. Res. Trends **5**(2) (2018)
13. Tadesse, M.M., Lin, H., Xu, B., Yang, L.: Detection of suicide ideation in social media forums using deep learning. Algorithms **13**(1), 7 (2019)
14. Devlin, J., Chang, M.W., Lee, K., Toutanova, K.: BERT: pre-training of deep bidirectional transformers for language understanding. arXiv preprint arXiv:1810.04805 (2018)
15. Kowsari, K., Jafari Meimandi, K., Heidarysafa, M., Mendu, S., Barnes, L., Brown, D.: Text classification algorithms: a survey. Information **10**(4), 150 (2019)
16. Hann, D., Winter, K., Jacobsen, P.: Measurement of depressive symptoms in cancer patients: evaluation of the Center for Epidemiological Studies Depression Scale (CES-D). J. Psychosom. Res. **46**(5), 437–443 (1999)
17. Manne, S., Schnoll, R.: Measuring cancer patients' psychological distress and well-being: a factor analytic assessment of the Mental Health Inventory. Psychol. Assess. **13**(1), 99 (2001)
18. Cassileth, B.R., Lusk, E.J., Strouse, T.B., Miller, D.S., Brown, L.L., Cross, P.A.: A psychological analysis of cancer patients and their next-of-kin. Cancer **55**(1), 72–76 (1985)
19. Mystakidou, K., Tsilika, E., Parpa, E., Galanos, A., Vlahos, L.: Brief cognitive assessment of cancer patients: evaluation of the mini-mental state examination (MMSE) psychometric properties. Psycho-Oncol. J. Psychol. Soc. Behav. Dimensions Cancer **16**(4), 352–357 (2007)
20. Oh, S.L., Ng, E.Y., San Tan, R., Acharya, U.R.: Automated diagnosis of arrhythmia using combination of CNN and LSTM techniques with variable length heart beats. Comput. Biol. Med. **102**, 278–287 (2018)
21. Mental health in tech survey. https://www.kaggle.com/datasets/osmi/mental-health-in-tech-survey. Accessed Sept 2023
22. Iandola, F.N., Han, S., Moskewicz, M.W., Ashraf, K., Dally, W.J., Keutzer, K.: SqueezeNet: AlexNet-level accuracy with 50x fewer parameters and <0.5 MB model size. arXiv preprint arXiv:1602.07360 (2016)
23. Chen, H.Y., Su, C.Y.: An enhanced hybrid MobileNet. In: Proceedings of 2018 9th International Conference on Awareness Science and Technology (iCAST), pp. 308–312 (2018)

24. Fei, N., Gao, Y., Lu, Z., Xiang, T.: Z-score normalization, hubness, and few-shot learning. In: Proceedings of the IEEE/CVF International Conference on Computer Vision, pp. 142–151 (2021)
25. Khan, S.I., Hoque, A.S.M.L.: SICE: an improved missing data imputation technique. J. Big Data **7**(1), 1–21 (2020)
26. Feng, L., Yang, G.: Deep Kronecker network. arXiv preprint arXiv:2210.13327 (2022)

Exploring the Usability of Quantum Machine Learning for EEG Signal Classification

Devansh Singh[1], Yashasvi Kanathey[1], Yoginii Waykole[1],
Rohit Kumar Mishra[2], Rahee Walambe[1,3]([✉]), Khan Hassan Aqeel[4],
and Ketan Kotecha[1,3]

[1] Symbiosis Institute of Technology, Symbiosis International University, Pune, India
devansh.singh.btech2021@sipune.edu.in, rahee.walambe@sitpune.edu.in,
director@sitpune.edu.in
[2] Centre for Development of Advanced Computing, Delhi, India
rohitm@cdac.in
[3] Symbiosis Centre for Applied, AI (SCAAI), SIU, Pune, India
[4] Department of Applied Artificial Intelligence and Robotics, Aston University,
Birmingham, UK
h.khan54@aston.ac.uk

Abstract. The classification of Electroencephalogram (EEG) signals into distinct frequency bands is a critical task in understanding brain function and diagnosing neurological disorders. The information obtained from frequency-specific classification has multiple applications, such as frequency-based wheelchair control, frequency-based 36-stroke brain operated keyboard for paralysed patients etc. In this work, a method based on machine learning to develop the frequency-based classification of EEG signals is proposed. The performance of Classical Machine Learning (CML) algorithms and Quantum Machine Learning (QML) techniques for the classification of EEG signals across four frequency bands are investigated. The primary objective is to evaluate the performance of QML models against traditional CML models in terms of computational efficiency, time efficiency and accuracy and uncover potential benefits offered by quantum computing for a particular task of classifying EEG signals. The goal is to assess the advantages of using quantum algorithms for classifying EEG signals. This includes improving accuracy and enhancing efficiency. These findings add to the existing knowledge about how quantum machine learning can benefit neuroscience in terms of enhancing methods that rely on EEG data.

Keywords: Electroencephalogram (EEG) · Quantum Machine Learning · Classical Machine Learning · Support Vector Machine · Random Forest Classifier · Quantum Support Vector Machine (QSVM) · Parameterized Quantum Circuit · Brain-Computer Interface (BCI)

© The Author(s), under exclusive license to Springer Nature Switzerland AG 2024
D. Garg et al. (Eds.): IACC 2023, CCIS 2053, pp. 427–438, 2024.
https://doi.org/10.1007/978-3-031-56700-1_34

1   Introduction

BCIs (Brain-Computer Inte¬rfaces) is an upcoming technology that stands to form a relationship between the human brain and computers [4]. One of the primary applications of BCIs is in assistive technology for people with disabilities or neurodegenerative diseases. BCIs provide a way to set up a direct communication channel between the brain and external devices [3] and can identify a user's intended commands or actions based on the brain activity patterns. Machine learning methods are primarily employed for BCI implementation [2]. However, the brain signals are nonlinear and highly unstructured in nature. Hence conventional ML algorithms may prove insufficient and computationally demanding [8]. Due to high computational costs, the porting of these techniques on edge devices also proves challenging. To that end, in this work, we propose to explore the use of Quantum Machine Learning for the classification of the BCI-generated EEG signals [5–7].

Both traditional ML and QML techniques for classification tasks are tested. Their performance is compared based on usability, and efficacy. The findings will guide¬ the development of QML-based BCIs to ensure re¬liable and efficient intention detection. Moreover, cross-disciplinary efforts will aid in creating BCIs that empower those with disabilities and open doors in cognitive¬ neuroscience and healthcare.

By merging principles derived from quantum physics and machine learning, the aim is to enhance the detection of intentions. Proposed are comparative assessments between QML and conventional machine learning algorithms in BCI applications. The objective is to assess the performance, computational efficiency, and practicality of QML in intention detection. The objective is to provide guidance for the future advancement of efficient and dependable QML-based BCIs. This progress will greatly benefit individuals with disabilities and drive advancements in multiple industries.

The paper is organized into five sections. Section 2 offers a concise summary of the dataset and the data preprocessing stage. In Sect. 3, the proposed framework and ML and QML methods employed in this work are discussed. Section 4 focuses on experimental results and discussion followed by Sect. 5 which concludes the paper.

2   The Data Set

2.1   Description

For this study, a secondary dataset named "A Dataset of EEG signals from a single-channel SSVEP-based Brain-Computer Interface" [20] available in the open domain was employed. This dataset consists of EEG readings from a portable BCI with Steady State Visual Evoked Potentials (SSVEP) technology. Experiments using repeating visual stimuli with four distinct flashing frequencies were used to get the data. The use of a single-channel dry-sensor collecting apparatus is the primary source of uniqueness for the proposed data set.

The Olimex EEG-SMT, a two-channel differential input 10-bit analog-to-digital converter (ADC) with a sampling frequency of 256 Hz, was used to collect data using a BCI headset. For the investigation, one of the two channels was employed.

Eleven volunteers were equipped with the data acquisition headset and asked to focus on the visual stimuli for 16 s each.

The subjects were positioned 70 cm from a 15.6-inch display with a resolution of 1024×768 pixels and a refresh rate of 60 Hz while seated in a chair. Four alternating black-and-white squares with relative frequencies of 8.57 Hz, 10 Hz, 12 Hz, and 15 Hz made up the visual stimuli shown on the monitor. According to the 10–20 system, the electrodes were placed on the midline sagittal plane in the Frontal Parietal area (Fpz) and the Occipital area (Oz).

	0	1	2	3	4	5	6	7	8	9	...
F1	410	513	511	492	472	451	487	498	499	488	...
F2	316	297	297	273	285	321	325	330	304	294	...
F3	749	739	738	733	710	752	767	758	737	695	...
F4	520	509	491	558	555	527	520	494	545	554	...

Fig. 1. First 9 EEG values for all 4 frequencies of visual stimuli.

mean	variance	skewness	kurtosis	psd	HHT_Component_1	frequency
425.906361	4637.904896	-0.009724	-0.826606	6410.837739	0.003950	0
371.164618	3345.082478	-0.015768	-0.815921	4649.264771	0.008611	1
317.140065	2280.162821	-0.023830	-0.801778	3193.285384	0.009391	2
264.527703	1444.901598	-0.034830	-0.782854	2045.632589	0.008352	3

Fig. 2. Extracted Features

The non-invasive neuroimaging method electroencephalography (EEG) [19] captures the electrical activity of the brain and offers important insights into cerebral function. Electrodes are affixed to the scalp during an EEG in order to identify and enhance electrical signals produced by brain neurons. Brainwaves, which are manifestations of these impulses at varying frequencies, are correlated

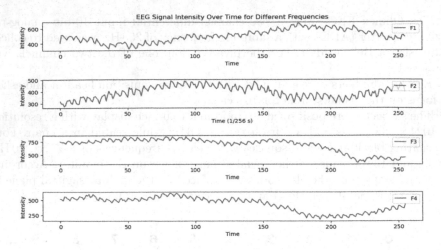

Fig. 3. Signal Visualisation

with various cognitive and physiological processes. The study of cognitive processes, event-related potentials (ERPs), neurofeedback, and the diagnosis and
monitoring of neurological illnesses are just a few of the many clinical and scientific settings where EEG is used [20]. Figure 1 are the actual EEG readings taken
256 times per second. Figure 2 depicts the extracted features from each segment
of 256 values in the whole dataset. Figure 3 visualizes the EEG signal values,
showcasing the characteristic electrical patterns recorded during cognitive tasks.

2.2   Data Preprocessing

In the data preprocessing stage of this intention detection pipeline, the focus was
on enhancing the quality and reliability of EEG signals. To achieve this, band-
pass filtering [12] was applied to eliminate unwanted noise and artefacts while
preserving the frequency components relevant to the intended brain activity.

Depending on the properties of the EEG signals, the band-pass filtering procedure required choosing the right parameters, such as the lower and upper
cutoff frequencies. It was essential to select the right filter design to obtain the
intended frequency response and reduce artefacts or distortions. Due to its consistent performance and smooth frequency response, the Butterworth filter was
used in our implementation [12].

The filter parameters are carefully adjusted to reduce any signals that fall
outside the desired range. These parameters consist of a cutoff frequency of
0.1 Hz, an upper cutoff frequency of 30 Hz, a sampling frequency of 1000 Hz and
a pad length of 27. This meticulous adjustment yields a set of EEG signals that
is perfect, for extracting features and conducting further analysis.

2.3 Feature Extraction

In signal processing the main goal of feature extraction is to identify patterns, from input signals [10,11]. This helps in analyzing signals in an efficient manner. These techniques assist in simplifying the data removing repetitive information and downplaying characteristics.

There are ways to represent EEG signals. For this study's purpose four key features Mean, variance, skewness and kurtosis Were extracted and evaluated.

Time Domain
The time-domain feature extraction method is based on the analysis of signals or data in respect to time [11]. Quantifying a signal's evolution over time is made feasible by this method, which is essential when working with EEG data because these recordings usually consist for several hours at a time. This section will look at a number of time-domain techniques particular to EEG.

1) Mean: The average electrical activity recorded from the brain establishes a baseline for EEG data [10]. Studying the central tendency of these signals provides insight into typical brain function during focus, relaxation, or cognitive¬ tasks. By calculating the mean, researchers ascertain normal brain waves over time, analyzing fluctuations across different mental states.
2) Variance: The variability (variance) of EEG data provides insight into the spread of electrical brain activity. Higher variance indicates more fluctuation in activity, while lower variance¬ suggests more stability. Assessing variance¬ helps detect shifts in brain patterns, including unusual variability associated with neurological conditions. Specifically, variance¬ measures the deviation of EEG signals from their average value¬. This statistic comprehensively depicts the distribution and diversity of electrical rhythms across the brain. In neurological assessments, variance offers a vital perspective for gauging stability versus volatility in recordings.
3) Skewness and Kurtosis: Skewness and Kurtosis shows if the brain's electrical activity differs from symmetry. Measuring skewness reveals abnormalities. Kurtosis describes the structure of the¬ brain's electrical activity. It finds tiny details and odd e-vents in the signals. Analyzing kurtosis helps classify brain signals. It also aids in diagnosing brain illnesses

2.4 Frequency-Domain Feature Extraction

To understand the aspects of a signal it's important to grasp the concept of the domain. Examining this domain provides information, about how energy's distributed across different frequencies in the signal. One significant piece of information recorded by domain characteristics is the power distribution within the signal. For instance, analyzing EEG data through power density (PSD) analysis can offer insights into both power distribution and frequency composition of captured brain signals [17]. The main objective of this work is to analyze EEG data using the Welch method [19] which predicts PSD. The use of Welch technique brings advantages such as its ability to handle stationary signals, resistance, against noise and reduced spectral leakage.

2.5   Time-Frequency Domain Feature Extraction

Instead of relying on analysis techniques that only consider the frequency content of a signal time frequency domain analysis examines how the frequency components change, over time providing a deeper understanding. Firstly, we utilized Independent Component Analysis (ICA) to prepare the EEG data. Subsequently, the EEG data was analyzed using the Hilbert Huang Transform (HHT). In order to distinguish between these underlying sources and locate independent components that correlate to various brain activities, we use ICA. After ICA, HHT was used to further analyze the retrieved independent components.

2.6   Feature Normalization

Feature normalization's [16] is used to modify the features of a dataset to a uniform scale, thus guaranteeing that all features have an equal impact on the learning process while preventing any specific feature from overpowering the model due to its larger size. In this study, features(x) were standardized (X) using mean (μ) and standard deviation (σ) as shown in Eq. 1:

$$X = \frac{x - \mu}{\sigma} \tag{1}$$

3   Proposed Framework

3.1   Support Vector Machine

In [1], an integration of quantum computing principles with SVM for BCI is proposed. For SVM implementation, the features were extracted using the scaled and preprocessed data. The 80/20 split for train:test data is used. For identifying the best hyperparameters for the SVM model, Grid-Search was used. SVM classifier is trained and validated through 5-fold cross- validation to get the optimal set of hyperparameters obtained through the grid search. Our experiments' outcomes showed that C = 100, gamma = "scale", and kernel = "linear" was the best parameter combination for the SVM classifier in sklearn library. It was discovered that these parameter values worked well for assisting our SVM classifier in achieving high accuracy and generalization capacity (Fig. 4).

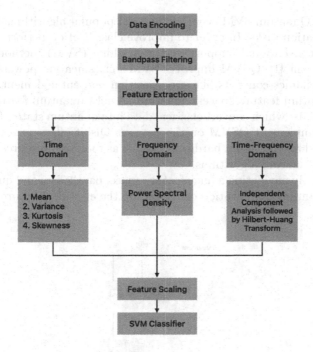

Fig. 4. Model pipeline for SVM Model

3.2   Random Forest

For random forest implementation, the standard techniques of data preprocessing, train:test split and grid search were employed as in the case of SVM
described in Sect. 4. The grid search helped in finding optimal values for the
primary hyperparameters such as the number of estimators (n estimators), the
maximum depth of the trees (max depth), and the least number of samples
required to split an internal node (min samples split) etc. The Random Forest
classifier was trained using these parameters. The F1-score and accuracy were
computed. The random Forest classifier yielded better results.

3.3   QSVM

The QML algorithms are highly effective in handling noisy, high-dimensional
data, resulting in more accurate feature extraction and classification. Quantum-
based feature extraction techniques may identify small correlations and patterns
in brain signals that are complex to identify. Due to the high computational
power offered by quantum computers, quantum machine learning may prove
more effective in handling complex EEG data. Quantum support vector machines
(QSVM) [1] and other quantum algorithms have been developed to explore these
goals and to understand if they offer more advantages as compared to traditional
ML for processing the EEG data for BCI tasks.

QSVM or Quantum SVM is one of the most popular algorithms used for handling classification tasks. In order to improve classification performance, QSVM extends the conventional support vector machine (SVM) method to a quantum environment [1]. QSVM improves SVM's classification powers by utilizing quantum mechanics concepts like superposition and entanglement. It does this by using quantum feature spaces, quantum kernels, quantum feature maps and quantum circuits, which convert classical data into quantum states. Qiskit library was used to implement QSVM on the dataset. Qiskit offers access to quantum simulators and real quantum hardware, as well as tools and resources for creating and running quantum algorithms.

By effectively navigating a huge feature space, parallelism and quantum interference in quantum computation can speed up the classification process (Fig. 5).

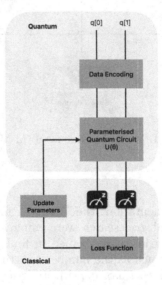

Fig. 5. Outline of a typical QML process

3.4   Trainable Parameterised Quantum Circuits

In neural networks, the model has weights as parameters. These weights can be trained to provide accurate output. Similarly [21], we can design parameterised quantum circuits (PQCs) [9] which have trainable parameters. The only difference is that PQCs work with qubits by having fixed rotation and entanglement gates which change the state of qubits. Broadly, Quantum Machine Learning requires us to perform three steps - data encoding, processing through a parameterised circuit and parameter updating after evaluation.

Data encoding is used to represent data as quantum states of qubits. Angle encoding is a simple type of data encoding technique wherein classical data is encoded as angular rotations of the qubit state. Another technique is using a feature map like the ZZFeatureMap as provided in qiskit. A quantum feature map $\Phi\colon \chi \to \mathcal{F}$ is a feature map where the vector space $\mathcal{F}$ is a Hilbert space and the feature vectors are quantum states. The map transforms $\chi \to |\Phi(\chi)\rangle$ by way of a unitary transformation $U_\Phi(\chi)$, which is typically a variational circuit whose parameters depend on the input data. While there are several others to experiment with, we have used both these techniques in different implementations.

The next step requires us to create a Parameterised Quantum Circuit (PQC) which will contain trainable parameters. In general, the number of qubits we have used is 2 or 3 depending on the implementation and number of features. Since there is no one prescribed way to define a PQC, we experiment with several combinations of rotation and CNOT gates. In the qiskit implementation we use TwoLocal which facilitates the creation of custom PQCs. The TwoLocal circuit having x and y rotation gates, cnot gates and 12 parameters in the 2 repetitions is visualized in Fig. 6.

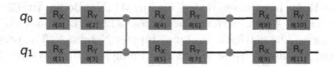

Fig. 6. Variational Circuit used in custom qiskit model

The final part requires us to measure the states of the qubits onto a classical bit. We then need to define a loss function and update parameters accordingly. In our qiskit implementation we define the cost function as the average of the cross-entropy loss of all predictions. The formula for cross entropy is given by:

$$CrossEntropy = -\sum_{i=1}^{n} y_i \log(p_i) \qquad (2)$$

where:

y_i : true probability of class i

p_i : predicted probability of class i

n : number of classes

The custom qiskit model uses Simultaneous Perturbation Stochastic Approximation (SPSA) optimizer to optimise the parameters using the cost function. The multi-class PennyLane models uses Square Loss to compute loss and Nesterov Momentum Optimizer for optimisation while the PennyLane binary classifier uses average Multiclass SVM Loss in association with Adam optimiser. Multi-class SVM Loss is inspired by (Linear) SVMs, which uses a scoring function 'f' to map our data points to numerical scores for each class label. The formula for multiclass SVM loss is given by:

$$MulticlassSVMLoss = \frac{1}{N} \sum_{i=1}^{N} \sum_{j \neq y_i} \max(0, s_j - s_{y_i} + \Delta) \qquad (3)$$

y_i : true probability of class i

p_i : predicted probability of class i

n : number of classes

Suppose we have three classes (A, B, C) and the respective predicted scores by a model (A: 3.2, B: 2.2, C: 1.2). The true class is A. We calculate the margins: margin_A = 1.0 (margin between A and B), margin_C = 2.7 (margin between A and C). Apply loss function: $L(A) = \max(0, 1.4 - 2.7 + 1) = 0$. We calculate loss for B and C similarly and sum all losses to get the final Multi-class SVM loss.

The algorithms have been tested on an M1 MacBook Air (2020) with 8 GB of RAM having 4 high-performance cores (3228 MHz) and 4 high-efficiency (2064 MHz) cores. The platform used was Jupyter Notebook. The programs have been built and simulated using Qiskit and Pennylane in a Python 3.9.13 environment.

4   Results and Analysis

In our research, in order to compare the performance of classical and quantum machine learning approaches, we utilized different feature sets. These feature sets consisted of two options: one with four features (mean, variance, skewness, kurtosis) and another with six features(mean, variance, skewness, kurtosis, power spectral density, ICA). We proceeded to train and test various quantum machine learning models, including QSVM, using the identical dataset.

Our findings demonstrated that classical machine learning algorithms consistently outperformed their quantum counterparts in terms of accuracy. Specifically, the Random Forest algorithm displayed higher efficiency in distinguishing between different cognitive states, resulting in superior classification outcomes when compared to the quantum models.

Additionally, classical machine learning algorithms exhibited an advantage in terms of training and testing time. Quantum machine learning techniques often necessitate intricate quantum computations, which can be both computationally expensive and time-consuming. On the other hand, classical algorithms like Random Forest offered faster training and testing times while still maintaining excellent classification performance (Tables 1 and 2).

Table 1. Performance Metrics for Machine Learning Models

Model Type	Classification Type	Class Labels	No. of Features	Accuracy	F1 Score	Training Time (per sample)	Testing Time
SVM Classifier	Multiclass	F1, F2, F3, F4	4	0.6536	0.6083	0.0173	0.0016
SVM Classifier	Multiclass	F1, F2, F3, F4	6	0.6241	0.6265	1.5930	0.0020
Random Forest Classifier	Multiclass	F1, F2, F3, F4	4	0.6950	0.7304	0.4131	0.0177
Random Forest Classifier	Multiclass	F1, F2, F3, F4	6	0.6950	0.7304	0.4131	0.0177

Table 2. Performance Metrics for Various Quantum ML Models

Model Type	Classification Type	Class Labels	No. of Features	Accuracy	F1 Score	Training Time (per sample)	Testing Time
Qiskit QSVC	Multiclass	F1, F2, F3, F4	6	60.28	0.603	2.66	5
Custom Model (PennyLane)	Multiclass	F1, F2, F3, F4	4	25	0.19	0.007	0.03
Custom Model (PennyLane)	Multiclass	F1, F2, F3, F4	6	31.91	0.21	0.177	0.06
Custom Model (PennyLane)	Binary	F1, F2	2	48.8	0.22	0.022	0.007
Custom Model (Qiskit)	Binary	F1, F2	6	55	0.44	0.45	0.008

5   Conclusion and Future Work

The results show that relatively less-researched Quantum Machine Learning methods produce comparable results to Classical Machine Learning models. Although QML techniques did not surpass the classification accuracies or efficiencies of classical ML, the research reflects that QML is a promising field that may lead to improvements as compared to traditional ML methods. Further research into developing more advanced and well-suited algorithms might harvest the benefits of quantum computing to a greater extent.

Acknowledgement. This work was part of the project titled "Industry-inspired Transnational Education in Artificial Intelligence / Machine Learning" (Project ID 877629610) under the British Council-funded Going Global Partnerships Programme (Top-up Grant).

References

1. Li, Y., Zhou, R.G., Xu, R., Luo, J., Jiang, S.X.: A quantum mechanics-based framework for EEG signal feature extraction and classification. IEEE Trans. Emerg. Top. Comput. **10**(1), 211–222 (2020)
2. Lotte, F., et al.: A review of classification algorithms for EEG-based brain-computer interfaces: a 10 year update. J. Neural Eng. **15**(3), 031005 (2018)

3. Xie, Y., Oniga, S.: A review of processing methods and classification algorithm for EEG signal. Carpath. J. Electron. Comput. Eng. **13**(1), 23–29 (2020)
4. Nicolas-Alonso, L.F., Gomez-Gil, J.: Brain computer interfaces, a review. Sensors **12**(2), 1211–1279 (2012)
5. Zhang, Y., Ni, Q.: Recent advances in quantum machine learning. Quantum Eng. **2**(1), e34 (2020)
6. Rakotomamonjy, A., Guigue, V.: BCI competition III: dataset II-ensemble of SVMs for BCI P300 speller. IEEE Trans. Biomed. Eng. **55**(3), 1147–1154 (2008)
7. Lal, T.N., et al.: Support vector channel selection in BCI. IEEE Trans. Biomed. Eng. **51**(6), 1003–1010 (2004)
8. Barnova, K., et al.: Implementation of artificial intelligence and machine learning-based methods in brain-computer interaction. Comput. Biol. Med. 107135 (2023)
9. Benedetti, M., Lloyd, E., Sack, S., Fiorentini, M.: Parameterized quantum circuits as machine learning models. Quantum Sci. Technol. **4**(4), 043001 (2019)
10. Panat, A., Patil, A., Deshmukh, G.: Feature extraction of EEG signals in different emotional states. In: IRAJ Conference (2014)
11. Singh, A.K., Krishnan, S.: Trends in EEG signal feature extraction applications. Front. Artif. Intell. **5**, 1072801 (2023)
12. Hussin, S.F., Birasamy, G., Hamid, Z.: Design of Butterworth band-pass filter. Politeknik Kolej Komuniti J. Eng. Technol. **1**(1) (2016)
13. Adcock, J., et al.: Advances in quantum machine learning. arXiv preprint arXiv:1512.02900 (2015)
14. Abohashima, Z., Elhosen, M., Houssein, E.H., Mohamed, W.M.: Classification with quantum machine learning: a survey. arXiv preprint arXiv:2006.12270 (2020)
15. Khan, T.M., Robles-Kelly, A.: Machine learning: quantum vs classical. IEEE Access **8**, 219275–219294 (2020)
16. Amin, H.U., Mumtaz, W., Subhani, A.R., Saad, M.N.M., Malik, A.S.: Classification of EEG signals based on pattern recognition approach. Front. Comput. Neurosci. **11**, 103 (2017)
17. Alam, M.N., Ibrahimy, M.I., Motakabber, S.M.A.: Feature extraction of EEG signal by power spectral density for motor imagery based BCI. In: 2021 8th International Conference on Computer and Communication Engineering (ICCCE), pp. 234–237). IEEE (2021)
18. Bergholm, V., et al.: PennyLane: automatic differentiation of hybrid quantum-classical computations (2018). arXiv:1811.04968
19. Khosla, A., Khandnor, P., Chand, T.: A comparative analysis of signal processing and classification methods for different applications based on EEG signals. Biocybern. Biomed. Eng. **40**(2), 649–690 (2020)
20. Yi, Y., Billor, N., Liang, M., Cao, X., Ekstrom, A., Zheng, J.: Classification of EEG signals: an interpretable approach using functional data analysis. J. Neurosci. Methods **376**, 109609 (2022)
21. Rudolph, M.S., Miller, J., Motlagh, D., Chen, J., Acharya, A., Perdomo-Ortiz, A.: Synergy between quantum circuits and tensor networks: short-cutting the race to practical quantum advantage. arXiv preprint arXiv:2208.13673 (2022)

Adaptive Coronavirus Mask Protection Algorithm Enabled Deep Learning for Brain Tumor Detection and Classification

Kalyani Ashok Bedekar[1,2](✉) [ID] and Anupama Sanjay Awati[1] [ID]

[1] KLS Gogte Institute of Technology, Affiliated to VTU, Belagavi, India
asawati@git.edu
[2] SIT College of Engg, Yadrav, India
kalyanibedekar@sitcoe.org.in

Abstract. Brain tumor (BT) is a dangerous disease and the process of detecting BT is difficult. Early detection of this disease plays a critical role in protecting the life of humans. Hence, this paper introduced an Adaptive Coronavirus Mask Protection Algorithm (ACMPA)-enabled deep learning technique for detecting and categorizing BT. First, the Magnetic Resonance Image (MRI) brain images are pre-processed using Kalman filtering. After that, BT is segmented by utilizing LadderNet, and the features are extracted which include mean, tumor size, entropy, kurtosis, variance, Haralick texture features, namely Angular second moment (ASM), contrast and Spider Local Image Feature (SLIF). Following this, BT is detected by the Deep Kronecker Network (DKN), where BT is categorized into normal or abnormal. If the detection is abnormal, then BT is categorized into Meningiomas, Gliomas, and pituitary tumors using DKN, which is tuned by the ACMPA. The ACMPA is obtained by integrating the Adaptive concept and Coronavirus Mask Protection Algorithm (CMPA). Furthermore, the proposed ACMPA_DKN acquired the value of accuracy to 90.4%, and obtained the value of TPR and TNR to 91.6% and 92.5%.

Keywords: Brain tumor · Coronavirus Mask Protection Algorithm · Adaptive concept · Deep Kronecker Network · Deep Learning

1 Introduction

In the human body, the brain is the significant and intricately structured organ. The presence of a skull around the brain makes it challenging to study the brain's behavior, and also makes disease detection complicated [1]. Tumors that are produced from brain cells or that cover the brain are called primary BTs. The initial cancer cells spreading to the brain from another part of the body results in secondary [2]. A high-quality brain image acquired by MRI is commonly used for analyzing tumors [1]. MRI is a popular medical tool that is employed to detect and examine various diseases, like epilepsy, neurological conditions, BT, and so on. Generally, a computer-aided method assists in modernizing the process for acquiring correct and quick results [3, 4]. Unlike,

D. Garg et al. (Eds.): IACC 2023, CCIS 2053, pp. 439–451, 2024.
https://doi.org/10.1007/978-3-031-56700-1_35

Computerized Tomography (CT), the parameters of MRI images can be changed to provide high-contrast images with several gray levels for many types of neuropathology [5, 6].

BT segmentation is mandatory and usually managed by factors, like, low contrast, noise and missing boundaries. BT detection is difficult because of the composite formation of the brain. At present, Deep Learning (DL) plays an important role in the medical field for detecting many types of diseases. DL techniques are also known as hierarchical learning, Deep structured network learning, and Deep Neural Network (DNN) [7, 8]. Moreover, one of the DL algorithms is the Convolutional Neural Network (CNN) [9]. Furthermore, a fine-tuned approach regarding Transfer learning in terms of the Visual Geometry Group (VGG16) model is utilized for categorizing abnormal or normal images of the brain [10]. In order to detect and segment medical images, the LeU-Net method is developed and it is motivated by the techniques of U-Net and LeNet. Here, LeNet is more rapid and has a small dataset which offers better accuracy with a suitable activation function whereas U-Net includes an up-sampling layer which is employed to enhance the resolutions of the output layer [9].

BT is a collection of abnormal cells in the brain and these cells develop and cause BT. The shape of BT is irregular which makes detecting tumors at an early stage difficult. Moreover, the existing techniques consume more time and are affected by overfitting. Hence, this work introduces an effective approach of ACMPA_DKN for identifying and categorizing BT. The goal of this work is to enhance BT classification by the newly introduced ACMPA_DKN approach.

The contribution of the research is:

- *ACMPA_DKN for BT classification:* If the detection is found as abnormal, then BT is classified into pituitary, Meningiomas, and Gliomas tumors. The categorization is done by employing DKN which is trained by ACMPA. The obtained ACMPA method is created by combining the Adaptive concept and CMPA.

The remaining section in the paper is illustrated below: The existing methods and their challenges are explained in Sect. 2, the introduced ACMPA_DKN for classifying BT is detailed in Sect. 3, the results of the research are explained in Sect. 4 and Sect. 5 shows the conclusion.

2   Literature Review

Khairandish, M.O., et al. [1] devised a Hybrid Support Vector Machine (SVM) and CNN and method for categorizing Malignant and Benign tumors. The features in this technique were extracted with high speed and effectiveness due to the model's distinctive aspects. However, it failed to consider the dimension and accurate position of tumor. The LeU-Net technique was presented by Rai, H.M. and Chatterjee, K., [9] for identifying BT from MRI images. This LeU-Net model acquired low complexity and performed well with excellent simulation time. However, this method was only used with a small database and failed to produce a better performance in a large amount of training data.

Sharif, M.I., et al. [11] presented a You Only Look Once v2-inceprion v3 (YOLOv2-inceptionv3) approach for classifying BT. This method perfectly identified the regions affected by tumors and attained competitive results. However, it was unsuccessful in incorporating quantum computation algorithms to investigate BT more effectively. The Deep Wavelet Autoencoder Model (DWAE) was formulated by Abd El Kader, I., *et al.* [3] to categorize input images into normal or abnormal. This model had outstanding capability for evaluating huge data from MRI without any technical issues. Nevertheless, the DWAE method suffered from low speed.

The challenges in this work are explained below,

- In [1], the hybrid SVM and CNN approach was introduced for BT classification. It attained a high rate however, it was challenging to take better decisions and in faster CNN with SVM to articulate superior improvement.
- In [9], the LeU-Net model delivered desirable accuracy on uncropped and cropped images which provided quick processing time. Nevertheless, it was challenging to implement a huge MRI image database for detecting and segmenting the BTs.
- In [3], the DWAE technique demonstrated highly accurate outcomes with a minimal loss. However, it was futile to improve the hidden layer parameters to enhance the performance.
- Though numerous methods have been created for classifying BT, the low contrast and similarities make BT classification a complex task. In addition to this, the growth of the tumor and its orientation adds to the complexity.

3   Proposed ACMPA_DKN for Brain Tumor Classification

BT is generated by the expansion of irregular tissues or cells in the brain. It is a hazardous disease because of the sudden expansion of tissues in the skull. In order to detect BT, the ACMPA_DKN model is developed to detect and classify BT. At first, an MRI brain image is considered as input to the pre-processing phase, and Kalman filtering [10] is employed to eliminate the noise from the image. After that, BT segmentation is carried out by LadderNet [12] for isolating the tumor region from the image. Then, features, like mean, tumor size, kurtosis, variance, entropy, and Haralick texture features [13] namely contrast, and ASM and SLIF [14] are mined. Following this, BT is detected by employing DKN [15, 16], and it is categorized as normal or abnormal. Later, if the detection is found as abnormal, then BT is categorized as pituitary tumor, Meningioma, or Glioma. Here, BT is classified by employing DKN and the structural optimization is obtained by the proposed ACMPA. The proposed ACMPA is acquired by integrating the Adaptive concept and CMPA [17]. Figure 1 illustrates the schematic view of the ACMPA_DKN for BT classification.

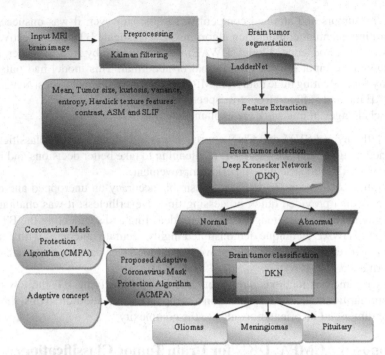

Fig. 1. Schematic view of proposed ACMPA_DKN for BT classification

3.1 Image Acquisition

An image attained from datasets [18, 19] is used to classify BT and the dataset is indicated in Eq. (1).

$$X = \{X_1, X_2, ..., X_r, ..., X_v\} \tag{1}$$

where, X specifies databases, the total quantity of images is denoted as v and X_r signifies v^{th} data which is employed for the following process.

3.2 Pre-processing Using Kalman Filter

For pre-processing the input is considered as X_r and the Kalman filter [10] is employed to eliminate the noise present in the image. These filters are largely exploited as the variant of Bayes filters. The approximate beliefs are found based on the unimodal Gaussian representation and it is formulated in Eq. (2).

$$G(u_g) \approx \aleph(u_g; \eta_g, \sum_g) = \frac{1}{(2\pi)^{j/2} \left|\sum_g\right|^{1/2}} \exp\left[-\frac{1}{2}(u_g - \eta_g)^D \sum_g^{-1}(u_g - \eta_g)\right] \tag{2}$$

where, mean of the distribution is signified as η_g, the covariance matrix is represented as $\sum_g$, the dimension of state is designated as j, probability of u_g with mean η_g and covariance $\sum_g$ is indicated as $\aleph(u_g; \eta_g, \sum_g)$. Here, the output obtained in the pre-processed image is mentioned as ϑ.

3.3 Brain Tumor Segmentation with Laddernet

The segmentation of BT is carried out to detect the position and expansion of tumor regions, namely edema tissue, necrotic tissue, and timorous tissues. For segmenting BT, LadderNet [12] is employed and output (ϑ) from the pre-processed image is taken as the input. It consists of many layers, such as Convolutional 2-Dimension, Batch normalization, activation, and transpose. Here the Conv layer generates a feature map and the transpose layer converts the features into a higher spatial dimension. The output acquired from LadderNet is portrayed as λ.

3.4 Feature Extraction

The features are mined to decrease the amount of redundant data from the MRI image and here the outcome from LadderNet is used as the input (λ). The feature extraction is executed by altering the MRI image into a set of features. The features to be extracted include SLIF, statistical, and the Haralick features.

SLIF Feature. SLIF [14] distributes an equal set of features by mining the data from the nearest pixels. It comprises bright shifts, scaling, and rotation. Furthermore, the SLIF feature is specified as N_1.

Statistical Features. The statistical features [20] are employed to obtain a feature vector.

Mean: It is enumerated as the average of the quantity of image pixels and it is articulated in Eq. (3).

$$N_2 = \sum_{p=0}^{F-1} p * K(p) \tag{3}$$

Here, p represents the image grey level, the overall quantity of grey levels is denoted as F, $K(p)$ specifies the probability of p and N_2 mentions mean.

Variance: Variance is termed as the variations of grey levels in an image related to the mean grey level which is demonstrated in Eq. (4).

$$N_3 = \sum_{p=0}^{F-1} (p - N_2)^2 * K(p) \tag{4}$$

where, variance is indicated as N_3.

Kurtosis: It is expressed as the quantity of distribution level with regards to the normal distribution and it is formulated in Eq. (5).

$$N_4 = N_2^{-4} \left[\sum_{p=0}^{F-1} (p - N_2)^4 * K(p) \right] \tag{5}$$

Here, kurtosis is represented as N_4.

Haralick Features. In this newly introduced ACMPA_DKN method, two haralick features [13], such as contrast and ASM are explained below.

Contrast: The amount or gray level dissimilarities among reference pixel and the neighbouring pixel is termed as contrast, which is given in Eq. (6).

$$N_5 = \sum_z \sum_v (z - v)^2 L_I(z, v) \tag{6}$$

Here, N_5 is mentioned as contrast, $L_I(z, v)$ denotes $(z, v)^{th}$ element of the segmented image.

ASM: It is utilized to compute the local uniformity of gray levels. If the similarity between pixels exists, then ASM will have a large value. This is given in Eq. (7).

$$N_6 = \sum_z \sum_v L_I^2(z, v) \tag{7}$$

where, N_6 is specified as ASM.

The final feature vector is determined using Eq. (8).

$$N = \{N_1, N_2, ..., N_6\} \tag{8}$$

Furthermore, the obtained feature vector N is used for BT detection.

3.5 Brain Tumor Detection Using DKN

Here, DKN [15, 16] is employed to identify the brain tumor by taking the feature vector N as input. DKN is produced on a structure of Kronecker product which completely requires a piece-wise even assets on coefficients.

The matrix signified images $J_e \in R_e^{c \times x}$ and scalar response d_e are taken into consideration with q samples, where $e = 1, 2, ..., q$. The response d_e is expressed in Eq. (9).

$$d_e|J_e \sim H(d_e|J_e) = \alpha(d_e) \exp\{d_e \langle J_e, E \rangle - \tau(\langle J_e, E \rangle)\} \tag{9}$$

Here, the target of the unknown coefficients matrix is denoted as $E \in R_e^{c \times x}$, and the definite known univariate functions are represented as $\alpha(\cdot)$ and $\tau(\cdot)$. Furthermore, the definite known link function $s(\cdot)$ is articulated in Eq. (10).

$$s(M(d_e)) = \langle J_e, E \rangle \tag{10}$$

The coefficient of E with the Kronecker product decomposition with $V(\geq 2)$ factor is demonstrated in Eq. (11).

$$E = \sum_{h=1}^T W_m^h \otimes W_{m-1}^h \otimes ... \otimes W_1^h \tag{11}$$

where, unknown matrix are mentioned as $W_m^h \in R_e^{em \times x_m}$, $m = 1, ..., V$, $h = 1, ..., T$ and the dimensions of W_m^h are not specified. The Kronecker product is required to satisfy $c = \prod_{m=1}^{V} c_m$ and $x = \prod_{m=1}^{V} x_m$ and it is represented in Eqs. (12) and (13).

$$W_{m'} \otimes W_{m'-1} \otimes \cdots W_{m''} = \overset{m''}{\underset{m=m'}{\otimes}} W_m \tag{12}$$

$$\sum_{h=1}^{T} \otimes_{m=V}^{1} W_m^h \tag{13}$$

For every matrix $W_{m'}, ..., W_{m''}$ with $m' \geq m''$. Hence the decomposition of E is articulated by the above expression (13). The output acquired in brain tumor detecting by DKN is specified as K_t.

3.6 Brain Tumor Classification

Here, input for classifying BT is taken from the output of BT detection K_t. Furthermore, ACMPA is employed to train DKN, and it is formed by integrating the Adaptive concept and CMPA.

Brain Tumor Classification Using DKN. In this sector, the BT is categorized by employing DKN [15] using the input K_t from BT detection. Furthermore, a detailed explanation of DKN is mentioned in the above Sect. 3.6. Here, DKN classifies brain tumors, and the output obtained in classifying the brain tumor by DKN is designated as Z_n.

Training of DKN Using ACMPA. By integrating the Adaptive concept and CMPA, the overall performance is improved by classifying BT. The algorithmic measures of the ACMPA approach are explained as follows

Initialization: In this initial step, the population is initialized randomly and it is demonstrated in Eq. (14).

$$H = \{H_1, H_2, ..., H_w, ..., H_l\} \tag{14}$$

where, H_w represents the wth solution and l mentions the size of the population.

Fitness measure: The fitness is exploited to measure the finest value based on Mean Square Error (MSE). Here, the solution providing low MSE is specified as the best solution and it is represented in Eq. (15).

$$MSE = \frac{1}{P} \sum_{n=1}^{P} \left(Z_n^* - Z_n \right)^2 \tag{15}$$

Here, the outcome of DKN is signified as Z_n, the expected output is termed as Z_n^*, and the entire sample count is indicated as P.

Infection stage: In this stage, if the distance between vulnerable and infected persons is less then the vulnerable person gets affected. The formulation of this stage is specified in Eqs. (16) and (17).

$$a_o(y + 1) = S(a_o(y)) \tag{16}$$

$$S(a_o(y)) = a_o(y) + \lambda_o(y) \times k(y) \times \|a_o(y) - a_f(y)\| \tag{17}$$

Here, the location of infected people in y^{th} public contact is mentioned as $a_f(t)$, the safety factor of masks for o^{th} person in y^{th} public contact is represented as $\lambda_o(y)$, and social distance is specified as k, $a_o(y+1)$ is the health of oth individual in $(y+1)$.

Diffusion stage: The expression for this diffusion is signified in Eqs. (18) and (19).

$$a_o(y+1) = B(a_o(y)) \tag{18}$$

$$B(a_o(y)) = (a_o(y) + \Gamma_o(y) \times k(y) \times \|a_o(y) - a_b(y)\|) \times \frac{\phi^{(\varsigma/\rho+1)} - 1}{\phi - 1} \tag{19}$$

Here, the time of virus spread and social actions are signified as ς and ρ, infection factor is mentioned as ϕ, location of the immune person in y^{th} public interaction is denoted as $a_b(y)$ and o^{th} the person in y^{th} public interaction is termed as $\Gamma_o(y)$.

Immune stage: If one person gets affected by a disease, maintaining distance from that person requires more awareness. In this stage, the expression is formulated in Eqs. (20) and (21).

$$a_o(y+1) = P(a_o(y)) \tag{20}$$

$$P(a_o(y)) = (a_o(y) + \lambda_o(y) \times k(y) \times \|a_o(y) - a_z(y)\|) \times \varpi i^\upsilon \tag{21}$$

where, the happiness index is specified as υ, coefficient of substantial fitness is mentioned as ϖ. The above equation is simplified in Eq. (22).

$$a_o(y+1) = Q + \Im \times (A - Q) \tag{22}$$

Furthermore, by applying the adaptive concept the performance is enhanced and a random number $\Im$ is made adaptive, which is given in Eq. (23).

$$\Im = U - \upsilon\left(\frac{\max .itr - y}{l}\right) \tag{23}$$

where, denotes lower bound, signifies upper bound, rand is made adaptive, parameter constant is denoted as, happiness index is specified as, maximum iteration is represented as, the current iteration is designated as and size of the population is indicated as

Re-evaluating fitness: The efficient solution of fitness is assessed from the resolution, in which the least value of fitness is deliberated as the best possible solution.

Termination: The process illustrated in this technique is made frequently till the ideal solution is attained.

4 Result and Discussion

The results of ACMPA_DKN for classifying BTs are illustrated and discussed in this part along with the datasets used.

Table 1. Parameter details

Parameter	Value
Epoch	20
Learning rate	0.01
Batch size	32

4.1 Experimental Setup

The newly suggested ACMPA_DKN is executed using the PYTHON tool. The experimental parameter details are given in Table 1.

4.2 Dataset Description

In this work, BRATS 2020 and Figshare datasets are employed. BRATS 2020 [18] employs multi-institutional pre-operative MRI images and mostly concentrates on segmentation task which is essentially heterogeneous in shape and appearance, like gliomas. Figshare [19] consists of T1-weighted contrast-enhanced images with three types of brain tumors. The entire dataset is divided into four groups in 4.zip files where each.zip file includes 766 slices. The dataset details are tabulated in Table 2.

Table 2. Dataset details

BRATS 2020 dataset	
Format	hdf5
Features	volume no, slice no, and target of that slice
Figshare dataset	
Total images	3064
Patients	233
meningioma	708 slices
pituitary	930 slices
glioma	1426 slices

4.3   Evaluation Metrics

The evaluation measures of BT are measured by using the TNR, TPR, and accuracy.

4.4   Experimental Results

The sample results by employing images are portrayed in Fig. 2. In Fig. 2(a) the input image is shown, the pre-processed outcome is illustrated in Fig. 2(b) and Fig. 2(c) exhibits the segmented outcome.

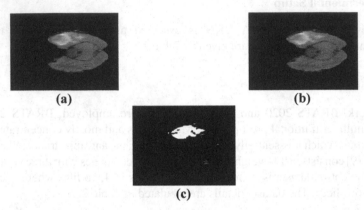

(a)   **(b)**

(c)

Fig. 2. Experimental outcomes of (a) Input image (b) pre-processed image (c) Segmented image

4.5   Comparative Methods

The techniques, such as CNN-SVM [1], LeU-Net [9], YOLOv2-inceptionv3 [11], and DWAE [3] are utilized to compare with newly established ACMPA_DKN.

4.6   Comparative Analysis

The estimation of models investigating ACMPA_DKN is estimated with BRATS 2020 and Figshare datasets.

Evaluation with BRATS 2020 Dataset. Figure 3 portrays the examination of ACMPA_DKN with other models regarding the BRATS 2020 dataset. The investigation of ACMPA_DKN with accuracy is shown in Fig. 3(a). At 70% of training data, ACMPA_DKN acquired an accuracy value of 86.5% and other models, like CNN-SVM, LeU-Net, YOLOv2-inceptionv3 and DWAE attained the TPR values of 72.2%, 75.0%, 78.3% and 82.6%. Figure 3(b), reveals investigation in terms of ACMPA_DKN with TPR. When training data is 60%, the TNR value of CNN-SVM is 74.0%, LeU-Net is 76.2%, YOLOv2-inceptionv3 is 78.9%, DWAE is 82.5%, and the proposed ACMPA_DKN is 85.5%. In Fig. 3(c), the analysis of ACMPA_DKN with TNR is displayed. When training data is 80%, the TNR value obtained by ACMPA_DKN is 89.4% while the existing models acquired the TNR value of 73.9%, 76.1%, 79.7% and 84.3%.

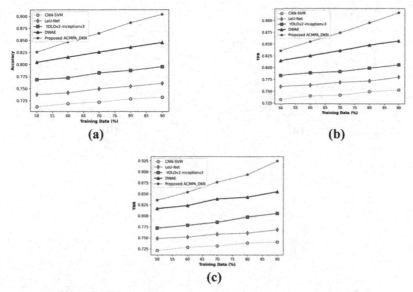

Fig. 3. Analysis using BRATS 2020 (a) accuracy (b) TPR (c) TNR

Evaluation with Figshare Dataset.   Figure 4 reveals the investigation of ACMPA_DKN with other models Figshare dataset. Figure 4(a) shows the examination of ACMPA_DKN based on accuracy. When training data is 70%, the accuracy value of CNN-SVM is 73.2%, LeU-Net is 75.9%, YOLOv2-inceptionv3 is 78.4%, DWAE is 83.3%, and proposed ACMPA_DKN is 87.3%. In Fig. 4(b), the investigation of ACMPA_DKN in terms of TPR is deliberated. Here, when training data is 60%, the TPR value obtained by ACMPA_DKN is 85.4% while the existing models acquired the TPR value of 73.9%, 76.1%, 78.9%, and 82.8%. The assessment of ACMPA_DKN based on TNR is demonstrated in Fig. 4(c). At 80% of training data, ACMPA_DKN attained the TNR value of 90.7% and other methods, namely CNN-SVM, LeU-Net, YOLOv2-inceptionv3, and DWAE attained the TNR values of 73.1%, 76.2%, 78.9%, and 82.5%.

4.7   Comparative Discussion

The performance measures utilized for comparing the methods based on training data are accuracy, TPR, and TNR. In the proposed method, Kalman filtering is used in the pre-processing, which efficiently improves the image quality and removes the noise present in the input image. Also, LadderNet is used for BT segmentation, which has many pathways of information flow. Moreover, BT is detected successfully using the DKN, which is trained by the proposed ACMPA. Thus, the proposed method achieves better results than the comparative methods.

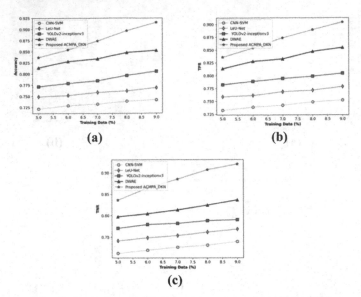

Fig. 4. Analysis using Figshare (a) accuracy (b) TPR (c) TNR

5 Conclusion

In this paper, an ACMPA_DKN model is employed for detecting and categorizing BTs. For that, input is pre-processed and BT is segmented by utilizing LadderNet. Then, the important features are extracted. After that, the BT detection is carried out by DKN which is classified into normal or abnormal. If it is identified as abnormal, the BT is classified. Moreover, BT is categorized by employing DKN which is tuned by ACMPA by integrating of Adaptive concept and CMPA. BT is classified with the ACMPA_DKN which attained the value of accuracy to 90.4%, the value of TPR and TNR to 91.6% and 92.5% with the BRATS 2020 dataset. The future work aims to work on both Machine Learning (ML) and image processing approaches with many images for categorizing BT from MRI and it also aims in categorizing BT in 3-Dimensional images.

References

1. Khairandish, M.O., Sharma, M., Jain, V., Chatterjee, J.M., Jhanjhi, N.Z.: A hybrid CNN-SVM threshold segmentation approach for tumor detection and classification of MRI brain images. Irbm **43**(4), 290–299 (2022)
2. Bhattacharyya, D., Kim, T.H.: Brain tumor detection using MRI image analysis. In: Proceedings of Ubiquitous Computing and Multimedia Applications: Second International Conference (UCMA 2011), Daejeon, Korea, 13–15 April 2011, Proceedings, Part II, Springer, Heidelberg, pp. 307–314 (2011)
3. Abd El Kader, I., et al.: Brain tumor detection and classification on MR images by a deep wavelet auto-encoder model. Diagnostics **11**(9), 1589 (2021)
4. Rahman, T., Saiful Islam, M.: MRI brain tumor detection and classification using parallel deep convolutional neural networks. Meas. Sens. **26** (2023)

5. Tian, D., Fan, L.: A brain MR images segmentation method based on SOM neural network. In: Proceedings of 2007 1st International Conference on Bioinformatics and Biomedical Engineering, IEEE, pp. 686–689 (2007)
6. Bandhyopadhyay, D.S.K., Paul, T.U.: Segmentation of brain MRI image–a review. Int. J. Adv. Res. Comput. Sci. Softw. Eng. **2**(3) (2012)
7. Muhammad Arif, F., Ajesh, S.S., Geman, O., Izdrui, D., Vicoveanu, D.: Brain tumor detection and classification by MRI using biologically inspired orthogonal wavelet transform and deep learning techniques. Advances in Feature Transformation based Medical Decision Support Systems for Health Informatics (2022)
8. Kumar Gupta, R., Bharti, S., Kunhare, N., Sahu, Y., Pathik, N.: Brain tumor detection and classification using cycle generative adversarial networks. Interdiscip. Sci. Comput. Life Sci. **14**, 485–502 (2022)
9. Rai, H.M., Chatterjee, K.: 2D MRI image analysis and brain tumor detection using deep learning CNN model LeU-Net. Multimed. Tools Appl. **80**, 36111–36141 (2021)
10. Fox, V., Hightower, J., Liao, L., Schulz, D., Borriello, G.: Bayesian filtering for location estimation. IEEE Pervasive Comput. **2**(3), 24–33 (2003)
11. Sharif, M.I., Li, J.P., Amin, J., Sharif, A.: An improved framework for brain tumor analysis using MRI based on YOLOv2 and convolutional neural network. Complex Intell. Systems **7**, 2023–2036 (2021)
12. Zhuang, J.: LadderNet: multi-path networks based on U-Net for medical image segmentation. arXiv preprint arXiv:1810.07810 (2018)
13. Zayed, N., Elnemr, H.A.: Statistical analysis of haralick texture features to discriminate lung abnormalities. J. Biomed. Imaging **2015**, 12 (2015)
14. Fausto, F., Cuevas, E., Gonzales, A.: A new descriptor for image matching based on bionic principles. Pattern Anal. Appl. **20**, 1245–1259 (2017)
15. Jagtap, A.D., Shin, Y., Kawaguchi, K., Karniadakis, G.E.: Deep Kronecker neural networks: a general framework for neural networks with adaptive activation functions. Neurocomputing **468**, 165–180 (2022)
16. Feng, L., Yang, G.: Deep Kronecker Network. arXiv preprint arXiv:2210.13327 (2022)
17. Yuan, Y., et al.: Coronavirus mask protection algorithm: a new bio-inspired optimization algorithm and its applications. J. Bionic Eng. 1–19 (2023)
18. BRATS 2020 dataset will be taken from https://www.kaggle.com/datasets/awsaf49/brats2 020-training-data?select=BraTS20+Training+Metadata.csv. Accessed Oct 2023
19. Figshare dataset will be taken from https://figshare.com/articles/brain_tumor_dataset/151 2427. Accessed Oct 2023
20. Lessa, V., Marengoni, M.: Applying artificial neural network for the classification of breast cancer using infrared thermographic images. In: Chmielewski, L., Datta, A., Kozera, R., Wojciechowski, K. (eds.) Computer Vision and Graphics (ICCVG 2016). LNCS, vol. 9972, pp. 429–438. Springer, Cham (2016). https://doi.org/10.1007/978-3-319-46418-3_38

Enhancing Hex Strategy: AI Based Two-Distance Pruning Approach with Pattern-Enhanced Alpha-Beta Search

Saatvik Saradhi Inampudi[✉] ⓘ

Fr. Conceicao Rodrigues Institute of Technology (FCRIT), Navi Mumbai 400073, India
isaatvik@gmail.com

Abstract. This paper introduces an effective algorithm designed for creating AI systems for the Hex board strategy game. The core algorithm, developed, employs the two-distance method for both board evaluation and for sorting of the moves. For empty board positions, the sum of two-distances from both ends is calculated to indicate the position's weight and is used for sorting. Additionally, the Pattern Search algorithm enhances efficiency by prioritizing moves in crucial regions. The algorithm demonstrated consistent performance across various board sizes, including 7×7, 9×9, and 11×11. When implemented as an Android game, this algorithm maintained excellent performance in the given board sizes.

Keywords: Game playing · Applications of AI · Logic

1 Introduction

Hex is a classic two-player board game, invented by Piet Hein in 1942 [1]. Hex is played on a hexagonal grid with a goal to connect opposite sides before the opponent. While simple in rules, it offers deep strategy and is used in AI research. There are no draws [2] and a winning strategy exists for the first player. It has been proven to be PSpace complete [3].

The intricate and complex nature of Hex has been a compelling source of motivation for the interest in the game. As I delved into this captivating world, I discovered a plethora of fascinating theorems that further ignited my curiosity. The theorems, outlined below, offer a glimpse into the rich landscape of Hex and serve as a prelude to the purpose behind the contributions from the author for this paper.

1. One of the earliest theorems asserts that on any board of regular size, there exists a winning opening move [1].
2. Another fundamental result establishes that adding a friendly piece or removing an enemy piece is never disadvantageous [4].
3. Beck's theorem reveals that, on any board size, there exists a losing opening move. Beck has found two opening moves that proved to be losses [5].

© The Author(s), under exclusive license to Springer Nature Switzerland AG 2024
D. Garg et al. (Eds.): IACC 2023, CCIS 2053, pp. 452–465, 2024.
https://doi.org/10.1007/978-3-031-56700-1_36

4. In the realm of 7×7 Hex, researchers have made significant strides in uncovering winning strategies, as well as identifying certain positions that the first player constantly avoids occupying [6].

This paper presents a new algorithm developed for Hex game strategy for three board sizes 7×7, 9×9, and 11×11. The algorithm is developed in easy, medium, and hard modes and depth of the search tree is increased as we move from easy to hard mode thereby the number of move combinations assessed by AI increases. This paper discusses the attempt made for improving the game performance by introducing bi-directional two-distance sum as weights for move sorting followed by pruning. This has reduced the move list which AI computes enabling it to find a move in less time. The performance efficiency of the algorithm is tested without degrading the quality of next move selection.

The literature review of different methods used for solving Hex are discussed in Sect. 2. The proposed algorithm and working are presented in Sect. 3 and 4 respectively. Section 5 evaluates the efficiency analysis of the proposed algorithm and Sect. 6 discusses the different test cases on a 7×7 board highlighting the moves played by AI in different modes. Section 7 present the final conclusion and future scope.

2 Related Work

Jack Van Rijswijck developed a program known as Queenbee [7] where he introduced the concept of two-distance evaluation function. The Queenbee uses iterative deepening α–β search with pruning at different depths followed by two-distance evaluation capturing the second-best alternative.

Young and Hayward [8] developed a strategy for playing Reverse Hex, a variant in which a player who connects two sides loses. Fabiano and Hayward [9] have introduced new Hex fill patterns (mutual and near dead) which has reduced the solving time on 8 × 8 opening.

Broderick, Hayward, and Philip [10] developed a Monte Carlo Tree Search in Hex. They developed the Monte Carlo Tree Search algorithm which is guided by the outcome of random game simulations. MoHex's MCTS is built on the code base of Fuego, the Go program developed by Martin Muller et al., at the University of Alberta.

Chao, Hayward and Müller [3] have used Deep Convolutional Neural Network for move prediction in Hex. They have used the self-play games of MoHex 2.0 neural network for training by canonical Max Likelihood and the trained model was evaluated by Wolve and MoHex 2.0. The improved version MoHex 2.0 uses a virtual connection engine that finds the smaller connection sets in half the time. Also, MoHex 2.0 introduces an optimization tool CLOP to tune parameters, extend unstable search and improve MCTS formula. MoHex 2.0 [11] an improved algorithm using MCTS is the current champion in the Hex game winning the latest competition.

Young, Vasan and Hayward [12] developed a Deep Q Learning (DQL) algorithm to train NeuroHex and with two weeks training NeuroHex achieved a success rate of 20.4% as first player and 21% as second player against MoHex, the IGCA Olympiad Hex Champion.

Apart from these, there are many algorithms and concepts for solving Hex and making a good move selection. These include popular Hex programs like Queenbee [7] and Hexy [13].

Chao, Siqi, Hayward, and Müller [14] have tested transferring of neural net knowledge learned in one board size to the other. They have shown that when only board independent neurons are used, the trained neural net is effectively used for other board sizes, larger or smaller.

Woodcok, Uscategui, and Corrales [15] evaluated the Hex game through game theory and graph theory by analyzing the short term and long term strategies, method of attacking and discussed several important proofs. They have shown the existence of weakly dominated and strongly dominated strategies within the game.

Hedan Liu and Xiaofu Du [16] have developed strategies based on cell geometry and chessboard region for Hex game and combined them with Monte Carlo tree search to achieve optimal results at the current level for reducing the scope of search space. They have developed human-AI and AI-AI interface to the Hex game.

3   Proposed Algorithm for Hex Board

The algorithms developed for the Hex game primarily concentrated on board evaluation [7] and pruning of search tree [1]. In this paper attempt has been made to use two-distance heuristic based sorting of the moves before board evaluation thereby improving the quality significantly. The core algorithm, developed, employs the two-distance method for both board evaluation and for sorting of the moves. For empty board positions, the sum of two-distances from both ends is calculated to indicate the position's weight and is used for sorting.

The two-distance concept is a unique way to measure distances between cells on a board for the Hex game. In contrast to conventional distance metrics, which measure the number of free moves needed to connect a cell to the edge, two-distance provides a more sophisticated approach. It calculates distances by considering not only the direct path but also the best second-best alternative, allowing it to account for strategic depth. This means it factors in how a player can block their opponent's optimal path, forcing them into a less advantageous position. Two-distance considers the whole neighborhood of a cell, accommodating different perspectives for White and Black due to existing game pieces. This nuanced approach is invaluable for evaluating moves and developing AI for Hex.

At the start of the game, AI is biased to play at the central region by giving more weight to board positions using $|i - j|$ and $|(i + j/2)\text{-mid}|$, where i and j being the horizontal and vertical coordinates of the board (Fig. 1)[1]. Center of the Hex board and thus the central region is important as it takes the advantage of the symmetry properties [17].

---

[1] All figures in this manuscript are from the "Simple Hex Board game with AI". Link: https://play. google.com/store/apps/details?id=com.SamgoGames.SimpleHex. The game can be installed and played on android based mobile devices with OS 7.0 and above.

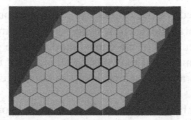

Fig. 1. The Central Region on 7 × 7 Hex Board

At every depth two-distance pruning is used. The details are further given in subsequent section. Pattern alpha beta search based pruning is used for simplifying the move search [18]. Depth represents the current depth of the search or recursion in the algorithm. This is often used to limit the depth of search or to determine when to stop recursive calls. The given algorithm performs two-distance based ranked heuristic sorting on every depth and two-distance board evaluation at the zeroth depth after which the AI picks the move to play. In easy mode the algorithm searches for the best possible move up to two depths, whereas in medium mode, algorithm searches up to four depths and in hard mode up to six depths. By increasing the depth, the accuracy and quality of the move is improved at the cost of processing time by AI.

At each level of depth in the algorithm, a strategy is employed to select a limited number of sorted moves. This strategic move selection process serves the purpose of narrowing down the set of potential moves, effectively reducing the overall count of moves considered. The selection criteria vary depending on the game board size and the difficulty mode.

For instance, when playing on a 7 × 7 board, at each of the available depths (2 depths for easy mode, 4 depths for medium mode and 6 depths for hard mode), the first 11 sorted moves for the initial 2 moves are considered. Similarly, on a 9 × 9 board, this strategy is extended to the first 4 moves, again choosing the top 11 sorted moves at each of the available depths depending on the difficulty of the mode and for 11 × 11 board, 11-sorted moves are picked at each depth for the first 8 moves. After these initial moves, first 21 sorted moves are picked at each depth for any mode and board size except that in hard mode.

For example, in the easy mode of the game, when the user makes a move on the board, the AI begins by selecting a limited number of moves from the total available moves during the first depth of the search. Then, it proceeds to the second depth, focusing on the selected moves from the previous step. Next, the AI changes its perspective as if it were the user and once again assesses the remaining moves on the board from that position. It then sorts through these moves and chooses a few. Following this process, the board is evaluated at the zeroth depth. Finally, the AI makes its move based on the position that gives it the most favourable outcome.

In the algorithm, regardless of the board size and difficulty mode, the AI computes several move calculations equal to fanOut raised to the power of depth in order to sort and select a move to play. The term fanOut in the algorithm refers to the maximum number of sorted moves selected at each depth.

As previously discussed, the performance of the Hex algorithm is notably influenced by several crucial hyperparameters. These hyperparameters include factors like Pruning Cutoff (fanOut), the dimensions of the game board, and the game depth. For instance, opting for an 11 × 11 game board may pose challenges for newcomers, thus reducing accessibility. Conversely, a 7 × 7 game board is considered more user-friendly and inclusive.

The selection of these hyperparameters is done with a goal to improve the strategic decision-making process of the Hex algorithm. It is essential to recognize that, despite the focus on these key hyperparameters in this study, there is a need for further comprehensive exploration, and certain parameters have not undergone thorough investigation due to limitations in time and scope.

The android game released is available in three board sizes: 7 × 7, 9 × 9, and 11 × 11. The algorithm discussed here works for any board size and offers easy, medium, and hard modes.

4 Working of Key Algorithms

4.1 TwoDistanceRankAndPrune

This method is responsible for ranking and sorting potential moves based on two-distance heuristic evaluation (Algorithm 1) which is the primary contribution to the Hex game. The heuristic aims to estimate the desirability of a given move.

It first calculates distances and scores for various game board cells using the twoDistanceForBoardPositions function (refer Sect. 4.2). Specifically, it calculates distances for the cell's reachability towards opposite ends of the board and is summed up. This is done both for the player and the opponent. The function then initializes a priority queue (a data structure that keeps elements in priority order). It uses a custom comparison function to order elements based on their heuristic scores. This allows the AI to prioritize moves with higher scores. It considers a certain number of moves (controlled by the fanOut variable) and returns this sorted list. Overall, the algorithm plays a crucial role in the AI's decision-making process by evaluating the game state and by selecting the most promising moves.

4.2 TwoDistanceForBoardPositions

This function applies the concept of two-distance in the Hex game [7]. It works by systematically exploring the game board and keeping track of distances from various cells to potential winning conditions. Below is how this function works:

It initializes two important data structures: isTwoDistance (a boolean array) and twoDistance (an integer array). These arrays are used to mark visited cells and store distances, respectively. Initially, all cells are marked as unvisited, and their distances are set to a large value.

The function uses a breadth-first search (BFS) approach. It starts by adding certain initial cells to a queue for exploration. It then enters a loop where it dequeues cells from the queue one by one and explores their neighbors. For each neighbor, it checks if it has been visited and if it is a valid move according to the game rules. If the neighbor has not been visited, it updates its distance and marks it as visited. If it belongs to the player, it sets the distance to be the same as the previous cell's distance. If it is a neutral cell (white), it increments the distance by one. This process continues until all relevant cells have been visited and distances calculated.

Finally, the function returns the twoDistance array, which contains the calculated distances for each cell on the board. These distances are crucial for AI to assess the game state which is used in the TwoDistanceRankAndPrune method for sorting moves.

This TwoDistanceRankAndPrune method is called by the Alpha Beta MiniMax method (Algorithm 2). The Algorithm 2 is similar to the algorithm developed by Rasmussen [18] where line 12 is the main contribution of the paper.

Algorithm 1. TwoDistanceRankAndPrune(moves, board, modeColour, depth)

1: playerWinDistance1 ← twoDistanceForBoardPositions(board, color, rotateView, true)
2: opponentWinDistance1 ← twoDistanceForBoardPositions(board, reverseColor, !rotateView, true)
3: playerWinDistance2 ← twoDistanceForBoardPositions(board, color, rotateView, false)
4: opponentWinDistance2 ← twoDistanceForBoardPositions(board, reverseColor, !rotateView, false)
5: for i ← 0 to boardSize - 1 do
6:   for j ← 0 to boardSize - 1 do
7:     if board[i, j] ≠ CellColor.White then continue
8:     opponentScore ← opponentWinDistance1[i, j] + opponentWinDistance2[i, j]
9:     playerScore ← playerWinDistance1[i, j] + playerWinDistance2[i, j]
10:    finalScore ← min(playerScore, opponentScore)
11:    n ← Node with (HexCoordinates (j, i), finalScore)
12:    enqueue n into queue
13: sortedList ← empty List of strings
14: fanOut ← 20 // This logic varies in the actual game but that is not relevant in understanding the algorithm
15: while queue is not empty AND size of sortedList < fanOut do
16:   n ← dequeue from queue
17:   move ← n.Row + ":" + n.Col
18:   if size of sortedList < fanOut
19:     add move to sortedList
20: return sortedList

Algorithm 2. Pattern_ αβ_Search (board, α, β, depth)

1: carrier ← Ø
2: modeColour ← board.notTurn
3: if board.isTerminal then
4: modeColour ← board.winningPlayer
5: return (carrier,modeColour)
6: end if
7: if depth = 0 then
8: modeColour ← Evaluate(board)
9: return (Ø, modeColour)
10: end if
11: moves ← board.emptyCells {The initial must-play region}
12: moves ← TwoDistanceRankAndPrune(moves, board, modeColour, depth)
{Update moves based on the two-distance heuristic ranking}
13: for m ∈ moves do
14:    board.playMove(m)
15:    (C, modeColour) ← Pattern_ αβ_Search (board, -β, -α, depth-1)
16:    board.undoMove(m)
17:    if modeColour = board.turn then
18:        carrier ← {m} U C {carrier, is now a weak threat pattern carrier.}
19:        return(carrier, modeColour}
20:    else if modeColour = board.notTurn then
21:        carrier ← carrier U C {The union of carriers.}
22:        moves ← moves ∩ C {Update the, must-play region.}
23:    end if
24:    α ← max (α, -modeColour)
25:    if -modeColour ≥ β then
26:        return (Ø, α)
27:    end if
28: end for
29: if moves ≠ Ø then
30:    return (Ø, α)
31: end if
32: return (carrier, modeColour) {Successful OR deduction}

Source: 13-Rasmussen 2007; Line 12 is the main contribution of this paper.

The primary functional variables used in the TwoDistanceRankAndPrune function are moves, board, modeColor, and depth, while for the Pattern_αβ_Search function, the variables are board, α, β, and depth. They are explained as follows:

1. moves: A list of potential moves to be ranked and sorted
2. board: The current game board state
3. modeColor: The color of the current player (with blue indicating the user, red indicating the AI)
4. depth: The current depth in the search tree

5 Efficiency Analysis: Impact of fanOut Strategy on Move Calculation Reduction and Computational Time

To assess the computational impact of the algorithm, a comparative analysis has been carried out, albeit with a simplification, temporarily disregarding the effects of alpha-beta pruning. This analysis focuses on a scenario in which the AI meticulously calculates its moves on a 7×7 Hex board across all difficulty modes.

In context of the Hex game made, considering game depths, this would entail an exhaustive exploration of approximately a total of 19,000 move possibilities in easy mode, 22,738,504 move calculations in medium mode, and a staggering 33,278,810,400 move calculations in hard mode. These calculations are shown in Table 1 where the first column represents the "Move Number", ranging from 1 to 49, reflecting the 7×7 board's dimensions. The second column represents the total number of moves without fanOut. For example, for move number 2 in 7×7 board easy mode, AI needs to calculate all 48 moves available after playing first move at depth 1 and 47 moves at depth 2, resulting in assessment of $48 \times 47 = 2256$ moves. The third column in the table represents the total number of moves using fanOut parameter, which is fanOut$^{(\text{game depth})}$. For example, as described above for move number 2 in 7×7 board easy mode, the AI selects 11 moves in the sorted list of 48 moves and 11 moves out of 47 moves in depth 2 resulting in assessment of $11*11 = 121$ move combinations for the best move. Additionally, after first 3 moves, fanOut is set to 20, selecting 21 moves from the sorted list of all available moves on the board. Similar calculations can be done for medium and hard modes on the 7×7 board.

To summarize, with the integration of fanOut strategy, which adopts a selective approach to move selection, this extensive calculation is significantly reduced. Instead of the initial 19,000 calculations, AI only considers 7,284 moves in easy mode on the 7×7 board as shown in the table. This reduction, stemming from the strategy, represents a remarkable 61.66% decrease in computational workload estimated using the Eq. 1 given below. Similarly, in total, the AI computes only 2,793,061 moves, down from the initial 22,738,504 moves, in medium mode on the 7×7 board, representing an 87.7% decrease in computational workload. In hard mode on the 7×7 board, the AI considers 81,157,945 moves, a significant reduction from the initial 33,278,810,400 moves, making it 99.755% more efficient in terms of the number of calculations. This substantial enhancement in computational efficiency, without accounting for the benefits of alpha-beta pruning, serves as a clear testament to the practicality and impact of the algorithm on the Hex game's artificial intelligence.

$$\text{Percentage Reduction} = \frac{(\text{Total moves without FanOut}) - (\text{moves using FanOut})}{(\text{Total moves without FanOut})} \times 100\% \qquad (1)$$

Further, the algorithm's performance in terms of computing time has been studied with and without fanOut parameter. Under without fanOut conditions the AI took significantly longer time to complete the game with a total execution time of 2 min. And 28 s in medium mode of 7×7 board. Whereas, by using fanOut parameter the AI was able to complete the same move sequence with a significantly reduced execution time of only 58 s. The time taken in each case is recorded using a laptop with i5 processor. However, it may be noted that the above timings are recorded where the AI has already ranked and

Table 1. Estimated number of moves required to be assessed with and without fanOut parameter and the RankAndPrune concept in easy mode of 7 × 7 Board

Move No.	Total No. of moves without fanOut	No. of moves with fanOut	Played by
1	49 × 48 = 2352	11 × 11 = 121	User
2	48 × 47 = 2256	11 × 11 = 121	AI
3	47 × 46 = 2162	11 × 11 = 121	User
4	46 × 45 = 2070	21 × 21 = 441	AI
5	45 × 44 = 1980	21 × 21 = 441	User
6	44 × 43 = 1892	21 × 21 = 441	AI
7	43 × 42 = 1806	21 × 21 = 441	User
8	42 × 41 = 1722	21 × 21 = 441	AI
9	41 × 40 = 1640	21 × 21 = 441	User
10	40 × 39 = 1560	21 × 21 = 441	AI
11	39 × 38 = 1482	21 × 21 = 441	User
12	38 × 37 = 1406	21 × 21 = 441	User
13	37 × 36 = 1332	21 × 21 = 441	AI
14	36 × 35 = 1260	21 × 21 = 441	User
15	35 × 34 = 1190	21 × 21 = 441	AI
16	34 × 33 = 1122	21 × 21 = 441	User
17	33 × 32 = 1056	21 × 21 = 441	AI
18	32 × 31 = 992	21 × 21 = 441	User
19	31 × 30 = 930	21 × 21 = 441	AI
20	30 × 29 = 870	21 × 21 = 441	User
21	29 × 28 = 812	21 × 21 = 441	AI
22	28 × 27 = 756	21 × 21 = 441	User
23	27 × 26 = 702	21 × 21 = 441	User
24	26 × 25 = 650	21 × 21 = 441	AI
25	25 × 24 = 600	21 × 21 = 441	User
26	24 × 23 = 552	21 × 21 = 441	AI
27	23 × 22 = 506	21 × 21 = 441	User
28	22 × 21 = 462	21 × 21 = 441	AI
29	21 × 20 = 420	420	User
30	20 × 19 = 380	380	AI
.	.	.	.

(*continued*)

Table 1. (*continued*)

Move No.	Total No. of moves without fanOut	No. of moves with fanOut	Played by
47	$3 \times 2 = 6$	6	User
48	$2 \times 1 = 2$	2	AI
49	0	0	User
Total moves by AI	19000	7284	

Note: After move no. 28 the number of move possibilities are equal for with and without fanOut parameter being used. This is because the number of moves would be less than 441

sorted the moves. The computing time of algorithm and results would change when the moves are not ranked and sorted. Figure 2 presented below shows the game with specific sequence of moves played by both the user and AI where first move was played by user. The same sequence is played by AI in both cases (with and without fanOut parameter and RankAndPrune). This demonstrates the contribution of TwoDistanceRankAndPrune function (In Sect. 4.1) which makes the AI computation significantly faster.

Fig. 2. Move sequence played for demonstration of computation time with and without "fanOut" and RankAndPrune concept in medium mode and 7×7 board size

This experiment underscores the crucial role of fanOut and rankAndPrune in optimizing the performance of the algorithm. By limiting the number of considered moves and employing a ranking mechanism, the algorithm effectively narrows down the set of potential moves, reducing the computational load and speeding up the AI's decision-making process. The results highlight the effectiveness of these strategies in achieving a balance between computational efficiency and quality gameplay. This finding provides valuable insights into the practical implications of these components in the algorithm's design, their impact on overall gameplay speed and importance of hyper parameter tuning to evaluate optimal AI performance. Similar results are observed in all modes across different board sizes.

6   Test Cases on 7 × 7 Board

In this section, a few examples for 7×7 board size detailing the functioning of algorithms at different depths are presented.

In 7 × 7 board size the moves played by AI Algorithm (Red Tiles) in response to the player moves (Blue Tile) in easy mode (depth 2) and the hard mode (depth 6) are discussed here to evaluate the performance of the algorithm. As shown in Fig. 3 the AI played the same first two moves for a similar set of moves played by the opponent (Blue Tile) in both easy and hard modes. The move no.4 played by AI is the same in both modes. In this case, two-distance sorting and two-distance board evaluation used in both easy and hard modes has resulted in the same move in spite of different depths. The board evaluation after searching up to depth 2 in easy mode and board evaluation after searching up to depth 6 in hard mode has yielded the same move. It may be noted that the game goes considerably faster in the easy mode compared to the hard mode.

Further continuing the same game to the sixth move (Red Tile No.6 in Fig. 4a and 4b), AI played different positions in easy and hard modes in response to the fifth move (Blue Tile No.5) by the player. An entirely different move played in hard mode is due to computation of a large number of move combinations at greater depths, which should have resulted in better move.

The following explanation provides the reasons for choosing move no. 6 by AI in hard mode as shown in Fig. 4b.

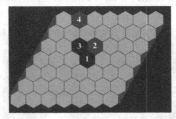

Fig. 3. Initial Moves of both Player and AI Algorithm in easy and hard Modes (Total four moves: Blue moves by player – Move no. 1 and 3; Red moves by AI Algorithm – Move no. 2 and 4) (Color figure online)

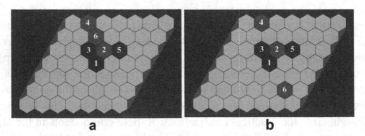

a   b

Fig. 4. Sixth move played by AI in response to fifth move by the player in easy (4a) and hard modes (4b) (Color figure online)

- As shown in Fig. 4a, in easy mode AI played a move (Red Tile 6) which would eventually give advantage to the opponent for connecting blue to the top of the board and this should have resulted in wastage of the move played by AI. Figure 5a and 5b presents the two combinations in which the opponent (Blue Tiles) connects to the top of the board.

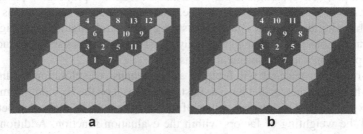

Fig. 5. Demonstration of Player (Blue Tile) connecting to top of the board in response to move no.6 by AI in easy Mode (Color figure online)

- Also, even if AI played move no.6 as shown below in Fig. 6a then also the blue player connecting to the top of the board cannot be avoided.

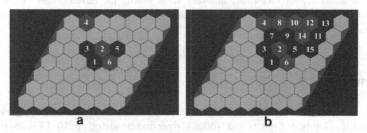

Fig. 6. Demonstration of Player (Blue Tile) connecting to top of the board in response to move no.6 by AI in easy Mode (Color figure online)

This shows the player (Blue Tile) by playing move no.5 ensured connection to the top of the board irrespective of AI (Red Tile) playing any position. Easy Mode could not evaluate this as it is computing move combinations only up to depth 2. Whereas, AI in hard mode, by estimating move combinations up to depth 6, has chosen to play move no.6 in the lower portion of the board (Fig. 4b) to prevent the blue from connecting to the bottom of the board. The two-distance board evaluation and two-distance sorting with depth 6 has helped the AI to choose a good move.

7 Conclusion and Future Scope

In this paper, a novel two-distance-based algorithm for Hex board strategy game has been successfully implemented across various board sizes, including 7×7, 9×9, and 11×11. The algorithm developed not only employs the two-distance method for board evaluation but also for move sorting and combines it with efficient fanOut parameter. The results of the efficiency analysis clearly demonstrate the algorithm's ability to reduce computational load and expedite the AI's decision-making process. Furthermore, the integrated alpha-beta pruning and pattern search-based must-play region pruning in the algorithm, enhanced its overall performance. This comprehensive approach has proven to be a valuable addition to the Hex game's AI strategy. The study highlights the significance of these innovations in advancing game-playing AI and provides a strong foundation for further exploration and improvement in this field.

In the future, the research will focus on a comprehensive exploration and fine-tuning of critical hyperparameters that have a substantial impact on the Hex algorithm's performance. Experiments with varying values of fanOut, game depth, alpha and beta parameters, and the weighting of factors within the evaluation function. Additionally, it is planned to extend algorithm's applicability to larger board sizes, such as 13×13, to assess its scalability and strategic capabilities. Also, applying the concepts of reinforcement learning like AlphaZero [19] to the hex game and making AI learn on its own and beat its own algorithm sounds quite interesting.

Acknowledgments. This work has been carried out as part of Summer Internship under the guidance of Mr. Naga Srinivas Vemuri, Google IT Services India Pvt Ltd, Hyderabad in his personal capacity. The author is deeply indebted to Dr. Naga Srinivas Vemuri, who is the primary developer of the code, for mentoring at every stage during the development of algorithm for building AI for the Hex board strategy game and for support during testing and performance evaluation.

References

1. Hayward, R.B., Toft, B.: HEX the full story. CRC Recreational Mathematics Series (2019)
2. Pierce, J.R.: Symbols, Signals and Noise. Harper and Brothers, pp. 10–13 (1961)
3. Chao, G., Hayward, R., Müller, M.: Move prediction using deep convolutional neural networks in Hex. IEEE Trans. Games **10**(4), 336–343 (2017)
4. Rijswijck, J.V.: Set colouring games. PhD Thesis, Department of Computing Science, University of Alberta, Canada (2006)
5. Beck, A., Bleicher, M.N., Crowe, D.W.: Excursions into Mathematics, pp. 317–387. Chapter Games, New York (1969)
6. Yang, J., Liao, S., Pawlak, M.: New winning and losing positions for 7×7 Hex. In: Schaeffer, J., Müller, M., Björnsson, Y. (eds.) Computers and Games (CG 2002). LNCS, vol. 2883, pp. 230–248. Springer, Heidelberg (2003). https://doi.org/10.1007/978-3-540-40031-8_16
7. Rijswijck, J.V.: Computer Hex: are bees better than fruitflies? Thesis of Master of Science, p. 37, Department of Computing Science, University of Alberta, Canada (2000)
8. Young, K., Hayward, R.B.: A reverse Hex solver. In: Plaat, A., Kosters, W., van den Herik, J. (eds.) Computers and Games (CG 2016), LNCS, vol. 10068, pp. 137–148. Springer, Cham (2016). https://doi.org/10.1007/978-3-319-50935-8_13
9. Fabiano, N., Hayward, R.: New Hex patterns for fill and prune. In: Cazenave, T., van den Herik, J., Saffidine, A., Wu, I.C. (eds.) Advances in Computer Games (ACG 2019). LNCS, vol. 12516, pp. 79–90. Springer, Cham (2020). https://doi.org/10.1007/978-3-030-65883-0_7
10. Broderick, A., Hayward, R.B., Philip, H.: Monte Carlo tree search in Hex. IEEE Trans. Comput. Intel. AI Games **2**(4), 251–258 (2010)

11. Huang, S.C., Arneson, B., Hayward, R.B., Müller, M., Pawlewicz, J.: MOHEX 2.0: a pattern-based MCTS Hex player. In: International Conference on Computers and Games, Computers and Games (CG 2013), pp. 60–71 (2013)

12. Young, K., Vasan, G., Hayward, R.: NeuroHex: a deep q-learning Hex agent. In: Workshop on Computer Games, International Workshop on General Intelligence in Game Playing Agents (CGW 2016, GIGA 2016), Computer Games (2016)

13. Anshelevich, V.V.: A hierarchical approach to computer Hex. Artif. Intell. **134**(1–2), 101–120 (2002). https://doi.org/10.1016/S0004-3702(01)00154-0

14. Chao, G., Siqi, Y., Hayward, R., Müller, M.: A transferable neural network for Hex. ICGA J. **40**(3), 224–233 (2018)

15. Woodcok, M., Uscategui, F., Corrales, D.: Basic analysis of Hex game. Econógrafos, Escuela de Economía 13417, Universidad Nacional de Colombia, FCE, CID (2015)

16. Liu, H., Du, X.: Strategy and implementation of Hex. In: Proceedings of the 2020 4th International Conference on Electronic Information Technology and Computer Engineering (EITCE 2020), pp. 800–805 (2020)

17. Yang, J., Simon, L., Mirek, P.: A new solution for a 7×7 Hex game (2002)

18. Rasmussen, R.: Algorithmic approaches for playing and solving Shannon games. PhD Dissertation, Faculty of Information Technology, Queensland University of Technology, pp. 24–26, 49–52, 108–111 (2007)

19. David, S., et al.: A general reinforcement learning algorithm that masters chess, shogi, and Go through self-play. Science **362**, 1140–1144 (2018). https://doi.org/10.1126/science.aar6404

IRBM: Incremental Restricted Boltzmann Machines for Concept Drift Detection and Adaption in Evolving Data Streams

Shubhangi Suryawanshi[1,2]([✉]), Anurag Goswami[1], and Pramod Patil[2]

[1] Bennett University, Greater Noida, India
{ss5683,anurag.goswami}@bennett.edu.in
[2] Dr. D. Y. Patil Institute of Technology, Pimpri, Pune, India

Abstract. In today's dynamically evolving data landscapes, detecting and adapting to concept drifts in streaming data is imperative. Concept drift occurs when there's a shift in the statistical characteristics of input features, like their mean or variance, or when the relationship between these features and the target label changes over time. This drift can decrease a model's accuracy because the model is trained on older data. As the data evolves, the model becomes outdated, which can lead to incorrect predictions and reduced performance. This paper introduces the Incremental Restricted Boltzmann Machine (IRBM), an approach designed to address these challenges. The IRBM adapts the traditional architecture and learning paradigms of Restricted Boltzmann Machines (RBMs) to incrementally process and learn from evolving data streams, ensuring model efficacy and accuracy over time. Through extensive experiments, we demonstrate the IRBM's ability to swiftly detect concept drifts, adapt its internal representations, and maintain robust performance even when confronted with significant data evolutions. The proposed approach outperforms existing methods with an accuracy of 77.42%, 75.32%, 92.12% and 89.21% for electricity, phishing, weather, and rotating hyperplane respectively. Our findings suggest that the IRBM not only offers an effective approach to understanding and adapting to changing patterns in streaming data but also outperforms the other state-of-the-art techniques.

Keywords: Incremental Learning · Restricted Boltzmann Machine · Concept Drift · Data Streams

1 Introduction

In today's big data era, advanced applications like weather forecasting, e-commerce, fraud detection, and telecommunications produce vast amounts of real-time data, often referred to as data streams [1–4]. These streams, owing to their sheer volume, require real-time processing. However, they can be affected by "concept drifts" that either alter the data distribution or the relationship between target labels and input features [3,5,6]. Two categories of concept drift are present. In the first, known as 'real drift', the relationship between the target label and input features changes, affecting decision boundaries. The second, 'virtual drift', only involves changes in the feature distribution. Drift can occur in various patterns, including sudden, gradual, incremental, or recurrent [1,3,4]. If drifts are left unaddressed, they can compromise the performance and reliability of a Machine Learning (ML) model, leading to degraded performance over time.

Traditional ML and deep learning methods (e.g. Naive Bayes, SVM, Decision Tree, Long Short Term Memory, OzaBagging) [7–11,18–21] are built on the assumption that data remains consistent over time, resulting in static model structures. These structures can become less accurate when data evolves. Given the changing nature of data streams, there's a pressing need for adaptable models that maintain consistent performance even when the data changes over time. There are numerous significant advantages of using Restricted Boltzmann Machines (RBMs) [12–15] for drift detection in changing data streams. Fundamentally, RBMs are designed to model the underlying probability distribution of their input data. This property, combined with their free energy metric, offers a direct and intuitive means to access the consistency of new data against this learned distribution. When the data starts to change or drift from the original patterns, this causes noticeable shifts in the free energy. Unlike traditional drift detection methods, which frequently rely on predetermined statistical tests or sliding windows, RBMs inherently detect drift without the need for arbitrarily chosen parameters or thresholds. The generative capabilities of RBMs also enable them to adapt to evolving data trends.

The contributions can be summarized in the following points:

– Presents a restricted boltzmann machine (RBM) for concept drift detection.
– Introduces the incremental RBM for adapting internal representations and maintaining model performance, with a focus on handling evolving data streams to ensure sustained accuracy.
– Demonstrated the ability to rapidly detect concept drifts, maintaining robust performance.
– Compares the current methodologies and the proposed approach across a range of diverse datasets.

The remaining paper is structured as follows: Sect. 2 presents the Literature Review, while Sect. 3 provides an in-depth explanation of the Methodology. In Sect. 4, we delve into the Experimental Design, focusing on the datasets used. Section 5 encompasses the Results and Analysis, and the paper concludes in the subsequent section.

2   Literature Survey

Data streams inherently impose numerous challenges due to their evolving characteristics and the emergence of concept drift [2–4]. In this context, concept drift signifies the moments of distribution shift of input feature attributes, like means and standard deviations, or when relationships between target labels and features evolve.

These challenges have opened the way for a variety of research opportunities and led to the focus of researchers in this area. Over the years, both machine learning Naive Bayes [6,8], Support Vector Machine (SVM) [7,8], Decision Tree [8,10], Incremental OzaBagging [20] and deep learning methodologies such as Incremental LSTM [20], and Extreme Learning Machine [6,8,10,18,19] have been explored extensively for drift detection and adaptation. Extreme Learning Machine (ELM) is distinguished by its efficiency, broad approximation capabilities, generalization, and straightforwardness, leading to the development of several ELM-centric techniques for identifying and adapting to concept drift [18,19].

Amongst the wide range of methodologies, Restricted Boltzmann Machines (RBMs) have gained notable attention [12–15]. Their intrinsic ability to address drift without extensive parameter optimization makes them a favoured choice. This literature review aims to delve into the various approaches and the prominence of using RBMs to overcome the difficulties presented by dynamic streams.

The study [13] proposes the application of Restricted Boltzmann Machines (RBMs) to detect drifts in the mining of time-varying data streams. RBMs can learn joint probability distributions of attribute values and classes, providing a condensed representation of the data distribution. Training an RBM on a portion of the data stream allows the identification of potential changes in the probability distribution. Two assessment measures are utilized to detect sudden or gradual shifts in the data stream. The efficacy of these techniques for detecting concept drift is demonstrated by experimental results on synthetic datasets. This paper [14] introduced a new drift detection by using the Restricted Boltzmann Machine (RBM). This detector is, capable of monitoring multiple classes, independently recognizing changes, managing imbalanced distributions, and adjusting to local concept drifts in underrepresented classes. By employing a skew-insensitive loss function, the detector efficiently works with multiple imbalanced distributions. Leveraging the reconstruction error of the RBM, it detects the changes within individual classes, thus facilitating adjustments to shifting class dynamics and localized drifts in minority classes.

The study [15] presented the Restricted Boltzmann Machine (RBM) can be optimized for data stream mining with incomplete datasets. By introducing two novel modifications to the RBM algorithm, missing values are managed efficiently. Experimental validation shows their effectiveness in detecting concept drift in incomplete data streams. The study [16] presented an anomaly detection system for video surveillance that is trained on unlabeled raw pixels while avoiding conventional obstacles. Anomalies are found by contrasting input videos with model reconstructions using RBMs and Deep Boltzmann Machines (DBMs). The results demonstrate their ability in detection as well as simultaneous scene clustering and reconstruction. The study [17] presented a concept drift detection and adaptation algorithm that was proposed using an online RBM. The integration of an attention mechanism within the RBM allows for targeted updating of the model's parameters based on essential data identified by the mechanism. This method enhances both drift detection capabilities and the adaptability of the model. Among the numerous approaches developed to address the concept drift issue, (RBMs) have emerged as the most promising solutions. Their distinct architecture, which is based on deep learning, has the potential benefit of detecting and adapting to drifts.

Motivated by the insights garnered from our exploration of existing literature, developed an RBM-based drift detection mechanism. When a drift is detected, an incremental RBM is trained using the most recent data to keep the model current and relevant.

3 Methodology

A detailed explanation of the methodology depicted in Fig. 1 is provided in this section.

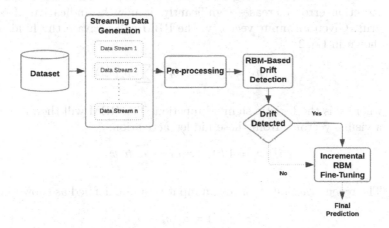

Fig. 1. IRBM: Incremental Restricted Boltzmann Machines for Concept Drift Detection and Adaption

Step 1 **Streaming Data Generation**

The dataset has been segmented into equal-sized chunks to facilitate incremental streaming. This partitioning improves processing efficiency, suits real-time data scenarios, and maintains structured organization, ensuring streamlined handling of continuous and large datasets.

Step 2 **Pre-processing**

In the pre-processing stage, all features are normalized to fit within a 0 to 1 range using the MinMax scaler. To maintain data consistency, missing values and several entries are removed. Following this preprocessing, the data becomes ready for the next processing steps. Additionally, a label encoder is used to process target labels.

Step 3 RBM-based drift detection

Restricted Boltzmann Machines (RBMs) [12] are generative stochastic artificial neural networks that can learn a probability distribution over their set of inputs. Utilizing RBMs (Restricted Boltzmann Machines) for identifying drifts in data streams can be depicted as follows:

An RBM has two layers: a visible layer v and a hidden layer h. Connections exist between visible and hidden units, but not within units in the same layer.

The energy of the system, given a state as shown in Eq. 1

$$E(v, h) = \sum_s a_s v_s - \sum_t b_s h_s - \sum_s^t v_s w_{st} h_s \tag{1}$$

where: a_s and b_t are the biases. w_{st} is the weight between visible unit s and hidden unit t.

For drift detection, the key idea is to monitor how well the RBM can reconstruct new incoming data compared to previous data. If the reconstruction error increases significantly, it may be indicative of concept drift. Given an input vector v, the RBM will activate the hidden units shown in Eq. 2

$$P(h_t = 1|v) = \sigma(b_t + \sum_s v_s w_{st}) \tag{2}$$

where σ is the logistic sigmoid function. The RBM will then reconstruct a visible vector v from these hidden activation:

$$P(v_t = 1\,h) = \sigma(a_t + \sum_t h_s w_{st}) \tag{3}$$

The reconstruction error for an input v can be defined as shown in Eq. 4:

$$P(v, v') = \sigma_t(v_s - v'_s)^2 \tag{4}$$

Train the RBM on a batch of data. As new data comes in, pass it through the RBM and compute the reconstruction error. If the error exceeds a predefined threshold or shows a consistent increasing trend, it can be taken as an indication of concept drift. if error (v_b, v'_b)-error(v_{b-1}, v'_{b-1}) $> \delta$

For a set of consecutive b (time steps or data batches), we might infer a drift. Here, δ is a predefined threshold.

Step 4 Incremental RBM Fine-tuning

- If drift is detected, the RBM can be retrained or fine-tuned on the most recent data to capture the new concept.
- The weight and bias are updated as follows by considering Eq. 2 and 3:
  Modify the weights and biases using the differences between the input and reconstruction errors as shown in Eq. 5, 6 and 7:

$$\Delta w_{st} = \alpha(v * p(h|v)) - (p(v'|h) * h') \tag{5}$$

$$\Delta a_s = \alpha(v_s - v'_s) \tag{6}$$

$$\Delta b_s = \alpha(h_s - h'_s) \tag{7}$$

where α is the learning rate, and primes indicate reconstructed values. When a drift is detected, an incremental RBM is trained using the most recent data

– Use the current weights and biases as starting points.
– Apply the above steps only on the new data batch.

Step 5 **Final Prediction**

When drift is identified, we train an incremental RBM with the latest data. This updated model is then employed for subsequent predictions.

4   Experiment Design

The section provides a detailed description of the datasets employed for testing and the evaluation metrics applied.

4.1   Dataset

Below is a detailed overview of the datasets used for the study:

– The electricity dataset has 45,312 instances. The dataset contains 8 attributes, with a target label describing the UP and DOWN in electricity prices. Prices are influenced by supply and demand [22].
– This dataset includes harmful web pages as well as the nslkdd dataset. It was primarily utilized to develop an intrusion detection system capable of discriminating between malicious (attack) and benign (regular) connections. It has two target label categories: 'attack' and 'normal'. It consists of 46 features and 11,055 instances [25].
– The dataset weather dataset is a real-world concept drift dataset that contains 18159 features with labels on whether there will be rain or not [24].
– In the synthetic dataset rotating hyperplane the position and orientation of a hyperplane are continuously adjusted. The dataset contains ten features and a class label [23].

4.2   Evaluation Measures

The evaluation measures used for the experimentation are described below:

– Accuracy:- It measures the ratio of correct predictions to the total prediction.
– F1 Score:- It is the harmonic mean of Precision and Recall, providing a balance between them.
F1 Score = 2 (Precision × Recall/Precision + Recall)
– Precision:- It quantifies the number of correct positive predictions out of all positive predictions.
– Recall:- It measures the number of correct positive predictions out of all actual positives.

5   Results and Analysis

In the experimentation, the performance of the proposed Incremental RBM approach was evaluated against established state-of-the-art methods like ILSTM and incremental OzaBagging. This comparison was carried out using four diverse datasets: real-world datasets such as electricity, weather, and phishing, and a synthetic dataset named Rotating Hyperplane. To evaluate their performance, we employed evaluation metrics, including accuracy, F1 score, precision, and recall. The outcomes of this comparative analysis are summarized in Table 1.

As illustrated in Table 1, the proposed method demonstrates superior performance on real-world datasets. Specifically, it achieved an accuracy of 77.42% for the electricity dataset, 75.32% for the weather dataset, and an impressive 92.12% for the phishing dataset. Additionally, when tested on the rotating hyperplane dataset, the method attained an accuracy of 89.21%.

Table 1. Comparison of different techniques with the proposed approach

Dataset	Models	Accuracy	F1-Score	Precision	Recall
Electricity	Proposed Approach	**77.42**	**77.12**	**79.32**	**73.95**
	Incremental OzaBagging	65.32	66.65	67.21	67.12
	ILSTM	72.43	73.87	76.40	72.65
Weather	Proposed Approach	**75.32**	**74.11**	**77.49**	**77.76**
	Incremental OzaBagging	72.44	72.01	73.98	70.86
	ILSTM	70.12	66.43	68.75	67.03
Phishing	Proposed Approach	**92.12**	**93.44**	**93.21**	**93.23**
	Incremental OzaBagging	88.47	84.21	88.54	85.63
	ILSTM	86.23	84.21	85.32	84.22
Rotating Hyperplane	Proposed Approach	**89.21**	**88.34**	**85.38**	**86.31**
	Incremental OzaBagging	73.21	72.90	73.76	72.97
	ILSTM	85.42	83.76	83.21	84.65

In Fig. 2, the datasets are plotted along the x-axis, and their corresponding accuracy is on the y-axis. This figure differentiates the performance of several methodologies, with each method represented by its unique color. Additionally, when compared to existing approaches, Fig. 2 indicates significant improvements of 5% for electricity, 3% for weather, 4% for phishing, and another 4% for rotating hyperplane datasets. While accuracy is essential, other metrics such as precision, recall, and the F1 score are also used to assess a model's true efficiency. The proposed approach method not only shows better accuracy but also shows outstanding performance across different measures such as Precision, Recall and F1 score, promising an efficient and robust model. In comparison with other existing techniques, our approach outperforms them. Its inherent strength lies in its

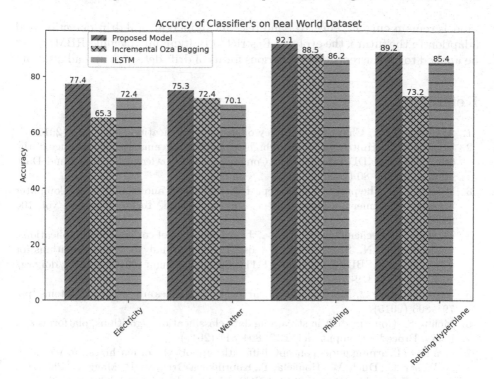

Fig. 2. Accuracy of Classifiers on Real World and Synthetic Dataset

adeptness at identifying drifts. Furthermore, when drift is detected, it incrementally adapts and trains depending on current data, assuring its continued relevance and adaptability in dynamic circumstances.

6 Conclusion and Future Scope

The proposed approach Incremental Restricted Boltzmann Machines for Concept Drift Detection and Adaptation in Evolving Data Streams was evaluated on real-world and synthetic datasets and compared with state-of-the-art methods. The proposed approach outperformed, with an accuracy of 77.42%, 75.32%, and 92.12% on the electricity, weather, and phishing datasets, respectively, and 89.21% on the rotating hyperplane dataset.

The proposed model performed better in terms of accuracy, F1 score, precision, and recall. Extensive experiments show that the IRBM can detect concept drifts efficiently, adapt its internal representations, and maintain high accuracy even when presented with evolving data streams.

The IRBM's ability to recognize and respond to concept drifts demonstrates its efficacy as a significant approach in the world of dynamic data streams. As data keeps on growing and changing in unanticipated ways, incrementally restricted boltzmann machines will become more significant in ensuring that models remain current, effective, and relevant in incremental drift detection and adaption.In the future, the evolving Restricted Boltzmann Machine (RBM) could be applied to concurrently tackle various forms of drift detection and adaptation.

References

1. Aggarwal, C.C.: Chapter 9 A survey of stream classification algorithms (2015)
2. Domingos, P., Hulten, G.: Mining high-speed data streams. In: Proceedings of the 6th ACM SIGKDD International Conference on Knowledge Discovery and Data Mining, pp. 71–80 (2000)
3. Tsymbal, A.: The problem of concept drift: definitions and related work. Computer Science Department, Trinity College, Dublin, Ireland, Technical report, vol. 106 (2004)
4. Žliobaitė, I., Pechenizkiy, M., Gama, J.: An overview of concept drift applications. In: Japkowicz, N., Stefanowski, J. (eds.) Big Data Analysis: New Algorithms for a New Society. SBD, vol. 16, pp. 91–114. Springer, Cham (2016). https://doi.org/10.1007/978-3-319-26989-4_4
5. Hesse, G., Lorenz, M.: Conceptual survey on data stream processing systems, pp. 798–803 (2015)
6. Mehta, S.: Concept drift in streaming data classification algorithms, platforms and issues. Procedia Comput. Sci. **122**, 804–811 (2017)
7. Ayad, O.: Learning under concept drift with support vector machines. In: Wermter, S., Weber, C., Duch, W., Honkela, T., Koprinkova-Hristova, P., Magg, S., Palm, G., Villa, A.E.P. (eds.) ICANN 2014. LNCS (LNAI and LNB), vol. 8681, pp. 587–594. Springer, Cham (2014). https://doi.org/10.1007/978-3-319-11179-7_74
8. Gama, J., Žliobaite, I., Bifet, A., Pechenizkiy, M., Bouchachia, A.: A survey on concept drift adaptation. ACM Comput. Surv. **46**(4), 44 (2014)
9. Cohen, L., Avrahami-Bakish, G., Last, M., Kandel, A., Kipersztok, O.: Real-time data mining of non-stationary data streams from sensor networks. Inform. Fusion **9**(3), 344–353 (2008)
10. Lu, J., Liu, A., Dong, F., Gu, F., Gama, J., Zhang, G.: Learning under concept drift: a review. IEEE Trans. Knowl. Data Eng. **31**, 2346–2363 (2018)
11. Ditzler, G., Roveri, M., Alippi, C., Polikar, R.: Learning in nonstationary environments: a survey. IEEE Comput. Intell. Mag. **10**(4), 12–25 (2015). https://doi.org/10.1109/MCI.2015.2471196
12. Fischer, A., Igel, C.: An introduction to restricted Boltzmann machines. In: Alvarez, L., Mejail, M., Gomez, L., Jacobo, J. (eds.) CIARP 2012. LNCS, vol. 7441, pp. 14–36. Springer, Heidelberg (2012). https://doi.org/10.1007/978-3-642-33275-3_2. ISBN 978-3-642-33274-6
13. Jaworski, M., Duda, P., Rutkowski, L.: On applying the restricted Boltzmann machine to active concept drift detection (2017). https://doi.org/10.1109/SSCI.2017.8285409
14. Korycki, Ł., Krawczyk, B.: Concept drift detection from multi-class imbalanced data streams. arXiv Learning (2021)
15. Jaworski, M., Duda, P., Rutkowska, D., Rutkowski, L.: On handling missing values in data stream mining algorithms based on the restricted Boltzmann machine. In: Gedeon, T., Wong, K.W., Lee, M. (eds.) ICONIP 2019. CCIS, vol. 1143, pp. 347–354. Springer, Cham (2019). https://doi.org/10.1007/978-3-030-36802-9_37

16. Vu, H., Nguyen, T.D., Phung, D.: Detection of unknown anomalies in streaming videos with generative energy-based Boltzmann models. arXiv Computer Vision and Pattern Recognition (2018)

17. Zhu, Q., Zhou, J., Wang, W.: Concept drift detection and update algorithm based on online restricted Boltzmann machine. In: Liang, Q., Wang, W., Mu, J., Liu, X., Na, Z. (eds.) AIC 2022. LNEE, vol. 871, pp. 305–311. Springer, Singapore (2023). https://doi.org/10.1007/978-981-99-1256-8_36

18. Xu, S., Wang, J.: Dynamic extreme learning machine for data stream classification. Neurocomputing **238**, 433–449 (2017)

19. Xiulin, Z., Peipei, L., Xindong, W.: Data stream classification based on extreme learning machine: a review. Big Data Res. **30**, 100356 (2022). https://doi.org/10.1016/j.bdr.2022.100356

20. Neto, Á.C.L., Coelho, R.A., de Castro, C.L.: An incremental learning approach using long short-term memory neural networks. J. Control Autom. Electr. Syst. **33**, 1457–1465 (2020)

21. Oza, N.C., Russell, S.J.: Online bagging and boosting. In: Richardson, T.S., Jaakkola, T.S. (eds.) Proceedings of the Eighth International Workshop on Artificial Intelligence and Statistics, pp. 229–236. PMLR (2001). https://proceedings.mlr.press/r3/oza01a.html

22. Dataset. Electricity dataset (2014). https://github.com/scikit-multiflow/streaming-datasets/blob/master/elec.csv. Accessed September 2023

23. Dataset. Rotating hyperplane dataset (2014). https://github.com/scikit-multiflow/streaming-datasets/blob/master/hyperplane.csv. Accessed September 2023

24. Dataset. Weather dataset (2014). https://github.com/scikit-multiflow/streaming-datasets/blob/master/weather.csv. Accessed September 2023

25. Dataset. Phishing dataset (2014). https://github.com/ogozuacik/concept-drift-datasets-scikit-multiflow/tree/master/real-world/phishing.csv. Accessed September 2023

Revisiting Class Imbalance: A Generalized Notion for Oversampling

Purushoth Velayuthan[1]([✉])(iD), Navodika Karunasingha[2](iD),
Hasalanka Nagahawaththa[2](iD), Buddhi G. Jayasekara[2](iD),
and Asela Hevapathige[3](iD)

[1] BPH 200 PTE. LTD., Singapore, Singapore
vpurushoth97@gmail.com
[2] Department of Electrical and Information Engineering, University of Ruhuna,
Galle, Sri Lanka
[3] College of Engineering, Computing and Cybernetics, The Australian National
University, Canberra, Australia
asela.hevapathige@anu.edu.au

Abstract. Class imbalance is a salient problem in both machine learning and data mining realms. Sampling techniques have become a cornerstone in solving this challenge, as they enable the creation of class-balanced datasets that is essential for robust model training. Addressing class imbalance not only enhances the predictive accuracy of machine learning algorithms but also ensures fair and unbiased decision-making across various applications, making it a critical aspect of research and development in various sectors. Through this work, we introduce the concept of a generalized oversampling function, unifying existing synthetic oversampling approaches. We explore diverse design decisions for such a function, presenting six functions categorized as linear and non-linear variants. We provide extensive experiments with these functions to gain an in-depth understanding of their behavior. Through our experiments, we observe that the best-performing function is primarily data-driven. Also, it is perceived that non-linear functions like minimum and maximum often depict higher learning capacity and steady performance in comparison to their linear counterparts mainly due to their ability in modelling non-trivial patterns. While moderate input counts would yield desirable performance in these functions, we can see varying robustness from these functions for distorted input data.

Keywords: Class imbalance · Statistics · Data mining · Classification

1 Introduction

The realm of machine learning prominently features classification as one of its central themes. Various classification algorithms including classical machine learning approaches and deep learning architectures have been developed and widely embraced across multiple domains. However, a common challenge pervades almost all these algorithms, which is the issue of imbalanced datasets, where certain classes contain more data instances than others. This imbalance often introduces biases into the model training process, leading to a subpar performance in inference [1,10].

The imbalance classification problem has been explored in various aspects in recent times. Many traditional approaches aim to solve this problem by employing sampling techniques. These sampling techniques augment the instances in the data set to achieve a better balance in class distribution [9,14]. From the sampling techniques, oversampling achieves class balance by magnifying the number of minority instances. Synthetic Minority Oversampling TEchnique (SMOTE) [3] is one of the prominent oversampling approaches used for this task. SMOTE balances the class distribution frequency of the dataset by populating synthetic minority samples using linear interpolation. There has been a line of works [6,7,13,19,30] proposed to enhance the oversampling process in SMOTE by introducing additional constraints and learning procedures. However, the quality of the oversampling process and its overall impact on imbalanced classification performance is under-explored.

After reviewing existing synthetic oversampling approaches, we observe that these methods generate new synthetic data using a transformation process that takes existing data instances as the input. Also, we notice that the properties of this transformation process govern the quality of the generated synthetic data and the performance of the imbalanced classification. Inspired by this observation, we intend to explore the prospect of introducing a generalized notion for this transformation process to understand the imbalanced classification process in a better way. We formulate this transformation process as a function that is dedicated to oversampling and explore the design options for such a function. Furthermore, we show that the intriguing properties of these design options have a non-trivial impact on the performance of the imbalanced classification. We outline the research contributions of our paper as follows.

- We introduce the generalized notion of the oversampling function and show that the existing synthetic oversampling functions like SMOTE can be formulated as an instance of the proposed notion.
- We explore potential design choices for the oversampling function by proposing six functions with diverse properties. We split these functions into two categories, namely, *linear functions*, and *non-linear functions*.
- We integrate the proposed design choices into the oversampling process and provide experiments on several datasets to evaluate their effectiveness of on the imbalanced classification process.

The rest of the paper is presented as follows: Sect. 2 describes the related work; Sect. 3 elaborates on the proposed methodology; Sect. 4 describes the experimental setup; Sect. 5 consists of the results and discussion; Sect. 6 explains the conclusion and future work.

2   Related Work

Sampling approaches intend to balance the class distribution by either increasing the minority class data instances (i.e. oversampling), decreasing majority class data instances (i.e. undersampling), or achieving a trade-off by combining both oversampling and undersampling approaches (i.e. hybrid sampling) [4,24]. We provide a brief overview of these sampling approaches below.

Oversampling Approaches: Chawla et al. [3] introduced SMOTE, which is a novel approach to generating synthetic instances by interpolating minority data instances in the dataset. It produces synthetic samples by blending attributes from minority samples with their neighbors, resulting in enhanced generalizability compared to random oversampling methods. The rising acclaim for this technique has led numerous subsequent studies to adopt SMOTE as their foundational methodology. The method presented in [18] integrates the widely recognized k-means clustering algorithm with SMOTE oversampling to tackle the issue of imbalanced datasets. This sets itself apart with both simplicity and strategic sample distribution: a clustering phase segments the input space, followed by a meticulous cluster selection for oversampling, demonstrating a unique and effective methodology. He et al. [8] introduced a pioneering method called Adaptive Synthetic Sampling (ADASYN) to tackle minority oversampling using density distribution. They assign varying weights to different minority instances, considering their complexity in discrimination. Concentrating on the difficult classification instances, ADASYN carefully generates synthetic data, improving dataset representation with precision and effectiveness. Two innovative extensions to SMOTE were presented by Han et al. [7], namely borderline-SMOTE1 and borderline-SMOTE2. These adaptations focus exclusively on oversampling minority instances located near the borderline. These selective approaches target instances that are inherently challenging for machine learning algorithms to distinguish.

Other Sampling Approaches: While much attention has traditionally been devoted to oversampling techniques, some research studies have diverged from this by focusing on the reduction of majority data instances to achieve class balance. These works concentrate on imbalanced classification through undersampling techniques [2,21,27,28]. Some works explore a combined approach that incorporates both oversampling and undersampling methods [4,12,16].

Our work is essentially dissimilar to existing sampling approaches in the literature owing to the fact that we focus on introducing a generalized notion for the oversampling process rather than limiting to a specific technique. Our method can accommodate a wide variety of oversampling functions.

3   Methodology

3.1   Preliminaries

We begin by introducing the notation that will be used throughout the paper. Let $D = \{X, Y\}$ be a dataset. $X = \{x_1, \ldots x_n\}$ is a set of data instances where each data instance x in X is a $(1 \times d)$ vector; i.e. $x \in \mathbf{R}^{1 \times d}$. $Y \in \mathbf{R}^n$ is the class labels for data instances in X. We consider there are m class labels in total, $\{C_1, \dots C_m\}$. For $1 \leq j \leq m$, we identify C_j as a *minority class* if it makes up a smaller proportion of D.

Let k be an integer and $dist(p, q)$ is the distance between p and q data instances under a given distance measure. Also, we define $L(x) \subseteq X$ to be the set of all data instances that has same class label as $x \in X$. We denote the set of the *k-nearest neighbors* of x as $N(x)$. Formally, $N(x)$ is defined as $N(x) \subseteq L(X)$, such that $|N(x)| = k$ and $\forall x' \in L(X) \backslash N(x)$, $dist(x, x') \geq \max_{x'' \in N(x)} dist(x, x'')$. Further, we use $\hat{N}(x) = x \cup N(x)$ for brevity.

3.2   Generalized Notion for the Oversampling Function

In this section, we first introduce a generalized notion for the oversampling function in imbalance classification. We define d_f as an oversampling function that takes a set of data instances $S \subseteq X$ as the input and aggregates the information of these instances into a single feature vector.

$$d_f : S \to \mathbf{R}^d \tag{1}$$

We identify the ability of d_f to generate synthetic minority data instances to balance the dataset. For a given minority data point x, we can generate a synthetic minority data instance $\tilde{x}$ as follows.

$$\tilde{x} = d_f \left(\hat{N}(x) \right) \tag{2}$$

Synthetic samples generated by different oversampling functions would be divergent containing disparate semantics (Fig. 1).

There can be many choices for d_f ranging from simple choices such as sum, and mean to functions with complex behaviors such as polynomial aggregation. We split these functions into two broad categories, namely, *linear functions* and *non-linear functions*. We define what a linear function is below.

Definition 1. *(Linear Function): Let U and V be vector spaces over the same field. $f : U \to V$ is defined as a linear function if for any $u_1, u_2 \in U$ and any scalar λ the following conditions are satisfied.*

$$f(u_1 + u_2) = f(u_1) + f(u_2)$$

$$f(\lambda u_1) = \lambda f(u_1)$$

Any function that does not satisfy the above definition falls into the category of a non-linear function. When compared with linear functions, non-linear functions are known to have the ability to model more complex relationships between data instances due to their high capacity [29]. To evaluate the impact of the oversampling function on the performance of imbalance classification, we select a subset of linear and non-linear functions. To retain simplicity, we omit complex functions and only focus on simple ones.

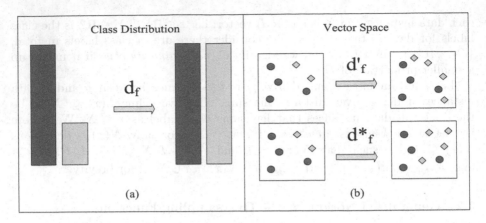

Fig. 1. (a) Oversampling function balances the class distribution (b) Different functions (i.e. d'_f and d^*_f) generate samples with different characteristics

3.3 Linear Functions for Information Aggregation

Sum. The sum function is the total of all input data points. Under sum, we can define $\tilde{x}$ as follows.

$$\tilde{x} = \sum_{x' \in N(x)} x' \tag{3}$$

Mean. Calculation of $\tilde{x}$ using mean values takes the average value of the function over its domain.

$$\tilde{x} = \frac{\sum_{x' \in N(x)} x'}{|N(x)|} \tag{4}$$

Weighted Arithmetic Mean. The weighted arithmetic mean function takes the sum of the input values multiplied by their weights divided by the sum of their weights. Formally, the weighted arithmetic mean-based oversampling function can be defined as,

$$\tilde{x} = \frac{\sum_{x' \in N(x)} w_{x'} \times x'}{\sum_{x' \in N(x)} w_{x'}} \tag{5}$$

3.4 Non-linear Functions for Information Aggregation

Maximum. The maximum function takes the element-wise maximum of vector elements. Let $x = (x_{1,r})_{1 \leq r \leq d}$. The maximum function takes the maximum of each column in data points given in $N(x)$ and forms the $(1 \times d)$ vector for $\tilde{x}$ defined by,

$$\tilde{x}_{1,r} := \text{MAX}\left(x'_{1,r} | x' \in N(x)\right) \tag{6}$$

Minimum. The minimum function works similarly to the maximum function where it takes the element-wise minimum of vector elements. Given $x = (x_{1,r})_{1 \leq r \leq d}$, the minimum function takes the minimum of each column in data points given in $N(\hat{x})$ and form the $(1 \times d)$ vector for $\tilde{x}$ defined by,

$$\tilde{x}_{1,r} := \text{MIN} \left(x'_{1,r} | x' \in N(\hat{x}) \right) \tag{7}$$

Standard Deviation. Standard deviation functions measure the dispersion of the input data concerning the mean. It is often used to quantify the information spread and the diversity of inputs. Let $x = (x_{1,r})_{1 \leq r \leq d}$. We formulate the standard deviation-based oversampling function as follows.

$$\mu_r = \frac{\sum_{x' \in N(\hat{x})} x'_{1,r}}{|N(\hat{x})|} \tag{8}$$

$$\tilde{x}_{1,r} := \sqrt{\frac{\sum_{x' \in N(\hat{x})} \left(x'_{1,r} - \mu_r \right)^2}{|N(\hat{x})|}} \tag{9}$$

3.5 SMOTE as an Instance of the Proposed Oversampling Function

Oversampling in SMOTE can be expressed as the following function. Let $x_{minority}$ and $x_{neighbor}$ be the considered minority data instance to be oversampled and the selected neighboring data instance, respectively. For a given threshold $\lambda \in [0,1]$, we can define the populated synthetic data instance $\tilde{x}$ as follows.

$$\tilde{x} = \lambda \times x_{minority} + (1 - \lambda) \times x_{neighbor} \tag{10}$$

We identify this as an instance of our generalized notion. Let $S \subseteq N(x), |S| - 1$. Also, $\mathbb{1}$ denotes the indicator function. We can define $\tilde{x}$ using the weighted arithmetic mean function.

$$\tilde{x} = \frac{\sum_{x' \in N(\hat{x})} (w_{x'} \times \mathbb{1}_{x' \in S \cup x}) \times x'}{\sum_{x' \in N(\hat{x})} (w_{x'} \times \mathbb{1}_{x' \in S \cup x})} \tag{11}$$

4 Experimental Design

Through our experiments, we seek to answer the following questions.

- To which extent do the proposed oversampling functions perform well to alleviate the class imbalance problem?
- Is there any impact from the input size on the performance of these functions?
- How well do these functions work with noisy input data?

In this section, we describe the datasets, training algorithms, and the implementation details of our experiments.

4.1 Datasets

In our experiments, we utilize six datasets with diverse characteristics. We divide each dataset into an 80:20 ratio where 80% and 20% of the dataset is used for model training and testing, respectively. A concise overview of each dataset can be found in Table 1.

Table 1. Comprehensive summary of the datasets used in experiments

Type	Name	Dataset Size	# of Features	Imbalanced Ratio
Binary	Thyroid [25]	7,200	21	12.5
	Wisconsin [23]	569	30	1.7
	Pima Diabetes [20]	768	8	1.9
Multi-Class	Page Blocks [26]	5,473	10	175.5
	Pen Digits [26]	1,100	16	2.2
	Glass [5]	214	9	6.4

4.2 Training Algorithm

We use a neural network as our discriminator model alongside cross-entropy loss [22] as the objective function. Algorithm 1 describes our training procedure.

Algorithm 1 Training Algorithm

1: **Input:** Training instances N_{train}, oversampling function d_f, number of epoch n_{epoch}, labels Y
2: **Output:** Predicted labels Y_{pred}
3: **for** $i = 1, 2, \ldots, n_{epoch}$ **do**
4:     $N_{updated} \leftarrow N_{train}$
5:     **for each** class c in minority classes **do**
6:         Select a set of data instances D_c to oversample
7:         **for each** data instance x in D_c **do**
8:             $\tilde{x} \leftarrow d_f(\hat{N(x)})$
9:             $N_{updated} \leftarrow N_{updated} \cup \tilde{x}$
10:        **end for**
11:    **end for**
12:    Infer Y' by feeding $N_{train-updated}$ to the neural network
13:    Update the weight matrices in the neural network using backpropagation
14: **end for**
15: **return** Trained neural network model

4.3 Evaluation Metrics

We employ precision, balanced accuracy, and F1-score to evaluate the model performance for binary datasets. For multi-class classification, we opt for the macro versions of these metrics. Notably, we exclude widely known evaluation measures such as accuracy and ROC AUC score because they do not effectively capture the nuances of imbalanced classification scenarios.

$$Precision = \frac{TP}{TP + FP} \tag{12}$$

$$Balanced - Accuracy = 0.5 \times \left(\frac{TN}{TP + FN} + \frac{TP}{TP + FN} \right) \tag{13}$$

$$F1 - score = \frac{TP}{TP + \frac{1}{2}(FP + FN)} \tag{14}$$

$$Precision_{macro} = \sum_{class} \frac{\text{Precision of class}}{\text{Number of classes}} \tag{15}$$

$$Balanced - Accuracy_{macro} = \sum_{class} \frac{\text{Balanced accuracy of class}}{\text{Number of classes}} \tag{16}$$

$$F1 - score_{macro} = \sum_{class} \frac{\text{F1-score of class}}{\text{Number of classes}} \tag{17}$$

In this context, TP stands for true positives, TN represents true negatives, FP denotes false positives, and FN indicates false negatives.

4.4   System Resources and Implementation Details

We have used Python programming language with PyTorch [11] and Scikit-learn [17] libraries for our implementation. All models are trained and tested on a computer with Core i7 CPU, 16 GB RAM and 8 GB GPU.

We use a multi-layer Perceptron (MLP) with 64 hidden layer neurons as our discriminator. Hyperparameters for model training are as follows; number of epochs: 200, learning rate: 0.05, optimizer: Adam [15]. Batch size for each dataset is selected from [100, 500, 5000]. We repeat each experimental run 30 times with different seed values in order to retain statistical significance and record the average test results. Further, we observe that the performance of the oversampling process highly depends on the number of selected neighbors. To achieve a fair comparison, we run each model under the number of selected neighbors from 2 to 6 and record the best result.

5   Results and Discussion

5.1   Performance Comparison Between Different Oversampling Functions

We compare the classification performance of the above-discussed functions in Table 2. Note that the SUM, MEAN, WAM, MIN, MAX, and STD denote the sum, mean, weighted arithmetic mean, minimum, maximum, and standard deviation functions, respectively.

Table 2. Classification performance (%) comparison of the oversampling functions. (Note: The best model under each evaluation metric is highlighted in **bold**)

Dataset	Method	Precision	F1-Score	Balanced Accuracy
Thyroid	SMOTE	88.71	92.25	97.55
	SUM	87.95	91.81	**97.55**
	MEAN	87.95	91.81	97.55
	WAM	**93.42**	**93.33**	93.64
	MIN	87.95	91.81	97.55
	MAX	89.76	92.38	96.47
	STD	46.28	48.07	50.00
Wisconsin	SMOTE	96.92	96.80	96.80
	SUM	97.02	96.89	96.85
	MEAN	97.02	96.89	96.85
	WAM	96.71	96.62	96.64
	MIN	**97.09**	**96.92**	**96.86**
	MAX	97.02	96.89	96.85
	STD	96.72	96.68	96.72
Pima Diabetes	SMOTE	**74.92**	**74.11**	**73.99**
	SUM	74.77	73.90	73.77
	MEAN	74.77	73.90	73.77
	WAM	72.45	70.89	70.56
	MIN	74.77	73.90	73.77
	MAX	74.77	73.90	73.77
	STD	32.47	39.37	50.00
Page Blocks	SMOTE	49.17	**55.41**	**77.98**
	SUM	**58.97**	50.13	52.84
	MEAN	45.51	45.48	68.37
	WAM	49.23	47.17	68.41
	MIN	45.31	45.43	68.25
	MAX	46.43	45.53	67.68
	STD	41.89	30.61	32.32
Pen Digits	SMOTE	99.07	99.06	99.06
	SUM	99.07	99.06	99.06
	MEAN	99.07	99.06	99.06
	WAM	99.07	99.06	99.06
	MIN	**99.09**	**99.08**	**99.08**
	MAX	99.07	99.06	99.06
	STD	98.94	98.93	98.93
Glass	SMOTE	68.81	67.14	67.14
	SUM	68.21	67.28	**70.35**
	MEAN	68.21	67.28	70.35
	WAM	66.41	64.82	66.74
	MIN	**70.30**	**67.93**	69.11
	MAX	68.21	67.28	70.35
	STD	60.09	59.05	60.73

From the results, it is evident that there is no single function that performs well for every dataset. The best-performing function always depends on the dataset characteristics. However, non-linear functions such as minimum and maximum show solid performance in all datasets compared to linear functions. We attribute this to the high capacity of these functions as they can model complex relationships between data instances using non-linearity. Weighted arithmetic mean consistently outperforms other linear functions such as mean, and SMOTE. Mean and SMOTE are special instances of weighted arithmetic mean. Therefore, the weighted average mean inherently contains higher modeling capacity and, thus performs comparably or better. Standard deviation is the worst-performing model. We believe this is mainly due to its inability to capture data distribution accurately, especially when the data distributions are skewed.

5.2 Ablation Studies

In this subsection, we provide additional experiments and further analysis on the behavior of oversampling functions.

Input Size of the Oversampling Function vs Classification Performance. Through this ablation study, we investigate the impact of the input size in the oversampling function on the classification performance. We evaluate each model's performance with different input sizes. To change the input size, we change the number of selected neighbors in the function. The results for Wisconsin and Diabetes are summarized in Fig. 2.

Lower input size means the oversampling is primarily done using more closer data instances whereas higher input size considers more distant neighbours to the oversampling process. We can see that there is a performance improvement when we increase the input size. However, this improvement seems to stabilize in all functions after a certain threshold and there is not much decline or enhancement in the performance with further input size increase. Therefore, we can deduce that a moderate neighborhood count (i.e. 4-6) would be enough to capture predominant information around a given data instance to achieve better performance in the oversampling process.

Robustness to Noise. To test the robustness of the oversampling functions, we conduct the following ablation study where we inject Gaussian noise into input data instances and evaluate the classification performance. The performance comparison between with and without noise for Glass and Thyroid datasets is depicted in Fig. 3.

As expected, random noise decreases the performance of the oversampling functions. Linear functions show a higher performance decline compared to non-linear functions. Standard deviation is less affected by the noise compared to other functions. The reason is standard deviation primarily measures the dispersion around data instances and this dispersion is less likely to be affected by outliers and noise.

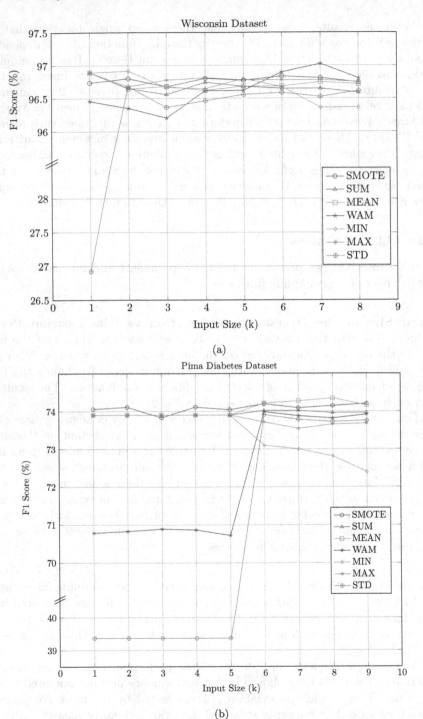

Fig. 2. Classification performance (F1-Score) against input size for (a) Wisconsin and (b) Diabetes datasets

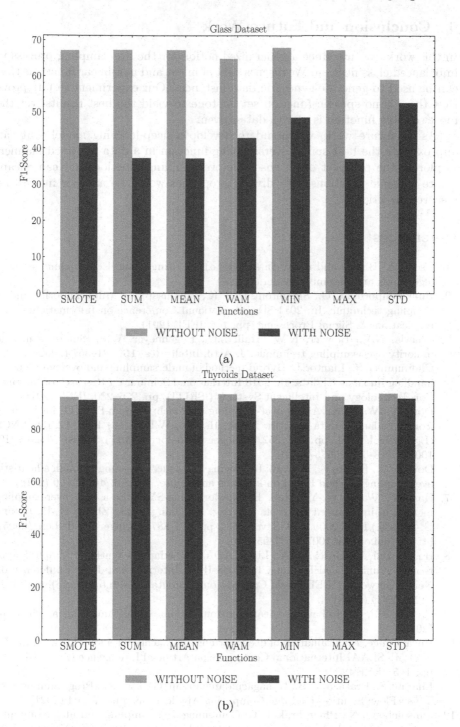

Fig. 3. Noise robustness for (a) Glass and (b) Thyroid datasets

6   Conclusion and Future Work

In this work, we introduce a generalized notion for the oversampling process in imbalanced classification. We discuss a set of linear and non-linear functions that can be used to generate synthetic data instances. Our experiment results prove that there is no specific function set in stone to yield the best results, yet the most suitable function is always data-driven.

As for future work, we intend to develop a deep-learning model that can approximate the best-suited oversampling function in a data-informed manner. Exploring the prospect of an ensemble oversampling function that can encapsulate multiple functions with diverse properties would be another interesting research direction.

References

1. Asela, H.: Binary and multi-class classification using supervised machine learning algorithms and ensemble model (2021)
2. Bunkhumpornpat, C., Sinapiromsaran, K., Lursinsap, C.: Mute: majority under-sampling technique. In: 2011 8th International Conference on Information, Communications & Signal Processing, pp. 1–4. IEEE (2011)
3. Chawla, N.V., Bowyer, K.W., Hall, L.O., Kegelmeyer, W.P.: Smote: synthetic minority over-sampling technique. J. Artif. Intell. Res. **16**, 321–357 (2002)
4. Choirunnisa, S., Lianto, J.: Hybrid method of undersampling and oversampling for handling imbalanced data. In: 2018 International Seminar on Research of Information Technology and Intelligent Systems (ISRITI), pp. 276–280. IEEE (2018)
5. Dong, Y., Wang, X.: A new over-sampling approach: random-SMOTE for learning from imbalanced data sets. In: Xiong, H., Lee, W.B. (eds.) KSEM 2011. LNCS (LNAI), vol. 7091, pp. 343–352. Springer, Heidelberg (2011). https://doi.org/10.1007/978-3-642-25975-3_30
6. Douzas, G., Bacao, F., Last, F.: Improving imbalanced learning through a heuristic oversampling method based on k-means and smote. Inf. Sci. **465**, 1–20 (2018)
7. Han, H., Wang, W.-Y., Mao, B.-H.: Borderline-SMOTE: a new over-sampling method in imbalanced data sets learning. In: Huang, D.-S., Zhang, X.-P., Huang, G.-B. (eds.) ICIC 2005. LNCS, vol. 3644, pp. 878–887. Springer, Heidelberg (2005). https://doi.org/10.1007/11538059_91
8. He, H., Bai, Y., Garcia, E.A., Li, S.: ADASYN: adaptive synthetic sampling approach for imbalanced learning. In: 2008 IEEE International Joint Conference on Neural Networks (IEEE World Congress on Computational Intelligence), pp. 1322–1328. IEEE (2008)
9. He, H., Ma, Y.: Imbalanced learning: foundations, algorithms, and applications (2013)
10. Hevapathige, A.: Evaluation of deep learning approaches for anomaly detection. In: 2021 5th SLAAI International Conference on Artificial Intelligence (SLAAI-ICAI), pp. 1–5. IEEE (2021)
11. Imambi, S., Prakash, K.B., Kanagachidambaresan, G.: Pytorch. Programming with TensorFlow: Solution for Edge Computing Applications, pp. 87–104 (2021)
12. Junsomboon, N., Phienthrakul, T.: Combining over-sampling and under-sampling techniques for imbalance dataset. In: Proceedings of the 9th International Conference on Machine Learning and Computing, pp. 243–247 (2017)

13. Karunasingha, N., Jayasekara, B.G., Hevapathige, A.: OC-SMOTE-NN: a deep learning-based approach for imbalanced classification. In: 2023 IEEE 13th Annual Computing and Communication Workshop and Conference (CCWC), pp. 0943–0948. IEEE (2023)
14. Kim, M., Hwang, K.B.: An empirical evaluation of sampling methods for the classification of imbalanced data. PLoS ONE **17**(7), e0271260 (2022)
15. Kingma, D.P., Ba, J.: Adam: a method for stochastic optimization. arXiv preprint arXiv:1412.6980 (2014)
16. Koziarski, M.: CSMOUTE: combined synthetic oversampling and undersampling technique for imbalanced data classification. In: 2021 International Joint Conference on Neural Networks (IJCNN), pp. 1–8. IEEE (2021)
17. Kramer, O., Kramer, O.: Scikit-Learn. Machine Learning for Evolution Strategies, pp. 45–53. Springer, Switzerland (2016). https://doi.org/10.1007/978-3-319-33383-0
18. Last, F., Douzas, G., Bacao, F.: Oversampling for imbalanced learning based on k-means and smote. arXiv preprint arXiv:1711.00837 (2017)
19. Liu, D., Zhong, S., Lin, L., Zhao, M., Fu, X., Liu, X.: Deep attention smote: data augmentation with a learnable interpolation factor for imbalanced anomaly detection of gas turbines. Comput. Ind. **151**, 103972 (2023)
20. Majumder, A., Dutta, S., Kumar, S., Behera, L.: A method for handling multi-class imbalanced data by geometry based information sampling and class prioritized synthetic data generation (gicaps). arXiv preprint arXiv:2010.05155 (2020)
21. Mani, I., Zhang, I.: KNN approach to unbalanced data distributions: a case study involving information extraction. In: Proceedings of the Workshop on Learning from Imbalanced Datasets, vol. 126, pp. 1–7. ICML (2003)
22. Mao, A., Mohri, M., Zhong, Y.: Cross-entropy loss functions: theoretical analysis and applications. arXiv preprint arXiv:2304.07288 (2023)
23. Mohammad, W.T., Teete, R., Al-Aaraj, H., Rubbai, Y.S.Y., Arabyat, M.M., et al.: Diagnosis of breast cancer pathology on the wisconsin dataset with the help of data mining classification and clustering techniques. Appl. Bionics Biomech. **2022** (2022)
24. Mohammed, R., Rawashdeh, J., Abdullah, M.: Machine learning with oversampling and undersampling techniques: overview study and experimental results. In: 2020 11th International Conference on Information and Communication Systems (ICICS), pp. 243–248. IEEE (2020)
25. Pang, G., Shen, C., van den Hengel, A.: Deep anomaly detection with deviation networks. In: Proceedings of the 25th ACM SIGKDD International Conference on Knowledge Discovery & Data Mining, pp. 353–362 (2019)
26. Tanha, J., Abdi, Y., Samadi, N., Razzaghi, N., Asadpour, M.: Boosting methods for multi-class imbalanced data classification: an experimental review. J. Big Data **7**(1), 1–47 (2020)
27. Tomek, I.: Two modifications of CNN (1976)
28. Vuttipittayamongkol, P., Elyan, E.: Neighbourhood-based undersampling approach for handling imbalanced and overlapped data. Inf. Sci. **509**, 47–70 (2020)
29. Wang, B., Jiang, B., Tang, J., Luo, B.: Generalizing aggregation functions in GNNs: building high capacity and robust GNNs via nonlinear aggregation. IEEE Trans. Pattern Anal. Mach. Intell. (2023)
30. Wang, Q., Luo, Z., Huang, J., Feng, Y., Liu, Z., et al.: A novel ensemble method for imbalanced data learning: bagging of extrapolation-smote SVM. Comput. Intell. Neurosci. **2017** (2017)

Unveiling AI Efficiency: Loan Application Process Optimization Using PM4PY Tool

Anukriti Tripathi[(✉)] [iD], Aditi Rai [iD], Uphar Singh [iD], Ranjana Vyas [iD],
and O. P. Vyas [iD]

Indian Institute of Information Technology Allahabad, Allahabad, India
{rsi2023003,ids2021902,pse2017003,ranjana,opvyas}@iiita.ac.in

Abstract. These days, financial institutions strive to streamline their
loan processes for cost reduction, improved customer satisfaction, and
enhanced overall efficiency. Process Mining (PM) offers a data-driven
approach that identifies bottlenecks, delays, and unnecessary steps within
the loan process. By leveraging event logs from these financial institution processes, PM facilitates optimization and automation, resulting
in faster loan approvals. Analyzing event logs can create a comprehensive process model representing the institution's workflow. This study
aims to create a process model specifically tailored for the loan application domain by utilizing the advantages offered by the discovery and
conformance steps of PM. The algorithms associated with the discovery and conformance steps are analyzed using two datasets related to
the loan application process to identify the most suitable model for the
loan application process Optimization. The analysis demonstrates the
significance of discovery and conformance algorithms for different quality matrices while generating an effective process model. The proposed
methodology reveals that each discovery algorithm comes with its own
set of advantages and disadvantages, characterized by varying values of
quality metrics. Consequently, the selection of a discovery algorithm is
based on the specific quality criteria needed for the task at hand.

Keywords: Process Mining · Loan Process Mining · Process
Discovery · Process Conformance Checking · PM4PY Tool

1 Introduction

A financial institution (FI) plays a crucial role in providing loans to individuals and businesses, helping them to meet their financial needs and achieve
their goals. Automation brings efficiency and convenience to FIs, prioritizing
customer service and ensuring customers' personalized assistance. It has been
widely known that FIs consist of complex and time-consuming structures to
provide loan solutions [9,14]. Hence, it is required to optimize these complex
structures by enhancing the experience and maximizing revenue generation.

Process mining is a technology that uses event data generated during process
execution, to learn and gain insights about the processes. The foundation of PM

D. Garg et al. (Eds.): IACC 2023, CCIS 2053, pp. 490–499, 2024.
https://doi.org/10.1007/978-3-031-56700-1_39

is the event log, which contains information such as activities, timestamps, and unique identifiers for each event. PM encompasses three main building blocks: process discovery, process conformance, and process enhancement. The **process discovery** uncovers the underlying process model without any prior knowledge, by analyzing the event logs to extract the process structure and behavior. **Process conformance** focuses on comparing an existing process model with the event log to evaluate their alignment by assessing the degree of conformity between the observed behavior in the event log and the expected behavior outlined in the process model. Finally, **process enhancement** improves and optimizes the overall process by incorporating insights from the event logs [1–3]. By employing these building blocks in organizations' functioning, identification of inefficiencies, and deviations from usual behavior, bottleneck identification etc can be achieved. The organization can gain valuable insights, behavior, and pattern for the smooth functioning.

Hence, the work proposes to use process mining for optimization of the loan application process in the financial application domain. Through this approach, various challenges like delayed loan approval, difficulty in fraud detection, etc can be resolved. The proposed work focuses on developing a process model by employing various process discovery algorithm using loan datasets [17,18]. The developed model is checked for its different parameter using different process conformance algorithms. The entire execution is deployed on PM4PY tool [8]. Figure 1 represents the workflow of the proposed approach, which develops a model, representing the actual activities being performed for the loan application initiation to its final acceptance or rejection stage.

In the rest of the paper, Sect. 2 delves into reviewing the existing research works on process mining in the loan application process domain. Section 3 provides essential background for the process mining by exploring the different algorithms of process discovery and conformance. Similarly, Sect. 4 outlines the proposed methodology and execution of process models on PM4PY tool. Section 5 provides the results of proposed implementation along with analyzing the obtained results. At last, Sect. 6 discusses the conclusion of the work by outlining the future scope of the proposed work.

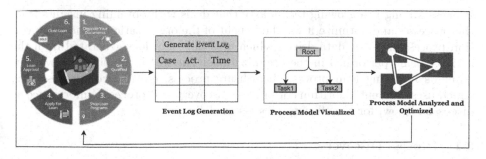

Fig. 1. Overview of the proposed workflow

2 Related Work

The proposed work focuses on applying process mining for the optimization of the loan application process. In this regard the work [13], focused on developing a process model for the loan application process by using *BPI challenge 2017 dataset* [17]. The process models are developed through four PM tool named SQL, Power BI, Disco, and ProM. Similarly, Authors in [15], applied PM to analyze the loan application process using *BPI Challenge 2017 dataset* and provided the critical analysis about the frequencies of accepted, approved, and cancelled loans either by user or bank along with denied applications, representing the relative analysis of all above frequencies. In [14], the author modeled the real-life financial loan application process of the Netherlands that can accurately represent the loan application tasks. For the deployment and analysis, the *BPI Challenge 2012 dataset* [18] is used which consists of 262,200 event logs from 13,087 credit applications.

The work [16], employed PM techniques, spreadsheet-based approaches, Disco for PM capabilities, and Classification and Regression Tree (CART) for exploratory analytics using *BPI Challenge 2012 dataset*. The analysis findings are presented, highlighting a deep understanding of the process gained from the event log data. The study identifies potential areas for operational efficiency improvements within the bank and explores the use of process execution knowledge to predict loan application outcomes.

The work has explored the state-of-the-art for the loan application process and it has been observed that a very limited research work is performed on the loan application process in the financial domain. Hence, it is very much required to perform a significant study on the loan application process, so that the banking processes can be standardized up to a significant level. Additionally, none of the previous research work has performed an exploratory analysis of possible PM models corresponding to the loan application process. Therefore, the analysis of different possible models through different available algorithms is performed using the PM4PY tool on the loan application event log in this proposed work.

3 Background

Process Mining is a growing technology that deals with obtaining insights from the processes and optimize it for the benefit of the organizations. The optimization process in PM is data-driven which uses the event logs generated from the activity being performed in the organizations. The PM is applicable in various domains including loan process, healthcare process, e-commerce process etc., which uses different algorithms of process discovery and process conformance as discussed below, for the efficient process modelling.

3.1 Process Discovery

Process Discovery (PD) marks the first stage in the PM journey, which generates the visual process model from the event logs captured in an organization [2]. There are four discovery algorithms for generating a process model as follows:

1. **Alpha Miner Algorithm:** It is an early method for PD which works on a workflow model that is retrieved from event log traces and generates the Petri net model. The α-algorithm or α-miner is a PM approach that specifically concentrates on deducing causation from sequences of events. By examining the connections between the activities documented in the log, the algorithm converts event logs to traces and then into workflow net. [11].

2. **Heuristic Miner Algorithm:** To improve the alpha method in the perspective of concurrency, the heuristic miner was introduced as the second algorithm in line. The heuristic miner algorithm considers the frequencies of events while disregarding uncommon patterns such as infrequent events, sequences, single events, and short loops (which can be seen as isolated events at various levels, including higher levels) [5].

3. **Inductive Miner Algorithm:** The main focus of the inductive miner algorithm is to identify cuts in the directly follows graph derived from the event log. Within this context, a directed graph serves as a representation of the directly follows graph. The core concept of the inductive miner revolves around identifying multiple divisions within the graph's arcs, which indicates immediate followed relationships. Once these divisions are established, the smaller components can be utilized to illustrate the order in which tasks are executed.

4. **Inductive Logic Programming (ILP) Algorithm:** This algorithm is employed to automatically infer process models from event logs by combining machine learning, logic programming, and PM principles. It establishes a hypothesis space comprising potential process models by using an event log as an input. It incorporates domain-specific background knowledge and constraints. Through an iterative process, it searches for the most fitting process model that aligns with the observed event sequences while adhering to the imposed constraints [12].

3.2 Process Conformance (PC)

In process conformance, the visual workflow is checked by comparing with the theoretical event log to determine if it accurately captures the expected behavior [3]. The PC algorithm uses four quality criteria matrices i.e. fitness, precision, simplicity, and generalization. The proposed work compares different process conformance algorithms to check the model derived in the process discovery stage as follows.

1. **Token-replay Algorithm:** The token replay algorithm involves replaying actual event logs on a process model to assess alignment. Tokens represent case instances moving through the model, and the method checks how well the model matches real executions. Key steps include event log extraction, process model definition, token initialization, movement, alignment checking, and performance analysis. This technique helps identify deviations, assess conformance, and improve process efficiency [7]. The conformance checking of a trace is mathematically evaluated using Eq. 1. By applying this equation

to each trace and aggregating the results, the overall conformance of the event log with the Petri net model can be established.

$$Fitness(petrinets, trace) = \frac{1}{2}(1 - \frac{rts}{pts}) + \frac{1}{2}(1 - \frac{mts}{cts}) \qquad (1)$$

Where, rts is the **remaining tokens**, pts is the **processed tokens**, mts is the **missing token**, and cts is **consumed token.**

2. **Alignment Algorithm:** Alignment involves the task of matching an actual trace with a process model to find the best possible match between the model and traces. The purpose of employing this algorithm-based replay is to determine the optimal pair between model and traces, which yields a collection of pairs for each trace. Each pair consists of a trace event or ≫ (representing the absence of an event) and a model transition.

3. **Footprint Algorithm:** Footprints are matrices that depict the causal relationships between activities. Likewise, a process model also acquires a footprint through its execution and recording of activity sequences. To ensure thoroughness, all activities that can transpire consecutively should correspond with the footprints matrix. Through a comparison of the footprints from the event log to the discovered process model, discrepancies can be identified and conformance between the event log and model can be evaluated.

4   Methodology and Experiment

The proposed work deals with the development of process model for loan application process by applying the process discovery algorithms on the loan application domain for generating a process model, so that smooth conduction of the loan approval process can be performed. The work is conducted on PM4PY Python-based tool which consists of the functionality to execute alpha, inductive, heuristic, and ILP algorithms for discovery and Footprint Matrix, Token Replay, and alignment algorithm for conformance checking.

4.1   Dataset

In the proposed work, BPI Challange 2017 [17] (2016 to 2017) and BPI Challange 2012 [18] (October 2011 to March 2012), datasets are employed to generate loan applications process models. Table 1 represents the technical specifications of these datasets.

4.2   PM4PY Tool

PM4Py is a powerful PM library that provides various functionalities for analyzing event data and extracting important insights. It offers many PM techniques, including discovery, conformance checking, and process enhancement. PM4PY supports different process notations such as Petri nets [4] and Directly-Follows Graphs and provides capabilities for visualizing and analyzing process models.

Table 1. Statistical Details of Datasets Used in the Proposed Work

Availability of Log	Log Name	Total events	Total traces	Dist. events (%)	Dist. traces (%)	Tr. length		
						avg	min	max
Public	BPI Challenge 2012	262200	13087	36%	33.4%	20	3	175
Public	BPI Challenge 2017	714198	21861	41%	40.1%	33	11	113

It is an open-source tool that allows researchers, practitioners, and organizations to leverage PM techniques for improving processes and making data-driven decisions. The proposed work uses the PM4PY tool for developing and analyzing the performance of different discovery and conformance algorithms [8, 10].

4.3 Selection of Algorithms

In the proposed work, four process discovery algorithms, such as the Alpha Miner, Inductive Miner, Heuristic Miner, and ILP, to generate process models from loan application event logs. The process conformance algorithms, including token replay, alignment, and footprint matrix, are employed to validate the generated model against the event logs.

4.4 Model Evaluation Quality Criteria

In process mining, the process models generated for any application domain undergoes for testing using four quality metrics: *simplicity, fitness, generalization,* and *precision,* discussed as follows. The evaluation of the model is based on the values obtained for these metrics, ranges between 0 and 1 [6].

1. **Fitness Metric:** As its name suggests, it specifies how much the model fits with the event log. Here, Fitness expresses if every possible trace is covered by the process model.
2. **Precision Metric:** It illustrates the concept of underfitting, emphasizing that the model should not excessively fit to the new traces generating in event log and should only accept the already available traces.
3. **Generalization Metric:** It expresses that, the model may be overfitted with the event log, measuring the presence of those activities that are valid but are not recorded in a generated event logs. It is completely the opposite of precision. It evaluates how well the process model generalizes the observed behavior in the event log.
4. **Simplicity Metric:** Simplicity is a measure that quantifies the complexity of a discovered model. A good process model should aim to minimize unnecessary complexities and entities, keeping the model as simple as possible.

5   Results and Analysis

The experiments are conducted to develop and evaluate the process models for the loan application process. The models for loan event logs are developed using four discovery algorithms **alpha miner, inductive miner, heuristics miner**, and **ILP** on **BPI Challenge 2012** and **BPI Challenge 2017** datasets. Figure 2 and 3 represents the model obtained for alpha miner algorithms for dataset BPI Challenge 2012 and BPI Challenge 2017 respectively. The models obtained from other algorithms are too large and complex which can not be accommodated in this paper.

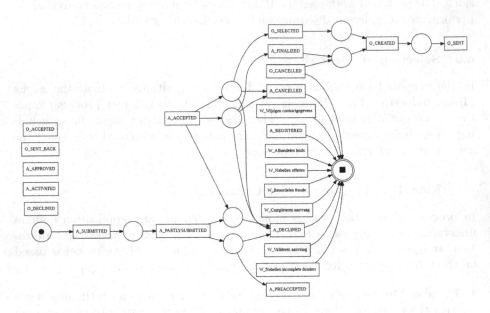

Fig. 2. Loan Process Model of BPI Challenge 2012 with Alpha Miner

The generated models using discovery algorithms are gone through conformance checking where it is re-validated with event logs. To perform this, three conformance-checking algorithms, e.g. **Footprint matrix** (FP), **alignment** (ALT), and **token replay** (TR), were used in which four quality metrics i.e. Fitness (FT), precision (PR), generalization (GN), and simplicity (SM), are employed to show the performance. The corresponding obtained results are shown in table 2, which represents the comparative results of all three conformance algorithms, drawing the following inferences.

i For the simplicity of the model, the **alpha Miner algorithm** performs well as compared to other discovery algorithm e.g. token replay, alignment, and footprint matrix algorithms. showing the significantly higher value for both the datasets.

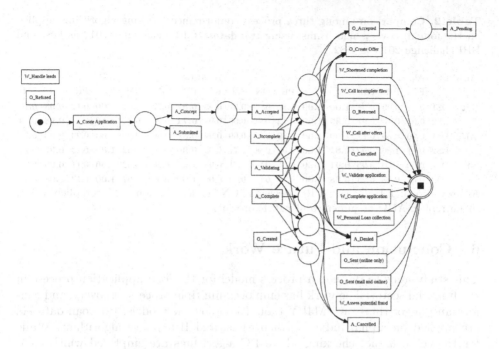

Fig. 3. Loan Process Model BPI Challenge 2017 with Alpha Miner

ii For the model's fitness, the algorithms **inductive miner** and **ILP** outperform others with a value of 1.0 in every case.

iii For the precision of models, the heuristic miner algorithm has shown its super capability more than others in both datasets.

iv For the generalization, it has been observed that alpha, inductive and heuristic algorithms have shown almost similar performance, but the ILP algorithm shows its best performance, compared with other algorithms in both the employed datasets.

Finally, after analyzing all the algorithms of process discovery and process conformance, it has been observed that the discovery algorithms are successful in generating the process model for the loan application process and the process conformance verifies the model by checking the event logs and the model for the conformance between them. All the algorithms have shown their capability in generating a process model for loan application approval systems with their significant strength. To evaluate the quality of the model generated by each algorithm, 4 quality metrics fitness, precision, simplicity, and generalization are used and their individual value corresponding to each algorithm is calculated. Since all 4 quality metrics have their significant importance and none of them can be prioritized, therefore choosing the best algorithm for model generation depends on what kind of quality metrics should be in the model. Hence, based on such quality metrics a specific algorithm can be selected.

Table 2. Comparison among three process conformance checking algorithms applied on the four discovery algorithms, using two datasets BPI challenge 2012 as DS1 and BPI challenge 2017 as DS2.

Algo	DS	Alpha				Inductive				Heuristic				ILP			
		FT	PR	GN	SM	FT	PR	GN	SM	FT	PR	GN	SM	FT	PR	GR	SM
TR	DS1	0.55	0.09	0.98	**1.00**	**1.00**	0.10	0.90	0.57	0.95	**0.87**	0.92	0.51	**1.00**	0.11	**0.98**	0.13
	DS2	0.67	0.10	0.97	**0.89**	**1.00**	0.12	0.96	0.56	0.97	**0.71**	0.92	0.56	**1.00**	0.13	**0.98**	0.10
ALT	DS1	0.20	0.60	0.88	**1.00**	**1.00**	0.80	0.95	0.69	0.99	**0.88**	0.90	0.62	**1.00**	0.23	**0.98**	0.21
	DS2	0.51	1.00	0.95	**0.81**	**1.00**	0.90	0.96	0.71	0.99	**0.96**	0.861	0.62	**1.00**	0.13	**0.97**	0.14
FP	DS1	0.50	1.00	0.95	**0.91**	**1.00**	0.66	0.96	0.71	0.98	**1.00**	0.86	0.62	**1.00**	0.11	**0.99**	0.29
	DS2	0.31	0.28	0.28	**0.88**	**1.00**	0.84	0.95	0.69	0.99	**1.00**	0.90	0.62	**1.00**	0.13	**0.98**	0.24

Abbreviations: FT: fitness, PR: precision, GN: generalization, SM: simplicity, TR: token replay, ALT: alignment and FP: Footprint.

6   Conclusion and Future Work

This study aims to develop a process model for the loan application process in the financial sector. The work has employed multiple process discovery, and conformance algorithms on PM4PY tool. To deploy the models, two loan datasets are applied on alpha, inductive, heuristics, and ILP miner algorithms. While for the conformance-checking, three PC algorithms are employed which compares the discovered model with the event log and evaluates the model's fitness. The experimental analysis reveals that, the alpha miner exhibited superior simplicity, the inductive algorithm excelled in fitness value, the heuristic algorithm displayed excellent precision, and the ILP algorithm demonstrated exceptional fitness and generalization values. For future research, the work can be extended to delve into additional PM algorithms to enhance the proposed work. Furthermore, it is crucial to investigate the significance of specific quality matrices to improve the accuracy of identifying appropriate process models. Additionally, we can validate the findings by conducting comparative analyses using other tools on the same datasets.

Acknowledgement. The work acknowledges the NewGen IEDC, Indian Institute of Information Technology Allahabad, India, for the partial funding support.

References

1. Book: Process Mining Wil van der Aalst Data Science. Accessed 28 Sep 2023
2. Aalst, W.: Process discovery: capturing the invisible. IEEE Comput. Intell. Mag. **5**, 28–41 (2010)
3. Carmona, J., Dongen, B., Solti, A., Weidlich, M.: Conformance Checking, p. 56. Springer, Switzerland (2018). https://doi.org/10.1007/978-3-319-99414-7
4. Leemans, S.J.J., Fahland, D., van der Aalst, W.M.P.: Discovering block-structured process models from event logs – a constructive approach. In: Colom, J.M., Desel, J. (eds.) Application and Theory of Petri Nets and Concurrency. PETRI NETS 2013. LNCS, vol. 7927, pp 311–329. Springer, Berlin, Heidelberg (2013). https://doi.org/10.1007/978-3-642-38697-8_17

5. Weijters, A.J.M.M., Van der Aalst, W.M., Alves De Medeiros, A.K.: Process mining with the heuristics miner-algorithm. Technische Universiteit Eindhoven, pp. 1–34 (2006). Technical report. WP 166.July 2017

6. Buijs, J.C.A.M., van Dongen, B.F., van der Aalst, W.M.P.: On the role of fitness, precision, generalization and simplicity in process discovery. In: Meersman, R., et al. (eds.) OTM 2012. LNCS, vol. 7565, pp. 305–322. Springer, Heidelberg (2012). https://doi.org/10.1007/978-3-642-33606-5_19

7. Berti, A., van der Aalst, W.M.P.: A novel token-based replay technique to speed up conformance checking and process enhancement. In: Koutny, M., Kordon, F., Pomello, L. (eds.) Transactions on Petri Nets and Other Models of Concurrency XV. LNCS, vol. 12530, pp. 1–26. Springer, Heidelberg (2021). https://doi.org/10.1007/978-3-662-63079-2_1

8. Berti, A., Van Zelst, S.J., van der Aalst, W.: Process mining for python (pm4py): bridging the gap between process-and data science (2019). arXiv preprint arXiv:1905.06169

9. Werner, M., Wiese, M., Maas, A.: Embedding process mining into financial statement audits. Int. J. Account. Inf. Syst. **41**, 100514 (2021)

10. F. I. for Applied Information Technology, pm4py - Process Mining for Python. https://pm4py.fit.fraunhofer.de/docs. Accessed 28 Dec 2022

11. Van der Aalst, W., Weijters, T., Maruster, L.: Workflow mining: discovering process models from event logs. IEEE Trans. Knowl. Data Eng. **16**(9), 1128–1142 (2004)

12. Verbeek, H., Aalst, W.: Decomposed process mining: the ILP case. In: Business Process Management Workshops: BPM 2014 International Workshops, Eindhoven, The Netherlands, 7–8 September 2014, Revised Papers 12, pp. 264–276 (2015)

13. Blevi, L., Delporte, L., Robbrecht, J.: Process mining on the loan application process of a Dutch Financial Institute. BPI Challenge, pp. 328–343 (2017)

14. Moreira, C., Haven, E., Sozzo, S., Wichert, A.: Process mining with real world financial loan applications: improving inference on incomplete event logs. PLoS ONE **13**, e0207806 (2018)

15. Carvallo, A., et al.: Applying Process Mining for Loan Approvals in a Banking Institution. Computer Science Department, School Of Engineering Pontificia Universidad Catolica De Chile, Santiago, Chile (2017)

16. Bautista, A., Wangikar, L., Akbar, S.: Process mining-driven optimization of a consumer loan approvals process. BPI Challenge (2012)

17. van Dongen, B.: BPI Challenge 2017. Version 1. 4TU.ResearchData. dataset (2017). https://doi.org/10.4121/uuid:5f3067df-f10b-45da-b98b-86ae4c7a310b

18. van Dongen, B.: BPI Challenge 2012. Version 1. 4TU.ResearchData. dataset (2012). https://doi.org/10.4121/uuid:3926db30-f712-4394-aebc-75976070e91f

Author Index

Printed in the United States
by Baker & Taylor Publisher Services